# Śrī Caitanya-caritāmṛta

**BOOKS by**
**His Divine Grace A.C. Bhaktivedanta Swami Prabhupāda**

Bhagavad-gītā As It Is
Śrīmad-Bhāgavatam, Cantos 1-5 (15 Vols.)
Śrī Caitanya-caritāmṛta (17 Vols.)
Teachings of Lord Caitanya
The Nectar of Devotion
Śrī Īśopaniṣad
Easy Journey to Other Planets
Kṛṣṇa Consciousness: The Topmost Yoga System
Kṛṣṇa, The Supreme Personality of Godhead (3 Vols.)
Transcendental Teachings of Prahlād Mahārāja
Kṛṣṇa, the Reservoir of Pleasure
The Perfection of Yoga
Beyond Birth and Death
On the Way to Kṛṣṇa
Rāja-vidyā: The King of Knowledge
Elevation to Kṛṣṇa Consciousness
Kṛṣṇa Consciousness: The Matchless Gift
Back to Godhead Magazine (Founder)

*A complete catalogue is available upon request*

International Society for Krishna Consciousness
3764 Watseka Avenue
Los Angeles, California 90034

All Glory to Śrī Guru and Gaurāṅga

# ŚRĪ CAITANYA-CARITĀMṚTA

of Kṛṣṇadāsa Kavirāja Gosvāmī



*Madhya-līlā*
*Volume Eight*

**"The Lord's Teachings to Śrīla Sanātana Gosvāmī"**

*with the original Bengali text, Roman transliterations, synonyms, translation and elaborate purports*

*by*

**HIS DIVINE GRACE**
**A.C. Bhaktivedanta Swami Prabhupāda**
*Founder-Ācārya of the International Society for Krishna Consciousness*

THE BHAKTIVEDANTA BOOK TRUST
New York · Los Angeles · London · Bombay

Readers interested in the subject matter of this book
are invited by the International Society for Krishna Consciousness
to correspond with its Secretary.

**International Society for Krishna Consciousness**
**3764 Watseka Avenue**
**Los Angeles, California 90034**



Library of Congress Catalogue Card Number: 73-93206
International Standard Book Number: 0-912776-70-6

First printing, 1975: 20,000 copies

Printed in the United States of America

# Contents

# Introduction

*Śrī Caitanya-caritāmṛta* is the principal work on the life and teachings of Śrī Kṛṣṇa Caitanya. Śrī Caitanya is the pioneer of a great social and religious movement which began in India a little less than five hundred years ago and which has directly and indirectly influenced the subsequent course of religious and philosophical thinking not only in India but in the recent West as well.

Caitanya Mahāprabhu is regarded as a figure of great historical significance. However, our conventional method of historical analysis—that of seeing a man as a product of his times—fails here. Śrī Caitanya is a personality who transcends the limited scope of historical settings.

At a time when, in the West, man was directing his explorative spirit toward studying the structure of the physical universe and circumnavigating the world in search of new oceans and continents, Śrī Kṛṣṇa Caitanya, in the East, was inaugurating and masterminding a revolution directed inward, toward a scientific understanding of the highest knowledge of man's spiritual nature.

The chief historical sources for the life of Śrī Kṛṣṇa Caitanya are the *kaḍacās* (diaries) kept by Murāri Gupta and Svarūpa Dāmodara Gosvāmī. Murāri Gupta, a physician and close associate of Śrī Caitanya's, recorded extensive notes on the first twenty-four years of Śrī Caitanya's life, culminating in his initiation into the renounced order, *sannyāsa*. The events of the rest of Caitanya Mahāprabhu's forty-eight years are recorded in the diary of Svarūpa Dāmodora Gosvāmī, another of Caitanya Mahāprabhu's intimate associates.

*Śrī Caitanya-caritāmṛta* is divided into three sections called *līlās,* which literally means "pastimes"—*Ādi-līlā* (the early period), *Madhya-līlā* (the middle period) and *Antya-līlā* (the final period). The notes of Murāri Gupta form the basis of the *Ādi-līlā,* and Svarūpa Dāmodara's diary provides the details for the *Madhya-* and *Antya-līlās.*

The first twelve of the seventeen chapters of *Ādi-līlā* constitute the preface for the entire work. By referring to Vedic scriptural evidence, this preface establishes Śrī Caitanya as the *avatāra* (incarnation) of Kṛṣṇa (God) for the age of Kali—the current epoch, beginning five thousand years ago and characterized by materialism, hypocrisy and dissension. In these descriptions, Caitanya Mahāprabhu, who is identical with Lord Kṛṣṇa, descends to liberally grant pure love of God to the fallen souls of this degraded age by propagating *saṅkīrtana*—literally, "congregational glorification of God"—especially by organizing massive public chanting of the *mahā-mantra* (Great Chant for Deliverance). The esoteric purpose of Lord Caitanya's appearance in the world is revealed, his co-*avatāras* and principal devotees are described and his teachings are summarized. The remaining portion of *Ādi-līlā,* chapters thirteen through seventeen, briefly recounts his divine birth and his life until he accepted the renounced order. This includes his childhood miracles, schooling, marriage and early philosophical confrontations, as well as his organization of a widespread *saṅkīrtana* movement and his civil disobedience against the repression of the Mohammedan government.

## Śrī Caitanya-caritāmṛta

The subject of *Madhya-līlā,* the longest of the three divisions, is a detailed narration of Lord Caitanya's extensive and eventful travels throughout India as a renounced mendicant, teacher, philosopher, spiritual preceptor and mystic. During this period of six years, Śrī Caitanya transmits his teachings to his principal disciples. He debates and converts many of the most renowned philosophers and theologians of his time, including Śaṅkarites, Buddhists and Muslims, and incorporates their many thousands of followers and disciples into his own burgeoning numbers. A dramatic account of Caitanya Mahāprabhu's miraculous activities at the giant Jagannātha Cart Festival in Orissa is also included in this section.

*Antya-līlā* concerns the last eighteen years of Śrī Caitanya's manifest presence, spent in semiseclusion near the famous Jagannātha temple at Jagannātha Purī in Orissa. During these final years, Śrī Caitanya drifted deeper and deeper into trances of spiritual ecstasy unparalleled in all of religious and literary history, Eastern or Western. Śrī Caitanya's perpetual and ever-increasing religious beatitude, graphically described in the eyewitness accounts of Svarūpa Dāmodara Gosvāmī, his constant companion during this period, clearly defy the investigative and descriptive abilities of modern psychologists and phenomenologists of religious experience.

The author of this great classic, Kṛṣṇadāsa Kavirāja Gosvāmī, born in the year 1507, was a disciple of Raghunātha dāsa Gosvāmī, a confidential follower of Caitanya Mahāprabhu. Raghunātha dāsa, a renowned ascetic saint, heard and memorized all the activities of Caitanya Mahāprabhu told to him by Svarūpa Dāmodara. After the passing away of Śrī Caitanya and Svarūpa Dāmodara, Raghunātha dāsa, unable to bear the pain of separation from these objects of his complete devotion, traveled to Vṛndāvana, intending to commit suicide by jumping from Govardhana Hill. In Vṛndāvana, however, he encountered Rūpa Gosvāmī and Sanātana Gosvāmī, the most confidential disciples of Caitanya Mahāprabhu. They convinced him to give up his plan of suicide and impelled him to reveal to them the spiritually inspiring events of Lord Caitanya's later life. Kṛṣṇadāsa Kavirāja Gosvāmī was also residing in Vṛndāvana at this time, and Raghunātha dāsa Gosvāmī endowed him with a full comprehension of the transcendental life of Śrī Caitanya.

By this time, several biographical works had already been written on the life of Śrī Caitanya by contemporary and near-contemporary scholars and devotees. These included *Śrī Caitanya-carita* by Murāri Gupta, *Caitanya-maṅgala* by Locana dāsa Ṭhākura and *Caitanya-bhāgavata.* This latter text, a work by Vṛndāvana dāsa Ṭhākura, who was then considered the principal authority on Śrī Caitanya's life, was highly revered. While composing his important work, Vṛndāvana dāsa, fearing that it would become too voluminous, avoided elaborately describing many of the events of Śrī Caitanya's life, particulary the later ones. Anxious to hear of these later pastimes, the devotees of Vṛndāvana requested Kṛṣṇadāsa Kavirāja Gosvāmī, whom they respected as a great saint, to compose a book to narrate these episodes in detail. Upon this request, and with the permission and blessings of the Madana-mohana Deity of Vṛndāvana, he began compiling *Śrī Caitanya-caritāmṛta,* which, due to its biographical excellence and thorough exposition of Lord Caitanya's profound philosophy and teachings, is regarded as the most significant of biographical works on Śrī Caitanya.

He commenced work on the text while in his late nineties and in failing health, as he vividly describes in the text itself: "I have now become too old and disturbed in invalidity. While writing, my hands tremble. I cannot remember anything, nor can I see or hear properly. Still I write, and this is a great wonder." That he nevertheless completed, under such debilitating conditions, the greatest literary gem of medieval India is surely one of the wonders of literary history.

This English translation and commentary is the work of His Divine Grace A. C. Bhaktivedanta Swami Prabhupāda, the world's most distinguished teacher of Indian religious and philosophical thought. His commentary is based upon two Bengali commentaries, one by his teacher Śrīla Bhaktisiddhānta Sarasvatī Gosvāmī, the eminent Vedic scholar who predicted, "The time will come when the people of the world will learn Bengali to read *Śrī Caitanya-caritāmṛta,*" and the other by Śrīla Bhaktisiddhānta's father, Bhaktivinoda Ṭhākura.

His Divine Grace A. C. Bhaktivedanta Swami Prabhupāda is himself a disciplic descendant of Śrī Caitanya Mahāprabhu, and he is the first scholar to execute systematic English translations of the major works of Śrī Caitanya's followers. His consummate Bengali and Sanskrit scholarship and intimate familiarity with the precepts of Śrī Kṛṣṇa Caitanya are a fitting combination that eminently qualifies him to present this important classic to the English-speaking world. The ease and clarity with which he expounds upon difficult philosophical concepts lures even a reader totally unfamiliar with Indian religious tradition into a genuine understanding and appreciation of this profound and monumental work.

The entire text, with commentary, presented in seventeen lavishly illustrated volumes by the Bhaktivedanta Book Trust, represents a contribution of major importance to the intellectual, cultural and spiritual life of contemporary man.

—The Publishers

*His Divine Grace*
A. C. Bhaktivedanta Swami Prabhupāda
*Founder-Ācārya of the International Society for Krishna Consciousness*

PLATE ONE

"As soon as Śrī Caitanya Mahāprabhu saw Sanātana Gosvāmī in the courtyard, He immediately went up to him with great haste. After embracing him, the Lord was overwhelmed with ecstatic love. As soon as Śrī Caitanya Mahāprabhu touched Sanātana Gosvāmī, Sanātana was also overwhelmed with ecstatic love. In a faltering voice, he said, 'O my Lord, do not touch me.' Shoulder to shoulder, Śrī Caitanya Mahāprabhu and Sanātana Gosvāmī began to cry unlimitedly. Candraśekhara was very astonished to see this." (*p.25*)

PLATE TWO

"Śrī Caitanya Mahāprabhu, the Supreme Personality of Godhead, personally told Sanātana Gosvāmī about Lord Kṛṣṇa's real identity. He also told him about the Lord's conjugal love, His personal opulence and the mellows of devotional service. All these truths were explained to Sanātana Gosvāmī by the Lord Himself out of His causeless mercy. Putting a straw in his mouth and bowing down, Sanātana Gosvāmī clasped the lotus feet of Śrī Caitanya Mahāprabhu and humbly spoke as follows. Sanātana Gosvāmī said, 'I was born in a low family, and my associates are all low-class men. I myself am fallen in the well of sinful materialism. I do not know what is beneficial for me and what is detrimental. Nonetheless, in ordinary dealings people consider me a learned scholar, and I am also thinking of myself as such. Out of Your causeless mercy, You have delivered me from the materialistic path. Now, by the same causeless mercy, please tell me what my duty is. Who am I? Why do the threefold miseries always give me trouble? If I do not know this, how can I be benefited? Actually, I do not know how to inquire about the goal of life and the process for obtaining it. Being merciful upon me, please explain all these truths.' " (*pp.48-51*)

PLATE THREE

"Kṛṣṇa is the original source of everything and the sum total of everything. He appears as the supreme youth, and His whole body is composed of spiritual bliss. He is the shelter and master of everyone. 'Kṛṣṇa, who is known as Govinda, is the supreme controller. He has an eternal, blissful, spiritual body. He is the origin of all. He has no other origin, for He is the prime cause of all causes.' 'The original Supreme Personality of Godhead is Kṛṣṇa. His original name is Govinda. He is full of all opulences, and His eternal abode is known as Goloka Vṛndāvana.' " (*pp.85-86*)

PLATE FOUR

"When Lord Kṛṣṇa took His birth, He appeared outside the womb as four-handed Viṣṇu. Then Devakī and Vasudeva offered their prayers to Him and asked Him to assume His two-armed form. The Lord immediately assumed His two-armed form and ordered that He be transferred to Gokula on the other side of the River Yamunā." (*p.99*)

PLATE FIVE

"The Lord is situated in all the universes in different forms just to please His devotees. Thus the Lord destroys irreligious principles and establishes religious principles. My dear Sanātana, just hear from Me as I tell you how the different *viṣṇu-mūrtis* hold Their weapons, beginning with the disc, and how They are named differently according to the placement of objects in Their hands. The procedure for counting begins with the lower right hand and goes to the upper right hand, the upper left hand, and the lower left hand. Lord Viṣṇu is named according to the order the objects are held in His hands." (*pp.122-123*)

PLATE SIX

"The first form of Lord Viṣṇu is called Mahā-Viṣṇu. He is the original creator of the total material energy. The innumerable universes emanate from the pores of His body. These universes are understood to be floating in air as the Mahā-Viṣṇu exhales. They are like atomic particles that float in sunshine and pass through the holes of a screen. All these universes are thus created by the exhalation of Mahā-Viṣṇu, and when Mahā-Viṣṇu inhales, they return to His body. The unlimited opulences of Mahā-Viṣṇu are completely beyond material conception.

After creating the total number of universes, which are unlimited, the Mahā-Viṣṇu expanded Himself into unlimited forms and entered into each of them. When Mahā-Viṣṇu entered each of the limitless universes, He saw that there was darkness all around and that there was no place to stay. He therefore began to consider the situation. With the perspiration produced from His own body, the Lord filled half the universe with water. He then lay down on that water on the bed of Lord Śeṣa. A lotus flower then sprouted from the lotus navel of that Garbhodakaśāyī Viṣṇu. That lotus flower became Lord Brahmā's birthplace. In the stem of that lotus flower the fourteen worlds were generated. Then He became Lord Brahmā and created the entire universe. In this way, the Supreme Personality of Godhead in His form of Viṣṇu maintains the entire material world. Since He is always beyond the material qualities, the material nature cannot touch Him." (*pp.157-162*)

PLATE SEVEN

"The third expansion of Viṣṇu is the Kṣīrodakaśāyī Viṣṇu, who is the incarnation of the quality of goodness. He is to be counted within the two types of incarnations (*puruṣa-avatāras* and *guṇa-avatāras*). This Kṣīrodakaśāyī Viṣṇu is the universal form of the Lord and is the Supersoul within every living entity. He is known as Kṣīrodakaśāyī, or the Lord who lies on the ocean of milk. He is the maintainer and master of the universe." (*p.165*)

PLATE EIGHT

"When Lord Kṛṣṇa was present in the earthly Vṛndāvana, Lord Brahmā, taking Him to be an ordinary cowherd boy, wanted to test His potency. Therefore Lord Brahmā stole all the cows, calves and cowherd boys from Kṛṣṇa and hid them by his illusory energy. When Kṛṣṇa saw that Brahmā had stolen His cows, calves and cowherd boys, He immediately created many material and spiritual planets in Lord Brahmā's presence. Within a moment, cows, cowherd boys, calves and unlimited Vaikuṇṭhas—all expansions of the Lord's spiritual energy—were manifested. The cowherd boys then became four-handed Nārāyaṇas, predominating Deities of the Vaikuṇṭha planets. All the separate Brahmās from different universes began to offer their prayers unto the Lord. All these transcendental bodies emanated from the body of Kṛṣṇa, and within a second They all entered again into His body. When the Lord Brahmā of this universe saw this pastime, he was astonished and struck with wonder." (*pp.241-245*)

PLATE NINE

"The primary predominating deities of this material creation are Lord Brahmā, Lord Śiva and Lord Viṣṇu. Nonetheless, they simply carry out the orders of Lord Kṛṣṇa, who is the master of them all. Following the will of the Supreme Personality of Godhead, Lord Brahmā creates, Lord Śiva destroys, and Kṛṣṇa Himself in the form of Kṣīrodakaśāyī Viṣṇu maintains all the affairs of material nature. Thus the supreme controller of material nature is Lord Viṣṇu." (*pp.251-252*)

PLATE TEN

"Upon hearing this, Śrī Kṛṣṇa smiled and immediately meditated. Unlimited Brahmās arrived instantly. These Brahmās had different numbers of heads. Some had ten heads, some had twenty, some a hundred, some a thousand, some ten thousand, some a hundred thousand, some ten million and others a hundred million. No one can count the number of faces they had. There also arrived many Lord Śivas with various heads numbering one hundred thousand and ten million. Many Indras also arrived, and they had hundreds of thousands of eyes all over their bodies. When the four-headed Brahmā of this universe saw all these opulences of Kṛṣṇa, he became very bewildered and considered himself a rabbit among many elephants. All the Brahmās who came to see Kṛṣṇa offered their respects at His lotus feet, and when they did this, their helmets touched His lotus feet. No one can estimate the inconceivable potency of Kṛṣṇa. All the Brahmās who were there were resting in the one body of Kṛṣṇa." (*pp.267-270*)

PLATE ELEVEN

"The sound of Kṛṣṇa's flute spreads in four directions. Even though Kṛṣṇa vibrates His flute within this universe, its sound pierces the universal covering and goes to the spiritual sky. Thus the vibration enters the ears of all inhabitants. It especially enters Goloka Vṛndāvana-dhāma and attracts the minds of the young damsels of Vrajabhūmi, bringing them forcibly to where Kṛṣṇa is present. The vibration of Kṛṣṇa's flute is very aggressive, and it breaks the vows of all chaste women. Indeed, its vibration takes them forcibly from the laps of their husbands. The vibration of His flute attracts even the goddesses of fortune in the Vaikuṇṭha planets, to say nothing of the poor damsels of Vṛndāvana. The vibration of His flute is just like a bird that creates a nest within the ears of the *gopīs* and always remains prominent there, not allowing any other sound to enter their ears. Indeed, the *gopīs* cannot hear anything else, nor are they able to concentrate on anything else, nor even give a suitable reply. Such are the effects of the vibration of Lord Kṛṣṇa's flute." (*pp.142-143*)

CHAPTER 20

# Lord Śrī Caitanya Mahāprabhu Instructs Sanātana Gosvāmī in the Science of the Absolute Truth

The following summary study of this chapter is given by Bhaktivinoda Ṭhākura in his *Amṛta-pravāha-bhāṣya.* When Śrīla Sanātana Gosvāmī was imprisoned by Nawab Hussain Shah, he received news from Rūpa Gosvāmī that Śrī Caitanya Mahāprabhu had gone to Mathurā. Sanātana Gosvāmī thereafter satisfied the superintendent of the jail by sweet solicitations and bribery. After giving the jailer seven thousand gold coins, Sanātana Gosvāmī was released. He then crossed the Ganges and fled. One of his servants, Īśāna, followed him, carrying eight gold coins. Sanātana Gosvāmī and his servant then spent the night in a small hotel on the way to Benares. The hotel owner knew that Sanātana Gosvāmī and his servant had eight gold coins, and he decided to kill them and take the money. Making plans in this way, the hotel owner received them as honorable guests. Sanātana Gosvāmī, however, asked his servant how much money he had, and, taking seven of the gold coins, Sanātana offered them to the hotel owner. Thus the owner helped them reach the hilly tract toward Vārāṇasī. On the way, Sanātana Gosvāmī met his brother-in-law, Śrīkānta, at Hājipura, and Śrīkānta helped him after he had heard about all Sanātana's troubles. Thus Sanātana Gosvāmī finally arrived at Vārāṇasī and stood before the door of Candraśekhara. Caitanya Mahāprabhu called him in and ordered him to change his dress so that he could look like a gentleman. For his garment, he used an old cloth of Tapana Miśra's. Later, he exchanged his valuable blanket for a torn quilt. At this time Caitanya Mahāprabhu was very pleased with him, and thus Śrī Sanātana Gosvāmī received knowledge of the Absolute Truth from the Lord Himself.

First they discussed the constitutional position of the living entities, and Śrī Caitanya Mahāprabhu explained to Sanātana Gosvāmī how the living entity is one of Lord Kṛṣṇa's energies. After this, the Lord explained the way of devotional service. While discussing the Absolute Truth, Śrī Kṛṣṇa, the Lord analyzed Brahman, Paramātmā and Bhagavān, as well as the expansions of the Lord called *svayaṁ-rūpa, tad-ekātma* and *āveśa,* which are divided into various branches known as *vaibhava* and *prābhava.* Thus the Lord described the many forms of the Supreme Personality of Godhead. He also described the incarnations of God within the material world, incarnations such as the *puruṣa-avatāras, manvantara-avatāras, guṇa-avatāras* and *saktyāveśa-avatāras.* The Lord also discussed the divisions of Kṛṣṇa's different ages, such as *bālya* and *paugaṇḍa,* and the different pastimes of the different ages. He explained how Kṛṣṇa attained His permanent form when He reached youth. In this way Śrī Caitanya Mahāprabhu explained and described everything to Sanātana Gosvāmī.

### TEXT 1

বন্দেঽনন্তাদ্ভুতৈশ্বর্যং শ্রীচৈতন্যমহাপ্রভুম্ ।
নীচোঽপি যৎপ্রসাদাৎ স্যাদ্ভক্তিশাস্ত্রপ্রবর্তকঃ ॥ ১ ॥

*vande 'nantādbhutaiśvaryaṁ*
*śrī-caitanya-mahāprabhum*
*nīco 'pi yat-prasādāt syād*
*bhakti-śāstra-pravartakaḥ*

### SYNONYMS

*vande*—I offer my respectful obeisances; *ananta*—unlimited; *adbhuta*—wonderful; *aiśvaryam*—possessing opulences; *śrī-caitanya-mahāprabhum*—unto Śrī Caitanya Mahāprabhu; *nīcaḥ api*—even a person in the lowest status of life; *yat-prasādāt*—by whose mercy; *syāt*—may become; *bhakti-śāstra*—of the science of devotional service; *pravartakaḥ*—an inaugurator.

### TRANSLATION

**Let me offer my respectful obeisances unto Śrī Caitanya Mahāprabhu, who has unlimited, wonderful opulences. By His mercy, even a person born as the lowest of men can spread the science of devotional service.**

### TEXT 2

জয় জয় শ্রীচৈতন্য জয় নিত্যানন্দ ।
জয়াদ্বৈতচন্দ্র জয় গৌরভক্তবৃন্দ ॥ ২ ॥

*jaya jaya śrī-caitanya jaya nityānanda*
*jayādvaita-candra jaya gaura-bhakta-vṛnda*

### SYNONYMS

*jaya jaya*—all glories; *śrī-caitanya*—to Lord Śrī Caitanya Mahāprabhu; *jaya*—all glories; *nityānanda*—to Nityānanda; *jaya*—all glories; *advaita-candra*—to Advaita Ācārya; *jaya*—all glories; *gaura-bhakta-vṛnda*—to all devotees of Lord Śrī Caitanya Mahāprabhu.

### TRANSLATION

**All glories to Śrī Caitanya Mahāprabhu! All glories to Nityānanda Prabhu! All glories to Advaita Ācārya! And all glories to all the devotees of Śrī Caitanya Mahāprabhu!**

### TEXT 3

এথা গৌড়ে সনাতন আছে বন্দিশালে ।
শ্রীরূপ-গোসাঞীর পত্রী আইল হেনকালে ॥ ৩ ॥

*ethā gauḍe sanātana āche bandi-śāle*
*śrī-rūpa-gosāñīra patrī āila hena-kāle*

### SYNONYMS

*ethā*—here; *gauḍe*—in Bengal; *sanātana*—Sanātana Gosvāmī; *āche*—was; *bandi-śāle*—in prison; *śrī-rūpa-gosāñīra*—of Śrīla Rūpa Gosvāmī; *patrī*—the letter; *āila*—came; *hena-kāle*—at that time.

### TRANSLATION

**While Sanātana Gosvāmī was imprisoned in Bengal, a letter arrived from Śrīla Rūpa Gosvāmī.**

### PURPORT

Śrīla Bhaktivinoda Ṭhākura informs us that this letter from Rūpa Gosvāmī to Sanātana Gosvāmī is mentioned by the annotator of *Udbhaṭa-candrikā*. Śrīla Rūpa Gosvāmī wrote a note to Sanātana Gosvāmī from Bāklā. This note indicated that Śrī Caitanya Mahāprabhu was coming to Mathurā, and it stated:

*yadu-pateḥ kva gatā mathurā-purī*
*raghu-pateḥ kva gatottara-kośalā*
*iti vicintya kurusva manaḥ sthiraṁ*
*na sad idaṁ jagad ity avadhāraya*

"Where has the Mathurā Purī of Yadupati gone? Where has the northern Kośalā of Raghupati gone? By reflection, make the mind steady, thinking, 'This universe is not eternal.' "

### TEXT 4

পত্রী পাঞা সনাতন আনন্দিত হৈলা ।
যবন-রক্ষক-পাশ কহিতে লাগিলা ॥ ৪ ॥

*patrī pāñā sanātana ānandita hailā*
*yavana-rakṣaka-pāśa kahite lāgilā*

## SYNONYMS

*patrī pāñā*—receiving the note; *sanātana*—Sanātana Gosvāmī; *ānandita hailā*—became very pleased; *yavana*—meat-eater; *rakṣaka*—the superintendent of the jail; *pāśa*—before; *kahite lāgilā*—began to say.

## TRANSLATION

**When Sanātana Gosvāmī received this note from Rūpa Gosvāmī, he became very pleased. He immediately went to the jail superintendent, who was a meat-eater, and spoke as follows.**

## TEXT 5

**"তুমি এক জিন্দাপীর মহাভাগ্যবান্‌।**
**কেতাব-কোরাণ-শাস্ত্রে আছে তোমার জ্ঞান ॥ ৫ ॥**

*"tumi eka jindā-pīra mahā-bhāgyavān*
*ketāba-korāṇa-śāstre āche tomāra jñāna*

## SYNONYMS

*tumi*—you; *eka jindā-pīra*—a living saint; *mahā-bhāgyavān*—very fortunate; *ketāba*—books; *korāṇa*—the Koran; *śāstre*—in the scripture; *āche*—there is; *tomāra*—your; *jñāna*—knowledge.

## TRANSLATION

**Sanātana Gosvāmī told the Mohammedan jailkeeper, "Dear sir, you are a saintly person and are very fortunate. You have full knowledge of the revealed scriptures such as the Koran and similar books.**

## TEXT 6

**এক বন্দী ছাড়ে যদি নিজ-ধর্ম দেখিয়া।**
**সংসার হইতে তারে মুক্ত করেন গোসাঞা ॥ ৬ ॥**

*eka bandī chāḍe yadi nija-dharma dekhiyā*
*saṁsāra ha-ite tāre mukta karena gosāñā*

## SYNONYMS

*eka bandī*—one imprisoned person; *chāḍe*—one releases; *yadi*—if; *nija-dharma*—one's own religion; *dekhiyā*—consulting; *saṁsāra ha-ite*—from material bondage; *tāre*—him; *mukta karena*—releases; *gosāñā*—the Supreme Personality of Godhead.

### TRANSLATION

**"If one releases a conditioned soul or imprisoned person according to religious principles, he himself is also released from material bondage by the Supreme Personality of Godhead."**

### PURPORT

It appears from this statement that Sanātana Gosvāmī, who was formerly a minister of the Nawab, was trying to cheat the Mohammedan superintendent. A jail superintendent had only an ordinary education, or practically no education, and he was certainly not supposed to be very advanced in spiritual knowledge. However, just to satisfy him, Sanātana Gosvāmī praised him as a very learned scholar of the scriptures. The jailkeeper could not deny that he was a learned scholar because when one is elevated to an exalted position, one thinks oneself fit for that position. Sanātana Gosvāmī was correctly explaining the effects of spiritual activity, and the jailkeeper connected his statement with his release from jail. There are innumerable conditioned souls rotting in the material world, imprisoned by *māyā* under the spell of sense gratification. The living entity is so entranced by the spell of *māyā* that in conditioned life even a pig feels satisfied.

There are two kinds of covering powers exhibited by *māyā*. One is called *prakṣepātmikā,* and the other is called *āvaraṇātmikā.* When one is determined to get out of material bondage, the *prakṣepātmikā-śakti,* the spell of diversion, impels one to remain in conditioned life fully satisfied by sense gratification. Due to the other power (*āvaraṇātmikā*), a conditioned soul feels satisfied even if he is rotting in the body of a pig or a worm in stool. To release a conditioned soul from material bondage is very difficult because the spell of *māyā* is so strong. Even when the Supreme Personality of Godhead Himself descends to deliver conditioned souls, asking them to surrender unto Him, the conditioned souls do not agree to the Lord's proposals. Therefore Śrī Sanātana Gosvāmī said, "Somehow or other, if one helps another gain release from the bondage of *māyā,* he is certainly recognized immediately by the Supreme Personality of Godhead." As stated in *Bhagavad-gītā* (18.69):

*na ca tasmān manuṣyeṣu*
*kaścin me priya-kṛttamaḥ*
*bhavitā na ca me tasmād*
*anyaḥ priyataro bhuvi*

The greatest service one can render to the Lord is to try to infuse devotional service into the heart of the conditioned soul so that the conditioned soul may be released from conditional life. Śrīla Bhaktivinoda Ṭhākura has said that a Vaiṣṇava is recognized by his preaching work—that is, by convincing the conditioned soul about his eternal position, which is explained here as *nija-dharma*. It is the living entity's eternal position to serve the Lord; therefore to help one get release from material bondage is to awaken one to the dormant understanding that he is the eternal servant of Kṛṣṇa. *Jīvera 'svarūpa' haya——kṛṣṇera 'nitya-dāsa'*. This will be further explained by the Lord Himself to Sanātana Gosvāmī.

### TEXT 7

পূর্বে আমি তোমার করিয়াছি উপকার ।
তুমি আমা ছাড়ি' কর প্রত্যুপকার ॥ ৭ ॥

*pūrve āmi tomāra kariyāchi upakāra*
*tumi āmā chāḍi' kara pratyupakāra*

### SYNONYMS

*pūrve*—formerly; *āmi*—I; *tomāra*—your; *kariyāchi*—have done; *upakāra*—welfare; *tumi*—you; *āmā*—me; *chāḍi'*—releasing; *kara*—do; *prati-upakāra*—return welfare.

### TRANSLATION

**Sanātana Gosvāmī continued, "Previously I have done much for you. Now I am in difficulty. Please return my goodwill by releasing me.**

### TEXT 8

পাঁচ সহস্র মুদ্রা তুমি কর অঙ্গীকার ।
পুণ্য, অর্থ,—দুই লাভ হইবে তোমার ॥" ৮ ॥

*pāñca sahasra mudrā tumi kara aṅgīkāra*
*puṇya, artha,——dui lābha ha-ibe tomāra"*

### SYNONYMS

*pāñca sahasra*—five thousand; *mudrā*—golden coins; *tumi*—you; *kara aṅgīkāra*—please accept; *puṇya*—pious activity; *artha*—material gain; *dui lābha*—two kinds of achievement; *ha-ibe*—will be; *tomāra*—yours.

### TRANSLATION

**"Here are five thousand gold coins. Please accept them. By releasing me, you will receive the results of pious activities and gain material profit as well. Thus you will profit in two ways simultaneously."**

### TEXT 9

তবে সেই যবন কহে,—"শুন, মহাশয়।
তোমারে ছাড়িব, কিন্তু করি রাজভয়॥" ৯ ॥

*tabe sei yavana kahe,——"śuna, mahāśaya*
*tomāre chāḍiba, kintu kari rāja-bhaya"*

### SYNONYMS

*tabe*—thereafter; *sei*—that; *yavana*—meat-eater; *kahe*—says; *śuna*—just hear; *mahāśaya*—my dear sir; *tomāre*—you; *chāḍiba*—I would release; *kintu*—but; *kari rāja-bhaya*—I am afraid of the government.

### TRANSLATION

**In this way Sanātana Gosvāmī convinced the jailkeeper, who replied, "Please hear me, my dear sir. I am willing to release you, but I am afraid of the government."**

### TEXTS 10-11

সনাতন কহে,—"তুমি না কর রাজ-ভয়।
দক্ষিণ গিয়াছে যদি লেউটি' আওয়য়॥ ১০ ॥
তাঁহারে কহিও - সেই বাহ্যকৃত্যে গেল।
গঙ্গার নিকট গঙ্গা দেখি' ঝাঁপ দিল॥ ১১ ॥

*sanātana kahe,——"tumi nā kara rāja-bhaya*
*dakṣiṇa giyāche yadi leuṭi' āoyaya*

*tāṅhāre kahio——sei bāhya-kṛtye gela*
*gaṅgāra nikaṭa gaṅgā dekhi' jhāṅpa dila*

### SYNONYMS

*sanātana kahe*—Sanātana replied; *tumi*—you; *nā*—not; *kara*—do; *rāja-bhaya*—fear of the government; *dakṣiṇa*—to the south; *giyāche*—has gone; *yadi*—if; *leuṭi'*—returning; *āoyaya*—comes; *tāṅhāre*—to him; *kahio*—you say; *sei*—he; *bāhya-kṛtye*—to evacuate; *gela*—went; *gaṅgāra nikaṭa*—near the bank of the Ganges; *gaṅgā dekhi'*—seeing the Ganges; *jhāṅpa dila*—jumped.

### TRANSLATION

**Sanātana replied, "There is no danger. The Nawab has gone to the south. If he returns, tell him that Sanātana went to pass stool near the bank of the Ganges and that as soon as he saw the Ganges, he jumped in.**

## TEXT 12

অনেক দেখিল, তার লাগ্ না পাইল।
দাড়ুকা-সহিত ডুবি কাহাঁ বহি' গেল ॥ ১২ ॥

*aneka dekhila, tāra lāg nā pāila*
*dāḍukā-sahita ḍubi kāhāṅ vahi' gela*

### SYNONYMS

*aneka*—for a long time; *dekhila*—I looked; *tāra*—of him; *lāg*—contact; *nā pāila*—could not obtain; *dāḍukā-sahita*—with the shackles; *ḍubi*—drowning; *kāhāṅ*—somewhere; *vahi' gela*—washed away.

### TRANSLATION

**"Tell him, 'I looked for him a long time, but I could not find any trace of him. He jumped in with his shackles, and therefore he was drowned and washed away by the waves.'**

## TEXT 13

কিছু ভয় নাহি, আমি এ-দেশে না রব।
দরবেশ হঞা আমি মক্কাকে যাইব ॥" ১৩ ॥

*kichu bhaya nāhi, āmi e-deśe nā raba*
*daraveśa hañā āmi makkāke yāiba"*

### SYNONYMS

*kichu*—any; *bhaya*—fear; *nāhi*—there is not; *āmi*—I; *e-deśe*—in this country; *nā raba*—shall not remain; *daraveśa hañā*—becoming a mendicant; *āmi*—I; *makkāke yāiba*—shall go to Mecca.

### TRANSLATION

**"There is no reason for you to be afraid, for I shall not remain in this country. I shall become a mendicant and go to the holy city of Mecca."**

## TEXT 14

তথাপি যবন-মন প্রসন্ন না দেখিলা।
সাত-হাজার মুদ্রা তার আগে রাশি কৈলা ॥ ১৪ ॥

*tathāpi yavana-mana prasanna nā dekhilā*
*sāta-hājāra mudrā tāra āge rāśi kailā*

### SYNONYMS

*tathāpi*—still; *yavana-mana*—the mind of the meat-eater; *prasanna*—satisfied; *nā*—not; *dekhilā*—he saw; *sāta-hājāra*—seven thousand; *mudrā*—golden coins; *tāra*—of him; *āge*—in front; *rāśi kailā*—made a stack.

### TRANSLATION

**Sanātana Gosvāmī could see that the mind of the meat-eater was still not satisfied. He then stacked seven thousand gold coins before him.**

### TEXT 15

লোভ হইল যবনের মুদ্রা দেখিয়া।
রাত্রে গঙ্গাপার কৈল দাড়ুকা কাটিয়া ॥ ১৫ ॥

*lobha ha-ila yavanera mudrā dekhiyā*
*rātre gaṅgā-pāra kaila dāḍukā kāṭiyā*

### SYNONYMS

*lobha ha-ila*—there was attraction for the money; *yavanera*—of the meat-eater; *mudrā dekhiyā*—seeing the golden coins; *rātre*—at night; *gaṅgā-pāra kaila*—he got him across the Ganges; *dāḍukā*—shackles; *kāṭiyā*—breaking.

### TRANSLATION

**When the meat-eater saw the coins, he was attracted to them. He then agreed, and that night he cut Sanātana's shackles and let him cross the Ganges.**

### TEXT 16

গড়দ্বার-পথ ছাড়িলা, নারে তাহাঁ যাইতে।
রাত্রি-দিন চলি' আইলা পাতড়া-পর্বতে ॥ ১৬ ॥

*gaḍa-dvāra-patha chāḍilā, nāre tāhāṅ yāite*
*rātri-dina cali' āilā pātaḍā-parvate*

### SYNONYMS

*gaḍa-dvāra-patha*—the path of the fortress; *chāḍilā*—gave up; *nāre*—not able; *tāhāṅ*—there; *yāite*—to go; *rātri-dina*—night and day; *cali'*—walking; *āilā*—arrived; *pātaḍā-parvate*—in the hilly tract of land known as Pātaḍā.

### TRANSLATION

**In this way, Sanātana Gosvāmī was released. However, he was not able to walk along the path of the fortress. Walking day and night, he finally arrived at the hilly tract of land known as Pātaḍā.**

### TEXT 17

তথা এক ভৌমিক হয়, তার ঠাঞি গেলা ।
'পর্বত পার কর আমা'—বিনতি করিলা ॥ ১৭ ॥

*tathā eka bhaumika haya, tāra ṭhāñi gelā*
*'parvata pāra kara āmā'——vinati karilā*

### SYNONYMS

*tathā*—there; *eka bhaumika*—one landowner; *haya*—there is; *tāra ṭhāñi*—unto him; *gelā*—he went; *parvata*—the hilly tract; *pāra kara*—cross over; *āmā*—me; *vinati*—submission; *karilā*—he made.

### TRANSLATION

**After reaching Pātaḍā, he met a landholder and submissively requested him to get him across that hilly tract of land.**

### TEXT 18

সেই ভূঞার সঙ্গে হয় হাতগণিতা ।
ভূঞার কাণে কহে সেই জানি' এই কথা ॥ ১৮ ॥

*sei bhūñāra saṅge haya hāta-gaṇitā*
*bhūñāra kāṇe kahe sei jāni' ei kathā*

### SYNONYMS

*sei bhūñāra*—the landlord; *saṅge*—with; *haya*—there is; *hāta-gaṇitā*—an expert in palmistry; *bhūñāra*—of the landlord; *kāṇe*—in the ear; *kahe*—says; *sei*—that man; *jāni'*—knowing; *ei kathā*—this statement.

### TRANSLATION

**A man who was expert in palmistry was at that time staying with the landlord. Knowing about Sanātana, he whispered the following in the landlord's ear.**

### TEXT 19

'ইঁহার ঠাঞি সুবর্ণের অষ্ট মোহর হয়'।
শুনি' আনন্দিত ভূঞা সনাতনে কয়॥ ১৯॥

*'iṅhāra ṭhāñi suvarṇera aṣṭa mohara haya'*
*śuni' ānandita bhūñā sanātane kaya*

### SYNONYMS

*iṅhāra ṭhāñi*—in the possession of this man; *suvarṇera*—of gold; *aṣṭa*—eight; *mohara*—coins; *haya*—there are; *śuni'*—hearing; *ānandita*—pleased; *bhūñā*—the landlord; *sanātane*—to Sanātana; *kaya*—says.

### TRANSLATION

**The palmist said, "This man Sanātana possesses eight gold coins." Hearing this, the landlord was very pleased and spoke the following to Sanātana Gosvāmī.**

### TEXT 20

"রাত্র্যে পর্বত পার করিব নিজ-লোক দিয়া।
ভোজন করহ তুমি রন্ধন করিয়া॥" ২০॥

*"rātrye parvata pāra kariba nija-loka diyā*
*bhojana karaha tumi randhana kariyā"*

### SYNONYMS

*rātrye*—at night; *parvata*—the hilly tract; *pāra kariba*—I shall cross; *nija-loka diyā*—with my own men; *bhojana karaha*—just take your meal; *tumi*—you; *randhana kariyā*—cooking.

### TRANSLATION

**The landlord said, "I shall get you across that hilly tract at night with my own men. Now just take your lunch and cook for yourself."**

### TEXT 21

এত বলি' অন্ন দিল করিয়া সম্মান।
সনাতন আসি' তবে কৈল নদীস্নান॥ ২১॥

*eta bali' anna dila kariyā sammāna*
*sanātana āsi' tabe kaila nadī-snāna*

### SYNONYMS

*eta bali'*—saying this; *anna dila*—supplied food grains; *kariyā sammāna*—showing great respect; *sanātana*—Sanātana Gosvāmī; *āsi'*—coming; *tabe*—then; *kaila*—did; *nadī-snāna*—bathing in the river.

### TRANSLATION

**Saying this, the landlord offered Sanātana grains to cook. Sanātana then went to the riverside and took his bath.**

### TEXT 22

দুই উপবাসে কৈলা রন্ধন-ভোজনে ।
রাজমন্ত্রী সনাতন বিচারিলা মনে ॥ ২২ ॥

*dui upavāse kailā randhana-bhojane*
*rāja-mantrī sanātana vicārilā mane*

### SYNONYMS

*dui upavāse*—fasting for two days; *kailā*—performed; *randhana-bhojane*—cooking and eating; *rāja-mantrī*—the former minister of the Nawab; *sanātana*—Sanātana; *vicārilā*—considered; *mane*—in the mind.

### TRANSLATION

**Because Sanātana had been fasting for two days, he cooked the food and ate it. However, having formerly been a minister of the Nawab, he began to contemplate the situation.**

### TEXT 23

'এই ভূঞা কেনে মোরে সন্মান করিল ?'
এত চিন্তি' সনাতন ঈশানে পুছিল ॥ ২৩ ॥

*'ei bhūñā kene more sammāna karila?'*
*eta cinti' sanātana īśāne puchila*

### SYNONYMS

*ei bhūñā*—this landlord; *kene*—why; *more*—unto me; *sammāna karila*—offered so much respect; *eta cinti'*—thinking this; *sanātana*—Sanātana; *īśāne*—from Īśāna, his servant; *puchila*—inquired.

### TRANSLATION

**As a former minister for the Nawab, Sanātana could certainly understand diplomacy. He therefore thought, "Why is this landlord offering me such respect?" Thinking in this way, he questioned his servant, whose name was Īśāna.**

### TEXT 24

‘তোমার ঠাঞি জানি কিছু দ্রব্য আছয়’ ।
ঈশান কহে,—‘মোর ঠাঞি সাত মোহর হয়’ ॥২৪॥

*'tomāra ṭhāñi jāni kichu dravya āchaya'*
*īśāna kahe,——'mora ṭhāñi sāta mohara haya'*

### SYNONYMS

*tomāra ṭhāñi*—in your possession; *jāni*—I understand; *kichu*—some; *dravya*—valuable thing; *āchaya*—there is; *īśāna kahe*—Īśāna replied; *mora ṭhāñi*—in my possession; *sāta mohara*—seven gold coins; *haya*—there are.

### TRANSLATION

**Sanātana asked his servant, "Īśāna, I think you have some valuable things with you." Īśāna replied, "Yes, I have seven gold coins."**

### TEXT 25

শুনি’ সনাতন তারে করিলা ভর্ৎসন ।
‘সঙ্গে কেনে আনিয়াছ এই কাল-যম ?’ ২৫ ॥

*śuni' sanātana tāre karilā bhartsana*
*'saṅge kene āniyācha ei kāla-yama?'*

### SYNONYMS

*śuni'*—hearing; *sanātana*—Sanātana Gosvāmī; *tāre*—him; *karilā bhartsana*—chastised; *saṅge*—with you; *kene*—why; *āniyācha*—have you brought; *ei*—this; *kāla-yama*—death knell.

### TRANSLATION

**Hearing this, Sanātana Gosvāmī chastised his servant, saying, "Why have you brought this death knell with you?"**

### TEXT 26

তবে সেই সাত মোহর হস্তেতে করিয়া।
ভূঞার কাছে যাঞা কহে মোহর ধরিয়া ॥ ২৬ ॥

*tabe sei sāta mohara hastete kariyā*
*bhūñāra kāche yāñā kahe mohara dhariyā*

### SYNONYMS

*tabe*—thereafter; *sei sāta mohara*—these seven golden coins; *hastete kariyā*—taking in the hands; *bhūñāra kāche*—to the landlord; *yāñā*—going; *kahe*—says; *mohara dhariyā*—holding the golden coins.

### TRANSLATION

**Thereupon, Sanātana Gosvāmī took the seven gold coins in his hands and went to the landlord. Holding the gold coins before him, he spoke as follows.**

### TEXT 27

"এই সাত সুবর্ণ মোহর আছিল আমার।
ইহা লঞা ধর্ম দেখি' পর্বত কর পার ॥ ২৭ ॥

*"ei sāta suvarṇa mohara āchila āmāra*
*ihā lañā dharma dekhi' parvata kara pāra*

### SYNONYMS

*ei sāta*—these seven; *suvarṇa mohara*—golden coins; *āchila*—were; *āmāra*—mine; *ihā lañā*—accepting them; *dharma dekhi'*—observing religious principles; *parvata*—the hilly tract of land; *kara pāra*—kindly get me across.

### TRANSLATION

**"I have these seven gold coins with me. Please accept them, and from a religious point of view please get me across that hilly tract of land.**

### TEXT 28

রাজবন্দী আমি, গড়দ্বার যাইতে না পারি।
পুণ্য হবে, পর্বত আমা দেহ' পার করি ॥" ২৮ ॥

*rāja-bandī āmi, gaḍa-dvāra yāite nā pāri*
*puṇya habe, parvata āmā deha' pāra kari"*

### SYNONYMS

*rāja-bandī*—a prisoner of the government; *āmi*—I; *gaḍa-dvāra yāite*—to go openly on the road by the ramparts; *nā pāri*—I am not able; *puṇya*—pious activity; *habe*—there will be; *parvata*—the hilly tract of land; *āmā*—to me; *deha'*—give help; *pāra kari*—by crossing over.

### TRANSLATION

**"I am a prisoner of the government, and I cannot go along the way of the ramparts. It will be very pious of you to take this money and kindly get me across this hilly tract of land."**

## TEXT 29

ভূঞা হাসি' কহে,—"আমি জানিয়াছি পহিলে।
অষ্ট মোহর হয় তোমার সেবক-আঁচলে ॥ ২৯ ॥

*bhūñā hāsi' kahe,—"āmi jāniyāchi pahile*
*aṣṭa mohara haya tomāra sevaka-āṅcale*

### SYNONYMS

*bhūñā*—the landlord; *hāsi'*—smiling; *kahe*—said; *āmi*—I; *jāniyāchi*—knew; *pahile*—before this; *aṣṭa mohara*—eight golden coins; *haya*—there are; *tomāra*—your; *sevaka-āṅcale*—in the pocket of the servant.

### TRANSLATION

**Smiling, the landlord said, "Before you offered them, I already knew that there were eight gold coins in your servant's possession.**

## TEXT 30

তোমা মারি' মোহর লইতাম আজিকার রাত্র্যে।
ভাল হৈল, কহিলা তুমি, ছুটিলাঙ পাপ হৈতে ॥৩০॥

*tomā māri' mohara la-itāma ājikāra rātrye*
*bhāla haila, kahilā tumi, chuṭilāṅa pāpa haite*

### SYNONYMS

*tomā māri'*—killing you; *mohara*—golden coins; *la-itāma*—I would have taken; *ājikāra rātrye*—on this night; *bhāla haila*—it was very good; *kahilā tumi*—you have spoken; *chuṭilāṅa*—I am relieved; *pāpa haite*—from such a sin.

### TRANSLATION

**"On this very night I would have killed you and taken your coins. It is very good that you have voluntarily offered them to me. I am now relieved from such a sinful activity.**

### TEXT 31

সন্তুষ্ট হইলাঙ আমি, মোহর না লইব ।
পুণ্য লাগি' পর্বত তোমা' পার করি' দিব ॥" ৩১ ॥

*santuṣṭa ha-ilāṅa āmi, mohara nā la-iba*
*puṇya lāgi' parvata tomā' pāra kari' diba"*

### SYNONYMS

*santuṣṭa*—satisfied; *ha-ilāṅa*—have become; *āmi*—I; *mohara*—the golden coins; *nā la-iba*—I shall not take; *puṇya lāgi'*—simply for pious activity; *parvata*—the hilly tract of land; *tomā'*—you; *pāra kari' diba*—I shall get across.

### TRANSLATION

**"I am very satisfied with your behavior. I shall not accept these gold coins, but I shall get you across that hilly tract of land simply to perform a pious activity."**

### TEXT 32

গোসাঞি কহে,— "কেহ দ্রব্য লইবে আমা মারি' ।
আমার প্রাণ রক্ষা কর দ্রব্য অঙ্গীকরি' ॥" ৩২ ॥

*gosāñi kahe,——"keha dravya la-ibe āmā māri'*
*āmāra prāṇa rakṣā kara dravya aṅgīkari' "*

### SYNONYMS

*gosāñi kahe*—Sanātana Gosvāmī said; *keha*—someone else; *dravya*—the valuable coins; *la-ibe*—will take; *āmā māri'*—killing me; *āmāra*—my; *prāṇa*—life; *rakṣā kara*—save; *dravya aṅgīkari'*—by accepting these coins.

### TRANSLATION

**Sanātana Gosvāmī replied, "If you do not accept these coins, someone else will kill me for them. It is better that you save me from the danger by accepting the coins."**

### TEXT 33

তবে ভুঞা গোসাঞির সঙ্গে চারি পাইক দিল।
রাত্র্যে রাত্র্যে বনপথে পর্বত পার কৈল ॥ ৩৩ ॥

*tabe bhūñā gosāñira saṅge cāri pāika dila*
*rātrye rātrye vana-pathe parvata pāra kaila*

### SYNONYMS

*tabe*—thereupon; *bhūñā*—the landlord; *gosāñira saṅge*—with Sanātana Gosvāmī; *cāri pāika*—four watchmen; *dila*—gave; *rātrye rātrye*—during the whole night; *vana-pathe*—on the jungle path; *parvata*—the hilly tract of land; *pāra kaila*—took him across.

### TRANSLATION

**After this settlement was made, the landlord gave Sanātana Gosvāmī four watchmen to accompany him. They went through the forest path for the whole night and thus brought him over the hilly tract of land.**

### TEXT 34

তবে পার হঞা গোসাঞি পুছিলা ঈশানে।
"জানি,—শেষ দ্রব্য কিছু আছে তোমা স্থানে" ॥৩৪॥

*tabe pāra hañā gosāñi puchilā īśāne*
*"jāni,——śeṣa dravya kichu āche tomā sthāne"*

### SYNONYMS

*tabe*—thereafter; *pāra hañā*—after crossing; *gosāñi*—Sanātana Gosvāmī; *puchilā*—asked; *īśāne*—Īśāna; *jāni*—I know; *śeṣa dravya*—something valuable left; *kichu*—some; *āche*—there is; *tomā sthāne*—with you.

### TRANSLATION

**After crossing the hills, Sanātana Gosvāmī told his servant, "Īśāna, I think you still have some balance left from the gold coins."**

### TEXT 35

ঈশান কহে,—"এক মোহর আছে অবশেষ।"
গোসাঞি কহে,—"মোহর লঞা যাহ' তুমি দেশ॥"

*īśāna kahe,——"eka mohara āche avaśeṣa"*
*gosāñi kahe,——"mohara lañā yāha' tumi deśa"*

### SYNONYMS

*īśāna kahe*—Īśāna replied; *eka*—one; *mohara*—gold coin; *āche*—is; *avaśeṣa*—left; *gosāñi*—Sanātana Gosvāmī; *kahe*—replied; *mohara lañā*—taking this gold coin; *yāha*—return; *tumi*—you; *deśa*—to your country.

### TRANSLATION

**Īśāna replied, "I still have one gold coin in my possession." Sanātana Gosvāmī then said, "Take the coin and return to your home."**

## TEXT 36

তারে বিদায় দিয়া গোসাঞি চলিলা একলা ।
হাতে করোঁয়া, ছিঁড়া কান্থা, নির্ভয় হইলা ॥ ৩৬ ॥

*tāre vidāya diyā gosāñi calilā ekalā*
*hāte karoṅyā, chiṅḍā kānthā, nirbhaya ha-ilā*

### SYNONYMS

*tāre vidāya diyā*—bidding him farewell; *gosāñi*—Sanātana Gosvāmī; *calilā ekalā*—began to travel alone; *hāte*—in the hand; *karoṅyā*—a beggar's pot; *chiṅḍā kānthā*—a torn quilt; *nirbhaya ha-ilā*—he became free from all anxiety.

### TRANSLATION

**After departing from Īśāna, Sanātana Gosvāmī began traveling alone with a waterpot in his hand. Simply covered with a torn quilt, he thus lost all his anxiety.**

## TEXT 37

চলি' চলি' গোসাঞি তবে আইলা হাজিপুরে ।
সন্ধ্যাকালে বসিলা এক উদ্যান-ভিতরে ॥ ৩৭ ॥

*cali' cali' gosāñi tabe āilā hājipure*
*sandhyā-kāle vasilā eka udyāna-bhitare*

### SYNONYMS

*cali' cali'*—walking and walking; *gosāñi*—Sanātana Gosvāmī; *tabe*—then; *āilā*—arrived; *hājipure*—at Hājipura; *sandhyā-kāle*—in the evening; *vasilā*—sat down; *eka*—one; *udyāna-bhitare*—within a garden.

### TRANSLATION

**Walking and walking, Sanātana Gosvāmī finally arrived at a place called Hājipura. That evening he sat down within a garden.**

### TEXT 38

সেই হাজিপুরে রহে—শ্রীকান্ত তার নাম ।
গোসাঞির ভগিনীপতি, করে রাজকাম ॥ ৩৮ ॥

*sei hājipure rahe——śrīkānta tāra nāma*
*gosāñira bhaginī-pati, kare rāja-kāma*

### SYNONYMS

*sei*—that; *hājipure*—in Hājipura; *rahe*—there is; *śrī-kānta*—Śrīkānta; *tāra*—his; *nāma*—name; *gosāñira*—of Sanātana Gosvāmī; *bhaginī-pati*—sister's husband; *kare*—executes; *rāja-kāma*—government service.

### TRANSLATION

**In Hājipura there was a gentleman named Śrīkānta, who happened to be the husband of Sanātana Gosvāmī's sister. He was engaged there in government service.**

### TEXT 39

তিন লক্ষ মুদ্রা রাজা দিয়াছে তার স্থানে ।
ঘোড়া মূল্য লঞা পাঠায় পাৎসার স্থানে ॥ ৩৯ ॥

*tina lakṣa mudrā rājā diyāche tāra sthāne*
*ghoḍā mūlya lañā pāṭhāya pātsāra sthāne*

### SYNONYMS

*tina lakṣa*—300,000; *mudrā*—golden coins; *rājā*—the king or nawab; *diyāche*—has given; *tāra sthāne*—in his custody; *ghoḍā*—of horses; *mūlya lañā*—taking the price; *pāṭhāya*—sends; *pātsāra sthāne*—to the care of the emperor.

### TRANSLATION

**Śrīkānta had 300,000 gold coins with him, which had been given to him by the emperor for the purchase of horses. Thus Śrīkānta was buying horses and dispatching them to the emperor.**

## TEXT 40

টুঙ্গি উপর বসি' সেই গোসাঞিরে দেখিল ।
রাত্র্যে একজন-সঙ্গে গোসাঞি-পাশ আইল ॥ ৪০ ॥

*ṭuṅgi upara vasi' sei gosāñire dekhila*
*rātrye eka-jana-saṅge gosāñi-pāśa āila*

## SYNONYMS

*ṭuṅgi upara vasi'*—sitting in an elevated place; *sei*—that Śrīkānta; *gosāñire*—Sanātana Gosvāmī; *dekhila*—saw; *rātrye*—at night; *eka-jana-saṅge*—with a servant; *gosāñi-pāśa*—near Sanātana Gosvāmī; *āila*—he came.

## TRANSLATION

**When Śrīkānta was sitting in an elevated place, he could see Sanātana Gosvāmī. That night he took a servant and went to see Sanātana Gosvāmī.**

## TEXT 41

দুইজন মিলি' তথা ইষ্টগোষ্ঠী কৈল ।
বন্ধন-মোক্ষণ-কথা গোসাঞি সকলি কহিল ॥ ৪১ ॥

*dui-jana mili' tathā iṣṭa-goṣṭhī kaila*
*bandhana-mokṣaṇa-kathā gosāñi sakali kahila*

## SYNONYMS

*dui-jana mili'*—meeting together; *tathā*—there; *iṣṭa-goṣṭhī*—various types of conversation; *kaila*—did; *bandhana-mokṣaṇa*—of the arrest and release; *kathā*—the story; *gosāñi*—Sanātana Gosvāmī; *sakali*—everything; *kahila*—narrated.

## TRANSLATION

**When they met, they had many conversations. Sanātana Gosvāmī told him in detail about his arrest and release.**

## TEXT 42

তেঁহো কহে,—"দিন-দুই রহ এইস্থানে ।
ভদ্র হও, ছাড়' এই মলিন বসনে ॥" ৪২ ॥

*teṅho kahe,—"dina-dui raha ei-sthāne*
*bhadra hao, chāḍa' ei malina vasane"*

### SYNONYMS

*teṅho kahe*—he said; *dina-dui*—at least for two days; *raha*—stay; *ei-sthāne*—in this place; *bhadra hao*—become like a gentleman in appearance; *chāḍa'*—give up; *ei*—this; *malina*—dirty; *vasane*—dress.

### TRANSLATION

**Śrīkānta then told Sanātana Gosvāmī, "Stay here for at least two days and dress up like a gentleman. Abandon these dirty garments."**

## TEXT 43

**গোসাঞি কহে,—"একক্ষণ ইহা না রহিব ।**
**গঙ্গা পার করি' দেহ', এক্ষণে চলিব ॥" ৪৩ ॥**

*gosāñi kahe,——'eka-kṣaṇa ihā nā rahiba*
*gaṅgā pāra kari' deha', e-kṣaṇe caliba"*

### SYNONYMS

*gosāñi kahe*—Sanātana Gosvāmī said; *eka-kṣaṇa*—even for one moment; *ihā*—here; *nā rahiba*—I shall not stay; *gaṅgā pāra kari' deha'*—help me cross the River Ganges; *e-kṣaṇe*—immediately; *caliba*—I shall go.

### TRANSLATION

**Sanātana Gosvāmī replied, "I shall not stay here even for a moment. Please help me cross the Ganges. I shall leave immediately."**

## TEXT 44

**যত্ন করি' তেঁহো এক ভোটকম্বল দিল ।**
**গঙ্গা পার করি' দিল—গোসাঞি চলিল ॥ ৪৪ ॥**

*yatna kari' teṅho eka bhoṭa-kambala dila*
*gaṅgā pāra kari' dila——gosāñi calila*

### SYNONYMS

*yatna kari'*—with great care; *teṅho*—he (Śrīkānta); *eka*—one; *bhoṭa-kambala*—woolen blanket; *dila*—gave; *gaṅgā pāra kari' dila*—got him across the River Ganges; *gosāñi calila*—Sanātana Gosvāmī departed.

### TRANSLATION

**With great care, Śrīkānta gave him a woolen blanket and helped him cross the Ganges. Thus Sanātana Gosvāmī departed again.**

### TEXT 45

তবে বারাণসী গোসাঞি আইলা কতদিনে ।
শুনি আনন্দিত হইলা প্রভুর আগমনে ॥ ৪৫ ॥

*tabe vārāṇasī gosāñi āilā kata-dine*
*śuni ānandita ha-ilā prabhura āgamane*

### SYNONYMS

*tabe*—in this way; *vārāṇasī*—to Vārāṇasī; *gosāñi*—Sanātana Gosvāmī; *āilā*—came; *kata-dine*—after a few days; *śuni*—hearing; *ānandita*—very pleased; *ha-ilā*—he became; *prabhura*—of Śrī Caitanya Mahāprabhu; *āgamane*—about the arrival.

### TRANSLATION

**After a few days, Sanātana Gosvāmī arrived at Vārāṇasī. He was very pleased to hear about Śrī Caitanya Mahāprabhu's arrival there.**

### TEXT 46

চন্দ্রশেখরের ঘরে আসি' দ্বারেতে বসিলা ।
মহাপ্রভু জানি' চন্দ্রশেখরে কহিলা ॥ ৪৬ ॥

*candraśekharera ghare āsi' dvārete vasilā*
*mahāprabhu jāni' candraśekhare kahilā*

### SYNONYMS

*candraśekharera ghare*—to the house of Candraśekhara; *āsi'*—going; *dvārete*—at the door; *vasilā*—sat down; *mahāprabhu*—Śrī Caitanya Mahāprabhu; *jāni'*—knowing; *candraśekhare*—to Candraśekhara; *kahilā*—said.

### TRANSLATION

**Sanātana Gosvāmī then went to the house of Candraśekhara and sat down by the door. Understanding what was happening, Śrī Caitanya Mahāprabhu spoke to Candraśekhara.**

## TEXT 47

'দ্বারে এক 'বৈষ্ণব' হয়, বোলাহ তাঁহারে'।
চন্দ্রশেখর দেখে—'বৈষ্ণব' নাহিক দ্বারে ॥ ৪৭ ॥

*'dvāre eka 'vaiṣṇava' haya, bolāha tāṅhāre'*
*candraśekhara dekhe——'vaiṣṇava' nāhika dvāre*

### SYNONYMS

*dvāre*—at your door; *eka vaiṣṇava*—one Vaiṣṇava devotee; *haya*—there is; *bolāha tāṅhāre*—please call him; *candraśekhara*—Candraśekhara; *dekhe*—sees; *vaiṣṇava*—a devotee; *nāhika*—there is not; *dvāre*—at the door.

### TRANSLATION

**Śrī Caitanya Mahāprabhu said, "There is a devotee at your door. Please call him in." Going outside, Candarśekhara could not see a Vaiṣṇava at his door.**

## TEXT 48

'দ্বারেতে বৈষ্ণব নাহি'—প্রভুরে কহিল।
'কেহ হয়' করি' প্রভু তাহারে পুছিল ॥ ৪৮ ॥

*'dvārete vaiṣṇava nāhi'——prabhure kahila*
*'keha haya' kari' prabhu tāhāre puchila*

### SYNONYMS

*dvārete*—at my door; *vaiṣṇava nāhi*—there is no Vaiṣṇava; *prabhure kahila*—he informed Śrī Caitanya Mahāprabhu; *keha haya*—is there anyone; *kari'*—in this way; *prabhu*—Śrī Caitanya Mahāprabhu; *tāhāre puchila*—inquired from him.

### TRANSLATION

**When Candraśekhara informed the Lord that no Vaiṣṇava was at his door, the Lord asked him, "Is there anyone at your door at all?"**

## TEXT 49

তেঁহো কহে,—এক 'দরবেশ' আছে দ্বারে।
'তাঁরে আন' প্রভুর বাক্যে কহিল তাঁহারে ॥ ৪৯ ॥

*teṅho kahe,——eka 'daraveśa' āche dvāre*
*'tāṅre āna' prabhura vākye kahila tāṅhāre*

### SYNONYMS

*teṅho kahe*—he replied; *eka daraveśa*—one Muslim mendicant; *āche*—there is; *dvāre*—at the door; *tāṅre āna*—bring him; *prabhura*—of Śrī Caitanya Mahāprabhu; *vākye*—the order; *kahila*—said; *tāṅhāre*—unto him.

### TRANSLATION

**Candraśekhara replied, "There is a Muslim mendicant." Śrī Caitanya Mahāprabhu immediately said, "Please bring him here." Candraśekhara then spoke to Sanātana Gosvāmī, who was still sitting beside the door.**

### TEXT 50

'প্রভু তোমায় বোলায়, আইস, দরবেশ !'
শুনি' আনন্দে সনাতন করিলা প্রবেশ ॥ ৫০ ॥

*'prabhu tomāya bolāya, āisa, daraveśa!'*
*śuni' ānande sanātana karilā praveśa*

### SYNONYMS

*prabhu*—Śrī Caitanya Mahāprabhu; *tomāya*—unto you; *bolāya*—calls; *āisa*—come here; *daraveśa*—O Muslim mendicant; *śuni'*—hearing; *ānande*—in great pleasure; *sanātana*—Sanātana Gosvāmī; *karilā praveśa*—entered.

### TRANSLATION

**"O Muslim mendicant, please come in. The Lord is calling you." Sanātana Gosvāmī was very pleased to hear this order, and he entered Candraśekhara's house.**

### TEXT 51

তাঁহারে অঙ্গনে দেখি' প্রভু ধাঞা আইলা ।
তাঁরে আলিঙ্গন করি' প্রেমাবিষ্ট হৈলা ॥ ৫১ ॥

*tāṅhāre aṅgane dekhi' prabhu dhāñā āilā*
*tāṅre āliṅgana kari' premāviṣṭa hailā*

### SYNONYMS

*tāṅhāre*—him; *aṅgane*—in the courtyard; *dekhi'*—seeing; *prabhu*—Śrī Caitanya Mahāprabhu; *dhāñā āilā*—came to see him with great haste; *tāṅre*—him; *āliṅgana kari'*—embracing; *prema-āviṣṭa hailā*—became overwhelmed with ecstatic love.

### TRANSLATION

**As soon as Śrī Caitanya Mahāprabhu saw Sanātana Gosvāmī in the courtyard, He immediately went up to him with great haste. After embracing him, the Lord was overwhelmed with ecstatic love.**

### TEXT 52

প্রভুস্পর্শে প্রেমাবিষ্ট হইলা সনাতন ।
'মোরে না ছুঁইহ' —কহে গদ্‌গদ-বচন ॥ ৫২ ॥

*prabhu-sparśe premāviṣṭa ha-ilā sanātana*
*'more nā chuṅiha'——kahe gadgada-vacana*

### SYNONYMS

*prabhu-sparśe*—by the touch of Śrī Caitanya Mahāprabhu; *prema-āviṣṭa*—overwhelmed with ecstatic love; *ha-ilā*—became; *sanātana*—Sanātana Gosvāmī; *more*—me; *nā*—do not; *chuṅiha*—touch; *kahe*—says; *gadgada-vacana*—in a faltering voice.

### TRANSLATION

**As soon as Śrī Caitanya Mahāprabhu touched Sanātana Gosvāmī, Sanātana was also overwhelmed with ecstatic love. In a faltering voice, he said, "O my Lord, do not touch me."**

### TEXT 53

দুইজনে গলাগলি রোদন অপার ।
দেখি' চন্দ্রশেখরের হইল চমৎকার ॥ ৫৩ ॥

*dui-jane galāgali rodana apāra*
*dekhi' candraśekharera ha-ila camatkāra*

### SYNONYMS

*dui-jane*—the two persons; *galāgali*—shoulder to shoulder; *rodana*—crying; *apāra*—unlimited; *dekhi'*—seeing; *candraśekharera*—of Candraśekhara; *ha-ila*—there was; *camatkāra*—astonishment.

### TRANSLATION

**Shoulder to shoulder, Śrī Caitanya Mahāprabhu and Sanātana Gosvāmī began to cry unlimitedly. Candarśekhara was very astonished to see this.**

### TEXT 54

তবে প্রভু তাঁর হাত ধরি' লঞা গেলা ।
পিণ্ডার উপরে আপন-পাশে বসাইলা ॥ ৫৪ ॥

*tabe prabhu tāṅra hāta dhari' lañā gelā*
*piṇḍāra upare āpana-pāśe vasāilā*

### SYNONYMS

*tabe*—thereafter; *prabhu*—Śrī Caitanya Mahāprabhu; *tāṅra*—of Sanātana Gosvāmī; *hāta dhari'*—catching the hand; *lañā gelā*—took him inside; *piṇḍāra upare*—in an elevated place; *āpana-pāśe*—near Him; *vasāilā*—made Sanātana Gosvāmī sit down.

### TRANSLATION

**Catching his hand, Śrī Caitanya Mahāprabhu took Sanātana Gosvāmī inside and made him sit in an elevated place next to Him.**

### TEXT 55

শ্রীহস্তে করেন তাঁর অঙ্গ সম্মার্জন ।
তেঁহো কহে,—'মোরে, প্রভু, না কর স্পর্শন' ॥ ৫৫ ॥

*śrī-haste karena tāṅra aṅga sammārjana*
*teṅho kahe,—'more, prabhu, nā kara sparśana'*

### SYNONYMS

*śrī-haste*—by the spiritual hand; *karena*—does; *tāṅra aṅga*—of his body; *sammārjana*—cleansing; *teṅho kahe*—he said; *more*—me; *prabhu*—my Lord; *nā kara sparśana*—do not touch.

### TRANSLATION

**When Śrī Caitanya Mahāprabhu began cleansing Sanātana Gosvāmī's body with His own transcendental hand, Sanātana Gosvāmī said, "O my Lord, please do not touch me."**

### TEXT 56

প্রভু কহে,—"তোমা স্পর্শি আত্ম পবিত্রিতে ।
ভক্তি-বলে পার তুমি ব্রহ্মাণ্ড শোধিতে ॥ ৫৬ ॥

*prabhu kahe,——"tomā sparśi ātma pavitrite*
*bhakti-bale pāra tumi brahmāṇḍa śodhite*

## SYNONYMS

*prabhu kahe*—Lord Caitanya Mahāprabhu replied; *tomā sparśi*—I touch you; *ātma pavitrite*—to purify Myself; *bhakti-bale*—the strength of your devotional service; *pāra*—are able; *tumi*—you; *brahmāṇḍa*—the whole universe; *śodhite*—to purify.

## TRANSLATION

**The Lord replied, "I am touching you just to purify Myself because by the force of your devotional service you can purify the whole universe.**

## TEXT 57

ভবদ্বিধা ভাগবতাস্তীর্থভূতাঃ স্বয়ং প্রভো ।
তীর্থীকুর্বন্তি তীর্থানি স্বান্তঃস্থেন গদাভৃতা ॥ ৫৭ ॥

*bhavad-vidhā bhāgavatās*
*tīrtha-bhūtāḥ svayaṁ prabho*
*tīrthī-kurvanti tīrthāni*
*svāntaḥ-sthena gadā-bhṛtā*

## SYNONYMS

*bhavat-vidhāḥ*—like you; *bhāgavatāḥ*—advanced devotees; *tīrtha-bhūtāḥ*—personified holy places of pilgrimage; *svayam*—personally; *prabho*—my lord; *tīrthī-kurvanti*—make into holy places; *tīrthāni*—all the holy places of pilgrimage; *sva-antaḥ-sthena*—situated within their hearts; *gadā-bhṛtā*—by Lord Viṣṇu, who carries a club.

## TRANSLATION

**" 'Saints of your caliber are themselves places of pilgrimage. Because of their purity, they are constant companions of the Lord, and therefore they can purify even the places of pilgrimage.'**

## PURPORT

This verse was spoken by Mahārāja Yudhiṣṭhira to Vidura in *Śrīmad-Bhāgavatam* (1.13.10). Vidura was returning home after visiting sacred places of pilgrimage, and Mahārāja Yudhiṣṭhira was receiving his saintly uncle. In essence, Mahārāja Yudhiṣṭhira was saying, "My dear Lord Vidura, you yourself are a holy place because you are an advanced devotee. People like you always carry Lord Viṣṇu in their hearts. You can revitalize all holy places after they have been polluted by the pilgrimages of sinners."

A sinful person goes to a holy place of pilgrimage to be purified. In a holy place, there are many saintly people and temples of Lord Viṣṇu; however, the holy place becomes infected with the sins of many visitors. When an advanced devotee goes to a holy place, he counteracts all the sins of the pilgrims. Therefore Mahārāja Yudiṣṭhira addressed Vidura in this way.

Since an advanced devotee carries Lord Viṣṇu within his heart, he is a moving temple and a moving Viṣṇu. An advanced devotee does not need to go to holy places, for wherever he stays is a holy place. In this connection, Narottama dāsa Ṭhākura states, *tīrtha-yātrā pariśrama, kevala manera bhrama:* visiting holy places is simply another type of bewilderment. Since an advanced devotee does not need to go to a holy place, why does he go? The answer is that he goes simply to purify the place.

### TEXT 58

ন মেঽভক্তশ্চতুর্বেদী মদ্ভক্তঃ শ্বপচঃ প্রিয়ঃ ।
তস্মৈ দেয়ং ততো গ্রাহ্যং স চ পূজ্যো যথা হ্যহম্ ॥ ৫৮ ॥

*na me 'bhaktaś catur-vedī*
*mad-bhaktaḥ śva-pacaḥ priyaḥ*
*tasmai deyaṁ tato grāhyaṁ*
*sa ca pūjyo yathā hy aham*

### SYNONYMS

*na*—not; *me*—My; *abhaktaḥ*—devoid of pure devotional service; *catuḥ-vedī*—a scholar in the four *Vedas; mat-bhaktaḥ*—My devotee; *śva-pacaḥ*—even from a family of dog-eaters; *priyaḥ*—very dear; *tasmai*—to him (a pure devotee, even though born in a very low family); *deyam*—should be given; *tataḥ*—from him; *grāhyam*—should be accepted (remnants of food); *saḥ*—that person; *ca*—also; *pūjyaḥ*—worshipable; *yathā*—as much as; *hi*—certainly; *aham*—I.

### TRANSLATION

**" 'Even though a person is a very learned scholar of the Sanskrit Vedic literatures, he is not accepted as My devotee unless he is pure in devotional service. However, even though a person is born in a family of dog-eaters, he is very dear to Me if he is a pure devotee who has no motive to enjoy fruitive activity or mental speculation. Indeed, all respects should be given to him, and whatever he offers should be accepted. Such devotees are as worshipable as I am.'**

### PURPORT

This verse is included in the *Hari-bhakti-vilāsa* (10.127) compiled by Sanātana Gosvāmī.

### TEXT 59

বিপ্রাদ্দ্বিষড়্গুণযুতাদরবিন্দনাভ-
পাদারবিন্দবিমুখাৎ শ্বপচং বরিষ্ঠম্ ।
মন্যে তদর্পিত-মনোবচনেহিতার্থ-
প্রাণং পুনাতি স কুলং ন তু ভূরিমানঃ ॥ ৫৯ ॥

*viprād dviṣaḍ-guṇa-yutād aravinda-nābha-*
*pādāravinda-vimukhāt śva-pacaṁ variṣṭham*
*manye tad-arpita-mano-vacanehitārtha-*
*prāṇaṁ punāti sa kulaṁ na tu bhūri-mānaḥ*

### SYNONYMS

*viprāt*—than a *brāhmaṇa; dvi-ṣaṭ-guṇa-yutāt*—who is qualified with twelve brahminical qualifications; *aravinda-nābha*—of Lord Viṣṇu, who has a lotuslike navel; *pāda-aravinda*—unto the lotus feet; *vimukhāt*—than a person bereft of devotion; *śva-pacam*—a *caṇḍāla,* or a person accustomed to eating dogs; *variṣṭham*—more glorified; *manye*—I think; *tat-arpita*—dedicated unto Him; *manaḥ*—mind; *vacana*—words; *īhita*—activities; *artha*—wealth; *prāṇam*—life; *punāti*—purifies; *saḥ*—he; *kulam*—his family; *na tu*—but not; *bhūri-mānaḥ*—a *brāhmaṇa* proud of possessing such qualities.

### TRANSLATION

**" 'One may be born in a brāhmaṇa family and have all twelve brahminical qualities, but if he is not devoted to the lotus feet of Lord Kṛṣṇa, who has a navel shaped like a lotus, he is not as good as a caṇḍāla who has dedicated his mind, words, activities, wealth and life to the service of the Lord. Simply to take birth in a brāhmaṇa family or to have brahminical qualities is not sufficient. One must become a pure devotee of the Lord. If a śva-paca or caṇḍāla is a devotee, he delivers not only himself but his whole family, whereas a brāhmaṇa who is not a devotee but simply has brahminical qualifications cannot even purify himself, not to speak of his family.' "**

### PURPORT

This verse is spoken by Prahlāda Mahārāja in *Śrīmad-Bhāgavatam* (7.9.10). A *brāhmaṇa* is supposed to be qualified with twelve quaiities. As stated in the *Mahābhārata:*

*dharmaś ca satyaṁ ca damas tapaś ca*
*amātsaryaṁ hrīs titikṣānasūyā*
*yajñaś ca dānaṁ ca dhṛtiḥ śrutaṁ ca*
*vratāni vai dvādaśa brāhmaṇasya*

"A *brāhmaṇa* must be perfectly religious. He must be truthful, and he must be able to control his senses. He must execute severe austerities, and he must be detached, humble and tolerant. He must not envy anyone, and he must be expert in performing sacrifices and giving whatever he has in charity. He must be fixed in devotional service and expert in the knowledge of the *Vedas.* These are the twelve qualifications for a *brāhmaṇa.*"

*Bhagavad-gītā* describes the brahminical qualities in this way:

*śamo damas tapaḥ śaucaṁ*
*kṣāntir ārjavam eva ca*
*jñānaṁ vijñānam āstikyaṁ*
*brahma-karma svabhāva-jam*

"Peacefulness, self-control, austerity, purity, tolerance, honesty, wisdom, knowledge, and religiousness—these are the qualities by which the *brāhmaṇas* work." (Bg. 18.42)

In the *Muktāphala-ṭīkā,* it is said:

*śamo damas tapaḥ śaucaṁ*
*kṣānty-ārjava-viraktayaḥ*
*jñāna-vijñāna-santoṣāḥ*
*satyāstikye dviṣaḍ guṇāḥ*

"Mental equilibrium, sense control, austerity, cleanliness, tolerance, simplicity, detachment, theoretical and practical knowledge, satisfaction, truthfulness and firm faith in the *Vedas* are the twelve qualities of a *brāhmaṇa.*"

### TEXT 60

**তোমা দেখি, তোমা স্পর্শি, গাই তোমার গুণ ।**
**সর্বেন্দ্রিয়-ফল,—এই শাস্ত্র-নিরূপণ ॥ ৬০ ॥**

*tomā dekhi, tomā sparśi, gāi tomāra guṇa*
*sarvendriya-phala,——ei śāstra-nirūpaṇa*

### SYNONYMS

*tomā dekhi*—by seeing you; *tomā sparśi*—by touching you; *gāi tomāra guṇa*—praising your transcendental qualities; *sarva-indriya-phala*—the fulfillment of the activities of all the senses; *ei*—this; *śāstra-nirūpaṇa*—the verdict of the revealed scriptures.

### TRANSLATION

**Śrī Caitanya Mahāprabhu continued, "By seeing you, by touching you and by glorifying your transcendental qualities, one can perfect the purpose of all sense activity. This is the verdict of the revealed scriptures.**

### PURPORT

This is confirmed in the following verse from the *Hari-bhakti-sudhodaya* (13.2).

## TEXT 61

অক্ষ্ণোঃ ফলং ত্বাদৃশ-দর্শনং হি
তনোঃ ফলং ত্বাদৃশ-গাত্রসঙ্গঃ।
জিহ্বা-ফলং ত্বাদৃশ-কীর্তনং হি
সুদুর্লভা ভাগবতা হি লোকে ॥ ৬১ ॥

*akṣṇoḥ phalaṁ tvādṛśa-darśanaṁ hi*
*tanoḥ phalaṁ tvādṛśa-gātra-saṅgaḥ*
*jihvā-phalaṁ tvādṛśa-kīrtanaṁ hi*
*sudurlabhā bhāgavatā hi loke*

### SYNONYMS

*akṣṇoḥ*—of the eyes; *phalam*—the perfect result of the action; *tvā-dṛśa*—a person like you; *darśanam*—to see; *hi*—certainly; *tanoḥ*—of the body; *phalam*—the perfection of activities; *tvā-dṛśa*—of a person like you; *gātra-saṅgaḥ*—touching the body; *jihvā-phalam*—the perfection of the tongue; *tvā-dṛśa*—a person like you; *kīrtanam*—glorifying; *hi*—certainly; *su-durlabhāḥ*—very rare; *bhāgavatāḥ*—pure devotees of the Lord; *hi*—certainly; *loke*—in this world.

### TRANSLATION

**" 'My dear Vaiṣṇava, seeing a person like you is the perfection of one's eyesight. Touching your lotus feet is the perfection of the sense of touch. Glorifying your good qualities is the tongue's real activity, for in the material world it is very difficult to find a pure devotee of the Lord.' "**

### TEXT 62

এত কহি কহে প্রভু,—"শুন, সনাতন ।
কৃষ্ণ—বড় দয়াময়, পতিত-পাবন ॥ ৬২ ॥

*eta kahi kahe prabhu,—"śuna, sanātana*
*kṛṣṇa—baḍa dayāmaya, patita-pāvana*

### SYNONYMS

*eta kahi*—saying this; *kahe*—continued to speak; *prabhu*—Lord Śrī Caitanya Mahāprabhu; *śuna*—please hear; *sanātana*—My dear Sanātana; *kṛṣṇa*—Lord Kṛṣṇa; *baḍa*—very much; *dayā-maya*—merciful; *patita-pāvana*—deliverer of the fallen souls.

### TRANSLATION

**Śrī Caitanya Mahāprabhu continued, "My dear Sanātana, please hear from Me. Kṛṣṇa is very merciful, and He is the deliverer of all fallen souls.**

### TEXT 63

মহা-রৌরব হৈতে তোমা করিলা উদ্ধার ।
কৃপার সমুদ্র কৃষ্ণ গম্ভীর অপার ॥" ৬৩ ॥

*mahā-raurava haite tomā karilā uddhāra*
*kṛpāra samudra kṛṣṇa gambhīra apāra"*

### SYNONYMS

*mahā-raurava haite*—from the deepest hellish condition of life; *tomā*—you; *karilā uddhāra*—has delivered; *kṛpāra samudra*—the ocean of mercy; *kṛṣṇa*—Kṛṣṇa; *gambhīra*—very grave; *apāra*—unlimitedly.

### TRANSLATION

**"My dear Sanātana, Kṛṣṇa has saved you from Mahāraurava, life's deepest hell. He is an ocean of mercy, and His activities are very grave."**

### PURPORT

As stated in *Bhagavad-gītā, īśvaraḥ sarva-bhūtānāṁ hṛd-deśe 'rjuna tiṣṭhati.* Staying within everyone's heart, Lord Kṛṣṇa works very gravely. No one can understand how He is working, but as soon as the Lord understands the sincere activity of a person in devotional service, He helps him in such a way that the devotee cannot understand how things are happening. If the devotee is determined to serve the Lord, the Lord is always prepared to help him (*dadāmi buddhi-yogaṁ taṁ yena mām upayānti te*). Śrī Caitanya Mahāprabhu is telling Sanātana Gosvāmī how merciful the Lord is. Sanātana Gosvāmī was a minister in the service of Nawab Hussain Shah. He was always mixing with people materially inclined, particularly with Mohammedans, meat-eaters. Although he was in intimate touch with them, by Kṛṣṇa's mercy he came to find such association distasteful. Therefore he left them. As stated by Śrīnivāsa Ācārya: *tyaktvā tūrṇam aśeṣa-maṇḍala-pati-śreṇīṁ sadā tucchavat.* Kṛṣṇa enlightened Sanātana Gosvāmī in such a way that he was able to give up his exalted post as minister. Thinking his material position insignificant, Sanātana was prepared to become a mendicant. Appreciating the activities of Sanātana Gosvāmī, Śrī Caitanya Mahāprabhu praised his action and thanked Kṛṣṇa for His mercy upon him.

## TEXT 64

সনাতন কহে,—'কৃষ্ণ আমি নাহি জানি।
আমার উদ্ধার-হেতু তোমার কৃপা মানি॥' ৬৪ ॥

*sanātana kahe,——'kṛṣṇa āmi nāhi jāni*
*āmāra uddhāra-hetu tomāra kṛpā māni'*

## SYNONYMS

*sanātana kahe*—Sanātana Gosvāmī said; *kṛṣṇa*—Lord Kṛṣṇa; *āmi*—I; *nāhi jāni*—do not know; *āmāra*—my; *uddhāra-hetu*—the cause of release; *tomāra*—Your; *kṛpā*—mercy; *māni*—I accept.

## TRANSLATION

**Sanātana replied, "I do not know who Kṛṣṇa is. As far as I am concerned, I have been released from prison only by Your mercy."**

## TEXT 65

'কেমনে ছুটিলা' বলি প্রভু প্রশ্ন কৈলা।
আদ্যোপান্ত সব কথা তেঁহো শুনাইলা ॥ ৬৫ ॥

*'kemane chuṭilā' bali prabhu praśna kailā*
*ādyopānta saba kathā teṅho śunāilā*

## SYNONYMS

*kemane chuṭilā*—how were you released; *bali*—saying; *prabhu*—Śrī Caitanya Mahāprabhu; *praśna kailā*—inquired; *ādya-upānta*—from beginning to the end; *saba*—all; *kathā*—the narration; *teṅho*—he; *śunāilā*—described.

### TRANSLATION

**Śrī Caitanya Mahāprabhu then asked Sanātana Gosvāmī, "How were you released from prison?" Sanātana then described the story from beginning to end.**

### TEXT 66

প্রভু কহে,—"তোমার দুইভাই প্রয়াগে মিলিলা।
রূপ, অনুপম—দুঁহে বৃন্দাবন গেলা" ॥ ৬৬ ॥

*prabhu kahe,—"tomāra dui-bhāi prayāge mililā*
*rūpa, anupama—duṅhe vṛndāvana gelā"*

### SYNONYMS

*prabhu kahe*—Śrī Caitanya Mahāprabhu said; *tomāra*—your; *dui-bhāi*—two brothers; *prayāge mililā*—met Me at Prayāga; *rūpa*—Rūpa Gosvāmī; *anupama*—his brother Anupama; *duṅhe*—both of them; *vṛndāvana gelā*—have gone to Vṛndāvana.

### TRANSLATION

**Śrī Caitanya Mahāprabhu said, "I met your two brothers, Rūpa and Anupama, at Prayāga. They have now gone to Vṛndāvana."**

### TEXT 67

তপনমিশ্রেরে আর চন্দ্রশেখরেরে।
প্রভু-আজ্ঞায় সনাতন মিলিলা দোঁহারে ॥ ৬৭ ॥

*tapana-miśrere āra candraśekharere*
*prabhu-ājñāya sanātana mililā doṅhāre*

### SYNONYMS

*tapana-miśrere*—unto Tapana Miśra; *āra*—and; *candraśekharere*—unto Candraśekhara; *prabhu-ājñāya*—by the order of Śrī Caitanya Mahāprabhu; *sanātana*—Sanātana; *mililā*—met; *doṅhāre*—both of them.

### TRANSLATION

**By the order of Śrī Caitanya Mahāprabhu, Sanātana Gosvāmī met both Tapana Miśra and Candraśekhara.**

### TEXT 68

তপনমিশ্র তবে তাঁরে কৈলা নিমন্ত্রণ ।
প্রভু কহে,—'ক্ষৌর করাহ, যাহ, সনাতন ॥' ৬৮ ॥

*tapana-miśra tabe tāṅre kailā nimantraṇa*
*prabhu kahe,—'kṣaura karāha, yāha, sanātana'*

### SYNONYMS

*tapana—miśra*—Tapana Miśra; *tabe*—then; *tāṅre*—unto him (Sanātana Gosvāmī); *kailā*—made; *nimantraṇa*—invitation; *prabhu kahe*—Caitanya Mahāprabhu said; *kṣaura karāha*—get shaved; *yāha*—go; *sanātana*—My dear Sanātana.

### TRANSLATION

**Tapana Miśra then extended an invitation to Sanātana, and Lord Caitanya Mahāprabhu asked Sanātana to go get a shave.**

### TEXT 69

চন্দ্রশেখরেরে প্রভু কহে বোলাঞা ।
'এই বেষ দূর কর, যাহ ইঁহারে লঞা' ॥ ৬৯ ॥

*candraśekharere prabhu kahe bolāñā*
*'ei veṣa dūra kara, yāha iṅhāre lañā'*

### SYNONYMS

*candraśekharere*—unto Candraśekhara; *prabhu kahe*—Śrī Caitanya Mahāprabhu said; *bolāñā*—calling; *ei veṣa*—this kind of dress; *dūra kara*—take away; *yāha*—go; *iṅhāre lañā*—taking him with you.

### TRANSLATION

**After this, Śrī Caitanya Mahāprabhu called Candraśekhara and asked him to take Sanātana Gosvāmī with him. He also asked him to take away Sanātana's present dress.**

### TEXT 70

ভদ্র করাঞা তাঁরে গঙ্গাস্নান করাইল ।
শেখর আনিয়া তাঁরে নূতন বস্ত্র দিল ॥ ৭০ ॥

*bhadra karāñā tāṅre gaṅgā-snāna karāila*
*śekhara āniyā tāṅre nūtana vastra dila*

### SYNONYMS

*bhadra karāñā*—making gentle; *tāṅre*—him; *gaṅgā-snāna*—bathing in the Ganges; *karāila*—caused to do; *śekhara*—Candraśekhara; *āniyā*—bringing; *tāṅre*—to him; *nūtana*—new; *vastra*—clothing; *dila*—delivered.

### TRANSLATION

**Candraśekhara then made Sanātana Gosvāmī look like a gentleman. He took him to bathe in the Ganges, and afterwards he brought him a new set of clothes.**

### PURPORT

The words *bhadra karāñā* are significant in this verse. Due to his long hair, moustache and beard, Sanātana Gosvāmī looked like a *daraveśa,* or hippie. Since Śrī Caitanya Mahāprabhu did not like Sanātana Gosvāmī's hippie features, he immediately asked Candraśekhara to get him shaved clean. If anyone with long hair or a beard wants to join this Kṛṣṇa consciousness movement and live with us, he must similarly shave himself clean. The followers of Śrī Caitanya Mahāprabhu consider long hair objectionable. Sanātana Gosvāmī was saved from a hellish condition (Mahāraurava) by the grace of Śrī Caitanya Mahāprabhu. Mahāraurava is a hell wherein animal killers are placed. In this regard, refer to *Śrīmad-Bhāgavatam* (5.26.10-12).

## TEXT 71

সেই বস্ত্র সনাতন না কৈল অঙ্গীকার ।
শুনিয়া প্রভুর মনে আনন্দ অপার ॥ ৭১ ॥

*sei vastra sanātana nā kaila aṅgīkāra*
*śuniyā prabhura mane ānanda apāra*

### SYNONYMS

*sei vastra*—that new dress; *sanātana*—Sanātana Gosvāmī; *nā kaila*—did not; *aṅgīkāra*—accept; *śuniyā*—hearing; *prabhura*—of Śrī Caitanya Mahāprabhu; *mane*—in the mind; *ānanda apāra*—unlimited happiness.

### TRANSLATION

**Candraśekhara offered a new set of garments to Sanātana Gosvāmī, but Sanātana did not accept them. When Śrī Caitanya Mahāprabhu heard news of this, he became unlimitedly happy.**

### TEXT 72

মধ্যাহ্ন করিয়া প্রভু গেলা ভিক্ষা করিবারে ।
সনাতনে লঞা গেলা তপনমিশ্রের ঘরে ॥ ৭২ ॥

*madhyāhna kariyā prabhu gelā bhikṣā karibāre*
*sanātane lañā gelā tapana-miśrera ghare*

### SYNONYMS

*madhyāhna kariyā*—finishing bathing at noon; *prabhu*—Śrī Caitanya Mahāprabhu; *gelā*—went; *bhikṣā karibāre*—to accept lunch; *sanātane*—Sanātana Gosvāmī; *lañā*—taking; *gelā*—went; *tapana-miśrera ghare*—to the house of Tapana Miśra.

### TRANSLATION

**After bathing at noon, Śrī Caitanya Mahāprabhu went to the house of Tapana Miśra for lunch. He took Sanātana Gosvāmī with Him.**

### TEXT 73

পাদপ্রক্ষালন করি' ভিক্ষাতে বসিলা ।
'সনাতনে ভিক্ষা দেহ'—মিশ্রেরে কহিলা ॥ ৭৩ ॥

*pāda-prakṣālana kari' bhikṣāte vasilā*
*'sanātane bhikṣā deha'——miśrere kahilā*

### SYNONYMS

*pāda-prakṣālana*—washing the feet; *kari'*—doing; *bhikṣāte*—to lunch; *vasilā*—sat down; *sanātane bhikṣā deha*—give Sanātana also lunch; *miśrere kahilā*—He asked Tapana Miśra.

### TRANSLATION

**After washing His feet, Śrī Caitanya Mahāprabhu sat down for lunch. He asked Tapana Miśra to supply Sanātana Gosvāmī lunch also.**

### TEXT 74

মিশ্র কহে,—'সনাতনের কিছু কৃত্য আছে ।
তুমি ভিক্ষা কর, প্রসাদ তাঁরে দিব পাছে ॥' ৭৪ ॥

*miśra kahe,——'sanātanera kichu kṛtya āche*
*tumi bhikṣā kara, prasāda tāṅre diba pāche'*

## SYNONYMS

*miśra kahe*—Tapana Miśra said; *sanātanera*—of Sanātana Gosvāmī; *kichu*—some; *kṛtya*—duty; *āche*—there is; *tumi bhikṣā kara*—You take Your lunch; *prasāda*—the remnants of Your food; *tāṅre*—unto him; *diba*—I shall deliver; *pāche*—at the end.

## TRANSLATION

**Tapana Miśra then said, "Sanātana has some duty to perform; therefore he cannot accept lunch now. At the conclusion of the meal, I shall supply Sanātana with some remnants."**

## TEXT 75

ভিক্ষা করি' মহাপ্রভু বিশ্রাম করিল ।
মিশ্র প্রভুর শেষপাত্র সনাতনে দিল ॥ ৭৫ ॥

*bhikṣā kari' mahāprabhu viśrāma karila*
*miśra prabhura śeṣa-pātra sanātane dila*

## SYNONYMS

*bhikṣā kari'*—after taking His lunch; *mahāprabhu*—Śrī Caitanya Mahāprabhu; *viśrāma karila*—took rest; *miśra*—Tapana Miśra; *prabhura*—of Śrī Caitanya Mahāprabhu; *śeṣa-pātra*—the plate of remnants; *sanātane dila*—delivered to Sanātana.

## TRANSLATION

**After eating, Śrī Caitanya Mahāprabhu took rest for a while. Tapana Miśra then gave Sanātana Gosvāmī the remnants of food left by Caitanya Mahāprabhu.**

## TEXT 76

মিশ্র সনাতনে দিলা নূতন বসন ।
বস্ত্র নাহি নিলা, তেঁহো কৈল নিবেদন ॥ ৭৬ ॥

*miśra sanātane dilā nūtana vasana*
*vastra nāhi nilā, teṅho kaila nivedana*

## SYNONYMS

*miśra*—Tapana Miśra; *sanātane*—unto Sanātana; *dilā*—delivered; *nūtana vasana*—new cloth; *vastra*—the cloth; *nāhi nilā*—he did not accept; *teṅho*—he; *kaila*—made; *nivedana*—submission.

### TRANSLATION

**When Tapana Miśra offered Sanātana Gosvāmī a new cloth, he did not accept it. Instead, he spoke as follows.**

### TEXT 77

“মোরে বস্ত্র দিতে যদি তোমার হয় মন ।
নিজ পরিধান এক দেহ’ পুরাতন ॥” ৭৭ ॥

*"more vastra dite yadi tomāra haya mana*
*nija paridhāna eka deha' purātana"*

### SYNONYMS

*more*—unto me; *vastra dite*—to offer cloth; *yadi*—if; *tomāra*—your; *haya*—there is; *mana*—mind; *nija*—own; *paridhāna*—cloth; *eka*—one; *deha'*—give; *purātana*—old.

### TRANSLATION

**"If you want to give me some cloth according to your desire, please give me an old cloth you have used."**

### TEXT 78

তবে মিশ্র পুরাতন এক ধুতি দিল ।
তেঁহো দুই বহির্বাস-কৌপীন করিল ॥ ৭৮ ॥

*tabe miśra purātana eka dhuti dila*
*teṅho dui bahirvāsa-kaupīna karila*

### SYNONYMS

*tabe*—thereafter; *miśra*—Tapana Miśra; *purātana*—old; *eka*—one; *dhuti*—dhoti; *dila*—delivered; *teṅho*—he (Sanātana Gosvāmī); *dui*—two; *bahirvāsa*—outer coverings; *kaupīna*—underwear; *karila*—made.

### TRANSLATION

**When Tapana Miśra gave Sanātana Gosvāmī a used dhoti, Sanātana immediately tore it in pieces to make two sets of outer cloth and underwear.**

### TEXT 79

মহারাষ্ট্রীয় দ্বিজে প্রভু মিলাইলা সনাতনে ।
সেই বিপ্র তাঁরে কৈল মহা-নিমন্ত্রণে ॥ ৭৯ ॥

*mahārāṣṭrīya dvije prabhu milāilā sanātane*
*sei vipra tāṅre kaila mahā-nimantraṇe*

### SYNONYMS

*mahā-rāṣṭrīya*—from Mahārāṣṭra; *dvije*—the *brāhmaṇa; prabhu*—Śrī Caitanya Mahāprabhu; *milāilā*—introduced; *sanātane*—unto Sanātana Gosvāmī; *sei*—that; *vipra*—*brāhmaṇa; tāṅre*—unto him; *kaila*—did; *mahā*—full; *nimantraṇe*—invitation.

### TRANSLATION

**When Caitanya Mahāprabhu introduced the Mahārāṣṭrīya brāhmaṇa to Sanātana, the brāhmaṇa immediately invited Sanātana Gosvāmī for full meals.**

### TEXT 80

**"সনাতন, তুমি যাবৎ কাশীতে রহিবা।**
**তাবৎ আমার ঘরে ভিক্ষা যে করিবা॥" ৮০ ॥**

*"sanātana, tumi yāvat kāśīte rahibā*
*tāvat āmāra ghare bhikṣā ye karibā"*

### SYNONYMS

*sanātana*—O Sanātana; *tumi*—you; *yāvat*—as long as; *kāśīte*—in Benares; *rahibā*—will remain; *tāvat*—so long; *āmāra*—my; *ghare*—at the home; *bhikṣā*—lunch; *ye*—that; *karibā*—please accept.

### TRANSLATION

**The brāhmaṇa said, "My dear Sanātana, as long as you remain at Kāśī, please accept lunch at my place."**

### TEXT 81

**সনাতন কহে,—"আমি মাধুকরী করিব।**
**ব্রাহ্মণের ঘরে কেনে একত্র ভিক্ষা লব?" ৮১ ॥**

*sanātana kahe,—"āmi mādhukarī kariba*
*brāhmaṇera ghare kene ekatra bhikṣā laba?"*

### SYNONYMS

*sanātana kahe*—Sanātana replied; *āmi*—I; *mādhukarī kariba*—shall practice acceptance of food by *mādhukarī* means; *brāhmaṇera ghare*—in the house of a *brāhmaṇa; kene*—why; *ekatra*—in one place; *bhikṣā laba*—I should accept lunch.

## TRANSLATION

**Sanātana replied, "I shall practice the process of mādhukarī. Why should I accept full meals in the house of a brāhmaṇa?"**

## PURPORT

The word *mādhukarī* comes from the word *madhukara,* which refers to bees collecting honey from flower to flower. A *mādhukarī* is a saintly person or a mendicant who does not accept a full meal at one house but begs from door to door, taking a little food from each householder's place. In this way he does not overeat or give householders unnecessary trouble. A person in the renounced order may beg but not cook. His begging should not be a burden for the householders. The *mādhukarī* process is strictly to be followed by a *bābājī,* that is, one who has attained the *paramahaṁsa* stage. This practice is still current in Vṛndāvana, and there are many places where alms are offered. Unfortunately, there are many beggars who have come to Vṛndāvana to accept alms but not follow the principles of Sanātana Gosvāmī. People try to imitate him and lead an idle life by practicing *mādhukarī.* It is almost impossible to strictly follow Sanātana Gosvāmī or Rūpa Gosvāmī. It is better to accept food offered to Kṛṣṇa in the temple than to try to imitate Sanātana Gosvāmī and Rūpa Gosvāmī.

*yuktāhāra-vihārasya*
*yukta-ceṣṭasya karmasu*
*yukta-svapnāvabodhasya*
*yogo bhavati duḥkha-hā*

"He who is temperate in his habits of eating, sleeping, working and recreation can mitigate all material pains by practicing the *yoga* system." (Bg. 6.17)

The ideal *sannyāsī* strictly follows the ways practiced by the Gosvāmīs.

## TEXT 82

সনাতনের বৈরাগ্যে প্রভুর আনন্দ অপার ।
ভোটকম্বল পানে প্রভু চাহে বারে বার ॥ ৮২ ॥

*sanātanera vairāgye prabhura ānanda apāra*
*bhoṭa-kambala pāne prabhu cāhe bāre bāra*

## SYNONYMS

*sanātanera*—of Sanātana Gosvāmī; *vairāgye*—by the renunciation; *prabhura*—of Śrī Caitanya Mahāprabhu; *ānanda*—happiness; *apāra*—unlimited; *bhoṭa-kambala*—the woolen blanket; *pāne*—towards; *prabhu*—Śrī Caitanya Mahāprabhu; *cāhe*—looks; *bāre bāra*—repeatedly.

### TRANSLATION

**Śrī Caitanya Mahāprabhu felt unlimited happiness to observe Sanātana Gosvāmī's strict following of the principles of sannyāsa. However, He repeatedly glanced at the woolen blanket Sanātana Gosvāmī was wearing.**

### TEXT 83

সনাতন জানিল এই প্রভুরে না ভায় ।
ভোট ত্যাগ করিবারে চিন্তিলা উপায় ॥ ৮৩ ॥

*sanātana jānila ei prabhure nā bhāya*
*bhoṭa tyāga karibāre cintilā upāya*

### SYNONYMS

*sanātana jānila*—Sanātana Gosvāmī could understand; *ei*—this; *prabhure*—by Śrī Caitanya Mahāprabhu; *nā bhāya*—is not approved; *bhoṭa*—the woolen blanket; *tyāga*—giving up; *karibāre*—to do; *cintilā*—considered; *upāya*—a means.

### TRANSLATION

**Because Śrī Caitanya Mahāprabhu was repeatedly glancing at this valuable woolen blanket, Sanātana Gosvāmī could understand that the Lord did not approve of it. He then began to consider a way to give it up.**

### TEXT 84

এত চিন্তি' গেলা গঙ্গায় মধ্যাহ্ন করিতে ।
এক গৌড়িয়া কান্থা ধুঞা দিয়াছে শুকাইতে ॥ ৮৪ ॥

*eta cinti' gelā gaṅgāya madhyāhna karite*
*eka gauḍiyā kānthā dhuñā diyāche śukāite*

### SYNONYMS

*eta cinti'*—thinking this; *gelā*—went; *gaṅgāya*—to the bank of the Ganges; *madhyāhna*—bathing at noon; *karite*—to do; *eka*—one; *gauḍiyā*—Bengali Vaiṣṇava; *kānthā*—quilt; *dhuñā*—washing; *diyāche*—spread out; *śukāite*—to dry.

### TRANSLATION

**Thinking in this way, Sanātana went to the bank of the Ganges to bathe. While there, he saw that a mendicant from Bengal had washed his quilt and had spread it out to dry.**

### TEXT 85

তারে কহে,—"ওরে ভাই, কর উপকারে।
এই ভোট লঞা এই কাঁথা দেহ' মোরে ॥" ৮৫ ॥

*tāre kahe,——"ore bhāi, kara upakāre*
*ei bhoṭa lañā ei kāṅthā deha' more"*

### SYNONYMS

*tāre kahe*—he said to him; *ore bhāi*—O my brother; *kara upakāre*—kindly do a favor; *ei bhoṭa*—this woolen blanket; *lañā*—taking; *ei*—this; *kāṅthā*—quilt; *deha'*—give; *more*—to me.

### TRANSLATION

**Sanātana Gosvāmī then told the Bengali mendicant, "My dear brother, please do me a favor. Trade me your quilt for this woolen blanket."**

### TEXT 86

সেই কহে,—"রহস্য কর প্রামাণিক হঞা?
বহুমূল্য ভোট দিবা কেন কাঁথা লঞা?" ৮৬ ॥

*sei kahe,——"rahasya kara prāmāṇika hañā?*
*bahu-mūlya bhoṭa dibā kena kāṅthā lañā?"*

### SYNONYMS

*sei kahe*—he said; *rahasya*—joking; *kara*—you do; *prāmāṇika hañā*—although being a man of authority; *bahu-mūlya*—very valuable; *bhoṭa*—woolen blanket; *dibā*—you would give; *kena*—why; *kāṅthā lañā*—taking this quilt.

### TRANSLATION

**The mendicant replied, "Sir, you are a respectable gentleman. Why are you joking with me? Why would you trade your valuable blanket for my torn quilt?"**

### TEXT 87

তেঁহো কহে,—"রহস্য নহে, কহি সত্যবাণী।
ভোট লহ, তুমি দেহ' মোরে কাঁথাখানি ॥" ৮৭ ॥

*teṅho kahe,——"rahasya nahe, kahi satya-vāṇī*
*bhoṭa laha, tumi deha' more kāṅthā-khāni"*

### SYNONYMS

*teṅho kahe*—he said; *rahasya nahe*—there is no joking; *kahi satya-vāṇī*—I am speaking the truth; *bhoṭa laha*—take this blanket; *tumi*—you; *deha'*—give; *more*—to me; *kāṅthā-khāni*—the quilt.

### TRANSLATION

**Sanātana said, "I am not joking; I am speaking the truth. Kindly take this blanket in exchange for your torn quilt."**

### TEXT 88

এত বলি' কাঁথা লইল, ভোট তাঁরে দিয়া।
গোসাঞির ঠাঁই আইলা কাঁথা গলে দিয়া ॥ ৮৮ ॥

*eta bali' kāṅthā la-ila, bhoṭa tāṅre diyā*
*gosāñira ṭhāṅi āilā kāṅthā gale diyā*

### SYNONYMS

*eta bali'*—saying this; *kāṅthā la-ila*—he took the quilt; *bhoṭa*—the blanket; *tāṅre*—unto him; *diyā*—giving; *gosāñira ṭhāṅi*—to Caitanya Mahāprabhu; *āilā*—returned; *kāṅthā*—quilt; *gale*—onto the shoulder; *diyā*—keeping.

### TRANSLATION

**Saying this, Sanātana Gosvāmī exchanged the blanket for the quilt. He then returned to Śrī Caitanya Mahāprabhu with the quilt on his shoulder.**

### TEXT 89

প্রভু কহে,—'তোমার ভোটকম্বল কোথা গেল ?'
প্রভুপদে সব কথা গোসাঞি কহিল ॥ ৮৯ ॥

*prabhu kahe,—'tomāra bhoṭa-kambala kothā gela?'*
*prabhu-pade saba kathā gosāñi kahila*

### SYNONYMS

*prabhu kahe*—Śrī Caitanya Mahāprabhu said; *tomāra*—your; *bhoṭa-kambala*—woolen blanket; *kothā gela*—where did it go; *prabhu-pade*—unto the lotus feet of Lord Caitanya; *saba*—all; *kathā*—narration; *gosāñi*—Sanātana Gosvāmī; *kahila*—said.

### TRANSLATION

**When Sanātana Gosvāmī returned, the Lord asked, "Where is your woolen blanket?" Sanātana Gosvāmī then narrated the whole story to the Lord.**

### TEXTS 90-91

প্রভু কহে,—"ইহা আমি করিয়াছি বিচার ।
বিষয়-রোগ খণ্ডাইল কৃষ্ণ যে তোমার ॥ ৯০ ॥
সে কেনে রাখিবে তোমার শেষ বিষয়-ভোগ ?
রোগ খণ্ডি' সদ্বৈদ্য না রাখে শেষ রোগ ॥ ৯১ ॥

*prabhu kahe,——"ihā āmi kariyāchi vicāra*
*viṣaya-roga khaṇḍāila kṛṣṇa ye tomāra*

*se kene rākhibe tomāra śeṣa viṣaya-bhoga?*
*roga khaṇḍi' sad-vaidya nā rākhe śeṣa roga*

### SYNONYMS

*prabhu kahe*—Śrī Caitanya Mahāprabhu said; *ihā*—this; *āmi*—I; *kariyāchi vicāra*—considered deliberately; *viṣaya-roga*—the disease of material attraction; *khaṇḍāila*—has now nullified; *kṛṣṇa*—Lord Kṛṣṇa; *ye*—since; *tomāra*—your; *se*—Lord Kṛṣṇa; *kene*—why; *rākhibe*—should allow you to keep; *tomāra*—your; *śeṣa*—last; *viṣaya-bhoga*—attraction for material things; *roga khaṇḍi'*—vanquishing the disease; *sat-vaidya*—a good physician; *nā rākhe*—does not keep; *śeṣa*—the last part; *roga*—disease.

### TRANSLATION

**Śrī Caitanya Mahāprabhu then said, "I have already deliberately considered this matter. Since Lord Kṛṣṇa is very merciful, He has nullified your attachment for material things. Why should Kṛṣṇa allow you to maintain a last bit of material attachment? After vanquishing a disease, a good physician does not allow any of the disease to remain.**

### TEXT 92

তিন মুদ্রার ভোট গায়, মাধুকরী গ্রাস ।
ধর্মহানি হয়, লোক করে উপহাস ॥" ৯২ ॥

*tina mudrāra bhoṭa gāya, mādhukarī grāsa*
*dharma-hāni haya, loka kare upahāsa"*

### SYNONYMS

*tina mudrāra bhoṭa*—a woolen blanket costing three gold coins; *gāya*—on the body; *mādhukarī grāsa*—and practicing the *mādhukarī* system; *dharma-hāni haya*—that is a religious discrepancy; *loka kare upahāsa*—people will joke.

### TRANSLATION

**"It is contradictory to practice mādhukarī and at the same time wear a valuable blanket. One loses his spiritual strength by doing this, and one will also become an object for jokes."**

### TEXT 93

গোসাঞি কহে,—'যে খণ্ডিল কুবিষয়-ভোগ ।
তাঁর ইচ্ছায় গেল মোর শেষ বিষয়-রোগ ॥" ৯৩ ॥

*gosāñi kahe,——'ye khaṇḍila kuviṣaya-bhoga*
*tāṅra icchāya gela mora śeṣa viṣaya-roga"*

### SYNONYMS

*gosāñi kahe*—Sanātana Gosvāmī said; *ye khaṇḍila*—the person who has vanquished; *ku-viṣaya-bhoga*—enjoyment of sinful material life; *tāṅra icchāya*—by His desire; *gela*—has gone; *mora*—my; *śeṣa*—last bit; *viṣaya-roga*—material disease.

### TRANSLATION

**Sanātana Gosvāmī replied, "The Supreme Personality of Godhead has saved me from the sinful life of material existence. By His desire, my last piece of material attraction is now gone."**

### TEXT 94

প্রসন্ন হঞা প্রভু তাঁরে কৃপা কৈল ।
তাঁর কৃপায় প্রশ্ন করিতে তাঁর শক্তি হৈল ॥ ৯৪ ॥

*prasanna hañā prabhu tāṅre kṛpā kaila*
*tāṅra kṛpāya praśna karite tāṅra śakti haila*

### SYNONYMS

*prasanna hañā*—being very pleased; *prabhu*—Śrī Caitanya Mahāprabhu; *tāṅre*—unto him; *kṛpā kaila*—offered His causeless mercy; *tāṅra kṛpāya*—by His mercy; *praśna karite*—to inquire; *tāṅra*—his; *śakti haila*—there was strength.

### TRANSLATION

**Being pleased with Sanātana Gosvāmī, Śrī Caitanya Mahāprabhu bestowed His causeless mercy upon him. By the Lord's mercy, Sanātana Gosvāmī received the spiritual strength to inquire from Him.**

### TEXTS 95-96

**পূর্বে যৈছে রায়-পাশে প্রভু প্রশ্ন কৈলা ।**
**তাঁর শক্ত্যে রামানন্দ তাঁর উত্তর দিলা ॥ ৯৫ ॥**
**ইহাঁ প্রভুর শক্ত্যে প্রশ্ন করে সনাতন ।**
**আপনে মহাপ্রভু করে 'তত্ত্ব'-নিরূপণ ॥ ৯৬ ॥**

*pūrve yaiche rāya-pāśe prabhu praśna kailā*
*tāṅra śaktye rāmānanda tāṅra uttara dilā*

*ihāṅ prabhura śaktye praśna kare sanātana*
*āpane mahāprabhu kare 'tattva'-nirūpaṇa*

### SYNONYMS

*pūrve*—formerly; *yaiche*—as; *rāya-pāśe*—unto Rāmānanda Rāya; *prabhu*—Śrī Caitanya Mahāprabhu; *praśna kailā*—inquired; *tāṅra śaktye*—only by His mercy; *rāmānanda*—Rāmānanda Rāya; *tāṅra*—his; *uttara*—answers; *dilā*—gave; *ihāṅ*—here; *prabhura*—of Śrī Caitanya Mahāprabhu; *śaktye*—by the strength; *praśna*—questions; *kare*—puts; *sanātana*—Sanātana Gosvāmī; *āpane*—personally; *mahāprabhu*—Śrī Caitanya Mahāprabhu; *kare*—does; *tattva*—the truth; *nirūpaṇa*—discerning.

### TRANSLATION

**Formerly, Śrī Caitanya Mahāprabhu asked Rāmānanda Rāya spiritual questions, and by the Lord's causeless mercy, Rāmānanda Rāya could properly reply. Now, by the Lord's mercy, Sanātana Gosvāmī questioned the Lord, and Śrī Caitanya Mahāprabhu personally supplied the truth.**

### TEXT 97

**কৃষ্ণস্বরূপমাধুর্যৈশ্বর্যভক্তিরসাশ্রয়ম্ ।**
**তত্ত্বং সনাতনায়েশঃ কৃপয়োপদিদেশ সঃ ॥ ৯৭ ॥**

*kṛṣṇa-svarūpa-mādhuryaiś-*
*varya-bhakti-rasāśrayam*

*tattvaṁ sanātanāyeśaḥ*
*kṛpayopadideśa saḥ*

### SYNONYMS

*kṛṣṇa-svarūpa*—of the real identity of Śrī Kṛṣṇa; *mādhurya*—of conjugal love; *aiśvarya*—of opulence; *bhakti*—of devotional service; *rasa*—of transcendental mellows; *āśrayam*—the shelter; *tattvam*—the truth; *sanātanāya*—unto Śrī Sanātana; *īśaḥ*—Śrī Caitanya Mahāprabhu, the Supreme Lord; *kṛpayā*—by His causeless mercy; *upadideśa*—instructed; *saḥ*—He.

### TRANSLATION

**Śrī Caitanya Mahāprabhu, the Supreme Personality of Godhead, personally told Sanātana Gosvāmī about Lord Kṛṣṇa's real identity. He also told him about the Lord's conjugal love, His personal opulence and the mellows of devotional service. All these truths were explained to Sanātana Gosvāmī by the Lord Himself out of His causeless mercy.**

### TEXT 98

তবে সনাতন প্রভুর চরণে ধরিয়া ।
দৈন্য বিনতি করে দন্তে তৃণ লঞা ॥ ৯৮ ॥

*tabe sanātana prabhura caraṇe dhariyā*
*dainya vinati kare dante tṛṇa lañā*

### SYNONYMS

*tabe*—thereafter; *sanātana*—Sanātana Gosvāmī; *prabhura*—of Śrī Caitanya Mahāprabhu; *caraṇe*—the lotus feet; *dhariyā*—catching; *dainya*—humility; *vinati*—bowing; *kare*—does; *dante*—in the teeth; *tṛṇa*—a straw; *lañā*—taking.

### TRANSLATION

**Putting a straw in his mouth and bowing down, Sanātana Gosvāmī clasped the lotus feet of Śrī Caitanya Mahāprabhu and humbly spoke as follows.**

### TEXT 99

"নীচ জাতি, নীচ-সঙ্গী, পতিত অধম ।
কুবিষয়-কূপে পড়ি' গোঙাইনু জনম ! ৯৯ ॥

*"nīca jāti, nīca-saṅgī, patita adhama*
*kuviṣaya-kūpe paḍi' goṅāinu janama!*

### SYNONYMS

*nīca jāti*—born of a low family; *nīca-saṅgī*—associated with low men; *patita*—fallen; *adhama*—the lowest; *ku-viṣaya-kūpe*—in a well of material enjoyment; *paḍi'*—having fallen down; *goṅāinu*—I have passed; *janama*—my life.

### TRANSLATION

**Sanātana Gosvāmī said, "I was born in a low family, and my associates are all low-class men. I myself am fallen and am the lowest of men. Indeed, I have passed my whole life falien in the well of sinful materialism.**

### PURPORT

Actually Śrī Sanātana Gosvāmī belonged to a *brāhmaṇa* family because he belonged to the Sārasvata division of the *brāhmaṇas* and was well cultured and well educated. Somehow or other he accepted a ministership in the Muslim government; therefore he had to associate with meat-eaters, drunkards and gross materialists. Sanātana Gosvāmī considered himself fallen, for in the association of such men, he also fell victim to material enjoyment. Having passed his life in that way, he considered that he had wasted his valuable time. This statement about how one can become fallen in this material world is made by the greatest authority in the Gauḍīya Vaiṣṇava-sampradāya. Actually the whole world is presently fallen into material existence. Everyone is a meat-eater, drunkard, woman hunter, gambler and whatnot. People are enjoying material life by committing the four basic sins. Although they are fallen, if they simply submit themselves at the lotus feet of Śrī Caitanya Mahāprabhu, they will be saved from sinful reactions.

### TEXT 100

আপনার হিতাহিত কিছুই না জানি !
গ্রাম্য-ব্যবহারে পণ্ডিত, তাই সত্য মানি ॥ ১০০ ॥

*āpanāra hitāhita kichui nā jāni!*
*grāmya-vyavahāre paṇḍita, tāi satya māni*

### SYNONYMS

*āpanāra*—of my personal self; *hita*—welfare; *ahita*—inauspiciousness; *kichui*—anything; *nā jāni*—I do not know; *grāmya-vyavahāre*—in ordinary dealings; *paṇḍita*—a learned man; *tāi satya māni*—I accept that as truth.

### TRANSLATION

**"I do not know what is beneficial for me and what is detrimental. Nonetheless, in ordinary dealings people consider me a learned scholar, and I am also thinking of myself as such.**

## TEXT 101

কৃপা করি' যদি মোরে করিয়াছ উদ্ধার ।
আপন-কৃপাতে কহ 'কর্তব্য' আমার ॥ ১০১ ॥

*kṛpā kari' yadi more kariyācha uddhāra*
*āpana-kṛpāte kaha 'kartavya' āmāra*

### SYNONYMS

*kṛpā kari'*—by Your causeless mercy; *yadi*—if; *more*—unto me; *kariyācha*—You have done; *uddhāra*—deliverance; *āpana-kṛpāte*—by Your own mercy; *kaha*—please speak; *kartavya āmāra*—my duty.

### TRANSLATION

**"Out of Your causeless mercy, You have delivered me from the materialistic path. Now, by the same causeless mercy, please tell me what my duty is.**

## TEXT 102

'কে আমি', 'কেনে আমায় জারে তাপত্রয়' ।
ইহা নাহি জানি—'কেমনে হিত হয়' ॥ ১০২ ॥

*'ke āmi', 'kene āmāya jāre tāpa-traya'*
*ihā nāhi jāni——'kemane hita haya'*

### SYNONYMS

*ke āmi*—who am I; *kene*—why; *āmāya*—unto me; *jāre*—give trouble; *tāpa-traya*—the three kinds of miserable conditions; *ihā*—this; *nāhi jāni*—I do not know; *kemane*—how; *hita*—my welfare; *haya*—there is.

### TRANSLATION

**"Who am I? Why do the threefold miseries always give me trouble? If I do not know this, how can I be benefited?**

### PURPORT

The threefold material miseries are miseries arising from the body and the mind, miseries arising from dealings with other living entities, and miseries arising from natural disturbances. Sometimes we suffer bodily when we are attacked by a fever, and sometimes we suffer mentally when a close relative dies. Other living entities also cause us misery. There are living entities born of the human embryo, of eggs, perspiration and vegetation. Miserable conditions brought about by natural catastrophes are controlled by the higher demigods. There may be severe cold or thunderbolts, or a person may be haunted by ghosts. These threefold miseries are always before us, and they entrap us in a dangerous situation. *Padaṁ padaṁ yad vipadām.* There is danger in every step of life.

### TEXT 103

'সাধ্য'-'সাধন'-তত্ত্ব পুছিতে না জানি ।
কৃপা করি' সব তত্ত্ব কহ ত' আপনি ॥" ১০৩ ॥

*'sādhya'-'sādhana'-tattva puchite nā jāni*
*kṛpā kari' saba tattva kaha ta' āpani"*

### SYNONYMS

*sādhya*—of the goal of spiritual life; *sādhana*—of the process of obtaining that goal; *tattva*—truth; *puchite*—to inquire; *nā jāni*—I do not know; *kṛpā kari'*—by Your causeless mercy; *saba tattva*—all such truths; *kaha ta' āpani*—please personally explain to me.

### TRANSLATION

**"Actually I do not know how to inquire about the goal of life and the process for obtaining it. Being merciful upon me, please explain all these truths."**

### TEXT 104

প্রভু কহে,—"কৃষ্ণ-কৃপা তোমাতে পূর্ণ হয় ।
সব তত্ত্ব জান, তোমার নাহি তাপত্রয় ॥ ১০৪ ॥

*prabhu kahe,——"kṛṣṇa-kṛpā tomāte pūrṇa haya*
*saba tattva jāna, tomāra nāhi tāpa-traya*

### SYNONYMS

*prabhu*—Śrī Caitanya Mahāprabhu; *kahe*—said; *kṛṣṇa-kṛpā*—the mercy of Kṛṣṇa; *tomāte*—on you; *pūrṇa*—full; *haya*—there is; *saba tattva*—all truths; *jāna*—you know; *tomāra*—of you; *nāhi*—there is not; *tāpa-traya*—the threefold miseries.

### TRANSLATION

**Śrī Caitanya Mahāprabhu said, "Lord Kṛṣṇa has bestowed His full mercy upon you so that all these things are known to you. For you, the threefold miseries certainly do not exist.**

## TEXT 105

কৃষ্ণশক্তি ধর তুমি, জান তত্ত্বভাব।
জানি' দার্ঢ্য লাগি' পুছে,—সাধুর স্বভাব॥ ১০৫॥

*kṛṣṇa-śakti dhara tumi, jāna tattva-bhāva*
*jāni' dārḍhya lāgi' puche,——sādhura svabhāva*

## SYNONYMS

*kṛṣṇa-śakti*—the energy of Lord Kṛṣṇa; *dhara*—process; *tumi*—you; *jāna*—know; *tattva-bhāva*—the factual position; *jāni'*—although knowing all these things; *dārḍhya lāgi'*—for the sake of strictness; *puche*—he inquires; *sādhura*—of the saintly persons; *sva-bhāva*—the nature.

## TRANSLATION

**"Since you possess Lord Kṛṣṇa's potency, you certainly know these things. However, it is the nature of a sādhu to inquire. Although he knows these things, the sādhu inquires for the sake of strictness.**

## TEXT 106

অচিরাদেব সর্বার্থঃ সিধ্যত্যেষামভীপ্সিতঃ।
সদ্ধর্মস্যাববোধায় যেষাং নির্বন্ধিনী মতিঃ॥ ১০৬॥

*acirād eva sarvārthaḥ*
*sidhyaty eṣām abhīpsitaḥ*
*sad-dharmasyāvabodhāya*
*yeṣāṁ nirbandhinī matiḥ*

## SYNONYMS

*acirāt*—very soon; eva—certainly; *sarva-arthaḥ*—the goal of life; *sidhyati*—becomes fulfilled; *eṣām*—of these persons; *abhīpsitaḥ*—desired; *sat-dharmasya*—of the path of progressive devotional service; *avabodhāya*—for understanding; *yeṣām*—those whose; *nirbandhinī*—unflinching; *matiḥ*—intelligence.

## TRANSLATION

**" 'Those who are anxious to awaken their spiritual consciousness, who have unflinching intelligence and who are not deviated, certainly attain the desired goal.'**

## PURPORT

This verse, quoted from the *Nāradīya Purāṇa,* is found in *Bhakti-rasāmṛta-sindhu* (1.2.103).

## TEXT 107

যোগ্যপাত্র হও তুমি ভক্তি প্রবর্তাইতে।
ক্রমে সব তত্ত্ব শুন, কহিয়ে তোমাতে ॥ ১০৭ ॥

*yogya-pātra hao tumi bhakti pravartāite*
*krame saba tattva śuna, kahiye tomāte*

## SYNONYMS

*yogya-pātra*—fit person; *hao*—are; *tumi*—you; *bhakti*—devotional service; *pravartāite*—to propagate; *krame*—one after another; *saba*—all; *tattva*—truths; *śuna*—please hear; *kahiye*—I shall speak; *tomāte*—to you.

## TRANSLATION

**"You are fit to propagate the cult of devotional service. Therefore gradually hear all the truths about it from Me. I shall tell you about them.**

## TEXTS 108-109

জীবের 'স্বরূপ' হয়—কৃষ্ণের 'নিত্যদাস'।
কৃষ্ণের 'তটস্থা-শক্তি', 'ভেদাভেদ-প্রকাশ' ॥ ১০৮ ॥
সূর্যাংশ-কিরণ, যৈছে অগ্নিজ্বালাচয়।
স্বাভাবিক কৃষ্ণের তিনপ্রকার 'শক্তি' হয় ॥ ১০৯ ॥

*jīvera 'svarūpa' haya——kṛṣṇera 'nitya-dāsa'*
*kṛṣṇera 'taṭasthā-śakti', 'bhedābheda-prakāśa'*

*sūryāṁśa-kiraṇa, yaiche agni-jvālā-caya*
*svābhāvika kṛṣṇera tina-prakāra 'śakti' haya*

## SYNONYMS

*jīvera*—of the living entity; *sva-rūpa*—the constitutional position; *haya*—is; *kṛṣṇera*—of Lord Kṛṣṇa; *nitya-dāsa*—eternal servant; *kṛṣṇera*—of Lord Kṛṣṇa; *taṭa-sthā*—marginal; *śakti*—potency; *bheda-abheda*—one and different; *prakāśa*—manifestation; *sūrya-aṁśa*—part and parcel of the sun; *kiraṇa*—a ray of sunshine;

*yaiche*—as; *agni-jvālā-caya*—molecular particle of fire; *svābhāvika*—naturally; *kṛṣṇera*—of Lord Kṛṣṇa; *tina-prakāra*—three varieties; *śakti*—energies; *haya*—there are.

## TRANSLATION

**"It is the living entity's constitutional position to be an eternal servant of Kṛṣṇa because he is the marginal energy of Kṛṣṇa and a manifestation simultaneously one and different from the Lord, like a molecular particle of sunshine or fire. Kṛṣṇa has three varieties of energy.**

## PURPORT

Śrīla Bhaktivinoda Ṭhākura paraphrases these verses as follows: Śrī Sanātana Gosvāmī asked Śrī Caitanya Mahāprabhu, "Who am I?" In answer, the Lord replied, "You are a pure living entity. You are neither the material body nor the subtle body composed of mind and intelligence. Actually you are a spirit soul, eternal part and parcel of the Supreme Soul, Kṛṣṇa. Therefore you are His eternal servant. You belong to Kṛṣṇa's marginal potency. There are two worlds—the spiritual world and the material world—and you are situated between the material and spiritual potencies. You have a relationship with both the material and spiritual worlds; therefore you are called the marginal potency. You are related with Kṛṣṇa as one and simultaneously different. Because you are spirit soul, you are one in quality with the Supreme Personality of Godhead, but because you are a very minute particle of spirit soul, you are different from the Supreme Soul. Therefore your position is simultaneously one with and different from the Supreme Soul. The examples given are those of the sun itself and the small particles of sunshine and of a blazing fire and the small particles of fire." Another explanation of these verses can be found in *Ādi-līlā* (Chapter Two, verse 96).

## TEXT 110

একদেশস্থিতস্যাগ্নের্জ্যোৎস্না বিস্তারিণী যথা।
পরস্য ব্রহ্মণঃ শক্তিস্তথেদমখিলং জগৎ ॥ ১১০ ॥

*eka-deśa-sthitasyāgner*
*jyotsnā vistāriṇī yathā*
*parasya brahmaṇaḥ śaktis*
*tathedam akhilaṁ jagat*

## SYNONYMS

*eka-deśa*—in one place; *sthitasya*—being situated; *agneḥ*—of fire; *jyotsnā*—the illumination; *vistāriṇī*—expanded everywhere; *yathā*—just as; *parasya*—of the Supreme; *brahmaṇaḥ*—of the Absolute Truth; *śaktiḥ*—the energy; *tathā*—similarly; *idam*—this; *akhilam*—entire; *jagat*—universe.

### TRANSLATION

**" 'Just as the illumination of a fire, which is situated in one place, is spread all over, the energies of the Supreme Personality of Godhead, Parabrahman, are spread all over this universe.'**

### PURPORT

This is a quotation from the *Viṣṇu Purāṇa* (1.22.53).

### TEXT 111

**কৃষ্ণের স্বাভাবিক তিনশক্তি-পরিণতি ।**
**চিচ্ছক্তি, জীবশক্তি, আর মায়াশক্তি ॥ ১১১ ॥**

*kṛṣṇera svābhāvika tina-śakti-pariṇati*
*cic-chakti, jīva-śakti, āra māyā-śakti*

### SYNONYMS

*kṛṣṇera*—of Lord Kṛṣṇa; *svābhāvika*—natural; *tina*—three; *śakti*—of energies; *pariṇati*—transformations; *cit-śakti*—spiritual potency; *jīva-śakti*—spiritual sparks, living entities; *āra*—and; *māyā-śakti*—illusory energy.

### TRANSLATION

**"Lord Kṛṣṇa naturally has three energetic transformations, and these are known as the spiritual potency, the living entity potency and the illusory potency.**

### TEXT 112

বিষ্ণুশক্তিঃ পরা প্রোক্তা ক্ষেত্রজ্ঞাখ্যা তথাপরা ।
অবিদ্যা-কর্মসংজ্ঞান্যা তৃতীয়া শক্তিরিষ্যতে ॥ ১১২ ॥

*viṣṇu-śaktiḥ parā proktā*
*kṣetrajñākhyā tathā parā*
*avidyā-karma-saṁjñānyā*
*tṛtīyā śaktir iṣyate*

### SYNONYMS

*viṣṇu-śaktiḥ*—the potency of Lord Viṣṇu; *parā*—spiritual; *proktā*—it is said; *kṣetra-jña-ākhyā*—the potency known as *kṣetrajña; tathā*—as well as; *parā*—spiritual; *avidyā*—ignorance; *karma*—fruitive activities; *saṁjñā*—known as; *anyā*—other; *tṛtīyā*—third; *śaktiḥ*—potency; *iṣyate*—known thus.

### TRANSLATION

**" 'Originally, Kṛṣṇa's energy is spiritual, and the energy known as the living entity is also spiritual. However, there is another energy, called illusion, which consists of fruitive activity. That is the Lord's third potency.'**

### PURPORT

For a further explanation of this verse, refer to the *Ādi-līlā,* Chapter Seven, verse 119.

### TEXT 113

শক্তয়ঃ সর্বভাবানামচিন্ত্যজ্ঞানগোচরাঃ ।
যতোঽতো ব্রহ্মণস্তাস্তু সর্গাদ্যা ভাবশক্তয়ঃ ।
ভবন্তি তপতাং শ্রেষ্ঠ পাবকস্য যথোষ্ণতা ॥ ১১৩ ॥

*śaktayaḥ sarva-bhāvānām*
*acintya-jñāna-gocarāḥ*
*yato 'to brahmaṇas tās tu*
*sargādyā bhāva-śaktayaḥ*
*bhavanti tapatāṁ śreṣṭha*
*pāvakasya yathoṣṇatā*

### SYNONYMS

*śaktayaḥ*—energies; *sarva-bhāvānām*—of all types of creation; *acintya*—inconceivable; *jñāna-gocarāḥ*—by the range of man's knowledge; *yataḥ*—from whom; *ataḥ*—therefore; *brahmaṇaḥ*—from the Absolute Truth; *tāḥ*—those; *tu*—but; *sarga-ādyāḥ*—bringing about creation, maintenance and annihilation; *bhāva-śaktayaḥ*—the creative energies; *bhavanti*—are; *tapatām*—of all the ascetics; *śreṣṭha*—O chief; *pāvakasya*—of fire; *yathā*—as; *uṣṇatā*—heat.

### TRANSLATION

**" 'All the creative energies, which are inconceivable to a common man, exist in the Supreme Absolute Truth. These inconceivable energies act in the process of creation, maintenance and annihilation. O chief of the ascetics, just**

**as there are two energies possessed by fire—namely heat and light—these inconceivable creative energies are the natural characteristics of the Absolute Truth.'**

## PURPORT

This is a quotation from the *Viṣṇu Purāṇa* (1.3.2).

## TEXT 114

যয়া ক্ষেত্রজ্ঞশক্তিঃ সা বেষ্টিতা নৃপ সর্বগা ।
সংসারতাপানখিলানবাপ্নোত্যত্র সন্ততান্ ॥ ১১৪ ॥

*yayā kṣetra-jña-śaktiḥ sā*
*veṣṭitā nṛpa sarva-gā*
*saṁsāra-tāpān akhilān*
*avāpnoty atra santatān*

## SYNONYMS

*yayā*—by which; *kṣetra-jña-śaktiḥ*—the living entities, known as the *kṣetra-jña* potency; *sā*—that potency; *veṣṭitā*—covered; *nṛpa*—O King; *sarva-gā*—capable of going anywhere in the spiritual or material worlds; *saṁsāra-tāpān*—miseries due to the cycle of repeated birth and death; *akhilān*—all kinds of; *avāpnoti*—obtains; *atra*—in this material world; *santatān*—arising from suffering or enjoying various kinds of reactions to fruitive activities.

## TRANSLATION

**" 'O King, the kṣetra-jña-śakti is the living entity. Although he has the facility to live in either the material or spiritual world, he suffers the threefold miseries of material existence because he is influenced by the avidyā [nescience] potency, which covers his constitutional position.**

## PURPORT

This and the following verse are also quoted from the *Viṣṇu Purāṇa* (6.7.62-63).

## TEXT 115

তয়া তিরোহিতত্বাচ্চ শক্তিঃ ক্ষেত্রজ্ঞ-সংজ্ঞিতা ।
সর্বভূতেষু ভূপাল তারতম্যেন বর্ততে ॥ ১১৫ ॥

*tayā tirohitatvāc ca*
*śaktiḥ kṣetra-jña-saṁjñitā*

*sarva-bhūteṣu bhū-pāla*
*tāratamyena vartate*

## SYNONYMS

*tayā*—by her; *tiraḥ-hitatvāt*—from being freed from the influence; *ca*—also; *śaktiḥ*—the potency; *kṣetra-jña*—*kṣetra-jña; saṁjñitā*—known by the name; *sarva-bhūteṣu*—in different types of bodies; *bhū-pāla*—O King; *tāratamyena*—in different degrees; *vartate*—exists.

## TRANSLATION

**" 'This living entity, covered by the influence of nescience, exists in different forms in the material condition. O King, he is thus proportionately freed from the influence of material energy, to greater or lesser degrees.'**

## TEXT 116

অপরেয়মিতস্ত্বন্যাং প্রকৃতিং বিদ্ধি মে পরাম্‌।
জীবভূতাং মহাবাহো যয়েদং ধার্যতে জগৎ ॥ ১১৬ ॥

*apareyam itas tv anyāṁ*
*prakṛtiṁ viddhi me parām*
*jīva-bhūtāṁ mahā-bāho*
*yayedaṁ dhāryate jagat*

## SYNONYMS

*aparā*—inferior energy; *iyam*—this material world; *itaḥ*—beyond this; *tu*—but; *anyām*—another; *prakṛtim*—energy; *viddhi*—you must know; *me*—of Me; *parām*—which is superior energy; *jīva-bhūtām*—they are the living entities; *mahā-bāho*—O mighty-armed; *yayā*—by which; *idam*—this material world; *dhāryate*—is being conducted; *jagat*—the cosmic manifestation.

## TRANSLATION

**" 'Besides this inferior nature, O mighty-armed Arjuna, there is a superior energy of Mine, which consists of all living entities who are struggling with material nature and are sustaining the universe.'**

## PURPORT

This is a verse from *Bhagavad-gītā* (7.5). It is also quoted in the *Ādi-līlā* (Chapter Seven, verse 118).

## TEXT 117

**কৃষ্ণ ভুলি' সেই জীব অনাদি-বহির্মুখ।**
**অতএব মায়া তারে দেয় সংসার-দুঃখ॥ ১১৭॥**

*kṛṣṇa bhuli' sei jīva anādi-bahirmukha*
*ataeva māyā tāre deya saṁsāra-duḥkha*

### SYNONYMS

*kṛṣṇa bhuli'*—forgetting Kṛṣṇa; *sei jīva*—that living entity; *anādi*—from time immemorial; *bahiḥ-mukha*—attracted by the external feature; *ataeva*—therefore; *māyā*—illusory energy; *tāre*—to him; *deya*—gives; *saṁsāra-duḥkha*—miseries of material existence.

### TRANSLATION

**"Forgetting Kṛṣṇa, the living entity has been attracted by the external feature from time immemorial. Therefore the illusory energy [māyā] gives him all kinds of misery in his material existence.**

### PURPORT

When the living entity forgets his constitutional position as an eternal servant of Kṛṣṇa, he is immediately entrapped by the illusory, external energy. The living entity is originally part and parcel of Kṛṣṇa and is therefore the superior energy of Kṛṣṇa. He is endowed with inconceivable minute energy that works inconceivably within the body. However, the living entity, forgetting his position, is situated in material energy. The living entity is called the marginal energy because by nature he is spiritual but by forgetfulness he is situated in the material energy. Thus he has the power to live either in the material energy or in the spiritual energy, and for this reason he is called marginal energy. He is sometimes attracted by the external illusory energy when he stays in the marginal position, and this is the beginning of his material life. When he enters the material energy, he is subjected to the threefold time measurement—past, present and future. Past, present and future belong only to the material world; they do not exist in the spiritual world. The living entity is eternal, and he existed before the creation of this material world. Unfortunately he has forgotten his relationship with Kṛṣṇa. The living entity's forgetfulness is described herein as *anādi,* which indicates that it has existed since time immemorial. One should understand that due to his desire to enjoy himself in competition with Kṛṣṇa, the living entity comes into material existence.

## TEXT 118

**কভু স্বর্গে উঠায়, কভু নরকে ডুবায়।**
**দণ্ড্যজনে রাজা যেন নদীতে চুবায়॥ ১১৮॥**

*kabhu svarge uṭhāya, kabhu narake ḍubāya*
*daṇḍya-jane rājā yena nadīte cubāya*

## SYNONYMS

*kabhu*—sometimes; *svarge*—to higher planetary systems; *uṭhāya*—he rises; *kabhu*—sometimes; *narake*—in hellish conditions of life; *ḍubāya*—he is drowned; *daṇḍya-jane*—a criminal; *rājā*—a king; *yena*—as; *nadīte*—in the river; *cubāya*—dunks.

## TRANSLATION

**"In the material condition, the living entity is sometimes raised to higher planetary systems and material prosperity and sometimes drowned in a hellish situation. His state is exactly like that of a criminal whom a king punishes by submerging him in water and then raising him again from the water.**

## PURPORT

In the *Vedas* it is stated, *asaṅgo 'yaṁ puruṣaḥ:* the living entity is always free from the contamination of the material world. One who is not materially infected and who does not forget Kṛṣṇa as his master is called *nitya-mukta.* In other words, one who is eternally liberated from material contamination is called *nitya-mukta.* From time immemorial the *nitya-mukta* living entity has always been a devotee of Kṛṣṇa, and his only attempt has been to serve Kṛṣṇa. Thus he never forgets his eternal servitorship to Kṛṣṇa. Any living entity who forgets his eternal relationship with Kṛṣṇa is under the sway of the material condition. Bereft of the Lord's transcendental loving service, he is subjected to the reactions of fruitive activity. When he is elevated to the higher planetary systems due to worldly pious activities, he considers himself well situated, but when he is subjected to punishment, he thinks himself improperly situated. Thus material nature awards and punishes the living entity. When the living entity is materially opulent, material nature is rewarding him. When he is materially embarrassed, material nature is punishing him.

## TEXT 119

ভয়ং দ্বিতীয়াভিনিবেশতঃ স্যা-
দীশাদপেতস্য বিপর্যয়োঽস্মৃতিঃ।
তন্মায়য়াতো বুধ আভজেত্তং
ভক্ত্যৈকয়েশং গুরুদেবতাত্মা॥ ১১৯ ॥

*bhayaṁ dvitīyābhiniveśataḥ syād*
*īśād apetasya viparyayo 'smṛtiḥ*

*tan-māyayāto budha ābhajet taṁ*
*bhaktyaikayeśaṁ guru-devatātmā*

## SYNONYMS

*bhayam*—fear; *dvitīya-abhiniveśataḥ*—from the misconception of being a product of material energy; *syāt*—arises; *īśāt*—from the Supreme Personality of Godhead, Kṛṣṇa; *apetasya*—of one who has withdrawn (the conditioned soul); *viparyayaḥ*—reversal of the position; *asmṛtiḥ*—no conception of his relationship with the Supreme Lord; *tat-māyayā*—because of the illusory energy of the Supreme Lord; *ataḥ*—therefore; *budhaḥ*—one who is wise; *ābhajet*—must worship; *tam*—Him; *bhaktyā*—by devotional service; *ekayā*—undiverted to *karma* and *jñāna; īśam*—the Supreme Personality of Godhead; *guru*—as the spiritual master; *devatā*—the worshipable Lord; *ātmā*—the Supersoul.

## TRANSLATION

**" 'When the living entity is attracted by the material energy, which is separate from Kṛṣṇa, he is overpowered by fear. Because he is separated from the Supreme Personality of Godhead by the material energy, his conception of life is reversed. In other words, instead of being the eternal servant of Kṛṣṇa, he becomes Kṛṣṇa's competitor. This is called viparyayo 'smṛtiḥ. To nullify this mistake, one who is actually learned and advanced worships the Supreme Personality of Godhead as his spiritual master, worshipful Deity and source of life. He thus worships the Lord by the process of unalloyed devotional service.'**

## PURPORT

This is a quotation from *Śrīmad-Bhāgavatam* (11.2.37). It is an instruction given by Kavi Ṛṣi, one of the nine saintly personalities called the nine Yogendras. When Vasudeva, Kṛṣṇa's father, asked Devarṣi Nārada in Dvārakā about devotional service, it was mentioned that previously King Nimi, who was the King of Videha, was instructed by the nine Yogendras. When Śrī Nārada Muni discoursed on *bhāgavata-dharma,* devotional service, he indicated how a conditioned soul can be liberated by engaging in the loving transcendental service of the Lord. The Lord is the Supersoul, spiritual master and worshipable Deity of all conditioned souls. Not only is Kṛṣṇa the supreme worshipful Deity for all living entities, but He is also the *guru,* or *caitya-guru,* the Supersoul who always gives the living entity good counsel. Unfortunately the living entity neglects the Supreme Person's instructions. He thus identifies with material energy and is consequently overpowered by a kind of fear resulting from accepting himself as the material body and considering paraphernalia related to the material body to be his property. All types of fruitive results actually come from the spirit soul, but because he has forgotten his real duty, he is embarrassed by many material consequences such as fear and attachment. The only remedy is to revert to the service of the Lord and thus be saved from material nature's unwanted harassment.

### TEXT 120

সাধু-শাস্ত্র-কৃপায় যদি কৃষ্ণোন্মুখ হয়।
সেই জীব নিস্তরে, মায়া তাহারে ছাড়য় ॥ ১২০ ॥

*sādhu-śāstra-kṛpāya yadi kṛṣṇonmukha haya*
*sei jīva nistare, māyā tāhāre chāḍaya*

### SYNONYMS

*sādhu*—of saintly persons; *śāstra*—of scriptures; *kṛpāya*—by the mercy; *yadi*—if; *kṛṣṇa-unmukha haya*—one becomes Kṛṣṇa conscious; *sei*—that; *jīva*—living entity; *nistare*—becomes liberated; *māyā*—the illusory energy; *tāhāre*—him; *chāḍaya*—gives up.

### TRANSLATION

**"If the conditioned soul becomes Kṛṣṇa conscious by the mercy of saintly persons who voluntarily preach scriptural injunctions and help him to become Kṛṣṇa conscious, the conditioned soul is liberated from the clutches of māyā, who gives him up.**

### PURPORT

A conditioned soul is one who has forgotten Kṛṣṇa as his eternal master. Thinking that he is enjoying the material world, the conditioned soul suffers the threefold miseries of material existence. Saintly persons (*sādhus*), Vaiṣṇava devotees of the Lord, preach Kṛṣṇa consciousness on the basis of Vedic literature. It is only by their mercy that the conditioned soul is awakened to Kṛṣṇa consciousness. When awakened, he is no longer eager to enjoy the materialistic way of life. Instead, he devotes himself to the loving transcendental service of the Lord. When one engages in the Lord's devotional service, he becomes detached from material enjoyment.

*bhaktiḥ pareśānubhavo viraktir*
*anyatra caiṣa trika eka-kālaḥ*
(*Bhāg.* 11.2.42)

This is the test by which one can tell whether he is advancing in devotional service. One must be detached from material enjoyment. Such detachment means that *māyā* has actually given the conditioned soul liberation from illusory enjoyment. When one is advanced in Kṛṣṇa consciousness, he does not consider himself as good as Kṛṣṇa. Whenever he thinks that he is the enjoyer of material advantages, he is imprisoned in the bodily conception. However, when he is freed from the bodily conception, he can engage in devotional service, which is his actual position of freedom from the clutches of *māyā*. This is all explained in the following verse from *Bhagavad-gītā* (7.14).

## TEXT 121

দৈবী হ্যেষা গুণময়ী মম মায়া দুরত্যয়া।
মামেব যে প্রপদ্যন্তে মায়ামেতাং তরন্তি তে ॥ ১২১ ॥

*daivī hy eṣā guṇamayī*
*mama māyā duratyayā*
*mām eva ye prapadyante*
*māyām etāṁ taranti te*

### SYNONYMS

*daivī*—belonging to the Supreme Lord; *hi*—certainly; *eṣā*—this; *guṇa-mayī*—made of the three modes; *mama*—My; *māyā*—external energy; *duratyayā*—very difficult to surpass; *mām*—unto Me; *eva*—certainly; *ye*—those who; *prapadyante*—surrender fully; *māyām*—illusory energy; *etām*—this; *taranti*—cross over; *te*—they.

### TRANSLATION

**" 'This divine energy of Mine, consisting of the three modes of material nature, is difficult to overcome. But those who have surrendered unto Me can easily cross beyond it.'**

## TEXT 122

**মায়ামুগ্ধ জীবের নাহি স্বতঃ কৃষ্ণজ্ঞান।**
**জীবেরে কৃপায় কৈলা কৃষ্ণ বেদ-পুরাণ ॥ ১২২ ॥**

*māyā-mugdha jīvera nāhi svataḥ kṛṣṇa-jñāna*
*jīvere kṛpāya kailā kṛṣṇa veda-purāṇa*

### SYNONYMS

*māyā-mugdha*—enchanted by the illusory energy; *jīvera*—of the conditioned soul; *nāhi*—there is not; *svataḥ*—automatically; *kṛṣṇa-jñāna*—knowledge of

Kṛṣṇa; *jīvere*—unto the conditioned soul; *kṛpāya*—out of mercy; *kailā*—presented; *kṛṣṇa*—Lord Kṛṣṇa; *veda-purāṇa*—the Vedic literature and the *Purāṇas* (supplements to the Vedic literature).

## TRANSLATION

**"The conditioned soul cannot revive his Kṛṣṇa consciousness by his own effort. But out of causeless mercy, Lord Kṛṣṇa compiled the Vedic literature and its supplements, the Purāṇas.**

## PURPORT

A conditioned soul is bewildered by the Lord's illusory energy (*māyā*). *Māyā's* business is to keep the conditioned soul forgetful of his real relationship with Kṛṣṇa. Thus the living entity forgets his real identity as spirit soul, Brahman, and instead of realizing his factual position thinks himself the product of the material energy. According to *Śrīmad-Bhāgavatam* (1.7.5):

*yayā sammohito jīva*
*ātmānaṁ tri-guṇātmakam*
*paro 'pi manute 'narthaṁ*
*tat-kṛtaṁ cābhipadyate*

"Due to this external energy, the living entity, although transcendental to the three modes of material nature, thinks of himself as a material product and thus undergoes the reactions of material miseries."

This is a description of *māyā's* action upon the conditioned soul. Thinking himself a product of the material energy, the conditioned soul engages in the service of material energy in so many ways. He becomes the servant of lust, anger, greed and envy. In this way one totally becomes a servant of the illusory energy. Later, the bewildered soul becomes a servant of mental speculation, but in any case he is simply covered by the illusory energy. Out of his causeless mercy and compassion, Kṛṣṇa has compiled various Vedic literatures in His incarnation as Vyāsadeva. Vyāsadeva is a *śaktyāveśa-avatāra* of Lord Kṛṣṇa. He has very kindly presented these literatures to awaken the conditioned soul to his senses. Unfortunately, at the present moment the conditioned souls are guided by demons who do not care to read the Vedic literatures. Although there is an immense treasure-house of knowledge, people are engaged in reading useless literature that will give them no information on how to get out of the clutches of *māyā*. The purpose of the Vedic literatures is explained in the following verses.

## TEXT 123

'শাস্ত্র-গুরু-আত্ম'-রূপে আপনারে জানান ।
'কৃষ্ণ মোর প্রভু, ত্রাতা'—জীবের হয় জ্ঞান ॥ ১২৩ ॥

*'śāstra-guru-ātma'-rūpe āpanāre jānāna*
*'kṛṣṇa mora prabhu, trātā'——jīvera haya jñāna*

## SYNONYMS

*śāstra-guru-ātma-rūpe*—in the form of Vedic literature, the spiritual master and the Supersoul; *āpanāre jānāna*—informs about Himself; *kṛṣṇa*—Lord Kṛṣṇa; *mora*—my; *prabhu*—Lord; *trātā*—deliver; *jīvera*—of the conditioned soul; *haya*—there is; *jñāna*—knowledge.

## TRANSLATION

**"The forgetful conditioned soul is educated by Kṛṣṇa through the Vedic literatures, the realized spiritual master and the Supersoul. Through these, he can understand the Supreme Personality of Godhead as He is, and he can understand that Lord Kṛṣṇa is his eternal master and deliverer from the clutches of māyā. In this way one can acquire real knowledge of his conditioned life and can come to understand how to attain liberation.**

## PURPORT

Being forgetful of his real position, the conditioned soul may take help from *śāstra, guru* and the Supersoul within his heart. Kṛṣṇa is situated within everyone's heart as the Supersoul. As stated in *Bhagavad-gītā:*

*īśvaraḥ sarva-bhūtānāṁ*
*hṛd-deśe 'rjuna tiṣṭhati*
*bhrāmayan sarva-bhūtāni*
*yantrārūḍhāni māyayā*

"The Supreme Lord is situated in everyone's heart, O Arjuna, and is directing the wanderings of all living entities, who are seated as on a machine, made of the material energy." (Bg. 18.61)

As the *śaktyāveśa-avatāra* Vyāsadeva, Kṛṣṇa teaches the conditioned soul through Vedic literatures. Kṛṣṇa externally appears as the spiritual master and trains the conditioned soul to come to Kṛṣṇa consciousness. When his original Kṛṣṇa consciousness is revived, the conditioned soul is delivered from the material clutches. Thus a conditioned soul is always helped by the Supreme Personality of

Godhead in three ways—by the scriptures, the spiritual master and the Supersoul within the heart. The Lord is the deliverer of the conditioned soul and is accepted as the Supreme Lord of all living entities. Kṛṣṇa says in *Bhagavad-gītā* (18.66):

*sarva-dharmān parityajya*
*mām ekaṁ śaraṇaṁ vraja*
*ahaṁ tvāṁ sarva-pāpebhyo*
*mokṣayiṣyāmi mā śucaḥ*

This same instruction is found throughout all Vedic literature. *Sādhu, śāstra* and *guru* act as the representatives of Kṛṣṇa, and the Kṛṣṇa consciousness movement is also taking place all over the universe. Whoever takes advantage of this opportunity becomes liberated.

### TEXT 124

**বেদশাস্ত্র কহে—'সম্বন্ধ', 'অভিধেয়', 'প্রয়োজন'।**
**'কৃষ্ণ'—প্রাপ্য সম্বন্ধ,'ভক্তি'—প্রাপ্ত্যের সাধন ॥১২৪॥**

*veda-śāstra kahe——'sambandha', 'abhidheya', 'prayojana'*
*'kṛṣṇa'——prāpya sambandha, 'bhakti'——prāptyera sādhana*

### SYNONYMS

*veda-śāstra kahe*—the Vedic literature instructs; *sambandha*—the conditioned soul's relationship with the Lord; *abhidheya*—the regulated activities of the conditioned soul for reviving that relationship; *prayojana*—and the ultimate goal of life to be attained by the conditioned soul; *kṛṣṇa*—Lord Kṛṣṇa; *prāpya*—to be awakened; *sambandha*—the original relationship; *bhakti*—devotional service; *prāptyera sādhana*—the means of attaining Kṛṣṇa.

### TRANSLATION

**"The Vedic literatures give information about the living entity's eternal relationship with Kṛṣṇa, which is called sambandha. The living entity's understanding of this relationship and acting accordingly is called abhidheya. Returning home, back to Godhead, is the ultimate goal of life and is called prayojana.**

### TEXT 125

**অভিধেয়-নাম 'ভক্তি', 'প্রেম'—প্রয়োজন।**
**পুরুষার্থ-শিরোমণি প্রেম মহাধন ॥ ১২৫ ॥**

*abhidheya-nāma 'bhakti', 'prema'——prayojana*
*puruṣārtha-śiromaṇi prema mahā-dhana*

## SYNONYMS

*abhidheya*—activities to revive one's relationship; *nāma*—named; *bhakti*—devotional service; *prema*—love of Godhead; *prayojana*—the ultimate goal of life; *puruṣa-artha-śiromaṇi*—the topmost interest of the living entity; *prema*—love of Godhead; *mahā-dhana*—the greatest wealth.

## TRANSLATION

**"Devotional service, or sense activity for the satisfaction of the Lord, is called abhidheya because it can develop one's original love of Godhead, which is the goal of life. This goal is the living entity's topmost interest and greatest wealth. Thus one attains the platform of transcendental loving service unto the Lord.**

## PURPORT

The conditioned soul is bewildered by the external material energy, which fully engages him in a variety of sense gratification. Due to engagement in material activities, one's original Kṛṣṇa consciousness is covered. However, as the supreme father of all living entities, Kṛṣṇa wants His sons to return home, back to Godhead; therefore He personally comes to deliver Vedic literatures like *Bhagavad-gītā*. He engages His confidential servants who serve as spiritual masters and enlighten the conditioned living entities. Being present in everyone's heart, the Lord gives the living entities the conscience whereby they can accept the *Vedas* and the spiritual master. In this way the living entity can understand his constitutional position and his relationship with the Supreme Lord. As personally enunciated by the Lord Himself in *Bhagavad-gītā* (15.15), *vedaiś ca sarvair aham eva vedyaḥ:* through the study of Vedānta, one may become fully aware of his relationship with the Supreme Lord and act accordingly. In this way one may ultimately attain the platform of loving service to the Lord. It is in the living entity's best interest to understand the Supreme Lord. Unfortunately, the living entities have forgotten; therefore *Śrīmad-Bhāgavatam* says: *na te viduḥ svārtha-gatiṁ hi viṣṇum* (*Bhāg.* 7.5.31).

Everyone wants to achieve life's ultimate goal, but due to being absorbed in the material energy, we waste our time with sense gratification. Through the study of Vedic literatures—of which the essence is *Bhagavad-gītā*—one comes to Kṛṣṇa consciousness. Thus one engages in devotional service, called *abhidheya*. When actually developed, love of Godhead is called *prayojana,* the living entity's ultimate goal. When one becomes fully Kṛṣṇa conscious, he has attained the perfection of life.

### TEXT 126

**কৃষ্ণমাধুর্য-সেবানন্দ-প্রাপ্তির কারণ।**
**কৃষ্ণ-সেবা করে, আর কৃষ্ণরস-আস্বাদন ॥ ১২৬ ॥**

*kṛṣṇa-mādhurya-sevānanda-prāptira kāraṇa*
*kṛṣṇa-sevā kare, āra kṛṣṇa-rasa-āsvādana*

### SYNONYMS

*kṛṣṇa-mādhurya*—of an intimate relationship with Kṛṣṇa; *sevā-ānanda*—of pleasure from rendering service unto Him; *prāptira*—of achievement; *kāraṇa*—because; *kṛṣṇa-sevā kare*—one renders service to Kṛṣṇa; *āra*—and; *kṛṣṇa-rasa*—of the mellows of such service; *āsvādana*—tasting.

### TRANSLATION

**"When one attains the transcendental bliss of an intimate relationship with Kṛṣṇa, he renders service to Him and tastes the mellows of Kṛṣṇa consciousness.**

### TEXT 127

**ইহাতে দৃষ্টান্ত—যৈছে দরিদ্রের ঘরে।**
**'সর্বজ্ঞ' আসি' দুঃখ দেখি' পুছয়ে তাহারে ॥ ১২৭ ॥**

*ihāte dṛṣṭānta——yaiche daridrera ghare*
*'sarvajña' āsi' duḥkha dekhi' puchaye tāhāre*

### SYNONYMS

*ihāte*—in this connection; *dṛṣṭānta*—the example; *yaiche*—just as; *daridrera ghare*—in the house of a poor man; *sarva-jña*—an astrologer; *āsi'*—coming; *duḥkha*—distressed condition; *dekhi'*—seeing; *puchaye tāhāre*—inquires from him.

### TRANSLATION

**"The following example may be given. Once a learned astrologer came to the house of a poor man and, seeing his distressed condition, questioned him.**

### PURPORT

Sometimes we go to an astrologer or palmist when we are in a distressed condition or when we want to know the future. The living entity in conditioned life is always distressed by the threefold miseries of material existence. Under the circumstances, he is inquisitive about his position. For instance, Sanātana Gosvāmī approached the Supreme Personality of Godhead, Śrī Caitanya Mahāprabhu, to ask Him why he was in a distressed condition. This is the position of all conditioned souls. We are always in a distressed condition, and an intelligent man naturally becomes inquisitive. This position is called *brahma-jijñāsā. Athāto brahma-jijñāsā* (*Vedānta-sūtra* 1.1.1). *Brahma* here refers to Vedic literature. One should consult Vedic literature to know why the conditioned soul is always in a distressed condition. Vedic literatures are meant to free the conditioned soul from the miserable conditions of material existence. In this chapter, the story of the astrologer Sarvajña and the poor man is very instructive.

## TEXT 128

**'তুমি কেনে দুঃখী, তোমার আছে পিতৃধন।**
**তোমারে না কহিল, অন্যত্র ছাড়িল জীবন॥" ১২৮॥**

*'tumi kene duḥkhī, tomāra āche pitṛ-dhana*
*tomāre nā kahila, anyatra chāḍila jīvana"*

### SYNONYMS

*tumi*—you; *kene*—why; *duḥkhī*—distressed; *tomāra*—your; *āche*—there is; *pitṛ-dhana*—the riches of your father; *tomāre*—unto you; *nā kahila*—he did not disclose; *anyatra*—somewhere else; *chāḍila*—gave up; *jīvana*—his life.

### TRANSLATION

**"The astrologer asked, 'Why are you unhappy? Your father was very wealthy, but he did not disclose his wealth to you because he died elsewhere?'**

## TEXT 129

**সর্বজ্ঞের বাক্যে করে ধনের উদ্দেশে।**
**ঐছে বেদ-পুরাণ জীবে 'কৃষ্ণ' উপদেশে॥ ১২৯॥**

*sarvajñera vākye kare dhanera uddeśe*
*aiche veda-purāṇa jīve 'kṛṣṇa' upadeśe*

### SYNONYMS

*sarvajñera*—of the astrologer; *vākye*—the words; *kare*—make; *dhanera*—of the riches; *uddeśe*—news; *aiche*—similarly; *veda-purāṇa*—Vedic literatures; *jīve*—unto the living entity, the conditioned soul; *kṛṣṇa*—of Lord Kṛṣṇa; *upadeśe*—instructs.

### TRANSLATION

**"Just as the words of the astrologer Sarvajña gave news of the poor man's treasure, Vedic literatures advise one about Kṛṣṇa consciousness when one is inquisitive to know why he is in a distressed material condition.**

### TEXT 130

সর্বজ্ঞের বাক্যে মূলধন অনুবন্ধ ।
সর্বশাস্ত্রে উপদেশে, 'শ্রীকৃষ্ণ'—সম্বন্ধ ॥ ১৩০ ॥

*sarvajñera vākye mūla-dhana anubandha*
*sarva-śāstre upadeśe, 'śrī-kṛṣṇa'——sambandha*

### SYNONYMS

*sarvajñera*—of the astrologer; *vākye*—by the assurance; *mūla-dhana*—with the treasure; *anubandha*—connection; *sarva-śāstre*—all Vedic literatures; *upadeśe*—instruct; *śrī-kṛṣṇa*—Lord Śrī Kṛṣṇa, the Supreme Personality of Godhead; *sambandha*—the central connection.

### TRANSLATION

**"By the words of the astrologer, the poor man's connection with the treasure was established. Similarly, Vedic literature advises us that our real connection is with Śrī Kṛṣṇa, the Supreme Personality of Godhead.**

### PURPORT

In *Bhagavad-gītā* (7.26), Śrī Kṛṣṇa says:

*vedāhaṁ samatītāni*
*vartamānāni cārjuna*
*bhaviṣyāṇi ca bhūtāni*
*māṁ tu veda na kaścana*

"O Arjuna, as the Supreme Personality of Godhead, I know everything that has happened in the past, all that is happening in the present, and all things that are yet to come. I also know all living entities, but Me no one knows."

Thus Kṛṣṇa knows the cause of the distressed condition of the conditioned soul. He therefore descends from His original position to instruct the conditioned soul and inform him about his forgetfulness of his relationship with Kṛṣṇa. Kṛṣṇa exhibits Himself in His relationships in Vṛndāvana and at the Battle of Kurukṣetra so that people will be attracted to Him and will again return home, back to Godhead. Kṛṣṇa also says in *Bhagavad-gītā* that He is the proprietor of all universes, the enjoyer of everything that be and the friend of everyone. *Suhṛdaṁ sarva-bhūtānāṁ jñātvā māṁ śāntim ṛcchati* (Bg. 5.29). If we revive our original intimate relationship with Kṛṣṇa, our distressed condition in the material world will be mitigated. Everyone is trying to adjust to the distressed conditions of material existence, but the basic problems cannot be solved unless one is in an intimate relationship with Kṛṣṇa.

## TEXT 131

**'বাপের ধন আছে'—জ্ঞানে ধন নাহি পায় ।**
**তবে সর্বজ্ঞ কহে তারে প্রাপ্তির উপায় ॥ ১৩১ ॥**

*'bāpera dhana āche'——jñāne dhana nāhi pāya*
*tabe sarvajña kahe tāre prāptira upāya*

### SYNONYMS

*bāpera dhana āche*—the father has some treasure; *jñāne*—by this knowledge; *dhana*—treasure; *nāhi pāya*—one does not get; *tabe*—then; *sarvajña*—the astrologer; *kahe*—says; *tāre*—unto the poor man; *prāptira upāya*—the means of getting the treasure.

### TRANSLATION

**"Although being assured of his father's treasure, the poor man cannot acquire this treasure by such knowledge alone. Therefore the astrologer had to inform him of the means whereby he could actually find the treasure.**

## TEXT 132

**'এই স্থানে আছে ধন'—যদি দক্ষিণে খুদিবে ।**
**'ভীমরুল-বরুলী' উঠিবে, ধন না পাইবে ॥ ১৩২ ॥**

*'ei sthāne āche dhana'——yadi dakṣiṇe khudibe*
*'bhīmarula-barulī' uṭhibe, dhana nā pāibe*

### SYNONYMS

*ei sthāne*—at this place; *āche*—is; *dhana*—treasure; *yadi*—if; *dakṣiṇe*—on the southern side; *khudibe*—you will dig; *bhīmarula-barulī*—wasps and drones; *uṭhibe*—will rise; *dhana*—the riches; *nā pāibe*—you will not get.

### TRANSLATION

**"The astrologer said, 'The treasure is in this place, but if you dig toward the southern side, the wasps and drones will rise, and you will not get your treasure.**

### TEXT 133

'পশ্চিমে' খুদিবে, তাহা 'যক্ষ' এক হয়।
সে বিঘ্ন করিবে,—ধনে হাত না পড়য় ॥ ১৩৩ ॥

*'paścime' khudibe, tāhā 'yakṣa' eka haya*
*se vighna karibe,——dhane hāta nā paḍaya*

### SYNONYMS

*paścime*—on the western side; *khudibe*—if you dig; *tāhā*—there; *yakṣa*—ghost; *eka*—one; *haya*—there is; *se*—he; *vighna karibe*—will create disturbances; *dhane*—on the treasure; *hāta*—hand; *nā*—not; *paḍaya*—touches.

### TRANSLATION

**" 'If you dig on the western side, there is a ghost who will create such a disturbance that your hands will not even touch the treasure.**

### TEXT 134

'উত্তরে' খুদিলে আছে কৃষ্ণ 'অজগরে'।
ধন নাহি পাবে, খুদিতে গিলিবে সবারে ॥ ১৩৪ ॥

*'uttare' khudile āche kṛṣṇa 'ajagare'*
*dhana nāhi pābe, khudite gilibe sabāre*

### SYNONYMS

*uttare*—on the northern side; *khudile*—if you dig; *āche*—there is; *kṛṣṇa*—black; *ajagare*—snake; *dhana*—treasure; *nāhi*—not; *pābe*—you will get; *khudite*—digging; *gilibe*—will devour; *sabāre*—everyone.

### TRANSLATION

**" 'If you dig on the northern side, there is a big black snake that will devour you if you attempt to dig up the treasure.**

### TEXT 135

পূর্বদিকে তাতে মাটী অল্প খুদিতে।
ধনের ঝারি পড়িবেক তোমার হাতেতে ॥ ১৩৫ ॥

*pūrva-dike tāte māṭī alpa khudite*
*dhanera jhāri paḍibeka tomāra hātete*

### SYNONYMS

*pūrva-dike*—on the eastern side; *tāte*—there; *māṭī*—the dirt; *alpa*—small quantity; *khudite*—digging; *dhanera*—of the treasure; *jhāri*—the pot; *paḍibeka*—you will get; *tomāra*—your; *hātete*—in the hands.

### TRANSLATION

**" 'However, if you dig up a small quantity of dirt on the eastern side, your hands will immediately touch the pot of treasure.'**

### PURPORT

The Vedic literatures, including the *Purāṇas,* state that according to the position of the conditioned soul, there are different processes—*karma-kāṇḍa, jñāna-kāṇḍa,* the yogic process and the *bhakti-yoga* process. *Karma-kāṇḍa* is compared to wasps and drones that will simply bite if one takes shelter of them. *Jñāna-kāṇḍa,* the speculative process, is simply like a ghost who creates mental disturbances. *Yoga,* the mystic process, is compared to a black snake that devours people by the impersonal cultivation of *kaivalya.* However, if one takes to *bhakti-yoga,* he becomes quickly successful. In other words, through *bhakti-yoga,* one's hands touch the hidden treasure without difficulty.

Therefore it is said in *Bhagavad-gītā: vedaiś ca sarvair aham eva vedyaḥ.* One has to take to devotional service. Although the *Vedas* enjoin one to search out Kṛṣṇa and take shelter at His lotus feet, other Vedic processes will not help. According to *Bhagavad-gītā,* only the *bhakti* process is said to be definitive. *Bhaktyā mām abhijānāti.* This is the conclusive statement of the *Vedas,* and one has to accept this process if one is serious in searching for Kṛṣṇa, the Supreme Personality of Godhead. In this connection, Śrīla Bhaktisiddhānta Sarasvatī Ṭhākura gives the following statement. The eastern side represents devotional service to Lord Kṛṣṇa. The southern side represents the process of fruitive activity (*karma-kāṇḍa*), which ends in material gain. The western side represents *jñāna-kāṇḍa,* the process of mental speculation, sometimes called *siddhi-kāṇḍa.* The northern side represents the speculative method sometimes known as the mystic *yoga* system. It is only the eastern side, devotional service, that enables one to attain life's real goal. On the southern side, there are fruitive activities by which one is subject to the punishment of Yamarāja. When one follows the system of fruitive activity, his material desires remain prominent. Consequently the results of this process are compared to wasps and drones. The living entity is bitten by the wasps and drones of fruitive activity and thus suffers in material existence birth after birth. One cannot be free from material desires by following this process. The propensity for material enjoyment never ends. Therefore the cycle of birth and death continues, and the spirit soul suffers perpetually.

The mystic *yoga* process is compared to a black snake that devours the living entity and injects him with poison. The ultimate goal of the *yoga* system is to become one with the Absolute. This means finishing one's personal existence. However, the spiritual part and parcel of the Supreme Personality of Godhead has an eternal individual existence. *Bhagavad-gītā* confirms that the individual soul existed in the past, is existing in the present and will continue to exist as an individual in the future. Artificially trying to become one with the Absolute is suicidal. One cannot annihilate his natural condition.

A *yakṣa,* a protector of riches, will not allow anyone to take away riches for enjoyment. Such a demon will simply create disturbances. In other words, a devotee will not depend on his material resources but on the mercy of the Supreme Personality of Godhead, who can give real protection. This is called *rakṣiṣyatīti viśvāsaḥ* or (in the Bengali poetry of Bhaktivinoda Ṭhākura's *Śaraṇāgati*), *'avaśya rakṣibe kṛṣṇa'—viśvāsa pālana.* The surrendered soul must accept the fact that his real protector is Kṛṣṇa, not his material acquisitions.

Considering all these points, devotional service to Kṛṣṇa is the real treasure-house for the living entity. When one comes to the platform of devotional service, he always remains opulent in the association of the Supreme Personality of Godhead. One who is bereft of devotional service is swallowed by the black snake of the *yoga* system and bitten by the wasps and drones of fruitive activity, and he suffers consequent material miseries. Sometimes the living entity is misled into trying to merge into spiritual existence, thinking himself as good as the Supreme Personality of Godhead. This means that when he comes to the spiritual platform, he will be disturbed and will again return to the material platform. According to *Śrīmad-Bhāgavatam* (10.2.32):

*ye 'nye 'ravindākṣa vimukta-māninas*
*tvayy asta-bhāvād aviśuddha-buddhayaḥ*
*āruhya kṛcchreṇa paraṁ padaṁ tataḥ*
*patanty adho 'nādṛta-yuṣmad-aṅghrayaḥ*

Such people may become *sannyāsīs,* but unless they take shelter of Kṛṣṇa's lotus feet, they will return to the material platform to perform philanthropic activities. In this way, one's spiritual life is lost. This is to be understood as being devoured by the black snake.

## TEXT 136

**ঐছে শাস্ত্র কহে,—কর্ম, জ্ঞান, যোগ ত্যজি' ।**
**'ভক্ত্যে' কৃষ্ণ বশ হয়, ভক্ত্যে তাঁরে ভজি ॥ ১৩৬ ॥**

*aiche śāstra kahe,—karma, jñāna, yoga tyaji'*
*'bhaktye' kṛṣṇa vaśa haya, bhaktye tāṅre bhaji*

## SYNONYMS

*aiche*—in that way; *śāstra kahe*—Vedic literatures confirm; *karma*—fruitive activities; *jñāna*—speculative knowledge; *yoga*—the mystic *yoga* system; *tyaji'*—giving up; *bhaktye*—by devotional service; *kṛṣṇa*—the Supreme Absolute Personality of Godhead; *vaśa haya*—becomes satisfied; *bhaktye*—by devotional service; *tāṅre*—Him; *bhaji*—we worship.

## TRANSLATION

**"Revealed scriptures conclude that one should give up fruitive activity, speculative knowledge and the mystic yoga system and instead take to devotional service, by which Kṛṣṇa can be fully satisfied.**

## TEXT 137

ন সাধয়তি মাং যোগো ন সাংখ্যং ধর্ম উদ্ধব ।
ন স্বাধ্যায়স্তপস্ত্যাগো যথা ভক্তির্মমোর্জিতা ॥ ১৩৭ ॥

*na sādhayati māṁ yogo*
*na sāṅkhyaṁ dharma uddhava*
*na svādhyāyas tapas tyāgo*
*yathā bhaktir mamorjitā*

## SYNONYMS

*na*—never; *sādhayati*—causes to remain satisfied; *mām*—Me; *yogaḥ*—the process of control; *na*—nor; *sāṅkhyam*—the process of gaining philosophical knowledge about the Absolute Truth; *dharmaḥ*—such an occupation; *uddhava*—My dear Uddhava; *na*—nor; *svādhyāyaḥ*—study of the *Vedas; tapaḥ*—austerities; *tyāgaḥ*—renunciation, acceptance of *sannyāsa,* or charity; *yathā*—as much as; *bhaktiḥ*—devotional service; *mama*—unto Me; *ūrjitā*—developed.

## TRANSLATION

**[The Supreme Personality of Godhead, Kṛṣṇa, said:] " 'My dear Uddhava, neither through aṣṭāṅga-yoga [the mystic yoga system to control the senses], nor through impersonal monism or an analytical study of the Absolute Truth, nor through study of the Vedas, nor through practice of austerities, nor through charity, nor through acceptance of sannyāsa can one satisfy Me as much as one can by developing unalloyed devotional service unto Me.'**

## PURPORT

This is a quotation from *Śrīmad-Bhāgavatam* (11.14.20). The explanation for this verse is given in *Ādi-līlā* (17.76).

## TEXT 138

ভক্ত্যাহমেকয়া গ্রাহ্যঃ শ্রদ্ধয়াত্মা প্রিয়ঃ সতাম্।
ভক্তিঃ পুনাতি মন্নিষ্ঠা শ্বপাকানপি সম্ভবাৎ ॥ ১৩৮ ॥

*bhaktyāham ekayā grāhyaḥ*
*śraddhayātmā priyaḥ satām*
*bhaktiḥ punāti man-niṣṭhā*
*śva-pākān api sambhavāt*

## SYNONYMS

*bhaktyā*—by devotional service; *aham*—I, the Supreme Personality of Godhead; *ekayā*—unflinching; *grāhyaḥ*—obtainable; *śraddhayā*—by faith; *ātmā*—the most dear; *priyaḥ*—to be served; *satām*—by the devotees; *bhaktiḥ*—the devotional service; *punāti*—purifies; *mat-niṣṭhā*—fixed only on Me; *śva-pākān*—the lowest of human beings, who are accustomed to eat dogs; *api*—certainly; *sambhavāt*—from all faults due to birth and other circumstances.

## TRANSLATION

**" 'Being very dear to the devotees and sādhus, I am attained through unflinching faith and devotional service. This bhakti-yoga system, which gradually increases attachment for Me, purifies even a human being born among dog-eaters. That is to say, everyone can be elevated to the spiritual platform by the process of bhakti-yoga.'**

## PURPORT

This verse is from *Śrīmad-Bhāgavatam* (11.14.21).

## TEXT 139

অতএব 'ভক্তি'—কৃষ্ণপ্রাপ্ত্যের উপায়।
'অভিধেয়' বলি' তারে সর্বশাস্ত্রে গায় ॥ ১৩৯ ॥

*ataeva 'bhakti'——kṛṣṇa-prāptyera upāya*
*'abhidheya' bali' tāre sarva-śāstre gāya*

## SYNONYMS

*ataeva*—therefore; *bhakti*—devotional service; *kṛṣṇa-prāptyera*—of achieving the lotus feet of Kṛṣṇa; *upāya*—the only means; *abhidheya*—*abhidheya; bali'*—calling; *tāre*—this system; *sarva-śāstre*—in all revealed scriptures; *gāya*—is described.

## TRANSLATION

**"The conclusion is that devotional service is the only means to approach the Supreme Personality of Godhead. This system is therefore called abhidheya. This is the verdict of all revealed scriptures.**

## PURPORT

As stated in *Bhagavad-gītā* (18.55):

*bhaktyā mām abhijānāti*
*yāvān yaś cāsmi tattvataḥ*
*tato māṁ tattvato jñātvā*
*viśate tad-anantaram*

"One can understand the Supreme Personality as He is only by devotional service. And when one is in full consciousness of the Supreme Lord by such devotion, he can enter the kingdom of God."

The aim of life is to get rid of the material conditioning and enter into spiritual existence. Although the *śāstras* prescribe different methods for different men, the Supreme Personality of Godhead says that one ultimately must accept the path of devotional service as the assured path of spiritual advancement. Devotional service to the Lord is the only process actually confirmed by the Lord. *Sarva-dharmān parityajya mām ekaṁ śaraṇaṁ vraja* (Bg. 18.66). One must become a devotee if one wants to return home, back to Godhead, and become eternally blissful.

## TEXT 140

**ধন পাইলে যৈছে সুখভোগ ফল পায় ।**
**সুখভোগ হৈতে দুঃখ আপনি পলায় ॥ ১৪০ ॥**

*dhana pāile yaiche sukha-bhoga phala pāya*
*sukha-bhoga haite duḥkha āpani palāya*

## SYNONYMS

*dhana pāile*—when one gets riches; *yaiche*—just as; *sukha-bhoga*—enjoyment of happiness; *phala*—result; *pāya*—one gets; *sukha-bhoga*—real enjoyment of happiness; *haite*—from; *duḥkha*—all distresses; *āpani*—themselves; *palāya*—run away.

## TRANSLATION

**"When one actually becomes rich, he naturally enjoys all kinds of happiness. When one is actually in a happy mood, all distressful conditions go away by themselves. No extraneous endeavor is needed.**

## TEXT 141

তৈছে ভক্তি-ফলে কৃষ্ণে প্রেম উপজয় ।
প্রেমে কৃষ্ণাস্বাদ হৈলে ভব নাশ পায় ॥ ১৪১ ॥

*taiche bhakti-phale kṛṣṇe prema upajaya*
*preme kṛṣṇāsvāda haile bhava nāśa pāya*

### SYNONYMS

*taiche*—similarly; *bhakti-phale*—by the result of devotional service; *kṛṣṇe*—unto Lord Kṛṣṇa; *prema*—love; *upajaya*—arises; *preme*—in devotional love; *kṛṣṇa-āsvāda*—tasting the association of Lord Kṛṣṇa; *haile*—when there is; *bhava*—the distress of the repetition of birth and death; *nāśa*—annihilation; *pāya*—obtains.

### TRANSLATION

**"Similarly, as a result of bhakti, one's dormant love for Kṛṣṇa awakens. When one is so situated that he can taste the association of Lord Kṛṣṇa, material existence, the repetition of birth and death, comes to an end.**

## TEXT 142

দারিদ্র্য-নাশ, ভবক্ষয়,—প্রেমের 'ফল' নয় ।
প্রেমসুখ-ভোগ—মুখ্য প্রয়োজন হয় ॥ ১৪২ ॥

*dāridrya-nāśa, bhava-kṣaya,——premera 'phala' naya*
*prema-sukha-bhoga——mukhya prayojana haya*

### SYNONYMS

*dāridrya-nāśa*—the end of poverty-stricken life; *bhava-kṣaya*—annihilation of material existence; *premera*—of love of Godhead; *phala*—the result; *naya*—certainly is not; *prema-sukha-bhoga*—enjoyment of the happiness of love of God; *mukhya*—chief; *prayojana*—goal of life; *haya*—is.

### TRANSLATION

**"The goal of love of Godhead is not to become materially rich or free from material bondage. The real goal is to be situated in devotional service to the Lord and to enjoy transcendental bliss.**

### PURPORT

The results of devotional service are certainly not material benefits or liberation from material bondage. The goal of devotional service is to be eternally situated in the loving service of the Lord and to enjoy spiritual bliss from that service. One is said to be in a poverty-stricken condition when one forgets the Supreme Personality of Godhead. One has to end such a life of poverty in order to automatically end the miserable conditions of material existence. One is automatically liberated from material enjoyment when one tastes the service of Kṛṣṇa. One does not have to endeavor separately for opulence. Opulence automatically comes to the pure devotee, even though he does not desire material happiness.

### TEXT 143

**বেদশাস্ত্রে কহে সম্বন্ধ, অভিধেয়, প্রয়োজন ।**
**কৃষ্ণ, কৃষ্ণভক্তি, প্রেম, – তিন মহাধন ॥ ১৪৩ ॥**

*veda-śāstre kahe sambandha, abhidheya, prayojana*
*kṛṣṇa, kṛṣṇa-bhakti, prema,——tina mahā-dhana*

### SYNONYMS

*veda-śāstre*—in Vedic literature; *kahe*—it is said; *sambandha*—relationship; *abhidheya*—execution; *prayojana*—goal; *kṛṣṇa*—Lord Kṛṣṇa; *kṛṣṇa-bhakti*—devotional service to the Lord; *prema*—love of Godhead; *tina*—these three; *mahā-dhana*—the supreme treasure.

### TRANSLATION

**"In Vedic literatures, Kṛṣṇa is the central point of attraction, and His service is our activity. To attain the platform of love of Kṛṣṇa is life's ultimate goal. Therefore Kṛṣṇa, Kṛṣṇa's service and love of Kṛṣṇa are the three great riches of life.**

### TEXT 144

**বেদাদি সকল শাস্ত্রে কৃষ্ণ—মুখ্য সম্বন্ধ ।**
**তাঁর জ্ঞানে আনুষঙ্গে যায় মায়াবন্ধ ॥ ১৪৪ ॥**

*vedādi sakala śāstre kṛṣṇa——mukhya sambandha*
*tāṅra jñāne ānuṣaṅge yāya māyā-bandha*

### SYNONYMS

*veda-ādi*—beginning with the *Vedas; sakala*—all; *śāstre*—in the revealed scriptures; *kṛṣṇa*—Lord Kṛṣṇa; *mukhya*—chief; *sambandha*—central point or central attraction; *tāṅra jñāne*—by knowledge of Him; *ānuṣaṅge*—simultaneously; *yāya*—goes away; *māyā-bandha*—the bondage of material existence.

## TRANSLATION

**"In all revealed scriptures, beginning with the Vedas, the central point of attraction is Kṛṣṇa. When complete knowledge of Him is realized, the bondage of māyā, the illusory energy, is automatically broken.**

## TEXT 145

ব্যামোহায় চরাচরস্য জগতস্তে তে পুরাণাগমা-
স্তাং তামেব হি দেবতাং পরমিকাং জল্পন্তু কল্পাবধি।
সিদ্ধান্তে পুনরেক এব ভগবান্ বিষ্ণুঃ সমস্তাগম-
ব্যাপারেষু বিবেচনব্যতিকরং নীতেষু নিশ্চীয়তে ॥ ১৪৫ ॥

*vyāmohāya carācarasya jagatas te te purāṇāgamās*
*tāṁ tām eva hi devatāṁ paramikāṁ jalpantu kalpāvadhi*
*siddhānte punar eka eva bhagavān viṣṇuḥ samastāgama-*
*vyāpāreṣu vivecana-vyatikaraṁ nīteṣu niścīyate*

## SYNONYMS

*vyāmohāya*—to increase the illusion and ignorance; *cara-acarasya*—of all living entities, moving and nonmoving; *jagataḥ*—of the world; *te te*—those respective; *purāṇa*—the supplementary Vedic literatures called the *Purāṇas; āgamāḥ*—and *Vedas; tām tām*—that respective; *eva hi*—certainly; *devatām*—demigod; *paramikām*—as supreme; *jalpantu*—let them speak about; *kalpa-avadhi*—until the end of the millenium; *siddhānte*—in conclusion; *punaḥ*—but; *ekaḥ*—one; *eva*—only; *bhagavān*—Supreme Personality of Godhead; *viṣṇuḥ*—Lord Viṣṇu; *samasta*—all; *āgama*—of the *Vedas; vyāpāreṣu*—in the dealings; *vivecana-vyatikaram*—to collective consideration; *nīteṣu*—when forcibly brought; *niścīyate*—is established.

## TRANSLATION

**" 'There are many types of Vedic literatures and supplementary Purāṇas. In each of them there are particular demigods who are spoken of as the chief demigods. This is just to create an illusion for moving and nonmoving living entities. Let them perpetually engage in such imaginations. However, when one analytically studies all these Vedic literatures collectively, he comes to the conclusion that Lord Viṣṇu is the one and only Supreme Personality of Godhead.'**

## PURPORT

This is a verse from the *Padma Purāṇa.*

## TEXT 146

**মুখ্য-গৌণ-বৃত্তি, কিংবা অন্বয়-ব্যতিরেকে ।**
**বেদের প্রতিজ্ঞা কেবল কহয়ে কৃষ্ণকে ॥ ১৪৬ ॥**

*mukhya-gauṇa-vṛtti, kiṁvā anvaya-vyatireke*
*vedera pratijñā kevala kahaye kṛṣṇake*

### SYNONYMS

*mukhya*—chief; *gauṇa*—secondary; *vṛtti*—meaning; *kiṁvā*—or; *anvaya-vyatireke*—directly or indirectly; *vedera pratijñā*—ultimate declaration of the *Vedas; kevala*—only; *kahaye*—speaks; *kṛṣṇake*—about Kṛṣṇa.

### TRANSLATION

**"When one accepts Vedic literature by interpretation or even by dictionary meaning, directly or indirectly the ultimate declaration of Vedic knowledge points to Lord Kṛṣṇa.**

## TEXTS 147-148

কিং বিধত্তে কিমাচষ্টে কিমনূদ্য বিকল্পয়েৎ ।
ইত্যস্যা হৃদয়ং লোকে নান্যো মদ্বেদ কশ্চন ॥ ১৪৭ ॥
মাং বিধত্তেঽভিধত্তে মাং বিকল্প্যাপোহ্যতে হ্যহম্ ।
এতাবান্ সর্ববেদার্থঃ শব্দ আস্থায় মাং ভিদাম্ ।
মায়ামাত্রমনূদ্যান্তে প্রতিষিধ্য প্রসীদতি ॥ ১৪৮ ॥

*kiṁ vidhatte kim ācaṣṭe*
*kim anūdya vikalpayet*
*ity asyā hṛdayaṁ loke*
*nānyo mad veda kaścana*

*māṁ vidhatte 'bhidhatte māṁ*
*vikalpyāpohyate hy aham*
*etāvān sarva-vedārthaḥ*
*śabda āsthāya māṁ bhidām*
*māyā-mātram anūdyānte*
*pratiṣidhya prasīdati*

### SYNONYMS

*kim*—what; *vidhatte*—direct; *kim*—what; *ācaṣṭe*—declare; *kim*—what; *anūdya*—taking as the object; *vikalpayet*—may conjecture; *iti*—thus; *asyāḥ*—of the Vedic literature; *hṛdayam*—intention; *loke*—in this world; *na*—not; *anyaḥ*—other; *mat*—than Me; *veda*—knows; *kaścana*—anyone; *mām*—Me; *vidhatte*—they ordain; *abhidhatte*—set forth; *mām*—Me; *vikalpya*—speculating; *aphyate*—am fixed; *hi*—certainly; *aham*—I; *etāvān*—of such measures; *sarva-veda-arthaḥ*—the purport of the *Vedas; śabdaḥ*—the *Vedas; āsthāya*—taking shelter of; *mām*—Me; *bhidām*—different; *māyā*—illusory energy; *mātram*—only; *anūdya*—saying; *ante*—at the end; *pratiṣidhya*—driving away; *prasīdati*—gets satisfaction.

## TRANSLATION

**" 'What is the direction of all Vedic literatures? On whom do they set focus? Who is the purpose of all speculation? Outside of Me no one knows these things. Now you should know that all these activities are aimed at ordaining and setting forth Me. The purpose of Vedic literature is to know Me by different speculations, either by indirect understanding or by dictionary understanding. Everyone is speculating about Me. The essence of all Vedic literatures is to distinguish Me from māyā. By considering the illusory energy, one comes to the platform of understanding Me. In this way one becomes free from speculation about the Vedas and comes to Me as the conclusion. Thus one is satisfied.'**

## PURPORT

These two verses are quoted from *Śrīmad-Bhāgavatam* (11.21.42, 43). When Uddhava asked Kṛṣṇa about the purpose of Vedic speculation, the Lord informed him of the process of understanding Vedic literature. The *Vedas* are composed of *karma-kāṇḍa, jñāna-kāṇḍa* and *upāsanā-kāṇḍa.* If one analytically studies the purpose of the *Vedas,* he understands that by *karma-kāṇḍa,* sacrificial activity, one comes to the conclusion of *jñāna-kāṇḍa,* speculative knowledge. After speculation, one comes to the conclusion that worship of the Supreme Personality of Godhead is the ultimate. When one comes to this conclusion, he becomes fully satisfied.

## TEXT 149

**কৃষ্ণের স্বরূপ—অনন্ত, বৈভব—অপার ।**
**চিচ্ছক্তি, মায়াশক্তি, জীবশক্তি আর ॥ ১৪৯ ॥**

*kṛṣṇera svarūpa——ananta, vaibhava——apāra*
*cic-chakti, māyā-śakti, jīva-śakti āra*

## SYNONYMS

*kṛṣṇera sva-rūpa*—the transcendental form of Kṛṣṇa; *ananta*—unlimitedly expanded; *vaibhava*—opulence; *apāra*—unlimited; *cit-śakti*—internal potency; *māyā-śakti*—external potency; *jīva-śakti*—marginal potency; *āra*—and.

### TRANSLATION

**"The transcendental form of Lord Kṛṣṇa is unlimited and also has unlimited opulence. He possesses the internal potency, external potency and marginal potency.**

### TEXT 150

বৈকুণ্ঠ, ব্রহ্মাণ্ডগণ—শক্তি-কার্য হয়।
স্বরূপশক্তি শক্তি-কার্যের—কৃষ্ণ সমাশ্রয় ॥ ১৫০ ॥

*vaikuṇṭha, brahmāṇḍa-gaṇa——śakti-kārya haya*
*svarūpa-śakti śakti-kāryera——kṛṣṇa samāśraya*

### SYNONYMS

*vaikuṇṭha*—the spiritual world; *brahmāṇḍa-gaṇa*—universes of the material world; *śakti-kārya haya*—they are all activities of Kṛṣṇa's potencies; *svarūpa-śakti*—of the internal potency; *śakti-kāryera*—of the activities of the external potency; *kṛṣṇa*—Lord Kṛṣṇa; *samāśraya*—the original source.

### TRANSLATION

**"Both the material and spiritual world are transformations of Kṛṣṇa's internal and external potencies. Therefore Kṛṣṇa is the original source of both material and spiritual manifestations.**

### TEXT 151

দশমে দশমং লক্ষ্যমাশ্রিতাশ্রয়-বিগ্রহম্।
শ্রীকৃষ্ণাখ্যং পরং ধাম জগদ্ধাম নমামি তৎ ॥ ১৫১ ॥

*daśame daśamaṁ lakṣyam*
*āśritāśraya-vigraham*
*śrī-kṛṣṇākhyaṁ paraṁ dhāma*
*jagad-dhāma namāmi tat*

### SYNONYMS

*daśame*—in the Tenth Canto; *daśamam*—the tenth subject matter; *lakṣyam*—to be seen; *āśrita*—of the sheltered; *āśraya*—of the shelter; *vigraham*—who is the form; *śrī-kṛṣṇa-ākhyam*—known as Lord Śrī Kṛṣṇa; *param*—supreme; *dhāma*—abode; *jagat-dhāma*—the abode of the universes; *namāmi*—I offer my obeisances; *tat*—to Him.

## TRANSLATION

**" 'The Tenth Canto of Śrīmad-Bhāgavatam reveals the tenth object, the Supreme Personality of Godhead, who is the shelter of all surrendered souls. He is known as Śrī Kṛṣṇa, and He is the ultimate source of all the universes. Let me offer my obeisances unto Him.'**

## PURPORT

This is a quotation from *Bhāvārtha-dīpikā,* Śrīdhara Svāmī's commentary on the *Śrīmad-Bhāgavatam* (10.1.1). In the Tenth Canto of *Śrīmad-Bhāgavatam* there is a description of the *āśraya-tattva,* Śrī Kṛṣṇa. There are two *tattvas—āśraya-tattva* and *āśrita-tattva. Āśraya-tattva* is the objective, and *āśrita-tattva* is the subjective. Since the lotus feet of Lord Śrī Kṛṣṇa are the shelter of all devotees, Śrī Kṛṣṇa is called *paraṁ dhāma.* in *Bhagavad-gītā* it is stated: *paraṁ brahma paraṁ dhāma pavitraṁ paramaṁ bhavān.* Everything is resting under the lotus feet of Kṛṣṇa. In *Śrīmad-Bhāgavatam* (10.14.58) it is stated:

*samāśritā ye pada-pallava-plavaṁ*
*mahat-padaṁ puṇya-yaśo-murāreḥ*

Under the lotus feet of Śrī Kṛṣṇa, the entire *mahat-tattva* is existing. Since everything is under Śrī Kṛṣṇa's protection, Śrī Kṛṣṇa is called *āśraya-tattva.* Everything else is called *āśrita-tattva.* The material creation is also called *āśrita-tattva.* Liberation from material bondage and the attainment of the spiritual platform are also *āśrita-tattva.* Kṛṣṇa is the only *āśraya-tattva.* In the beginning of the creation there are Mahā-Viṣṇu, Garbhodakaśāyī Viṣṇu and Kṣīrodakaśāyī Viṣṇu. They are also *āśraya-tattva.* Kṛṣṇa is the cause of all causes (*sarva-kāraṇa-kāraṇam*). To understand Kṛṣṇa perfectly, one has to make an analytical study of *āśraya-tattva* and *āśrita-tattva.*

## TEXT 152

**কৃষ্ণের স্বরূপ-বিচার শুন, সনাতন ।**
**অদ্বয়জ্ঞান-তত্ত্ব, ব্রজে ব্রজেন্দ্রনন্দন ॥ ১৫২ ॥**

*kṛṣṇera svarūpa-vicāra śuna, sanātana*
*advaya-jñāna-tattva, vraje vrajendra-nandana*

## SYNONYMS

*kṛṣṇera*—of Lord Kṛṣṇa; *svarūpa-vicāra*—consideration of the eternal form; *śuna*—please hear; *sanātana*—My dear Sanātana; *advaya-jñāna-tattva*—the Absolute Truth without duality; *vraje*—in Vṛndāvana; *vrajendra-nandana*—the son of Nanda Mahārāja.

### TRANSLATION

**"O Sanātana, please hear about the eternal form of Lord Kṛṣṇa. He is the Absolute Truth, devoid of duality but present in Vṛndāvana as the son of Nanda Mahārāja.**

### TEXT 153

**সর্ব-আদি, সর্ব-অংশী, কিশোর-শেখর ।**
**চিদানন্দ-দেহ, সর্বাশ্রয়, সর্বেশ্বর ॥ ১৫৩ ॥**

*sarva-ādi, sarva-aṁśī, kiśora-śekhara*
*cid-ānanda-deha, sarvāśraya, sarveśvara*

### SYNONYMS

*sarva-ādi*—origin of everything; *sarva-aṁśī*—sum total of all parts and parcels; *kiśora-śekhara*—the supreme youth; *cit-ānanda-deha*—a body of spiritual blissfulness; *sarva-āśraya*—shelter of everyone; *sarva-īśvara*—master of everyone.

### TRANSLATION

**"Kṛṣṇa is the original source of everything and the sum total of everything. He appears as the supreme youth, and His whole body is composed of spiritual bliss. He is the shelter of everything and master of everyone.**

### PURPORT

Kṛṣṇa is the origin of all *viṣṇu-tattvas,* including Mahā-Viṣṇu, Garbhodakaśāyī Viṣṇu and Kṣīrodakaśāyī Viṣṇu. He is the ultimate goal of Vaiṣṇava philosophy. Everything emanates from Him. His body is completely spiritual and is the source of all spiritual being. Although He is the source of everything, He Himself has no source. *Advaitam acyutam anādim ananta-rūpaṁ, ādyaṁ purāṇa-puruṣaṁ nava-yauvanaṁ* ca. Although He is the supreme source of everyone, He is still always a fresh youth.

### TEXT 154

ঈশ্বরঃ পরমঃ কৃষ্ণঃ সচ্চিদানন্দবিগ্রহঃ ।
অনাদিরাদির্গোবিন্দঃ সর্বকারণকারণম্ ॥ ১৫৪ ॥

*īśvaraḥ paramaḥ kṛṣṇaḥ*
*sac-cid-ānanda-vigrahaḥ*
*anādir ādir govindaḥ*
*sarva-kāraṇa-kāraṇam*

### SYNONYMS

*īśvaraḥ*—the controller; *paramaḥ*—supreme; *kṛṣṇaḥ*—Lord Kṛṣṇa; *sat*—eternal existence; *cit*—absolute knowledge; *ānanda*—absolute bliss; *vigrahaḥ*—whose form; *anādiḥ*—without beginning; *ādiḥ*—the origin; *govindaḥ*—Lord Govinda; *sarva-kāraṇa-kāraṇam*—the cause of all causes.

### TRANSLATION

**" 'Kṛṣṇa, who is known as Govinda, is the supreme controller. He has an eternal, blissful, spiritual body. He is the origin of all. He has no other origin, for He is the prime cause of all causes.'**

### PURPORT

This is the first verse of the Fifth Chapter of *Brahma-saṁhitā.*

### TEXT 155

**স্বয়ং ভগবান্ কৃষ্ণ, 'গোবিন্দ' পর নাম ।**
**সর্বৈশ্বর্যপূর্ণ যাঁর গোলোক—নিত্যধাম ॥ ১৫৫ ॥**

*svayaṁ bhagavān kṛṣṇa, 'govinda' para nāma*
*sarvaiśvarya-pūrṇa yāṅra goloka——nitya-dhāma*

### SYNONYMS

*svayam*—personally; *bhagavān*—the Supreme Personality of Godhead; *kṛṣṇa*—Kṛṣṇa; *govinda*—Govinda; *para nāma*—another name; *sarva-aiśvarya-pūrṇa*—full of all opulences; *yāṅra*—whose; *goloka*—Goloka Vṛndāvana; *nitya-dhāma*—eternal abode.

### TRANSLATION

**"The original Supreme Personality of Godhead is Kṛṣṇa. His original name is Govinda. He is full of all opulences, and His eternal abode is known as Goloka Vṛndāvana.**

### TEXT 156

এতে চাংশকলাঃ পুংসঃ কৃষ্ণস্তু ভগবান্ স্বয়ম্ ।
ইন্দ্রারিব্যাকুলং লোকং মৃড়য়ন্তি যুগে যুগে ॥ ১৫৬ ॥

*ete cāṁśa-kalāḥ puṁsaḥ*
*kṛṣṇas tu bhagavān svayam*
*indrāri-vyākulaṁ lokaṁ*
*mṛḍayanti yuge yuge*

### SYNONYMS

*ete*—these; *ca*—and; *aṁśa*—plenary portions; *kalāḥ*—parts of plenary portions; *puṁsaḥ*—of the *puruṣa-avatāras; kṛṣṇaḥ*—Lord Kṛṣṇa; *tu*—but; *bhagavān*—the Supreme Personality of Godhead; *svayam*—Himself; *indra-ari*—the enemies of Lord Indra; *vyākulam*—full of; *lokam*—the world; *mṛḍayanti*—make happy; *yuge yuge*—at the right time in each age.

### TRANSLATION

**" 'All these incarnations of Godhead are either plenary portions or parts of the plenary portions of the puruṣa-avatāras. But Kṛṣṇa is the Supreme Personality of Godhead Himself. In every age He protects the world through His different features when the world is disturbed by the enemies of Indra.'**

### PURPORT

This is a quotation from *Śrīmad-Bhāgavatam* (1.3.28). See also *Ādi-līlā,* Chapter Two, verse 67.

## TEXT 157

**জ্ঞান, যোগ, ভক্তি,—তিন সাধনের বশে ।**
**ব্রহ্ম, আত্মা, ভগবান্—ত্রিবিধ প্রকাশে ॥ ১৫৭ ॥**

*jñāna, yoga, bhakti,——tina sādhanera vaśe*
*brahma, ātmā, bhagavān——trividha prakāśe*

### SYNONYMS

*jñāna*—knowledge; *yoga*—mystic power; *bhakti*—devotional service; *tina*—three; *sādhanera*—of the processes of spiritual life; *vaśe*—under the control; *brahma*—impersonal Brahman; *ātmā*—localized Paramātmā; *bhagavān*—the Supreme Personality of Godhead; *tri-vidha prakāśe*—three kinds of manifestation.

### TRANSLATION

**"There are three kinds of spiritual processes for understanding the Absolute Truth—the processes of speculative knowledge, mystic yoga and bhakti-yoga. According to these three processes, the Absolute Truth is manifested as Brahman, Paramātmā and Bhagavān.**

## TEXT 158

বদন্তি তত্তত্ত্ববিদস্তত্ত্বং যজ্ জ্ঞানমদ্বয়ম্ ।
ব্রহ্মেতি পরমাত্মেতি ভগবানিতি শব্দ্যতে ॥ ১৫৮ ॥

*vadanti tat tattva-vidas*
*tattvaṁ yaj jñānam advayam*
*brahmeti paramātmeti*
*bhagavān iti śabdyate*

### SYNONYMS

*vadanti*—they say; *tat*—that; *tattva-vidaḥ*—learned souls; *tattvam*—the Absolute Truth; *yat*—which; *jñānam*—knowledge; *advayam*—nondual; *brahma*—Brahman; *iti*—thus; *paramātmā*—Paramātmā; *iti*—thus; *bhagavān*—Bhagavān; *iti*—thus; *śabdyate*—is known.

### TRANSLATION

**" 'Learned transcendentalists who know the Absolute Truth call this nondual substance Brahman, Paramātmā or Bhagavān.'**

### PURPORT

This is a quotation from *Śrīmad-Bhāgavatam* (1.2.11). For an explanation, see also *Ādi-līlā,* Chapter Two, verse 11.

Those who are interested in the impersonal Brahman effulgence which is not different from the Supreme Personality of Godhead, can attain that goal by speculative knowledge. Those who are interested in practicing mystic *yoga* can attain the localized aspect of Paramātmā. As stated in *Bhagavad-gītā, īśvaraḥ sarva-bhūtānāṁ hṛd-deśe 'rjuna tiṣṭhati:* the Supreme Personality of Godhead is situated within the heart as Paramātmā. He witnesses the activities of the living entities and gives them permission to act.

### TEXT 159

ব্রহ্ম – অঙ্গকান্তি তাঁর, নির্বিশেষ প্রকাশে ।
সূর্য যেন চর্মচক্ষে জ্যোতির্ময় ভাসে ॥ ১৫৯ ॥

*brahma——aṅga-kānti tāṅra, nirviśeṣa prakāśe*
*sūrya yena carma-cakṣe jyotirmaya bhāse*

### SYNONYMS

*brahma*—the impersonal Brahman effulgence; *aṅga-kānti*—the bodily rays; *tāṅra*—of Him; *nirviśeṣa*—without varieties; *prakāśe*—manifestation; *sūrya yena*—exactly like the sun; *carma-cakṣe*—with our ordinary material eyes; *jyotiḥ-maya*—simply effulgent; *bhāse*—appears.

### TRANSLATION

**"The manifestation of the impersonal Brahman effulgence, which is without variety, is the rays of Kṛṣṇa's bodily effulgence. It is exactly like the sun. When the sun is seen by our ordinary eyes, it simply appears to consist of effulgence.**

### TEXT 160

যস্য প্রভা প্রভবতো জগদণ্ডকোটি-
কোটিষ্বশেষবসুধাদিবিভূতিভিন্নম্ ।
তদ্ব্রহ্ম নিষ্কলমনন্তমশেষভূতং
গোবিন্দমাদিপুরুষং তমহং ভজামি ॥ ১৬০ ॥

*yasya prabhā prabhavato jagad-aṇḍa-koṭi-*
*koṭiṣv aśeṣa-vasudhādi-vibhūti-bhinnam*
*tad brahma niṣkalam anantam aśeṣa-bhūtaṁ*
*govindam ādi-puruṣaṁ tam ahaṁ bhajāmi*

### SYNONYMS

*yasya*—of whom; *prabhā*—the effulgence; *prabhavataḥ*—of one who excels in power; *jagat-aṇḍa*—of universes; *koṭi-koṭiṣu*—in millions and millions; *aśeṣa*—unlimited; *vasudhā-ādi*—with planets and other manifestations; *vibhūti*—with opulences; *bhinnam*—becoming variegated; *tat*—that; *brahma*—Brahman; *niṣkalam*—without parts; *anantam*—unlimited; *aśeṣa-bhūtam*—being complete; *govindam*—Lord Govinda; *ādi-puruṣam*—the original person; *tam*—Him; *aham*—I; *bhajāmi*—worship.

### TRANSLATION

**" 'I worship Govinda, the primeval Lord, who is endowed with great power. The glowing effulgence of His transcendental form is the impersonal Brahman, which is absolute, complete and unlimited and which displays the varieties of countless planets, with their different opulences, in millions and millions of universes.'**

### PURPORT

This verse is quoted from *Brahma-saṁhitā* (5.40). For an explanation, refer to *Ādi-līlā,* Chapter Two, verse 14.

### TEXT 161

**পরমাত্মা যেঁহো, তেঁহো কৃষ্ণের এক অংশ ।**
**আত্মার 'আত্মা' হয় কৃষ্ণ সর্ব-অবতংস ॥ ১৬১ ॥**

*paramātmā yeṅho, teṅho kṛṣṇera eka aṁśa*
*ātmāra 'ātmā' haya kṛṣṇa sarva-avataṁsa*

### SYNONYMS

*paramātmā*—the Supersoul within the heart; *yeṅho*—who; *teṅho*—He; *kṛṣṇera*—of Lord Kṛṣṇa; *eka*—one; *aṁśa*—plenary portion; *ātmāra*—of the soul; *ātmā*—the soul; *haya*—is; *kṛṣṇa*—Lord Kṛṣṇa; *sarva*—of everything; *avataṁsa*—source.

### TRANSLATION

**"The Paramātmā, the Supersoul feature, is the partial plenary portion of the Supreme Personality of Godhead, who is the original source of all living entities. It is also Kṛṣṇa who is the original source of Paramātmā.**

### TEXT 162

কৃষ্ণমেনমবেহি ত্বমাত্মানমখিলাত্মনাম্ ।
জগদ্ধিতায় সোঽপ্যত্র দেহীবাভাতি মায়য়া ১৬২ ॥

*kṛṣṇam enam avehi tvam*
*ātmānam akhilātmanām*
*jagad-dhitāya so 'py atra*
*dehīvābhāti māyayā*

### SYNONYMS

*kṛṣṇam*—in the Supreme Personality of Godhead; *enam*—this; *avehi*—just try to understand; *tvam*—you; *ātmānam*—the soul; *akhila-ātmanām*—of all living entities; *jagat-hitāya*—the benefit of the whole universe; *saḥ*—He; *api*—certainly; *atra*—here; *dehī*—a human being; *iva*—like; *ābhāti*—appears; *māyayā*—by His internal potency.

### TRANSLATION

**" 'You should know Kṛṣṇa as the original soul of all ātmās [living entities]. For the benefit of the whole universe, He has, out of His causeless mercy, appeared as an ordinary human being. He has done this with the strength of His own internal potency.'**

### PURPORT

This is a quotation from *Śrīmad-Bhāgavatam* (10.14.55). Parīkṣit Mahārāja asked Śukadeva Gosvāmī why Kṛṣṇa was so beloved by the residents of Vṛndāvana, who loved Him even more than their own offspring or life itself. At that time Śukadeva Gosvāmī replied that everyone's *ātmā,* or soul, is very, very dear, especially to all living entities who have accepted material bodies. However, that *ātmā,* the spirit soul, is part and parcel of Kṛṣṇa. For this reason, Kṛṣṇa is very dear to every living entity. Everyone's body is very dear to oneself, and one wants to protect the body by all means because within the body the soul is living. Due to the intimate relationship between the soul and the body, the body is important and dear to everyone. Similarly, the soul, being part and parcel of Kṛṣṇa, the Supreme Lord, is very, very dear to all living entities. Unfortunately, the soul forgets his constitutional position and thinks he is only the body (*deha-ātma-buddhi*). Thus the soul is subjected to the rules and regulations of material nature. When a living entity, by his intelligence, reawakens his attraction for Kṛṣṇa, he can understand that he is not the body but part and parcel of Kṛṣṇa. Thus filled with knowledge, he no longer labors under attachment to the body and everything related to the body. *Janasya moho 'yam aham mameti.* Material existence, wherein one thinks, "I am the body, and this belongs to me," is also illusory. One must redirect his attraction to Kṛṣṇa. *Śrīmad-Bhāgavatam* (1.2.7) states:

*vāsudeve bhagavati*
*bhakti-yogaḥ prayojitaḥ*
*janayaty āśu vairāgyaṁ*
*jñānaṁ ca yad ahaitukam*

"By rendering devotional service unto the Personality of Godhead, Śrī Kṛṣṇa, one immediately acquires causeless knowledge and detachment from the world."

## TEXT 163

অথবা বহুনৈতেন কিং জ্ঞাতেন তবার্জুন ।
বিষ্টভ্যাহমিদং কৃৎস্নমেকাংশেন স্থিতো জগৎ ॥ ১৬৩ ॥

*athavā bahunaitena*
*kiṁ jñātena tavārjuna*
*viṣṭabhyāham idaṁ kṛtsnam*
*ekāṁśena sthito jagat*

### SYNONYMS

*athavā*—or; *bahunā*—much; *etena*—with this; *kim*—what use; *jñātena*—being known; *tava*—by you; *arjuna*—O Arjuna; *viṣṭabhya*—pervading; *aham*—I; *idam*—this; *kṛtsnam*—entire; *eka-aṁśena*—with one portion; *sthitaḥ*—situated; *jagat*—universe.

### TRANSLATION

**" 'But what need is there, Arjuna, for all this detailed knowledge? With a single fragment of Myself, I pervade and support this entire universe.'**

### PURPORT

This is a quotation from *Bhagavad-gītā* (10.42).

### TEXT 164

'ভক্ত্যে' ভগবানের অনুভব—পূর্ণরূপ ।
একই বিগ্রহে তাঁর অনন্ত স্বরূপ ॥ ১৬৪ ॥

*'bhaktye' bhagavānera anubhava——pūrṇa-rūpa*
*eka-i vigrahe tāṅra ananta svarūpa*

### SYNONYMS

*bhaktye*—by devotional service; *bhagavānera*—of the Supreme Personality of Godhead; *anubhava*—perception; *pūrṇa-rūpa*—perfectly; *eka-i*—one; *vigrahe*—in the transcendental form; *tāṅra*—His; *ananta*—unlimited; *sva-rūpa*—expansions of plenary portions.

### TRANSLATION

**"Only by devotional activity can one understand the transcendental form of the Lord, which is perfect in all respects. Although His form is one, He can expand His form into unlimited numbers by His supreme will.**

### TEXT 165

স্বয়ংরূপ, তদেকাত্মরূপ, আবেশ—নাম ।
প্রথমেই তিনরূপে রহেন ভগবান্ ॥ ১৬৫ ॥

*svayaṁ-rūpa, tad-ekātma-rūpa, āveśa——nāma*
*prathamei tina-rūpe rahena bhagavān*

### SYNONYMS

*svayam-rūpa*—the personal form; *tat-ekātma-rūpa*—the same form, non-different from *svayaṁ-rūpa; āveśa*—especially empowered; *nāma*—named; *prathamei*—in the beginning; *tina-rūpe*—in three forms; *rahena*—remains; *bhagavān*—the Supreme Personality of Godhead.

## TRANSLATION

**"The Supreme Personality of Godhead exists in three principal forms—svayaṁ-rūpa, tad-ekātma-rūpa, and āveśa-rūpa.**

## PURPORT

Śrīla Rūpa Gosvāmī has described *svayaṁ-rūpa* in his *Laghu-bhāgavatāmṛta, Pūrva-khaṇḍa,* verse 12, *ananyāpekṣi yad rūpaṁ svayaṁ-rūpaḥ sa ucyate:* the original form of the Supreme Personality of Godhead does not depend on other forms. The original form is called *svayaṁ-rūpa,* and it is described in *Śrīmad-Bhāgavatam: kṛṣṇas tu bhagavān svayam* (1.3.28). Kṛṣṇa's original form as a cowherd boy in Vṛndāvana is called *svayaṁ-rūpa.* It is confirmed in *Brahma-saṁhitā* (5.1):

*īśvaraḥ paramaḥ kṛṣṇaḥ*
*sac-cid-ānanda-vigrahaḥ*
*anādir ādir govindaḥ*
*sarva-kāraṇa-kāraṇam*

There is nothing superior to Govinda. He is the ultimate source and the cause of all causes. In *Bhagavad-gītā* (7.7) the Lord says, *mattaḥ parataraṁ nānyat:* "There is no truth superior to Me."

The *tad-ekātma-rūpa* is also described in the *Laghu-bhāgavatāmṛta, Pūrva-khaṇḍa,* verse 14:

*yad rūpaṁ tad-abhedena*
*svarūpeṇa virājate*
*ākṛtyādibhir anyādṛk*
*sa tad-ekātma-rūpakaḥ*

The *tad-ekātma-rūpa* forms exist simultaneously with the *svayaṁ-rūpa* form and are nondifferent. At the same time, the bodily features and specific activities appear to be different. This *tad-ekātma-rūpa* is also divided into two categories—*svāṁśa* and *vilāsa.*

His *āveśa* form is also explained in the *Laghu-bhāgavatāmṛta,* verse 18:

*jñāna-śaktyādi-kalayā*
*yatrāviṣṭo janārdanaḥ*
*ta āveśā nigadyante*
*jīvā eva mahattamāḥ*

A living entity who is specifically empowered by the Lord with knowledge or strength is technically called *āveśa-rūpa.* As stated in the *Caitanya-caritāmṛta* (*An-*

*tya* 7.11), *kṛṣṇa-śakti vinā nahe tāra pravartana:* unless a devotee is specifically empowered by the Lord, he cannot preach the holy name of the Lord all over the world. This is an explanation of the word *āveśa-rūpa.*

### TEXT 166

**'স্বয়ংরূপ' 'স্বয়ংপ্রকাশ',—দুই রূপে স্ফূর্তি।**
**স্বয়ংরূপে—এক 'কৃষ্ণ' ব্রজে গোপমূর্তি ॥ ১৬৬ ॥**

*'svayaṁ-rūpa' 'svayaṁ-prakāśa',——dui rūpe sphūrti*
*svayaṁ-rūpe——eka 'kṛṣṇa' vraje gopa-mūrti*

#### SYNONYMS

*svayam-rūpa*—the original form of the Lord; *svayam-prakāśa*—the personal manifestation; *dui rūpe*—in two forms; *sphūrti*—exhibition; *svayam-rūpe*—in the original form; *eka*—one; *kṛṣṇa*—Kṛṣṇa, the Supreme Personality of Godhead; *vraje*—in Vṛndāvana; *gopa-mūrti*—the cowherd boy.

#### TRANSLATION

**"The original form of the Lord [svayaṁ-rūpa] is exhibited in two forms—svayaṁ-rūpa and svayaṁ-prakāśa. In His original form as svayaṁ-rūpa, Kṛṣṇa is observed as a cowherd boy in Vṛndāvana.**

### TEXT 167

**'প্রাভব-বৈভব'-রূপে দ্বিবিধ প্রকাশে।**
**এক-বপু বহু রূপ যৈছে হৈল রাসে ॥ ১৬৭ ॥**

*'prābhava-vaibhava'-rūpe dvividha prakāśe*
*eka-vapu bahu rūpa yaiche haila rāse*

#### SYNONYMS

*prābhava*—*prābhava; vaibhava*—*vaibhava; rūpe*—in forms; *dvi-vidha prakāśe*—twofold manifestations; *eka-vapu*—the same original form; *bahu rūpa*—expanded into unlimited numbers; *yaiche*—like; *haila*—it was; *rāse*—while dancing in the *rāsa* dance with the *gopīs.*

#### TRANSLATION

**"In His original form, Kṛṣṇa manifests Himself in two features—prābhava and vaibhava. He expands His one original form into many, as He did during the rāsa-līlā dance.**

### TEXT 168

মহিষী-বিবাহে হৈল বহুবিধ মূর্তি ।
'প্রাভব প্রকাশ'—এই শাস্ত্র-পরসিদ্ধি ॥ ১৬৮ ॥

*mahiṣī-vivāhe haila bahu-vidha mūrti*
*'prābhava prakāśa'——ei śāstra-parasiddhi*

### SYNONYMS

*mahiṣī-vivāhe*—in the matter of marrying 16,108 wives at Dvārakā; *haila*—there were; *bahu-vidha mūrti*—many forms; *prābhava prakāśa*—called *prābhava-prakāśa; ei*—this; *śāstra-parasiddhi*—determined by reference to the revealed scriptures.

### TRANSLATION

**"When the Lord married 16,108 wives at Dvārakā, He expanded Himself into many forms. These expansions and the expansions at the rāsa dance are called prābhava-prakāśa, according to the directions of revealed scriptures.**

### TEXT 169

সৌভর্যাদি-প্রায় সেই কায়ব্যূহ নয় ।
কায়ব্যূহ হৈলে নারদের বিস্ময় না হয় ॥ ১৬৯ ॥

*saubhary-ādi-prāya sei kāya-vyūha naya*
*kāya-vyūha haile nāradera vismaya nā haya*

### SYNONYMS

*saubhari-ādi*—beginning with the sage named Saubhari; *prāya*—like; *sei*—that; *kāya-vyūha*—the expansion of one's body; *naya*—is not; *kāya-vyūha*—expansions of the body; *haile*—if there are; *nāradera*—of Nārada Muni; *vismaya*—the astonishment; *nā haya*—there cannot be.

### TRANSLATION

**"The prābhava-prakāśa expansions of Lord Kṛṣṇa are not like the expansions of the sage Saubhari. Had they been so, Nārada would not have been astonished to see them.**

### TEXT 170

চিত্রং বতৈতদেকেন বপুষা যুগপৎ পৃথক্ ।
গৃহেষু দ্ব্যষ্টসাহস্রং স্ত্রিয় এক উদাবহৎ ॥ ১৭০ ॥

*citraṁ bataitad ekena*
*vapuṣā yugapat pṛthak*
*gṛheṣu dvy-aṣṭa-sāhasraṁ*
*striya eka udāvahat*

### SYNONYMS

*citram*—wonderful; *bata*—oh; *etat*—this; *ekena*—with one; *vapuṣā*—form; *yugapat*—simultaneously; *pṛthak*—separately; *gṛheṣu*—in the houses; *dvi-aṣṭa-sāhasram*—sixteen thousand; *striyaḥ*—all the queens; *ekaḥ*—the one Śrī Kṛṣṇa; *udāvahat*—married.

### TRANSLATION

**" 'It is astounding that Lord Śrī Kṛṣṇa, who is one without a second, expanded Himself in sixteen thousand similar forms to marry sixteen thousand queens in their respective homes.'**

### PURPORT

This verse is spoken by Nārada Muni in *Śrīmad-Bhāgavatam* (10.69.2).

## TEXT 171

সেই বপু, সেই আকৃতি পৃথক্ যদি ভাসে ।
ভাবাবেশ-ভেদে নাম 'বৈভবপ্রকাশে' ॥ ১৭১ ॥

*sei vapu, sei ākṛti pṛthak yadi bhāse*
*bhāvāveśa-bhede nāma 'vaibhava-prakāśe'*

### SYNONYMS

*sei vapu*—that form; *sei ākṛti*—that feature; *pṛthak*—different; *yadi*—if; *bhāse*—appears; *bhāva-āveśa*—of the ecstatic emotion; *bhede*—according to varieties; *nāma*—named; *vaibhava-prakāśe*—*vaibhava-prakāśa.*

### TRANSLATION

**"If one form or feature is differently manifested according to different emotional features, it is called vaibhava-prakāśa.**

## TEXT 172

অনন্ত প্রকাশে কৃষ্ণের নাহি মূর্তিভেদ ।
আকার-বর্ণ-অস্ত্র-ভেদে নাম-বিভেদ ॥ ১৭২ ॥

*ananta prakāśe kṛṣṇera nāhi mūrti-bheda*
*ākāra-varṇa-astra-bhede nāma-vibheda*

## SYNONYMS

*ananta prakāśe*—in innumerable manifestations; *kṛṣṇera*—of Lord Kṛṣṇa; *nāhi*—there is not; *mūrti-bheda*—difference of form; *ākāra*—of features; *varṇa*—of color; *astra*—of weapons; *bhede*—according to differentiation; *nāma-vibheda*—difference of names.

## TRANSLATION

**"When the Lord expands Himself in innumerable forms, there is no difference in the forms, but due to different features, bodily colors and weapons, the names are different.**

## TEXT 173

অন্যে চ সংস্কৃতাত্মানো বিধিনাভিহিতেন তে।
যজন্তি ত্বন্ময়াস্ত্বাং বৈ বহুমূর্ত্ত্যেকমূর্ত্তিকম্ ॥ ১৭৩ ॥

*anye ca saṁskṛtātmāno*
*vidhinābhihitena te*
*yajanti tvan-mayās tvāṁ vai*
*bahu-mūrtyeka-mūrtikam*

## SYNONYMS

*anye*—different persons; *ca*—also; *saṁskṛta-ātmānaḥ*—persons who are purified; *vidhinā*—by the regulative principles; *abhihitena*—stated in the revealed scriptures; *te*—such persons; *yajanti*—worship; *tvat-mayāḥ*—being absorbed in You; *tvām*—You; *vai*—certainly; *bahu-mūrti*—having many forms; *eka-mūrtikam*—although one.

## TRANSLATION

**" 'In different Vedic scriptures, there are prescribed rules and regulative principles for worshiping different types of forms. When one is purified by these rules and regulations, he worships You, the Supreme Personality of Godhead. Although manifest in many forms, You are one.'**

## PURPORT

This verse is quoted from *Śrīmad-Bhāgavatam* (10.40.7). In the *Vedas* it is stated that the one becomes many (*eko bahu syām*). The Supreme Personality of Godhead expands Himself in various forms—*viṣṇu-tattva, jīva-tattva* and *śakti-tattva.*

According to the Vedic literatures, there are different regulative principles for the worship of each of these forms. If one takes advantage of the Vedic literatures and purifies himself by following the rules and regulations, ultimately he worships the Supreme Personality of Godhead, Kṛṣṇa. Kṛṣṇa says in *Bhagavad-gītā* (4.11): *mama vartmānuvartante manuṣyāḥ pārtha sarvaśaḥ.* Worship of the demigods is in a sense worship of the Supreme Personality of Godhead, but such worship is said to be *avidhi-pūrvakam,* improper. Actually demigod worship is meant for unintelligent men. One who is intelligent considers the words of the Supreme Personality of Godhead: *sarva dharmān parityajya mām ekaṁ śaraṇaṁ vraja.* One who worships demigods worships the Supreme Lord indirectly, but according to the revealed scriptures, there is no need to worship Him indirectly. One can worship Him directly.

## TEXT 174

**বৈভবপ্রকাশ কৃষ্ণের—শ্রীবলরাম ।**
**বর্ণমাত্র-ভেদ, সব —কৃষ্ণের সমান ॥ ১৭৪ ॥**

*vaibhava-prakāśa kṛṣṇera——śrī-balarāma*
*varṇa-mātra-bheda, saba——kṛṣṇera samāna*

## SYNONYMS

*vaibhava-prakāśa*—manifestation of the *vaibhava* feature; *kṛṣṇera*—of Lord Kṛṣṇa; *śrī-balarāma*—Śrī Balarāma; *varṇa-mātra*—color only; *bheda*—difference; *saba*—everything; *kṛṣṇera samāna*—equal to Kṛṣṇa.

## TRANSLATION

**"The first manifestation of the vaibhava feature of Kṛṣṇa is Śrī Balarāmajī. Śrī Balarāma and Kṛṣṇa have different bodily colors, but otherwise Śrī Balarāma is equal to Kṛṣṇa in all respects.**

## PURPORT

To understand the difference between *svayaṁ-rūpa, tad-ekātma-rūpa, āveśa, prābhava* and *vaibhava,* Śrīla Bhaktivinoda Ṭhākura has given the following description. In the beginning, Kṛṣṇa has three bodily features: (1) *svayaṁ-rūpa,* as a cowherd boy in Vṛndāvana; (2) *tad-ekātma-rūpa,* which is divided into *svāṁśaka* and *vilāsa;* and (3) *āveśa-rūpa.* The *svāṁśaka,* or expansions of the personal potency, are (1) Kāraṇodakaśāyī, Garbhodakaśāyī, Kṣīrodakaśāyī and (2) incarnations such as the fish, tortoise, boar and Nṛsiṁha. The *vilāsa-rūpa* has a *prābhava* division, including Vāsudeva, Saṅkarṣaṇa, Pradyumna and Aniruddha. There is also a *vaibhava* division in which there are twenty-four forms, including the second Vāsudeva, Saṅkarṣaṇa, Pradyumna and Aniruddha. For each of these, there are three forms; therefore there are twelve forms altogether. These twelve forms constitute the predominant names for the twelve months of the year as well as the twelve *tilaka* marks on the body. Each of the four Personalities of Godhead expands into two other forms; thus there are eight forms, such as Puruṣottama, Acyuta, etc. The four forms (Vāsudeva, etc.), the twelve (Keśava, etc.), and the eight (Puruṣottama, etc.) all together constitute twenty-four forms. All the forms are differently named in accordance with the weapons They hold in Their four hands.

## TEXT 175

**বৈভবপ্রকাশ যৈছে দেবকী-তনুজ ।**
**দ্বিভুজ-স্বরূপ কভু, কভু হয় চতুর্ভুজ ॥ ১৭৫ ॥**

*vaibhava-prakāśa yaiche devakī-tanuja*
*dvibhuja-svarūpa kabhu, kabhu haya caturbhuja*

## SYNONYMS

*vaibhava-prakāśa*—the feature of *vaibhava-prakāśa; yaiche*—just as; *devakī-tanuja*—the son of Devakī; *dvi-bhuja*—two-handed; *svarūpa*—form; *kabhu*—sometimes; *kabhu*—sometimes; *haya*—is; *catuḥ-bhuja*—four-handed.

## TRANSLATION

**"An example of vaibhava-prakāśa is the son of Devakī. He sometimes has two hands and sometimes four hands.**

## PURPORT

When Lord Kṛṣṇa took His birth, He appeared outside the womb as four-handed Viṣṇu. Then Devakī and Vasudeva offered their prayers to Him and asked Him to assume His two-handed form. The Lord immediately assumed His two-handed form and ordered that He be transferred to Gokula on the other side of the River Yamunā.

## TEXT 176

**যে-কালে দ্বিভুজ, নাম—বৈভবপ্রকাশ ।**
**চতুর্ভুজ হৈলে, নাম—প্রাভবপ্রকাশ ॥ ১৭৬ ॥**

*ye-kāle dvibhuja, nāma——vaibhava-prakāśa*
*caturbhuja haile, nāma——prābhava-prakāśa*

### SYNONYMS

*ye-kāle dvi-bhuja*—when the Lord appears as two-handed; *nāma*—named; *vaibhava-prakāśa—vaibhava-prakāśa; catuḥ-bhuja haile*—when He becomes four-handed; *nāma*—named; *prābhava-prakāśa—prābhava-prakāśa.*

### TRANSLATION

**"When the Lord is two-handed, He is called vaibhava-prakāśa, and when He is four-handed He is called prābhava-prakāśa.**

### TEXT 177

**স্বয়ংরূপের গোপবেশ, গোপ-অভিমান।**
**বাসুদেবের ক্ষত্রিয়-বেশ, 'আমি—ক্ষত্রিয়'-জ্ঞান ॥১৭৭॥**

*svayaṁ-rūpera gopa-veśa, gopa-abhimāna*
*vāsudevera kṣatriya-veśa, 'āmi——kṣatriya'-jñāna*

### SYNONYMS

*svayam-rūpera*—of the original form; *gopa-veśa*—the dress of a cowherd boy; *gopa-abhimāna*—thinking Himself a cowherd boy; *vāsudevera*—of Vāsudeva, the son of Vasudeva and Devakī; *kṣatriya-veśa*—the dress is like that of a *kṣatriya; āmi*—I; *kṣatriya*—a *kṣatriya; jñāna*—knowledge.

### TRANSLATION

**"In His original form, the Lord dresses like a cowherd boy and thinks Himself one of them. When He appears as Vāsudeva, the son of Vasudeva and Devakī, His dress and consciousness are those of a kṣatriya, a warrior.**

### TEXT 178

**সৌন্দর্য, ঐশ্বর্য, মাধুর্য, বৈদগ্ধ্য-বিলাস।**
**ব্রজেন্দ্রনন্দনে ইহা অধিক উল্লাস ॥ ১৭৮ ॥**

*saundarya, aiśvarya, mādhurya, vaidagdhya-vilāsa*
*vrajendra-nandane ihā adhika ullāsa*

### SYNONYMS

*saundarya*—the beauty; *aiśvarya*—the opulence; *mādhurya*—the sweetness; *vaidagdhya-vilāsa*—the intellectual pastimes; *vrajendra-nandane*—of the son of Nanda Mahārāja and Yaśodā; *ihā*—all these; *adhika ullāsa*—more jubilant.

### TRANSLATION

**"When one compares the beauty, opulence, sweetness and intellectual pastimes of Vāsudeva, the warrior, to Kṛṣṇa, the cowherd boy, son of Nanda Mahārāja, one sees that Kṛṣṇa's attributes are more pleasant.**

### TEXT 179

গোবিন্দের মাধুরী দেখি' বাসুদেবের ক্ষোভ।
সে মাধুরী আস্বাদিতে উপজয় লোভ॥ ১৭৯ ॥

*govindera mādhurī dekhi' vāsudevera kṣobha*
*se mādhurī āsvādite upajaya lobha*

### SYNONYMS

*govindera*—of Lord Govinda; *mādhurī*—the sweetness; *dekhi'*—seeing; *vāsudevera*—of Vāsudeva; *kṣobha*—agitation; *se*—that; *mādhurī*—sweetness; *āsvādite*—to taste; *upajaya*—awakens; *lobha*—greed.

### TRANSLATION

**"Indeed, Vāsudeva is agitated just to see the sweetness of Govinda, and a transcendental greed awakens in Him to enjoy that sweetness.**

### TEXT 180

উদ্গীর্ণাদ্ভুত-মাধুরী-পরিমলস্যাভীরলীলস্য মে
দ্বৈতং হন্ত সমীক্ষয়ন্ মুহুরসৌ চিত্রীয়তে চারণঃ।
চেতঃ কেলি-কুতূহলোত্তরলিতং সত্যং সখে মামকং
যস্য প্রেক্ষ্য স্বরূপতাং ব্রজবধূসারূপ্যমন্বিচ্ছতি ॥ ১৮০ ॥

*udgīrṇādbhuta-mādhurī-parimalasyābhīra-līlasya me*
*dvaitaṁ hanta samīkṣayan muhur asau citrīyate cāraṇaḥ*
*cetaḥ keli-kutūhalottaralitaṁ satyaṁ sakhe māmakaṁ*
*yasya prekṣya svarūpatāṁ vraja-vadhū-sārūpyam anvicchati*

### SYNONYMS

*udgīrṇa*—overflowing; *adbhuta*—wonderful; *mādhurī*—sweetness; *parimalasya*—whose fragrance; *ābhīra*—of a cowherd boy; *līlasya*—who has pastimes; *me*—My; *dvaitam*—second form; *hanta*—alas; *samīkṣayan*—showing; *muhuḥ*—again and again; *asau*—that; *citrīyate*—is acting like a picture;

*cāraṇaḥ*—dramatic actor; *cetaḥ*—heart; *keli-kutūhala*—by longing for pastimes; *uttaralitam*—greatly excited; *satyam*—actually; *sakhe*—O dear friend; *māmakam*—My; *yasya*—of whom; *prekṣya*—by seeing; *sva-rūpatām*—similarity to My form; *vraja-vadhū*—of the damsels of Vrajabhūmi; *sārūpyam*—a form like the forms; *anvicchati*—desires.

### TRANSLATION

**" 'My dear friend, this dramatic actor appears like a second form of My own self. Like a picture, He displays My pastimes as a cowherd boy overflowing with wonderfully attractive sweetness and fragrance, which are so dear to the damsels of Vraja. When I see such a display, My heart becomes greatly excited. I long for such pastimes and desire a form exactly like the damsels of Vraja.'**

### PURPORT

This verse is found in the *Lalita-mādhava* (4.19).

### TEXT 181

**মথুরায় যৈছে গন্ধর্বনৃত্য-দরশনে ।**
**পুনঃ দ্বারকাতে যৈছে চিত্র-বিলোকনে ॥ ১৮১ ॥**

*mathurāya yaiche gandharva-nṛtya-daraśane*
*punaḥ dvārakāte yaiche citra-vilokane*

### SYNONYMS

*mathurāya*—at Mathurā; *yaiche*—just as; *gandharva-nṛtya*—the dance of the Gandharvas; *daraśane*—by seeing; *punaḥ*—again; *dvārakāte*—at Dvārakā; *yaiche*—just as; *citra-vilokane*—by seeing a picture of Kṛṣṇa.

### TRANSLATION

**"One instance of Vāsudeva's attraction to Kṛṣṇa occurred when Vāsudeva saw the Gandharva dance at Mathurā. Another instance occurred in Dvārakā when Vāsudeva was surprised to see a picture of Kṛṣṇa.**

### TEXT 182

অপরিকলিতপূর্বঃ কশ্চমৎকারকারী
স্ফুরতু মম গরীয়ানেষ মাধুর্যপূরঃ ।
অয়মহমপি হন্ত প্রেক্ষ্য যং লুব্ধচেতাঃ
সরভসমুপভোক্তুং কাময়ে রাধিকেব ॥ ১৮২ ॥

*aparikalita-pūrvaḥ kaś camatkāra-kārī*
*sphuratu mama garīyān eṣa mādhurya-pūraḥ*
*ayam aham api hanta prekṣya yaṁ lubdha-cetāḥ*
*sarabhasam upabhoktuṁ kāmaye rādhikeva*

### SYNONYMS

*aparikalita*—not experienced; *pūrvaḥ*—previously; *kaḥ*—who; *camatkāra-kārī*—causing wonder; *sphuratu*—manifests; *mama*—My; *garīyān*—more great; *eṣaḥ*—this; *mādhurya-pūraḥ*—abundance of sweetness; *ayam*—this; *aham*—I; *api*—even; *hanta*—alas; *prekṣya*—seeing; *yam*—which; *lubdha-cetāḥ*—My mind being bewildered; *sa-rabhasam*—impetuously; *upabhoktum*—to enjoy; *kāmaye*—desire; *rādhikā iva*—like Śrīmatī Rādhārāṇī.

### TRANSLATION

**" 'Who manifests an abundance of sweetness greater than Mine, which has never been experienced before and which causes wonder to all? Alas, I Myself, My mind bewildered upon seeing this beauty, impetuously desire to enjoy it like Śrīmatī Rādhārāṇī.'**

### PURPORT

This verse spoken by Vāsudeva in Dvārakā is recorded by Śrīla Rūpa Gosvāmī in his *Lalita-mādhava* (8.34).

## TEXT 183

**সেই বপু ভিন্নাভাসে কিছু ভিন্নাকার ।**
**ভাবাবেশাকৃতি-ভেদে 'তদেকাত্ম' নাম তাঁর ॥১৮৩ ॥**

*sei vapu bhinnābhāse kichu bhinnākāra*
*bhāvāveśākṛti-bhede 'tad-ekātma' nāma tāṅra*

### SYNONYMS

*sei vapu*—that body; *bhinna-ābhāse*—manifested differently; *kichu*—some; *bhinna-ākāra*—bodily differences; *bhāva-āveśa-ākṛti*—forms and transcendental emotions; *bhede*—by different; *tat-ekātma nāma*—the name is *tad-ekātma; tāṅra*—of Kṛṣṇa.

### TRANSLATION

**"When that body is a little differently manifest and its features a little different in transcendental emotion and form, it is called tad-ekātma.**

### TEXT 184

তদেকাত্মরূপে 'বিলাস', 'স্বাংশ'—দুই ভেদ।
বিলাস, স্বাংশের ভেদে বিবিধ বিভেদ ॥ ১৮৪ ॥

*tad-ekātma-rūpe 'vilāsa', 'svāṁśa'——dui bheda*
*vilāsa, svāṁśera bhede vividha vibheda*

### SYNONYMS

*tat-ekātma-rūpe*—in the form of *tad-ekātma; vilāsa*—pastime; *svāṁśa*—personal expansion; *dui bheda*—two divisions; *vilāsa*—of the pastime expansion; *svāṁśera*—of the personal expansion; *bhede*—by differences; *vividha*—various; *vibheda*—distinctions.

### TRANSLATION

**"In the tad-ekātma-rūpa there are pastime expansions [vilāsa] and personal expansions [svāṁśa]. Consequently there are two divisions. According to pastime and personal expansion, there are various differences.**

### TEXT 185

প্রাভব-বৈভব-ভেদে বিলাস—দ্বিধাকার।
বিলাসের বিলাস-ভেদ—অনন্ত প্রকার ॥ ১৮৫ ॥

*prābhava-vaibhava-bhede vilāsa——dvidhākāra*
*vilāsera vilāsa-bheda——ananta prakāra*

### SYNONYMS

*prābhava-vaibhava-bhede*—by the differences between *prābhava* and *vaibhava; vilāsa*—pastime expansion; *dvidhā-ākāra*—twofold; *vilāsera*—of pastime forms; *vilāsa-bheda*—by the different pastimes; *ananta prakāra*—unlimited varieties.

### TRANSLATION

**"Again the vilāsa forms are divided into twofold categories—prābhava and vaibhava. Again the pastimes of these forms are of unlimited variety.**

### PURPORT

In the *Laghu-bhāgavatāmṛta, Pūrva-khaṇḍa,* verse 17, it is stated:

*tādṛśo nyūna-śaktiṁ yo*
*vyanakti svāṁśa īritaḥ*
*saṅkarṣaṇādir matsyādir*
*yathā tat-tat-svadhāmasu*

When a form of Kṛṣṇa is nondifferent from the original form but is less important and exhibits less potency, it is called *svāṁśa*. Examples of the *svāṁśa* expansion can be found in the quadruple forms of the Lord residing in their respective places, beginning with Saṅkarṣaṇa, Pradyumna and Aniruddha and including the *puruṣa-avatāras, līlā-avatāras, manvantara-avatāras* and *yuga-avatāras*.

## TEXT 186

প্রাভববিলাস—বাসুদেব, সঙ্কর্ষণ।
প্রদ্যুম্ন, অনিরুদ্ধ,—মুখ্য চারিজন ॥ ১৮৬ ॥

*prābhava-vilāsa——vāsudeva, saṅkarṣaṇa*
*pradyumna, aniruddha,——mukhya cāri-jana*

### SYNONYMS

*prābhava-vilāsa*—the *prābhava-vilāsa* forms; *vāsudeva*—Vāsudeva; *saṅkarṣaṇa*—Saṅkarṣaṇa; *pradyumna*—Pradyumna; *aniruddha*—Aniruddha; *mukhya cāri-jana*—the four chief expansions.

### TRANSLATION

**"The chief quadruple expansions are named Vāsudeva, Saṅkarṣaṇa, Pradyumna and Aniruddha. These are called prābhava-vilāsa.**

## TEXT 187

ব্রজে গোপভাব রামের, পুরে ক্ষত্রিয়-ভাবন।
বর্ণ-বেশ-ভেদ, তাতে 'বিলাস' তাঁর নাম ॥ ১৮৭ ॥

*vraje gopa-bhāva rāmera, pure kṣatriya-bhāvana*
*varṇa-veśa-bheda, tāte 'vilāsa' tāṅra nāma*

### SYNONYMS

*vraje*—in Vṛndāvana; *gopa-bhāva*—emotion of a cowherd boy; *rāmera*—of Balarāma; *pure*—in Dvārakā; *kṣatriya-bhāvana*—the emotion of a *kṣatriya; varṇa-veśa-bheda*—by differences of dress and color; *tāte*—therefore; *vilāsa*—pastime expansion; *tāṅra nāma*—His name.

### TRANSLATION

**"Balarāma, who has the same original form of Kṛṣṇa, is Himself a cowherd boy in Vṛndāvana, and He also considers Himself to belong to the kṣatriya race in Dvārakā. Thus His color and dress are different, and He is called a pastime form of Kṛṣṇa.**

### TEXT 188

বৈভবপ্রকাশে আর প্রাভববিলাসে।
একই মূর্ত্যে বলদেব ভাব-ভেদে ভাসে ॥ ১৮৮ ॥

*vaibhava-prakāśe āra prābhava-vilāse*
*eka-i mūrtye baladeva bhāva-bhede bhāse*

### SYNONYMS

*vaibhava-prakāśe*—in *vaibhava* manifestation; *āra*—and; *prābhava-vilāse*—in the *prābhava* pastime form; *eka-i mūrtye*—in one form; *baladeva*—Lord Baladeva; *bhāva-bhede*—according to different emotions; *bhāse*—exists.

### TRANSLATION

**"Śrī Balarāma is a vaibhava-prakāśa manifestation of Kṛṣṇa. He is also manifest in the original quadruple expansion of Vāsudeva, Saṅkarṣaṇa, Pradyumna and Aniruddha. These are prābhava-vilāsa expansions with different emotions.**

### TEXT 189

আদি-চতুর্ব্যূহ—ইঁহার কেহ নাহি সম।
অনন্ত চতুর্ব্যূহগণের প্রাকট্য-কারণ ॥ ১৮৯ ॥

*ādi-catur-vyūha——iṅhāra keha nāhi sama*
*ananta caturvyūha-gaṇera prākaṭya-kāraṇa*

### SYNONYMS

*ādi-catuḥ-vyūha*—the original quadruple group; *iṅhāra*—of this; *keha nāhi*—no one; *sama*—equal; *ananta*—unlimited; *catuḥ-vyūha-gaṇera*—of the quadruple expansions; *prākaṭya*—of manifestation; *kāraṇa*—the cause.

### TRANSLATION

**"The first expansion of the caturvyūha, quadruple forms, is unique. There is nothing to compare with Them. These quadruple forms are the source of unlimited quadruple forms.**

### TEXT 190

কৃষ্ণের এই চারি প্রাভববিলাস।
দ্বারকা-মথুরা-পুরে নিত্য ইঁহার বাস ॥ ১৯০ ॥

*kṛṣṇera ei cāri prābhava-vilāsa*
*dvārakā-mathurā-pure nitya iṅhāra vāsa*

### SYNONYMS

*kṛṣṇera*—of Lord Kṛṣṇa; *ei*—these; *cāri*—four; *prābhava-vilāsa*—*prābhava* pastime forms; *dvārakā-mathurā-pure*—in the two cities Dvārakā and Mathurā; *nitya*—eternal; *iṅhāra*—of Them; *vāsa*—the residential quarters.

### TRANSLATION

**"These four prābhava pastime forms of Lord Kṛṣṇa reside eternally in Dvārakā and Mathurā.**

### TEXT 191

এই চারি হৈতে চব্বিশ মূর্তি পরকাশ।
অস্ত্রভেদে নাম-ভেদ—বৈভববিলাস ॥ ১৯১ ॥

*ei cāri haite cabbiśa mūrti parakāśa*
*astra-bhede nāma-bheda——vaibhava-vilāsa*

### SYNONYMS

*ei cāri haite*—from these four; *cabbiśa*—twenty-four; *mūrti*—forms; *parakāśa*—manifestation; *astra-bhede*—according to the different weapons; *nāma-bheda*—the difference of names; *vaibhava-vilāsa*—the *vaibhava* pastime expansions.

### TRANSLATION

**"From the original quadruple expansion, twenty-four forms are manifest. They differ according to the placement of weapons in Their four hands. They are called vaibhava-vilāsa.**

### TEXT 192

পুনঃ কৃষ্ণ চতুর্ব্যূহ লঞা পূর্বরূপে।
পরব্যোম-মধ্যে বৈসে নারায়ণরূপে ॥ ১৯২ ॥

*punaḥ kṛṣṇa catur-vyūha lañā pūrva-rūpe*
*paravyoma-madhye vaise nārāyaṇa-rūpe*

## SYNONYMS

*punaḥ*—again; *kṛṣṇa*—Kṛṣṇa; *catuḥ-vyūha*—the quadruple expansions; *lañā*—taking; *pūrva-rūpe*—as previously; *paravyoma-madhye*—in the *paravyoma* area; *vaise*—resides; *nārāyaṇa-rūpe*—in the form of four-handed Nārāyaṇa.

## TRANSLATION

**"Lord Kṛṣṇa again expands, and within the paravyoma, the spiritual sky, He is situated in fullness as the four-handed Nārāyaṇa, accompanied by expansions of the original quadruple form.**

## PURPORT

At the top of the *paravyoma,* the spiritual sky, there is Goloka Vṛndāvana, which is divided into three parts. Two of the parts, called Mathurā and Dvārakā, are the residences of Kṛṣṇa in His *prābhava-vilāsa* forms. Balarāma, Kṛṣṇa's *vaibhava-prakāśa,* is eternally situated in Gokula. From the quadruple *prābhava-vilāsa,* twenty-four forms of the *vaibhava-vilāsa* are expanded. Each has four hands holding weapons in different positions. The topmost planet in the spiritual sky is Goloka Vṛndāvana, and below that planet is the spiritual sky itself. In that spiritual sky, Kṛṣṇa Himself is four-handed and is situated as Nārāyaṇa.

## TEXT 193

তাঁহা হৈতে পুনঃ চতুর্ব্যূহ-পরকাশ ।
আবরণরূপে চারিদিকে যাঁর বাস ॥ ১৯৩ ॥

*tāṅhā haite punaḥ catur-vyūha-parakāśa*
*āvaraṇa-rūpe cāri-dike yāṅra vāsa*

## SYNONYMS

*tāṅhā haite*—from that original *catur-vyūha; punaḥ*—again; *catuḥ-vyūha-parakāśa*—manifestation of quadruple expansions; *āvaraṇa-rūpe*—in the form of a covering; *cāri-dike*—in four directions; *yāṅra*—whose; *vāsa*—residence.

## TRANSLATION

**"Thus the original quadruple forms again manifest Themselves in a second quadruple expansion. The residences of these second quadruple expansions cover the four directions.**

### TEXT 194

চারিজনের পুনঃ পৃথক্ তিন তিন মূর্তি ।
কেশবাদি যাহা হৈতে বিলাসের পূর্তি ॥ ১৯৪ ॥

*cāri-janera punaḥ pṛthak tina tina mūrti*
*keśavādi yāhā haite vilāsera pūrti*

### SYNONYMS

*cāri-janera*—of the original of the four expansions; *punaḥ*—again; *pṛthak*—separate; *tina tina*—three each; *mūrti*—forms; *keśava-ādi*—beginning with Lord Keśava; *yāhā haite*—from which; *vilāsera pūrti*—the *vilāsa* expansions are fulfilled.

### TRANSLATION

**"Again these quadruple forms expand three times, beginning with Keśava. That is the fulfillment of the pastime forms.**

### TEXT 195

চক্রাদি-ধারণ-ভেদে নাম-ভেদ সব ।
বাসুদেবের মূর্তি—কেশব, নারায়ণ, মাধব ॥ ১৯৫ ॥

*cakrādi-dhāraṇa-bhede nāma-bheda saba*
*vāsudevera mūrti——keśava, nārāyaṇa, mādhava*

### SYNONYMS

*cakra-ādi*—of the disc and other weapons; *dhāraṇa*—of holding; *bhede*—by differences; *nāma*—of names; *bheda*—differences; *saba*—all; *vāsudevera mūrti*—the expansions of Vāsudeva; *keśava*—Keśava; *nārāyaṇa*—Nārāyaṇa; *mādhava*—Mādhava.

### TRANSLATION

**"Out of the catur-vyūha, there are three expansions of each and every form, and they are named differently according to the position of the weapons. The Vāsudeva expansions are Keśava, Nārāyaṇa and Mādhava.**

### TEXT 196

সঙ্কর্ষণের মূর্তি—গোবিন্দ, বিষ্ণু, মধুসূদন ।
এ অন্য গোবিন্দ—নহে ব্রজেন্দ্রনন্দন ॥ ১৯৬ ॥

*saṅkarṣaṇera mūrti——govinda, viṣṇu, madhusūdana*
*e anya govinda——nahe vrajendra-nandana*

### SYNONYMS

*saṅkarṣaṇera mūrti*—the expansions of Saṅkarṣaṇa; *govinda*—Govinda; *viṣṇu*—Viṣṇu; *madhu-sūdana*—Madhusūdana; *e*—this; *anya*—another; *govinda*—Govinda; *nahe vrajendra-nandana*—not the son of Nanda Mahārāja.

### TRANSLATION

**"The expansions of Saṅkarṣaṇa are Govinda, Viṣṇu and Madhusūdana. This Govinda is different from the original Govinda, for He is not the son of Mahārāja Nanda.**

## TEXT 197

প্রদ্যুম্নের মূর্তি—ত্রিবিক্রম, বামন, শ্রীধর ।
অনিরুদ্ধের মূর্তি – হৃষীকেশ, পদ্মনাভ, দামোদর ॥১৯৭

*pradyumnera mūrti——trivikrama, vāmana, śrīdhara*
*aniruddhera mūrti——hṛṣīkeśa, padmanābha, dāmodara*

### SYNONYMS

*pradyumnera mūrti*—expansions of the form of Pradyumna; *tri-vikrama*—Trivikrama; *vāmana*—Vāmana; *śrīdhara*—Śrīdhara; *aniruddhera mūrti*—expansions of Aniruddha; *hṛṣīkeśa*—Hṛṣīkeśa; *padmanābha*—Padmanābha; *dāmodara*—Dāmodara.

### TRANSLATION

**"The expansions of Pradyumna are Trivikrama, Vāmana and Śrīdhara. The expansions of Aniruddha are Hṛṣīkeśa, Padmanābha and Dāmodara.**

## TEXT 198

দ্বাদশ-মাসের দেবতা—এইবার জন ।
মার্গশীর্ষে—কেশব, পৌষে –নারায়ণ ॥ ১৯৮ ॥

*dvādaśa-māsera devatā——ei-bāra jana*
*mārga-śīrṣe——keśava, pauṣe——nārāyaṇa*

### SYNONYMS

*dvādaśa-māsera*—of the twelve months; *devatā*—predominating Deities; *ei*—these; *bāra jana*—twelve Personalities of Godhead; *mārga-śīrṣe*—the month of

Agrahāyana (November-December); *keśava*—Keśava; *pauṣe*—the month of Pauṣa (December-January); *nārāyaṇa*—Nārāyaṇa.

### TRANSLATION

**"These twelve are the predominating Deities of the twelve months. Keśava is the predominating Deity of Agrahāyana, and Nārāyaṇa is the predominating Deity of Pauṣa.**

### TEXT 199

মাঘের দেবতা – মাধব, গোবিন্দ—ফাল্গুনে ।
চৈত্রে – বিষ্ণু, বৈশাখে – শ্রীমধুসূদন ॥ ১৯৯ ॥

*māghera devatā——mādhava, govinda——phālgune*
*caitre——viṣṇu, vaiśākhe——śrī-madhusūdana*

### SYNONYMS

*māghera devatā*—the predominating Deity of the month of Māgha (January-February); *mādhava*—Mādhava; *govinda*—Govinda; *phālgune*—in the month of Phālguna (February-March); *caitre*—in the month of Caitra (March-April); *viṣṇu*—Lord Viṣṇu; *vaiśākhe*—in the month of Vaiśākha (April-May); *śrī-madhusūdana*—Madhusūdana.

### TRANSLATION

**"The predominating Deity for the month of Māgha is Mādhava, and the predominating Deity for the month of Phālguna is Govinda. Viṣṇu is the predominating Deity for Caitra, and Madhusūdana is the predominating Deity for Vaiśākha.**

### TEXT 200

জ্যৈষ্ঠে – ত্রিবিক্রম, আষাঢ়ে—বামন দেবেশ ।
শ্রাবণে—শ্রীধর, ভাদ্রে—দেব হৃষীকেশ ॥ ২০০ ॥

*jyaiṣṭhe——trivikrama, āṣāḍhe——vāmana deveśa*
*śrāvaṇe——śrīdhara, bhādre——deva hṛṣīkeśa*

### SYNONYMS

*jyaiṣṭhe*—in the month of Jyaiṣṭha (May-June); *trivikrama*—Trivikrama; *āṣāḍhe*—in the month of Āṣāḍha (June-July); *vāmana deva-īśa*—Lord Vāmana; *śrāvaṇe*—in the month of Śrāvaṇa (July-August); *śrīdhara*—Śrīdhara; *bhādre*—in the month of Bhādra (August-September); *deva hṛṣīkeśa*—Lord Hṛṣīkeśa.

### TRANSLATION

**"In the month of Jyaiṣṭha, the predominating Deity is Trivikrama. In Āṣāḍha the Deity is Vāmana, in Śrāvaṇa the Deity is Śrīdhara, and in Bhādra the Deity is Hṛṣīkeśa.**

### TEXT 201

**আশ্বিনে—পদ্মনাভ, কার্তিকে দামোদর ।**
**'রাধা-দামোদর' অন্য ব্রজেন্দ্র-কোঙর ॥ ২০১ ॥**

*āśvine——padmanābha, kārtike dāmodara*
*'rādhā-dāmodara' anya vrajendra-koṅara*

### SYNONYMS

*āśvine*—in the month of Āśvina (September-October); *padma-nābha*—Padmanābha; *kārtike*—in the month of Kārttika (October-November); *dāmodara*—Dāmodara; *rādhā-dāmodara*—the Dāmodara of Śrīmatī Rādhārāṇī; *anya*—another; *vrajendra-koṅara*—the son of Mahārāja Nanda.

### TRANSLATION

**"In the month of Āśvina, the predominating Deity is Padmanābha, and in Kārttika it is Dāmodara. This Dāmodara is different from Rādhā-Dāmodara, the son of Nanda Mahārāja in Vṛndāvana.**

### TEXT 202

**দ্বাদশ-তিলক-মন্ত্র এই দ্বাদশ নাম ।**
**আচমনে এই নামে স্পর্শি তত্তৎস্থান ॥ ২০২ ॥**

*dvādaśa-tilaka-mantra ei dvādaśa nāma*
*ācamane ei nāme sparśi tat-tat-sthāna*

### SYNONYMS

*dvādaśa-tilaka*—for twelve marks of *tilaka; mantra*—the *mantra; ei*—these; *dvādaśa nāma*—twelve names; *ācamane*—in washing with water; *ei nāme*—with these names; *sparśi*—we touch; *tat-tat-sthāna*—the respective places.

### TRANSLATION

**"When putting the twelve tilaka marks on the twelve places of the body, one has to chant the mantra consisting of these twelve Viṣṇu names. After**

**daily worship, when one anoints the different parts of the body with water, these names should be chanted as one touches each part of the body.**

### PURPORT

While marking the body with *tilaka,* one should chant the following *mantra,* which consists of the twelve names of Lord Viṣṇu.

*lalāṭe keśavaṁ dhyāyen*
*nārāyaṇam athodare*
*vakṣaḥ-sthale mādhavaṁ tu*
*govindaṁ kaṇṭha-kūpake*

*viṣṇuṁ ca dakṣiṇe kukṣau*
*bāhau ca madhusūdanam*
*trivikramaṁ kandhare tu*
*vāmanaṁ vāma-pārśvake*

*śrīdharaṁ vāma-bāhau tu*
*hṛṣīkeśaṁ tu kandhare*
*pṛṣṭhe ca padmanābhaṁ ca*
*kaṭyāṁ dāmodaraṁ nyaset*

"When one marks the forehead with *tilaka,* he must remember Keśava. When one marks the lower abdomen, he must remember Nārāyaṇa. For the chest, one should remember Mādhava, and when marking the hollow of the neck one should remember Govinda. Lord Viṣṇu should be remembered while marking the right side of the belly, and Madhusūdana should be remembered when marking the right arm. Trivikrama should be remembered when marking the right shoulder, and Vāmana should be remembered when marking the left side of the belly. Śrīdhara should be remembered while marking the left arm, and Hṛṣīkeśa should be remembered when marking the left shoulder. Padmanābha and Dāmodara should be remembered when marking the back."

### TEXT 203

**এই চারিজনের বিলাস-মূর্তি আর অষ্ট জন ।**
**তাঁ সবার নাম কহি, শুন সনাতন ॥ ২০৩ ॥**

*ei cāri-janera vilāsa-mūrti āra aṣṭa jana*
*tāṅ sabāra nāma kahi, śuna sanātana*

### SYNONYMS

*ei cāri-janera*—of the four personalities; *vilāsa-mūrti*—pastime forms; *āra*—more; *aṣṭa jana*—eight personalities; *tāṅ sabāra*—of all of them; *nāma*—the holy names; *kahi*—I shall mention; *śuna*—hear; *sanātana*—O Sanātana.

### TRANSLATION

**"From Vāsudeva, Saṅkarṣaṇa, Pradyumna and Aniruddha, there are eight additional pastime expansions. O Sanātana, please hear Me as I mention Their names.**

### TEXT 204

পুরুষোত্তম, অচ্যুত, নৃসিংহ, জনার্দন ।
হরি, কৃষ্ণ,অধোক্ষজ, উপেন্দ্র,—অষ্টজন ॥ ২০৪ ॥

*puruṣottama, acyuta, nṛsiṁha, janārdana*
*hari, kṛṣṇa, adhokṣaja, upendra,——aṣṭa-jana*

### SYNONYMS

*puruṣottama*—Puruṣottama; *acyuta*—Acyuta; *nṛsiṁha*—Nṛsiṁha; *janārdana*—Janārdana; *hari*—Hari; *kṛṣṇa*—Kṛṣṇa; *adhokṣaja*—Adhokṣaja; *upendra*—Upendra; *aṣṭa-jana*—eight persons.

### TRANSLATION

**"The eight pastime expansions are Puruṣottama, Acyuta, Nṛsiṁha, Janārdana, Hari, Kṛṣṇa, Adhokṣaja and Upendra.**

### TEXT 205

বাসুদেবের বিলাস দুই—অধোক্ষজ, পুরুষোত্তম ।
সঙ্কর্ষণের বিলাস—উপেন্দ্র, অচ্যুত দুইজন ॥ ২০৫ ॥

*vāsudevera vilāsa dui——adhokṣaja, puruṣottama*
*saṅkarṣaṇera vilāsa——upendra, acyuta dui-jana*

### SYNONYMS

*vāsudevera vilāsa*—the pastime expansions of Vāsudeva; *dui*—two; *adhokṣaja*—Adhokṣaja; *puruṣottama*—Puruṣottama; *saṅkarṣaṇera vilāsa*—the pastime expansions of Saṅkarṣaṇa; *upendra*—Upendra; *acyuta*—Acyuta; *dui-jana*—the two persons.

### TRANSLATION

**"Of these eight expansions, two are pastime forms of Vāsudeva. Their names are Adhokṣaja and Puruṣottama. The two pastime forms of Saṅkarṣaṇa are Upendra and Acyuta.**

### TEXT 206

প্রদ্যুম্নের বিলাস – নৃসিংহ, জনার্দন ।
অনিরুদ্ধের বিলাস—হরি, কৃষ্ণ দুইজন ॥ ২০৬ ॥

*pradyumnera vilāsa——nṛsiṁha, janārdana*
*aniruddhera vilāsa——hari, kṛṣṇa dui-jana*

### SYNONYMS

*pradyumnera vilāsa*—the pastime forms of Pradyumna; *nṛsiṁha*—Nṛsiṁha; *janārdana*—Janārdana; *aniruddhera vilāsa*—the pastime forms of Aniruddha; *hari*—Hari; *kṛṣṇa*—Kṛṣṇa; *dui-jana*—the two persons.

### TRANSLATION

**"The pastime forms of Pradyumna are Nṛsiṁha and Janārdana, and the pastime forms of Aniruddha are Hari and Kṛṣṇa.**

### TEXT 207

এই চব্বিশ মূর্তি—প্রাভব-বিলাস প্রধান ।
অস্ত্রধারণ-ভেদে ধরে ভিন্ন ভিন্ন নাম ॥ ২০৭ ॥

*ei cabbiśa mūrti——prābhava-vilāsa pradhāna*
*astra-dhāraṇa-bhede dhare bhinna bhinna nāma*

### SYNONYMS

*ei cabbiśa mūrti*—all of these twenty-four forms; *prābhava-vilāsa*—pastime forms of the *prābhava* expansions; *pradhāna*—chief; *astra-dhāraṇa*—of holding the weapons; *bhede*—in terms of differences; *dhare*—accept; *bhinna bhinna*—separate from one another; *nāma*—names.

### TRANSLATION

**"All these twenty-four forms constitute the chief prābhava-vilāsa pastime forms of the Lord. They are named differently according to the position of weapons in Their hands.**

### TEXT 208

**ইঁহার মধ্যে যাহার হয় আকার-বেশ-ভেদ ।**
**সেই সেই হয় বিলাস-বৈভব-বিভেদ ॥ ২০৮ ॥**

*iṅhāra madhye yāhāra haya ākāra-veśa-bheda*
*sei sei haya vilāsa-vaibhava-vibheda*

### SYNONYMS

*iṅhāra madhye*—out of Them all; *yāhāra*—of whom; *haya*—there is; *ākāra*—of bodily features; *veśa*—of dress; *bheda*—difference; *sei sei haya*—they are; *vilāsa-vaibhava*—of *vaibhava-vilāsa; vibheda*—the difference.

### TRANSLATION

**"Of all these, the forms that differ in dress and features are distinguished as vaibhava-vilāsa.**

### TEXT 209

**পদ্মনাভ, ত্রিবিক্রম, নৃসিংহ, বামন ।**
**হরি, কৃষ্ণ আদি হয় 'আকারে' বিলক্ষণ ॥ ২০৯ ॥**

*padmanābha, trivikrama, nṛsiṁha, vāmana*
*hari, kṛṣṇa ādi haya 'ākāre' vilakṣaṇa*

### SYNONYMS

*padmanābha*—Padmanābha; *trivikrama*—Trivikrama; *nṛsiṁha*—Nṛsiṁha; *vāmana*—Vāmana; *hari*—Hari; *kṛṣṇa*—Kṛṣṇa; *ādi*—and so on; *haya*—are; *ākāre vilakṣaṇa*—different in bodily feature.

### TRANSLATION

**"Of them, Padmanābha, Trivikrama, Nṛsiṁha, Vāmana, Hari, Kṛṣṇa, and so on all have different bodily features.**

### TEXT 210

**কৃষ্ণের প্রাভববিলাস—বাসুদেবাদি চারি জন ।**
**সেই চারিজনার বিলাস—বিংশতি গণন ॥ ২১০ ॥**

*kṛṣṇera prābhava-vilāsa——vāsudevādi cāri jana*
*sei cāri-janāra vilāsa——viṁśati gaṇana*

### SYNONYMS

*kṛṣṇera*—of Lord Kṛṣṇa; *prābhava-vilāsa*—*prābhava* pastime forms; *vāsudeva-ādi*—Vāsudeva and others; *cāri jana*—quadruple expansions; *sei*—those; *cāri-janāra*—of the four personalities; *vilāsa*—pastime forms; *viṁśati gaṇana*—counted as twenty.

### TRANSLATION

**"Vāsudeva and the three others are direct prābhava pastime forms of Lord Kṛṣṇa. Of these quadruple forms, the pastime expansions are twenty in number.**

### TEXT 211

ইঁহা-সবার পৃথক্ বৈকুণ্ঠ—পরব্যোম-ধামে।
পূর্ব্বাদি অষ্টদিকে তিন তিন ক্রমে ॥ ২১১ ॥

*iṅhā-sabāra pṛthak vaikuṇṭha——paravyoma-dhāme*
*pūrvādi aṣṭa-dike tina tina krame*

### SYNONYMS

*iṅhā*—of them; *sabāra*—of all; *pṛthak*—separate; *vaikuṇṭha*—a Vaikuṇṭha planet; *paravyoma-dhāme*—in the spiritual world; *pūrva-ādi*—beginning from the east; *aṣṭa-dike*—in the eight directions; *tina tina*—three in each; *krame*—in consecutive order.

### TRANSLATION

**"All these forms preside over different Vaikuṇṭha planets in the spiritual world, beginning from the east in consecutive order. In each of eight directions, there are three different forms.**

### TEXT 212

যদ্যপি পরব্যোম সবাকার নিত্যধাম।
তথাপি ব্রহ্মাণ্ডে কারো কাঁহো সন্নিধান ॥ ২১২ ॥

*yadyapi paravyoma sabākāra nitya-dhāma*
*tathāpi brahmāṇḍe kāro kāṅho sannidhāna*

### SYNONYMS

*yadyapi*—although; *paravyoma*—the spiritual sky; *sabākāra*—of all of Them; *nitya-dhāma*—the eternal abode; *tathāpi*—still; *brahmāṇḍe*—in the material universes; *kāro*—of some of Them; *kāṅho*—somewhere; *sannidhāna*—the residential places.

### TRANSLATION

**"Although They all have Their residences eternally in the spiritual sky, some of Them are situated within the material universes.**

### TEXT 213

পরব্যোম-মধ্যে নারায়ণের নিত্য-স্থিতি ।
পরব্যোম-উপরি কৃষ্ণলোকের বিভুতি ॥ ২১৩ ॥

*paravyoma-madhye nārāyaṇera nitya-sthiti*
*paravyoma-upari kṛṣṇalokera vibhuti*

### SYNONYMS

*paravyoma-madhye*—in the spiritual sky; *nārāyaṇera*—of Nārāyaṇa; *nitya-sthiti*—eternal residence; *paravyoma-upari*—in the upper portion of the spiritual sky; *kṛṣṇa-lokera vibhuti*—the opulence of the Kṛṣṇaloka planet.

### TRANSLATION

**"There is an eternal residence of Nārāyaṇa in the spiritual sky. In the upper portion of the spiritual sky is a planet known as Kṛṣṇaloka, which is filled with all opulences.**

### TEXT 214

এক 'কৃষ্ণলোক' হয় ত্রিবিধপ্রকার ।
গোকুলাখ্য, মথুরাখ্য, দ্বারকাখ্য আর ॥ ২১৪ ॥

*eka 'kṛṣṇaloka' haya trividha-prakāra*
*gokulākhya, mathurākhya, dvārakākhya āra*

### SYNONYMS

*eka*—one; *kṛṣṇa-loka*—the planet known as Kṛṣṇaloka; *haya*—there is; *tri-vidha-prakāra*—in three different divisions; *gokula-ākhya*—Gokula; *mathurā-ākhya*—Mathurā; *dvārakā-ākhya*—Dvārakā; *āra*—and.

### TRANSLATION

**"The planet of Kṛṣṇaloka is divided into three sections—Gokula, Mathurā and Dvārakā.**

## TEXT 215

মথুরাতে কেশবের নিত্য সন্নিধান ।
নীলাচলে পুরুষোত্তম—'জগন্নাথ' নাম ॥ ২১৫ ॥

*mathurāte keśavera nitya sannidhāna*
*nīlācale puruṣottama——'jagannātha' nāma*

### SYNONYMS

*mathurāte*—in Mathurā; *keśavera*—of Lord Keśava; *nitya*—eternal; *sannidhāna*—residence; *nīlācale*—in Nīlācala (Jagannātha Purī); *puruṣottama*—Puruṣottama; *jagannātha nāma*—also known as Jagannātha.

### TRANSLATION

**"Lord Keśava eternally resides at Mathurā, and Lord Puruṣottama, known by the name Jagannātha, eternally resides at Nīlācala.**

## TEXT 216

প্রয়াগে মাধব, মন্দারে শ্রীমধুসূদন ।
আনন্দারণ্যে বাসুদেব, পদ্মনাভ জনার্দন ॥ ২১৬ ॥

*prayāge mādhava, mandāre śrī-madhusūdana*
*ānandāraṇye vāsudeva, padmanābha janārdana*

### SYNONYMS

*prayāge*—at Prayāga; *mādhava*—Bindu Mādhava; *mandāre*—at Mandāra-parvata; *śrī-madhusūdana*—Śrī Madhusūdana; *ānanda-araṇye*—at the place known as Ānandāraṇya; *vāsudeva*—Lord Vāsudeva; *padmanābha*—Lord Padmanābha; *janārdana*—Lord Janārdana.

### TRANSLATION

**"At Prayāga, the Lord is situated as Bindu Mādhava, and at Mandāra-parvata, the Lord is known as Madhusūdana. Vāsudeva, Padmnābha and Janārdana reside at Ānandāraṇya.**

## TEXT 217

বিষ্ণুকাঞ্চীতে বিষ্ণু, হরি রহে, মায়াপুরে ।
ঐছে আর নানা মূর্তি ব্রহ্মাণ্ড-ভিতরে ॥ ২১৭ ॥

*viṣṇu-kāñcīte viṣṇu, hari rahe, māyāpure*
*aiche āra nānā mūrti brahmāṇḍa-bhitare*

## SYNONYMS

*viṣṇu-kāñcīte*—at Viṣṇu-kāñcī; *viṣṇu*—Lord Viṣṇu; *hari*—Lord Hari; *rahe*—remains; *māyāpure*—at Māyāpur; *aiche*—similarly; *āra*—also; *nānā*—various; *mūrti*—forms; *brahmāṇḍa-bhitare*—throughout the universe.

## TRANSLATION

**"At Viṣṇu-kāñcī there is Lord Viṣṇu, at Māyāpur Lord Hari, and throughout the universe a variety of other forms.**

## PURPORT

All of these forms are *mūrti* forms, and They are worshiped in the temples. Their names are Keśava at Mathurā, Puruṣottama or Jagannātha at Nīlācala, Śrī Bindu Mādhava at Prayāga, Madhusūdana at Mandāra, and Vāsudeva, Padmanābha and Janārdana at Ānandāraṇya, which is situated in Kerala, South India. At Viṣṇu-kāñcī, which is situated in the Barada state, there is Lord Viṣṇu, and Hari is situated at Māyāpur, Lord Caitanya's birthsite. Thus in different places throughout the universe there are various Deities in temples bestowing Their causeless mercy upon the devotees. All these Deity forms are nondifferent from the *mūrtis* in the spiritual world of the Vaikuṇṭhas. Although the *arcā-mūrti,* the worshipable Deity form of the Lord, appears to be made of material elements, it is as good as the spiritual forms found in the spiritual Vaikuṇṭhalokas. The Deity in the temple, however, is visible to the material eyes of the devotee. It is not possible for one in material conditional life to see the spiritual form of the Lord. To bestow causeless mercy upon us, the Lord appears as *arcā-mūrti* so that we can see Him. It is forbidden to consider the *arcā-mūrti* to be made of stone or wood. In the *Padma Purāṇa* it is said:

*arcye viṣṇau śilā-dhīr guruṣu nara-matir vaiṣṇave jāti-buddhir*
*viṣṇor vā vaiṣṇavānāṁ kali-mala-mathane pāda-tīrthe 'mbu-buddhiḥ*
*śrī-viṣṇor nāmni mantre sakala-kaluṣa-he śabde-sāmānya-buddhir*
*viṣṇau sarveśvareśe tad-itara-sama-dhīr yasya vā nārakī saḥ*

No one should consider the Deity in the temple to be made of stone or wood, nor should one consider the spiritual master an ordinary human being. No one should consider a Vaiṣṇava to belong to a particular caste or creed, and no one should consider *caraṇāmṛta* or Ganges water to be like ordinary water. Nor should anyone consider the Hare Kṛṣṇa *mahā-mantra* to be a material vibration. All these expansions of Kṛṣṇa in the material world are simply demonstrations of the Lord's mercy and willingness to give facility to His devotees who are engaged in His devotional service within the material world.

### TEXT 218

এইমত ব্রহ্মাণ্ড-মধ্যে সবার 'পরকাশ' ।
সপ্তদ্বীপে নবখণ্ডে যাঁহার বিলাস ॥ ২১৮ ॥

*ei-mata brahmāṇḍa-madhye sabāra 'parakāśa'*
*sapta-dvīpe nava-khaṇḍe yāṅhāra vilāsa*

### SYNONYMS

*ei-mata*—in this way; *brahmāṇḍa-madhye*—within this universe; *sabāra*—of all of Them; *parakāśa*—manifestations; *sapta-dvīpe*—on seven islands; *nava-khaṇḍe*—in different sections, nine in number; *yāṅhāra vilāsa*—the pastimes of whom.

### TRANSLATION

**"Within the universe the Lord is situated in different spiritual manifestations. These are situated on seven islands in nine sections. Thus Their pastimes are going on.**

### PURPORT

The seven islands are mentioned in the *Siddhānta-śiromaṇi:*

*bhūmer ardhaṁ kṣīra-sindhor udaka-sthaṁ*
*jambu-dvīpaṁ prāhur ācārya-varyāḥ*
*ardhe 'nyasmin dvīpa-ṣaṭkasya yāmye*
*kṣāra-kṣīrādy-ambudhīnāṁ niveśaḥ*

*śākaṁ tataḥ śālmala-matra kauśaṁ*
*krauñcaṁ ca go-medaka-puṣkare ca*
*dvayor dvayor antaram ekam ekaṁ*
*samudrayor dvīpam udāharanti*

The seven islands (*dvīpas*) are known as (1) Jambu, (2) Śāka, (3) Śālmalī, (4) Kuśa, (5) Krauñca, (6) Gomeda, or Plakṣa, and (7) Puṣkara. The planets are called *dvīpa.* Outer space is like an ocean of air. Just as there are islands in the watery ocean, these planets in the ocean of space are called *dvīpas,* or islands in outer space. There are nine *khaṇḍas,* known as (1) Bhārata, (2) Kinnara, (3) Hari, (4) Kuru, (5) Hiraṇmaya, (6) Ramyaka, (7) Ilāvṛta, (8) Bhadrāśva and

(9) Ketumāla. These are different parts of the Jambudvīpa. A valley between two mountains is called a *khaṇḍa* or *varṣa.*

### TEXT 219

**সর্বত্র প্রকাশ তাঁর—ভক্তে সুখ দিতে।**
**জগতের অধর্ম নাশি' ধর্ম স্থাপিতে ॥ ২১৯ ॥**

*sarvatra prakāśa tāṅra——bhakte sukha dite*
*jagatera adharma nāśi' dharma sthāpite*

### SYNONYMS

*sarvatra*—everywhere; *prakāśa*—manifestations; *tāṅra*—His; *bhakte*—to the devotees; *sukha dite*—to give happiness; *jagatera*—of the material world; *adharma*—irreligious principles; *nāśi'*—destroying; *dharma*—religious principles; *sthāpite*—to establish.

### TRANSLATION

**"The Lord is situated in all the universes in different forms just to please His devotees. Thus the Lord destroys irreligious principles and establishes religious principles.**

### PURPORT

In the material world the Lord is situated in different *arcā-mūrtis* (Deities) in the temples, just to decrease the material activities of the conditioned soul and increase his spiritual activities. Particularly in India there are many temples throughout the country. Devotees may take advantage of them and go see the Lord at Jagannātha Purī, Vṛndāvana, Prayāga, Mathurā, Hardwar and Viṣṇu-kāñcī. When the devotees travel to these places and see the Lord, they become very happy in devotional service.

### TEXT 220

**ইঁহার মধ্যে কারো হয় 'অবতারে' গণন।**
**যৈছে বিষ্ণু, ত্রিবিক্রম, নৃসিংহ, বামন ॥ ২২০ ॥**

*iṅhāra madhye kāro haya 'avatāre' gaṇana*
*yaiche viṣṇu, trivikrama, nṛsiṁha, vāmana*

### SYNONYMS

*iṅhāra madhye*—of Them; *kāro*—of some; *haya*—there is; *avatāre*—as incarnations; *gaṇana*—counting; *yaiche*—as; *viṣṇu*—Lord Viṣṇu; *trivikrama*—Lord Trivikrama; *nṛsiṁha*—Lord Nṛsiṁha; *vāmana*—Lord Vāmana.

## TRANSLATION

**"Of these forms, some are considered incarnations. Examples are Lord Viṣṇu, Lord Trivikrama, Lord Nṛsiṁha and Lord Vāmana.**

## TEXT 221

অস্ত্রধৃতি-ভেদ—নাম-ভেদের কারণ ।
চক্রাদি-ধারণ-ভেদ শুন, সনাতন ॥ ২২১ ॥

*astra-dhṛti-bheda——nāma-bhedera kāraṇa*
*cakrādi-dhāraṇa-bheda śuna, sanātana*

## SYNONYMS

*astra-dhṛti*—of holding the weapon; *bheda*—difference; *nāma-bhedera*—of differences of names; *kāraṇa*—the cause; *cakra-ādi*—of weapons, beginning with the disc; *dhāraṇa*—of holding; *bheda*—differences; *śuna*—please hear; *sanātana*—O Sanātana.

## TRANSLATION

**"My dear Sanātana, just hear from Me as I tell you how the different viṣṇu-mūrtis hold Their weapons, beginning with the disc, and how They are named differently according to the placement of objects in Their hands.**

## TEXT 222

দক্ষিণাধো হস্ত হৈতে বামাধঃ পর্যন্ত ।
চক্রাদি অস্ত্রধারণ-গণনার অন্ত ॥ ২২২ ॥

*dakṣiṇādho hasta haite vāmādhaḥ paryanta*
*cakrādi astra-dhāraṇa-gaṇanāra anta*

## SYNONYMS

*dakṣiṇa-adhaḥ*—the lower right; *hasta*—hand; *haite*—from; *vāma-adhaḥ*—the lower left hand; *paryanta*—up to; *cakra-ādi*—beginning with the disc; *astra-dhāraṇa*—of holding the weapons; *gaṇanāra*—of counting; *anta*—the end.

## TRANSLATION

**"The procedure for counting begins with the lower right hand and goes to the upper right hand, the upper left hand, and the lower left hand. Lord Viṣṇu is named according to the order the objects are held in His hands.**

## TEXT 223

সিদ্ধার্থ-সংহিতা করে চব্বিশ মূর্তি গণন।
তার মতে কহি আগে চক্রাদি-ধারণ ॥ ২২৩ ॥

*siddhārtha-saṁhitā kare cabbiśa mūrti gaṇana*
*tāra mate kahi āge cakrādi-dhāraṇa*

### SYNONYMS

*siddhārtha-saṁhitā*—the revealed scripture named *Siddhārtha-saṁhitā; kare*—does; *cabbiśa*—twenty-four; *mūrti*—forms; *gaṇana*—counting; *tāra mate*—according to the opinion of *Siddhārtha-saṁhitā; kahi*—I shall describe; *āge*—first; *cakra-ādi-dhāraṇa*—holding of the weapons, beginning with the disc.

### TRANSLATION

**"According to the Siddhārtha-saṁhitā there are twenty-four forms of Lord Viṣṇu. First I shall describe, according to the opinion of that book, the location of the weapons, beginning with the disc.**

### PURPORT

The twenty-four forms are (1) Vāsudeva, (2) Saṅkarṣaṇa, (3) Pradyumna, (4) Aniruddha, (5) Keśava, (6) Nārāyaṇa, (7) Mādhava, (8) Govinda, (9) Viṣṇu, (10) Madhusūdana, (11) Trivikrama, (12) Vāmana, (13) Śrīdhara, (14) Hṛṣīkeśa, (15) Padmanābha, (16) Dāmodara, (17) Puruṣottama, (18) Acyuta, (19) Nṛsiṁha, (20) Janārdana, (21) Hari, (22) Kṛṣṇa, (23) Adhokṣaja and (24) Upendra.

## TEXT 224

বাসুদেব – গদাশঙ্খচক্রপদ্মধর।
সঙ্কর্ষণ—গদাশঙ্খপদ্মচক্রকর ॥ ২২৪ ॥

*vāsudeva——gadā-śaṅkha-cakra-padma-dhara*
*saṅkarṣaṇa——gadā-śaṅkha-padma-cakra-kara*

### SYNONYMS

*vāsudeva*—Vāsudeva; *gadā*—club; *śaṅkha*—conchshell; *cakra*—disc; *padma*—lotus flower; *dhara*—holding; *saṅkarṣaṇa*—Saṅkarṣaṇa; *gadā*—club; *śaṅkha*—conchshell; *padma*—lotus flower; *cakra-kara*—the disc in the hand.

### TRANSLATION

**"In His lower right hand, Lord Vāsudeva holds a club, in the upper right hand a conchshell, in the upper left hand a disc and in the lower left hand a lotus flower. In His lower right hand, Saṅkarṣaṇa holds a club, in His upper right hand a conchshell, in His upper left hand a lotus flower and in His lower left hand a disc.**

### TEXT 225

প্রদ্যুম্ন—চক্রশঙ্খগদাপদ্মধর ।
অনিরুদ্ধ—চক্রগদাশঙ্খপদ্মকর ॥ ২২৫ ॥

*pradyumna——cakra-śaṅkha-gadā-padma-dhara*
*aniruddha——cakra-gadā-śaṅkha-padma-kara*

### SYNONYMS

*pradyumna*—Lord Pradyumna; *cakra*—disc; *śaṅkha*—conch; *gadā*—club; *padma*—lotus; *dhara*—holding; *aniruddha*—Lord Aniruddha; *cakra*—disc; *gadā*—club; *śaṅkha*—conch; *padma-kara*—lotus flower in hand.

### TRANSLATION

**"Pradyumna holds the disc, conch, club and lotus. Aniruddha holds the disc, club, conch and lotus.**

### TEXT 226

পরব্যোমে বাসুদেবাদি—নিজ নিজ অস্ত্রধর ।
তাঁর মত কহি, যে-সব অস্ত্রকর ॥ ২২৬ ॥

*paravyome vāsudevādi——nija nija astra-dhara*
*tāṅra mata kahi, ye-saba astra-kara*

### SYNONYMS

*para-vyome*—in the spiritual sky; *vāsudeva-ādi*—beginning with Lord Vāsudeva; *nija nija*—Their own respective; *astra-dhara*—holding of different weapons; *tāṅra mata kahi*—I am speaking the opinion of *Siddhārtha-saṁhitā; ye-saba*—all; *astra-kara*—weapons in the different hands.

### TRANSLATION

**"Thus in the spiritual sky the expansions, headed by Vāsudeva, hold weapons in Their own respective order. I am repeating the opinion of Siddhārtha-saṁhitā in describing Them.**

### TEXT 227

শ্রীকেশব—পদ্মশঙ্খচক্রগদাধর ।
নারায়ণ—শঙ্খপদ্মগদাচক্রধর ॥ ২২৭ ॥

*śrī-keśava——padma-śaṅkha-cakra-gadā-dhara*
*nārāyaṇa——śaṅkha-padma-gadā-cakra-dhara*

### SYNONYMS

*śrī-keśava*—Lord Keśava; *padma*—lotus; *śaṅkha*—conch; *cakra*—disc; *gadā*—club; *dhara*—holding; *nārāyaṇa*—Lord Nārāyaṇa; *śaṅkha*—conch; *padma*—lotus; *gadā*—club; *cakra*—disc; *dhara*—holding.

### TRANSLATION

**"Lord Keśava holds the lotus, conch, disc and club. Lord Nārāyaṇa holds the conch, lotus, club and disc.**

### TEXT 228

শ্রীমাধব—গদাচক্রশঙ্খপদ্মকর ।
শ্রীগোবিন্দ—চক্রগদাপদ্মশঙ্খধর ॥ ২২৮ ॥

*śrī-mādhava——gadā-cakra-śaṅkha-padma-kara*
*śrī-govinda——cakra-gadā-padma-śaṅkha-dhara*

### SYNONYMS

*śrī-mādhava*—Lord Mādhava; *gadā*—club; *cakra*—disc; *śaṅkha*—conch; *padma*—lotus; *kara*—in the hands; *śrī-govinda*—Lord Govinda; *cakra*—disc; *gadā*—club; *padma*—lotus; *śaṅkha*—conch; *dhara*—holding.

### TRANSLATION

**"Lord Mādhava holds the club, disc, conch and lotus. Lord Govinda holds the disc, club, lotus and conch.**

### TEXT 229

বিষ্ণুমূর্তি—গদাপদ্মশঙ্খচক্রকর ।
মধুসূদন—চক্রশঙ্খপদ্মগদাধর ॥ ২২৯ ॥

*viṣṇu-mūrti——gadā-padma-śaṅkha-cakra-kara*
*madhusūdana——cakra-śaṅkha-padma-gadā-dhara*

### SYNONYMS

*viṣṇu-mūrti*—Lord Viṣṇu; *gadā*—club; *padma*—lotus; *śaṅkha*—conch; *cakra*—disc; *kara*—in the hands; *madhusūdana*—Lord Madhusūdana; *cakra*—disc; *śaṅkha*—conch; *padma*—lotus; *gadā*—club; *dhara*—holding.

### TRANSLATION

**"Lord Viṣṇu holds the club, lotus, conch and disc. Lord Madhusūdana holds the disc, conch, lotus and club.**

### TEXT 230

ত্রিবিক্রম—পদ্মগদাচক্রশঙ্খকর ।
শ্রীবামন—শঙ্খচক্রগদাপদ্মধর ॥ ২৩০ ॥

*trivikrama——padma-gadā-cakra-śaṅkha-kara*
*śrī-vāmana——śaṅkha-cakra-gadā-padma-dhara*

### SYNONYMS

*trivikrama*—Lord Trivikrama; *padma*—lotus; *gadā*—club; *cakra*—disc; *śaṅkha*—conch; *kara*—in the hands; *śrī-vāmana*—Lord Vāmana; *śaṅkha*—conch; *cakra*—disc; *gadā*—club; *padma*—lotus; *dhara*—holding.

### TRANSLATION

**"Lord Trivikrama holds the lotus, club, disc and conch. Lord Vāmana holds the conch, disc, club and lotus.**

### TEXT 231

শ্রীধর—পদ্মচক্রগদাশঙ্খকর ।
হৃষীকেশ—গদাচক্রপদ্মশঙ্খধর ॥ ২৩১ ॥

*śrīdhara——padma-cakra-gadā-śaṅkha-kara*
*hṛṣīkeśa——gadā-cakra-padma-śaṅkha-dhara*

### SYNONYMS

*śrīdhara*—Lord Śrīdhara; *padma*—lotus; *cakra*—disc; *gadā*—club; *śaṅkha*—conch; *kara*—in the hands; *hṛṣīkeśa*—Lord Hṛṣīkeśa; *gadā*—club; *cakra*—disc; *padma*—lotus; *śaṅkha*—conch; *dhara*—holding.

### TRANSLATION

**"Lord Śrīdhara holds the lotus, disc, club and conch. Lord Hṛṣīkeśa holds the club, disc, lotus and conch.**

### TEXT 232

পদ্মনাভ- শঙ্খপদ্মচক্রগদাকর ।
দামোদর - পদ্মচক্রগদাশঙ্খধর ॥ ২৩২ ॥

*padmanābha——śaṅkha-padma-cakra-gadā-kara*
*dāmodara——padma-cakra-gadā-śaṅkha-dhara*

### SYNONYMS

*padmanābha*—Lord Padmanābha; *śaṅkha*—conch; *padma*—lotus; *cakra*—disc; *gadā*—club; *kara*—in the hands; *dāmodara*—Lord Dāmodara; *padma*—lotus; *cakra*—disc; *gadā*—club; *śaṅkha*—conch; *dhara*—holding.

### TRANSLATION

**"Lord Padmanābha holds the conch, lotus, disc and club. Lord Dāmodara holds the lotus, disc, club and conch.**

### TEXT 233

পুরুষোত্তম— চক্রপদ্মশঙ্খগদাধর ।
শ্রীঅচ্যুত - গদাপদ্মচক্রশঙ্খধর ॥ ২৩৩ ॥

*puruṣottama——cakra-padma-śaṅkha-gadā-dhara*
*śrī-acyuta——gadā-padma-cakra-śaṅkha-dhara*

### SYNONYMS

*puruṣottama*—Lord Puruṣottama; *cakra*—disc; *padma*—lotus; *śaṅkha*—conch; *gadā*—club; *dhara*—holding; *śrī-acyuta*—Lord Acyuta; *gadā*—club; *padma*—lotus; *cakra*—disc; *śaṅkha*—conch; *dhara*—holding.

### TRANSLATION

**"Lord Puruṣottama holds the disc, lotus, conch and club. Lord Acyuta holds the club, lotus, disc and conch.**

### TEXT 234

শ্রীনৃসিংহ – চক্রপদ্মগদাশঙ্খধর ।
জনার্দন—পদ্মচক্রশঙ্খগদাকর ॥ ২৩৪ ॥

*śrī-nṛsiṁha——cakra-padma-gadā-śaṅkha-dhara*
*janārdana——padma-cakra-śaṅkha-gadā-kara*

### SYNONYMS

*śrī-nṛsiṁha*—Lord Nṛsiṁha; *cakra*—disc; *padma*—lotus; *gadā*—club; *śaṅkha*—conch; *dhara*—holding; *janārdana*—Lord Janārdana; *padma*—lotus; *cakra*—disc; *śaṅkha*—conch; *gadā*—club; *kara*—in the hands.

### TRANSLATION

**"Lord Nṛsiṁha holds the disc, lotus, club and conch. Lord Janārdana holds the lotus, disc, conch and club.**

### TEXT 235

শ্রীহরি – শঙ্খচক্রপদ্মগদাকর ।
শ্রীকৃষ্ণ –শঙ্খগদাপদ্মচক্রকর ॥ ২৩৫ ॥

*śrī-hari——śaṅkha-cakra-padma-gadā-kara*
*śrī-kṛṣṇa——śaṅkha-gadā-padma-cakra-kara*

### SYNONYMS

*śrī-hari*—Lord Hari; *śaṅkha*—conch; *cakra*—disc; *padma*—lotus; *gadā*—club; *kara*—in the hand; *śrī-kṛṣṇa*—Lord Kṛṣṇa; *śaṅkha*—conch; *gadā*—club; *padma*—lotus; *cakra*—disc; *kara*—in the hands.

### TRANSLATION

**"Śrī Hari holds the conch, disc, lotus and club. Lord Śrī Kṛṣṇa holds the conch, club, lotus and disc.**

### TEXT 236

অধোক্ষজ—পদ্মগদাশঙ্খচক্রকর ।
উপেন্দ্র –শঙ্খগদাচক্রপদ্মকর ॥ ২৩৬ ॥

*adhokṣaja——padma-gadā-śaṅkha-cakra-kara*
*upendra——śaṅkha-gadā-cakra-padma-kara*

### SYNONYMS

*adhokṣaja*—Lord Adhokṣaja; *padma*—lotus; *gadā*—club; *śaṅkha*—conch; *cakra*—disc; *kara*—in hand; *upendra*—Lord Upendra; *śaṅkha*—conch; *gadā*—club; *cakra*—disc; *padma*—lotus; *kara*—in hand.

## TRANSLATION

**"Lord Adhokṣaja holds the lotus, club, conch and disc. Lord Upendra holds the conch, club, disc and lotus.**

## TEXT 237

হয়শীর্ষ-পঞ্চরাত্রে কহে ষোলজন।
তার মতে কহি এবে চক্রাদি-ধারণ॥ ২৩৭॥

*hayaśīrṣa-pañcarātre kahe ṣola-jana*
*tāra mate kahi ebe cakrādi-dhāraṇa*

## SYNONYMS

*hayaśīrṣa-pañcarātre*—the revealed scripture named the *Hayaśīrṣa-pañcarātra; kahe*—says; *ṣola-jana*—sixteen personalities; *tāra mate*—according to this opinion; *kahi*—I shall describe; *ebe*—now; *cakra-ādi-dhāraṇa*—the holding of weapons, beginning with the disc.

## TRANSLATION

**"According to the Hayaśīrṣa-pañcarātra, there are sixteen personalities. I shall now describe that opinion of how They hold the weapons.**

## PURPORT

The sixteen personalities are as follows: (1) Vāsudeva, (2) Saṅkarṣaṇa, (3) Pradyumna, (4) Aniruddha, (5) Keśava, (6) Nārāyaṇa, (7) Mādhava, (8) Govinda, (9) Viṣṇu, (10) Madhusūdana, (11) Trivikrama, (12) Vāmana, (13) Śrīdhara, (14) Hṛṣīkeśa, (15) Padmanābha, (16) Dāmodara.

## TEXT 238

কেশব-ভেদে পদ্মশঙ্খগদাচক্রধর।
মাধব-ভেদে চক্রগদাশঙ্খপদ্মকর॥ ২৩৮॥

*keśava-bhede padma-śaṅkha-gadā-cakra-dhara*
*mādhava-bhede cakra-gadā-śaṅkha-padma-kara*

## SYNONYMS

*keśava-bhede*—according to the different opinion about Lord Keśava; *padma*—lotus; *śaṅkha*—conch; *gadā*—club; *cakra*—and disc; *dhara*—holding; *mādhava-bhede*—according to the different opinion about the bodily features of

Lord Mādhava; *cakra*—disc; *gadā*—club; *śaṅkha*—conch; *padma*—lotus; *kara*—in the hands.

### TRANSLATION

**"Keśava is described differently as holding the lotus, conch, club and disc, and Mādhava is described as holding disc, club, conch and lotus in His hands.**

### TEXT 239

নারায়ণ-ভেদে নানা অস্ত্র-ভেদ-ধর ।
ইত্যাদিক ভেদ এই সব অস্ত্রকর ॥ ২৩৯ ॥

*nārāyaṇa-bhede nānā astra-bheda-dhara*
*ityādika bheda ei saba astra-kara*

### SYNONYMS

*nārāyaṇa-bhede*—according to the different opinion about the bodily features of Lord Nārāyaṇa; *nānā*—various; *astra*—of weapons; *bheda-dhara*—differences in holding; *iti-ādika*—in this way; *bheda*—differentiated; *ei saba*—all these; *astra-kara*—weapons in the hands.

### TRANSLATION

**"According to the Hayaśīrṣa Pañcarātra, Nārāyaṇa and others are also presented differently as holding the weapons in different hands.**

### TEXT 240

'স্বয়ং ভগবান্', আর 'লীলা-পুরুষোত্তম' ।
এই দুই নাম ধরে ব্রজেন্দ্রনন্দন ॥ ২৪০ ॥

*'svayaṁ bhagavān', āra 'līlā-puruṣottama'*
*ei dui nāma dhare vrajendra-nandana*

### SYNONYMS

*svayam bhagavān*—the Supreme Personality of Godhead; *āra*—and; *līlā-puruṣottama*—the Lord Puruṣottama of pastimes; *ei dui*—these two; *nāma*—names; *dhare*—takes; *vrajendra-nandana*—Kṛṣṇa, the son of Nanda Mahārāja.

### TRANSLATION

**"Kṛṣṇa, the original Supreme Personality of Godhead, indicated as the son of Mahārāja Nanda, has two names. One is svayaṁ bhagavān, and the other is līlā-puruṣottama.**

### TEXT 241

পুরীর আবরণরূপে পুরীর নবদেশে ।
নবব্যূহরূপে নবমূর্তি পরকাশে ॥ ২৪১ ॥

*purīra āvaraṇa-rūpe purīra nava-deśe*
*nava-vyūha-rūpe nava-mūrti parakāśe*

### SYNONYMS

*purīra*—of Dvārakā Purī; *āvaraṇa-rūpe*—as a covering for the four sides; *purīra nava-deśe*—in nine different parts of the city; *nava-vyūha-rūpe*—in nine Deities; *nava-mūrti*—nine forms; *parakāśe*—manifests.

### TRANSLATION

**"Lord Kṛṣṇa personally surrounds Dvārakā Purī as its protector. In different parts of the Purī, in nine places, He expands in nine different forms.**

### TEXT 242

চত্বারো বাসুদেবাদ্যা নারায়ণনৃসিংহকৌ ।
হয়গ্রীবো মহাক্রোড়ো ব্রহ্মা চেতি নবোদিতাঃ ॥২৪২॥

*catvāro vāsudevādyā*
*nārāyaṇa-nṛsiṁhakau*
*hayagrīvo mahākroḍo*
*brahmā ceti navoditāḥ*

### SYNONYMS

*catvāraḥ*—four principal protectors; *vāsudeva-ādyāḥ*—Vāsudeva, Saṅkarṣaṇa, Pradyumna and Aniruddha; *nārāyaṇa*—including Lord Nārāyaṇa; *nṛsiṁhakau*—as well as Lord Nṛsiṁha; *hayagrīvaḥ*—Lord Hayagrīva; *mahākroḍaḥ*—Lord Varāha; *brahmā*—Lord Brahmā; *ca*—also; *iti*—thus; *nava-uditāḥ*—nine personalities.

### TRANSLATION

**" 'The nine personalities mentioned are Vāsudeva, Saṅkarṣaṇa, Pradyumna, Aniruddha, Nārāyaṇa, Nṛsiṁha, Hayagrīva, Varāha and Brahmā.'**

### PURPORT

This verse is found in the *Laghu-bhāgavatāmṛta* (1.451). The Brahmā mentioned herein is not a living entity. Sometimes, when there is a scarcity of living entities to take charge of Brahmā's post, Mahā-Viṣṇu expands Himself as Lord Brahmā. This Brahmā is not considered to be a living entity; He is an expansion of Viṣṇu.

### TEXT 243

প্রকাশ-বিলাসের এই কৈলুঁ বিবরণ ।
স্বাংশের ভেদ এবে শুন, সনাতন ॥ ২৪৩ ॥

*prakāśa-vilāsera ei kailuṅ vivaraṇa*
*svāṁśera bheda ebe śuna, sanātana*

### SYNONYMS

*prakāśa-vilāsera*—of pastime forms and manifestations; *ei*—this; *kailuṅ*—I have made; *vivaraṇa*—description; *svāṁśera*—of personal expansions; *bhede*—the differences; *ebe*—now; *śuna*—please hear; *sanātana*—O Sanātana Gosvāmī.

### TRANSLATION

**"I have already described the pastime and prakāśa forms. Now please hear about the different personal expansions.**

### TEXT 244

সঙ্কর্ষণ, মৎস্যাদিক,—দুই ভেদ তাঁর ।
সঙ্কর্ষণ - পুরুষাবতার, লীলাবতার আর ॥ ২৪৪ ॥

*saṅkarṣaṇa, matsyādika,——dui bheda tāṅra*
*saṅkarṣaṇa——puruṣāvatāra, līlāvatāra āra*

### SYNONYMS

*saṅkarṣaṇa*—Saṅkarṣaṇa; *matsya-ādika*—and incarnations such as the fish; *dui*—two; *bheda*—differentiations; *tāṅra*—His; *saṅkarṣaṇa*—Saṅkarṣaṇa; *puruṣa-avatāra*—incarnations of Viṣṇu; *līlā-avatāra*—pastime incarnations; *āra*—and.

### TRANSLATION

**"The first personal expansion is Saṅkarṣaṇa, and the others are incarnations like the fish incarnation. Saṅkarṣaṇa is an expansion of the Puruṣa, or Viṣṇu. The incarnations such as Matsya, the fish incarnation, appear in different yugas for specific pastimes.**

### PURPORT

The *puruṣa-avatāras* are the Lords of the universal creation. These are the Kāraṇodakaśāyī Viṣṇu, Garbhodakaśāyī Viṣṇu and Kṣīrodakaśāyī Viṣṇu. There are also *līlā-avatāras,* and these include (1) Catuḥsana, (2) Nārada, (3) Varāha, (4) Matsya, (5) Yajña, (6) Nara-Nārāyaṇa, (7) Kārdami Kapila, (8) Dattātreya, (9) Hayaśīrṣā, (10) Haṁsa, (11) Dhruvapriya, or Pṛśnigarbha, (12) Ṛṣabha, (13) Pṛthu, (14) Nṛsiṁha, (15) Kūrma, (16) Dhanvantari, (17) Mohinī, (18) Vāmana, (19) Bhārgava Paraśurāma, (20) Rāghavendra, (21) Vyāsa, (22) Pralambāri Balarāma, (23) Kṛṣṇa, (24) Buddha and (25) Kalkī.

These twenty-five Personalities of Godhead are known as *līlā-avatāras.* Because they appear in each day of Brahmā, or in each *kalpa* (millennium), they are sometimes known as *kalpa-avatāras.* Of these incarnations, Haṁsa and Mohinī are not very permanent or well known, but They are listed among the *prābhava-avatāras.* Kapila, Dattātreya, Ṛṣabha, Dhanvantari and Vyāsa are eternally situated and very widely known. They are also counted among the *prābhava* incarnations. Kūrma, Matsya, Nārāyaṇa, Varāha, Hayagrīva, Pṛśnigarbha, and Baladeva, the killer of Pralambāsura, are counted among the *vaibhava-avatāras.*

### TEXT 245

**অবতার হয় কৃষ্ণের ষড়্‌বিধ প্রকার ।**
**পুরুষাবতার এক, লীলাবতার আর ॥ ২৪৫ ॥**

*avatāra haya kṛṣṇera ṣaḍ-vidha prakāra*
*puruṣāvatāra eka, līlāvatāra āra*

### SYNONYMS

*avatāra*—incarnations; *haya*—there are; *kṛṣṇera*—of Lord Kṛṣṇa; *ṣaṭ-vidha prakāra*—six kinds; *puruṣa-avatāra*—incarnations of Viṣṇu; *eka*—one; *līlā-avatāra*—incarnations for the execution of pastimes; *āra*—also.

### TRANSLATION

**"There are six types of incarnations [avatāras] of Kṛṣṇa. One is the incarnations of Viṣṇu [puruṣa-avatāras], and another is the incarnations meant for the performance of pastimes [līlā-avatāras].**

### TEXT 246

**গুণাবতার, আর মন্বন্তরাবতার ।**
**যুগাবতার, আর শক্ত্যাবেশাবতার ॥ ২৪৬ ॥**

*guṇāvatāra, āra manvantarāvatāra*
*yugāvatāra, āra śaktyāveśāvatāra*

## SYNONYMS

*guṇa-avatāra*—the incarnations to control the material qualities; *āra*—also; *manu-antara-avatāra*—the incarnations of the Manus; *yuga-avatāra*—the incarnations according to different *yugas; āra*—and; *śakti-āveśa-avatāra*—empowered incarnations.

## TRANSLATION

**"There are incarnations that control the material qualities [guṇa-avatāras], incarnations of the Manus [manvantara-avatāras], incarnations in different millenniums [yuga-avatāras] and incarnations of empowered living entities [śaktyāveśa-avatāras].**

## PURPORT

The *guṇa-avatāras* are three—Lord Brahmā, Lord Śiva and Lord Viṣṇu (*Bhāg.* 10.88.3). The *avatāras* of Manu, or *manvantara-avatāras,* are listed as follows in *Śrīmad-Bhāgavatam* (8.1.5,13): (1) Yajña, (2) Vibhu, (3) Satyesena, (4) Hari, (5) Vaikuṇṭha, (6) Ajita, (7) Vāmana, (8) Sārvabhauma, (9) Ṛṣabha, (10) Viṣvaksena, (11) Dharmasetu, (12) Sudhāmā, (13) Yogeśvara and (14) Bṛhadbhānu. Altogether these are fourteen in number, and of these, both Yaja and Vāmana are also counted among the *līlā-avatāras.* All these Manu incarnations are sometimes called *vaibhava-avatāras.*

The four *yuga-avatāras* are (1) *śukla* (white) in the Satya-yuga (*Bhāg.* 11.5.21), (2) *rakta* (red) in the Tretā-yuga (*Bhag.* 11.5.24), (3) *śyāma* (dark blue) in the Dvāpara-yuga (*Bhāg.* 11.5.27), and (4) generally *kṛṣṇa* (black) but in special cases *pīta* (yellow) as Caitanya Mahāprabhu in the Kali-yuga, (*Bhāg.* 11.5.32 and 10.8.13).

The *śaktyāveśa-avatāra* is categorized into (1) forms of divine absorption (*bhagavad-āveśa*) like Kapiladeva or Ṛṣabhadeva and (2) divinely empowered forms (*śaktyāveśa*), of whom there are seven: (1) Śeṣa Nāga in the Vaikuṇṭha world, empowered for the personal service of the Supreme Lord (*sva-sevana-śakti*), (2) Anantadeva, empowered to bear all the planets within the universe (*bhū-dhāraṇa-śakti*), (3) Lord Brahmā, empowered with the energy to create the cosmic manifestation (*sṛṣṭi-śakti*), (4) Catuḥsana, or the Kumāras, specifically empowered to distribute transcendental knowledge (*jñāna-śakti*), (5) Nārada Muni, empowered to distribute devotional service (*bhakti-śakti*), (6) Mahārāja Pṛthu, specifically empowered to rule and maintain the living entities (*pālana-śakti*) and (7) Paraśurāma, specifically empowered to cut down rogues and demons (*duṣṭa-damana-śakti*).

### TEXT 247

বাল্য, পৌগণ্ড হয় বিগ্রহের ধর্ম ।
এতরূপে লীলা করেন ব্রজেন্দ্রনন্দন ॥ ২৪৭ ॥

*bālya, paugaṇḍa haya vigrahera dharma*
*eta-rūpe līlā karena vrajendra-nandana*

### SYNONYMS

*bālya*—childhood; *paugaṇḍa*—boyhood; *haya*—there are; *vigrahera*—of the Deity; *dharma*—characteristics; *eta-rūpe*—in so many forms; *līlā*—pastimes; *karena*—executes; *vrajendra-nandana*—Kṛṣṇa, the son of Nanda Mahārāja.

### TRANSLATION

**"Childhood and boyhood are the typical ages of the Deity. Kṛṣṇa, the son of Mahārāja Nanda, performed His pastimes as a child and as a boy.**

### TEXT 248

অনন্ত অবতার কৃষ্ণের, নাহিক গণন ।
শাখা-চন্দ্র-ন্যায় করি দিগ্‌দরশন ॥ ২৪৮ ॥

*ananta avatāra kṛṣṇera, nāhika gaṇana*
*śākhā-candra-nyāya kari dig-daraśana*

### SYNONYMS

*ananta*—unlimited; *avatāra*—incarnations; *kṛṣṇera*—of Lord Kṛṣṇa; *nāhika gaṇana*—there is no possibility of counting; *śākhā-candra-nyāya*—by the analogy of the moon and the branches of a tree; *kari*—I make; *dik-daraśana*—a slight indication.

### TRANSLATION

**"There are innumerable incarnations of Kṛṣṇa, and there is no possibility of counting them. We can simply indicate them by giving the example of the moon and the branches of a tree.**

### PURPORT

Although the moon appears to be located in the branches of a tree, it is actually situated very far away. Similarly, none of the *avatāras,* or incarnations, of Lord Kṛṣṇa are within this material world, but they are visible by the causeless mercy of the Lord. We should not consider them to belong to this material world. As stated in *Bhagavad-gītā:*

*avajānanti māṁ mūḍhā*
*mānuṣīṁ tanum āśritam*
*paraṁ bhāvam ajānanto*
*mama bhūta-maheśvaram*

"Fools deride Me when I descend in the human form. They do not know My transcendental nature and My supreme dominion over all that be." (Bg. 9.11)

*Avatāras* descend of their own free will, and although they may act like ordinary human beings, they do not belong to this material world. Lord Kṛṣṇa and His *avatāras* can be understood only by the grace of the Lord.

*nāyam ātmā pravacanena labhyo*
*na medhayā na bahunā śrutena*
*yam evaiṣa vṛṇute tena labhyas*
*tasyaiṣa ātmā vivṛṇute tanūṁ svām*
(*Kaṭha Upaniṣad* 1.2.23)

*athāpi te deva padāmbuja-dvaya-*
*prasāda-leśānugṛhīta eva hi*
*janāti tattvaṁ bhagavan-mahimno*
*na cānya eko 'pi ciraṁ vicinvan*
(*Bhāg.* 10.14.29)

## TEXT 249

অবতারা হ্যসংখ্যেয়া হরেঃ সত্ত্বনিধের্দ্বিজাঃ ।
যথাঽবিদাসিনঃ কুল্যাঃ সরসঃ স্যুঃ সহস্রশঃ ॥ ২৪৯ ॥

*avatārā hy asaṅkhyeyā*
*hareḥ sattva-nidher dvijāḥ*
*yathā 'vidāsinaḥ kulyāḥ*
*sarasaḥ syuḥ sahasraśaḥ*

## SYNONYMS

*avatārāḥ*—all the incarnations; *hi*—certainly; *asaṅkhyeyāḥ*—beyond counting; *hareḥ*—from the Supreme Personality of Godhead; *sattva-nidheḥ*—who is the reservoir of spiritual energy; *dvijāḥ*—O *brāhmaṇas; yathā*—as; *avidāsinaḥ*—containing a great reservoir of water; *kulyāḥ*—small ponds; *sarasaḥ*—from a lake; *syuḥ*—must be; *sahasraśaḥ*—by hundreds and thousands of times.

### TRANSLATION

**"'O learned brāhmaṇas, just as hundreds and thousands of small ponds issue from great reservoirs of water, innumerable incarnations flow from Śrī Hari, the Supreme Personality of Godhead and the reservoir of all power.'**

### PURPORT

This verse is quoted from *Śrīmad-Bhāgavatam* (1.3.26).

### TEXT 250

**প্রথমেই করে কৃষ্ণ 'পুরুষাবতার'।**
**সেইত পুরুষ হয় ত্রিবিধ প্রকার ॥ ২৫০ ॥**

*prathamei kare kṛṣṇa 'puruṣāvatāra'*
*seita puruṣa haya trividha prakāra*

### SYNONYMS

*prathamei*—in the beginning; *kare*—does; *kṛṣṇa*—Lord Kṛṣṇa; *puruṣa-avatāra*—the incarnation of the three Viṣṇus (Mahā-Viṣṇu, Garbhodakaśāyī Viṣṇu and Kṣīrodakaśāyī Viṣṇu); *seita*—that; *puruṣa*—Viṣṇu; *haya*—becomes; *tri-vidha prakāra*—three different manifestations.

### TRANSLATION

**"In the beginning, Kṛṣṇa incarnates Himself as puruṣa-avatāras, or Viṣṇu incarnations. These are of three types.**

### PURPORT

Up to this verse, the many types of expansions have been described. Now the manifestations of the Lord's different potencies will be described.

### TEXT 251

বিষ্ণোস্তু ত্রীণি রূপাণি পুরুষাখ্যান্যথো বিদুঃ।
একন্তু মহতঃ স্রষ্টৃ দ্বিতীয়ং ত্বণ্ডসংস্থিতম্।
তৃতীয়ং সর্বভূতস্থং তানি জ্ঞাত্বা বিমুচ্যতে ॥ ২৫১ ॥

*viṣṇos tu trīṇi rūpāṇi*
*puruṣākhyāny atho viduḥ*

*ekaṁ tu mahataḥ sraṣṭṛ*
*dvitīyaṁ tv aṇḍa-saṁsthitam*
*tṛtīyaṁ sarva-bhūta-sthaṁ*
*tāni jñātvā vimucyate*

## SYNONYMS

*viṣṇoḥ*—of Lord Viṣṇu; *tu*—certainly; *trīṇi*—three; *rūpāṇi*—forms; *puruṣa-ākhyāni*—celebrated as the *puruṣa; atho*—how; *viduḥ*—they know; *ekam*—one of them; *tu*—but; *mahataḥ sraṣṭṛ*—the creator of the total material energy; *dvitīyam*—the second; *tu*—but; *aṇḍa-saṁsthitam*—situated within the universe; *tṛtīyam*—the third; *sarva-bhūta-stham*—within the hearts of all living entities; *tāni*—these three; *jñātvā*—knowing; *vimucyate*—one becomes liberated.

## TRANSLATION

**" 'Viṣṇu has three forms called puruṣas. The first, Mahā-Viṣṇu, is the creator of the total material energy [mahat], the second is Garbhodaśāyī, who is situated within each universe, and the third is Kṣīrodaśāyī, who lives in the heart of every living being. He who knows these three becomes liberated from the clutches of māyā.'**

## PURPORT

This verse appears in the *Laghu-bhāgavatāmṛta* (*Pūrva-khaṇḍa* 33), where it has been quoted from the *Sātvata-tantra.*

## TEXT 252

**অনন্তশক্তি-মধ্যে কৃষ্ণের তিন শক্তি প্রধান ।**
**'ইচ্ছাশক্তি', 'জ্ঞানশক্তি', 'ক্রিয়াশক্তি' নাম ॥ ২৫২ ॥**

*ananta-śakti-madhye kṛṣṇera tina śakti pradhāna*
*'icchā-śakti', 'jñāna-śakti', 'kriyā-śakti' nāma*

## SYNONYMS

*ananta-śakti*—of unlimited potencies; *madhye*—in the midst; *kṛṣṇera*—of Lord Kṛṣṇa; *tina*—three; *śakti*—potencies; *pradhāna*—are chief; *icchā-śakti*—willpower; *jñāna-śakti*—the power of knowledge; *kriyā-śakti*—the creative energy; *nāma*—named.

## TRANSLATION

**"Kṛṣṇa has unlimited potencies, out of which three are chief—willpower, the power of knowledge and the creative energy.**

### TEXT 253

ইচ্ছাশক্তিপ্রধান কৃষ্ণ—ইচ্ছায় সর্বকর্তা ।
জ্ঞানশক্তিপ্রধান বাসুদেব অধিষ্ঠাতা ॥ ২৫৩ ॥

*icchā-śakti-pradhāna kṛṣṇa——icchāya sarva-kartā*
*jñāna-śakti-pradhāna vāsudeva adhiṣṭhātā*

### SYNONYMS

*icchā-śakti*—of willpower; *pradhāna*—predominator; *kṛṣṇa*—Lord Kṛṣṇa; *icchāya*—simply by willing; *sarva-kartā*—the creator of everything; *jñāna-śakti-pradhāna*—the predominator of the power of knowledge; *vāsudeva*—Lord Vāsudeva; *adhiṣṭhātā*—reservoir.

### TRANSLATION

**"The predominator of the willing potency is Lord Kṛṣṇa, for by His supreme will everything comes into existence. In willing, there is a need for knowledge, and that knowledge is expressed through Vāsudeva.**

### TEXT 254

ইচ্ছা-জ্ঞান-ক্রিয়া বিনা না হয় স্বজন ।
তিনের তিনশক্তি মেলি' প্রপঞ্চ-রচন ॥ ২৫৪ ॥

*icchā-jñāna-kriyā vinā nā haya sṛjana*
*tinera tina-śakti meli' prapañca-racana*

### SYNONYMS

*icchā-jñāna-kriyā*—thinking, feeling, willing, knowledge and activity; *vinā*—without; *nā*—not; *haya*—there is; *sṛjana*—creation; *tinera*—of the three; *tina-śakti*—three potencies; *meli'*—being amalgamated; *prapañca-racana*—there is the cosmic manifestation.

### TRANSLATION

**"There is no possibility of creation without thinking, feeling, willing, knowledge and activity. The combination of the supreme will, knowledge and action brings about the cosmic manifestation.**

### TEXT 255

ক্রিয়াশক্তিপ্রধান সঙ্কর্ষণ বলরাম ।
প্রাকৃতাপ্রাকৃত-সৃষ্টি করেন নির্মাণ ॥ ২৫৫ ॥

*kriyā-śakti-pradhāna saṅkarṣaṇa balarāma*
*prākṛtāprākṛta-sṛṣṭi karena nirmāṇa*

### SYNONYMS

*kriyā-śakti-pradhāna*—the predominator of the creative energy; *saṅkarṣaṇa*—Lord Saṅkarṣaṇa; *balarāma*—Lord Balarāma; *prākṛta*—material; *aprākṛta*—spiritual; *sṛṣṭi*—worlds; *karena*—does; *nirmāṇa*—creation.

### TRANSLATION

**"Lord Saṅkarṣaṇa is Lord Balarāma. Being the predominator of the creative energy, He creates both the material and spiritual worlds.**

## TEXT 256

অহঙ্কারের অধিষ্ঠাতা কৃষ্ণের ইচ্ছায় ।
গোলোক, বৈকুণ্ঠ সৃজে চিচ্ছক্তিদ্বারায় ॥ ২৫৬ ॥

*ahaṅkārera adhiṣṭhātā kṛṣṇera icchāya*
*goloka, vaikuṇṭha sṛje cic-chakti-dvārāya*

### SYNONYMS

*ahaṅkārera*—of egotism; *adhiṣṭhātā*—the source or predominating Deity; *kṛṣṇera*—of Lord Kṛṣṇa; *icchāya*—by the will; *goloka*—the supreme spiritual planet, known as Goloka; *vaikuṇṭha*—other, lower planets, known as Vaikuṇṭhas; *sṛje*—creates; *cit-śakti-dvārāya*—by the spiritual energy.

### TRANSLATION

**"That original Saṅkarṣaṇa [Lord Balarāma] is the cause of both the material and spiritual creation. He is the predominating deity of egotism, and by the will of Kṛṣṇa and the power of the spiritual energy, He creates the spiritual world, which consists of the planet Goloka Vṛndāvana and the Vaikuṇṭha planets.**

## TEXT 257

যদ্যপি অসৃজ্য নিত্য চিচ্ছক্তিবিলাস ।
তথাপি সঙ্কর্ষণ-ইচ্ছায় তাহার প্রকাশ ॥ ২৫৭ ॥

*yadyapi asṛjya nitya cic-chakti-vilāsa*
*tathāpi saṅkarṣaṇa-icchāya tāhāra prakāśa*

### SYNONYMS

*yadyapi*—although; *asṛjya*—there is no question of creation; *nitya*—eternal; *cit-śakti-vilāsa*—pastimes of the eternal spiritual energy; *tathāpi*—still; *saṅkarṣaṇa-icchāya*—by the will of Saṅkarṣaṇa; *tāhāra*—of the spiritual world; *prakāśa*—manifestation.

### TRANSLATION

**"Although there is no question of creation as far as the spiritual world is concerned, the spiritual world is nonetheless manifest by the supreme will of Saṅkarṣaṇa. The spiritual world is the abode of the pastimes of the eternal spiritual energy.**

## TEXT 258

সহস্রপত্রং কমলং গোকুলাখ্যং মহৎপদম্ ।
তৎকর্ণিকারং তদ্ধাম তদনন্তাংশসম্ভবম্ ॥ ২৫৮ ॥

*sahasra-patraṁ kamalaṁ*
*gokulākhyaṁ mahat-padam*
*tat-karṇikāraṁ tad-dhāma*
*tad anantāṁśa-sambhavam*

### SYNONYMS

*sahasra-patram*—with thousands of petals; *kamalam*—resembling a lotus flower; *gokula-ākhyam*—named Gokula; *mahat-padam*—the supreme abode; *tat-karṇikāram*—the whorl of that lotus flower; *tat-dhāma*—the abode of the Lord; *tat*—that; *ananta-aṁśa*—from the expansion of energy of Ananta; *sambhavam*—creation.

### TRANSLATION

**" 'Gokula, the supreme abode and planet, appears like a lotus flower that has a thousand petals. The whorl of that lotus is the abode of the Supreme Lord, Kṛṣṇa. This lotus-shaped supreme abode is created by the will of Lord Ananta.'**

### PURPORT

This verse is quoted from *Brahma-saṁhitā* (5.2)

## TEXT 259

**মায়া-দ্বারে সৃজে তেঁহো ব্রহ্মাণ্ডের গণ ।**
**জড়রূপা প্রকৃতি নহে ব্রহ্মাণ্ড-কারণ ॥ ২৫৯ ॥**

*māyā-dvāre sṛje teṅho brahmāṇḍera gaṇa*
*jaḍa-rūpā prakṛti nahe brahmāṇḍa-kāraṇa*

**SYNONYMS**

*māyā-dvāre*—by the agency of the external energy; *sṛje*—creates; *teṅho*—Lord Saṅkarṣaṇa; *brahmāṇḍera gaṇa*—all the groups of universes; *jaḍa-rūpā*—appearing dull; *prakṛti*—the material energy; *nahe*—is not; *brahmāṇḍa-kāraṇa*—the cause of the cosmic manifestation.

**TRANSLATION**

**"By the agency of the material energy, this same Lord Saṅkarṣaṇa creates all the universes. The dull material energy—known in modern language as nature—is not the cause of the material universe.**

**TEXT 260**

জড় হৈতে সৃষ্টি নহে ঈশ্বরশক্তি বিনে ।
তাহাতেই সঙ্কর্ষণ করে শক্তির আধানে ॥ ২৬০ ॥

*jaḍa haite sṛṣṭi nahe īśvara-śakti vine*
*tāhātei saṅkarṣaṇa kare śaktira ādhāne*

**SYNONYMS**

*jaḍa haite*—from the dull material energy; *sṛṣṭi nahe*—the cosmic manifestation is not possible; *īśvara-śakti vine*—without the help of the energy of the Supreme Lord, the Personality of Godhead; *tāhātei*—in the material energy; *saṅkarṣaṇa*—Lord Saṅkarṣaṇa; *kare*—does; *śaktira*—of the spiritual energy; *ādhāne*—empowering.

**TRANSLATION**

**"Without the Supreme Personality of Godhead's energy, dull matter cannot create the cosmic manifestation. Its power does not arise from the material energy itself but is endowed by Saṅkarṣaṇa.**

**TEXT 261**

ঈশ্বরের শক্ত্যে সৃষ্টি করয়ে প্রকৃতি ।
লৌহ যেন অগ্নিশক্ত্যে পায় দাহ-শক্তি ॥ ২৬১ ॥

*īśvarera śaktye sṛṣṭi karaye prakṛti*
*lauha yena agni-śaktye pāya dāha-śakti*

### SYNONYMS

*īśvarera śaktye*—by the energy of the Supreme Personality of Godhead; *sṛṣṭi*—creation; *karaye*—does; *prakṛti*—material energy; *lauha*—iron; *yena*—as; *agni-śaktye*—by the power of fire; *pāya*—gets; *dāha-śakti*—the power to burn.

### TRANSLATION

**"Dull matter alone cannot create anything. The material energy produces the creation by the power of the Supreme Personality of Godhead. Iron itself has no power to burn, but when iron is placed in fire, it is empowered to burn.**

## TEXT 262

এতৌ হি বিশ্বস্য চ বীজযোনী
রামো মুকুন্দঃ পুরুষঃ প্রধানম্।
অন্বীয় ভূতেষু বিলক্ষণস্য
জ্ঞানস্য চেশাত ইমৌ পুরাণৌ॥ ২৬২ ॥

*etau hi viśvasya ca bīja-yonī*
*rāmo mukundaḥ puruṣaḥ pradhānam*
*anvīya bhūteṣu vilakṣaṇasya*
*jñānasya ceśāta imau purāṇau*

### SYNONYMS

*etau*—these two, namely Rāma and Kṛṣṇa; *hi*—certainly; *viśvasya*—of the universe; *ca*—and; *bīja-yonī*—both the cause and ingredient; *rāmaḥ*—Balarāma; *mukundaḥ*—Kṛṣṇa; *puruṣaḥ*—the original Mahā-Viṣṇu; *pradhānam*—material energy; *anvīya*—after entering; *bhūteṣu*—into the material elements; *vilakṣaṇasya*—of varieties of manifestation; *jñānasya*—of knowledge; *ca*—also; *īśāte*—are the controlling power; *imau*—both of Them; *purāṇau*—are the original cause.

### TRANSLATION

**" 'Balarāma and Kṛṣṇa are the original efficient and material causes of the material world. As Mahā-Viṣṇu and the material energy, They enter into the material elements and create the diversities by multi-energies. Thus They are the cause of all causes.'**

### PURPORT

This verse is quoted from *Śrīmad-Bhāgavatam* (10.46.31).

### TEXT 263

**সৃষ্টি-হেতু যেই মূর্তি প্রপঞ্চে অবতরে ।
সেই ঈশ্বরমূর্তি 'অবতার' নাম ধরে ॥ ২৬৩ ॥**

*sṛṣṭi-hetu yei mūrti prapañce avatare
sei īśvara-mūrti 'avatāra' nāma dhare*

### SYNONYMS

*sṛṣṭi-hetu*—for the purpose of creation; *yei mūrti*—which form of the Lord; *prapañce*—in the material world; *avatare*—descends; *sei*—that; *īśvara-mūrti*—form of the Lord; *avatāra*—incarnation; *nāma dhare*—takes the name.

### TRANSLATION

**"The form of the Lord that descends into the material world to create is called an avatāra, or incarnation.**

### TEXT 264

**মায়াতীত পরব্যোমে সবার অবস্থান ।
বিশ্বে অবতরি' ধরে 'অবতার' নাম ॥ ২৬৪ ॥**

*māyātīta paravyome sabāra avasthāna
viśve avatari' dhare 'avatāra' nāma*

### SYNONYMS

*māyā-atīta*—beyond the material nature; *para-vyome*—in the spiritual sky; *sabāra*—all of them; *avasthāna*—residence; *viśve*—within the material universe; *avatari'*—coming down; *dhare*—take; *avatāra nāma*—the name *avatāra.*

### TRANSLATION

**"All the expansions of Lord Kṛṣṇa are actually residents of the spiritual world. However, when they descend into the material world, they are called incarnations [avatāras].**

### TEXT 265

**সেই মায়া অবলোকিতে শ্রীসঙ্কর্ষণ ।
পুরুষরূপে অবতীর্ণ হইলা প্রথম ॥ ২৬৫ ॥**

*sei māyā avalokite śrī-saṅkarṣaṇa
puruṣa-rūpe avatīrṇa ha-ilā prathama*

### SYNONYMS

*sei māyā*—that material energy; *avalokite*—just to glance over; *śrī-saṅkarṣaṇa*—Saṅkarṣaṇa; *puruṣa-rūpe*—in the original form of Mahā-Viṣṇu; *avatīrṇa*—incarnated; *ha-ilā*—became; *prathama*—at first.

### TRANSLATION

**"To glance over that material energy and empower her, Lord Saṅkarṣaṇa first incarnates as Lord Mahā-Viṣṇu.**

### TEXT 266

জগৃহে পৌরুষং রূপং ভগবান্মহদাদিভিঃ।
সম্ভূতং ষোড়শকলমাদৌ লোকসিসৃক্ষয়া ॥ ২৬৬ ॥

*jagṛhe pauruṣaṁ rūpaṁ*
*bhagavān mahad-ādibhiḥ*
*sambhūtaṁ ṣoḍaśa-kalam*
*ādau loka-sisṛkṣayā*

### SYNONYMS

*jagṛhe*—accepted; *pauruṣam rūpam*—the form of the *puruṣa* incarnation; *bhagavān*—the Supreme Personality of Godhead; *mahat-ādibhiḥ*—with the material energy, etc.; *sambhūtam*—created; *ṣoḍaśa*—sixteen; *kalam*—elements; *ādau*—in the beginning; *loka*—of the material worlds; *sisṛkṣayā*—with a desire for the creation.

### TRANSLATION

**" 'In the beginning of the creation, the Lord expanded Himself in the form of the puruṣa incarnation, accompanied by all the ingredients of material creation. First He created the sixteen principal energies suitable for creation. This was for the purpose of manifesting the material universes.'**

### PURPORT

This is a quotation from *Śrīmad-Bhāgavatam* (1.3.1). For an explanation, refer to *Ādi-līlā,* Chapter Five, verse 84.

### TEXT 267

আদ্যোঽবতারঃ পুরুষঃ পরস্য কালঃ স্বভাবঃ সদসন্মনশ্চ।
দ্রব্যং বিকারো গুণ ইন্দ্রিয়াণি বিরাট্ স্বরাট্ স্থাস্নু চরিষ্ণু ভূম্নঃ ॥ ২৬৭ ॥

*ādyo 'vatāraḥ puruṣaḥ parasya*
*kālaḥ svabhāvaḥ sad-asan-manaś ca*
*dravyaṁ vikāro guṇa indriyāṇi*
*virāṭ svarāṭ sthāsnu cariṣṇu bhūmnaḥ*

## SYNONYMS

*ādyaḥ avatāraḥ*—the original incarnation; *puruṣaḥ*—the Lord; *parasya*—of the Supreme; *kālaḥ*—time; *svabhāvaḥ*—nature; *sat-asat*—cause and effect; *manaḥ ca*—as well as the mind; *dravyam*—the five elements; *vikāraḥ*—transformation or the false ego; *guṇaḥ*—modes of nature; *indriyāṇi*—senses; *virāṭ*—the universal form; *svarāṭ*—complete independence; *sthāsnu*—immovable; *cariṣṇu*—movable; *bhūmnaḥ*—of the Supreme Personality of Godhead.

## TRANSLATION

**" 'Kāraṇābdhiśāyī Viṣṇu [Mahā-Viṣṇu] is the first incarnation of the Supreme Lord, and He is the master of eternal time, space, cause and effects, mind, elements, material ego, modes of nature, senses, the universal form of the Lord, Garbhodakaśāyī Viṣṇu, and the sum total of all living beings, both moving and nonmoving.'**

## PURPORT

This is a quotation from *Śrīmad-Bhāgavatam* (2.6.42). For an explanation, refer to *Ādi-līlā,* Chapter Five, verse 83.

## TEXT 268

সেই পুরুষ বিরজাতে করেন শয়ন ।
'কারণাব্ধিশায়ী' নাম জগৎকারণ ॥ ২৬৮ ॥

*sei puruṣa virajāte karena śayana*
*'kāraṇābdhiśāyī' nāma jagat-kāraṇa*

## SYNONYMS

*sei puruṣa*—the Supreme Personality of Godhead; *virajāte*—on the border known as Virajā; *karena śayana*—lies down; *kāraṇa-abdhi-śāyī*—Kāraṇābdhiśāyī; *nāma*—named; *jagat-kāraṇa*—is the original cause of material creation.

## TRANSLATION

**"That original Personality of Godhead, named Saṅkarṣaṇa, first lies down in the River Virajā, which serves as a border between the material and spiritual**

**worlds. As Kāraṇābdhiśāyī Viṣṇu, He is the original cause of the material creation.**

### TEXT 269

কারণাব্ধি-পারে মায়ার নিত্য অবস্থিতি।
বিরজার পারে পরব্যোমে নাহি গতি ॥ ২৬৯ ॥

*kāraṇābdhi-pāre māyāra nitya avasthiti*
*virajāra pāre paravyome nāhi gati*

### SYNONYMS

*kāraṇa-abdhi-pāre*—on one bank of the Causal Ocean; *māyāra*—of the material energy; *nitya*—eternal; *avasthiti*—position; *virajāra pāre*—on the other bank of the Virajā, or the Causal Ocean; *para-vyome*—in the spiritual world or sky; *nāhi*—there is not; *gati*—admission.

### TRANSLATION

**"The Virajā, or Causal Ocean, is the border between the spiritual and material worlds. The material energy is situated on one shore of that ocean, and it cannot enter onto the other shore, which is the spiritual sky.**

### TEXT 270

প্রবর্ততে যত্র রজস্তমস্তয়োঃ
সত্ত্বঞ্চ মিশ্রং ন চ কালবিক্রমঃ।
ন যত্র মায়া কিমুতাপরে হরে-
রনুব্রতা যত্র সুরাসুরার্চিতাঃ ॥ ২৭০ ॥

*pravartate yatra rajas tamas tayoḥ*
*sattvaṁ ca miśraṁ na ca kāla-vikramaḥ*
*na yatra māyā kim utāpare harer*
*anuvratā yatra surāsurārcitāḥ*

### SYNONYMS

*pravartate*—exists; *yatra*—where; *rajaḥ*—the mode of passion; *tamaḥ*—the mode of ignorance; *tayoḥ*—of both of them; *sattvam ca*—and the mode of goodness; *miśram*—mixture; *na*—not; *ca*—also; *kāla-vikramaḥ*—the influence of time or annihilation; *na*—not; *yatra*—where; *māyā*—external energy; *kim*—what; *uta*—to speak; *apare*—others; *hareḥ*—of the Supreme Personality of Godhead;

*anuvratāḥ*—strict followers; *yatra*—where; *sura*—by demigods; *asura*—and by demons; *arcitāḥ*—being worshiped.

## TRANSLATION

**" 'In the spiritual world, there is neither the mode of passion, the mode of ignorance nor a mixture of both, nor is there adulterated goodness, nor the influence of time or māyā itself. Only the pure devotees of the Lord, who are worshiped both by demigods and by demons, reside in the spiritual world as the Lord's associates.'**

## PURPORT

This verse from *Śrīmad-Bhāgavatam* (2.9.10) was spoken by Śrīla Śukadeva Gosvāmī. He was answering the questions of Parīkṣit Mahārāja, who asked how the living entity falls down into the material world. Śukadeva Gosvāmī explained the cream of *Śrīmad-Bhāgavatam* in four verses, which had been explained to Lord Brahmā at the end of the severe austerities he performed for one thousand celestial years. At that time, Brahmā was shown the spiritual world and its transcendental nature.

## TEXT 271

মায়ার যে দুই বৃত্তি—'মায়া' আর 'প্রধান'।
'মায়া' নিমিত্তহেতু, বিশ্বের উপাদান 'প্রধান' ॥২৭১॥

*māyāra ye dui vṛtti——'māyā' āra 'pradhāna'*
*'māyā' nimitta-hetu, viśvera upādāna 'pradhāna'*

## SYNONYMS

*māyāra*—of the material nature; *ye*—which; *dui*—two; *vṛtti*—functions; *māyā*—called *māyā; āra*—and; *pradhāna*—ingredients; *māyā*—the word *māyā; nimitta-hetu*—the efficient cause; *viśvera*—of the material universe; *upādāna*—ingredients; *pradhāna*—is called *pradhāna.*

## TRANSLATION

**"Māyā has two functions. One is called māyā, and the other is called pradhāna. Māyā refers to the efficient cause, and pradhāna refers to the ingredients that create the cosmic manifestation.**

## PURPORT

For a further explanation, see *Ādi-līlā,* Chapter Five, verse 58.

## TEXT 272

সেই পুরুষ মায়া-পানে করে অবধান ।
প্রকৃতি ক্ষোভিত করি' করে বীর্যের আধান ॥ ২৭২ ॥

*sei puruṣa māyā-pāne kare avadhāna*
*prakṛti kṣobhita kari' kare vīryera ādhāna*

## SYNONYMS

*sei puruṣa*—that Supreme Personality of Godhead; *māyā-pāne*—toward *māyā; kare avadhāna*—glances; *prakṛti*—the material nature; *kṣobhita kari'*—making agitated; *kare*—impregnates; *vīryera*—of the semina; *ādhāna*—injection.

## TRANSLATION

**"When the Supreme Personality of Godhead glances over the material energy, she becomes agitated. At that time, the Lord injects the original semina of the living entities.**

## PURPORT

In *Bhagavad-gītā* (7.10), Kṛṣṇa says, *bījaṁ māṁ sarva-bhūtānām:* "I am the original seed of all existences." This is also confirmed in another verse in *Bhagavad-gītā* (14.4):

*sarva-yoniṣu kaunteya*
*mūrtayaḥ sambhavanti yāḥ*
*tāsāṁ brahma mahad-yonir*
*ahaṁ bīja-pradaḥ pitā*

"It should be understood that all species of life, O son of Kuntī, are made possible by birth in this material nature, and that I am the seed-giving father."

For a further explanation, one may refer to *Brahmā-saṁhitā* (Chapter Five, verses 10-13). *Brahmā-saṁhitā* also states (5.51):

*agnir mahī gaganam ambu marud diśaś ca*
*kālas tathātma-manasīti jagat-trayāṇi*
*yasmād bhavanti vibhavanti viśanti yaṁ ca*
*govindam ādi-puruṣaṁ tam ahaṁ bhajāmi*

All material elements, as well as the spiritual sparks (individual souls), are emanating from the Supreme Personality of Godhead. This is also confirmed by the *Vedānta-sūtra* (1.1). *Janmādy asya yataḥ:* "The Absolute Truth is He from whom everything emanates." He is the Supreme Truth: *satyaṁ paraṁ dhīmahi* (*Bhāg.* 1.1.1). The absolute ultimate truth is Kṛṣṇa. *Oṁ namo bhagavate vāsudevāya/ janmādy asya yato 'nvayād itarataś cārtheṣv abhijñaḥ sva-rāṭ:* "The Absolute Truth is a person who is directly and indirectly cognizant of the entire cosmic manifestation." (*Bhāg.* 1.1.1)

The Absolute Truth, the Supreme Personality of Godhead, educated Lord Brahmā from the heart (*Bhāg.* 1.1.1): *tene brahma hṛdā ya ādi-kavaye.* Therefore the Absolute Truth cannot be dull matter; the Absolute Truth must be the Supreme Person Himself. *Sei puruṣa māyā-pāne kare avadhāna.* Simply by His glance, material nature is impregnated with all living entities. According to their *karma* and fruitive activity, they emerge in different bodies. That is the explanation given by *Bhagavad-gītā* (2.13):

*dehino 'smin yathā dehe*
*kaumāraṁ yauvanaṁ jarā*
*tathā dehāntara-prāptir*
*dhīras tatra na muḥyati*

"As the embodied soul continually passes, in this body, from boyhood to youth to old age, the soul similarly passes into another body at death. The self-realized soul is not bewildered by such a change."

## TEXT 273

**স্বাঙ্গ-বিশেষাভাসরূপে প্রকৃতি-স্পর্শন।**
**জীব-রূপ 'বীজ' তাতে কৈলা সমর্পণ ॥ ২৭৩ ॥**

*svāṅga-viśeṣābhāsa-rūpe prakṛti-sparśana*
*jīva-rūpa 'bīja' tāte kailā samarpaṇa*

## SYNONYMS

*sva-aṅga-viśeṣa-ābhāsa-rūpe*—in the form of a specific shadow from His personal body; *prakṛti-sparśana*—the Lord glances over the material nature; *jīva-rūpa*—having the form of the sparklike living entities, who are parts and parcels; *bīja*—semina; *tāte*—in that material nature; *kailā samarpaṇa*—impregnated.

## TRANSLATION

**"To impregnate with the seeds of living entities, the Lord Himself does not directly touch the material energy, but by His specific functional expansion, He touches the material energy, and thus the living entities, who are His parts and parcels, are impregnated into material nature.**

**PURPORT**

According to *Bhagavad-gītā:*

*mamaivāṁśo jīva-loke*
*jīva-bhūtaḥ sanātanaḥ*
*manaḥ ṣaṣṭhānīndriyāṇi*
*prakṛti-sthāni karṣati*

"The living entities in this conditioned world are My eternal, fragmental parts. Due to conditioned life, they are struggling very hard with the six senses, which include the mind." (Bg. 15.7)

The word *prakṛti-sparśana* is explained in *Caitanya-caritāmṛta* in reference to the way the living entities come in contact with dull matter. The glancing is performed by Mahā-Viṣṇu: *sa aikṣata lokān nu sṛjā iti* (*Aitareya Upaniṣad* 1.1.1). In the conditional stage we impregnate according to the bodily conception—that is, by sexual intercourse—but the Supreme Lord does not need sexual intercourse to impregnate. The impregnation is performed simply by His glance. This is also explained in *Brahma-saṁhitā* (5.32):

*aṅgāni yasya sakalendriya-vṛttimanti*
*paśyanti pānti kalayanti ciraṁ jaganti*
*ānanda-cinmaya-sad-ujjvala-vigrahasya*
*govindam ādi-puruṣaṁ tam ahaṁ bhājami*

Govinda can impregnate simply by glancing. In other words, His eyes can work as His genitals. He does not need genitals to beget a child. Indeed, Kṛṣṇa can beget any one of the living entities with any part of His body.

The word *svāṅga-viśeṣābhāsa-rūpe,* the form by which the Lord begets living entities in the material world, is explained herein. He is Lord Śiva. In *Brahma-saṁhitā* it is stated that Lord Śiva, who is another form of Mahā-Viṣṇu, is like yogurt. Yogurt is nothing but milk, yet it is not milk. Similarly, Lord Śiva is considered the father of this universe, and material nature is considered the mother. The father and mother are known as Lord Śiva and the goddess Durgā. Together, Lord Śiva's genitals and the vagina of goddess Durgā are worshiped as *śiva-liṅga.* This is the origin of the material creation. Thus Lord Śiva's position is between the living entity and the Supreme Lord. Lord Śiva is neither the Supreme Personality of Godhead nor the living entity. He is the form through which the Supreme Lord works to beget living entities within this material world. As yogurt is prepared when milk is mixed with a culture, the form of Lord Śiva expands when the Supreme Personality of Godhead is in touch with material nature. The impregnation of material nature by the father, Lord Śiva, is wonderful because at one time innumerable living entities are conceived. *Bhāgo jīvaḥ sa vijñeyaḥ sa cānantyāya kalpate* (*Śvetāśvatara Upaniṣad* 5.9). These living entities are very, very small.

*keśāgra-śata-bhāgasya*
*śatāṁśa-sadṛśātmakaḥ*
*jīvaḥ sūkṣma-svarūpo 'yaṁ*
*saṅkhyātīto hi cit-kaṇaḥ*

"If we divide the tip of a hair into a hundred parts and then take one of these parts and divide it again into a hundred parts, that very fine division is the size of but one of the numberless living entities. They are all *cit-kaṇa,* particles of spirit, not matter."

The innumerable *brahmāṇḍas,* or universes, come from the pores of the Lord's body, and innumerable living entities also come from the pores of the transcendental body of the Lord. This is the process of material creation. Without the living entity, this material nature has no value. Both emanate from the pores of the transcendental body of Lord Mahā-Viṣṇu. They are different energies. That is explained in *Bhagavad-gītā:*

*bhūmir āpo 'nalo vāyuḥ*
*khaṁ mano buddhir eva ca*
*ahaṅkāra itīyaṁ me*
*bhinnā prakṛtir aṣṭadhā*

"Earth, water, fire, air, ether, mind, intelligence and false ego—all together these eight comprise My separated material energies." (Bg. 7.4) The material elements also come from the body of the Supreme Personality of Godhead, and they are also a different type of energy. Although the living entities also come from the Lord's body, they are categorized as a superior energy.

*apareyam itas tv anyāṁ*
*prakṛtiṁ viddhi me parām*
*jīva-bhūtāṁ mahā-bāho*
*yayedaṁ dhāryate jagat*

"Besides this inferior nature, O mighty-armed Arjuna, there is a superior energy of Mine, which consists of all living entities who are struggling with material nature and are sustaining the universe." (Bg. 7.5) The inferior energy, matter, cannot act without the superior energy. All these things are very clearly explained in the *Vedas.* The materialistic theory that life develops from matter is incorrect. Life and matter come from the supreme living entity; therefore, being the source of both, that supreme living entity, Kṛṣṇa, is described in *Vedānta-sūtra* as *janmādy asya yataḥ* (1.1), or the original source of everything, *sarva-kāraṇa-kāraṇam.* This is further explained in the following verse.

## TEXT 274

দৈবাৎ ক্ষুভিতধর্মিণ্যাং স্বস্যাং যোনৌ পরঃ পুমান্।
আধত্ত বীর্যং সাঽসূত মহত্তত্ত্বং হিরণ্ময়ম্ ॥ ২৭৪ ॥

*daivāt kṣubhita-dharmiṇyāṁ*
*svasyāṁ yonau paraḥ pumān*
*ādhatta vīryaṁ sā 'sūta*
*mahat-tattvaṁ hiraṇmayam*

## SYNONYMS

*daivāt*—from time immemorial; *kṣubhita-dharmiṇyām*—the material nature, which is subjected to agitation; *svasyām*—which belongs to the Supreme as one of His energies; *yonau*—in the womb from which the living entity takes his birth; *paraḥ pumān*—the Supreme Brahman, the Personality of Godhead; *ādhatta*—impregnated; *vīryam*—semina; *sā*—that material nature; *asūta*—produced; *mahat-tattvam*—the total material energy; *hiraṇmayam*—the original source for the emanation of varieties of material things.

## TRANSLATION

**" 'From time immemorial, after agitating the material nature into three qualities, the Supreme Personality of Godhead places the semina of innumerable living entities within the womb of that material nature. Thus material nature gives birth to the total material energy known as the hiraṇmaya-mahat-tattva, the original symbolic representation of the cosmic manifestation.'**

## PURPORT

This is a quotation from *Śrīmad-Bhāgavatam* (3.26.19). Lord Kapila is explaining to His mother the relationship between the Supreme Personality of Godhead and material nature. He is informing her how the Supreme Personality of Godhead is the original cause of the living entities, who emanated from material nature. Over and above the twenty-eight elements of the material creation is the Supreme Personality of Godhead, the cause of all causes. Life comes not from matter but from life itself. As explained in the *Vedas: nityo nityānāṁ cetanaś cetanānām* (*Kaṭha Upaniṣad* 2.2.13). The Supreme Lord is the original source of life.

## TEXT 275

কালবৃত্ত্যা তু মায়ায়াং গুণময্যামধোক্ষজঃ ।
পুরুষেণাত্মভূতেন বীর্যমাধত্ত বীর্যবান্ ॥ ২৭৫ ॥

*kāla-vṛttyā tu māyāyāṁ*
*guṇamayyām adhokṣajaḥ*
*puruṣeṇātma-bhūtena*
*vīryam ādhatta vīryavān*

## SYNONYMS

*kāla-vṛttyā*—in due course of time, as the immediate cause of creation; *tu*—but; *māyāyām*—within the material nature; *guṇa-mayyām*—full of the three material modes of nature (*sattva-guṇa, rajo-guṇa* and *tamo-guṇa*); *adhokṣajaḥ*—the Supreme Personality of Godhead, who is beyond material conceptions; *puruṣeṇa*—by the enjoyer of material nature; *ātma-bhūtena*—who is an expansion of His personal self; *vīryam*—semina; *ādhatta*—placed; *vīryavān*—the omnipotent.

## TRANSLATION

**" 'In due course of time, the Supreme Personality of Godhead [Mahā-Viṣṇu or Mahā-Vaikuṇṭhanātha], by the agency of a further expansion of His personal self, places the seed of the living entities within the womb of material nature.'**

## PURPORT

This is a quotation from *Śrīmad-Bhāgavatam* (3.5.26). This verse tells how the living entities come in contact with material nature. Just as a woman cannot beget children without uniting with a man, material nature cannot beget living entities without being in union with the Supreme Personality of Godhead. There is a history of how the Absolute Lord becomes the father of all living entities. In every system of religion, it is accepted that God is the supreme father of all living entities. According to Christianity, the supreme father, God, provides the living entities with all of life's necessities. Therefore they pray, "Give us this day our daily bread." Any religion that does not accept the Supreme Lord as the absolute father is called *kaitava-dharma,* or a cheating religion. Such religious systems are rejected in *Śrīmad-Bhāgavatam* (1.1.2): *dharmaḥ projjhita-kaitavo 'tra.* Only an atheist does not accept the omnipotent supreme father. If one accepts the omnipotent supreme father, he abides by His orders and becomes a religious person.

### TEXT 276

তবে মহত্তত্ত্ব হৈতে ত্রিবিধ অহঙ্কার ।
যাহা হৈতে দেবতেন্দ্রিয়ভূতের প্রচার ॥ ২৭৬ ॥

*tabe mahat-tattva haite trividha ahaṅkāra*
*yāhā haite devatendriya-bhūtera pracāra*

### SYNONYMS

*tabe*—thereafter; *mahat-tattva haite*—from the total material energy; *trividha*—three kinds of; *ahaṅkāra*—egotism; *yāhā haite*—from which; *devatā*—of predominating deities; *indriya*—of the senses; *bhūtera*—and of material elements; *pracāra*—expansion.

### TRANSLATION

**"First the total material energy is manifest, and from this arise the three types of egotism, which are the original sources from which all demigods [controlling deities], senses and material elements expand.**

### PURPORT

The three types of egotism (*ahaṅkāra*) are technically known as *vaikārika, taijasa* and *tāmasa*. The *mahat-tattva* is situated within the heart, or *citta*, and the predominating Deity of the *mahat-tattva* is Lord Vāsudeva (*Bhāg.* 3.26.21). The *mahat-tattva* is transformed into three divisions: (1) *vaikārika*, egotism in goodness (*sāttvika-ahaṅkāra*), from which the eleventh sense organ, the mind, is manifest and whose predominating Deity is Aniruddha (*Bhāg.* 3.26.27-28); (2) *taijasa*, or egotism in passion (*rājasa-ahaṅkāra*), from which the senses and intelligence are manifest and whose predominating Deity is Lord Pradyumna (*Bhāg.* 3.26.29-31); (3) *tāmasa*, or egotism in ignorance, from which sound vibration (*śabda-tanmātra*) expands. From the sound vibration, the sky (*ākāśa*) is manifest and, the senses, beginning with the ear, are also manifest (*Bhāg.* 3.26.32). Of these three types of egotism, Lord Saṅkarṣaṇa is the predominating Deity. In the philosophical discourse known as the *Sāṅkhya-kārikā*, it is stated: *sāttvika ekādaśakaḥ pravartate vaikṛtād ahaṅkārāt——bhūtādes tanmātraṁ tāmasa-taijasādy-ubhayam.*

### TEXT 277

সর্ব তত্ত্ব মিলি' সৃজিল ব্রহ্মাণ্ডের গণ ।
অনন্ত ব্রহ্মাণ্ড, তার নাহিক গণন ॥ ২৭৭ ॥

*sarva tattva mili' sṛjila brahmāṇḍera gaṇa*
*ananta brahmāṇḍa, tāra nāhika gaṇana*

### SYNONYMS

*sarva tattva*—all different elements; *mili'*—combining; *sṛjila*—created; *brahmāṇḍera gaṇa*—all the universes; *ananta brahmāṇḍa*—those universes are unlimited in number; *tāra nāhika gaṇana*—there is no possibility of counting them.

### TRANSLATION

**"Combining all the different elements, the Supreme Lord created all the universes. Those universes are unlimited in number; there is no possibility of counting them.**

### TEXT 278

**ইঁহো মহৎস্রষ্টা পুরুষ—'মহাবিষ্ণু' নাম ।**
**অনন্ত ব্রহ্মাণ্ড তাঁর লোমকূপে ধাম ॥ ২৭৮ ॥**

*iṅho mahat-sraṣṭā puruṣa——'mahā-viṣṇu' nāma*
*ananta brahmāṇḍa tāṅra loma-kūpe dhāma*

### SYNONYMS

*iṅho*—He; *mahat-sraṣṭā*—the creator of the *mahat-tattva,* or total material energy; *puruṣa*—the person; *mahā-viṣṇu nāma*—called Lord Mahā-Viṣṇu; *ananta*—unlimited; *brahmāṇḍa*—universes; *tāṅra*—of His body; *loma-kūpe*—within the hair holes; *dhāma*—are situated.

### TRANSLATION

**"The first form of Lord Viṣṇu is called Mahā-Viṣṇu. He is the original creator of the total material energy. The innumerable universes emanate from the pores of His body.**

### TEXTS 279-280

**গবাক্ষে উড়িয়া যৈছে রেণু আসে যায় ।**
**পুরুষ-নিশ্বাস-সহ ব্রহ্মাণ্ড বাহিরায় ॥ ২৭৯ ॥**
**পুনরপি নিশ্বাস-সহ যায় অভ্যন্তর ।**
**অনন্ত ঐশ্বর্য তাঁর, সব—মায়া-পার ॥ ২৮০ ॥**

*gavākṣe uḍiyā yaiche reṇu āse yāya*
*puruṣa-niśvāsa-saha brahmāṇḍa bāhirāya*

*punarapi niśvāsa-saha yāya abhyantara*
*ananta aiśvarya tāṅra, saba——māyā-pāra*

## SYNONYMS

*gavākṣe*—from a hole at the top of a wall; *uḍiyā*—floating; *yaiche*—as; *reṇu*—atomic particles; *āse yāya*—come and go; *puruṣa-niśvāsa-saha*—with the exhaling of Mahā-Viṣṇu; *brahmāṇḍa*—the universes; *bāhirāya*—come outside; *punarapi*—again; *niśvāsa-saha*—by His inhalation; *yāya*—go; *abhyantara*—within; *ananta*—unlimited; *aiśvarya*—opulences; *tāṅra*—of Him; *saba*—everything; *māyā-pāra*—beyond the material conception.

## TRANSLATION

**"These universes are understood to be floating in air as the Mahā-Viṣṇu exhales. They are like atomic particles that float in sunshine and pass through the holes of a screen. All these universes are thus created by the exhalation of Mahā-Viṣṇu, and when Mahā-Viṣṇu inhales, they return to His body. The unlimited opulences of Mahā-Viṣṇu are completely beyond material conception.**

## TEXT 281

যস্যৈক-নিশ্বসিতকালমথাবলম্ব্য
জীবন্তি লোমবিলজা জগদণ্ডনাথাঃ ।
বিষ্ণুর্মহান্ স ইহ যস্য কলাবিশেষো
গোবিন্দমাদিপুরুষং তমহং ভজামি ॥ ২৮১ ॥

*yasyaika-niśvasita-kālam athāvalambya*
*jīvanti loma-vilajā jagad-aṇḍa-nāthāḥ*
*viṣṇur mahān sa iha yasya kalā-viśeṣo*
*govindam ādi-puruṣaṁ tam ahaṁ bhajāmi*

## SYNONYMS

*yasya*—whose; *eka*—one; *niśvasita*—of breath; *kālam*—time; *atha*—thus; *avalambya*—taking shelter of; *jīvanti*—live; *loma-vilajāḥ*—grown from the hair holes; *jagat-aṇḍa-nāthāḥ*—the masters of the universes (the Brahmās); *viṣṇuḥ mahān*—the Supreme Lord Mahā-Viṣṇu; *saḥ*—that; *iha*—here; *yasya*—whose; *kalā-viśeṣaḥ*—particular plenary portion or expansion; *govindam*—Lord Govinda; *ādi-puruṣam*—the original person; *tam*—Him; *aham*—I; *bhajāmi*—worship.

## TRANSLATION

**" 'The Brahmās and other lords of the mundane worlds appear from the pores of the Mahā-Viṣṇu and remain alive for the duration of His one exhala-**

**tion. I adore the primeval Lord, Govinda, for Mahā-Viṣṇu is a portion of His plenary portion.'**

### PURPORT

This is a quotation from *Brahma-saṁhitā* (5.48).

### TEXT 282

সমস্ত ব্রহ্মাণ্ডগণের ইঁহো অন্তর্যামী ।
কারণাব্ধিশায়ী – সব জগতের স্বামী ॥ ২৮২ ॥

*samasta brahmāṇḍa-gaṇera iṅho antaryāmī*
*kāraṇābdhiśāyī——saba jagatera svāmī*

### SYNONYMS

*samasta brahmāṇḍa-gaṇera*—of the aggregate of the *brahmāṇḍas,* or universes; *iṅho*—that Lord Mahā-Viṣṇu; *antaryāmī*—the Supersoul; *kāraṇa-abdhi-śāyī*—Lord Mahā-Viṣṇu, lying on the Causal Ocean; *saba jagatera*—of all the universes; *svāmī*—the Supreme Lord.

### TRANSLATION

**"Mahā-Viṣṇu is the Supersoul of all the universes. Lying on the Causal Ocean, He is the master of all material worlds.**

### TEXT 283

এইত কহিলুঁ প্রথম পুরুষের তত্ত্ব ।
দ্বিতীয় পুরুষের এবে শুনহ মহত্ত্ব ॥ ২৮৩ ॥

*eita kahiluṅ prathama puruṣera tattva*
*dvitīya puruṣera ebe śunaha mahattva*

### SYNONYMS

*eita*—thus; *kahiluṅ*—I have explained; *prathama puruṣera*—of the first incarnation of the Personality of Godhead; *tattva*—the truth; *dvitīya puruṣera*—of the second incarnation of the Personality of Godhead; *ebe*—now; *śunaha*—please hear; *mahattva*—glories.

### TRANSLATION

**"I have thus explained the truth of the first Personality of Godhead, Mahā-Viṣṇu. I shall now explain the glories of the second Personality of Godhead.**

### TEXT 284

সেই পুরুষ অনন্ত-কোটি ব্রহ্মাণ্ড স্বজিয়া ।
একৈক-মূর্ত্যে প্রবেশিলা বহু মূর্তি হঞা ॥২৮৪ ॥

*sei puruṣa ananta-koṭi brahmāṇḍa sṛjiyā*
*ekaika-mūrtye praveśilā bahu mūrti hañā*

### SYNONYMS

*sei puruṣa*—that Personality of Godhead, Mahā-Viṣṇu; *ananta-koṭi brahmāṇḍa*—millions and trillions of *brahmāṇḍas,* or universes; *sṛjiyā*—after creating; *eka-eka*—in each one of them; *mūrtye*—in a form; *praveśilā*—entered; *bahu mūrti hañā*—becoming many forms.

### TRANSLATION

**"After creating the total number of universes, which are unlimited, the Mahā-Viṣṇu expanded Himself into unlimited forms and entered into each of them.**

### TEXT 285

প্রবেশ করিয়া দেখে, সব – অন্ধকার ।
রহিতে নাহিক স্থান, করিলা বিচার ॥ ২৮৫ ॥

*praveśa kariyā dekhe, saba——andhakāra*
*rahite nāhika sthāna, karilā vicāra*

### SYNONYMS

*praveśa kariyā*—after entering; *dekhe*—He sees; *saba*—everywhere; *andhakāra*—complete darkness; *rahite*—to remain there; *nāhika sthāna*—there was no place; *karilā vicāra*—then He considered.

### TRANSLATION

**"When Mahā-Viṣṇu entered each of the limitless universes, He saw that there was darkness all around and that there was no place to stay. He therefore began to consider the situation.**

### TEXT 286

নিজাঙ্গ-স্বেদজলে ব্রহ্মাণ্ডার্ধ ভরিল ।
সেই জলে শেষ-শয্যায় শয়ন করিল ॥ ২৮৬ ॥

*nijāṅga-sveda-jale brahmāṇḍārdha bharila*
*sei jale śeṣa-śayyāya śayana karila*

### SYNONYMS

*nija-aṅga*—from His own personal body; *sveda-jale*—by emitting the water of perspiration; *brahmāṇḍa-ardha*—half of the universe; *bharila*—filled; *sei jale*—on that water; *śeṣa-śayyāya*—on the bed of Lord Śeṣa; *śayana karila*—lay down.

### TRANSLATION

**"With the perspiration produced from His own body, the Lord filled half the universe with water. He then lay down on that water on the bed of Lord Śeṣa.**

## TEXT 287

তাঁর নাভিপদ্ম হৈতে উঠিল এক পদ্ম ।
সেই পদ্মে হইল ব্রহ্মার জন্ম-সদ্ম ॥ ২৮৭ ॥

*tāṅra nābhi-padma haite uṭhila eka padma*
*sei padme ha-ila brahmāra janma-sadma*

### SYNONYMS

*tāṅra nābhi-padma haite*—from His lotus navel; *uṭhila*—grew; *eka*—one; *padma*—lotus flower; *sei padme*—on that lotus flower; *ha-ila*—there was; *brahmāra*—of Lord Brahmā; *janma-sadma*—the place of generation.

### TRANSLATION

**"A lotus flower then sprouted from the lotus navel of that Garbhodakaśāyī Viṣṇu. That lotus flower became Lord Brahmā's birthplace.**

## TEXT 288

সেই পদ্মনালে হইল চৌদ্দ ভুবন ।
তেঁহো 'ব্রহ্মা' হঞা সৃষ্টি করিল সৃজন ॥ ২৮৮ ॥

*sei padma-nāle ha-ila caudda bhuvana*
*teṅho 'brahmā' hañā sṛṣṭi karila sṛjana*

### SYNONYMS

*sei padma-nāle*—within the stem of that lotus; *ha-ila*—became manifested; *caudda*—fourteen; *bhuvana*—planetary systems; *teṅho*—He; *brahmā*—Lord

Brahmā; *hañā*—having become; *sṛṣṭi*—the material creation; *karila sṛjana*—created.

### TRANSLATION

**"In the stem of that lotus flower the fourteen worlds were generated. Then He became Lord Brahmā and created the entire universe.**

### TEXT 289

'বিষ্ণু'-রূপ হঞা করে জগৎ পালনে।
গুণাতীত বিষ্ণু—স্পর্শ নাহি মায়া-সনে ॥ ২৮৯ ॥

*'viṣṇu'-rūpa hañā kare jagat pālane*
*guṇātīta viṣṇu——sparśa nāhi māyā-sane*

### SYNONYMS

*viṣṇu-rūpa*—Lord Kṛṣṇa in His form as Viṣṇu; *hañā*—becoming; *kare*—does; *jagat pālane*—maintenance of the material world; *guṇa-atīta*—beyond the material qualities, transcendental; *viṣṇu*—Lord Viṣṇu; *sparśa*—touching; *nāhi*—there is not; *māyā-sane*—with *māyā*, the material energy.

### TRANSLATION

**"In this way, the Supreme Personality of Godhead in His form of Viṣṇu maintains the entire material world. Since He is always beyond the material qualities, the material nature cannot touch Him.**

### PURPORT

The influence of the material energy cannot touch Lord Viṣṇu as she touches Lord Brahmā and Lord Śiva. Therefore it is said that Lord Viṣṇu is transcendental to the material qualities. The incarnations of the material qualities—Lord Śiva and Lord Brahmā—are under the jurisdiction of the external energy. Lord Viṣṇu, however, is different. In the *mantras* of the *Ṛg Veda* it is said: *oṁ tad viṣṇoḥ paramaṁ padam* (*Ṛg Veda-saṁhitā* 1.22.20). The words *paramaṁ padam* indicate that He is transcendental to the material qualities. Because Lord Viṣṇu is not within the jurisdiction of the material qualities, He is always superior to the living entities who are controlled by material energy. This is one of the differences between the Supreme Lord and the living entities. Lord Brahmā is a very powerful living entity, and Lord Śiva is even more powerful. Therefore Lord Śiva is not accepted as a living entity, but at the same time is not considered to be on the level of Lord Viṣṇu.

### TEXT 290

'রুদ্র'রূপ ধরি করে জগৎ সংহার।
সৃষ্টি, স্থিতি, প্রলয় হয় ইচ্ছায় যাঁহার ॥ ২৯০ ॥

*'rudra'-rūpa dhari kare jagat saṁhāra*
*sṛṣṭi, sthiti, pralaya haya icchāya yāṅhāra*

### SYNONYMS

*rudra-rūpa dhari*—accepting the form of Lord Śiva; *kare*—performs; *jagat saṁhāra*—dissolution of the universal creation; *sṛṣṭi*—creation; *sthiti*—maintenance; *pralaya*—and dissolution; *haya*—take place; *icchāya*—by the will; *yāṅhāra*—of whom.

### TRANSLATION

**"The Supreme Lord, and His form of Rudra [Lord Śiva], brings about the dissolution of this material creation. In other words, by His will only, there is creation, maintenance and dissolution of the whole cosmic manifestation.**

### TEXT 291

ব্রহ্মা, বিষ্ণু, শিব - তাঁর গুণ-অবতার।
সৃষ্টি-স্থিতি-প্রলয়ের তিনের অধিকার ॥ ২৯১ ॥

*brahmā, viṣṇu, śiva——tāṅra guṇa-avatāra*
*sṛṣṭi-sthiti-pralayera tinera adhikāra*

### SYNONYMS

*brahmā*—Lord Brahmā; *viṣṇu*—Lord Viṣṇu; *śiva*—Lord Śiva; *tāṅra*—of Garbhodakaśāyī Viṣṇu; *guṇa-avatāra*—incarnations of the material qualities; *sṛṣṭi-sthiti-pralayera*—of the three functions, namely creation, maintenance and dissolution; *tinera adhikāra*—there is control by the three deities (Lord Brahmā, Lord Viṣṇu and Lord Śiva).

### TRANSLATION

**"Brahmā, Viṣṇu and Śiva are His three incarnations of the material qualities. Creation, maintenance and destruction respectively are under the charge of these three personalities.**

### TEXT 292

হিরণ্যগর্ভ-অন্তর্যামী—গর্ভোদকশায়ী।
'সহস্রশীর্ষাদি' করি' বেদে যাঁরে গাই ॥ ২৯২ ॥

*hiraṇyagarbha-antaryāmī——garbhodakaśāyī*
*'sahasra-śīrṣādi' kari' vede yāṅre gāi*

### SYNONYMS

*hiraṇyagarbha*—named Hiraṇyagarbha; *antaryāmī*—the Supersoul; *garbha-udaka-śāyī*—Lord Garbhodakaśāyī Viṣṇu; *sahasra-śīrṣā-ādi kari'*—by the Vedic hymns beginning with *sahasra-śīrṣā* (*Ṛg Veda-saṁhitā* 10.90); *vede yāṅre gāi*—unto whom the *Vedas* pray.

### TRANSLATION

**"Garbhodakaśāyī Viṣṇu, known within the universe as Hiraṇyagarbha and the antaryāmī, or Supersoul, is glorified in the Vedic hymns, beginning with the hymn that starts with the word sahasra-śīrṣā.**

### TEXT 293

**এই ত' দ্বিতীয়-পুরুষ—ব্রহ্মাণ্ডের ঈশ্বর ।**
**মায়ার 'আশ্রয়' হয়, তবু মায়া-পার ॥ ২৯৩ ॥**

*ei ta' dvitīya-puruṣa——brahmāṇḍera īśvara*
*māyāra 'āśraya' haya, tabu māyā-pāra*

### SYNONYMS

*ei ta'*—in this way; *dvitīya-puruṣa*—the second Personality of Godhead; *brahmāṇḍera īśvara*—the master of the universe; *māyāra*—of the external, material energy; *āśraya haya*—becomes the shelter; *tabu*—still; *māyā-pāra*—is beyond the touch of the material energy.

### TRANSLATION

**"This second Personality of Godhead, known as Garbhodakaśāyī Viṣṇu, is the master of each and every universe and the shelter of the external energy. Nonetheless, He remains beyond the touch of the external energy.**

### TEXT 294

**তৃতীয়-পুরুষ বিষ্ণু—'গুণ-অবতার' ।**
**দুই অবতার-ভিতর গণনা তাঁহার ॥ ২৯৪ ॥**

*tṛtīya-puruṣa viṣṇu——'guṇa-avatāra'*
*dui avatāra-bhitara gaṇanā tāṅhāra*

### SYNONYMS

*tṛtīya-puruṣa*—the third Personality; *viṣṇu*—Lord Viṣṇu; *guṇa-avatāra*—the incarnation of the material quality of goodness; *dui avatāra-bhitara*—within the two incarnations; *gaṇanā-tāṅhāra*—He is designated.

### TRANSLATION

**"The third expansion of Viṣṇu is the Kṣīrodakaśāyī Viṣṇu, who is the incarnation of the quality of goodness. He is to be counted within the two types of incarnations [puruṣa-avatāras and guṇa-avatāras].**

## TEXT 295

বিরাট্ ব্যষ্টি-জীবের তেঁহো অন্তর্যামী ।
ক্ষীরোদকশায়ী তেঁহো –পালনকর্তা, স্বামী ॥ ২৯৫ ॥

*virāṭ vyaṣṭi-jīvera teṅho antaryāmī*
*kṣīrodakaśāyī teṅho——pālana-kartā, svāmī*

### SYNONYMS

*virāṭ*—the universal form; *vyaṣṭi-jīvera*—of all other living entities; *teṅho*—He; *antaryāmī*—the Supersoul; *kṣīra-udaka-śāyī*—Lord Viṣṇu who lies down in the ocean of milk; *teṅho*—He; *pālana-kartā*—the maintainer; *svāmī*—the master.

### TRANSLATION

**"This Kṣīrodakaśāyī Viṣṇu is the universal form of the Lord and is the Supersoul within every living entity. He is known as Kṣīrodakaśāyī, or the Lord who lies on the ocean of milk. He is the maintainer and master of the universe.**

## TEXT 296

পুরুষাবতারের এই কৈলুঁ নিরূপণ ।
লীলাবতার এবে শুন, সনাতন ॥ ২৯৬ ॥

*puruṣāvatārera ei kailuṅ nirūpaṇa*
*līlāvatāra ebe śuna, sanātana*

### SYNONYMS

*puruṣa-avatārera*—of all the *puruṣa-avatāras;* *ei*—this; *kailuṅ nirūpaṇa*—I have described; *līlā-avatāra*—incarnations for pastimes; *ebe*—now; *śuna*—please hear; *sanātana*—O Sanātana.

### TRANSLATION

**"O Sanātana, I have definitively described the three puruṣa-avatāras of Viṣṇu. Now please hear from Me about the pastime incarnations.**

### TEXT 297

লীলাবতার কৃষ্ণের না যায় গণন।
প্রধান করিয়া কহি দিগ্‌দরশন ॥ ২৯৭ ॥

*līlāvatāra kṛṣṇera nā yāya gaṇana*
*pradhāna kariyā kahi dig-daraśana*

### SYNONYMS

*līlā-avatāra*—incarnations for pastimes; *kṛṣṇera*—of Lord Kṛṣṇa; *nā yāya gaṇana*—are not countable; *pradhāna kariyā*—chiefly; *kahi*—let me describe; *dik-daraśana*—by a sample direction.

### TRANSLATION

**"No one can count the innumerable pastime incarnations of Lord Kṛṣṇa, but I shall describe the principal ones.**

### TEXT 298

মৎস্য, কূর্ম, রঘুনাথ, নৃসিংহ, বামন।
বরাহাদি—লেখা যাঁর না যায় গণন ॥ ২৯৮ ॥

*matsya, kūrma, raghunātha, nṛsiṁha, vāmana*
*varāhādi——lekhā yāṅra nā yāya gaṇana*

### SYNONYMS

*matsya*—the fish incarnation; *kūrma*—the tortoise incarnation; *raghunātha*—Lord Rāmacandra; *nṛsiṁha*—the man-lion incarnation; *vāmana*—the dwarf incarnation; *varāha-ādi*—the hog incarnation and others; *lekhā*—describing; *yāṅra*—of which incarnations; *nā yāya gaṇana*—cannot be counted.

### TRANSLATION

**"Some of the pastime incarnations are the fish incarnation, the tortoise incarnation, Lord Rāmacandra, Lord Nṛsiṁha, Lord Vāmana, and Lord Varāha. There is no end to them.**

## TEXT 299

মৎস্যাশ্বকচ্ছপনৃসিংহ-বরাহ-হংস-
রাজন্যবিপ্রবিবুধেষু কৃতাবতারঃ ।
ত্বং পাসি নস্ত্রিভুবনঞ্চ তথাধুনেশ
ভারং ভুবো হর যদূত্তম বন্দনং তে ॥ ২৯৯ ॥

*matsyāśva-kacchapa-nṛsiṁha-varāha-haṁsa-*
*rājanya-vipra-vibudheṣu kṛtāvatāraḥ*
*tvaṁ pāsi nas tribhuvanaṁ ca tathādhuneśa*
*bhāraṁ bhuvo hara yadūttama vandanaṁ te*

## SYNONYMS

*matsya*—in the forms of a fish; *aśva*—of a horse; *kacchapa*—of a tortoise; *nṛsiṁha*—of Lord Nṛsiṁhadeva; *varāha*—of a boar; *haṁsa*—of a swan; *rājanya*—of Lord Rāmacandra; *vipra*—of Lord Paraśurāma; *vibudheṣu*—and of Vāmanadeva; *kṛta-avatāraḥ*—who have accepted incarnation; *tvam*—You; *pāsi*—please protect; *naḥ*—us demigods; *tri-bhuvanam ca*—and the three worlds; *tathā*—as well; *adhunā*—now; *īśa*—O Lord; *bhāram*—the burden; *bhuvaḥ*—of the universe; *hara*—kindly take away; *yadu-uttama*—O best of the Yadu dynasty; *vandanam te*—to You we offer our prayers.

## TRANSLATION

**" 'O Lord of the universe, best of the Yadu dynasty, we are offering our prayers unto You mainly to diminish the heavy burden of the universe. Indeed, You diminished this burden formerly by incarnating in the form of a fish, a horse [Hayagrīva], a tortoise, a lion [Lord Nṛsiṁha], a boar [Lord Varāha] and a swan. You also incarnated as Lord Rāmacandra, Paraśurāma and Vāmana the dwarf. You have always protected us demigods and the universe in this way. Now please continue.'**

## PURPORT

This is a quotation from *Śrīmad-Bhāgavatam* (10.2.40).

## TEXT 300

লীলাবতারের কৈলুঁ দিগ্‌দরশন ।
গুণাবতারের এবে শুন বিবরণ ॥ ৩০০ ॥

*līlāvatārera kailuṅ dig-daraśana*
*guṇāvatārera ebe śuna vivaraṇa*

### SYNONYMS

*līlā-avatārera*—of the incarnations of pastimes; *kailuṅ*—I have done; *dik-daraśana*—indicating the direction only; *guṇa-avatārera*—of incarnations of the material qualities; *ebe*—now; *śuna vivaraṇa*—hear the description.

### TRANSLATION

**"I have given a few examples of pastime incarnations. Now I will describe the guṇa-avatāras, the incarnations of the material qualities. Please listen.**

### TEXT 301

ব্রহ্মা, বিষ্ণু, শিব,– তিন গুণ অবতার ।
ত্রিগুণ অঙ্গীকরি' করে সৃষ্ট্যাদি-ব্যবহার ॥ ৩০১ ॥

*brahmā, viṣṇu, śiva,——tina guṇa avatāra*
*tri-guṇa aṅgīkari' kare sṛṣṭy-ādi-vyavahāra*

### SYNONYMS

*brahmā, viṣṇu, śiva*—Lord Brahmā, Lord Viṣṇu and Lord Śiva; *tina*—three; *guṇa avatāra*—the incarnations of the material qualities; *tri-guṇa*—the three qualities of material nature; *aṅgīkari'*—accepting; *kare*—does; *sṛṣṭi-ādi-vyavahāra*—transactions in reference to the creation, maintenance and dissolution.

### TRANSLATION

**"There are three functions within this material world. Everything here is created, everything is maintained for some time, and everything is finally dissolved. The Lord therefore incarnates Himself as the controllers of the three qualities—sattva-guṇa, rajo-guṇa and tamo-guṇa [goodness, passion and ignorance]. Thus the transactions of the material world take place.**

### TEXT 302

ভক্তিমিশ্রকৃতপুণ্যে কোন জীবোত্তম ।
রজোগুণে বিভাবিত করি' তাঁর মন ॥ ৩০২ ॥

*bhakti-miśra-kṛta-puṇye kona jīvottama*
*rajo-guṇe vibhāvita kari' tāṅra mana*

### SYNONYMS

*bhakti-miśra-kṛta-puṇye*—because of pious activities mixed with devotional service; *kona*—someone; *jīva-uttama*—the best of the living entities; *rajaḥ-guṇe*—by the mode of passion; *vibhāvita*—influenced; *kari'*—making; *tāṅra*—his; *mana*—mind.

### TRANSLATION

**"Because of his past pious activities mixed with devotional service, the first-class living entity is influenced by the mode of passion within his mind.**

### TEXT 303

গর্ভোদকশায়িদ্বারা শক্তি সঞ্চারি' ।
ব্যষ্টি সৃষ্টি করে কৃষ্ণ ব্রহ্মা-রূপ ধরি' ॥ ৩০৩ ॥

*garbhodakaśāyi-dvārā śakti sañcāri'*
*vyaṣṭi sṛṣṭi kare kṛṣṇa brahmā-rūpa dhari'*

### SYNONYMS

*garbha-udaka-śāyi-dvārā*—by Lord Garbhodakaśāyī Viṣṇu; *śakti sañcāri'*—giving him special powers; *vyaṣṭi*—total; *sṛṣṭi*—creation; *kare*—does; *kṛṣṇa*—Lord Kṛṣṇa; *brahmā-rūpa dhari'*—accepting the form of Lord Brahmā.

### TRANSLATION

**"Such a devotee is empowered by Garbhodakaśāyī Viṣṇu. In this way, an incarnation of Kṛṣṇa in the form of Brahmā engineers the total creation of the universe.**

### PURPORT

The Garbhodakaśāyī Viṣṇu *puruṣa-avatāra* expansion of Lord Viṣṇu accepts the material modes—*sattva-guṇa, rajo-guṇa* and *tamo-guṇa*— and thus incarnates as Lord Viṣṇu, Brahmā and Śiva. These are incarnations of the material qualities. Among the many superior living entities qualified with pious activities and devotional service, one, called Lord Brahmā, is infused with the quality of passion by the supreme will of Garbhodakaśāyī Viṣṇu. Thus Lord Brahmā becomes the incarnation of the creative energy of the Lord.

### TEXT 304

ভাস্বান্ যথাশ্মসকলেষু নিজেষু তেজঃ
স্বীয়ং কিয়ৎ প্রকটয়ত্যপি তদ্বদত্র ।

ব্রহ্মা য এষ জগদণ্ডবিধানকর্তা
গোবিন্দমাদিপুরুষং তমহং ভজামি ॥ ৩০৪ ॥

*bhāsvān yathāśma-sakaleṣu nijeṣu tejaḥ*
*svīyaṁ kiyat prakaṭayaty api tadvad atra*
*brahmā ya eṣa jagad-aṇḍa-vidhāna-kartā*
*govindam ādi-puruṣaṁ tam ahaṁ bhajāmi*

### SYNONYMS

*bhāsvān*—the illuminating sun; *yathā*—as; *aśma-sakaleṣu*—in various types of precious stones; *nijeṣu*—his own; *tejaḥ*—brilliance; *svīyam*—his own; *kiyat*—to some extent; *prakaṭayati*—manifests; *api*—also; *tadvat*—similarly; *atra*—here; *brahmā*—Lord Brahmā; *yaḥ*—who is; *eṣaḥ*—the Lord; *jagat-aṇḍa-vidhāna-kartā*—becomes the chief of the universe; *govindam ādi-puruṣam*—Lord Govinda, the original Supreme Personality of Godhead; *tam*—Him; *aham*—I; *bhajāmi*—worship.

### TRANSLATION

**" 'The sun manifests his brilliance in a gem, although it is stone. Similarly, the original Personality of Godhead, Govinda, manifests His special power in a pious living entity. Thus the living entity becomes Brahmā and manages the affairs of the universe. Let me worship Govinda, the original Personality of Godhead.'**

### PURPORT

This is a quotation from *Brahma-saṁhitā* (5.49).

## TEXT 305

**কোন কল্পে যদি যোগ্য জীব নাহি পায়।**
**আপনে ঈশ্বর তবে অংশে 'ব্রহ্মা' হয় ॥ ৩০৫ ॥**

*kona kalpe yadi yogya jīva nāhi pāya*
*āpane īśvara tabe aṁśe 'brahmā' haya*

### SYNONYMS

*kona kalpe*—in some lifetime of Brahmā; *yadi*—if; *yogya*—suitable; *jīva*—living entity; *nāhi*—not; *pāya*—is available; *āpane*—personally; *īśvara*—the Supreme Lord; *tabe*—then; *aṁśe*—by His plenary expansion; *brahmā haya*—becomes Lord Brahmā.

### TRANSLATION

**"If in a kalpa a suitable living entity is not available to take charge of Brahmā's post, the Supreme Personality of Godhead Himself personally expands and becomes Lord Brahmā.**

### PURPORT

One day of Brahmā consists of the four *yugas* multiplied a thousand times—or, according to solar calculations, 4,320,000,000 years—and such also is the duration of his night. One year of Brahmā's life consists of 360 days and nights, and Brahmā lives for one hundred such years. Such is the life of a Brahmā.

## TEXT 306

যস্যাঙ্ঘ্রিপঙ্কজরজোঽখিললোকপালৈ-
মৌর্ল্যুত্তমৈর্ধৃতমুপাসিত-তীর্থতীর্থম্ ।
ব্রহ্মা ভবোঽহমপি যস্য কলাঃ কলায়াঃ
শ্রীশ্চোদ্বহেম চিরমস্য নৃপাসনং ক্ব ॥ ৩০৬ ॥

*yasyāṅghri-paṅkaja-rajo 'khila-loka-pālair*
*mauly-uttamair dhṛtam upāsita-tīrtha-tīrtham*
*brahmā bhavo 'ham api yasya kalāḥ kalāyāḥ*
*śrīś codvahema ciram asya nṛpāsanaṁ kva*

### SYNONYMS

*yasya*—whose; *aṅghri-paṅkaja*—lotuslike feet; *rajaḥ*—the dust; *akhila-loka*—of the universal planetary systems; *pālaiḥ*—by the masters; *mauli-uttamaiḥ*—with valuable turbans on their heads; *dhṛtam*—accepted; *upāsita*—worshiped; *tīrtha-tīrtham*—the sanctifier of the holy places; *brahmā*—Lord Brahmā; *bhavaḥ*—Lord Śiva; *aham api*—even I; *yasya*—of whom; *kalāḥ*—portions; *kalāyāḥ*—of a plenary portion; *śrīḥ*—the goddess of fortune; *ca*—and; *udvahema*—we carry; *ciram*—eternally; *asya*—of Him; *nṛpa-āsanam*—the throne of a king; *kva*—where.

### TRANSLATION

**" 'What is the value of a throne to Lord Kṛṣṇa? The masters of the various planetary systems accept the dust of His lotus feet on their crowned heads. That dust makes the holy places sacred, and even Lord Brahmā, Lord Śiva, Lakṣmī and I myself, who are all portions of His plenary portion, eternally carry that dust on our heads.'**

### PURPORT

This is a quotation from *Śrīmad-Bhāgavatam* (10.68.37). When the Kauravas flattered Baladeva so that He would become their ally and spoke ill of Śrī Kṛṣṇa, Lord Baladeva was angry and spoke this verse.

### TEXT 307

নিজাংশ-কলায় কৃষ্ণ তমো-গুণ অঙ্গীকরি' ।
সংহারার্থে মায়া-সঙ্গে রুদ্র-রূপ ধরি ॥ ৩০৭ ॥

*nijāṁśa-kalāya kṛṣṇa tamo-guṇa aṅgīkari'*
*saṁhārārthe māyā-saṅge rudra-rūpa dhari*

### SYNONYMS

*nija-aṁśa*—of His personal plenary expansion; *kalāya*—by an expansion known as *kalā; kṛṣṇa*—Lord Kṛṣṇa; *tamaḥ-guṇa*—the material mode of darkness; *aṅgīkari'*—accepting; *saṁhāra-arthe*—for the purpose of dissolution; *māyā-saṅge*—in association with the external energy; *rudra-rūpa*—the form of Rudra; *dhari*—assumes.

### TRANSLATION

**"Lord Kṛṣṇa, the Supreme Personality of Godhead, expands a portion of His plenary portion and, accepting the association of the material mode of ignorance, assumes the form of Rudra to dissolve the cosmic manifestation.**

### PURPORT

This is a description of the Rudra form, which is another expansion of Kṛṣṇa. Only *viṣṇu-mūrtis* are expansions of Kṛṣṇa's personal and plenary portions. Mahā-Viṣṇu, who lies on the Causal Ocean, is an expansion of Saṅkarṣaṇa. When Garbhodakaśāyī Viṣṇu accepts the material modes of nature for the purpose of dissolving the cosmic manifestation, His form is called Rudra. As already explained, Lord Viṣṇu is the controller of *māyā.* How, then, can He associate with *māyā?* The conclusion is that the incarnation of Lord Śiva or Lord Brahmā indicates the absence of the supreme power of Viṣṇu. When the supreme power is not there, it is possible to associate with *māyā,* the external energy. Lord Brahmā and Lord Śiva are to be considered creations of *māyā.*

### TEXT 308

মায়াসঙ্গ-বিকারী রুদ্র—ভিন্নাভিন্ন রূপ ।
জীবতত্ত্ব নহে, নহে কৃষ্ণের 'স্বরূপ' ॥ ৩০৮ ॥

*māyā-saṅga-vikārī rudra——bhinnābhinna rūpa*
*jīva-tattva nahe, nahe kṛṣṇera 'svarūpa'*

## SYNONYMS

*māyā-saṅga*—by association with *māyā; vikārī*—transformed; *rudra*—the form of Rudra; *bhinna-abhinna rūpa*—having different types of forms; *jīva-tattva nahe*—still he is not called *jīva-tattva; nahe*—nor; *kṛṣṇera*—of Lord Kṛṣṇa; *sva-rūpa*—personal form.

## TRANSLATION

**"Rudra, Lord Śiva, has various forms, which are transformations brought about by association with māyā. Although Rudra is not on a level with the jīva-tattvas, he still cannot be considered a personal expansion of Lord Kṛṣṇa.**

## PURPORT

Rudra is simultaneously one with and different from the *viṣṇu-tattva.* Due to his association with *māyā,* he is different from the *viṣṇu-tattva,* but at the same time he is an expansion of Kṛṣṇa's personal form. This situation is called *bhedābheda-tattva,* or *acintya-bhedābheda-tattva,* simultaneously one and different.

## TEXT 309

দুগ্ধ যেন অম্লযোগে দধিরূপ ধরে ।
দুগ্ধান্তর বস্তু নহে, দুগ্ধ হৈতে নারে ॥ ৩০৯ ॥

*dugdha yena amla-yoge dadhi-rūpa dhare*
*dugdhāntara vastu nahe, dugdha haite nāre*

## SYNONYMS

*dugdha*—milk; *yena*—as; *amla-yoge*—in association with a sour substance; *dadhi-rūpa*—the form of yogurt; *dhare*—takes; *dugdha-antara*—something other than milk; *vastu*—substance; *nahe*—is not; *dugdha*—milk; *haite*—to be; *nāre*—is not able.

## TRANSLATION

**"Milk is transformed into yogurt when it associates with a yogurt culture. Thus yogurt is nothing but milk, but still it is not milk.**

## PURPORT

Of the three deities supervising the creation, maintenance and dissolution of the universe, Lord Viṣṇu is never separate from the original Viṣṇu. However, Lord Śiva and Brahmā, due to their association with *māya,* are different from Viṣṇu.

Viṣṇu cannot be transformed into any form of material energy. Whenever there is association with *māyā,* the personality involved must be different from Lord Viṣṇu. Therefore Lord Śiva and Lord Brahmā are called *guṇa-avatāras,* for they associate with the material qualities. The conclusion is that Rudra is a transformation of Viṣṇu, but he is not exactly Lord Viṣṇu. Therefore, he does not come within the category of the *viṣṇu-tattvas.* Thus he is inconceivably one with Viṣṇu and different from Him. The example given in this verse is very clear. Milk is compared to Viṣṇu. As soon as milk touches a sour substance, it becomes yogurt, or Lord Śiva. Although yogurt is constitutionally milk it cannot be used in place of milk.

### TEXT 310

ক্ষীরং যথা দধি বিকারবিশেষযোগাৎ
সংজায়তে ন তু ততঃ পৃথগস্তি হেতোঃ।
যঃ শম্ভুতামপি তথা সমুপৈতি কার্যাদ্
গোবিন্দমাদিপুরুষং তমহং ভজামি ॥ ৩১০ ॥

*kṣīraṁ yathā dadhi vikāra-viśeṣa-yogāt*
*sañjāyate na tu tataḥ pṛthag asti hetoḥ*
*yaḥ śambhutām api tathā samupaiti kāryād*
*govindam ādi-puruṣaṁ tam ahaṁ bhajāmi*

### SYNONYMS

*kṣīram*—milk; *yathā*—as; *dadhi*—yogurt; *vikāra-viśeṣa*—with a special transforming agent; *yogāt*—by mixing; *sañjāyate*—is transformed into; *na*—not; *tu*—but; *tataḥ*—from the milk; *pṛthak*—separated; *asti*—is; *hetoḥ*—which is the cause; *yaḥ*—who; *śambhutām*—the nature of Lord Śiva; *api*—even though; *tathā*—as; *samupaiti*—accepts; *kāryāt*—from the matter of some particular business; *govindam*—unto Govinda, the Supreme Personality of Godhead; *ādi-puruṣam*—the original person; *tam*—unto Him; *aham*—I; *bhajāmi*—offer my respectful obeisances.

### TRANSLATION

**" 'Milk changes into yogurt when mixed with a yogurt culture, but actually it is constitutionally nothing but milk. Similarly, Govinda, the Supreme Personality of Godhead, assumes the form of Lord Śiva [Śambhu] for the special purpose of material transactions. I offer my obeisances at His lotus feet.'**

### PURPORT

This is a quotation from *Brahma-saṁhitā* (5.45).

## TEXT 311

'শিব'—মায়াশক্তিসঙ্গী, তমোগুণাবেশ ।
মায়াতীত, গুণাতীত 'বিষ্ণু'— পরমেশ ॥ ৩১১ ॥

*'śiva'——māyā-śakti-saṅgī, tamo-guṇāveśa*
*māyātīta, guṇātīta 'viṣṇu'——parameśa*

## SYNONYMS

*śiva*—Lord Śiva; *māyā-śakti-saṅgī*—an associate of the external energy; *tamaḥ-guṇa-āveśa*—absorbed by the quality of ignorance; *māyā-atīta*—transcendental to the external energy; *guṇa-atīta*—transcendental to the qualities of matter; *viṣṇu*—Viṣṇu; *parama-īśa*—the Supreme Lord.

## TRANSLATION

**"Lord Śiva is an associate of the external energy; therefore he is absorbed in the material quality of darkness. Lord Viṣṇu is transcendental to māyā and the qualities of māyā. Therefore He is the Supreme Personality of Godhead.**

## PURPORT

Viṣṇu is beyond the range of the material manifestation, and He is not within the control of the material energy. He is the supreme independent Personality of Godhead. This is even admitted by Śaṅkarācārya: *nārāyaṇaḥ paro 'vyaktāt* (*Gīta-bhāṣya*). In his constitutional form, Śiva is a *mahā-bhāgavata,* a supreme devotee of the Lord, but because he accepts *māyā's* association—especially the quality of ignorance—he is not free from *māyā's* influence. Such an intimate association is completely absent in the Supreme Personality of Godhead, Viṣṇu. Lord Śiva accepts *māyā,* but in the presence of Lord Viṣṇu, *māyā* does not exist. Consequently Lord Śiva has to be considered a product of *māyā.* When Lord Śiva is free from *māyā's* influence, he is in the position of a *mahā-bhāgavata,* a supreme devotee of Lord Viṣṇu. *Vaiṣṇavānāṁ yathā śambhuḥ.*

## TEXT 312

শিবঃ শক্তিযুক্তঃ শশ্বৎ ত্রিলিঙ্গো গুণসংবৃতঃ ।
বৈকারিকস্তৈজসশ্চ তামসশ্চেত্যহং ত্রিধা ॥ ৩১২ ॥

*śivaḥ śakti-yuktaḥ śaśvat*
*triliṅgo guṇa-saṁvṛtaḥ*
*vaikārikas taijasaś ca*
*tāmasaś cety ahaṁ tridhā*

### SYNONYMS

*śivaḥ*—Lord Śiva; *śakti-yuktaḥ*—associated with material nature; *śaśvat*—eternally; *tri-liṅgaḥ*—in three features; *guṇa-saṁvṛtaḥ*—covered by the modes of nature; *vaikārikaḥ*—one is called *vaikārika; taijasaḥ ca*—another is called *taijasa; tāmasaḥ ca*—as well as *tāmasa; iti*—thus; *aham*—egotism; *tri-dhā*—three kinds.

### TRANSLATION

**" 'The truth about Lord Śiva is that he is always covered with three material coverings—vaikārika, taijasa and tāmasa. Because of these three modes of material nature, he always associates with the external energy and egotism itself.'**

### PURPORT

This is a quotation from *Śrīmad-Bhāgavatam* (10.88.3).

### TEXT 313

হরির্হি নির্গুণঃ সাক্ষাৎ পুরুষঃ প্রকৃতেঃ পরঃ।
স সর্বদৃগুপদ্রষ্টা তং ভজন্নির্গুণো ভবেৎ ॥ ৩১৩ ॥

*harir hi nirguṇaḥ sākṣāt*
*puruṣaḥ prakṛteḥ paraḥ*
*sa sarva-dṛg upadraṣṭā*
*taṁ bhajan nirguṇo bhavet*

### SYNONYMS

*hariḥ*—the Supreme Personality of Godhead, Viṣṇu; *hi*—certainly; *nirguṇaḥ*—transcendental to all material qualities; *sākṣāt*—directly; *puruṣaḥ*—the supreme enjoyer; *prakṛteḥ*—material nature; *paraḥ*—beyond; *saḥ*—He; *sarva-dṛk*—the seer of everything; *upadraṣṭā*—the overseer of everything; *tam*—Him; *bhajan*—by worshiping; *nirguṇaḥ*—transcendental to material qualities; *bhavet*—one becomes.

### TRANSLATION

**" 'Śrī Hari, the Supreme Personality of Godhead, is situated beyond the range of material nature; therefore He is the supreme transcendental person. He can see everything inside and outside; therefore He is the supreme overseer of all living entities. If someone takes shelter at His lotus feet and worships Him, he also attains a transcendental position.'**

### PURPORT

This is also a quotation from *Śrīmad-Bhāgavatam* (10.88.5).

### TEXT 314

পালনার্থ স্বাংশ বিষ্ণুরূপে অবতার ।
সত্ত্বগুণ দ্রষ্টা, তাতে গুণমায়া-পার ॥ ৩১৪ ॥

*pālanārtha svāṁśa viṣṇu-rūpe avatāra*
*sattva-guṇa draṣṭā, tāte guṇa-māyā-pāra*

### SYNONYMS

*pālana-artha*—for maintenance; *svāṁśa*—personal plenary expansion; *viṣṇu-rūpe*—in the form of Lord Viṣṇu; *avatāra*—incarnation; *sattva-guṇa*—of the mode of goodness; *draṣṭā*—director; *tāte*—therefore; *guṇa-māyā-pāra*—transcendental to the material modes of nature.

### TRANSLATION

**"For the maintenance of the universe, Lord Kṛṣṇa descends as His personal plenary expansion in the form of Viṣṇu. He is the director of the mode of goodness; therefore He is transcendental to the material energy.**

### TEXT 315

স্বরূপ—ঐশ্বর্যপূর্ণ, কৃষ্ণসম প্রায় ।
কৃষ্ণ অংশী, তেঁহো অংশ, বেদে হেন গায় ॥ ৩১৫ ॥

*svarūpa——aiśvarya-pūrṇa, kṛṣṇa-sama prāya*
*kṛṣṇa aṁśī, teṅho aṁśa, vede hena gāya*

### SYNONYMS

*sva-rūpa*—personal expansion; *aiśvarya-pūrṇa*—full of all opulences; *kṛṣṇa-sama*—equal to Kṛṣṇa; *prāya*—almost; *kṛṣṇa aṁśī*—Kṛṣṇa is the Supreme Personality of Godhead; *teṅho*—Lord Viṣṇu; *aṁśa*—personal expansion; *vede*—the *Vedas; hena*—thus; *gāya*—sing.

### TRANSLATION

**"Lord Viṣṇu is in the category of svāṁśa because He has opulences almost equal to Kṛṣṇa's. Kṛṣṇa is the original person, and Lord Viṣṇu is His personal expansion. This is the verdict of all Vedic literature.**

### PURPORT

Although an incarnation of the material energy, Lord Brahmā is nonetheless the director of the material mode of passion. Similarly, Lord Śiva, although simultaneously one with and different from Lord Kṛṣṇa, is still the incarnation of the mode of darkness. However, Lord Viṣṇu is Kṛṣṇa's personal expansion; therefore He is the director of the mode of goodness and is always transcendentally situated beyond the jurisdiction of the modes of material nature. Lord Viṣṇu is the original personal expansion of Kṛṣṇa, and Kṛṣṇa is the original source of all incarnations. As far as power is concerned, Lord Viṣṇu is as powerful as Lord Kṛṣṇa because He possesses all the opulences.

## TEXT 316

দীপার্চিরেব হি দশান্তরমভ্যুপেত্য
দীপায়তে বিবৃতহেতুসমানধর্মা ।
যস্তাদৃগেব হি চ বিষ্ণুতয়া বিভাতি
গোবিন্দমাদিপুরুষং তমহং ভজামি ॥ ৩১৬ ॥

*dīpārcir eva hi daśāntaram abhyupetya*
*dīpāyate vivṛta-hetu-samāna-dharmā*
*yas tādṛg eva hi ca viṣṇutayā vibhāti*
*govindam ādi-puruṣaṁ tam ahaṁ bhajāmi*

## SYNONYMS

*dīpa-arciḥ*—the flame of a lamp; *eva*—as; *hi*—certainly; *daśā-antaram*—another lamp; *abhyupetya*—expanding; *dīpāyate*—illuminates; *vivṛta-hetu*—with its expanded cause; *samāna-dharmā*—equally powerful; *yaḥ*—who; *tādṛk*—similarly; *eva*—certainly; *hi*—certainly; *ca*—also; *viṣṇutayā*—by His expansion as Lord Viṣṇu; *vibhāti*—illuminates; *govindam*—to Lord Kṛṣṇa; *ādi-puruṣam*—the supreme original person; *tam*—to Him; *aham*—I; *bhajāmi*—offer my worshipful respect.

## TRANSLATION

**" 'When the flame of one candle is expanded to another candle and placed in a different position, it burns separately, and its illumination is as powerful as the original candle. Similarly, the Supreme Personality of Godhead, Govinda, expands Himself in different forms as Viṣṇu, who is equally luminous, powerful and opulent. Let me worship that Supreme Personality of Godhead, Govinda.'**

## PURPORT

This is a quotation from *Brahma-saṁhitā* (5.46).

## TEXT 317

ব্রহ্মা, শিব—আজ্ঞাকারী ভক্ত-অবতার।
পালনার্থে বিষ্ণু—কৃষ্ণের স্বরূপ-আকার ॥ ৩১৭ ॥

*brahmā, śiva——ājñā-kārī bhakta-avatāra*
*pālanārthe viṣṇu——kṛṣṇera svarūpa-ākāra*

### SYNONYMS

*brahmā*—Lord Brahmā; *śiva*—Lord Śiva; *ājñā-kārī*—order carriers; *bhakta-avatāra*—incarnations of devotees; *pālana-arthe*—for maintenance; *viṣṇu*—Lord Viṣṇu; *kṛṣṇera*—of Lord Kṛṣṇa; *svarūpa-ākāra*—in the form of a personal feature.

### TRANSLATION

**"The conclusion is that Lord Brahmā and Lord Śiva are simply devotee incarnations who carry out orders. However, Lord Viṣṇu, the maintainer, is the personal feature of Lord Kṛṣṇa.**

## TEXT 318

সৃজামি তন্নিযুক্তোঽহং হরো হরতি তদ্বশঃ।
বিশ্বং পুরুষরূপেণ পরিপাতি ত্রিশক্তিধৃক্ ॥ ৩১৮ ॥

*sṛjāmi tan-niyukto 'haṁ*
*haro harati tad-vaśaḥ*
*viśvaṁ puruṣa-rūpeṇa*
*paripāti triśakti-dhṛk*

### SYNONYMS

*sṛjāmi*—create; *tat-niyuktaḥ*—engaged by Him; *aham*—I; *haraḥ*—Lord Śiva; *harati*—annihilates; *tat-vaśaḥ*—under His control; *viśvam*—the whole universe; *puruṣa-rūpeṇa*—in the form of Lord Viṣṇu; *paripāti*—maintains; *tri-śakti-dhṛk*—the controller of the three modes of material nature.

### TRANSLATION

**" 'Lord Brahmā said, "I am engaged by the Supreme Personality of Godhead to create. Following His orders, Lord Śiva dissolves everything. The Supreme Personality of Godhead, in His form of Kṣīrodakaśāyī Viṣṇu, maintains all the affairs of material nature. Thus the supreme controller of the three modes of material nature is Lord Viṣṇu." '**

### PURPORT

This is a quotation from *Śrīmad-Bhāgavatam* (2.6.32). Lord Brahmā gave this information to Devarṣi Nārada when he was receiving instructions from Lord Brahmā to understand the Supreme Personality of Godhead, Paramātmā. After describing the universal form of the Lord, Lord Brahmā explained that his position and Lord Śiva's position are controlled by Lord Viṣṇu.

### TEXT 319

**মন্বন্তরাবতার এবে শুন, সনাতন ।**
**অসংখ্য গণন তাঁর, শুনহ কারণ ॥ ৩১৯ ॥**

*manvantarāvatāra ebe śuna, sanātana*
*asaṅkhya gaṇana tāṅra, śunaha kāraṇa*

### SYNONYMS

*manu-antara-avatāra*—the Manu incarnations; *ebe*—now; *śuna*—hear; *sanātana*—O Sanātana Gosvāmī; *asaṅkhya*—unlimited; *gaṇana*—counting; *tāṅra*—of them; *śunaha*—just hear; *kāraṇa*—the cause.

### TRANSLATION

**"O Sanātana, just hear about the Manu incarnations [manvantara-avatāras]. They are unlimited, and no one can count them. Just hear of their source.**

### TEXT 320

**ব্রহ্মার একদিনে হয় চৌদ্দ মন্বন্তর ।**
**চৌদ্দ অবতার তাহাঁ করেন ঈশ্বর ॥ ৩২০ ॥**

*brahmāra eka-dine haya caudda manvantara*
*caudda avatāra tāhāṅ karena īśvara*

### SYNONYMS

*brahmāra eka-dine*—in one day of Brahmā; *haya*—there are; *caudda*—14; *manu-antara*—changes of Manu; *caudda*—14; *avatāra*—incarnations; *tāhāṅ*—in that time; *karena*—manifests; *īśvara*—the Supreme Personality of Godhead.

### TRANSLATION

**"In one day of Brahmā, there are fourteen changes of the Manus, and all those fourteen Manus are considered incarnations manifested by the Supreme Personality of Godhead.**

### PURPORT

In one day of Brahmā, there are 14 Manus, and all of them are considered to be *manvantara-avatāras* of the Supreme Personality of Godhead. Thus in one month of Brahmā's life, there are 420 *manvantara-avatāras,* or Manus. In one year (360 days) of Brahmā's life, there are 5,040 Manu incarnations. Thus for the one hundred years of Brahmā's life, there is a total of 504,000 *manvantara-avatāras.*

### TEXT 321

চৌদ্দ এক দিনে, মাসে চারিশত বিশ ।
ব্রহ্মার বৎসরে পঞ্চসহস্র চল্লিশ ॥ ৩২১ ॥

*caudda eka dine, māse cāri-śata biśa*
*brahmāra vatsare pañca-sahasra calliśa*

### SYNONYMS

*caudda*—14; *eka dine*—in one day; *māse*—in one month; *cāri-śata biśa*—420; *brahmāra vatsare*—in one year of Brahmā; *pañca-sahasra calliśa*—5,040 *avatāras.*

### TRANSLATION

**"There are 14 manvantara-avatāras in one day of Brahmā, 420 in one month, and 5,040 in one year.**

### TEXT 322

শতেক বৎসর হয় 'জীবন' ব্রহ্মার ।
পঞ্চলক্ষ চারিসহস্র মন্বন্তরাবতার ॥ ৩২২ ॥

*śateka vatsara haya 'jīvana' brahmāra*
*pañca-lakṣa cāri-sahasra manvantarāvatāra*

### SYNONYMS

*śateka vatsara haya*—there are one hundred years; *jīvana*—the duration of life; *brahmāra*—of Brahmā; *pañca-lakṣa*—500,000; *cāri-sahasra*—4,000; *manu-antara-avatāra*—incarnations of Manu.

### TRANSLATION

**"During the hundred years of Brahmā's life, there are 504,000 manvantara-avatarās.**

## TEXT 323

অনন্ত ব্রহ্মাণ্ডে ঐছে করহ গণন।
মহাবিষ্ণু একশ্বাসে ব্রহ্মার জীবন ॥ ৩২৩ ॥

*ananta brahmāṇḍe aiche karaha gaṇana*
*mahā-viṣṇu eka-śvāse brahmāra jīvana*

## SYNONYMS

*ananta brahmāṇḍe*—in innumerable universes; *aiche*—in that way; *karaha gaṇana*—just try to count; *mahā-viṣṇu*—Lord Mahā-Viṣṇu; *eka-śvāse*—by one exhalation; *brahmāra jīvana*—the duration of life of one Brahmā.

## TRANSLATION

**"The number of manvantara-avatāras for only one universe has been given. One can only imagine how many manvantara-avatāras exist in the innumerable universes. And all these universes and Brahmās exist only during one exhalation of Mahā-Viṣṇu.**

## TEXT 324

মহাবিষ্ণুর নিশ্বাসের নাহিক পর্যন্ত।
এক মন্বন্তরাবতারের দেখ লেখার অন্ত ॥ ৩২৪ ॥

*mahā-viṣṇura niśvāsera nāhika paryanta*
*eka manvantarāvatārera dekha lekhāra anta*

## SYNONYMS

*mahā-viṣṇura*—of Lord Mahā-Viṣṇu; *niśvāsera*—of the exhalations; *nāhika paryanta*—there is no limit; *eka manvantara-avatārera*—of only one feature of the Lord, namely the *manvantara-avatāra; dekha*—just see; *lekhāra anta*—it is beyond the power of writing.

## TRANSLATION

**"There is no limit to the exhalations of Mahā-Viṣṇu. Just see how impossible it is to speak or write of even only the manvantara-avatāra.**

## TEXT 325

স্বায়ংভুবে 'যজ্ঞ', স্বারোচিষে 'বিভু' নাম।
ঔত্তমে 'সত্যসেন', তামসে 'হরি' অভিধান ॥ ৩২৫ ॥

*svāyaṁbhuve 'yajña', svārociṣe 'vibhu' nāma*
*auttame 'satyasena', tāmase 'hari' abhidhāna*

### SYNONYMS

*svāyaṁbhuve*—in the Svāyambhuva-manvantara; *yajña*—the *avatāra* named Yajña; *svārociṣe*—in the Svārociṣa-manvantara; *vibhu*—the *avatāra* Vibhu; *nāma*—named; *auttame*—in the Auttama-manvantara; *satyasena*—the *avatāra* named Satyasena; *tāmase*—in the Tāmasa-manvantara; *hari*—Hari; *abhidhāna*—named.

### TRANSLATION

**"In the Svāyambhuva-manvantara, the avatāra was named Yajña. In the Svārociṣa-manvantara, he was named Vibhu. In the Auttama-manvantara, he was named Satyasena, and in the Tāmasa-manvantara he was named Hari.**

### TEXT 326

রৈবতে 'বৈকুণ্ঠ', চাক্ষুষে 'অজিত', বৈবস্বতে 'বামন' ।
সাবর্ণ্যে 'সার্বভৌম', দক্ষসাবর্ণ্যে 'ঋষভ' গণন ॥৩২৬॥

*raivate 'vaikuṇṭha', cākṣuṣe 'ajita', vaivasvate 'vāmana'*
*sāvarṇye 'sārvabhauma', dakṣa-sāvarṇye 'ṛṣabha' gaṇana*

### SYNONYMS

*raivate*—in the Raivata-manvantara; *vaikuṇṭha*—the *avatāra* named Vaikuṇṭha; *cākṣuṣe*—in the Cākṣuṣa-manvantara; *ajita*—the *avatāra* named Ajita; *vaivasvate*—in the Vaivasvata-manvantara; *vāmana*—the *avatara* named Vāmana; *sāvarṇye*—in the Sāvarṇya-manvantara; *sārvabhauma*—the *avatāra* named Sārvabhauma; *dakṣa-sāvarṇye*—in the Dakṣa-sāvarṇya-manvantara; *ṛṣabha*—the *avatāra* Ṛṣabha; *gaṇana*—named.

### TRANSLATION

**"In the Raivata-manvantara, the avatāra was named Vaikuṇṭha, and in the Cākṣuṣa-manvantara, he was named Ajita. In the Vaivasvata-manvantara, he was named Vāmana, and in the Sāvarṇya-manvantara, he was named Sārvabhauma. In the Dakṣa-sāvarṇya-manvantara, he was named Ṛṣabha.**

### TEXT 327

ব্রহ্মসাবর্ণ্যে 'বিষ্বক্সেন', 'ধর্মসেতু' ধর্মসাবর্ণ্যে ।
রুদ্রসাবর্ণ্যে 'সুধামা', 'যোগেশ্বর' দেবসাবর্ণ্যে ॥৩২৭॥

*brahma-sāvarṇye 'viṣvaksena', 'dharmasetu' dharma-sāvarṇye*
*rudra-sāvarṇye 'sudhāmā', 'yogeśvara' deva-sāvarṇye*

**SYNONYMS**

*brahma-sāvarṇye*—in the Brahma-sāvarṇya-manvantara; *viṣvaksena*—the *avatāra* named Viṣvaksena; *dharmasetu*—the *avatāra* named Dharmasetu; *dharma-sāvarṇye*—in the Dharma-sāvarṇya-manvantara; *rudra-sāvarṇye*—in the Rudra-sāvarṇya-manvantara; *sudhāmā*—the *avatāra* named Sudhāmā; *yogeśvara*—the *avatāra* named Yogeśvara; *deva-sāvarṇye*—in the Deva-sāvarṇya-manvantara.

**TRANSLATION**

**"In the Brahma-sāvarṇya-manvantara, the avatāra was named Viṣvaksena, and in the Dharma-sāvarṇya, he was named Dharmasetu. In the Rudra-sāvarṇya he was named Sudhāmā, and in the Deva-sāvarṇya, he was named Yogeśvara.**

**TEXT 328**

**ইন্দ্রসাবর্ণ্যে 'বৃহদ্ভানু' অভিধান ।**
**এই চৌদ্দ মন্বন্তরে চৌদ্দ 'অবতার' নাম ॥ ৩২৮ ॥**

*indra-sāvarṇye 'bṛhadbhānu' abhidhāna*
*ei caudda manvantare caudda 'avatāra' nāma*

**SYNONYMS**

*indra-sāvarṇye*—in the Indra-sāvarṇya-manvantara; *bṛhadbhānu*—the *avatāra* named Bṛhadbhānu; *abhidhāna*—named; *ei caudda manvantare*—in the fourteen *manvantaras; caudda*—fourteen; *avatāra*—of the incarnations; *nāma*—different names.

**TRANSLATION**

**"In the Indra-sāvarṇya-manvantara, the avatāra was named Bṛhadbhānu. These are the names of the fourteen avatāras in the fourteen manvantaras.**

**PURPORT**

Śrīla Bhaktisiddhānta Sarasvatī Ṭhākura, in his *Anubhāṣya,* gives a list of Manus and their fathers' names: (1) Svāyambhuva Manu, the son of Lord Brahmā; (2) Svārociṣa, the son of Svarociḥ, or Agni, the predominating deity of fire; (3) Uttama, the son of King Priyavrata; (4) Tāmasa, the brother of Uttama;

(5) Raivata, the twin brother of Tāmasa; (6) Cākṣuṣa, the son of the demigod Cakṣu; (7) Vaivasvata, the son of Vivasvān, the sun-god (whose name is also mentioned in *Bhagavad-gītā,* (4.1); (8) Sāvarṇi, a son born to the sun-god and wife named Chāyā; (9) Dakṣa-sāvarṇi, the son of the demigod Varuṇa; (10) Brahma-sāvarṇi, the son of Upaśloka; (11-14) Rudra-sāvarṇi, Dharma-sāvarṇi, Deva-sāvarṇi and Indra-sāvarṇi, the sons of Rudra, Ruci, Satyasahā and Bhūti respectively.

### TEXT 329

যুগাবতার এবে শুন, সনাতন ।
সত্য-ত্রেতা-দ্বাপর-কলি-যুগের গণন ॥ ৩২৯ ॥

*yugāvatāra ebe śuna, sanātana*
*satya-tretā-dvāpara-kali-yugera gaṇana*

### SYNONYMS

*yuga-avatāra*—incarnation of millenniums; *ebe*—now; *śuna*—hear; *sanātana*—O Sanātana Gosvāmī; *satya-tretā-dvāpara-kali-yugera*—of the Satya-yuga, Tretā-yuga, Dvāpara-yuga and Kali-yuga; *gaṇana*—the chronological order.

### TRANSLATION

**"O Sanātana, now hear from Me about the yuga-avatāras, the incarnations for the millenniums. First of all, there are four yugas—Satya-yuga, Tretā-yuga, Dvāpara-yuga and Kali-yuga.**

### TEXT 330

শুক্ল-রক্ত-কৃষ্ণ-পীত -- ক্রমে চারি বর্ণ ।
চারি বর্ণ ধরি' কৃষ্ণ করেন যুগধর্ম ॥ ৩৩০ ॥

*śukla-rakta-kṛṣṇa-pīta——krame cāri varṇa*
*cāri varṇa dhari' kṛṣṇa karena yuga-dharma*

### SYNONYMS

*śukla*—white; *rakta*—red; *kṛṣṇa*—black; *pīta*—yellow; *krame*—one after another; *cāri varṇa*—four colors; *cāri varṇa dhari'*—accepting these four colors; *kṛṣṇa*—Lord Kṛṣṇa; *karena yuga-dharma*—manifests His pastimes in different millenniums.

### TRANSLATION

**"In the four yugas—Satya, Tretā, Dvāpara and Kali—the Lord incarnates in four colors: white, red, black and yellow respectively. These are the colors of the incarnations in different millenniums.**

### TEXT 331

আসন্ বর্ণাস্ত্রয়ো হ্যস্য গৃহ্নতোঽনুযুগং তনূঃ ।
শুক্লো রক্তস্তথা পীত ইদানীং কৃষ্ণতাং গতঃ ॥ ৩৩১ ॥

*āsan varṇās trayo hy asya*
*gṛhṇato 'nuyugaṁ tanūḥ*
*śuklo raktas tathā pīta*
*idānīṁ kṛṣṇatāṁ gataḥ*

### SYNONYMS

*āsan*—there were; *varṇāḥ*—colors; *trayaḥ*—three; *hi*—certainly; *asya*—of your son; *gṛhṇataḥ*—accepting; *anuyugam*—according to the millennium; *tanūḥ*—body; *śuklaḥ*—white; *raktaḥ*—red; *tathā*—as well as; *pītaḥ*—yellow; *idānīm*—just now; *kṛṣṇatām gataḥ*—He has assumed a blackish hue.

### TRANSLATION

**" 'This child formerly had three colors according to the prescribed color for different millenniums. Formerly He was white, red and yellow, and now He has assumed a blackish color.'**

### PURPORT

This verse from *Śrīmad-Bhāgavatam* (10.8.13) was spoken by Gargamuni when performing the name-giving ceremony for Kṛṣṇa at the house of Nanda Mahārāja. The following two verses are also from *Śrīmad-Bhāgavatam* (11.5.21,24).

### TEXT 332

কৃতে শুক্লশ্চতুর্বাহুর্জটিলো বল্কলাম্বরঃ ।
কৃষ্ণাজিনোপবীতাক্ষান্ বিভ্রদ্দণ্ডকমণ্ডলূ ॥ ৩৩২ ॥

*kṛte śuklaś catur-bāhur*
*jaṭilo valkalāmbaraḥ*
*kṛṣṇājinopavītākṣān*
*bibhrad daṇḍa-kamaṇḍalū*

### SYNONYMS

*kṛte*—in the Satya-yuga; *śuklaḥ*—having a white color and bearing the name Śukla; *catuḥ-bāhuḥ*—having four arms; *jaṭilaḥ*—with a bunch of hair; *valkala-ambaraḥ*—wearing a garment made of tree bark; *kṛṣṇa-ajina*—black-colored antelope skin; *upavīta*—sacred thread; *akṣān*—a garland of beads for chanting; *bibhrat*—carried; *daṇḍa-kamaṇḍalū*—a rod and waterpot.

### TRANSLATION

**" 'In the Satya-yuga, the Lord appeared in a body colored white with four arms and matted hair. He wore tree bark and bore a black antelope skin. He wore a sacred thread and a garland of rudrākṣa beads. He carried a rod and a waterpot, and He was a brahmacārī.'**

## TEXT 333

ত্রেতায়াং রক্তবর্ণোঽসৌ চতুর্বাহুস্ত্রিমেখলঃ ।
হিরণ্যকেশস্ত্রয্যাত্মা স্রুক্স্রুবাদ্যুপলক্ষণঃ ॥ ৩৩৩ ॥

*tretāyāṁ rakta-varṇo 'sau*
*catur-bāhus trimekhalaḥ*
*hiraṇya-keśas trayy-ātmā*
*sruk-sruv-ādy-upalakṣaṇaḥ*

### SYNONYMS

*tretāyām*—in the Tretā-yuga; *rakta-varṇaḥ*—of a reddish color; *asau*—He; *catuḥ-bāhuḥ*—with four arms; *tri-mekhalaḥ*—having three circles on the abdomen; *hiraṇya-keśaḥ*—hair colored like gold; *trayī-ātmā*—whose form manifests the *Vedas; sruk-sruv-ādi-upalakṣaṇaḥ*—decorated with the sacrificial spoon, ladle and so on.

### TRANSLATION

**" 'In the Tretā-yuga, the Lord appeared in a body that had a reddish hue and four arms. There were three distinctive lines on His abdomen, and His hair was golden. His form manifested the Vedic knowledge, and He bore the symbols of a sacrificial spoon, ladle and so on.'**

## TEXT 334

**সত্যযুগে ধর্ম-ধ্যান করায় 'শুক্ল'-মূর্তি ধরি' ।**
**কর্দমকে বর দিলা যেঁহো কৃপা করি' ॥ ৩৩৪ ॥**

*satya-yuge dharma-dhyāna karāya 'śukla'-mūrti dhari'*
*kardamake vara dilā yeṅho kṛpā kari'*

### SYNONYMS

*satya-yuge*—in the millennium of Satya-yuga; *dharma-dhyāna*—religious principles and meditation; *karāya*—induces; *śukla*—whitish; *mūrti*—form; *dhari'*—accepting; *kardamake*—to Kardama Muni; *vara dilā*—gave benedictions; *yeṅho*—who; *kṛpā kari'*—out of causeless mercy.

### TRANSLATION

**"As the white incarnation, the Lord taught religion and meditation. He offered benedictions to Kardama Muni, and in this way He showed His causeless mercy.**

### PURPORT

Kardama Muni was one of the *prajāpatis*. He married Devahūti, the daughter of Manu, and their son was Kapiladeva. The Supreme Lord was very pleased with Kardama Muni's austerities, and He appeared before Kardama Muni in a whitish body. This happened in the Satya-yuga millennium, when people were accustomed to practicing meditation.

### TEXT 335

**কৃষ্ণ-'ধ্যান' করে লোক জ্ঞান-অধিকারী ।**
**ত্রেতার ধর্ম 'যজ্ঞ' করায় 'রক্ত'-বর্ণ ধরি' ॥ ৩৩৫ ॥**

*kṛṣṇa-'dhyāna' kare loka jñāna-adhikārī*
*tretāra dharma 'yajña' karāya 'rakta'-varṇa dhari'*

### SYNONYMS

*kṛṣṇa-dhyāna*—meditation upon Kṛṣṇa; *kare*—perform; *loka*—the people; *jñāna-adhikārī*—who are advanced in spiritual knowledge; *tretāra*—of the Tretā-yuga; *dharma*—the occupational duty; *yajña*—performance of sacrifices; *karāya*—induces; *rakta-varṇa dhari'*—assuming a reddish color.

### TRANSLATION

**"In the Satya-yuga the people were generally advanced in spiritual knowledge and could meditate upon Kṛṣṇa very easily. The people's occupational duty in Tretā-yuga was to perform great sacrifices. This was induced by the Personality of Godhead in His reddish incarnation.**

### TEXT 336

**'কৃষ্ণপদার্চন' হয় দ্বাপরের ধর্ম ।**
**'কৃষ্ণ'-বর্ণে করায় লোকে কৃষ্ণার্চন-কর্ম ॥ ৩৩৬ ॥**

*'kṛṣṇa-padārcana' haya dvāparera dharma*
*'kṛṣṇa'-varṇe karāya loke kṛṣṇārcana-karma*

### SYNONYMS

*kṛṣṇa-pada-arcana*—worshiping the lotus feet of Kṛṣṇa; *haya*—is; *dvāparera*—of the Dvāpara millennium; *dharma*—the occupational duty; *kṛṣṇa-varṇe*—in a blackish color; *karāya*—induces; *loke*—to the people; *kṛṣṇa-arcana-karma*—the activities of worshiping Lord Kṛṣṇa.

### TRANSLATION

**"In Dvāpara-yuga the people's occupational duty was to worship the lotus feet of Kṛṣṇa. Therefore Lord Kṛṣṇa, appearing in a blackish body, personally induced people to worship Him.**

### TEXT 337

দ্বাপরে ভগবান্ শ্যামঃ পীতবাসা নিজায়ুধঃ ।
শ্রীবৎসাদিভিরঙ্কৈশ্চ লক্ষণৈরুপলক্ষিতঃ ॥ ৩৩৭ ॥

*dvāpare bhagavān śyāmaḥ*
*pīta-vāsā nijāyudhaḥ*
*śrī-vatsādibhir aṅkaiś ca*
*lakṣaṇair upalakṣitaḥ*

### SYNONYMS

*dvāpare*—in the Dvāpara-yuga; *bhagavān*—the Supreme Personality of Godhead; *śyāmaḥ*—blackish; *pīta-vāsāḥ*—having yellow clothes; *nija*—own; *āyudhaḥ*—having weapons; *śrī-vatsa-ādibhiḥ*—such as Śrīvatsa; *aṅkaiḥ*—by bodily markings; *ca*—and; *lakṣaṇaiḥ*—by external characteristics such as the Kaustubha jewel; *upalakṣitaḥ*—characterized.

### TRANSLATION

**" 'In the Dvāpara-yuga the Personality of Godhead appears in a blackish hue. He is dressed in yellow, He holds His own weapons, and He is decorated with the Kaustubha jewel and marks of Śrīvatsa. That is how His symptoms are described.'**

## PURPORT

This is a quotation from *Śrīmad-Bhāgavatam* (11.5.27). The *śyāma* color is not exactly blackish. Śrīla Bhaktisiddhānta Sarasvatī Ṭhākura compares it to the color of the *atasī* flower. It is not that Lord Kṛṣṇa Himself appears in a blackish color in all the Dvāpara-yugas. In other Dvāpara-yugas, previous to Lord Kṛṣṇa's appearance, the Supreme Lord appeared in a greenish body by His own personal expansion. This is mentioned in the *Viṣṇu Purāṇa, Hari-vaṁśa* and *Mahābhārata.*

## TEXT 338

নমস্তে বাসুদেবায় নমঃ সঙ্কর্ষণায় চ ।
প্রদ্যুম্নায়ানিরুদ্ধায় তুভ্যং ভগবতে নমঃ ॥ ৩৩৮ ।

*namas te vāsudevāya*
*namaḥ saṅkarṣaṇāya ca*
*pradyumnāyāniruddhāya*
*tubhyaṁ bhagavate namaḥ*

## SYNONYMS

*namaḥ*—let me offer my respectful obeisances; *te*—unto You; *vāsudevāya*—Lord Vāsudeva; *namaḥ*—respectful obeisances; *saṅkarṣaṇāya ca*—also to Lord Saṅkarṣaṇa; *pradyumnāya*—to Lord Pradyumna; *aniruddhāya*—unto Aniruddha; *tubhyam*—unto You; *bhagavate*—unto the Supreme Personality of Godhead; *namaḥ*—my respectful obeisances.

## TRANSLATION

**" 'I offer my respectful obeisances unto the Supreme Personality of Godhead, expanded as Vāsudeva, Saṅkarṣaṇa, Pradyumna and Aniruddha.'**

## PURPORT

This is a prayer from *Śrīmad-Bhāgavatam* (11.5.29) spoken by Karabhājana Muni when he was questioned by Mahārāja Nimi, the King of Videha, about the incarnations in specific *yugas* and their method of worship. Karabhājana Muni was one of the nine Yogendras, and he met the King to inform him about future incarnations.

## TEXT 339

**এই মন্ত্রে দ্বাপরে করে কৃষ্ণার্চন ।**
**'কৃষ্ণনাম-সংকীর্তন'—কলিযুগের ধর্ম ॥ ৩৩৯ ॥**

*ei mantre dvāpare kare kṛṣṇārcana*
*'kṛṣṇa-nāma-saṅkīrtana'——kali-yugera dharma*

### SYNONYMS

*ei mantre*—by this *mantra; dvāpare*—in the age of Dvāpara; *kare*—perform; *kṛṣṇa-arcana*—the worship of Lord Kṛṣṇa; *kṛṣṇa-nāma-saṅkīrtana*—chanting of the holy name of Lord Kṛṣṇa; *kali-yugera dharma*—the occupational duty in the age of Kali.

### TRANSLATION

**"By this mantra, the people worship Lord Kṛṣṇa in the Dvāpara-yuga. In the Kali-yuga the occupational duty of the people is to chant congregationally the holy name of Kṛṣṇa.**

### PURPORT

As stated in *Śrīmad-Bhāgavatam* (12.3.51):

*kaler doṣa-nidhe rājann*
*asti hy eko mahān guṇaḥ*
*kīrtanād eva kṛṣṇasya*
*mukta-bandhaḥ paraṁ vrajet*

In Kali-yuga one worships Lord Kṛṣṇa by chanting Hare Kṛṣṇa, Hare Kṛṣṇa, Kṛṣṇa Kṛṣṇa, Hare Hare/ Hare Rāma, Hare Rāma, Rāma Rāma, Hare Hare. To propagate this movement, Lord Kṛṣṇa personally appeared as Lord Caitanya Mahāprabhu. That is described in the following verse.

### TEXT 340

**'পীত'-বর্ণ ধরি' তবে কৈলা প্রবর্তন।**
**প্রেমভক্তি দিলা লোকে লঞা ভক্তগণ ॥ ৩৪০ ॥**

*'pīta'-varṇa dhari' tabe kailā pravartana*
*prema-bhakti dilā loke lañā bhakta-gaṇa*

### SYNONYMS

*pīta-varṇa dhari'*—assuming the color yellow; *tabe*—thereafter; *kailā pravartana*—introduced the *saṅkīrtana* movement; *prema-bhakti dilā*—He distributed love of Kṛṣṇa; *loke*—to the people in general; *lañā bhakta-gaṇa*—accompanied by His devotees.

### TRANSLATION

**"Accompanied by His personal devotees, Lord Kṛṣṇa, assuming a golden color, introduces the hari-nāma-saṅkīrtana, the chanting of the Hare Kṛṣṇa mantra, in the age of Kali. By this process, He delivers love for Kṛṣṇa to the general populace.**

### TEXT 341

ধর্ম প্রবর্তন করে ব্রজেন্দ্রনন্দন ।
প্রেমে গায় নাচে লোক করে সঙ্কীর্তন ॥ ৩৪১ ॥

*dharma pravartana kare vrajendra-nandana*
*preme gāya nāce loka kare saṅkīrtana*

### SYNONYMS

*dharma pravartana kare*—introduces a particular type of religious activity; *vrajendra-nandana*—Kṛṣṇa Himself; *preme*—in love; *gāya*—chants; *nāce*—dances; *loka*—all people; *kare*—perform; *saṅkīrtana*—congregational chanting.

### TRANSLATION

**"Lord Kṛṣṇa, the son of Nanda Mahārāja, personally introduces the occupational duty of the age of Kali. He personally chants and dances in ecstatic love, and thus the entire world chants congregationally.**

### TEXT 342

কৃষ্ণবর্ণং ত্বিষাঽকৃষ্ণং সাঙ্গোপাঙ্গাস্ত্রপার্ষদম্ ।
যজ্ঞৈঃ সঙ্কীর্তন-প্রায়ৈর্যজন্তি হি সুমেধসঃ ॥ ৩৪২ ॥

*kṛṣṇa-varṇaṁ tviṣākṛṣṇaṁ*
*sāṅgopāṅgāstra-pārṣadam*
*yajñaiḥ saṅkīrtana-prāyair*
*yajanti hi sumedhasaḥ*

### SYNONYMS

*kṛṣṇa-varṇam*—repeating the syllables *kṛṣ-ṇa; tviṣā*—with a luster; *akṛṣṇam*—not black (golden); *sa-aṅga*—with associates; *upāṅga*—servitors; *astra*—weapons; *pārṣadam*—confidential companions; *yajñaiḥ*—by sacrifice; *saṅkīrtana-prāyaiḥ*—consisting chiefly of congregational chanting; *yajanti*—they worship; *hi*—certainly; *su-medhasaḥ*—intelligent persons.

### TRANSLATION

**" 'In the age of Kali, intelligent persons perform congregational chanting to worship the incarnation of Godhead who constantly sings the name of Kṛṣṇa. Although His complexion is not blackish, He is Kṛṣṇa Himself. He is accompanied by His associates, servants, weapons and confidential companions.'**

### PURPORT

This is a quotation from *Śrīmad-Bhāgavatam* (11.5.32). See also *Ādi-līlā,* Chapter Three, text 52.

### TEXT 343

আর তিনযুগে ধ্যানাদিতে যেই ফল হয়।
কলিযুগে কৃষ্ণনামে সেই ফল পায়॥ ৩৪৩॥

*āra tina-yuge dhyānādite yei phala haya*
*kali-yuge kṛṣṇa-nāme sei phala pāya*

### SYNONYMS

*āra tina-yuge*—in the three other *yugas; dhyāna-ādite*—by processes beginning with meditation; *yei*—whatever; *phala*—result; *haya*—there is; *kali-yuge*—in this age of Kali; *kṛṣṇa-nāme*—by chanting the Hare Kṛṣṇa *mahā-mantra; sei phala pāya*—one gets the same achievement.

### TRANSLATION

**"In the other three yugas—Satya, Tretā and Dvāpara—people perform different types of spiritual activities. Whatever results they achieve in that way, they can achieve in Kali-yuga simply by chanting the Hare Kṛṣṇa mahā-mantra.**

### TEXT 344

কলের্দোষনিধে রাজন্নস্তি হ্যেকো মহান্ গুণঃ।
কীর্তনাদেব কৃষ্ণস্য মুক্তবন্ধঃ পরং ব্রজেৎ॥ ৩৪৪॥

*kaler doṣa-nidhe rājann*
*asti hy eko mahān guṇaḥ*
*kīrtanād eva kṛṣṇasya*
*mukta-bandhaḥ paraṁ vrajet*

### SYNONYMS

*kaleḥ*—of the age of Kali; *doṣa-nidhe*—in the ocean of faults; *rājan*—O King; *asti*—there is; *hi*—certainly; *ekaḥ*—one; *mahān*—very great; *guṇaḥ*—good quality; *kīrtanāt*—by chanting; *eva*—certainly; *kṛṣṇasya*—of the holy name of Kṛṣṇa; *mukta-bandhaḥ*—liberated from material bondage; *param*—to the transcendental spiritual kingdom; *vrajet*—one can go.

### TRANSLATION

**" 'My dear King, although Kali-yuga is full of faults, there is still one good quality about this age. It is that simply by chanting the Hare Kṛṣṇa mahā-mantra, one can become free from material bondage and be promoted to the transcendental kingdom.**

### PURPORT

This is a verse from *Śrīmad-Bhāgavatam* (12.3.51).

### TEXT 345

ক্বতে যদ্ধ্যায়তো বিষ্ণুং ত্রেতায়াং যজতো মখৈঃ ।
দ্বাপরে পরিচর্যায়াং কলৌ তদ্ধরিকীর্তনাৎ ॥ ৩৪৫ ॥

*kṛte yad dhyāyato viṣṇuṁ*
*tretāyāṁ yajato makhaiḥ*
*dvāpare paricaryāyāṁ*
*kalau tad dhari-kīrtanāt*

### SYNONYMS

*kṛte*—in the Satya-yuga; *yat*—which; *dhyāyataḥ*—from meditation; *viṣṇum*—on Lord Viṣṇu; *tretāyām*—in the Tretā-yuga; *yajataḥ*—from worshiping; *makhaiḥ*—by performing sacrifices; *dvāpare*—in the age of Dvāpara; *paricaryāyām*—by worshiping the lotus feet of Kṛṣṇa; *kalau*—in the age of Kali; *tat*—that same result (can be achieved); *hari-kīrtanāt*—simply by chanting the Hare Kṛṣṇa *mahā-mantra.*

### TRANSLATION

**" 'Whatever result was obtained in Satya-yuga by meditating on Viṣṇu, in Tretā-yuga by performing sacrifices and in Dvāpara-yuga by serving the Lord's lotus feet can also be obtained in Kali-yuga simply by chanting the Hare Kṛṣṇa mahā-mantra.'**

### PURPORT

This verse is quoted from *Śrīmad-Bhāgavatam* (12.3.52). At the present moment in Kali-yuga there are many false meditators who concoct some imaginary form and try to meditate upon it. It has become fashionable to meditate, but people know nothing about the object of meditation. That is explained here. *Yad dhyāyato viṣṇum.* One has to meditate upon Lord Viṣṇu or Lord Kṛṣṇa. Without referring to the *śāstras,* so-called meditators aim at impersonal objects. Lord Kṛṣṇa has condemned them in *Bhagavad-gītā* (12.5):

*kleśo 'dhikataras teṣām*
*avyaktāsakta-cetasām*
*avyaktā hi gatir duḥkhaṁ*
*dehavadbhir avāpyate*

"For those whose minds are attached to the unmanifested, impersonal feature of the Supreme, advancement is very troublesome. To make progress in that discipline is always difficult for those who are embodied."

Not knowing how to meditate, foolish people simply suffer, and there is no benefit derived from their spiritual activities. The same reference can be found in the following verse from the *Viṣṇu Purāṇa* (6.2.17), *Padma Purāṇa* (*Uttara-khaṇḍa* 72.25) and *Bṛhan-nāradīya Purāṇa* (38.97).

## TEXT 346

ধ্যায়ন্ কৃতে যজন্ যজ্ঞৈস্ত্রেতায়াং দ্বাপরেঽর্চয়ন্ ।
যদাপ্নোতি তদাপ্নোতি কলৌ সঙ্কীর্ত্য কেশবম্ ॥ ৩৪৬ ॥

*dhyāyan kṛte yajan yajñais*
*tretāyāṁ dvāpare 'rcayan*
*yad āpnoti tad āpnoti*
*kalau saṅkīrtya keśavam*

## SYNONYMS

*dhyāyan*—meditating; *kṛte*—in the Satya-yuga; *yajan*—worshiping; *yajñaiḥ*—by the performance of great sacrifices; *tretāyām*—in the Tretā-yuga; *dvāpare*—in the Dvāpara-yuga; *arcayan*—worshiping the lotus feet; *yat*—whatever; *āpnoti*—is achieved; *tat*—that; *āpnoti*—is obtained; *kalau*—in the age of Kali; *saṅkīrtya*—simply by chanting; *keśavam*—the pastimes and qualities of Lord Keśava.

## TRANSLATION

**" 'Whatever is achieved by meditation in Satya-yuga, by the performance of yajña in Tretā-yuga or by the worship of Kṛṣṇa's lotus feet in Dvāpara-yuga is also obtained in the age of Kali simply by chanting and glorifying Lord Keśava.'**

## TEXT 347

কলিং সভাজয়ন্ত্যার্যা গুণজ্ঞাঃ সারভাগিনঃ ।
যত্র সঙ্কীর্তনেনৈব সর্বস্বার্থোঽভিলভ্যতে ॥ ৩৪৭ ॥

*kaliṁ sabhājayanty āryā*
*guṇa-jñāḥ sāra-bhāginaḥ*
*yatra saṅkīrtanenaiva*
*sarva-svārtho 'bhilabhyate*

### SYNONYMS

*kalim*—the Kali-yuga; *sabhājayanti*—worship; *āryāḥ*—advanced people; *guṇa-jñāḥ*—appreciating this good quality of Kali-yuga; *sāra-bhāginaḥ*—persons who accept the essence of life; *yatra*—in which age; *saṅkīrtanena*—simply by performing *saṅkīrtana-yajña,* the chanting of the Hare Kṛṣṇa *mantra; eva*—certainly; *sarva-sva-arthaḥ*—all interests of life; *abhilabhyate*—are achieved.

### TRANSLATION

**" 'Those who are advanced and highly qualified and are interested in the essence of life, know the good qualities of Kali-yuga. Such people worship the age of Kali because in this age, simply by chanting the Hare Kṛṣṇa mahā-mantra, one can advance in spiritual knowledge and attain life's goal.'**

### PURPORT

This is a quotation from *Śrīmad-Bhāgavatam* (11.5.36) spoken by the great sage Karabhājana Ṛṣi, one of the nine Yogendras. The sage was informing Mahārāja Nimi about the people's duty to worship the Supreme Personality of Godhead according to different processes in different *yugas.*

## TEXT 348

পূর্ববৎ লিখি যবে গুণাবতারগণ ।
অসংখ্য সংখ্যা তাঁর, না হয় গণন ॥ ৩৪৮ ॥

*pūrvavat likhi yabe guṇāvatāra-gaṇa*
*asaṅkhya saṅkhyā tāṅra, nā haya gaṇana*

### SYNONYMS

*pūrva-vat*—as previously; *likhi*—I write; *yabe*—when; *guṇa-avatāra-gaṇa*—incarnations of the material modes of nature; *asaṅkhya*—innumerable; *saṅkhyā*—counting; *tāṅra*—of them; *nā haya gaṇana*—not actually countable.

### TRANSLATION

**"As stated before when I described the incarnations of the material modes [guṇa-avatāras], one should consider that these incarnations also are unlimited and that no one can count them.**

### TEXT 349

চারিযুগাবতারে এই ত' গণন ।
শুনি' ভঙ্গি করি' তাঁরে পুছে সনাতন ॥ ৩৪৯ ॥

*cāri-yugāvatāre ei ta' gaṇana*
*śuni' bhaṅgi kari' tāṅre puche sanātana*

### SYNONYMS

*cāri-yuga-avatāre*—of the incarnations in the four different *yugas; ei ta' gaṇana*—such enumeration; *śuni'*—hearing; *bhaṅgi kari'*—giving a hint; *tāṅre*—unto Lord Śrī Caitanya Mahāprabhu; *puche*—inquired; *sanātana*—Sanātana Gosvāmī.

### TRANSLATION

**"Thus I have given a description of the incarnations of the four different yugas." After hearing all this, Sanātana Gosvāmī gave an indirect hint to the Lord.**

### TEXT 350

রাজমন্ত্রী সনাতন—বুদ্ধ্যে বৃহস্পতি ।
প্রভুর কৃপাতে পুছে অসঙ্কোচ-মতি ॥ ৩৫০ ॥

*rāja-mantrī sanātana——buddhye bṛhaspati*
*prabhura kṛpāte puche asaṅkoca-mati*

### SYNONYMS

*rāja-mantrī sanātana*—Sanātana Gosvāmī was formerly an intelligent minister for Nawab Hussain Shah; *buddhye*—in intelligence; *bṛhaspati*—exactly like Bṛhaspati, the priest in the heavenly kingdom; *prabhura kṛpāte*—because of the unlimited mercy of the Lord; *puche*—inquires; *asaṅkoca-mati*—without hesitation.

### TRANSLATION

**Sanātana Gosvāmī had been a minister under Nawab Hussain Shah, and he was undoubtedly as intelligent as Bṛhaspati, the chief priest of the heavenly**

**kingdom. Due to the Lord's unlimited mercy, Sanātana Gosvāmī questioned Him without hesitation.**

### TEXT 351

'অতি ক্ষুদ্র জীব মুঞি নীচ, নীচাচার ।
কেমনে জানিব কলিতে কোন্ অবতার ?' ৩৫১ ॥

*'ati kṣudra jīva muñi nīca, nīcācāra*
*kemane jāniba kalite kon avatāra?'*

### SYNONYMS

*ati*—very; *kṣudra*—unimportant, insignificant; *jīva*—living entity; *muñi*—I; *nīca*—low; *nīca-ācāra*—having very abominable behavior; *kemane*—how; *jāniba*—shall I know; *kalite*—in this age; *kon avatāra*—who is the incarnation.

### TRANSLATION

**Sanātana Gosvāmī said, "I am a very insignificant living entity. I am low and poorly behaved. How can I understand who is the incarnation for this age of Kali?"**

### PURPORT

This verse is very important in reference to the incarnations of God. At present there are especially many rascals prevalent in India who proclaim themselves incarnations of God or goddesses. Thus they are fooling and bluffing foolish people. On behalf of the general populace, Sanātana Gosvāmī presented himself as a foolish, lowborn, poorly behaved person, although he was a most exalted personality. Inferior people cannot accept the real God, yet they are very eager to accept an imitation God who can simply bluff foolish people. All this is going on in this age of Kali. To guide these foolish people, Śrī Caitanya Mahāprabhu answers the question as follows.

### TEXT 352

প্রভু কহে,—"অন্যাবতার শাস্ত্র-দ্বারে জানি ।
কলিতে অবতার তৈছে শাস্ত্রবাক্যে মানি ॥ ৩৫২ ॥

*prabhu kahe,—"anyāvatāra śāstra-dvāre jāni*
*kalite avatāra taiche śāstra-vākye māni*

### SYNONYMS

*prabhu kahe*—Lord Śrī Caitanya Mahāprabhu said; *anya-avatāra*—the incarnations in other *yugas; śāstra-dvāre jāni*—one has to accept by reference to the *śāstras; kalite*—in this age of Kali; *avatāra*—incarnation; *taiche*—similarly; *śāstra-vākye māni*—one has to accept according to the description of revealed scriptures.

### TRANSLATION

**Śrī Caitanya Mahāprabhu replied, "As in other ages an incarnation is accepted according to the directions of the śāstras, in this age of Kali an incarnation of God should be accepted in that way.**

### PURPORT

According to Śrī Caitanya Mahāprabhu, this is the way an incarnation should be accepted. Śrīla Narottama dāsa Ṭhākura says, *sādhu-śāstra-guru-vākya, cittete kariyā aikya.* One should accept a thing as genuine by studying the words of saintly people, the spiritual master and *śāstra.* The actual center is *śāstra,* the revealed scripture. If a spiritual master does not speak according to revealed scripture, he is not to be accepted. Similarly, if a saintly person does not speak according to the *śāstra,* he is not a saintly person. *Śāstra* is the center for all. Unfortunately, at the present moment, people do not refer to the *śāstras;* therefore they accept rascals as incarnations, and consequently they have made incarnations into a very cheap thing. Intelligent people who follow Śrī Caitanya Mahāprabhu's instructions and the instructions of the *ācārya,* the bona fide spiritual master, will not accept a pretender as an incarnation of God. In Kali-yuga, the only incarnation is Śrī Caitanya Mahāprabhu. Imitation incarnations take advantage of Śrī Caitanya Mahāprabhu. The Lord appeared within the past five hundred years, played as the son of a *brāhmaṇa* from Nadia and introduced the *saṅkīrtana* movement. Imitating Śrī Caitanya Mahāprabhu and ignoring the *śāstra,* rascals present themselves as incarnations and introduce their rascaldom as a religious process. As we have repeatedly said, religion can be given only by the Supreme Personality of Godhead. From the discussions in *Caitanya-caritāmṛta,* we can understand that in different ages the Supreme Lord introduces different systems and different religious duties. In this age of Kali, the only incarnation of Kṛṣṇa is Śrī Caitanya Mahāprabhu, and He introduced the religious duty of Kali-yuga, the chanting of the Hare Kṛṣṇa *mahā-mantra:* Hare Kṛṣṇa, Hare Kṛṣṇa, Kṛṣṇa Kṛṣṇa, Hare Hare/Hare Rāma, Hare Rāma, Rāma Rāma, Hare Hare.

### TEXT 353

**সর্বজ্ঞ মুনির বাক্য—শাস্ত্র-'পরমাণ' ।**
**আমা-সবা জীবের হয় শাস্ত্রদ্বারা 'জ্ঞান' ॥ ৩৫৩ ॥**

*sarvajña munira vākya——śāstra-'paramāṇa'*
*āmā-sabā jīvera haya śāstra-dvārā 'jñāna'*

## SYNONYMS

*sarva-jña munira vākya*—the words of the omniscient *muni* (Vyāsadeva); *śāstra-paramāṇa*—evidence of revealed scriptures; *āmā-sabā*—all of us; *jīvera*—of the conditioned souls; *haya*—there is; *śāstra-dvārā*—through the medium of revealed scriptures; *jñāna*—knowledge.

## TRANSLATION

**"The Vedic literatures composed by the omniscient Mahāmuni Vyāsadeva are evidence of all spiritual existence. Only through these revealed scriptures can all conditioned souls attain knowledge.**

## PURPORT

Foolish people try to concoct knowledge by manufacturing something in their brains. That is not the real way of knowledge. Knowledge is *śabda-pramāṇa*, evidence from Vedic literature. Śrīla Vyāsadeva is called Mahāmuni. He is also known as Vedavyāsa because he has compiled so many *śāstras*. He has divided the *Vedas* into four divisions—*Sāma, Ṛg, Yajur* and *Atharva*. He has expanded the *Vedas* into eighteen *Purāṇas* and has summarized Vedic knowledge in the *Vedānta-sūtra*. He also compiled the *Mahābhārata*, which is accepted as the fifth *Veda*. *Bhagavad-gītā* is contained within the *Mahābhārata*. Therefore *Bhagavad-gītā* is also Vedic literature (*smṛti*). Some of the Vedic literatures are called *śrutis*, and some are called *smṛtis*. Śrīla Rūpa Gosvāmī recommends in *Bhakti-rasāmṛta-sindhu* (1.2.101):

*śruti-smṛti-purāṇādi-*
*pañcarātra-vidhiṁ vinā*
*aikāntikī harer bhaktir*
*utpātāyaiva kalpate*

Unless one refers to *śāstra* (*śruti, smṛti* and *purāṇādi*), one's spiritual activity simply disturbs society. There is no king or government to check people, and therefore society has fallen into a chaotic condition as far as spiritual understanding is concerned. Taking advantage of this chaotic condition, many rascals have appeared and proclaimed themselves incarnations of God. As a result, the entire population is indulging in sinful activities such as illicit sex, intoxication, gambling and meat-eating. Out of many sinful people, many incarnations of God are emerging. This is a very regrettable situation, especially in India.

## TEXT 354

অবতার নাহি কহে—'আমি অবতার'।
মুনি সব জানি' করে লক্ষণ-বিচার ॥ ৩৫৪ ॥

*avatāra nāhi kahe——'āmi avatāra'*
*muni saba jāni' kare lakṣaṇa-vicāra*

## SYNONYMS

*avatāra*—the actual incarnation of Godhead; *nāhi*—never; *kahe*—says; *āmi avatāra*—I am an incarnation; *muni*—the great sage Mahāmuni Vyāsadeva; *saba jāni'*—knowing all (past, present and future); *kare lakṣaṇa-vicāra*—describes the symptoms of the *avatāras.*

## TRANSLATION

**"An actual incarnation of God never says, 'I am God,' or 'I am an incarnation of God.' The great sage Vyāsadeva, knowing all, has already recorded the characteristics of the avatāras in the śāstras.**

## PURPORT

In this verse it is clearly stated that a real incarnation of God never claims to be a real incarnation. According to the symptoms described in the *śāstra,* one can understand who is an *avatāra* and who is not.

## TEXT 355

যস্যাবতারা জ্ঞায়ন্তে শরীরিষ্বশরীরিণঃ।
তৈস্তৈরতুল্যাতিশয়ৈর্বীর্যৈর্দেহিষ্বসঙ্গতৈঃ ॥ ৩৫৫ ॥

*yasyāvatārā jñāyante*
*śarīriṣv aśarīriṇaḥ*
*tais tair atulyātiśayair*
*vīryair dehiṣv asaṅgataiḥ*

## SYNONYMS

*yasya*—whose; *avatārāḥ*—incarnations; *jñāyante*—can be known; *śarīriṣu*—among the living entities; *aśarīriṇaḥ*—of the Lord, who has no material body; *taiḥ taiḥ*—all those; *atulya*—incomparable; *atiśayaiḥ*—extraordinary; *vīryaiḥ*—by prowess; *dehiṣu*—among the living entities; *asaṅgataiḥ*—impossible.

### TRANSLATION

**" 'The Lord does not have a material body, yet He descends among human beings in His transcendental body as an incarnation. Therefore it is very difficult for us to understand who is an incarnation. Only by His extraordinary prowess and uncommon activities, which are impossible for embodied living entities, can one partially understand the incarnation of the Supreme Personality of Godhead.'**

### PURPORT

This is a quotation from *Śrīmad-Bhāgavatam* (10.10.34).

### TEXT 356

'স্বরূপ'-লক্ষণ, আর 'তটস্থ-লক্ষণ'।
এই দুই লক্ষণে 'বস্তু' জানে মুনিগণ ॥ ৩৫৬ ॥

*'svarūpa'-lakṣaṇa, āra 'taṭastha-lakṣaṇa'*
*ei dui lakṣaṇe 'vastu' jāne muni-gaṇa*

### SYNONYMS

*svarūpa-lakṣaṇa*—the personal characteristics; *āra*—and; *taṭastha-lakṣaṇa*—the marginal characteristics; *ei dui lakṣaṇe*—by these two symptoms; *vastu*—an object; *jāne*—know; *muni-gaṇa*—the great sages.

### TRANSLATION

**"By two symptoms—personal characteristics and marginal characteristics—the great sages can understand an object.**

### TEXT 357

আকৃতি, প্রকৃতি, স্বরূপ,—স্বরূপ-লক্ষণ।
কার্যদ্বারা জ্ঞান,—এই তটস্থ-লক্ষণ ॥ ৩৫৭ ॥

*ākṛti, prakṛti, svarūpa,——svarūpa-lakṣaṇa*
*kārya-dvārā jñāna,——ei taṭastha-lakṣaṇa*

### SYNONYMS

*ākṛti*—bodily features; *prakṛti*—nature; *svarūpa*—form; *svarūpa-lakṣaṇa*—personal symptoms; *kārya-dvārā*—by activities; *jñāna*—knowledge; *ei*—this; *taṭastha-lakṣaṇa*—the marginal symptom.

## TRANSLATION

**"Bodily features, nature and form are the personal characteristics. Knowledge of His activities provides the marginal characteristic.**

## TEXT 358

ভাগবতারম্ভে ব্যাস মঙ্গলাচরণে ।
'পরমেশ্বর' নিরূপিল এই দুই লক্ষণে ॥ ৩৫৮ ॥

*bhāgavatārambhe vyāsa maṅgalācaraṇe*
*'parameśvara' nirūpila ei dui lakṣaṇe*

## SYNONYMS

*bhāgavata-ārambhe*—in the beginning of the *Śrīmad-Bhāgavatam; vyāsa*—the great author Vyāsadeva; *maṅgala-ācaraṇe*—in the auspicious invocation; *parama-īśvara*—the Supreme Personality of Godhead; *nirūpila*—has described; *ei dui lakṣaṇe*—by these two characteristics, namely *svarūpa* (personal) and *taṭastha* (marginal) symptoms.

## TRANSLATION

**"In the auspicious invocation in the beginning of Śrīmad-Bhāgavatam, Śrīla Vyāsadeva has described the Supreme Personality of Godhead by these symptoms.**

## TEXT 359

জন্মাদ্যস্য যতোঽন্বয়াদিতরতশ্চার্থেষ্বভিজ্ঞঃ স্বরাট্
তেনে ব্রহ্ম হৃদা য আদিকবয়ে মুহ্যন্তি যৎ সূরয়ঃ ।
তেজোবারিমৃদাং যথা বিনিময়ো যত্র ত্রিসর্গোঽমৃষা
ধাম্না স্বেন সদা নিরস্তকুহকং সত্যং পরং ধীমহি ॥ ৩৫৯ ॥

*janmādy asya yato 'nvayād itarataś cārtheṣv abhijñaḥ svarāṭ*
*tene brahma hṛdā ya ādi-kavaye muhyanti yat sūrayaḥ*
*tejo-vāri-mṛdāṁ yathā vinimayo yatra tri-sargo 'mṛṣā*
*dhāmnā svena sadā nirasta-kuhakaṁ satyaṁ paraṁ dhīmahi*

## SYNONYMS

*janma-ādi*—creation, maintenance and dissolution; *asya*—of this (the universe); *yataḥ*—from whom; *anvayāt*—directly from the spiritual connection;

*itarataḥ*—indirectly from the lack of material contact; *ca*—also; *artheṣu*—in all affairs; *abhijñaḥ*—perfectly cognizant; *sva-rāṭ*—independent; *tene*—imparted; *brahma*—the Absolute Truth; *hṛdā*—through the heart; *yaḥ*—who; *ādi-kavaye*—unto Lord Brahmā; *muhyanti*—are bewildered; *yat*—in whom; *sūrayaḥ*—great personalities like Lord Brahmā and other demigods or great *brāhmaṇas; tejaḥ-vāri-mṛdām*—of fire, water and earth; *yathā*—as; *vinimayaḥ*—the exchange; *yatra*—in whom; *tri-sargaḥ*—the material creation of three modes; *amṛṣā*—factual; *dhāmnā*—with the abode; *svena*—His own personal; *sadā*—always; *nirasta-kuhakam*—devoid of all illusion; *satyam*—the truth; *param*—absolute; *dhīmahi*—let us meditate upon.

## TRANSLATION

**" 'I offer my obeisances unto Lord Śrī Kṛṣṇa, son of Vasudeva, who is the supreme all-pervading Personality of Godhead. I meditate upon Him, the transcendent reality, who is the primeval cause of all causes, from whom all manifested universes arise, in whom they dwell and by whom they are destroyed. I meditate upon that eternally effulgent Lord who is directly and indirectly conscious of all manifestations and yet is beyond them. It is He only who first imparted Vedic knowledge unto the heart of Brahmā, the first created being. Through Him this world, like a mirage, appears real even to great sages and demigods. Because of Him, the material universes, created by the three modes of nature, appear factual, although they are unreal. I meditate, therefore, upon Him, the Absolute Truth, who is eternally existent in His transcendental abode and who is forever free of illusion.'**

## PURPORT

This verse, quoted from *Śrīmad-Bhāgavatam* (1.1.1), links the *Śrīmad-Bhāgavatam* with the *Vedānta-sūtra* with the words *janmādy asya yataḥ*. It is stated that the Supreme Personality of Godhead, Vāsudeva, is the Absolute Truth beyond the material creation. This has been accepted by all *ācāryas*. Even Śaṅkarācārya, the most elevated impersonalist, says in the beginning of his commentary on *Bhagavad-gītā: nārāyaṇaḥ paro 'vyaktāt.* When this material creation is not yet manifested from the *mahat-tattva,* it is called *avyakta,* and when it is demonstrated from that total energy, it is called *vyakta*. Nārāyaṇa, the Supreme Personality of Godhead, is beyond this *vyakta-avyakta,* manifested and unmanifested material nature. This is the chief qualification of the Supreme Personality of Godhead when He assumes a particular incarnation. Kṛṣṇa tells Arjuna that they both took birth many, many times before. Kṛṣṇa remembers everything about His previous appearances, but Arjuna does not remember. Since Kṛṣṇa is beyond the cosmic creation, He is in the exalted position of being able to remember everything in the past. Everything within the cosmic creation has a material body, but Kṛṣṇa, being beyond the material cosmic creation, always has a spiritual body. He imparted Vedic knowledge into the heart of Brahmā. Although Brahmā is the most important and exalted personality within this universe, he could not remember what he did in his past life. Kṛṣṇa has to remind him through the heart. When Lord Brahmā was thus inspired, he was able to create the entire universe. Remembering everything about the past and inspiring Lord Brahmā to create are vivid examples of the characteristics called *svarūpa-lakṣaṇa* and *taṭastha-lakṣaṇa.*

### TEXT 360

**এই শ্লোকে 'পরং'-শব্দে 'কৃষ্ণ'-নিরূপণ ।**
**'সত্যং' শব্দে কহে তাঁর স্বরূপ-লক্ষণ ॥ ৩৬০ ॥**

*ei śloke 'paraṁ'-śabde 'kṛṣṇa'-nirūpaṇa*
*'satyaṁ' śabde kahe tāṅra svarūpa-lakṣaṇa*

### SYNONYMS

*ei śloke*—in this verse; *param-śabde*—by the word *param,* or supreme; *kṛṣṇa*—of Lord Kṛṣṇa; *nirūpaṇa*—there is an indication; *satyam śabde*—by the word *satyam,* or Absolute Truth; *kahe*—indicates; *tāṅra*—His; *svarūpa-lakṣaṇa*—personal characteristics.

### TRANSLATION

**"In this invocation from Śrīmad-Bhāgavatam, the word param indicates Lord Kṛṣṇa, the Supreme Personality of Godhead, and the word satyam indicates His personal characteristics.**

### TEXT 361

**বিশ্বসৃষ্ট্যাদি কৈল, বেদ ব্রহ্মাকে পড়াইল ।**
**অর্থাভিজ্ঞতা, স্বরূপশক্ত্যে মায়া দূর কৈল ॥ ৩৬১ ॥**

*viśva-sṛṣṭy-ādi kaila, veda brahmāke paḍāila*
*arthābhijñatā, svarūpa-śaktye māyā dūra kaila*

### SYNONYMS

*viśva-sṛṣṭi-ādi*—creation, maintenance and dissolution of the cosmic manifestation; *kaila*—performed; *veda*—the Vedic knowledge; *brahmāke*—unto Lord Brahmā; *paḍāila*—instructed; *artha-abhijñatā*—having full knowledge of past, present and future; *svarūpa-śaktye*—by His personal energy; *māyā*—the illusory energy; *dūra kaila*—separated.

### TRANSLATION

**"In that same verse it is stated that the Lord is the creator, maintainer and annihilator of the cosmic manifestation, and that He enabled Lord Brahmā to create the universe by infusing him with the knowledge of the Vedas. It is also stated that the Lord has full knowledge directly and indirectly, that He knows past, present and future and that His personal energy is separate from māyā, the illusory energy.**

### TEXT 362

এই সব কার্য—তাঁর তটস্থ-লক্ষণ ।
অন্য অবতার ঐছে জানে মুনিগণ ॥ ৩৬২ ॥

*ei saba kārya——tāṅra taṭastha-lakṣaṇa*
*anya avatāra aiche jāne muni-gaṇa*

### SYNONYMS

*ei saba kārya*—all these activities; *tāṅra*—His; *taṭastha-lakṣaṇa*—marginal characteristics; *anya avatāra*—another incarnation; *aiche*—in that same way; *jāne*—know; *muni-gaṇa*—the great saintly persons like Vyāsadeva.

### TRANSLATION

**"All these activities are His marginal characteristics. Great saintly persons understand the incarnations of the Supreme Personality of Godhead by the indications of the two characteristics known as svarūpa and taṭastha. All the incarnations of Kṛṣṇa should be understood in this way.**

### TEXT 363

অবতার-কালে হয় জগতে গোচর ।
এই দুই লক্ষণে কেহ জানয়ে ঈশ্বর ॥" ৩৬৩ ॥

*avatāra-kāle haya jagate gocara*
*ei dui lakṣaṇe keha jānaye īśvara"*

### SYNONYMS

*avatāra-kāle*—at the time of incarnation; *haya*—there is; *jagate*—in the world; *gocara*—information; *ei dui lakṣaṇe*—by these two characteristics, namely *svarūpa* and *taṭastha; keha*—some persons; *jānaye*—know; *īśvara*—the incarnation of the Supreme Lord.

### TRANSLATION

**"At the time of Their appearance, the incarnations of the Lord are known in the world because people can consult the śāstras to understand the incarnation's chief characteristics, known as svarūpa and taṭastha. In this way the incarnations become known to great saintly persons."**

### TEXT 364

**সনাতন কহে,—"যাতে ঈশ্বর-লক্ষণ ।**
**পীতবর্ণ, কার্য—প্রেমদান-সঙ্কীর্তন ॥ ৩৬৪ ॥**

*sanātana kahe,——"yāte īśvara-lakṣaṇa*
*pīta-varṇa, kārya——prema-dāna-saṅkīrtana*

### SYNONYMS

*sanātana kahe*—Sanātana said; *yāte*—in whom; *īśvara-lakṣaṇa*—the characteristics of the Lord are found; *pīta-varṇa*—yellowish color; *kārya*—activities; *prema-dāna*—distributing love of Godhead; *saṅkīrtana*—and chanting congregationally the holy name of the Lord.

### TRANSLATION

**Sanātana Gosvāmī, "The color of the personality in whom the characteristics of the Lord are found is yellowish. His activities include the distribution of love of Godhead and the chanting of the holy names of the Lord.**

### TEXT 365

**কলিকালে সেই 'কৃষ্ণাবতার' নিশ্চয় ।**
**সুদৃঢ় করিয়া কহ, যাউক সংশয় ॥" ৩৬৫ ॥**

*kali-kāle sei 'kṛṣṇāvatāra' niścaya*
*sudṛḍha kariyā kaha, yāuka saṁśaya"*

### SYNONYMS

*kali-kāle*—in the age of Kali; *sei*—that personality; *kṛṣṇa-avatāra*—the incarnation of Kṛṣṇa; *niścaya*—certainly; *su-dṛḍha kariyā*—firmly; *kaha*—kindly inform me; *yāuka saṁśaya*—so that all doubts may go away.

### TRANSLATION

**"The incarnation of Kṛṣṇa for this age is indicated by these symptoms. Please confirm this definitely so that all my doubts will go away."**

### PURPORT

Sanātana Gosvāmī wanted to confirm the fact that Śrī Caitanya Mahāprabhu is the incarnation of Kṛṣṇa for this age. According to *śāstra,* in Kali-yuga the Lord would assume a golden or yellow color and would distribute love of Kṛṣṇa and the *saṅkīrtana* movement. In accordance with *śāstra* and saintly persons, these characteristics were vividly displayed by Śrī Caitanya Mahāprabhu, and it was therefore clear that Śrī Caitanya Mahāprabhu was an incarnation of Kṛṣṇa. He was confirmed by the *śāstras,* and His characteristics were accepted by saintly people. Since Śrī Caitanya Mahāprabhu could not escape Sanātana Gosvāmī's argument, He remained silent on this point and thereby indirectly accepted Sanātana's statement. By this we can clearly understand that Śrī Caitanya Mahāprabhu was the direct incarnation of Lord Kṛṣṇa.

### TEXT 366

প্রভু কহে,—চতুরালি ছাড়, সনাতন।
শক্ত্যাবেশাবতারের শুন বিবরণ ॥ ৩৬৬ ॥

*prabhu kahe,——caturāli chāḍa, sanātana*
*śaktyāveśāvatārera śuna vivaraṇa*

### SYNONYMS

*prabhu kahe*—Śrī Caitanya Mahāprabhu replied; *caturāli*—very intelligent argument; *chāḍa*—give up; *sanātana*—O Sanātana; *śakti-āveśa-avatārera*—of the especially empowered incarnations; *śuna*—hear; *vivaraṇa*—the description.

### TRANSLATION

**Śrī Caitanya Mahāprabhu replied, "O Sanātana, you must give up your intelligent tricks. Just try to understand the meaning of the śaktyāveśa-avatāra.**

### TEXT 367

শক্ত্যাবেশাবতার কৃষ্ণের অসংখ্য গণন।
দিগ্‌দরশন করি মুখ্য মুখ্য জন ॥ ৩৬৭ ॥

*śaktyāveśāvatāra kṛṣṇera asaṅkhya gaṇana*
*dig-daraśana kari mukhya mukhya jana*

### SYNONYMS

*śakti-āveśa-avatāra*—incarnations especially empowered by the Lord; *kṛṣṇera*—of Lord Kṛṣṇa; *asaṅkhya gaṇana*—unlimited and innumerable; *dik-*

*daraśana kari*—let Me describe some of them; *mukhya mukhya jana*—who are counted as the chief.

### TRANSLATION

**"There are unlimited śaktyāveśa-avatāras of Lord Kṛṣṇa. Let Me describe the chief among them.**

### TEXT 368

শক্ত্যাবেশ দুইরূপ—'মুখ্য', 'গৌণ' দেখি।
সাক্ষাৎশক্ত্যে 'অবতার',আভাসে 'বিভূতি' লিখি॥৩৬৮

*śaktyāveśa dui-rūpa——'mukhya', 'gauṇa' dekhi*
*sākṣāt-śaktye 'avatāra', ābhāse 'vibhūti' likhi*

### SYNONYMS

*śakti-āveśa*—empowered incarnations; *dui-rūpa*—two categories; *mukhya*—primary; *gauṇa*—secondary; *dekhi*—I see; *sākṣāt-śaktye*—when there is direct power; *avatāra*—they are called incarnations; *ābhāse*—when there is indication; *vibhūti likhi*—they are called *vibhūti,* or possessing special favor.

### TRANSLATION

**"Empowered incarnations are of two types—primary and secondary. The primary one is directly empowered by the Supreme Personality of Godhead and is called an incarnation. The secondary one is indirectly empowered by the Supreme Personality of Godhead and is called vibhūti.**

### TEXT 369

'সনকাদি', 'নারদ', 'পৃথু', 'পরশুরাম'।
জীবরূপ 'ব্রহ্মার' আবেশাবতার-নাম ॥ ৩৬৯ ॥

*'sanakādi', 'nārada', 'pṛthu', 'paraśurāma'*
*jīva-rūpa 'brahmāra' āveśāvatāra-nāma*

### SYNONYMS

*sanaka-ādi*—the four Kumāras; *nārada*—Nārada; *pṛthu*—Mahārāja Pṛthu; *paraśurāma*—Paraśurāma; *jīva-rūpa*—as the living entity; *brahmāra*—of Lord Brahmā; *āveśa-avatāra-nāma*—all of them are called empowered incarnations.

### TRANSLATION

**"Some śaktyāveśa-avatāras are the four Kumāras, Nārada, Mahārāja Pṛthu and Paraśurāma. When a living being is empowered to act as Lord Brahmā, he is also considered a śaktyāveśa-avatāra.**

### TEXT 370

বৈকুণ্ঠে 'শেষ'—ধরা ধরয়ে 'অনন্ত'।
এই মুখ্যাবেশাবতার—বিস্তারে নাহি অন্ত ॥ ৩৭০ ॥

*vaikuṇṭhe 'śeṣa'—dharā dharaye 'ananta'*
*ei mukhyāveśāvatāra—vistāre nāhi anta*

### SYNONYMS

*vaikuṇṭhe*—in the spiritual world; *śeṣa*—Lord Śeṣa; *dharā dharaye*—carries innumerable planets; *ananta*—Ananta; *ei*—these; *mukhya-āveśa-avatāra*—primary directly empowered incarnations; *vistāre*—in expanding them; *nāhi*—there is not; *anta*—limit.

### TRANSLATION

**"Lord Śeṣa in the spiritual world of Vaikuṇṭha and, in the material world, Lord Ananta, who carries innumerable planets on His hood, are two primary empowered incarnations. There is no need to count the others, for they are unlimited.**

### TEXT 371

সনকাদ্যে 'জ্ঞান'-শক্তি, নারদে শক্তি 'ভক্তি'।
ব্রহ্মায় 'সৃষ্টি'-শক্তি, অনন্তে 'ভূ-ধারণ'-শক্তি ॥ ৩৭১ ॥

*sanakādye 'jñāna'-śakti, nārade śakti 'bhakti'*
*brahmāya 'sṛṣṭi'-śakti, anante 'bhū-dhāraṇa'-śakti*

### SYNONYMS

*sanaka-ādye*—in the four Kumāras; *jñāna-śakti*—the power of knowledge; *nārade*—in Nārada Muni; *śakti*—the power; *bhakti*—of devotional service; *brahmāya*—in Lord Brahmā; *sṛṣṭi-śakti*—the power of creation; *anante*—in Lord Ananta; *bhū-dhāraṇa-śakti*—the power to carry the planets.

### TRANSLATION

**"The power of knowledge was invested in the four Kumāras, and the power of devotional service was invested in Nārada. The power of creation was in-**

**vested in Lord Brahmā, and the power to carry innumerable planets was invested in Lord Ananta.**

### TEXT 372

শেষে 'স্ব-সেবন'-শক্তি, পৃথুতে 'পালন'।
পরশুরামে 'দুষ্টনাশক-বীর্যসঞ্চারণ' ॥ ৩৭২ ॥

*śeṣe 'sva-sevana'-śakti, pṛthute 'pālana'*
*paraśurāme 'duṣṭa-nāśaka-vīrya-sañcāraṇa'*

### SYNONYMS

*śeṣe*—in Lord Śeṣa; *sva-sevana śakti*—the power to serve the Lord personally; *pṛthute*—in King Pṛthu; *pālana*—the power to rule; *paraśurāme*—in Paraśurāma; *duṣṭa-nāśaka-vīrya*—the extraordinary power to kill rogues and miscreants; *sañcāraṇa*—empowering.

### TRANSLATION

**"The Supreme Personality of Godhead invested the power of personal service to Lord Śeṣa, and He invested the power to rule the earth in King Pṛthu. Lord Paraśurāma received the power to kill rogues and miscreants.**

### PURPORT

Kṛṣṇa says in *Bhagavad-gītā* (Bg. 4.8): *paritrāṇāya sādhūnāṁ vināśāya ca duṣkṛtām.* Sometimes the Lord invests His power to rule in a king like Pṛthu and enables such a king to kill rogues and miscreants. He also invests His power in incarnations like Paraśurāma.

### TEXT 373

জ্ঞানশক্ত্যাদিকলয়া যত্রাবিষ্টো জনার্দনঃ।
ত আবেশা নিগদ্যন্তে জীবা এব মহত্তমাঃ ॥ ৩৭৩ ॥

*jñāna-śakty-ādi-kalayā*
*yatrāviṣṭo janārdanaḥ*
*ta āveśā nigadyante*
*jīvā eva mahattamāḥ*

### SYNONYMS

*jñāna-śakti-ādi-kalayā*—by portions of the potencies of knowledge, devotional service, creation, personal service, ruling over the material world, carrying the different planets, and killing the rogues and miscreants; *yatra*—wherever; *āviṣṭaḥ*—is entered; *janārdanaḥ*—the Supreme Personality of Godhead, Viṣṇu; *te*—they; *āveśāḥ*—empowered; *nigadyante*—are called; *jīvāḥ*—living entities; *eva*—although; *mahat-tamāḥ*—most exalted devotees.

### TRANSLATION

**"'Whenever the Lord is present in someone by portions of His various potencies, the living entity representing the Lord is called śaktyāveśa-avatāra—that is, an incarnation invested with special power.'**

### PURPORT

This verse is found in the *Laghu-bhāgavatāmṛta* (1.18).

### TEXT 374

**'বিভূতি' কহিয়ে যৈছে গীতা-একাদশে ।**
**জগৎ ব্যাপিল কৃষ্ণশক্ত্যাভাসাবেশে ॥ ৩৭৪ ॥**

*'vibhūti' kahiye yaiche gītā-ekādaśe*
*jagat vyāpila kṛṣṇa-śakty-ābhāsāveśe*

### SYNONYMS

*vibhūti*—specific power; *kahiye*—we say; *yaiche*—just like; *gītā*—of *Bhagavad-gītā; ekādaśe*—in the Eleventh Chapter; *jagat*—throughout the whole universe; *vyāpila*—He expanded; *kṛṣṇa-śakti-ābhāsa-āveśe*—by the reflection of His power.

### TRANSLATION

**"As explained in the Eleventh Chapter of Bhagavad-gītā, Kṛṣṇa has spread Himself all over the universe in many personalities through specific powers, known as vibhūti.**

### PURPORT

The expansion of specific *māyā* powers is explained in *Śrīmad-Bhāgavatam* (2.7.39).

### TEXT 375

যদ্‌যদ্‌বিভূতিমৎ সত্ত্বং শ্রীমদূর্জিতমেব বা ।
তত্তদেবাবগচ্ছ ত্বং মম তেজোঽংশসম্ভবম্ ॥ ৩৭৫ ॥

*yad yad vibhūtimat sattvaṁ*
*śrīmad ūrjitam eva vā*
*tat tad evāvagaccha tvaṁ*
*mama tejo 'ṁśa-sambhavam*

### SYNONYMS

*yat yat*—whatever and wherever; *vibhūtimat*—extraordinarily opulent; *sattvam*—living entity; *śrīmat*—full of wealth; *ūrjitam*—full of power; *eva*—certainly; *vā*—or; *tat tat*—there; *eva*—certainly; *avagaccha*—should know; *tvam*—you; *mama*—of Me; *tejaḥ*—of power; *aṁśa*—of a part; *sambhavam*—exhibition.

### TRANSLATION

**" 'Know that all beautiful, glorious and mighty creations spring but from a spark of My splendor.**

### PURPORT

This is a statement made by Kṛṣṇa in *Bhagavad-gītā* (10.41).

## TEXT 376

অথবা বহুনৈতেন কিং জ্ঞাতেন তবার্জুন।
বিষ্টভ্যাহমিদং কৃৎস্নমেকাংশেন স্থিতো জগৎ ॥ ৩৭৬ ॥

*athavā bahunaitena*
*kiṁ jñātena tavārjuna*
*viṣṭabhyāham idaṁ kṛtsnam*
*ekāṁśena sthito jagat*

### SYNONYMS

*athavā*—or; *bahunā*—much; *etena*—with this; *kim*—what use; *jñātena*—being known; *tava*—by you; *arjuna*—O Arjuna; *viṣṭabhya*—pervading; *aham*—I; *idam*—this; *kṛtsnam*—entire; *eka-aṁśena*—with one portion; *sthitaḥ*—situated; *jagat*—universe.

### TRANSLATION

**" 'But what need is there, Arjuna, for all this detailed knowledge? With a single fragment of Myself I pervade and support this entire universe.'**

### PURPORT

This is also a statement made by Kṛṣṇa in *Bhagavad-gītā* (10.42).

### TEXT 377

এইত কহিলুঁ শক্ত্যাবেশ-অবতার ।
বাল্য-পৌগণ্ড-ধর্মের শুনহ বিচার ॥ ৩৭৭ ॥

*eita kahiluṅ śakty-āveśa-avatāra*
*bālya-paugaṇḍa-dharmera śunaha vicāra*

### SYNONYMS

*eita*—thus; *kahiluṅ*—I have explained; *śakti-āveśa-avatāra*—the incarnations specifically empowered; *bālya*—in childhood; *paugaṇḍa*—in boyhood; *dharmera*—of the characteristics; *śunaha*—now hear; *vicāra*—the consideration.

### TRANSLATION

**"Thus I have explained specifically empowered incarnations. Now please hear about the characteristics of Lord Kṛṣṇa's childhood, boyhood and youth.**

### TEXT 378

কিশোরশেখর-ধর্মী ব্রজেন্দ্রনন্দন ।
প্রকটলীলা করিবারে যবে করে মন ॥ ৩৭৮ ॥

*kiśora-śekhara-dharmī vrajendra-nandana*
*prakaṭa-līlā karibāre yabe kare mana*

### SYNONYMS

*kiśora-śekhara*—topmost of youth; *dharmī*—whose natural position; *vrajendra-nandana*—the son of Mahārāja Nanda; *prakaṭa-līlā*—manifested pastimes; *karibāre*—to perform; *yabe*—when; *kare*—makes; *mana*—mind.

### TRANSLATION

**"As the son of Mahārāja Nanda, Lord Kṛṣṇa is by nature the paragon of kiśora [youth]. He chooses to exhibit His pastimes at that age.**

### TEXT 379

আদৌ প্রকট করায় মাতা-পিতা-ভক্তগণে ।
পাছে প্রকট হয় জন্মাদিক-লীলাক্রমে ॥ ৩৭৯ ॥

*ādau prakaṭa karāya mātā-pitā-bhakta-gaṇe*
*pāche prakaṭa haya janmādika-līlā-krame*

### SYNONYMS

*ādau*—first; *prakaṭa*—manifest; *karāya*—He makes; *mātā-pitā*—His mother and father; *bhakta-gaṇe*—similar devotees; *pāche*—after that; *prakaṭa haya*—becomes manifest; *janma-ādika-līlā-krame*—such pastimes as birth, in order.

### TRANSLATION

**"Before His personal appearance, the Lord causes some of His devotees to appear as His mother, father and intimate associates. He then appears later as if He were taking birth and growing from a baby to a child and gradually into a youth.**

### TEXT 380

বয়সো বিবিধত্বেঽপি সর্বভক্তিরসাশ্রয়ঃ ।
ধর্মী কিশোর এবাত্র নিত্যলীলা-বিলাসবান্ ॥ ৩৮০ ॥

*vayaso vividhatve 'pi*
*sarva-bhakti-rasāśrayaḥ*
*dharmī kiśora evātra*
*nitya-līlā-vilāsavān*

### SYNONYMS

*vayasaḥ*—of age; *vividhatve*—in varieties; *api*—although; *sarva*—of all kinds; *bhakti-rasa-āśrayaḥ*—the shelter of devotional service; *dharmī*—whose constitutional nature; *kiśoraḥ*—in the age before youth; *eva*—certainly; *atra*—in this; *nitya-līlā*—of eternal pastimes; *vilāsavān*—the supreme enjoyer.

### TRANSLATION

**" 'The Supreme Personality of Godhead is eternally enjoying Himself, and He is the shelter of all kinds of devotional service. Although His ages are various, His age known as kiśora [pre-youth] is best of all.'**

### PURPORT

This verse is found in *Bhakti-rasāmṛta-sindhu* (2.1.63).

### TEXT 381

পূতনা-বধাদি যত লীলা ক্ষণে ক্ষণে ।
সব লীলা নিত্য প্রকট করে অনুক্রমে ॥ ৩৮১ ॥

*pūtanā-vadhādi yata līlā kṣaṇe kṣaṇe*
*saba līlā nitya prakaṭa kare anukrame*

### SYNONYMS

*pūtanā-vadha-ādi*—killing of the demons like Pūtanā; *yata*—all; *līlā*—pastimes; *kṣaṇe kṣaṇe*—one moment after another; *saba līlā*—all these pastimes; *nitya*—eternally; *prakaṭa*—manifesting; *kare*—does; *anukrame*—one after another.

### TRANSLATION

**"When Lord Kṛṣṇa appears, from moment to moment He exhibits His different pastimes, beginning with the killing of Pūtanā. All these pastimes are eternally being demonstrated one after another.**

### TEXT 382

অনন্ত ব্রহ্মাণ্ড, তার নাহিক গণন ।
কোন লীলা কোন ব্রহ্মাণ্ডে হয় প্রকটন ॥ ৩৮২ ॥

*ananta brahmāṇḍa, tāra nāhika gaṇana*
*kona līlā kona brahmāṇḍe haya prakaṭana*

### SYNONYMS

*ananta brahmāṇḍa*—innumerable universes; *tāra*—of which; *nāhika gaṇana*—there is no counting; *kona līlā*—some pastimes; *kona brahmāṇḍe*—in some universe; *haya*—there is; *prakaṭana*—manifestation.

### TRANSLATION

**"The consecutive pastimes of Kṛṣṇa are manifest in one of the innumerable universes moment after moment. There is no possibility of counting the universes, but in any case some pastime of the Lord is being manifest at every moment in one universe or another.**

### TEXT 383

এইমত সব লীলা—যেন গঙ্গাধার ।
সে-সে লীলা প্রকট করে ব্রজেন্দ্রকুমার ॥ ৩৮৩ ॥

*ei-mata saba līlā——yena gaṅgā-dhāra*
*se-se līlā prakaṭa kare vrajendra-kumāra*

### SYNONYMS

*ei-mata*—in this way; *saba līlā*—all pastimes; *yena*—like; *gaṅgā-dhāra*—the flowing of the water of the Ganges; *se-se*—those; *līlā*—pastimes; *prakaṭa kare*—demonstrates; *vrajendra-kumāra*—the son of Mahārāja Nanda.

### TRANSLATION

**"Thus the Lord's pastimes are like flowing Ganges water. In this way all the pastimes are manifested by the son of Nanda Mahārāja.**

### TEXT 384

ক্রমে বাল্য-পৌগণ্ড-কৈশোরতা-প্রাপ্তি ।
রাস-আদি লীলা করে, কৈশোরে নিত্যস্থিতি ॥৩৮৪॥

*krame bālya-paugaṇḍa-kaiśoratā-prāpti*
*rāsa-ādi līlā kare, kaiśore nitya-sthiti*

### SYNONYMS

*krame*—gradually; *bālya*—childhood; *paugaṇḍa*—boyhood; *kaiśoratā*—youth; *prāpti*—development; *rāsa*—dancing with the *gopīs; ādi*—and others; *līlā*—pastimes; *kare*—performs; *kaiśore*—in His age of pre-youth; *nitya-sthiti*—eternally existing.

### TRANSLATION

**"Lord Kṛṣṇa exhibits His pastimes of childhood, boyhood and pre-youth. When He reaches pre-youth, He continues to exist eternally to perform His rāsa dance and other pastimes.**

### PURPORT

The comparison made here is very interesting. Kṛṣṇa does not grow like an ordinary human being, even though He exhibits His pastimes of childhood, boyhood and pre-youth. When He reaches the age of pre-youth, *kaiśora,* He does not grow any older. He simply remains in His *kaiśora* age. He is therefore described in *Brahma-saṁhitā* (5.33) as *nava-yauvana.*

*advaitam acyutam anādim ananta-rūpam*
*ādyaṁ purāṇa-puruṣaṁ nava-yauvanaṁ ca*
*vedeṣu durlabham adurlabham ātma-bhaktau*
*govindam ādi-puruṣaṁ tam ahaṁ bhajāmi*

This *nava-yauvana,* or pre-youth, is the eternal transcendental form of Kṛṣṇa. Kṛṣṇa never grows older than *nava-yauvana.*

### TEXT 385

'নিত্যলীলা' কৃষ্ণের সর্বশাস্ত্রে কয়।
বুঝিতে না পারে লীলা কেমনে 'নিত্য' হয়॥ ৩৮৫॥

*'nitya-līlā' kṛṣṇera sarva-śāstre kaya*
*bujhite nā pāre līlā kemane 'nitya' haya*

### SYNONYMS

*nitya-līlā*—eternal pastimes; *kṛṣṇera*—of Lord Kṛṣṇa; *sarva-śāstre kaya*—described in every *śāstra; bujhite nā pāre*—not able to understand; *līlā*—pastimes; *kemane*—how; *nitya haya*—are eternal.

### TRANSLATION

**"Descriptions of Kṛṣṇa's eternal pastimes are in all revealed scriptures. But one cannot understand how they are continuing eternally.**

### TEXT 386

দৃষ্টান্ত দিয়া কহি তবে লোক যদি জানে।
কৃষ্ণলীলা—নিত্য, জ্যোতিশ্চক্র-প্রমাণে॥ ৩৮৬॥

*dṛṣṭānta diyā kahi tabe loka yadi jāne*
*kṛṣṇa-līlā—nitya, jyotiścakra-pramāṇe*

### SYNONYMS

*dṛṣṭānta diyā*—giving an example; *kahi*—let Me say; *tabe*—then; *loka*—people; *yadi*—if; *jāne*—can understand; *kṛṣṇa-līlā*—pastimes of Lord Kṛṣṇa; *nitya*—eternal; *jyotiḥ-cakra*—of the zodiac; *pramāṇe*—by evidence.

### TRANSLATION

**"Let me give an example by which people may understand Lord Kṛṣṇa's eternal pastimes. An example can be found in the zodiac.**

### TEXT 387

জ্যোতিশ্চক্রে সূর্য যেন ফিরে রাত্রি-দিনে।
সপ্তদ্বীপাম্বুধি লঙ্ঘি' ফিরে ক্রমে ক্রমে॥ ৩৮৭॥

*jyotiścakre sūrya yena phire rātri-dine*
*sapta-dvīpāmbudhi laṅghi' phire krame krame*

### SYNONYMS

*jyotiḥ-cakre*—in the zodiac; *sūrya*—of the sun; *yena*—as; *phire*—moves; *rātri-dine*—the day and night; *sapta-dvīpa-ambudhi*—the oceans of the islands; *laṅghi'*—crossing; *phire*—rotates; *krame krame*—one after another.

### TRANSLATION

**"The sun moves across the zodiac day and night and crosses the oceans between the seven islands one after the other.**

### TEXT 388

রাত্রি-দিনে হয় ষষ্টিদণ্ড-পরিমাণ ।
তিনসহস্র ছয়শত 'পল' তার মান ॥ ৩৮৮ ॥

*rātri-dine haya ṣaṣṭi-daṇḍa-parimāṇa*
*tina-sahasra chaya-śata 'pala' tāra māna*

### SYNONYMS

*rātri-dine*—during the whole day and night; *haya*—there is; *ṣaṣṭi-daṇḍa*—of sixty *daṇḍas* (a measure of time); *parimāṇa*—duration; *tina-sahasra*—three thousand; *chaya-śata*—six hundred; *pala*—*palas; tāra*—of that; *māna*—measurement.

### TRANSLATION

**"According to Vedic astronomical calculations, the rotation of the sun consists of sixty daṇḍas, and it is divided into thirty-six hundred palas.**

### TEXT 389

সূর্যোদয় হৈতে ষষ্টিপল-ক্রমোদয় ।
সেই এক দণ্ড, অষ্ট দণ্ডে 'প্রহর' হয় ॥ ৩৮৯ ॥

*sūryodaya haite ṣaṣṭi-pala-kramodaya*
*sei eka daṇḍa, aṣṭa daṇḍe 'prahara' haya*

### SYNONYMS

*sūrya-udaya haite*—beginning from the sunrise; *ṣaṣṭi-pala*—sixty *palas; krama-udaya*—gradually rising higher and higher; *sei*—that; *eka daṇḍa*—one *daṇḍa; aṣṭa daṇḍe*—in eight *daṇḍas; prahara haya*—there is a *prahara.*

### TRANSLATION

**"The sun rises in steps consisting of sixty palas. Sixty palas equal one daṇḍa, and eight daṇḍas comprise one prahara.**

### TEXT 390

এক-দুই-তিন-চারি প্রহরে অস্ত হয়।
চারিপ্রহর রাত্রি গেলে পুনঃ সূর্যোদয় ॥ ৩৯০ ॥

*eka-dui-tina-cāri prahare asta haya*
*cāri-prahara rātri gele punaḥ sūryodaya*

### SYNONYMS

*eka-dui-tina-cāri*—one, two, three, four; *prahare*—in *praharas; asta haya*—the sun sets in the evening; *cāri-prahara*—generally after four *praharas; rātri*—the night; *gele*—when it passes; *punaḥ*—again; *sūryodaya*—the sun rises.

### TRANSLATION

**"Day and night are divided into eight praharas—four belonging to the day and four belonging to the night. After eight praharas, the sun rises again.**

### TEXT 391

ঐছে কৃষ্ণের লীলা-মণ্ডল চৌদ্দমন্বন্তরে।
ব্রহ্মাণ্ডমণ্ডল ব্যাপি' ক্রমে ক্রমে ফিরে ॥ ৩৯১ ॥

*aiche kṛṣṇera līlā-maṇḍala caudda-manvantare*
*brahmāṇḍa-maṇḍala vyāpi' krame krame phire*

### SYNONYMS

*aiche*—in the same way; *kṛṣṇera*—of Lord Kṛṣṇa; *līlā-maṇḍala*—groups of different pastimes; *caudda-manvantare*—in the duration of fourteen Manus; *brahmāṇḍa-maṇḍala*—all of the universes; *vyāpi'*—spreading through; *krame krame*—gradually; *phire*—return.

### TRANSLATION

**"Just like the sun, there is an orbit to Kṛṣṇa's pastimes, which are manifest one after the other. During the lifetime of fourteen Manus, this orbit expands through all the universes, and gradually it returns. Thus Kṛṣṇa moves with His pastimes through all the universes, one after another.**

### TEXT 392

**সওয়াশত বৎসর কৃষ্ণের প্রকট-প্রকাশ।
তাহা যৈছে ব্রজ-পুরে করিলা বিলাস॥ ৩৯২॥**

*saoyāśata vatsara kṛṣṇera prakaṭa-prakāśa*
*tāhā yaiche vraja-pure karilā vilāsa*

### SYNONYMS

*saoyāśata*—125; *vatsara*—years; *kṛṣṇera*—of Lord Kṛṣṇa; *prakaṭa-prakāśa*—manifestation of the appearance; *tāhā*—that; *yaiche*—like; *vraja-pure*—in Vṛndāvana and Dvārakā; *karilā vilāsa*—enjoys the pastimes.

### TRANSLATION

**"Kṛṣṇa remains within a universe for 125 years, and He enjoys His pastimes both in Vṛndāvana and Dvārakā.**

### TEXT 393

**অলাতচক্রপ্রায় সেই লীলাচক্র ফিরে।
সব লীলা সব ব্রহ্মাণ্ডে ক্রমে উদয় করে॥ ৩৯৩॥**

*alāta-cakra-prāya sei līlā-cakra phire*
*saba līlā saba brahmāṇḍe krame udaya kare*

### SYNONYMS

*alāta-cakra-prāya*—exactly like a wheel of fire; *sei*—that; *līlā-cakra*—the cycle of Kṛṣṇa's pastimes; *phire*—turns; *saba līlā*—all these pastimes; *saba brahmāṇḍe*—in all the universes; *krame*—one after another; *udaya kare*—become manifest.

### TRANSLATION

**"The cycle of His pastimes turns like a wheel of fire. Thus Kṛṣṇa exhibits His pastimes one after the other in every universe.**

### TEXT 394

**জন্ম, বাল্য, পৌগণ্ড, কৈশোর প্রকাশ।
পূতনা-বধাদি করি' মৌষলান্ত বিলাস॥ ৩৯৪॥**

*janma, bālya, paugaṇḍa, kaiśora prakāśa*
*pūtanā-vadhādi kari' mauṣalānta vilāsa*

### SYNONYMS

*janma*—birth; *bālya*—childhood; *paugaṇḍa*—boyhood; *kaiśora*—pre-youth; *prakāśa*—manifestation; *pūtanā-vadha-ādi*—killing the demons, beginning from Pūtanā; *kari'*—manifesting; *mauṣalānta*—until the end of the *mauṣala* pastimes; *vilāsa*—pastimes.

### TRANSLATION

**"Kṛṣṇa's pastimes—appearance, childhood, boyhood and youth—are all manifest, beginning with the killing of Pūtanā and extending to the end of mauṣala-līlā, the annihilation of the Yadu dynasty. All of these pastimes are rotating in every universe.**

### TEXT 395

কোন ব্রহ্মাণ্ডে কোন লীলার হয় অবস্থান ।
তাতে লীলা 'নিত্য' কহে আগম-পুরাণ ॥ ৩৯৫ ॥

*kona brahmāṇḍe kona līlāra haya avasthāna*
*tāte līlā 'nitya' kahe āgama-purāṇa*

### SYNONYMS

*kona brahmāṇḍe*—in some universe; *kona līlāra*—some pastimes; *haya*—there is; *avasthāna*—the presence; *tāte*—therefore; *līlā*—pastimes; *nitya*—eternal; *kahe*—explains; *āgama-purāṇa*—the *Vedas* and *Purāṇas.*

### TRANSLATION

**"Since all Kṛṣṇa's pastimes are taking place continuously, at every moment some pastime is existing in one universe or another. Consequently these pastimes are called eternal by the Vedas and Purāṇas.**

### TEXT 396

গোলোক, গোকুল-ধাম—'বিভু' কৃষ্ণসম ।
কৃষ্ণেচ্ছায় ব্রহ্মাণ্ডগণে তাহার সংক্রম ॥ ৩৯৬ ॥

*goloka, gokula-dhāma—'vibhu' kṛṣṇa-sama*
*kṛṣṇecchāya brahmāṇḍa-gaṇe tāhāra saṅkrama*

### SYNONYMS

*goloka*—the planet known as Goloka; *gokula-dhāma*—the spiritual land, the pasturing fields for the *surabhi* cows; *vibhu*—opulent and powerful; *kṛṣṇa-sama*—as much as Kṛṣṇa; *kṛṣṇa-icchāya*—by the supreme will of Kṛṣṇa; *brahmāṇḍa-gaṇe*—in each of the universes; *tāhāra*—of the Goloka and Gokula *dhāmas; saṅkrama*—appearance.

### TRANSLATION

**"The spiritual abode known as Goloka, which is a pasturing land for surabhi cows, is as powerful and opulent as Kṛṣṇa. By the will of Kṛṣṇa, the original Goloka and Gokula dhāmas are manifest with Him in all the universes.**

### TEXT 397

অতএব গোলোকস্থানে নিত্য বিহার।
ব্রহ্মাণ্ডগণে ক্রমে প্রাকট্য তাহার ॥ ৩৯৭ ॥

*ataeva goloka-sthāne nitya vihāra*
*brahmāṇḍa-gaṇe krame prākaṭya tāhāra*

### SYNONYMS

*ataeva*—therefore; *goloka-sthāne*—in the original Goloka Vṛndāvana planet; *nitya vihāra*—eternal pastimes; *brahmāṇḍa-gaṇe*—within the material universes; *krame*—gradually; *prākaṭya*—manifestation; *tāhāra*—of them.

### TRANSLATION

**"The eternal pastimes of Kṛṣṇa are continuously taking place in the original Goloka Vṛndāvana planet. These same pastimes are gradually manifest within the material world, in each and every brahmāṇḍa.**

### PURPORT

Śrīla Bhaktisiddhānta Sarasvatī Ṭhākura elucidates this complicated explanation of Kṛṣṇa's pastimes. Kṛṣṇa's pastimes are always present in the material world in one of the many universes. These pastimes appear in the universes one after the other, just as the sun moves across the sky and measures the time. Kṛṣṇa's appearance may be manifest in this universe at one moment, and immediately after His birth, this pastime is manifest in the next universe. After His killing of Pūtanā is manifest in this universe, it is next manifest in another universe. Thus all the pastimes of Kṛṣṇa are eternally existing both in the original Goloka Vṛndāvana planet and in the material universes. The 125 years calculated in our solar system to be Kṛṣṇa's lifetime equal one moment for Kṛṣṇa. One moment these pastimes are manifest in one universe, and the next moment they are manifest in the next universe. There are unlimited universes, and Kṛṣṇa's pastimes are manifest one moment after the other in all of them. This rotation is explained through the example of the sun's moving across the sky. Kṛṣṇa appears and disappears in innumerable universes, just as the sun appears and disappears during the day. Although the sun appears to rise and set, it is continuously shining somewhere on the earth. Although Kṛṣṇa's pastimes seem to appear and disappear, they are continuously existing in one *brahmāṇḍa* (universe) or another. Thus all of Kṛṣṇa's *līlās* are present simultaneously throughout the innumerable universes. By our limited senses we cannot appreciate this; therefore Kṛṣṇa's eternal pastimes are very difficult for us to understand. One should try to understand how they are taking place by understanding the allegory of the sun. Although the Lord is appearing constantly in the material universes, His pastimes are eternally present in the original Goloka Vṛndāvana. Therefore these pastimes are called *nitya-līlā* (eternally present pastimes). Because we cannot see what is going on in other universes, it is a little difficult for us to understand how Kṛṣṇa is eternally manifesting His pastimes. There are fourteen Manus in one day of Brahmā, and this time calculation is also taking place in other universes. Kṛṣṇa's pastimes are manifest before fourteen Manus expire. Although it is a little difficult to understand the eternal pastimes of Kṛṣṇa in this way, we must accept the verdict of Vedic literatures.

There are two types of devotees—the *sādhaka,* who is preparing for perfection, and the *siddha,* who is already perfect. As far as those who are already perfect are concerned, *Bhagavad-gītā* says, *tyaktvā dehaṁ punar janma naiti mām eti so 'rjuna:* "After giving up this material body, such a devotee comes to Me." After leaving the material body, the perfect devotee takes birth in the womb of a *gopī* on a planet where Kṛṣṇa's pastimes are going on. This may be in this universe or another universe. This statement is found in the *Ujjvala-nīlamaṇi,* which is commented upon by Viśvanātha Cakravartī Ṭhākura. When a devotee becomes perfect, he is transferred to the universe where Kṛṣṇa's pastimes are taking place. Kṛṣṇa's eternal associates go wherever Kṛṣṇa manifests His pastimes. As stated before, first the father and mother of Kṛṣṇa appear, then the other associates. Quitting his material body, the perfect devotee also goes to associate with Kṛṣṇa and His other associates.

**TEXT 398**

ব্রজে কৃষ্ণ—সর্বৈশ্বর্যপ্রকাশে 'পূর্ণতম' ।
পুরীদ্বয়ে, পরব্যোমে—'পূর্ণতর', 'পূর্ণ' ॥ ৩৯৮ ॥

*vraje kṛṣṇa——sarvaiśvarya-prakāśe 'pūrṇatama'*
*purī-dvaye, paravyome——'pūrṇatara', 'pūrṇa'*

## SYNONYMS

*vraje*—in Vṛndāvana; *kṛṣṇa*—Lord Kṛṣṇa; *sarva-aiśvarya-prakāśe*—manifestation of His full opulence; *pūrṇa-tama*—most complete; *purī-dvaye*—in Dvārakā and Mathurā; *para-vyome*—and in the spiritual world; *pūrṇa-tara*—more complete; *pūrṇa*—complete.

## TRANSLATION

**"Kṛṣṇa is complete in the spiritual sky [Vaikuṇṭha]. He is more complete in Mathurā and Dvārakā, and He is most complete in Vṛndāvana, Vraja, due to His manifesting all His opulences.**

## PURPORT

This is confirmed in the following three verses from *Bhakti-rasāmṛta-sindhu* (2.1.221-223).

## TEXT 399

হরিঃ পূর্ণতমঃ পূর্ণতরঃ পূর্ণ ইতি ত্রিধা ।
শ্রেষ্ঠমধ্যাদিভিঃ শব্দৈর্নাট্যে যঃ পরিপঠ্যতে ॥ ৩৯৯ ॥

*hariḥ pūrṇatamaḥ pūrṇa-*
*taraḥ pūrṇa iti tridhā*
*śreṣṭha-madhyādibhiḥ śabdair*
*nāṭye yaḥ paripaṭhyate*

## SYNONYMS

*hariḥ*—the Supreme Personality of Godhead; *pūrṇa-tamaḥ*—most complete; *pūrṇa-taraḥ*—more complete; *pūrṇaḥ*—complete; *iti*—thus; *tri-dhā*—three stages; *śreṣṭha*—best; *madhya-ādibhiḥ*—middle, etc.; *śabdaiḥ*—by the words; *nāṭye*—in books on dramatics; *yaḥ*—who; *paripaṭhyate*—is proclaimed.

## TRANSLATION

**" 'This is stated in the dramatic literatures as "perfect," "more perfect," and "most perfect." Thus Lord Kṛṣṇa manifests Himself in three ways—perfect, more perfect and most perfect.**

## TEXT 400

প্রকাশিতাখিলগুণঃ স্মৃতঃ পূর্ণতমো বুধৈঃ ।
অসর্বব্যঞ্জকঃ পূর্ণতরঃ পূর্ণোঽল্পদর্শকঃ ॥ ৪০০ ॥

*prakāśitākhila-guṇaḥ*
*smṛtaḥ pūrṇatamo budhaiḥ*
*asarva-vyañjakaḥ pūrṇa-*
*taraḥ pūrṇo 'lpa-darśakaḥ*

## SYNONYMS

*prakāśita-akhila-guṇaḥ*—having all transcendental qualities manifested; *smṛtaḥ*—is understood; *pūrṇa-tamaḥ*—most perfect; *budhaiḥ*—by learned scholars; *asarva-vyañjakaḥ*—having qualities not fully manifested; *pūrṇa-taraḥ*—more perfect; *pūrṇaḥ*—perfect; *alpa-darśakaḥ*—still less fully manifested.

## TRANSLATION

**" 'When the Supreme Personality of Godhead does not manifest all His transcendental qualities, He is called complete. When all the qualities are manifest, but not fully, He is called more complete. When He manifests all His qualities in fullness, He is called most complete. This is the version of all learned scholars in the devotional science.**

## TEXT 401

কৃষ্ণস্য পূর্ণতমতা ব্যক্তাভূদ্‌গোকুলান্তরে।
পূর্ণতা পূর্ণতরতা দ্বারকা-মথুরাদিষু ॥ ৪০১ ॥

*kṛṣṇasya pūrṇatamatā*
*vyaktābhūd gokulāntare*
*pūrṇatā pūrṇataratā*
*dvārakā-mathurādiṣu*

## SYNONYMS

*kṛṣṇasya*—of Lord Kṛṣṇa; *pūrṇa-tamatā*—being most perfect; *vyaktā*—manifested; *abhūt*—became; *gokula-antare*—in the domain of Gokula Vṛndāvana; *pūrṇatā*—completeness; *pūrṇa-taratā*—more completeness; *dvārakā*—in Dvārakā; *mathurā-ādiṣu*—and Mathurā, and so on.

## TRANSLATION

**" 'The most complete qualities of Kṛṣṇa are manifest within Vṛndāvana, and His complete and more complete qualities are manifest in Dvārakā and Mathurā.'**

### TEXT 402

এই কৃষ্ণ—ব্রজে 'পূর্ণতম' ভগবান্।
আর সব স্বরূপ—'পূর্ণতর' 'পূর্ণ' নাম ॥ ৪০২ ॥

*ei kṛṣṇa——vraje 'pūrṇatama' bhagavān*
*āra saba svarūpa——'pūrṇatara' 'pūrṇa' nāma*

### SYNONYMS

*ei kṛṣṇa*—the same Kṛṣṇa; *vraje*—Vṛndāvana; *pūrṇa-tama bhagavān*—the most complete manifestation of the Supreme Personality of Godhead; *āra*—other; *saba*—all; *sva-rūpa*—forms; *pūrṇa-tara*—more complete; *pūrṇa*—complete; *nāma*—named.

### TRANSLATION

**"Lord Kṛṣṇa is the most complete Supreme Personality of Godhead in Vṛndāvana. Elsewhere all His expansions are either complete or more complete.**

### TEXT 403

সংক্ষেপে কহিলুঁ কৃষ্ণের স্বরূপ-বিচার।
'অনন্ত' কহিতে নারে ইহার বিস্তার ॥ ৪০৩ ॥

*saṅkṣepe kahiluṅ kṛṣṇera svarūpa-vicāra*
*'ananta' kahite nāre ihāra vistāra*

### SYNONYMS

*saṅkṣepe*—in brief; *kahiluṅ*—I have described; *kṛṣṇera*—of Lord Kṛṣṇa; *svarūpa-vicāra*—consideration of His different forms and features; *ananta*—Lord Ananta; *kahite nāre*—not able to describe; *ihāra*—of this; *vistāra*—the expanse.

### TRANSLATION

**"Thus I have briefly described Kṛṣṇa's manifestation of transcendental forms. This subject matter is so large that even Lord Ananta cannot describe it fully.**

### TEXT 404

অনন্ত স্বরূপ কৃষ্ণের নাহিক গণন।
শাখা-চন্দ্র-ন্যায়ে করি দিগ দরশন ॥ ৪০৪ ॥

*ananta svarūpa kṛṣṇera nāhika gaṇana*
*śākhā-candra-nyāye kari dig-daraśana*

**SYNONYMS**

*ananta*—unlimited; *svarūpa*—forms; *kṛṣṇera*—of Lord Kṛṣṇa; *nāhika gaṇana*—there is no counting; *śākhā-candra-nyāye*—by the logic of showing the moon through the branches of a tree; *kari*—I do; *dik-daraśana*—only partial showing.

**TRANSLATION**

**"In this way Kṛṣṇa's transcendental forms are expanded unlimitedly. No one can count them. Whatever I have explained is simply a little glimpse. It is like showing the moon through the branches of a tree."**

**TEXT 405**

ইহা যেই শুনে, পড়ে, সেই ভাগ্যবান্ ।
কৃষ্ণের স্বরূপতত্ত্বের হয় কিছু জ্ঞান ॥ ৪০৫ ॥

*ihā yei śune, paḍe, sei bhāgyavān*
*kṛṣṇera svarūpa-tattvera haya kichu jñāna*

**SYNONYMS**

*ihā*—this narration; *yei śune*—anyone who hears; *paḍe*—or reads; *sei*—such a person; *bhāgyavān*—is most fortunate; *kṛṣṇera*—of Lord Kṛṣṇa; *svarūpa-tattvera*—of personal bodily features; *haya*—there is; *kichu*—something; *jñāna*—knowledge.

**TRANSLATION**

**Whoever hears or recites these descriptions of the expansions of Kṛṣṇa's body is certainly a very fortunate man. Although this is very difficult to understand, one can nonetheless acquire some knowledge about the different features of Kṛṣṇa's body.**

**TEXT 406**

শ্রীরূপ-রঘুনাথ-পদে যার আশ ।
চৈতন্যচরিতামৃত কহে কৃষ্ণদাস ॥ ৪০৬ ॥

*śrī-rūpa-raghunātha pade yāra āśa*
*caitanya-caritāmṛta kahe kṛṣṇadāsa*

### SYNONYMS

*śrī-rūpa*—Śrīla Rūpa Gosvāmī; *raghunātha*—Śrīla Raghunātha dāsa Gosvāmī; *pade*—at the lotus feet; *yāra*—whose; *āśa*—expectation; *caitanya-caritāmṛta*—the book named *Caitanya-caritāmṛta; kahe*—describes; *kṛṣṇadāsa*—Śrīla Kṛṣṇadāsa Kavirāja Gosvāmī.

### TRANSLATION

**Praying at the lotus feet of Śrī Rūpa and Śrī Raghunātha, always desiring their mercy, I, Kṛṣṇadāsa, narrate Śrī Caitanya-caritāmṛta, following in their footsteps.**

*Thus end the Bhaktivedanta purports to the* Śrī Caitanya-caritāmṛta, Madhya-līlā, *Twentieth Chapter, describing how Sanātana Gosvāmī met the Lord at Vārāṇasī and received knowledge of the Absolute Truth.*

CHAPTER 21

# The Opulence and Sweetness of Lord Śrī Kṛṣṇa

Śrīla Bhaktivinoda Ṭhākura gives the following summary study of the Twenty-first Chapter. In this chapter Śrī Caitanya Mahāprabhu fully describes Kṛṣṇaloka, the spiritual sky, the Causal Ocean and the material world, which consists of innumerable universes. Śrī Caitanya Mahāprabhu then describes Lord Brahmā's interview with Kṛṣṇa at Dvārakā and the Lord's curbing the pride of Brahmā. There is also a description of one of Kṛṣṇa's pastimes with Brahmā. In this chapter the author of *Caitanya-caritāmṛta* has presented some nice poems about the pastimes of Kṛṣṇa and Kṛṣṇa's superexcellent beauty. Throughout the rest of the chapter, our intimate relationship (*sambandha*) with Kṛṣṇa is described.

### TEXT 1

অগত্যেকগতিং নত্বা হীনার্থাধিকসাধকম্ ।
শ্রীচৈতন্যং লিখাম্যস্য মাধুর্যৈশ্বর্য-শীকরম্ ॥ ১ ॥

*agaty-eka-gatiṁ natvā*
*hīnārthādhika-sādhakam*
*śrī-caitanyaṁ likhāmy asya*
*mādhuryaiśvarya-śīkaram*

### SYNONYMS

*agati-eka-gatim*—to the only shelter for the conditioned souls who do not know the goal of life; *natvā*—offering obeisances; *hīna-artha*—of the necessities of the conditioned souls, who are poor in spiritual knowledge; *adhika*—increase; *sādhakam*—bringing about; *śrī-caitanyam*—unto Lord Śrī Caitanya Mahāprabhu; *likhāmi*—I am writing; *asya*—of Him; *mādhurya-aiśvarya*—of the sweetness and opulence; *śīkaram*—a small portion.

### TRANSLATION

**Offering my obeisances unto Śrī Caitanya Mahāprabhu, let me describe a particle of His opulence and sweetness. He is most valuable for a fallen conditioned soul bereft of spiritual knowledge, and He is the only shelter for those who do not know the real goal of life.**

### TEXT 2

**জয় জয় শ্রীচৈতন্য জয় নিত্যানন্দ।**
**জয়াদ্বৈতচন্দ্র জয় গৌরভক্তবৃন্দ ॥ ২ ॥**

*jaya jaya śrī-caitanya jaya nityānanda*
*jayādvaita-candra jaya gaura-bhakta-vṛnda*

### SYNONYMS

*jaya*—all glories; *jaya*—all glories; *śrī-caitanya*—to Śrī Caitanya Mahāprabhu; *jaya*—all glories; *nityānanda*—to Nityānanda Prabhu; *jaya*—all glories; *advaita-candra*—to Advaita Ācārya; *jaya*—all glories; *gaura-bhakta-vṛnda*—to the devotees of Śrī Caitanya Mahāprabhu.

### TRANSLATION

**All glories to Śrī Caitanya Mahāprabhu! All glories to Nityānanda Prabhu! All glories to Advaita Ācārya! All glories to all the devotees of Śrī Caitanya Mahāprabhu!**

### TEXT 3

**সর্ব স্বরূপের ধাম—পরব্যোম-ধামে।**
**পৃথক্ পৃথক্ বৈকুণ্ঠ সব, নাহিক গণনে ॥ ৩ ॥**

*sarva svarūpera dhāma——paravyoma-dhāme*
*pṛthak pṛthak vaikuṇṭha saba, nāhika gaṇane*

### SYNONYMS

*sarva*—all; *svarūpera*—of the personal forms; *dhāma*—abode; *para-vyoma-dhāme*—in the spiritual sky; *pṛthak pṛthak*—separate; *vaikuṇṭha*—Vaikuṇṭha planets; *saba*—all; *nāhika gaṇane*—there is no counting.

### TRANSLATION

**Śrī Caitanya Mahāprabhu continued, "All the transcendental forms of the Lord are situated in the spiritual sky. They preside over spiritual planets in that abode, but there is no counting those Vaikuṇṭha planets.**

### TEXT 4

**শত, সহস্র, অযুত, লক্ষ, কোটী-যোজন।**
**এক এক বৈকুণ্ঠের বিস্তার বর্ণন ॥ ৪ ॥**

*śata, sahasra, ayuta, lakṣa, koṭī-yojana*
*eka eka vaikuṇṭhera vistāra varṇana*

## SYNONYMS

*śata*—a hundred; *sahasra*—a thousand; *ayuta*—ten thousand; *lakṣa*—a hundred thousand; *koṭī*—ten million; *yojana*—a distance of eight miles; *eka eka*—each and every one; *vaikuṇṭhera*—of the spiritual planets; *vistāra*—the breadth; *varṇana*—description.

## TRANSLATION

**"The breadth of each Vaikuṇṭha planet is described as eight miles multiplied by one hundred, by one thousand, by ten thousand, by one hundred thousand, and by ten million. In other words, each Vaikuṇṭha planet is expanded beyond our ability to measure.**

## TEXT 5

সব বৈকুণ্ঠ—ব্যাপক, আনন্দ-চিন্ময় ।
পারিষদ-ষড়ৈশ্বর্য-পূর্ণ সব হয় ॥ ৫ ॥

*saba vaikuṇṭha——vyāpaka, ānanda-cinmaya*
*pāriṣada-ṣaḍaiśvarya-pūrṇa saba haya*

## SYNONYMS

*saba*—all; *vaikuṇṭha*—the spiritual planets; *vyāpaka*—vast; *ānanda-cit-maya*—made of spiritual bliss; *pāriṣada*—associates; *ṣaṭ-aiśvarya*—six kinds of opulence; *pūrṇa*—in full; *saba*—all; *haya*—are.

## TRANSLATION

**"Each Vaikuṇṭha planet is very large, and each is made of spiritual bliss. The inhabitants are all associates of the Supreme Lord, and they have full opulence like the Lord Himself. Thus they are all situated.**

## TEXT 6

অনন্ত বৈকুণ্ঠ এক এক দেশে যার ।
সেই পরব্যোম-ধামের কে করু বিস্তার ॥ ৬ ॥

*ananta vaikuṇṭha eka eka deśe yāra*
*sei paravyoma-dhāmera ke karu vistāra*

### SYNONYMS

*ananta vaikuṇṭha*—unlimited Vaikuṇṭha planets; *eka eka*—certain; *deśe*—in a place; *yāra*—of which; *sei*—that; *para-vyoma*—of the spiritual sky; *dhāmera*—of the abode; *ke karu vistāra*—who can understand the breadth.

### TRANSLATION

**"Since all the Vaikuṇṭha planets are located in a certain corner of the spiritual sky, who can measure the spiritual sky?**

### TEXT 7

অনন্ত বৈকুণ্ঠ-পরব্যোম যার দলশ্রেণী ।
সর্বোপরি কৃষ্ণলোক 'কর্ণিকার' গণি ॥ ৭ ॥

*ananta vaikuṇṭha-paravyoma yāra dala-śreṇī*
*sarvopari kṛṣṇaloka 'karṇikāra' gaṇi*

### SYNONYMS

*ananta*—unlimited; *vaikuṇṭha*—Vaikuṇṭha planets; *para-vyoma*—the spiritual sky; *yāra*—of which; *dala-śreṇī*—the bunches of outlying petals; *sarva-upari*—in the topmost portion of the spiritual sky; *kṛṣṇa-loka*—the abode of Lord Kṛṣṇa; *karṇikāra gaṇi*—we consider the whorl of the lotus flower.

### TRANSLATION

**"The shape of the spiritual sky is compared to a lotus flower. The topmost region of that flower is called the whorl, and within that whorl is Kṛṣṇa's abode. The petals of the spiritual lotus flower consist of many Vaikuṇṭha planets.**

### TEXT 8

এইমত ষড়ৈশ্বর্য, স্থান, অবতার ।
ব্রহ্মা, শিব অন্ত না পায়—জীব কোন্ ছার ॥ ৮ ॥

*ei-mata ṣaḍ-aiśvarya, sthāna, avatāra*
*brahmā, śiva anta nā pāya—jīva kon chāra*

### SYNONYMS

*ei-mata*—such; *ṣaṭ-aiśvarya*—six opulences; *sthāna*—abode; *avatāra*—incarnations; *brahmā*—Lord Brahmā; *śiva*—Lord Śiva; *anta nā pāya*—cannot find the limit; *jīva*—a living entity; *kon*—what of; *chāra*—worthless.

## TRANSLATION

**"Each Vaikuṇṭha planet is full of spiritual bliss, complete opulence and space, and each is inhabited by incarnations. If Lord Brahmā and Lord Śiva cannot estimate the length and breadth of the spiritual sky and the Vaikuṇṭha planets, how can ordinary living entities begin to imagine them?**

## TEXT 9

কো বেত্তি ভূমন্ ভগবন্ পরাত্মন্
যোগেশ্বরোতীর্ভবতস্ত্রিলোক্যাম্ ।
ক্ব বা কথং বা কতি বা কদেতি
বিস্তারয়ন্ ক্রীড়সি যোগমায়াম্ ॥ ৯ ॥

*ko vetti bhūman bhagavan parātman*
*yogeśvarotīr bhavatas trilokyām*
*kva vā kathaṁ vā kati vā kadeti*
*vistārayan krīḍasi yoga-māyām*

## SYNONYMS

*kaḥ*—who; *vetti*—knows; *bhūman*—O supreme great one; *bhagavan*—O Supreme Personality of Godhead; *para-ātman*—O Supersoul; *yoga-īśvara*—O master of mystic power; *ūtīḥ*—pastimes; *bhavataḥ*—of Your Lordship; *tri-lokyām*—in the three worlds; *kva*—where; *vā*—or; *katham*—how; *vā*—or; *kati*—how many; *vā*—or; *kadā*—when; *iti*—thus; *vistārayan*—expanding; *krīḍasi*—You play; *yoga-māyām*—spiritual energy.

## TRANSLATION

**" 'O supreme great one! O Supreme Personality of Godhead! O Supersoul, master of all mystic power! Your pastimes are taking place continuously in these worlds, but who can estimate where, how and when You are employing Your spiritual energy and performing Your pastimes? No one can understand the mystery of these activities.'**

## PURPORT

This verse is quoted from *Śrīmad-Bhāgavatam* (10.14.21).

## TEXT 10

**এইমত কৃষ্ণের দিব্য সদ্‌গুণ অনন্ত ।**
**ব্রহ্মা-শিব-সনকাদি না পায় যাঁর অন্ত ॥ ১০ ॥**

*ei-mata kṛṣṇera divya sad-guṇa ananta*
*brahmā-śiva-sanakādi nā pāya yāṅra anta*

## SYNONYMS

*ei-mata*—in this way; *kṛṣṇera*—of Lord Kṛṣṇa; *divya*—transcendental; *sat-guṇa*—spiritual qualities; *ananta*—unlimited; *brahmā*—Lord Brahmā; *śiva*—Lord Śiva; *sanaka-ādi*—the four Kumāras and so on; *nā*—not; *pāya*—obtain; *yāṅra*—of which; *anta*—the limit.

## TRANSLATION

**"The spiritual qualities of Kṛṣṇa are also unlimited. Great personalities like Lord Brahmā, Lord Śiva and the four Kumāras cannot estimate the spiritual qualities of the Lord.**

## TEXT 11

গুণাত্মনস্তেঽপি গুণান্ বিমাতুং
হিতাবতীর্ণস্য ক ঈশিরেঽস্য ।
কালেন যৈর্বা বিমিতাঃ সুকল্পৈ-
র্ভূ-পাংশবঃ খে মিহিকা দ্যুভাসঃ ॥ ১১ ॥

*guṇātmanas te 'pi guṇān vimātuṁ*
*hitāvatīrṇasya ka īśire 'sya*
*kālena yair vā vimitāḥ sukalpair*
*bhū-pāṁśavaḥ khe mihikā dyubhāsaḥ*

## SYNONYMS

*guṇa-ātmanaḥ*—the overseer of the three qualities; *te*—of You; *api*—certainly; *guṇān*—the qualities; *vimātum*—to count; *hita-avatīrṇasya*—who have descended for the benefit of all living entities; *ke*—who; *īśire*—were able; *asya*—of the universe; *kālena*—in due course of time; *yaiḥ*—by whom; *vā*—or; *vimitāḥ*—counted; *su-kalpaiḥ*—by great scientists; *bhū-pāṁśavaḥ*—the atoms of the universe; *khe*—in the sky; *mihikāḥ*—particles of snow; *dyu-bhāsaḥ*—the illuminating stars and planets.

## TRANSLATION

**" 'In time, great scientists may be able to count all the atoms of the universe, all the stars and planets in the sky, and all the particles of snow, but who among them can count the unlimited transcendental qualities of the Supreme Personality of Godhead? He descends on the surface of the globe for the benefit of all living entities.'**

## PURPORT

This verse is quoted from *Śrīmad-Bhāgavatam* (10.14.7).

## TEXT 12

ব্রহ্মাদি রহু—সহস্রবদনে 'অনন্ত'।
নিরন্তর গায় মুখে, না পায় গুণের অন্ত ॥ ১২ ॥

*brahmādi rahu——sahasra-vadane 'ananta'*
*nirantara gāya mukhe, nā pāya guṇera anta*

## SYNONYMS

*brahmā-ādi rahu*—leave aside Lord Brahmā and others; *sahasra-vadane*—in thousands of mouths; *ananta*—Lord Ananta; *nirantara*—continuously; *gāya*—chants; *mukhe*—in the mouths; *nā pāya*—does not obtain; *guṇera*—of qualities of the Lord; *anta*—the end.

## TRANSLATION

**"To say nothing of Lord Brahmā, even Lord Ananta, who has thousands of heads, could not reach the end of the Lord's transcendental qualities, even though He is continuously chanting their praises.**

## TEXT 13

নান্তং বিদাম্যহমমী মুনয়োঽগ্রজাস্তে
মায়াবলস্য পুরুষস্য কুতোঽবরা যে।
গায়ন্ গুণান্ দশশতানন আদিদেবঃ
শেষোঽধুনাপি সমবস্যতি নাস্য পারম্ ॥ ১৩ ॥

*nāntaṁ vidāmy aham amī munayo 'grajās te*
*māyā-balasya puruṣasya kuto 'varā ye*
*gāyan guṇān daśa-śatānana ādi-devaḥ*
*śeṣo 'dhunāpi samavasyati nāsya pāram*

## SYNONYMS

*na antam*—no limit; *vidāmi*—know; *aham*—I; *amī*—those; *munayaḥ*—great saintly persons; *agrajāḥ*—brothers; *te*—of you; *māyā-balasya*—who has multi-energies; *puruṣasya*—of the Personality of Godhead; *kutaḥ*—how; *avarāḥ*—less intelligent; *ye*—those who; *gāyan*—chanting; *guṇān*—the qualities; *daśa-śata-ānanaḥ*—who has a thousand hoods; *ādi-devaḥ*—the Personality of Godhead; *śeṣaḥ*—Ananta Śeṣa; *adhunā api*—even until now; *samavasyati*—reaches; *na*—not; *asya*—of the Lord; *pāram*—limit.

### TRANSLATION

**" 'If I, Lord Brahmā, and your elder brothers, the great saints and sages, cannot understand the limits of the Supreme Personality of Godhead, who is full of various energies, who else can understand them? Although constantly chanting about His transcendental qualities, the thousand-hooded Lord Śeṣa has not yet reached the end of the Lord's activities.'**

### PURPORT

This verse, spoken to Nārada Muni, is from *Śrīmad-Bhāgavatam* (2.7.41).

### TEXT 14

**সেহো রহু—সর্বজ্ঞ-শিরোমণি শ্রীকৃষ্ণ ।**
**নিজ-গুণের অন্ত না পাঞা হয়েন সতৃষ্ণ ॥ ১৪ ॥**

*seho rahu——sarvajña-śiromaṇi śrī-kṛṣṇa*
*nija-guṇera anta nā pāñā hayena satṛṣṇa*

### SYNONYMS

*seho rahu*—let Him (Ananta) alone; *sarva-jña*—the omniscient; *śiromaṇi*—the topmost; *śrī-kṛṣṇa*—Lord Kṛṣṇa; *nija-guṇera*—of His personal qualities; *anta*—limit; *nā*—not; *pāñā*—getting; *hayena*—becomes; *sa-tṛṣṇa*—very inquisitive.

### TRANSLATION

**"To say nothing of Anantadeva, even Lord Kṛṣṇa Himself cannot find an end to His transcendental qualities. Indeed, He Himself is always eager to know them.**

### TEXT 15

দ্যুপতয় এব তে ন যযুরন্তমনন্তত্য়া
ত্বমপি যদন্তরাণ্ডনিচয়া নম্বু সাবরণাঃ ।
খ ইব রজাংসি বান্তি বয়সা সহ যচ্ছ্রুতয়-
স্ত্বয়ি হি ফলন্ত্যতন্নিরসনেন ভবন্নিধনাঃ ॥ ১৫ ॥

*dyu-pataya eva te na yayur antam anantatayā*
*tvam api yad antarāṇḍa-nicayā nanu sāvaraṇāḥ*
*kha iva rajāṁsi vānti vayasā saha yac chrutayas*
*tvayi hi phalanty atannirasanena bhavan-nidhanāḥ*

### SYNONYMS

*dyu-patayaḥ*—the predominating deities of higher planetary systems (Lord Brahmā and others); *eva*—also; *te*—Your; *na*—not; *yayuḥ*—could reach; *antam*—the limit of transcendental qualities; *anantatayā*—due to being unlimited; *tvam api*—You also; *yat*—since; *antara*—within You; *aṇḍa-nicayāḥ*—the groups of universes; *nanu*—O sir; *sāvaraṇāḥ*—having different coverings; *khe*—in the sky; *iva*—like; *rajāṁsi*—atoms; *vānti*—rotate; *vayasā*—the course of time; *saha*—with; *yat*—what; *śrutayaḥ*—great personalities who understand the *Vedas; tvayi*—in You; *hi*—certainly; *phalanti*—end in; *atannirasanena*—by refuting the inferior elements; *bhavat-nidhanāḥ*--whose conclusion is in You.

### TRANSLATION

**" 'My Lord, You are unlimited. Even the predominating deities of the higher planetary systems, including Lord Brahmā, could not find Your limitations. Nor could You Yourself ascertain the limit of Your qualities. Like atoms in the sky, there are multi-universes with seven coverings, and these are rotating in due course of time. All the experts in Vedic understanding are searching for You by eliminating the material elements. In this way, searching and searching, they come to the conclusion that everything is complete in You. Thus You are the resort of everything. This is the conclusion of all Vedic experts.'**

### PURPORT

This verse from *Śrīmad-Bhāgavatam* (10.87.41) is confirmed in *Bhagavad-gītā:*

*bahūnāṁ janmanām ante*
*jñānavān māṁ prapadyate*
*vāsudevaḥ sarvam iti*
*sa mahātmā sudurlabhaḥ*

"After many births and deaths, he who is actually in knowledge surrenders unto Me, knowing Me to be the cause of all causes and all that is. Such a great soul is very rare." (Bg. 7.19)

After searching for the Absolute Truth throughout the universe, learned scholars and Vedic experts cannot reach the ultimate goal. In this way they come to Kṛṣṇa.

When there is a discussion about the Absolute Truth, there are always various pros and cons. The purpose of such arguments is to come to the right conclusion. Such an argument is generally known as *neti neti* ("not this, not that"). Until one comes to the right conclusion, the process of thinking, "This is not the Absolute Truth, that is not the Absolute Truth," will continue. When we come to the right conclusion, we accept the Supreme Personality of Godhead, Kṛṣṇa, as the ultimate truth.

## TEXT 16

**সেহ রহু—ব্রজে যবে কৃষ্ণ অবতার ।**
**তাঁর চরিত্র বিচারিতে মন না পায় পার ॥ ১৬ ॥**

*seha rahu——vraje yabe kṛṣṇa avatāra*
*tāṅra caritra vicārite mana nā pāya pāra*

### SYNONYMS

*seha rahu*—leave aside such negative arguments; *vraje*—in Vṛndāvana; *yabe*—when; *kṛṣṇa*—Lord Kṛṣṇa; *avatāra*—incarnation; *tāṅra*—His; *caritra*—character; *vicārite*—to deliberate; *mana*—mind; *nā*—not; *pāya*—gets; *pāra*—the limit.

### TRANSLATION

**"Apart from all argument, logic and negative or positive processes, when Lord Śrī Kṛṣṇa was present as the Supreme Personality of Godhead at Vṛndāvana, one could not find a limit to His potencies by studying His characteristics and activities.**

## TEXT 17

**প্রাকৃতাপ্রাকৃত সৃষ্টি কৈলা একক্ষণে ।**
**অশেষ-বৈকুণ্ঠাজাণ্ড স্বস্বনাথ-সনে ॥ ১৭ ॥**

*prākṛtāprākṛta sṛṣṭi kailā eka-kṣaṇe*
*aśeṣa-vaikuṇṭhājāṇḍa svasvanātha-sane*

### SYNONYMS

*prākṛta-aprākṛta*—material and spiritual; *sṛṣṭi*—creation; *kailā*—did; *eka-kṣaṇe*—in one moment; *aśeṣa*—unlimited; *vaikuṇṭha*—Vaikuṇṭha planets; *aja-aṇḍa*—material planets; *sva-sva-nātha-sane*—with their own predominating deities.

### TRANSLATION

**"At Vṛndāvana, the Lord immediately created all material and spiritual planets in one moment. Indeed, all of them were created with their predominating deities.**

## TEXT 18

**এমত অন্যত্র নাহি শুনিয়ে অদ্ভুত ।
যাহার শ্রবণে চিত্ত হয় অবধূত ॥ ১৮ ॥**

*e-mata anyatra nāhi śuniye adbhuta*
*yāhāra śravaṇe citta haya avadhūta*

### SYNONYMS

*e-mata*—like this; *anyatra*—anywhere else; *nāhi*—not; *śuniye*—I hear; *adbhuta*—wonderful event; *yāhāra*—of which; *śravaṇe*—by hearing; *citta*—consciousness; *haya*—becomes; *avadhūta*—agitated and cleansed.

### TRANSLATION

**"We do not hear of such wonderful things anywhere. Simply by hearing of those incidents, one's consciousness is agitated and cleansed.**

### PURPORT

When Lord Kṛṣṇa was present in the earthly Vṛndāvana, Lord Brahmā, taking Him to be an ordinary cowherd boy, wanted to test His potency. Therefore Lord Brahmā stole all the cows, calves and cowherd boys from Kṛṣṇa and hid them by his illusory energy. When Kṛṣṇa saw that Brahmā had stolen His cows, calves and cowherd boys, He immediately created many material and spiritual planets in Lord Brahmā's presence. Within a moment, cows, cowherd boys, calves and unlimited Vaikuṇṭhas— all expansions of the Lord's spiritual energy—were manifested. As stated in the *Brahma-saṁhitā: ānanda-cinmaya-rasa-pratibhāvitābhiḥ.* Not only did Kṛṣṇa create all the paraphernalia of His spiritual energy, but He also created unlimited material universes with unlimited Brahmās. All these pastimes, which are described in *Śrīmad-Bhāgavatam,* will cleanse one's consciousness. In this way one can actually understand the Absolute Truth. The spiritual planets in the spiritual sky are called Vaikuṇṭhas, and each of them has a predominating Deity (Nārāyaṇa) with a specific name. Similarly, in the material sky there are innumerable universes, and each is dominated by a specific deity, a Brahmā. Kṛṣṇa simultaneously created all these Vaikuṇṭha planets and universes within a moment of Brahmā's return.

The word *avadhūta* means "rambling, agitating, moving, absorbed, defeated." In some readings of *Caitanya-caritāmṛta,* it is said: *yāhāra śravaṇe citta-mala haya dhūta.* Instead of the word *avadhūta,* the words *haya dhūta,* meaning that the heart or consciousness is cleansed, is used. When the consciousness is cleansed, one can understand what and who Kṛṣṇa is. This is also confirmed in *Bhagavad-gītā* (7.28):

*yeṣāṁ tv anta-gataṁ pāpaṁ*
*janānāṁ puṇya-karmaṇām*
*te dvandva-moha-nirmuktā*
*bhajante māṁ dṛḍha-vratāḥ*

"Persons who have acted piously in previous lives and in this life, whose sinful actions are completely eradicated and who are freed from the duality of delusion, engage themselves in My service with determination."

Unless one is freed from the reaction of sinful activities, one cannot understand Kṛṣṇa or engage in His transcendental loving service.

### TEXT 19

"কৃষ্ণবৎসৈরসংখ্যাতৈঃ"- শুকদেব-বাণী ।
কৃষ্ণ-সঙ্গে কত গোপ—সংখ্যা নাহি জানি ॥ ১৯ ॥

*"kṛṣṇa-vatsair asaṅkhyātaiḥ"——śukadeva-vāṇī*
*kṛṣṇa-saṅge kata gopa——saṅkhyā nāhi jāni*

### SYNONYMS

*kṛṣṇa-vatsaiḥ asaṅkhyātaiḥ*—Kṛṣṇa was accompanied by an unlimited number of calves and cowherd boys; *śukadeva-vāṇī*—the words of Śukadeva Gosvāmī; *kṛṣṇa-saṅge*—with Lord Kṛṣṇa; *kata gopa*—how many cowherd boys; *saṅkhyā*—the count; *nāhi jāni*—we do not know.

### TRANSLATION

**"According to Śukadeva Gosvāmī, Kṛṣṇa had unlimited cows and cowherd boys with Him. No one could count their actual number.**

### TEXT 20

এক এক গোপ করে যে বৎস চারণ ।
কোটি, অর্বুদ, শঙ্খ, পদ্ম, তাহার গণন ॥ ২০ ॥

*eka eka gopa kare ye vatsa cāraṇa*
*koṭi, arbuda, śaṅkha, padma, tāhāra gaṇana*

### SYNONYMS

*eka eka*—one after another; *gopa*—cowherd boys; *kare*—do; *ye*—whatever; *vatsa*—calves; *cāraṇa*—grazing; *koṭi*—ten millions; *arbuda*—a hundred million; *śaṅkha*—one trillion; *padma*—ten trillion; *tāhāra gaṇana*—the enumeration of that.

### TRANSLATION

**"Each of the cowherd boys was tending calves to the extent of a koṭi, arbuda, śaṅkha and padma. That is the way of counting.**

### PURPORT

According to Vedic mathematical calculations, the following enumeration system is used: units, tens (*daśa*), hundreds (*śata*), thousands (*sahasra*), ten thousands (*ayuta*) and hundred thousands (*lakṣa*). Ten times *lakṣa* is *niyuta*. Ten times *niyuta* is *koṭi*. Ten times *koṭi* is *arbuda*. Ten times *arbuda* is *vṛnda*. Ten times *vṛnda* is *kharva*. Ten times *kharva* is *nikharva*. Ten times *nikharva* is *śaṅkha*. Ten times *śaṅkha* is *padma*, and ten times *padma* is *sāgara*. Ten times *sāgara* is *antya*, and ten times *antya* is *madhya*, and ten times *madhya* is *parārdha*. Each item is ten times greater than the previous one. Thus all the cowherd boys who were companions of Kṛṣṇa had many calves to take care of.

### TEXT 21

**বেত্র, বেণু, দল, শৃঙ্গ, বস্ত্র, অলঙ্কার ।**
**গোপগণের যত, তার নাহি লেখা-পার ॥ ২১ ॥**

*vetra, veṇu, dala, śṛṅga, vastra, alaṅkāra*
*gopa-gaṇera yata, tāra nāhi lekhā-pāra*

### SYNONYMS

*vetra*—canes; *veṇu*—flutes; *dala*—lotus flowers; *śṛṅga*—horns; *vastra*—garments; *alaṅkāra*—ornaments; *gopa-gaṇera yata*—as many as are possessed by the cowherd boys; *tāra*—of them; *nāhi*—there is not; *lekhā-pāra*—limitation to writing.

### TRANSLATION

**"All the cowherd boys had unlimited calves. Similarly, their canes, flutes, lotus flowers, horns, garments and ornaments were all unlimited. They cannot be limited by writing about them.**

### TEXT 22

**সবে হৈলা চতুর্ভুজ বৈকুণ্ঠের পতি ।**
**পৃথক্ পৃথক্ ব্রহ্মাণ্ডের ব্রহ্মা করে স্তুতি ॥ ২২ ॥**

*sabe hailā caturbhuja vaikuṇṭhera pati*
*pṛthak pṛthak brahmāṇḍera brahmā kare stuti*

### SYNONYMS

*sabe*—all of them: *hailā*—became; *catuḥ-bhuja*—four-handed; *vaikuṇṭhera pati*—predominating Deities of the Vaikuṇṭha planets; *pṛthak pṛthak*—separately; *brahmāṇḍera*—of the universes; *brahmā*—the predominating deities known as Lord Brahmā; *kare stuti*—offer prayers.

### TRANSLATION

**"The cowherd boys then became four-handed Nārāyaṇas, predominating Deities of Vaikuṇṭha planets. All the separate Brahmās from different universes began to offer their prayers unto the Lords.**

### TEXT 23

এক কৃষ্ণদেহ হৈতে সবার প্রকাশে ।
ক্ষণেকে সবাই সেই শরীরে প্রবেশে ॥ ২৩ ॥

*eka kṛṣṇa-deha haite sabāra prakāśe*
*kṣaṇeke sabāi sei śarīre praveśe*

### SYNONYMS

*eka*—one; *kṛṣṇa-deha*—transcendental body of Kṛṣṇa; *haite*—from; *sabāra*—of everyone; *prakāśe*—the manifestation; *kṣaṇeke*—in a second; *sabāi*—every one of Them; *sei śarīre*—in that body of Kṛṣṇa; *praveśe*—enter.

### TRANSLATION

**"All these transcendental bodies emanated from the body of Kṛṣṇa, and within a second They all entered again into His body.**

### TEXT 24

ইহা দেখি' ব্রহ্মা হৈলা মোহিত, বিস্মিত ।
স্তুতি করি' এই পাছে করিলা নিশ্চিত ॥ ২৪ ॥

*ihā dekhi' brahmā hailā mohita, vismita*
*stuti kari' ei pāche karilā niścita*

### SYNONYMS

*ihā dekhi'*—seeing this; *brahmā*—Lord Brahmā; *hailā*—became; *mohita*—astonished; *vismita*—struck with wonder; *stuti kari'*—offering prayers; *ei*—this; *pāche*—at the end; *karilā*—made; *niścita*—conclusion.

### TRANSLATION

**"When the Lord Brahmā from this universe saw this pastime, he was astonished and struck with wonder. After offering his prayers, he gave the following conclusion.**

### TEXT 25

**"যে কহে—'কৃষ্ণের বৈভব মুঞি সব জানোঁ।'**
**সে জানুক,—কায়মনে মুঞি এই মানোঁ॥ ২৫ ॥**

*"ye kahe——'kṛṣṇera vaibhava muñi saba jānoṅ'*
*se jānuka,——kāya-mane muñi ei mānoṅ*

### SYNONYMS

*ye kahe*—if anyone says; *kṛṣṇera*—of Lord Kṛṣṇa; *vaibhava*—opulences; *muñi*—I; *saba*—all; *jānoṅ*—know; *se jānuka*—let him know; *kāya-mane*—by my body and mind; *muñi*—myself; *ei*—this; *mānoṅ*—accept.

### TRANSLATION

**"Lord Brahmā said, 'If someone says that he knows everything about Kṛṣṇa's opulence, let him think that way. However, as far as I am concerned, with my body and mind I consider it in this way.**

### TEXT 26

**এই যে তোমার অনন্ত বৈভবামৃতসিন্ধু।**
**মোর বাঙ্‌মনোগম্য নহে এক বিন্দু॥ ২৬ ॥**

*ei ye tomāra ananta vaibhavāmṛta-sindhu*
*mora vāṅ-mano-gamya nahe eka bindu*

### SYNONYMS

*ei ye*—all this; *tomāra*—Your; *ananta*—unlimited; *vaibhava-amṛta-sindhu*—ocean of the nectar of Your opulence; *mora*—my; *vāk-manaḥ-gamya*—within the reach of words and mind; *nahe*—not; *eka bindu*—even a drop.

### TRANSLATION

**" 'My Lord, Your opulence is like an unlimited ocean of nectar, and it is verbally and mentally impossible for me to realize even a drop of that ocean.**

## TEXT 27

জানন্ত এব জানন্তু কিং বহূক্ত্যা ন মে প্রভো ।
মনসো বপুষো বাচো বৈভবং তব গোচরঃ ॥" ২৭ ॥

*jānanta eva jānantu*
*kiṁ bahūktyā na me prabho*
*manaso vapuṣo vāco*
*vaibhavaṁ tava gocaraḥ"*

## SYNONYMS

*jānantaḥ*—persons who think they are aware of Your unlimited potency; *eva*—certainly; *jānantu*—let them think like that; *kim*—what is the use; *bahu-uktyā*—with many words; *na*—not; *me*—my; *prabho*—O Lord; *manasaḥ*—of the mind; *vapuṣaḥ*—of the body; *vācaḥ*—of the words; *vaibhavam*—opulences; *tava*—Your; *gocaraḥ*—within the range.

## TRANSLATION

**" 'There are people who say, "I know everything about Kṛṣṇa." Let them think that way. As far as I am concerned, I do not wish to speak very much about this matter. O my Lord, let me say this much. As far as Your opulences are concerned, they are all beyond the reach of my mind, body and words.'**

## PURPORT

This is a quotation from *Śrīmad-Bhāgavatam* (10.14.38), spoken by Lord Brahmā after he had stolen Lord Kṛṣṇa's cows, calves and cowherd boys and Kṛṣṇa had exhibited His transcendental opulence by re-creating all the stolen cows, calves and cowherd boys by His *viṣṇu-mūrti* expansions. After he had seen this, Brahmā offered the above prayer.

## TEXT 28

কৃষ্ণের মহিমা রহু—কেবা তার জ্ঞাতা ।
বৃন্দাবন-স্থানের দেখ আশ্চর্য বিভুতা ॥ ২৮ ॥

*kṛṣṇera mahimā rahu——kebā tāra jñātā*
*vṛndāvana-sthānera dekha āścarya vibhutā*

## SYNONYMS

*kṛṣṇera*—of Lord Kṛṣṇa; *mahimā*—glories; *rahu*—let be; *kebā*—who; *tāra*—of those; *jñātā*—a knower; *vṛndāvana-sthānera*—of the abode of Kṛṣṇa, Vṛndāvana; *dekha*—just see; *āścarya*—wonderful; *vibhutā*—opulences.

## TRANSLATION

**"Let the glories of Lord Kṛṣṇa be! Who could be aware of all of them? His abode, Vṛndāvana, has many wonderful opulences. Just try to see them all.**

## TEXT 29

ষোলক্রোশ বৃন্দাবন,—শাস্ত্রের প্রকাশে ।
তার একদেশে বৈকুণ্ঠাজাণ্ডগণ ভাসে ॥ ২৯ ॥

*ṣola-krośa vṛndāvana,——śāstrera prakāśe*
*tāra eka-deśe vaikuṇṭhājāṇḍa-gaṇa bhāse*

## SYNONYMS

*ṣola-krośa*—measuring sixteen *krośas* (thirty-two miles); *vṛndāvana*—Vṛndāvana-dhāma; *śāstrera prakāśe*—according to the revelation of revealed scripture; *tāra*—of Vṛndāvana; *eka-deśe*—in one corner; *vaikuṇṭha*—all the Vaikuṇṭha planets; *ajāṇḍa-gaṇa*—the innumerable universes; *bhāse*—are situated.

## TRANSLATION

**"According to the revelations of revealed scripture, Vṛndāvana extends only sixteen krośas [thirty-two miles]. Nonetheless, all the Vaikuṇṭha planets and innumerable universes are located in one corner of this tract.**

## PURPORT

In Vraja, the land is divided into various *vanas,* or forests. The forests total twelve, and their extension is estimated to be eighty-four *krośas.* Of these, the special forest known as Vṛndāvana is located from the present municipal city of Vṛndāvana to the village called Nanda-grāma. This distance is sixteen *krośas* (thirty-two miles).

## TEXT 30

অপার ঐশ্বর্য কৃষ্ণের—নাহিক গণন ।
শাখা-চন্দ্র-ন্যায়ে করি দিগ্‌দরশন ॥ ৩০ ॥

*apāra aiśvarya kṛṣṇera——nāhika gaṇana*
*śākhā-candra-nyāye kari dig-daraśana*

## SYNONYMS

*apāra*—unlimited; *aiśvarya*—opulence; *kṛṣṇera*—of Lord Kṛṣṇa; *nāhika gaṇana*—there is no estimation; *śākhā-candra-nyāye*—according to the logic of seeing the moon through the branches of a tree; *kari*—I make; *dik-daraśana*—an indication only.

### TRANSLATION

**"No one can estimate the opulence of Kṛṣṇa. That is unlimited. However, just as one sees the moon through the branches of a tree, I wish to give a little indication."**

### PURPORT

First a child is shown the branches of a tree, and then he is shown the moon through the branches. This is called *śākhā-candra-nyāya*. The idea is that first one must be given a simpler example. Then the more difficult background is explained.

### TEXT 31

**ঐশ্বর্য কহিতে স্ফুরিল ঐশ্বর্য-সাগর ।**
**মনেন্দ্রিয় ডুবিলা, প্রভু হইলা ফাঁপর ॥ ৩১ ॥**

*aiśvarya kahite sphurila aiśvarya-sāgara*
*manendriya ḍubilā, prabhu ha-ilā phāṅpara*

### SYNONYMS

*aiśvarya*—opulence; *kahite*—to describe; *sphurila*—there manifested; *aiśvarya-sāgara*—an ocean of opulence; *mana-indriya*—the chief sense, namely the mind; *ḍubilā*—immersed; *prabhu*—Śrī Caitanya Mahāprabhu; *ha-ilā*—became; *phāṅpara*—perplexed.

### TRANSLATION

**While describing the transcendental opulences of Kṛṣṇa, the ocean of opulence manifested in the mind of Śrī Caitanya Mahāprabhu, and His mind and senses were immersed in this ocean. Thus He was perplexed.**

### TEXT 32

**ভাগবতের এই শ্লোক পড়িলা আপনে ।**
**অর্থ আস্বাদিতে সুখে করেন ব্যাখ্যানে ॥ ৩২ ॥**

*bhāgavatera ei śloka paḍilā āpane*
*artha āsvādite sukhe karena vyākhyāne*

## SYNONYMS

*bhāgavatera*—of *Śrīmad-Bhāgavatam; ei*—this; *śloka*—verse; *paḍilā*—recited; *āpane*—personally; *artha*—the meaning; *āsvādite*—to taste; *sukhe*—in happiness; *karena vyākhyāne*—describes the meaning.

## TRANSLATION

**Śrī Caitanya Mahāprabhu personally recited the following verse from Śrīmad-Bhāgavatam, and to relish the meaning, He began to explain it Himself.**

## TEXT 33

স্বয়ন্ত্বসাম্যাতিশয়স্ত্র্যধীশঃ স্বারাজ্যলক্ষ্ম্যাপ্তসমস্তকামঃ।
বলিং হরদ্ভিশ্চিরলোকপালৈঃ কিরীটকোটীড়িতপাদপীঠঃ॥৩৩॥

*svayaṁ tv asāmyātiśayas tryadhīśaḥ*
*svārājya-lakṣmy-āpta-samasta-kāmaḥ*
*baliṁ haradbhiś cira-loka-pālaiḥ*
*kirīṭa-koṭīḍita-pāda-pīṭhaḥ*

## SYNONYMS

*svayam*—personally the Supreme Personality of Godhead; *tu*—but; *asāmya-atiśayaḥ*—who has no equal nor superior; *tri-adhīśaḥ*—the master of three places, namely Goloka Vṛndāvana, Vaikuṇṭhaloka and the material world, or the master of Mahā-Viṣṇu, Garbhodakaśāyī Viṣṇu and Kṣīrodakaśāyī Viṣṇu, or the master of Brahmā, Viṣṇu and Maheśvara, or the master of the three worlds (the higher, lower and middle planetary systems); *svārājya-lakṣmī*—by His personal spiritual potency; *āpta*—already achieved; *samasta-kāmaḥ*—all desirable objects; *balim*—a presentation or taxation; *haradbhiḥ*—who are offering; *cira-loka-pālaiḥ*—by the predominating deities of different planets; *kirīṭa-koṭi*—by millions of helmets; *īḍita*—being worshiped; *pāda-pīṭhaḥ*—whose lotus feet.

## TRANSLATION

**" 'The Supreme Personality of Godhead, Kṛṣṇa, is the master of the three worlds and the three principal demigods [Brahmā, Viṣṇu and Śiva]. No one is equal to or greater than Him. By His spiritual potency, known as svārājya-lakṣmī, all His desires are fulfilled. While offering their dues and presents in worship, the predominating deities of all the planets touch the lotus feet of the Lord with their helmets. Thus they offer prayers to the Lord.'**

## PURPORT

This quotation is verse 21 of the Second Chapter, Third Canto of *Śrīmad-Bhāgavatam.*

## TEXT 34

**পরম ঈশ্বর কৃষ্ণ স্বয়ং ভগবান্ ।**
**তাতে বড়, তাঁর সম কেহ নাহি আন ॥ ৩৪ ॥**

*parama īśvara kṛṣṇa svayaṁ bhagavān*
*tāte baḍa, tāṅra sama keha nāhi āna*

## SYNONYMS

*parama*—supreme; *īśvara*—controller; *kṛṣṇa*—Lord Kṛṣṇa; *svayam*—personally; *bhagavān*—the original Personality of Godhead; *tāte*—therefore; *baḍa*—most exalted; *tāṅra*—His; *sama*—equal; *keha*—anyone; *nāhi*—there is not; *āna*—else.

## TRANSLATION

**"Kṛṣṇa is the original Supreme Personality of Godhead; therefore He is the greatest of all. No one is equal to Him, nor is anyone greater than Him.**

## TEXT 35

ঈশ্বরঃ পরমঃ কৃষ্ণঃ সচ্চিদানন্দবিগ্রহঃ ।
অনাদিরাদির্গোবিন্দঃ সর্বকারণকারণম্ ॥ ৩৫ ॥

*īśvaraḥ paramaḥ kṛṣṇaḥ*
*sac-cid-ānanda-vigrahaḥ*
*anādir ādir govindaḥ*
*sarva-kāraṇa-kāraṇam*

## SYNONYMS

*īśvaraḥ*—the controller; *paramaḥ*—supreme; *kṛṣṇaḥ*—Lord Kṛṣṇa; *sat*—eternal existence; *cit*—absolute knowledge; *ānanda*—absolute bliss; *vigrahaḥ*—whose form; *anādiḥ*—without beginning; *ādiḥ*—the origin; *govindaḥ*—Lord Govinda; *sarva-kāraṇa-kāraṇam*—the cause of all causes.

## TRANSLATION

**" 'Kṛṣṇa, known as Govinda, is the supreme controller. He has an eternal, blissful, spiritual body. He is the origin of all. He has no other origin, for He is the prime cause of all causes.'**

### PURPORT

This is the first verse of the Fifth Chapter of *Brahma-saṁhitā.*

### TEXT 36

ব্রহ্মা, বিষ্ণু, হর,—এই সৃষ্ট্যাদি-ঈশ্বর ।
তিনে আজ্ঞাকারী কৃষ্ণের, কৃষ্ণ – অধীশ্বর ॥ ৩৬ ॥

*brahmā, viṣṇu, hara,——ei sṛṣṭyādi-īśvara*
*tine ājñākārī kṛṣṇera, kṛṣṇa——adhīśvara*

### SYNONYMS

*brahmā*—Lord Brahmā; *viṣṇu*—Lord Viṣṇu; *hara*—and Lord Śiva; *ei*—they; *sṛṣṭi-ādi-īśvara*—the masters of material creation, maintenance and dissolution; *tine*—all three of them; *ājñākārī*—order carriers; *kṛṣṇera*—of Lord Kṛṣṇa; *kṛṣṇa*—Lord Kṛṣṇa; *adhīśvara*—their master.

### TRANSLATION

**"The primary predominating deities of this material creation are Lord Brahmā, Lord Śiva and Lord Viṣṇu. Nonetheless, they simply carry out the orders of Lord Kṛṣṇa, who is master of them all.**

### TEXT 37

সৃজামি তন্নিযুক্তোঽহং হরো হরতি তদ্বশঃ ।
বিশ্বং পুরুষরূপেণ পরিপাতি ত্রিশক্তিধৃক্ ॥ ৭ ॥

*sṛjāmi tan-niyukto 'haṁ*
*haro harati tad-vaśaḥ*
*viśvaṁ puruṣa-rūpeṇa*
*paripāti triśakti-dhṛk*

### SYNONYMS

*sṛjāmi*—create; *tat-niyuktaḥ*—engaged by Him; *aham*—I; *haraḥ*—Lord Śiva; *harati*—annihilates; *tat-vaśaḥ*—under His control; *viśvam*—the whole universe; *puruṣa-rūpeṇa*—in the form of Lord Viṣṇu; *paripāti*—maintains; *tri-śakti-dhṛk*—the controller of the three modes of material nature.

### TRANSLATION

**"Lord Brahmā said, 'Following the will of the Supreme Personality of Godhead, I create, Lord Śiva destroys, and He Himself in the form of Kṣīrodakaśāyī**

**Viṣṇu maintains all the affairs of material nature. Thus the supreme controller of the three modes of material nature is Lord Viṣṇu.'**

### PURPORT

This is a quotation from *Śrīmad-Bhāgavatam* (2.6.32).

### TEXT 38

**এ সামান্য, ত্র্যধীশ্বরের শুন অর্থ আর ।**
**জগৎকারণ তিন পুরুষাবতার ॥ ৩৮ ॥**

*e sāmānya, tryadhīśvarera śuna artha āra*
*jagat-kāraṇa tina puruṣāvatāra*

### SYNONYMS

*e sāmānya*—this is a general description; *tri-adhīśvarera*—of the master of the three worlds; *śuna*—please hear; *artha*—meaning; *āra*—another; *jagat-kāraṇa*—the cause of the material creation; *tina*—three; *puruṣa-avatāra*—*puruṣa* incarnations of Viṣṇu.

### TRANSLATION

**"This is only a general description. Please try to understand another meaning of tryadhīśa. The three puruṣa incarnations of Viṣṇu are the original cause of the material creation.**

### TEXT 39

**মহাবিষ্ণু, পদ্মনাভ, ক্ষীরোদকস্বামী ।**
**এই তিন—স্থূল-সূক্ষ্ম-সর্ব-অন্তর্যামী ॥ ৩৯ ॥**

*mahā-viṣṇu, padmanābha, kṣīrodaka-svāmī*
*ei tina——sthūla-sūkṣma-sarva-antaryāmī*

### SYNONYMS

*mahā-viṣṇu*—Mahā-Viṣṇu; *padmanābha*—Padmanābha (Garbhodakaśāyī Viṣṇu); *kṣīra-udaka-svāmī*—Kṣīrodakaśāyī Viṣṇu; *ei tina*—all these three; *sthūla-sūkṣma*—gross and subtle; *sarva*—of all; *antaryāmī*—the Supersoul.

### TRANSLATION

**"Mahā-Viṣṇu, Padmanābha and Kṣīrodakaśāyī Viṣṇu are the Supersouls of all subtle and gross existences.**

### PURPORT

Lord Mahā-Viṣṇu is known as Kāraṇodakaśāyī Viṣṇu, the Supersoul of everything. Garbhodakaśāyī Viṣṇu, from whose lotus navel Brahmā was created, is also called Hiraṇyagarbha and is the total Supersoul and the subtle Supersoul. Kṣīrodakaśāyī Viṣṇu is the universal form and the gross Supersoul.

### TEXT 40

**এই তিন—সর্বাশ্রয়, জগৎ-ঈশ্বর ।**
**এহো সব কলা-অংশ, কৃষ্ণ—অধীশ্বর ॥ ৪০ ॥**

*ei tina——sarvāśraya, jagat-īśvara*
*eho saba kalā-aṁśa, kṛṣṇa——adhīśvara*

### SYNONYMS

*ei tina*—these three; *sarva-āśraya*—the shelter of the whole material creation; *jagat-īśvara*—supreme controllers of the universe; *eho saba*—all of Them; *kalā-aṁśa*—plenary portions, or portions of the plenary portions; *kṛṣṇa*—Lord Kṛṣṇa; *adhīśvara*—the Supreme Personality of Godhead.

### TRANSLATION

**"Although Mahā-Viṣṇu, Padmanābha and Kṣīrodakaśāyī Viṣṇu are all shelters and controllers of the entire universe, They are nonetheless but plenary portions or portions of the plenary portions of Kṛṣṇa. Therefore He is the original Personality of Godhead.**

### TEXT 41

যস্যৈকনিশ্বসিতকালমথাবলম্ব্য
জীবন্তি লোমবিলজা জগদণ্ডনাথাঃ ।
বিষ্ণুর্মহান্ স ইহ যস্য কলাবিশেষো
গোবিন্দমাদিপুরুষং তমহং ভজামি ॥ ৪১ ॥

*yasyaika-niśvasita-kālam athāvalambya*
*jīvanti loma-vilajā jagad-aṇḍa-nāthāḥ*
*viṣṇur mahān sa iha yasya kalā-viśeṣo*
*govindam ādi-puruṣaṁ tam ahaṁ bhajāmi*

### SYNONYMS

*yasya*—whose; *eka*—one; *niśvasita*—of breath; *kālam*—time; *atha*—thus; *avalambya*—taking shelter of; *jīvanti*—live; *loma-vilajāḥ*—grown from the hair holes; *jagat-aṇḍa-nāthāḥ*—the masters of the universes (the Brahmās); *viṣṇuḥ mahān*—the Supreme Lord Mahā-Viṣṇu; *saḥ*—that; *iha*—here; *yasya*—whose; *kalā-viśeṣaḥ*—particular plenary portion or expansion; *govindam*—Lord Govinda; *ādi-puruṣam*—the original person; *tam*—Him; *aham*—I; *bhajāmi*—worship.

### TRANSLATION

**" 'The Brahmās and other lords of the mundane worlds appear from the pores of the Mahā-Viṣṇu and remain alive for the duration of His one exhalation. I adore the primeval Lord, Govinda, for Mahā-Viṣṇu is a portion of His plenary portion.'**

### PURPORT

This is a quotation from *Brahma-saṁhitā* (5.48). See also *Ādi-līlā* (5.71).

## TEXT 42

এই অর্থ – মধ্যম, শুন 'গূঢ়' অর্থ আর ।
তিন আবাস-স্থান কৃষ্ণের শাস্ত্রে খ্যাতি যার ॥ ৪২ ॥

*ei artha——madhyama, śuna 'gūḍha' artha āra*
*tina āvāsa-sthāna kṛṣṇera śāstre khyāti yāra*

### SYNONYMS

*ei artha*—this explanation; *madhyama*—middle; *śuna*—please hear; *gūḍha*—confidential; *artha*—meaning; *āra*—another; *tina*—three; *āvāsa-sthāna*—residential places; *kṛṣṇera*—of Lord Kṛṣṇa; *śāstre*—in the revealed scriptures; *khyāti*—fame; *yāra*—of which.

### TRANSLATION

**"This is the middle meaning. Now please hear the confidential meaning. Lord Kṛṣṇa has three places of residence, which are well known from revealed scriptures.**

### PURPORT

Kṛṣṇa has three abodes—His internal abode (Goloka Vṛndāvana), His intermediate abode (the spiritual sky), and His external abode (this material world).

### TEXT 43

**'অন্তঃপুর'—গোলোক-শ্রীবৃন্দাবন ।**
**যাহাঁ নিত্যস্থিতি মাতাপিতা-বন্ধুগণ ॥ ৪৩ ॥**

*'antaḥpura'—goloka-śrī-vṛndāvana*
*yāhāṅ nitya-sthiti mātā-pitā-bandhu-gaṇa*

### SYNONYMS

*antaḥ-pura*—the internal abode; *goloka-śrī-vṛndāvana*—Goloka Vṛndāvana; *yāhāṅ*—where; *nitya-sthiti*—eternal residence; *mātā-pitā*—mother and father; *bandhu-gaṇa*—and friends.

### TRANSLATION

**"The internal abode is called Goloka Vṛndāvana. It is there that Lord Kṛṣṇa's personal friends, associates, father and mother live.**

### TEXT 44

**মধুরৈশ্বর্য-মাধুর্য-কৃপাদি-ভাণ্ডার ।**
**যোগমায়া দাসী যাহাঁ রাসাদি লীলা-সার ॥ ৪৪ ॥**

*madhuraiśvarya-mādhurya-kṛpādi-bhāṇḍāra*
*yogamāyā dāsī yāhāṅ rāsādi līlā-sāra*

### SYNONYMS

*madhura-aiśvarya*—of sweetness and opulence; *mādhurya*—of conjugal love; *kṛpā-ādi*—and of mercy and so on; *bhāṇḍāra*—storehouse; *yoga-māyā*—the spiritual energy; *dāsī*—maidservant; *yāhāṅ*—where; *rāsa-ādi*—the *rāsa* dance and other pastimes; *līlā-sāra*—the quintessence of all pastimes.

### TRANSLATION

**"Vṛndāvana is the storehouse of Kṛṣṇa's mercy and the sweet opulences of conjugal love. That is where the spiritual energy, working as a maidservant, exhibits the rāsa dance, the quintessence of all pastimes.**

### TEXT 45

করুণানিকুরম্বকোমলে মধুরৈশ্বর্যবিশেষশালিনি ।
জয়তি ব্রজরাজনন্দনে ন হি চিন্তাকণিকাভ্যুদেতি নঃ ॥৪৫॥

*karuṇā-nikuramba-komale*
*madhuraiśvarya-viśeṣa-śālini*
*jayati vraja-rāja-nandane*
*na hi cintā-kaṇikābhyudeti naḥ*

### SYNONYMS

*karuṇā-nikuramba-komale*—who is very soft because of great mercy; *madhura-aiśvarya-viśeṣa-śālini*—expecially by the opulence of conjugal love; *jayati*—all glories; *vraja-rāja-nandane*—to the son of Mahārāja Nanda; *na*—not; *hi*—certainly; *cintā*—of anxiety; *kaṇika*—even a particle; *abhyudeti*—awakens; *naḥ*—of us.

### TRANSLATION

**"Vṛndāvana-dhāma is very soft due to the mercy of the Supreme Lord, and it is especially opulent due to conjugal love. The transcendental glories of the son of Mahārāja Nanda are exhibited here. Under the circumstances, not the least anxiety is awakened within us.**

### TEXT 46

**তার তলে পরব্যোম—'বিষ্ণুলোক'-নাম ।**
**নারায়ণ-আদি অনন্ত স্বরূপের ধাম ॥ ৪৬ ॥**

*tāra tale paravyoma—'viṣṇuloka'-nāma*
*nārāyaṇa-ādi ananta svarūpera dhāma*

### SYNONYMS

*tāra tale*—below Vṛndāvana-dhāma; *para-vyoma*—the spiritual sky; *viṣṇu-loka-nāma*—known as Viṣṇuloka; *nārāyaṇa-ādi*—Nārāyaṇa and others; *ananta*—unlimited; *sva-rūpera*—of personal expansions; *dhāma*—the place.

### TRANSLATION

**"Below the Vṛndāvana planet is the spiritual sky, which is known as Viṣṇuloka. In Viṣṇuloka there are innumerable Vaikuṇṭha planets controlled by Nārāyaṇa and other innumerable expansions of Kṛṣṇa.**

### TEXT 47

**'মধ্যম-আবাস' কৃষ্ণের—ষড়ৈশ্বর্য-ভাণ্ডার ।**
**অনন্ত স্বরূপে যাহাঁ করেন বিহার ॥ ৪৭ ॥**

*'madhyama-āvāsa' kṛṣṇera——ṣaḍ-aiśvarya-bhāṇḍāra*
*ananta svarūpe yāhāṅ karena vihāra*

### SYNONYMS

*madhyama-āvāsa*—the middle residence; *kṛṣṇera*—of Lord Kṛṣṇa; *ṣaṭ-aiśvarya-bhāṇḍāra*—the storehouse of six opulences; *ananta sva-rūpe*—in unlimited forms; *yāhāṅ*—where; *karena vihāra*—enjoys His pastimes.

### TRANSLATION

**"The spiritual sky, which is full in all six opulences, is the interim residence of Lord Kṛṣṇa. It is there that an unlimited number of forms of Kṛṣṇa enjoy Their pastimes.**

### TEXT 48

অনন্ত বৈকুণ্ঠ যাহাঁ ভাণ্ডার-কোঠরি ।
পারিষদগণে ষড়ৈশ্বর্যে আছে ভরি' ॥ ৪৮ ॥

*ananta vaikuṇṭha yāhāṅ bhāṇḍāra-koṭhari*
*pāriṣada-gaṇe ṣaḍ-aiśvarye āche bhari'*

### SYNONYMS

*ananta*—unlimited; *vaikuṇṭha*—Vaikuṇṭha planets; *yāhāṅ*—where; *bhāṇḍāra-koṭhari*—like rooms of a treasure-house; *pāriṣada-gaṇe*—eternal associates; *ṣaṭ-aiśvarye*—with the six opulences; *āche*—are; *bhari'*—filling.

### TRANSLATION

**"Innumerable Vaikuṇṭha planets, which are just like different rooms of a treasure-house, are all there, filled with all opulences. Those unlimited planets house the Lord's eternal associates, who are also enriched with the six opulences."**

### TEXT 49

গোলোকনাম্নি নিজধাম্নি তলে চ তস্য
দেবী-মহেশ-হরিধামসু তেষু তেষু ।
তে তে প্রভাবনিচয়া বিহিতাশ্চ যেন
গোবিন্দমাদিপুরুষং তমহং ভজামি ॥ ৪৯ ॥

*goloka-nāmni nija-dhāmni tale ca tasya*
*devī-maheśa-hari-dhāmasu teṣu teṣu*

*te te prabhāva-nicayā vihitāś ca yena*
*govindam ādi-puruṣaṁ tam ahaṁ bhajāmi*

## SYNONYMS

*goloka-nāmni nija-dhāmni*—in the planet known as Goloka Vṛndāvana, the personal abode of the Supreme Personality of Godhead; *tale*—in the part underneath; *ca*—also; *tasya*—of that; *devī*—of the goddess Durgā; *maheśa*—of Lord Śiva; *hari*—of Nārāyaṇa; *dhāmasu*—in the planets; *teṣu teṣu*—in each of them; *te te*—those respective; *prabhāva-nicayāḥ*—opulences; *vihitāḥ*—established; *ca*—also; *yena*—by whom; *govindam*—unto that Govinda; *ādi-puruṣam*—the original Supreme Personality of Godhead; *tam*—unto Him; *aham*—I; *bhajāmi*—offer my obeisances.

## TRANSLATION

**" 'Below the planet named Goloka Vṛndāvana are the planets known as Devī-dhāma, Maheśa-dhāma and Hari-dhāma. These are opulent in different ways. They are managed by the Supreme Personality of Godhead, Govinda, the original Lord. I offer my obeisances unto Him.'**

## PURPORT

This is a quotation from *Brahma-saṁhitā* (5.43).

## TEXT 50

প্রধান-পরমব্যোম্নোরন্তরে বিরজা নদী ।
বেদাঙ্গস্বেদজনিতৈস্তোয়ৈঃ প্রস্রাবিতা শুভা ॥ ৫০ ॥

*pradhāna-parama-vyomnor*
*antare virajā nadī*
*vedāṅga-sveda-janitais*
*toyaiḥ prasrāvitā śubhā*

## SYNONYMS

*pradhāna-parama-vyomnoḥ antare*—between the material world and spiritual world; *virajā nadī*—is a river known as Virajā; *veda-aṅga*—of the transcendental body of the Supreme Personality of Godhead; *sveda-janitaiḥ*—produced from the perspiration; *toyaiḥ*—with water; *prasrāvitā*—flowing; *śubhā*—all-auspicious.

## TRANSLATION

**" 'Between the spiritual and material worlds is a body of water known as the River Virajā. This water is generated from the bodily perspiration of the**

**Supreme Personality of Godhead, who is known as Vedāṅga. Thus the river flows.'**

### PURPORT

This verse and the following verse are from the *Padma Purāṇa*.

### TEXT 51

তস্যাঃ পারে পরব্যোম ত্রিপাদ্‌ভূতং সনাতনম্ ।
অমৃতং শাশ্বতং নিত্যমনন্তং পরমং পদম্ ॥ ৫১ ॥

*tasyāḥ pāre paravyoma*
*tripād-bhūtaṁ sanātanam*
*amṛtaṁ śāśvataṁ nityam*
*anantaṁ paramaṁ padam*

### SYNONYMS

*tasyāḥ pāre*—on the other bank of the Virajā River; *para-vyoma*—the spiritual sky; *tri-pād-bhūtam*—existing as three fourths of the opulence of the Supreme Lord; *sanātanam*—eternal; *amṛtam*—without deterioration; *śāśvatam*—without being subjected to the control of time; *nityam*—constantly existing; *anantam*—unlimited; *paramam*—supreme; *padam*—abode.

### TRANSLATION

**" 'Beyond the River Virajā is a spiritual nature, which is indestructible, eternal, inexhaustible and unlimited. It is the supreme abode consisting of three fourths of the Lord's opulences. It is known as paravyoma, the spiritual sky.'**

### PURPORT

In the spiritual sky there is neither anxiety nor fear. It is eternally existing, and it consists of three fourths of the Lord's energy. The material world is an exhibition of only one fourth of the Lord's energy. Therefore it is called *eka-pāda-vibhūti*.

### TEXT 52

**তার তলে 'বাহ্যাবাস' বিরজার পার ।**
**অনন্ত ব্রহ্মাণ্ড যাহাঁ কোঠরি অপার ॥ ৫২ ॥**

*tāra tale 'bāhyāvāsa' virajāra pāra*
*ananta brahmāṇḍa yāhāṅ koṭhari apāra*

### SYNONYMS

*tāra tale*—below the spiritual world; *bāhya-āvāsa*—external abode; *virajāra pāra*—on the other side of the River Virajā; *ananta brahmāṇḍa*—unlimited number of universes; *yāhāṅ*—where; *koṭhari*—apartments; *apāra*—unlimited.

### TRANSLATION

**"On the other side of the River Virajā is the external abode, which is full of unlimited universes, each containing unlimited atmospheres.**

### TEXT 53

‘দেবীধাম’ নাম তার, জীব যার বাসী ।
জগল্লক্ষ্মী রাখি’ রহে যাহাঁ মায়া দাসী ॥ ৫৩ ॥

*'devī-dhāma' nāma tāra, jīva yāra vāsī*
*jagal-lakṣmī rākhi' rahe yāhāṅ māyā dāsī*

### SYNONYMS

*devī-dhāma*—the place of the external energy; *nāma*—named; *tāra*—its; *jīva*—the conditioned living entities; *yāra*—of which; *vāsī*—the inhabitants; *jagat-lakṣmī*—the material energy; *rākhi'*—keeping them; *rahe*—exists; *yāhāṅ*—wherein; *māyā*—the external energy; *dāsī*—maidservant.

### TRANSLATION

**"The abode of the external energy is called Devī-dhāma, and its inhabitants are conditioned souls. It is there that the material energy, Durgā, resides with many opulent maidservants.**

### PURPORT

Because he wants to enjoy the material energy, the conditioned soul is allowed to reside in Devī-dhāma, the external energy, where the goddess Durgā carries out the orders of the Supreme Lord as His maidservant. The material energy is called *jagal-lakṣmī* because she protects the bewildered conditioned souls. The goddess Durgā is therefore known as the mother, and Lord Śiva, her husband, is known as the father. Lord Śiva and goddess Durgā are therefore known as the material father and mother. Goddess Durgā is so named because this material world is like a big fort where the conditioned soul is placed under her care. For material facilities, the conditioned soul tries to please the goddess Durgā, and mother Durgā supplies all kinds of material facilities. Because of this, the conditioned souls are allured and do not wish to leave the external energy. Consequently they are continuously making plans to live here peacefully and happily. Such is the material world.

## TEXT 54

এই তিন ধামের হয় কৃষ্ণ অধীশ্বর ।
গোলোক-পরব্যোম – প্রকৃতির পর ॥ ৫৪ ॥

*ei tina dhāmera haya kṛṣṇa adhīśvara*
*goloka-paravyoma——prakṛtira para*

## SYNONYMS

*ei tina dhāmera*—of these three *dhāmas,* or residential places, namely Goloka Vṛndāvana-dhāma, Vaikuṇṭha-dhāma (Hari-dhāma) and Devī-dhāma (the material world); *haya*—is; *kṛṣṇa*—Lord Kṛṣṇa; *adhīśvara*—the supreme master; *goloka-paravyoma*—the spiritual planet Goloka and the spiritual sky; *prakṛtira para*—beyond this material energy.

## TRANSLATION

**"Kṛṣṇa is the supreme proprietor of all dhāmas, including Goloka-dhāma, Vaikuṇṭha-dhāma and Devī-dhāma. The paravyoma and Goloka-dhāma are beyond Devī-dhāma, this material world.**

## PURPORT

When a living entity is liberated from Devī-dhāma but does not know of the opulence of Hari-dhāma, he is placed in Maheśa-dhāma, which is between the other two *dhāmas.* The liberated soul does not get an opportunity to serve the Supreme Personality of Godhead there; therefore although this Maheśa-dhāma is Lord Śiva's *dhāma* and above the Devī-dhāma, it is not the spiritual world. The spiritual world begins with Hari-dhāma, or Vaikuṇṭhaloka.

## TEXT 55

চিচ্ছক্তিবিভূতি-ধাম—ত্রিপাদৈশ্বর্য-নাম ।
মায়িক বিভূতি- একপাদ অভিধান ॥ ৫৫ ॥

*cic-chakti-vibhūti-dhāma——tripād-aiśvarya-nāma*
*māyika vibhūti——eka-pāda abhidhāna*

## SYNONYMS

*cit-śakti*—of the spiritual energy; *vibhūti-dhāma*—opulent abode; *tri-pād*—three fourths; *aiśvarya*—opulence; *nāma*—named; *māyika vibhūti*—material opulence; *eka-pāda*—one fourth; *abhidhāna*—known.

### TRANSLATION

**"The spiritual world is considered to be three fourths of the energy and opulence of the Supreme Personality of Godhead, whereas this material world is only one fourth of that energy. That is our understanding.**

### PURPORT

Hari-dhāma (*paravyoma*) and Goloka Vṛndāvana are beyond the material cosmic manifestation. They are celebrated as three fourths of the Lord's energy. The material world, conducted by the Supreme Lord's external energy, is called Devī-dhāma and is a manifestation of one fourth of His energy.

### TEXT 56

ত্রিপাদ্বিভূতের্ধামত্বাৎ ত্রিপাদ্ভূতং হি তৎ পদম্ ।
বিভূতির্মায়িকী সর্বা প্রোক্তা পাদাত্মিকা যতঃ ॥ ৫৬ ॥

*tripād-vibhūter dhāmatvāt*
*tripād-bhūtaṁ hi tat padam*
*vibhūtir māyikī sarvā*
*proktā pādātmikā yataḥ*

### SYNONYMS

*tri-pād-vibhūteḥ*—of the three fourths of the energy; *dhāmatvāt*—because of being the abode; *tri-pād-bhūtam*—consisting of three fourths of the energy; *hi*—certainly; *tat padam*—that abode; *vibhūtiḥ*—the energy or potency; *māyikī*—material; *sarvā*—all; *proktā*—said; *pāda-ātmikā*—only one fourth; *yataḥ*—therefore.

### TRANSLATION

**" 'Because it consists of three fourths of the Lord's energy, the spiritual world is called tripād-bhūta. Being a manifestation of one fourth of the Lord's energy, the material world is called eka-pāda.'**

### PURPORT

This verse is found in *Laghu-bhāgavatāmṛta* (1.5.286).

### TEXT 57

**ত্রিপাদবিভূতি কৃষ্ণের—বাক্য-অগোচর ।**
**একপাদ বিভূতির শুনহ বিস্তার ॥ ৫৭ ॥**

*tripāda-vibhūti kṛṣṇera——vākya-agocara*
*eka-pāda vibhūtira śunaha vistāra*

### SYNONYMS

*tri-pāda-vibhūti kṛṣṇera*—three fourths of the energy of Lord Kṛṣṇa; *vākya-agocara*—beyond words; *eka-pāda vibhūtira*—of one fourth of the energy; *śunaha*—please hear; *vistāra*—breadth.

### TRANSLATION

**"The three-fourths part of Lord Kṛṣṇa's energy is beyond our speaking power. Let us therefore hear elaborately about the remaining one fourth of His energy.**

### TEXT 58

অনন্ত ব্রহ্মাণ্ডের যত ব্রহ্মা-রুদ্রগণ ।
চিরলোকপাল-শব্দে তাহার গণন ॥ ৫৮ ॥

*ananta brahmāṇḍera yata brahmā-rudra-gaṇa*
*cira-loka-pāla-śabde tāhāra gaṇana*

### SYNONYMS

*ananta*—unlimited; *brahmāṇḍera*—of the universes; *yata*—all; *brahmā*—Lord Brahmās; *rudra-gaṇa*—and Lord Śivas; *cira-loka-pāla*—permanent governors of the worlds; *śabde*—by the word; *tāhāra*—of them; *gaṇana*—counting.

### TRANSLATION

**"Actually it is very difficult to ascertain the number of universes. Every universe has its separate Lord Brahmā and Lord Śiva, who are known as permanent governors. Therefore there is also no counting of them.**

### PURPORT

Lord Brahmā and Lord Śiva are called *cira-loka-pāla,* permanent governors. This means that they govern the affairs of the universe from the beginning of the creation to the end. In the next creation, the same living entities may not be present, but because Brahmā and Śiva are existing from the beginning to the end, they are called *cira-loka-pāla,* permanent governors. *Loka-pāla* means "predominating deities." There are eight predominating deities of the prominent heavenly planets, and they are Indra, Agni, Yama, Varuṇa, Nirṛti, Vāyu, Kuvera and Śiva.

### TEXT 59

একদিন দ্বারকাতে কৃষ্ণ দেখিবারে ।
ব্রহ্মা আইলা,– দ্বারপাল জানাইল কৃষ্ণেরে ॥ ৫৯ ॥

*eka-dina dvārakāte kṛṣṇa dekhibāre*
*brahmā āilā,——dvāra-pāla jānāila kṛṣṇere*

### SYNONYMS

*eka-dina*—one day; *dvārakāte*—in Dvārakā; *kṛṣṇa dekhibāre*—to see Kṛṣṇa; *brahmā āilā*—Lord Brahmā came; *dvāra-pāla*—the doorman; *jānāila*—informed; *kṛṣṇere*—Lord Kṛṣṇa.

### TRANSLATION

**"Once, when Kṛṣṇa was ruling Dvārakā, Lord Brahmā came to see Him, and the doorman immediately informed Lord Kṛṣṇa of Brahmā's arrival.**

### TEXT 60

কৃষ্ণ কহেন –'কোন্ ব্রহ্মা, কি নাম তাহার ?'
দ্বারী আসি' ব্রহ্মারে পুছে আর বার ॥ ৬০ ॥

*kṛṣṇa kahena——'kon brahmā, ki nāma tāhāra?'*
*dvārī āsi' brahmāre puche āra bāra*

### SYNONYMS

*kṛṣṇa kahena*—Kṛṣṇa said; *kon brahmā*—which Brahmā; *ki nāma tāhāra*—what is his name; *dvārī āsi'*—the doorman, coming back; *brahmāre*—to Lord Brahmā; *puche*—inquires; *āra bāra*—again.

### TRANSLATION

**"When Kṛṣṇa was so informed, He immediately asked the doorman, 'Which Brahmā? What is his name?' The doorman therefore returned and questioned Lord Brahmā.**

### PURPORT

From this verse we can understand that Brahmā is the name of the post and that the person occupying the post has a particular name also. From *Bhagavad-gītā: imaṁ vivasvate yogam.* Vivasvān is the name of the present predominating deity of the sun. He is generally called Sūrya, the sun-god, but he also has his own particular name. The governor of the state is generally called *rāja-pāla,* but he also has his own individual name. Since there are hundreds and thousands of Brahmās with different names, Kṛṣṇa wanted to know which of them had come to see Him.

## TEXT 61

বিস্মিত হঞা ব্রহ্মা দ্বারীকে কহিলা।
'কহ গিয়া সনক-পিতা চতুর্মুখ আইলা' ॥ ৬১ ॥

*vismita hañā brahmā dvārīke kahilā*
*'kaha giyā sanaka-pitā caturmukha āilā'*

## SYNONYMS

*vismita hañā*—becoming surprised; *brahmā*—Lord Brahmā; *dvārīke*—unto the doorman; *kahilā*—replied; *kaha*—inform; *giyā*—going; *sanaka-pitā*—the father of the four Kumāras; *catuḥ-mukha*—four-headed; *āilā*—has come.

## TRANSLATION

**"When the doorman asked, 'Which Brahmā?' Lord Brahmā was surprised. He told the doorman, 'Please go inform Lord Kṛṣṇa that I am the four-headed Brahmā who is the father of the four Kumāras.'**

## TEXT 62

কৃষ্ণে জানাঞা দ্বারী ব্রহ্মারে লঞা গেলা।
কৃষ্ণের চরণে ব্রহ্মা দণ্ডবৎ কৈলা ॥ ৬২ ॥

*kṛṣṇe jānāñā dvārī brahmāre lañā gelā*
*kṛṣṇera caraṇe brahmā daṇḍavat kailā*

## SYNONYMS

*kṛṣṇe jānāñā*—informing Lord Kṛṣṇa; *dvārī*—the doorman; *brahmāre*—Lord Brahmā; *lañā*—taking; *gelā*—went; *kṛṣṇera caraṇe*—at the lotus feet of Kṛṣṇa; *brahmā*—Lord Brahmā; *daṇḍavat kailā*—offered obeisances.

## TRANSLATION

**"The doorman then informed Lord Kṛṣṇa of Lord Brahmā's description, and Lord Kṛṣṇa gave him permission to enter. The doorman escorted Lord Brahmā in, and as soon as Brahmā saw Lord Kṛṣṇa, he offered obeisances at His lotus feet.**

### TEXT 63

কৃষ্ণ মান্য-পূজা করি' তাঁরে প্রশ্ন কৈল।
'কি লাগি' তোমার ইহাঁ আগমন হৈল?' ৬৩ ॥

*kṛṣṇa mānya-pūjā kari' tāṅre praśna kaila*
*'ki lāgi' tomāra ihāṅ āgamana haila?'*

### SYNONYMS

*kṛṣṇa*—Lord Kṛṣṇa; *mānya-pūjā*—respect and worship; *kari'*—showing; *tāṅre*—to him; *praśna kaila*—put a question; *ki lāgi'*—for what reason; *tomāra*—your; *ihāṅ*—here; *āgamana haila*—there was arrival.

### TRANSLATION

**"After being worshiped by Lord Brahmā, Lord Kṛṣṇa also honored him with suitable words. Then Lord Kṛṣṇa asked him, 'Why have you come here?'**

### TEXT 64

ব্রহ্মা কহে,—'তাহা পাছে করিব নিবেদন।
এক সংশয় মনে হয়, করহ ছেদন ॥ ৬৪ ॥

*brahmā kahe,—'tāhā pāche kariba nivedana*
*eka saṁśaya mane haya, karaha chedana*

### SYNONYMS

*brahmā kahe*—Lord Brahmā said; *tāhā*—that; *pāche*—later; *kariba nivedana*—I shall submit unto You; *eka*—one; *saṁśaya*—doubt; *mane*—in the mind; *haya*—there is; *karaha chedana*—kindly dissipate it.

### TRANSLATION

**"Being questioned, Lord Brahmā immediately replied, 'I shall later tell You why I have come. First of all there is a doubt in my mind which I wish You would kindly dissipate.**

### TEXT 65

'কোন্ ব্রহ্মা?' পুছিলে তুমি কোন্ অভিপ্রায়ে?
আমা বই জগতে আর কোন্ ব্রহ্মা হয়ে?' ৬৫ ॥

*'kon brahmā?' puchile tumi kon abhiprāye?*
*āmā ba-i jagate āra kon brahmā haye?'*

### SYNONYMS

*kon brahmā*—which Brahmā; *puchile tumi*—You inquired; *kon abhiprāye*—by what intention; *āmā ba-i*—except me; *jagate*—within this universe; *āra*—other; *kon*—which; *brahmā*—Lord Brahmā; *haye*—is there.

### TRANSLATION

**" 'Why did you inquire which Brahmā had come to see You? What is the purpose of such an inquiry? Is there any other Brahmā besides me within this universe?'**

### TEXT 66

শুনি' হাসি' কৃষ্ণ তবে করিলেন ধ্যানে ।
অসংখ্য ব্রহ্মার গণ আইলা ততক্ষণে ॥ ৬৬ ॥

*śuni' hāsi' kṛṣṇa tabe karilena dhyāne*
*asaṅkhya brahmāra gaṇa āilā tata-kṣaṇe*

### SYNONYMS

*śuni'*—hearing; *hāsi'*—smilingly; *kṛṣṇa*—Lord Kṛṣṇa; *tabe*—then; *karilena*—did; *dhyāne*—meditation; *asaṅkhya*—unlimited; *brahmāra*—of Lord Brahmās; *gaṇa*—the group; *āilā*—arrived; *tata-kṣaṇe*—at that time.

### TRANSLATION

**"Upon hearing this, Śrī Kṛṣṇa smiled and immediately meditated. Unlimited Brahmās arrived instantly.**

### TEXT 67

দশ-বিশ-শত-সহস্র-অযুত-লক্ষ-বদন ।
কোট্যর্বুদ মুখ কারো, না যায় গণন ॥ ৬৭ ॥

*daśa-biśa-śata-sahasra-ayuta-lakṣa-vadana*
*koṭy-arbuda mukha kāro, nā yāya gaṇana*

### SYNONYMS

*daśa*—ten; *biśa*—twenty; *śata*—hundred; *sahasra*—thousand; *ayuta*—ten thousand; *lakṣa*—a hundred thousand; *vadana*—faces; *koṭi*—ten million; *ar-*

*buda*—a hundred million; *mukha*—faces; *kāro*—of some of them; *nā yāya gaṇana*—not possible to count.

### TRANSLATION

**"These Brahmās had different numbers of heads. Some had ten heads, some twenty, some a hundred, some a thousand, some ten thousand, some a hundred thousand, some ten million and others a hundred million. No one can count the number of faces they had.**

### TEXT 68

রুদ্রগণ আইলা লক্ষ কোটি-বদন ।
ইন্দ্রগণ আইলা লক্ষ কোটি-নয়ন ॥ ৬৮ ॥

*rudra-gaṇa āilā lakṣa koṭi-vadana*
*indra-gaṇa āilā lakṣa koṭi-nayana*

### SYNONYMS

*rudra-gaṇa*—the Śivas; *āilā*—arrived; *lakṣa koṭi-vadana*—possessing a hundred thousand and ten million faces; *indra-gaṇa*—the Indras; *āilā*—arrived; *lakṣa*—a hundred thousand; *koṭi*—ten million; *nayana*—eyes.

### TRANSLATION

**"There also arrived many Lord Śivas with various heads numbering one hundred thousand and ten million. Many Indras also arrived, and they had hundreds of thousands of eyes all over their bodies.**

### PURPORT

It is said that Indra, the King of heaven, is very lusty. Once he tactfully had sexual intercourse with the wife of a great sage, and when the sage learned about this, he cursed the lusty Indra with a curse that put vaginas all over his body. Being very ashamed, Indra fell down at the lotus feet of the great sage and begged his pardon. Being compassionate, the sage turned the vaginas into eyes; therefore Indra possesses hundreds and thousands of eyes all over his body. Just as Lord Brahmā and Lord Śiva have many faces, the King of heaven, Indra, has many eyes.

### TEXT 69

দেখি' চতুর্মুখ ব্রহ্মা ফাঁপর হইলা ।
হস্তিগণ-মধ্যে যেন শশক রহিলা ॥ ৬৯ ॥

*dekhi' caturmukha brahmā phāṅpara ha-ilā*
*hasti-gaṇa-madhye yena śaśaka rahilā*

### SYNONYMS

*dekhi'*—seeing; *catuḥ-mukha brahmā*—the four-faced Lord Brahmā of this universe; *phāṅpara ha-ilā*—became bewildered; *hasti-gaṇa-madhye*—in the midst of many elephants; *yena*—like; *śaśaka*—a rabbit; *rahilā*—remained.

### TRANSLATION

**"When the four-headed Brahmā of this universe saw all these opulences of Kṛṣṇa, he became very bewildered and considered himself a rabbit among many elephants.**

## TEXT 70

আসি' সব ব্রহ্মা কৃষ্ণ-পাদপীঠ-আগে ।
দণ্ডবৎ করিতে মুকুট পাদপীঠে লাগে ॥ ৭০ ॥

*āsi' saba brahmā kṛṣṇa-pāda-pīṭha-āge*
*daṇḍavat karite mukuṭa pāda-pīṭhe lāge*

### SYNONYMS

*āsi'*—coming; *saba brahmā*—all the Brahmās; *kṛṣṇa-pāda-pīṭha-āge*—before the lotus feet of Kṛṣṇa; *daṇḍavat karite*—offering their obeisances; *mukuṭa*—helmets; *pāda-pīṭhe*—at the lotus feet; *lāge*—touched.

### TRANSLATION

**"All the Brahmās who came to see Kṛṣṇa offered their respects at His lotus feet, and when they did this, their helmets touched His lotus feet.**

## TEXT 71

কৃষ্ণের অচিন্ত্য-শক্তি লখিতে কেহ নারে ।
যত ব্রহ্মা, তত মূর্তি একই শরীরে ॥ ৭১ ॥

*kṛṣṇera acintya-śakti lakhite keha nāre*
*yata brahmā, tata mūrti eka-i śarīre*

### SYNONYMS

*kṛṣṇera*—of Lord Kṛṣṇa; *acintya-śakti*—inconceivable potencies; *lakhite*—to observe; *keha*—anyone; *nāre*—not able; *yata brahmā*—all Brahmās; *tata mūrti*—so many forms; *eka-i śarīre*—in the same body.

### TRANSLATION

**"No one can estimate the inconceivable potency of Kṛṣṇa. All the Brahmās who were there were resting in the one body of Kṛṣṇa.**

### TEXT 72

পাদপীট-মুকুটাগ্র-সংঘট্টে উঠে ধ্বনি ।
পাদপীঠে স্তুতি করে মুকুট হেন জানি' ॥ ৭২ ॥

*pāda-pīṭa-mukuṭāgra-saṅghaṭṭe uṭhe dhvani*
*pāda-pīṭhe stuti kare mukuṭa hena jāni'*

### SYNONYMS

*pāda-pīṭa*—at Kṛṣṇa's lotus feet; *mukuṭa-agra*—of the tops of the helmets; *saṅghaṭṭe*—in the crowding together; *uṭhe dhvani*—there arose a sound; *pāda-pīṭhe stuti*—offering prayers unto the lotus feet; *kare*—do; *mukuṭa*—the helmets; *hena jāni'*—appearing as such.

### TRANSLATION

**"When all the helmets struck together at Kṛṣṇa's lotus feet, there was a tumultuous sound. It appeared that the helmets themselves were offering prayers unto Kṛṣṇa's lotus feet.**

### TEXT 73

যোড়-হাতে ব্রহ্মা-রুদ্রাদি করয়ে স্তবন ।
"বড় কৃপা করিলা প্রভু, দেখাইলা চরণ ॥ ৭৩ ॥

*yoḍa-hāte brahmā-rudrādi karaye stavana*
*"baḍa kṛpā karilā prabhu, dekhāilā caraṇa*

### SYNONYMS

*yoḍa-hāte*—with folded hands; *brahmā*—the Lord Brahmās; *rudra-ādi*—the Lord Śivas and others; *karaye stavana*—offered their prayers; *baḍa kṛpā*—great mercy; *karilā*—You have shown; *prabhu*—O Lord; *dekhāilā caraṇa*—You have shown Your lotus feet.

### TRANSLATION

**"With folded hands, all the Brahmās and Śivas began to offer prayers unto Lord Kṛṣṇa, saying, 'O Lord, You have shown me a great favor. I have been able to see Your lotus feet.'**

### TEXT 74

ভাগ্য, মোরে বোলাইলা 'দাস' অঙ্গীকরি'।
কোন্ আজ্ঞা হয়, তাহা করি শিরে ধরি' ॥" ৭৪ ॥

*bhāgya, more bolāilā 'dāsa' aṅgīkari'*
*kon ājñā haya, tāhā kari śire dhari' "*

### SYNONYMS

*bhāgya*—great fortune; *more*—me; *bolāilā*—You have called; *dāsa*—as a servant; *aṅgīkari'*—accepting; *kon ājñā haya*—what is Your order; *tāhā*—that; *kari*—let me accept; *śire dhari'*—holding it on my head.

### TRANSLATION

**"All of them then said, 'It is my great fortune, Lord, that You have called me, thinking of me as Your servant. Now let me know what Your order is so that I may carry it on my heads.'**

### TEXT 75

কৃষ্ণ কহে,– তোমা-সবা দেখিতে চিত্ত হৈল।
তাহা লাগি' এক ঠাঞি সবা বোলাইল ॥ ৭৫ ॥

*kṛṣṇa kahe,——tomā-sabā dekhite citta haila*
*tāhā lāgi' eka ṭhāñi sabā bolāila*

### SYNONYMS

*kṛṣṇa kahe*—Lord Kṛṣṇa said; *tomā-sabā*—all of you; *dekhite*—to see; *citta haila*—there was a desire; *tāhā lāgi'*—for that reason; *eka ṭhāñi*—in one place; *sabā*—all of you; *bolāila*—I called for.

### TRANSLATION

**"Lord Kṛṣṇa replied, 'Since I wanted to see all of you together, I have called all of you here.**

### TEXT 76

সুখী হও সবে, কিছু নাহি দৈত্য-ভয় ?
তারা কহে,—'তোমার প্রসাদে সর্বত্রই জয় ॥ ৭৬ ॥

*sukhī hao sabe, kichu nāhi daitya-bhaya?*
*tārā kahe,——'tomāra prasāde sarvatra-i jaya*

### SYNONYMS

*sukhī hao*—be happy; *sabe*—all of you; *kichu*—some; *nāhi*—there is not; *daitya-bhaya*—fear of the demons; *tārā kahe*—all of them replied; *tomāra prasāde*—by Your mercy; *sarvatra-i*—everywhere; *jaya*—victorious.

### TRANSLATION

**" 'All of you should be happy. Is there any fear from the demons?' They replied, 'By Your mercy, we are victorious everywhere.**

### TEXT 77

সম্প্রতি পৃথিবীতে যেবা হৈয়াছিল ভার ।
অবতীর্ণ হঞা তাহা করিলা সংহার ॥' ৭৭ ॥

*samprati pṛthivīte yebā haiyāchila bhāra*
*avatīrṇa hañā tāhā karilā saṁhāra'*

### SYNONYMS

*samprati*—presently; *pṛthivīte*—upon the earth; *yebā*—whatever; *haiyāchila*—there was; *bhāra*—burden; *avatīrṇa hañā*—descending; *tāhā*—that; *karilā saṁhāra*—You have taken away.

### TRANSLATION

**" 'Whatever burden was upon the earth You have taken away by descending on that planet.'**

### TEXT 78

দ্বারকাদি—বিভু, তার এই ত প্রমাণ ।
'আমারই ব্রহ্মাণ্ডে কৃষ্ণ' সবার হৈল জ্ঞান ॥ ৭৮ ॥

*dvārakādi——vibhu, tāra ei ta pramāṇa*
*'āmāra-i brahmāṇḍe kṛṣṇa' sabāra haila jñāna*

### SYNONYMS

*dvārakā-ādi*—Dvārakā-dhāma and other abodes; *vibhu*—transcendental abode; *tāra ei ta pramāṇa*—this is the evidence of that; *āmāra-i brahmāṇḍe*—in my *brahmāṇḍa; kṛṣṇa*—Kṛṣṇa is now present; *sabāra*—of all of them; *haila jñāna*—there was this knowledge.

### TRANSLATION

**"This is the proof of Dvārakā's opulence: all the Brahmās thought, 'Kṛṣṇa is now staying in my jurisdiction.'**

### TEXT 79

কৃষ্ণ-সহ দ্বারকা-বৈভব অনুভব হৈল ।
একত্র মিলনে কেহ কাহো না দেখিল ॥ ৭৯ ॥

*kṛṣṇa-saha dvārakā-vaibhava anubhava haila*
*ekatra milane keha kāho nā dekhila*

### SYNONYMS

*kṛṣṇa-saha*—with Kṛṣṇa; *dvārakā-vaibhava*—the opulence of Dvārakā; *anubhava haila*—there was perception; *ekatra milane*—although they came together; *keha*—someone; *kāho*—anyone else; *nā dekhila*—did not see.

### TRANSLATION

**"Thus the opulence of Dvārakā was perceived by each and every one of them. Although they were all assembled together, no one could see anyone but himself.**

### PURPORT

The four-headed Brahmā perceived the opulence of Dvārakā-dhāma where Kṛṣṇa was staying, and although there were Brahmās present having ten to ten million heads, and also many Lord Śivas were also assembled, only the four-headed Brahmā of this universe could see all of them. By the inconceivable potency of Kṛṣṇa, the others could not see one another. Althouth all the Brahmās and Śivas were assembled together, due to Kṛṣṇa's energy, they could not meet or talk among themselves individually.

### TEXT 80

তবে কৃষ্ণ সর্ব-ব্রহ্মাগণে বিদায় দিলা ।
দণ্ডবৎ হঞা সবে নিজ ঘরে গেলা ॥ ৮০ ॥

*tabe kṛṣṇa sarva-brahmā-gaṇe vidāya dilā*
*daṇḍavat hañā sabe nija ghare gelā*

### SYNONYMS

*tabe*—thereafter; *kṛṣṇa*—Lord Kṛṣṇa; *sarva-brahmā-gaṇe*—unto all the Brahmās; *vidāya dilā*—bade farewell; *daṇḍavat hañā*—offering obeisances; *sabe*—all of them; *nija ghare gelā*—returned to their respective homes.

### TRANSLATION

**"Lord Kṛṣṇa then bade farewell to all the Brahmās there, and after offering their obeisances, they all returned to their respective homes.**

### TEXT 81

দেখি' চতুর্মুখ ব্রহ্মার হৈল চমৎকার ।
কৃষ্ণের চরণে আসি' কৈলা নমস্কার ॥ ৮১ ॥

*dekhi' caturmukha brahmāra haila camatkāra*
*kṛṣṇera caraṇe āsi' kailā namaskāra*

### SYNONYMS

*dekhi'*—seeing; *catuḥ-mukha brahmāra*—of the four-headed Brahmā of this universe; *haila*—there was; *camatkāra*—astonishment; *kṛṣṇera caraṇe āsi'*—coming to the lotus feet of Lord Kṛṣṇa; *kailā namaskāra*—offered his respects.

### TRANSLATION

**"After observing all these opulences, the four-headed Brahmā of this universe was astonished. He again came before the lotus feet of Kṛṣṇa and offered Him obeisances.**

### TEXT 82

ব্রহ্মা বলে,—পূর্বে আমি যে নিশ্চয় করিলুঁ ।
তার উদাহরণ আমি আজি ত' দেখিলুঁ ॥ ৮২ ॥

*brahmā bale,——pūrve āmi ye niścaya kariluṅ*
*tāra udāharaṇa āmi āji ta' dekhiluṅ*

### SYNONYMS

*brahmā bale*—Brahmā said; *pūrve*—formerly; *āmi*—I; *ye*—whatever; *niścaya kariluṅ*—decided; *tāra*—of that; *udāharaṇa*—the example; *āmi*—I; *āji*—today; *ta'*—certainly; *dekhiluṅ*—have seen.

## TRANSLATION

**"Brahmā then said, 'Whatever I formerly decided about my knowledge, I have just now had personally verified.'**

## TEXT 83

জানন্ত এব জানন্তু কিং বহূক্ত্যা ন মে প্রভো ।
মনসো বপুষো বাচো বৈভবং তব গোচরঃ ॥ ৮৩ ॥

*jānanta eva jānantu*
*kiṁ bahūktyā na me prabho*
*manaso vapuṣo vāco*
*vaibhavaṁ tava gocaraḥ*

## SYNONYMS

*jānantaḥ*—persons who think they are aware of Your unlimited potency; *eva*—certainly; *jānantu*—let them think like that; *kim*—what is the use; *bahu-uktyā*—with many words; *na*—not; *me*—my; *prabho*—O my Lord; *manasaḥ*—of the mind; *vapuṣaḥ*—of the body; *vācaḥ*—of the words; *vaibhavam*—opulences; *tava*—Your; *gocaraḥ*—within the range.

## TRANSLATION

**" 'There are people who say, "I know everything about Kṛṣṇa." Let them think in that way. As far as I am concerned, I do not wish to speak very much about this matter. O my Lord, let me say this much. As far as your opulences are concerned, they are all beyond the reach of my mind, body and words.'**

## PURPORT

This is a quotation from *Śrīmad-Bhāgavatam* (10.14.38), spoken by Lord Brahmā.

## TEXT 84

কৃষ্ণ কহে,"এই ব্রহ্মাণ্ড পঞ্চাশৎ কোটি যোজন ।
অতি ক্ষুদ্র, তাতে তোমার চারি বদন ॥ ৮৪ ॥

*kṛṣṇa kahe,"ei brahmāṇḍa pañcāśat koṭi yojana*
*ati kṣudra, tāte tomāra cāri vadana*

### SYNONYMS

*kṛṣṇa kahe*—Kṛṣṇa said; *ei brahmāṇḍa*—this universe; *pañcāśat koṭi yojana*—four billion miles; *ati kṣudra*—very small; *tāte*—therefore; *tomāra*—your; *cāri vadana*—four faces.

### TRANSLATION

**"Kṛṣṇa said, 'Your particular universe extends four billion miles; therefore it is the smallest of all the universes. Consequently you have only four heads.**

### PURPORT

Śrīla Bhaktisiddhānta Sarasvatī Ṭhākura, one of the greatest astrologers of his time, gives information from *Siddhānta-śiromaṇi* that this universe measures 18,712,069,200,000,000 x 8 miles. This is the circumference of this universe. According to some, this is only half the circumference.

### TEXT 85

কোন ব্রহ্মাণ্ড শতকোটি, কোন লক্ষকোটি।
কোন নিযুতকোটি, কোন কোটি-কোটি ॥ ৮৫ ॥

*kona brahmāṇḍa śata-koṭi, kona lakṣa-koṭi*
*kona niyuta-koṭi, kona koṭi-koṭi*

### SYNONYMS

*kona brahmāṇḍa*—some universes; *śata-koṭi*—one billion *yojanas; kona*—some; *lakṣa-koṭi*—one trillion *yojanas; kona*—some; *niyuta-koṭi*—ten trillion; *kona*—some; *koṭi-koṭi*—one hundred trillion.

### TRANSLATION

**" 'Some of the universes are one billion yojanas, some one trillion, some ten trillion and some one hundred trillion yojanas. Thus they are almost unlimited in area.**

### PURPORT

A *yojana* equals eight miles.

### TEXT 86

ব্রহ্মাণ্ডানুরূপ ব্রহ্মার শরীর-বদন।
এইরূপে পালি আমি ব্রহ্মাণ্ডের গণ ॥ ৮৬ ॥

*brahmāṇḍānurūpa brahmāra śarīra-vadana*
*ei-rūpe pāli āmi brahmāṇḍera gaṇa*

### SYNONYMS

*brahmāṇḍa-anurūpa*—according to the size of a universe; *brahmāra*—of Lord Brahmā; *śarīra-vadana*—heads on the body; *ei-rūpe*—in this way; *pāli āmi*—I maintain; *brahmāṇḍera gaṇa*—all the innumerable groups of universes.

### TRANSLATION

**" 'According to the size of the universe, there are so many heads on the body of Brahmā. In this way I maintain innumerable universes [brahmāṇḍas].**

### TEXT 87

**'একপাদ বিভূতি' ইহার নাহি পরিমাণ ।**
**'ত্রিপাদ বিভূতি'র কেবা করে পরিমাণ ॥" ৮৭ ॥**

*'eka-pāda vibhūti' ihāra nāhi parimāṇa*
*'tripāda vibhūti'ra kebā kare parimāṇa"*

### SYNONYMS

*eka-pāda vibhūti*—a one-fourth manifestation of My opulence; *ihāra*—of this; *nāhi*—there is not; *parimāṇa*—measurement; *tri-pāda vibhūtira*—of the spiritual world, having three fourths of My energy; *kebā*—who; *kare*—can do; *parimāṇa*—measurement.

### TRANSLATION

**" 'No one can measure the length and breadth of one fourth of My energy. Who can measure the three fourths that is manifested in the spiritual world?'**

### TEXT 88

তস্যাঃ পারে পরব্যোম ত্রিপাদ্‌ভূতং সনাতনম্ ।
অমৃতং শাশ্বতং নিত্যমনন্তং পরমং পদম্ ॥ ৮৮ ॥

*tasyāḥ pāre paravyoma*
*tripād-bhūtaṁ sanātanam*
*amṛtaṁ śāśvataṁ nityam*
*anantaṁ paramaṁ padam*

### SYNONYMS

*tasyāḥ pāre*—on the other bank of the Virajā River; *para-vyoma*—the spiritual sky; *tri-pād-bhūtam*—existing as three fourths of the opulence of the Supreme Lord; *sanātanam*—eternal; *amṛtam*—without deterioration; *śāśvatam*—without being subjected to the control of time; *nityam*—constantly existing; *anantam*—unlimited; *paramam*—supreme; *padam*—abode.

### TRANSLATION

**" 'Beyond the River Virajā is a spiritual nature, which is indestructible, eternal, inexhaustible and unlimited. It is the supreme abode consisting of three fourths of the Lord's opulences. It is known as paravyoma, the spiritual sky.'**

### PURPORT

This is a verse from the *Padma Purāṇa,* recited here by Lord Kṛṣṇa.

### TEXT 89

**তবে কৃষ্ণ ব্রহ্মারে দিলেন বিদায়।**
**কৃষ্ণের বিভূতি-স্বরূপ জানান না যায় ৮৯ ॥**

*tabe kṛṣṇa brahmāre dilena vidāya*
*kṛṣṇera vibhūti-svarūpa jānāna nā yāya*

### SYNONYMS

*tabe*—thereafter; *kṛṣṇa*—Lord Kṛṣṇa; *brahmāre*—unto the Lord Brahmā of this universe; *dilena vidāya*—bade farewell; *kṛṣṇera*—of Lord Kṛṣṇa; *vibhūti-svarūpa*—spiritual verification of opulence; *jānāna nā yāya*—is not possible to understand.

### TRANSLATION

**"In this way Lord Kṛṣṇa bade farewell to the four-headed Brahmā of this universe. We may thus understand that no one can calculate the extent of Kṛṣṇa's energies.**

### TEXT 90

**'ত্র্যধীশ্বর'-শব্দের অর্থ 'গূঢ়' আর হয়।**
**'ত্রি'-শব্দে কৃষ্ণের তিন লোক কয় ॥ ৯০ ॥**

*'tryadhīśvara'-śabdera artha 'gūḍha' āra haya*
*'tri'-śabde kṛṣṇera tina loka kaya*

### SYNONYMS

*tri-adhīśvara*—*tryadhīśvara; śabdera*—of the word; *artha*—a meaning; *gūḍha*—confidential; *āra*—another; *haya*—there is; *tri-śabde*—by the word "three"; *kṛṣṇera*—of Kṛṣṇa; *tina loka kaya*—the three places or properties of Lord Kṛṣṇa.

### TRANSLATION

**"There is a very deep meaning in the word tryadhīśvara, which indicates that Kṛṣṇa possesses three different lokas, or natures.**

### PURPORT

The word *tryadhīśvara* means "proprietor of the three worlds." There are three worlds of which Kṛṣṇa is the supreme proprietor. This is explained in *Bhagavad-gītā:*

*bhoktāraṁ yajña-tapasāṁ*
*sarva-loka-maheśvaram*
*suhṛdaṁ sarva-bhūtānāṁ*
*jñātvā māṁ śāntim ṛcchati*

"The sages, knowing Me as the ultimate purpose of all sacrificies and austerities, the Supreme Lord of all planets and demigods and the benefactor and well-wisher of all living entities, attain peace from the pangs of material miseries." (Bg. 5.29)

The word *sarva-loka* means "all three worlds," and the word *maheśvara* means "the supreme proprietor." Kṛṣṇa is the proprietor of both material and spiritual worlds. The spiritual world is divided into two portions—Goloka Vṛndāvana and the Vaikuṇṭhas. The material world is a combination of universes unlimited in number.

### TEXT 91

গোলোকাখ্য গোকুল, মথুরা, দ্বারাবতী ।
এই তিন লোকে কৃষ্ণের সহজে নিত্যস্থিতি ॥ ৯১ ॥

*golokākhya gokula, mathurā, dvārāvatī*
*ei tina loke kṛṣṇera sahaje nitya-sthiti*

### SYNONYMS

*goloka-ākhya*—called Goloka; *gokula*—Gokula; *mathurā*—Mathurā; *dvārā-vatī*—Dvārakā; *ei tina loke*—all three of these places; *kṛṣṇera*—of Lord Kṛṣṇa; *sahaje*—naturally; *nitya-sthiti*—eternal residence.

### TRANSLATION

**"The three lokas are Gokula (Goloka), Mathurā and Dvārakā. Kṛṣṇa lives eternally in these three places.**

### PURPORT

Śrīla Bhaktisiddhānta Sarasvatī Ṭhākura comments that in the Goloka planet there are three divisions: Gokula, Mathurā and Dvārakā. In His incarnation as Gaurasundara, Lord Śrī Caitanya Mahāprabhu, the Lord conducts His pastimes in three areas: Navadvīpa, Jagannātha Purī (and South India) and Vraja-maṇḍala (the area of Vṛndāvana-dhāma).

### TEXT 92

অন্তরঙ্গ-পূর্ণৈশ্বর্যপূর্ণ তিন ধাম ।
তিনের অধীশ্বর—কৃষ্ণ স্বয়ং ভগবান্ ॥ ৯২ ॥

*antaraṅga-pūrṇaiśvarya-pūrṇa tina dhāma*
*tinera adhīśvara——kṛṣṇa svayaṁ bhagavān*

### SYNONYMS

*antaraṅga*—internal; *pūrṇa-aiśvarya-pūrṇa*—full of all opulences; *tina dhāma*—three abodes; *tinera adhīśvara*—the Lord of all three; *kṛṣṇa*—Lord Kṛṣṇa; *svayam bhagavān*—the Supreme Personality of Godhead.

### TRANSLATION

**"These three places are full of internal potencies, and Kṛṣṇa, the Supreme Personality of Godhead, is their sole proprietor.**

### TEXTS 93-94

পূর্ব-উক্ত ব্রহ্মাণ্ডের যত দিক্‌পাল ।
অনন্ত বৈকুণ্ঠাবরণ, চিরলোকপাল ॥ ৯৩ ॥
তাঁ-সবার মুকুট কৃষ্ণপাদপীঠ-আগে ।
দণ্ডবৎকালে তার মণি পীঠে লাগে ॥ ৯৪ ॥

*pūrva-ukta brahmāṇḍera yata dik-pāla*
*ananta vaikuṇṭhāvaraṇa, cira-loka-pāla*

*tāṅ-sabāra mukuṭa kṛṣṇa-pāda-pīṭha-āge*
*daṇḍavat-kāle tāra maṇi pīṭhe lāge*

### SYNONYMS

*pūrva-ukta*—as mentioned above; *brahmāṇḍera*—of all the universes; *yata*—all; *dik-pāla*—the governors of the directions; *ananta vaikuṇṭha-āvaraṇa*—the expansions surrounding the innumerable Vaikuṇṭhas; *cira-loka-pāla*—permanent governors of the universe; *tāṅ-sabāra*—of all of them; *mukuṭa*—helmets; *kṛṣṇa-pāda-pīṭha-āge*—in front of the lotus feet of Kṛṣṇa; *daṇḍavat-kāle*—at the time of offering obeisances; *tāra*—of them; *maṇi*—the jewels; *pīṭhe*—on the throne; *lāge*—touch.

### TRANSLATION

**"As previously mentioned, the jewels on the helmets of all the predominating deities of all the universes and Vaikuṇṭha planets touched the throne and the lotus feet of the Lord when they all offered obeisances.**

### TEXT 95

মণি-পীঠে ঠেকাঠেকি, উঠে ঝন্‌ঝনি ।
পীঠের স্তুতি করে মুকুট—হেন অনুমানি ॥ ৯৫ ॥

*maṇi-pīṭhe ṭhekāṭheki, uṭhe jhanjhani*
*pīṭhera stuti kare mukuṭa——hena anumāni*

### SYNONYMS

*maṇi-pīṭhe*—between the gems and the lotus feet or the throne; *ṭhekāṭheki*—collision; *uṭhe*—arises; *jhanjhani*—a jingling sound; *pīṭhera*—to the lotus feet or the throne; *stuti*—prayers; *kare*—offer; *mukuṭa*—all the helmets; *hena*—thus; *anumāni*—we can imagine.

### TRANSLATION

**"When the gems on the helmets of all the predominating deities collide before the throne and the Lord's lotus feet, there is a jingling sound, which seems like prayers offered by the helmets at Kṛṣṇa's lotus feet.**

### TEXT 96

নিজ-চিচ্ছক্তে কৃষ্ণ নিত্য বিরাজমান ।
চিচ্ছক্তি-সম্পত্তির 'ষড়ৈশ্বর্য' নাম ॥ ৯৬ ॥

*nija-cic-chakte kṛṣṇa nitya virājamāna*
*cic-chakti-sampattira 'ṣaḍ-aiśvarya' nāma*

### SYNONYMS

*nija*—His own; *cit-śakte*—in spiritual potency; *kṛṣṇa*—Lord Kṛṣṇa; *nitya*—eternally; *virājamāna*—existing; *cit-śakti*—of the spiritual potency; *sampattira*—of the opulence; *ṣaṭ-aiśvarya*—the six opulences; *nāma*—named.

### TRANSLATION

**"Kṛṣṇa is thus situated eternally in His spiritual potency, and the opulence of that spiritual potency is called ṣaḍ-aiśvarya, indicating six kinds of opulence.**

### TEXT 97

সেই স্বারাজ্যলক্ষ্মী করে নিত্য পূর্ণ কাম।
অতএব বেদে কহে 'স্বয়ং ভগবান্' ॥ ৯৭ ॥

*sei svārājya-lakṣmī kare nitya pūrṇa kāma*
*ataeva vede kahe 'svayaṁ bhagavān'*

### SYNONYMS

*sei svārājya-lakṣmī*—that personal opulence; *kare*—does; *nitya*—eternally; *pūrṇa*—fulfilling; *kāma*—all desires; *ataeva*—therefore; *vede*—in the *Vedas;* *kahe*—it is said; *svayam bhagavān*—Kṛṣṇa is the Supreme Personality of Godhead.

### TRANSLATION

**"Because He possesses the spiritual potencies which fulfill all His desires, Kṛṣṇa is accepted as the Supreme Personality of Godhead. This is the Vedic version.**

### TEXT 98

কৃষ্ণের ঐশ্বর্য—অপার অমৃতের সিন্ধু।
অবগাহিতে নারি, তার ছুইলঁ এক বিন্দু ॥ ৯৮ ॥

*kṛṣṇera aiśvarya——apāra amṛtera sindhu*
*avagāhite nāri, tāra chuilaṅ eka bindu*

### SYNONYMS

*kṛṣṇera aiśvarya*—the opulence of Kṛṣṇa; *apāra*—unlimited; *amṛtera sindhu*—an ocean of nectar; *avagāhite*—to bathe; *nāri*—I am unable; *tāra*—of that; *chuilaṅ*—I touched; *eka bindu*—only one drop.

### TRANSLATION

**"The unlimited potencies of Kṛṣṇa are just like an ocean of nectar. Since one cannot bathe within that ocean, I have only touched a drop of it."**

### TEXT 99

ঐশ্বর্য কহিতে প্রভুর কৃষ্ণস্ফূর্তি হৈল ।
মাধুর্যে মজিল মন, এক শ্লোক পড়িল ॥ ৯৯ ॥

*aiśvarya kahite prabhura kṛṣṇa-sphūrti haila*
*mādhurye majila mana, eka śloka paḍila*

### SYNONYMS

*aiśvarya kahite*—while describing the opulence; *prabhura*—of Śrī Caitanya Mahāprabhu; *kṛṣṇa-sphūrti*—awakening of love of Kṛṣṇa; *haila*—there was; *mādhurye*—in the sweetness of conjugal love; *majila mana*—the mind became immersed; *eka*—one; *śloka*—verse; *paḍila*—recited.

### TRANSLATION

**When Śrī Caitanya Mahāprabhu described the opulences and spiritual potencies of Kṛṣṇa in this way, there was an awakening of love of Kṛṣṇa within Him. His mind was immersed in the sweetness of conjugal love, and He quoted the following verse from Śrīmad-Bhāgavatam.**

### TEXT 100

যন্মর্ত্যলীলৌপয়িকং স্বযোগমায়াবলং দর্শয়তা গৃহীতম্ ।
বিস্মাপনং স্বস্য চ সৌভগর্ধেঃ পরং পদং ভূষণভূষণাঙ্গম্ ॥১০০॥

*yan martya-līlaupayikaṁ svayoga-*
*māyā-balaṁ darśayatā gṛhītam*
*vismāpanaṁ svasya ca saubhagardheḥ*
*paraṁ padaṁ bhūṣaṇa-bhūṣaṇāṅgam*

### SYNONYMS

*yat*—that which; *martya-līlā*—pastimes in the material world; *aupayikam*—just suitable for; *sva*—His own; *yoga-māyā*—of the spiritual potency; *balam*—the strength; *darśayatā*—showing; *gṛhītam*—accepted; *vismāpanam*—even producing wonder; *svasya*—for Himself; *ca*—also; *saubhaga-ṛdheḥ*—of abundant good fortune; *param*—supreme; *padam*—abode; *bhūṣaṇa*—of ornaments; *bhūṣaṇa-aṅgam*—the limbs of which were the ornaments.

### TRANSLATION

**"'To exhibit the strength of His own spiritual potency, Lord Kṛṣṇa manifested a suitable form just for His pastimes in the material world. This form was wonderful even for Him and was the supreme abode of the wealth of good fortune. Its limbs were so beautiful that they increased the beauty of the ornaments worn on different parts of His body.'**

### PURPORT

This verse from *Śrīmad-Bhāgavatam* (3.2.12) is stated in a conversation between Vidura and Uddhava. Uddhava thus begins his description of the pastimes of Śrī Kṛṣṇa in His form exhibited by *yogamāyā.*

### TEXT 101

**কৃষ্ণের যতেক খেলা, সর্বোত্তম নরলীলা,**
**নরবপু তাহার স্বরূপ ।**
**গোপবেশ, বেণুকর, নবকিশোর, নটবর,**
**নরলীলার হয় অনুরূপ ॥ ১০১ ॥**

*kṛṣṇera yateka khelā, sarvottama nara-līlā,*
*nara-vapu tāhāra svarūpa*
*gopa-veśa, veṇu-kara, nava-kiśora, naṭa-vara,*
*nara-līlāra haya anurūpa*

### SYNONYMS

*kṛṣṇera*—of Lord Kṛṣṇa; *yateka*—all; *khelā*—pastimes; *sarva-uttama*—the most attractive of all; *nara-līlā*—the pastimes as a human being; *nara-vapu*—a body just like that of a human being; *tāhāra*—of that; *sva-rūpa*—the real form; *gopa-veśa*—the dress of a cowherd boy; *veṇu-kara*—with a flute in the hands; *nava-kiśora*—newly youthful; *naṭa-vara*—an expert dancer; *nara-līlāra*—for exhibiting the pastimes as a human being; *haya*—is; *anurūpa*—suitable.

### TRANSLATION

**"Lord Kṛṣṇa has many pastimes, of which His pastimes as a human being are the best. His form as a human being is the supreme transcendental form. In this form He is a cowherd boy. He carries a flute in His hand, and His youth is new. He is also an expert dancer. All this is just suitable for His pastimes as a human being.**

## TEXT 102

কৃষ্ণের মধুর রূপ, শুন, সনাতন।
যে রূপের এক কণ, ডুবায় সব ত্রিভুবন,
সর্ব প্রাণী করে আকর্ষণ॥ ১০২ ॥ ধ্রু ॥

*kṛṣṇera madhura rūpa, śuna, sanātana*
*ye rūpera eka kaṇa, ḍubāya saba tribhuvana,*
*sarva prāṇī kare ākarṣaṇa*

### SYNONYMS

*kṛṣṇera*—of Lord Kṛṣṇa; *madhura*—sweet; *rūpa*—form; *śuna*—please hear; *sanātana*—O My dear Sanātana; *ye rūpera*—of which form; *eka kaṇa*—even a fraction; *ḍubāya*—floods; *saba*—all; *tri-bhuvana*—the three worlds; *sarva prāṇī*—all living entities; *kare*—does; *ākarṣaṇa*—attracting.

### TRANSLATION

**"My dear Sanātana, the sweet, attractive transcendental form of Kṛṣṇa is so nice. Just try to understand it. Even a fractional understanding of Kṛṣṇa's beauty can merge all three worlds in the ocean of love. He attracts all the living entities within the three worlds.**

## TEXT 103

যোগমায়া চিচ্ছক্তি, বিশুদ্ধসত্ত্ব-পরিণতি,
তার শক্তি লোকে দেখাইতে।
এই রূপ-রতন, ভক্তগণের গূঢ়ধন,
প্রকট কৈলা নিত্যলীলা হৈতে॥ ১০৩ ॥

*yogamāyā cic-chakti, viśuddha-sattva-pariṇati,*
*tāra śakti loke dekhāite*
*ei rūpa-ratana, bhakta-gaṇera gūḍha-dhana,*
*prakaṭa kailā nitya-līlā haite*

### SYNONYMS

*yoga-māyā*—internal energy; *cit-śakti*—spiritual potency; *viśuddha-sattva*—of transcendental pure goodness; *pariṇati*—a transformation; *tāra śakti*—the potency of such energy; *loke dekhāite*—to exhibit within the material world; *ei rūpa-ratana*—this beautiful, transcendental, jewellike form; *bhakta-gaṇera gūḍha-dhana*—the most confidential treasure of the devotees; *prakaṭa*—exhibition; *kailā*—made; *nitya-līlā haite*—from the eternal pastimes of the Lord.

*ratana*—this beautiful, transcendental, jewellike form; *bhakta-gaṇera gūḍha-dhana*—the most confidential treasure of the devotees; *prakaṭa*—exhibition; *kailā*—made; *nitya-līlā haite*—from the eternal pastimes of the Lord.

### TRANSLATION

**"The transcendental form of Kṛṣṇa is shown to the world by Lord Kṛṣṇa's internal spiritual energy, which is a transformation of pure goodness. This jewellike form is the most confidential treasure of the devotees. This form is manifest from Kṛṣṇa's eternal pastimes.**

### TEXT 104

রূপ দেখি' আপনার, কৃষ্ণের হৈল চমৎকার,
আস্বাদিতে মনে উঠে কাম।
'স্বসৌভাগ্য' যাঁর নাম, সৌন্দর্যাদি-গুণগ্রাম,
এইরূপ নিত্য তার ধাম ॥ ১০৪ ॥

*rūpa dekhi' āpanāra, kṛṣṇera haila camatkāra,*
*āsvādite mane uṭhe kāma*
*'svasaubhāgya' yāṅra nāma, saundaryādi-guṇa-grāma,*
*ei-rūpa nitya tāra dhāma*

### SYNONYMS

*rūpa dekhi'*—by seeing the form; *āpanāra*—His own; *kṛṣṇera*—of Lord Kṛṣṇa; *haila*—there was; *camatkāra*—wonder; *āsvādite*—to taste; *mane*—in the mind; *uṭhe*—arises; *kāma*—a desire; *sva-saubhāgya*—one's own good fortune; *yāṅra*—of which; *nāma*—the name; *saundarya-ādi-guṇa-grāma*—the transcendental qualities, headed by beauty; *ei rūpa*—this form; *nitya*—eternal; *tāra*—of them; *dhāma*—the abode.

### TRANSLATION

**"The wonder of Kṛṣṇa in His personal feature is so great that it attracts even Kṛṣṇa to taste His own association. Thus Kṛṣṇa becomes very eager to taste that wonder. Total beauty, knowledge, wealth, strength, fame and renunciation are the six opulences of Kṛṣṇa. He is eternally situated in His opulences.**

### PURPORT

Kṛṣṇa has many pastimes, of which His pastimes in Goloka Vṛndāvana (the *gokula-līlā*) are supreme. He also has pastimes in the Vaikuṇṭhas, the spiritual world, as Vāsudeva, Saṅkarṣaṇa, Pradyumna and Aniruddha. In His pastimes in the spiritual sky, He lies down in the Causal Ocean as Kāraṇārṇavaśāyī, the *puruṣa-avatāra.* His incarnations as a fish, tortoise and so on are called His causal incarnations. He incarnates in the modes of nature as Lord Brahmā, Lord Śiva and Lord Viṣṇu. He also incarnates as empowered living entities like Pṛthu and Vyāsa. The Supersoul is His localized incarnation, and His all-pervasive aspect is the impersonal Brahman.

When we consider impartially all the unlimited pastimes of the Lord, we find that His pastimes as a human being on this planet—wherein He sports as a cowherd boy with a flute in His hands and appears youthful and fresh like a ballet dancer—are pastimes and features that are never subjected to material laws and inebrieties. The wonderful beauty of Kṛṣṇa is presented in the supreme planet, Gokula (Goloka Vṛndāvana). Inferior to that is His representation in the spiritual sky, and inferior to that is His representation in the external energy (Devī-dhāma). A mere drop of Kṛṣṇa's sweetness can drown these three worlds—Goloka Vṛndāvana, Hari-dhāma (Vaikuṇṭhaloka), and Devī-dhāma (the material world). Everywhere, Kṛṣṇa's beauty merges everyone in the ecstasy of transcendental bliss. Actually the activities of *yogamāyā* are absent in the spiritual sky and the Vaikuṇṭha planets. She simply works in the supreme planet, Goloka Vṛndāvana, and she works to manifest the activities of Kṛṣṇa when He descends to the material universe to please His innumerable devotees within the material world. Thus a replica of the Goloka Vṛndāvana planet and the pastimes there are manifest on this planet on a specific tract of land—Bhauma Vṛndāvana, the Vṛndāvana-dhāma on this planet.

## TEXT 105

ভূষণের ভূষণ অঙ্গ, তাহেঁ ললিত ত্রিভঙ্গ,
তাহার উপর ভ্রূধনু-নর্তন।
তেরছে নেত্রান্ত বাণ, তার দৃঢ় সন্ধান,
বিন্ধে রাধা-গোপীগণ-মন ॥ ১০৫ ॥

*bhūṣaṇera bhūṣaṇa aṅga, tāheṅ lalita tribhaṅga,*
*tāhāra upara bhrūdhanu-nartana*
*terache netrānta bāṇa, tāra dṛḍha sandhāna,*
*vindhe rādhā-gopī-gaṇa-mana*

## SYNONYMS

*bhūṣaṇera*—of the ornament; *bhūṣaṇa*—the ornament; *aṅga*—the limbs of the body; *tāheṅ*—that feature; *lalita*—delicate; *tri-bhaṅga*—bent in three places;

*tāhāra upara*—above that; *bhrū-dhanu-nartana*—dancing of the eyebrows; *terache*—crooked; *netra-anta*—the end of the eye; *bāṇa*—arrow; *tāra*—of that arrow; *dṛḍha*—strong; *sandhāna*—fixing; *vindhe*—pierces; *rādhā*—of Śrīmatī Rādhārāṇī; *gopī-gaṇa*—of the *gopīs* also; *mana*—the minds.

### TRANSLATION

**"Ornaments caress that body, but the transcendental body of Kṛṣṇa is so beautiful that it beautifies the ornaments He wears. Therefore Kṛṣṇa's body is said to be the ornament of ornaments. Despite the wonderful beauty of Kṛṣṇa, there is His three-curved style of standing, which beautifies that form. Above all these beautiful features, Kṛṣṇa's eyes dance and move obliquely, acting like arrows to pierce the minds of Śrīmatī Rādhārāṇī and the gopīs. When the arrow succeeds in hitting its target, their minds become agitated.**

### TEXT 106

ব্রহ্মাণ্ডোপরি পরব্যোম, তাহাঁ যে স্বরূপগণ,
তাঁ-সবার বলে হরে মন ।
পতিব্রতা-শিরোমণি, যাঁরে কহে বেদবাণী,
আকর্ষয়ে সেই লক্ষ্মীগণ ॥ ১০৬ ॥

*brahmāṇḍopari paravyoma, tāhāṅ ye svarūpa-gaṇa,*
*tāṅ-sabāra bale hare mana*
*pati-vratā-śiromaṇi, yāṅre kahe veda-vāṇī,*
*ākarṣaye sei lakṣmī-gaṇa*

### SYNONYMS

*brahmāṇḍa-upari*—above all the universes; *para-vyoma*—the spiritual sky; *tāhāṅ*—there; *ye*—all those; *svarūpa-gaṇa*—transcendental personal expansions; *tāṅ-sabāra*—of all of Them; *bale*—by force; *hare mana*—it enchants the minds; *pati-vratā*—of those who are chaste and devoted to the husband; *śiromaṇi*—topmost; *yāṅre*—unto whom; *kahe*—describe; *veda-vāṇī*—hymns of the *Vedas; ākarṣaye*—it attracts; *sei*—those; *lakṣmī-gaṇa*—all the goddesses of fortune.

### TRANSLATION

**"The beauty of Kṛṣṇa's body is so attractive that it attracts not only the demigods and other living entities within this material world but the personalities of the spiritual sky as well, including the Nārāyaṇas, who are expansions of Kṛṣṇa's personality. The minds of the Nārāyaṇas are thus attracted by the beauty of Kṛṣṇa's body. In addition, the goddesses of fortune [Lakṣmīs]—**

**who are wives of the Nārāyaṇas and are the women described in the Vedas as most chaste—are also attracted by the wonderful beauty of Kṛṣṇa.**

## TEXT 107

চড়ি' গোপী-মনোরথে, মন্মথের মন মথে,
নাম ধরে 'মদনমোহন'।
জিনি' পঞ্চশর-দর্প, স্বয়ং নবকন্দর্প,
রাস করে লঞা গোপীগণ ॥ ১০৭ ॥

*caḍi' gopī-manorathe, manmathera mana mathe,*
*nāma dhare 'madana-mohana'*
*jini' pañcaśara-darpa, svayaṁ nava-kandarpa,*
*rāsa kare lañā gopī-gaṇa*

## SYNONYMS

*caḍi'*—riding; *gopī-manaḥ-rathe*—on the chariot of the minds of the *gopīs; manmathera*—of Cupid; *mana*—the mind; *mathe*—churns; *nāma*—the name; *dhare*—accepts; *madana-mohana*—Madana-mohana, the deluder of Cupid; *jini'*—conquering; *pañca-śara*—of Cupid, the master of the five arrows of the senses; *darpa*—the pride; *svayam*—personally; *nava*—new; *kandarpa*—Cupid; *rāsa*—*rāsa* dance; *kare*—performs; *lañā*—with; *gopī-gaṇa*—the *gopīs.*

## TRANSLATION

**"Favoring them, Kṛṣṇa rides on the chariot of the minds of the gopīs, and just to receive loving service from them, He attracts their minds like Cupid. Therefore He is also called Madana-mohana, the attractor of Cupid. Cupid has five arrows, representing form, taste, smell, sound and touch. Kṛṣṇa is the owner of these five arrows, and with His Cupid-like beauty, He conquers the minds of the gopīs, though they are very proud of their superexcellent beauty. Becoming a new Cupid, Kṛṣṇa attracts their minds and engages in the rāsa dance.**

## TEXT 108

নিজ-সম সখা-সঙ্গে, গোগণ-চারণ রঙ্গে,
বৃন্দাবনে স্বচ্ছন্দ বিহার।
যাঁর বেণু-ধ্বনি শুনি', স্থাবর-জঙ্গম প্রাণী,
পুলক, কম্প, অশ্রু বহে ধার ॥ ১০৮ ॥

*nija-sama sakhā-saṅge, go-gaṇa-cāraṇa raṅge,*
*vṛndāvane svacchanda vihāra*
*yāṅra veṇu-dhvani śuni' sthāvara-jaṅgama prāṇī,*
*pulaka, kampa, aśru vahe dhāra*

### SYNONYMS

*nija-sama*—equal to Himself; *sakhā-saṅge*—with the friends; *go-gaṇa*—an unlimited number of cows; *cāraṇa*—tending; *raṅge*—such pastimes; *vṛndāvane*—in Vṛndāvana; *svacchanda*—spontaneous; *vihāra*—blissful enjoyment; *yāṅra*—of whom; *veṇu-dhvani śuni'*—hearing the vibration of the flute; *sthāvara-jaṅgama prāṇī*—all living entities, moving and not moving; *pulaka*—jubilation; *kampa*—trembling; *aśru*—tears; *vahe*—flow; *dhāra*—streams.

### TRANSLATION

**"When Lord Kṛṣṇa wanders in the forest of Vṛndāvana with His friends on an equal level, there are innumerable cows grazing. This is another of the Lord's blissful enjoyments. When He plays on His flute, all living entities—including trees, plants, animals and human beings—tremble and are saturated with jubilation. Tears flow constantly from their eyes.**

### TEXT 109

**মুক্তাহার—বকপাঁতি, ইন্দ্রধনু-পিঞ্ছ ততি,**
**পীতাম্বর—বিজুরী-সঞ্চার ।**
**কৃষ্ণ নব-জলধর, জগৎ-শস্য-উপর,**
**বরিষয়ে লীলামৃত-ধার ॥ ১০৯ ॥**

*muktā-hāra——baka-pāṅti, indra-dhanu-piñcha tati,*
*pītāmbara——vijurī-sañcāra*
*kṛṣṇa nava-jaladhara, jagat-śasya-upara,*
*variṣaye līlāmṛta-dhāra*

### SYNONYMS

*muktā-hāra*—a necklace of pearls; *baka-pāṅti*—like a row of white ducks; *indra-dhanu*—like a rainbow; *piñcha*—a peacock feather; *tati*—there; *pīta-ambara*—yellow garments; *vijurī-sañcāra*—like the appearance of lightning in the sky; *kṛṣṇa*—Lord Kṛṣṇa; *nava*—new; *jala-dhara*—cloud carrying water; *jagat*—the universe; *śasya*—like crops of grains; *upara*—upon; *variṣaye*—rains; *līlā-amṛta*—the pastimes of Lord Kṛṣṇa; *dhāra*—like a shower.

### TRANSLATION

**"Kṛṣṇa wears a pearl necklace that appears like a chain of white ducks around His neck. The peacock feather in His hair appears like a rainbow, and His yellow garments appear like lightning in the sky. Kṛṣṇa appears like a newly risen cloud, and the gopīs appear like newly grown grains in the field. Constant rains of nectarean pastimes fall upon these newly grown grains, and it seems that the gopīs are receiving beams of life from Kṛṣṇa, exactly as grains receive life from the rains.**

### TEXT 110

**মাধুর্য ভগবত্তা-সার, ব্রজে কৈল পরচার,**
**তাহা শুক—ব্যাসের নন্দন ।**
**স্থানে স্থানে ভাগবতে, বর্ণিয়াছে জানাইতে,**
**তাহা শুনি' মাতে ভক্তগণ ॥ ১১০ ॥**

*mādhurya bhagavattā-sāra, vraje kaila paracāra,*
*tāhā śuka——vyāsera nandana*
*sthāne sthāne bhāgavate, varṇiyāche jānāite,*
*tāhā śuni' māte bhakta-gaṇa*

### SYNONYMS

*mādhurya*—sweetness; *bhagavattā-sāra*—the quintessence of the Supreme Personality of Godhead; *vraje*—in Vṛndāvana; *kaila*—did; *paracāra*—propagation; *tāhā*—that; *śuka*—Śukadeva Gosvāmī; *vyāsera nandana*—the son of Vyāsadeva; *sthāne sthāne*—in different places; *bhāgavate*—in *Śrīmad-Bhāgavatam; varṇiyāche*—has described; *jānāite*—in order to explain; *tāhā śuni'*—hearing those statements; *māte*—become maddened; *bhakta-gaṇa*—all the devotees.

### TRANSLATION

**"The Supreme Personality of Godhead, Kṛṣṇa, is full in all six opulences, including His attractive beauty, which engages Him in conjugal love with the gopīs. Such sweetness is the quintessence of His qualities. Śukadeva Gosvāmī, the son of Vyāsadeva, has described these pastimes of Kṛṣṇa throughout Śrīmad-Bhāgavatam. Hearing the descriptions, the devotees become mad with love of God."**

### TEXT 111

**কহিতে কৃষ্ণের রসে, শ্লোক পড়ে প্রেমাবেশে,**
**প্রেমে সনাতন-হাত ধরি' ।**

গোপী-ভাগ্য, কৃষ্ণ গুণ, যে করিল বর্ণন,
ভাবাবেশে মথুরা-নাগরী ॥ ১১১ ॥

*kahite kṛṣṇera rase, śloka paḍe premāveśe,*
*preme sanātana-hāta dhari'*
*gopī-bhāgya, kṛṣṇa guṇa, ye karila varṇana,*
*bhāvāveśe mathurā-nāgarī*

## SYNONYMS

*kahite*—to describe; *kṛṣṇera*—of Lord Kṛṣṇa; *rase*—the different types of mellows; *śloka*—a verse; *paḍe*—recites; *prema-āveśe*—absorbed in ecstatic love; *preme*—in such love; *sanātana-hāta dhari'*—catching the hand of Sanātana Gosvāmī; *gopī-bhāgya*—the fortune of the *gopīs; kṛṣṇa guṇa*—the transcendental qualities of Kṛṣṇa; *ye*—which; *karila varṇana*—described; *bhāva-āveśe*—in ecstatic love; *mathurā-nāgarī*—the women of the city of Mathurā.

## TRANSLATION

**Just as the women of Mathurā ecstatically described the fortune of the gopīs of Vṛndāvana and the transcendental qualities of Kṛṣṇa, Śrī Caitanya Mahāprabhu described the different mellows of Kṛṣṇa and became overwhelmed with ecstatic love. Grasping the hand of Sanātana Gosvāmī, He recited the following verse.**

## TEXT 112

গোপ্যস্তপঃ কিমচরন্ যদমুষ্য রূপং
লাবণ্যসারমসমোর্দ্ধমনন্যসিদ্ধম্ ।
দৃগ্‌ভিঃ পিবন্ত্যনুসবাভিনবং দুরাপ-
মেকান্তধাম যশসঃ শ্রিয় ঐশ্বরস্য ॥ ১১২ ॥

*gopyas tapaḥ kim acaran yad amuṣya rūpaṁ*
*lāvaṇya-sāram asamordhvam ananya-siddham*
*dṛgbhiḥ pibanty anusavābhinavaṁ durāpam*
*ekānta-dhāma yaśasaḥ śriya aiśvarasya*

## SYNONYMS

*gopyaḥ*—the *gopīs; tapaḥ*—austerities; *kim*—what; *acaran*—performed; *yat*—from which; *amuṣya*—of such a one (Lord Kṛṣṇa); *rūpam*—the form; *lāvaṇya-sāram*—the essence of loveliness; *asama-ūrdhvam*—not paralleled or surpassed;

*ananya-siddham*—not perfected by any other ornament (self-perfect); *dṛgbhiḥ*—by the eyes; *pibanti*—they drink; *anusava-abhinavam*—constantly new; *durāpam*—difficult to obtain; *ekānta-dhāma*—the only abode; *yaśasaḥ*—of fame; *śriyaḥ*—of beauty; *aiśvarasya*—of opulence.

## TRANSLATION

**" 'What austerities must the gopīs have performed? With their eyes they always drink the nectar of the face of Lord Kṛṣṇa, which is the essence of loveliness and is not to be equaled or surpassed. That loveliness is the only abode of beauty, fame and opulence. It is self-perfect, ever fresh and unique.'**

## PURPORT

This verse from *Śrīmad-Bhāgavatam* (10.44.14) was spoken by the women of Mathurā when they saw Kṛṣṇa in the wrestling arena.

## TEXT 113

**তারুণ্যামৃত – পারাবার, তরঙ্গ — লাবণ্যসার,**
**তাতে সে আবর্ত ভাবোদ্গম ।**
**বংশীধ্বনি — চক্রবাত, নারীর মন – তৃণপাত,**
**তাহা ডুবায়, না হয় উদ্গম ॥ ১১৩ ॥**

*tāruṇyāmṛta——pārāvāra, taraṅga——lāvaṇya-sāra,*
*tāte se āvarta bhāvodgama*
*vaṁśī-dhvani——cakravāta, nārīra mana——tṛṇa-pāta,*
*tāhā ḍubāya nā haya udgama*

## SYNONYMS

*tāruṇya-amṛta*—eternal youth; *pārāvāra*—like a great ocean; *taraṅga*—waves; *lāvaṇya-sāra*—the essence of bodily beauty; *tāte*—in that ocean; *se*—that; *āvarta*—like a whirlpool; *bhāva-udgama*—awakening of different ecstatic emotions; *vaṁśī-dhvani*—the vibration of the flute; *cakravāta*—a whirlwind; *nārīra*—of the women; *mana*—the minds; *tṛṇa-pāta*—leaves of grass; *tāhā*—that; *ḍubāya*—plunge down; *nā haya udgama*—never to come up again.

## TRANSLATION

**"The bodily beauty of Śrī Kṛṣṇa is like a wave in the ocean of eternal youth. In that great ocean is the whirlpool of the awakening of ecstatic love. The vibration of Kṛṣṇa's flute is like a whirlwind, and the flickering minds of the**

**gopīs are like straws and dry leaves. After they fall down in the whirlwind, they never rise again but remain eternally at the lotus feet of Kṛṣṇa.**

### TEXT 114

**সখি হে, কোন্ তপ কৈল গোপীগণ ।**
**কৃষ্ণরূপ-সুমাধুরী, পিবি' পিবি' নেত্র ভরি',**
**শ্লাঘ্য করে জন্ম-তনু-মন ॥ ১১৪ ॥ ধ্রু ॥**

*sakhi he, kon tapa kaila gopī-gaṇa*
*kṛṣṇa-rūpa-sumādhurī, pibi' pibi' netra bhari',*
*ślāghya kare janma-tanu-mana*

### SYNONYMS

*sakhi he*—My dear friend; *kon*—what; *tapa*—austerity; *kaila*—have executed; *gopī-gaṇa*—all the *gopīs; kṛṣṇa-rūpa*—of the beauty of Lord Kṛṣṇa; *su-mādhurī*—the essence of all sweetness; *pibi' pibi'*—drinking and drinking; *netra bhari'*—filling the eyes; *ślāghya kare*—they glorify; *janma-tanu-mana*—their births, bodies and minds.

### TRANSLATION

**"O my dear friend, what severe austerities have the gopīs performed to drink His transcendental beauty and sweetness through their eyes in complete fulfillment? Thus they glorify their births, bodies and minds.**

### TEXT 115

**যে মাধুরীর ঊর্ধ্ব আন, নাহি যার সমান,**
**পরব্যোমে স্বরূপের গণে ।**
**যেঁহো সব-অবতারী, পরব্যোম-অধিকারী,**
**এ মাধুর্য নাহি নারায়ণে ॥ ১১৫ ॥**

*ye mādhurīra ūrdhva āna, nāhi yāra samāna,*
*paravyome svarūpera gaṇe*
*yeṅho saba-avatārī, paravyoma-adhikārī,*
*e mādhurya nāhi nārāyaṇe*

### SYNONYMS

*ye mādhurīra*—that sweetness; *ūrdhva*—higher; *āna*—another; *nāhi*—there is not; *yāra samāna*—equal to which; *para-vyome*—the spiritual sky; *sva-rūpera gaṇe*—among the expansions of Kṛṣṇa's personality; *yeṅho*—who; *saba-avatārī*—the source of all the incarnations; *para-vyoma-adhikārī*—the predominating Deity of the Vaikuṇṭha planets; *e mādhurya*—this ecstatic sweetness; *nāhi*—is not; *nārāyaṇe*—even in Lord Nārāyaṇa.

## TRANSLATION

**"The sweetness of Kṛṣṇa's beauty enjoyed by the gopīs is unparalleled. Nothing is equal to or greater than such ecstatic sweetness. Even the predominating Deities of the Vaikuṇṭha planets, the Nārāyaṇas, do not possess such sweetness. Indeed, none of the incarnations of Kṛṣṇa up to Nārāyaṇa possess such transcendental beauty.**

## TEXT 116

তাতে সাক্ষী সেই রমা, নারায়ণের প্রিয়তমা,
পতিব্রতাগণের উপাস্যা ।
তিঁহো যে মাধুর্যলোভে, ছাড়ি' সব কামভোগে,
ব্রত করি' করিলা তপস্যা ॥ ১১৬ ॥

*tāte sākṣī sei ramā, nārāyaṇera priyatamā,*
*pativratā-gaṇera upāsyā*
*tiṅho ye mādhurya-lobhe, chāḍi' saba kāma-bhoge,*
*vrata kari' karilā tapasyā*

## SYNONYMS

*tāte*—in this regard; *sākṣī*—the evidence; *sei ramā*—that goddess of fortune; *nārāyaṇera priya-tamā*—the most dear consort of Nārāyaṇa; *pati-vratā-gaṇera*—of all chaste women; *upāsyā*—worshipable; *tiṅho*—she; *ye*—that; *mādhurya-lobhe*—being attracted by the same sweetness; *chāḍi'*—giving up; *saba*—all; *kāma-bhoge*—to enjoy with Kṛṣṇa; *vrata kari'*—taking a vow; *karilā tapasyā*—executed austerities.

## TRANSLATION

**"Even the dearest consort of Nārāyaṇa, the goddess of fortune, who is worshiped by all chaste women, is captivated by the unparalleled sweetness of Kṛṣṇa. She even gave up everything in her desire to enjoy Kṛṣṇa, and taking a great vow, she underwent severe austerities.**

## TEXT 117

সেই ত' মাধুর্য-সার, অন্য-সিদ্ধি নাহি তার,
তিঁহো—মাধুর্যাদি-গুণখনি।
আর সব প্রকাশে, তাঁর দত্ত গুণ ভাসে,
যাহাঁ যত প্রকাশে কার্য জানি॥ ১১৭॥

*sei ta' mādhurya-sāra, anya-siddhi nāhi tāra,*
*tiṅho——mādhuryādi-guṇa-khani*
*āra saba prakāśe, tāṅra datta guṇa bhāse,*
*yāhāṅ yata prakāśe kārya jāni*

## SYNONYMS

*sei ta' mādhurya-sāra*—that is the quintessence of sweetness; *anya-siddhi*—perfection due to anything else; *nāhi*—there is not; *tāra*—of that; *tiṅho*—Lord Kṛṣṇa; *mādhurya-ādi-guṇa-khani*—the mine of transcendental mellows, headed by sweetness; *āra saba*—all other; *prakāśe*—in manifestations; *tāṅra*—His; *datta*—given; *guṇa*—transcendental qualities; *bhāse*—are exhibited; *yāhaṅ*—where; *yata*—as much as; *prakāśe*—in that manifestation; *kārya*—to be done; *jāni*—I understand.

## TRANSLATION

**"The quintessence of Kṛṣṇa's sweet bodily luster is so perfect that there is no perfection above it. He is the immutable mine of all transcendental qualities. In His other manifestations and personal expansions, there is only a partial exhibition of such qualities. We understand all His personal expansions in this way.**

## TEXT 118

গোপীভাব-দরপণ, নব নব ক্ষণে ক্ষণ,
তার আগে কৃষ্ণের মাধুর্য।
দোঁহে করে হুড়াহুড়ি, বাড়ে, মুখ নাহি মুড়ি,
নব নব দোঁহার প্রাচুর্য॥ ১১৮॥

*gopī-bhāva-darapaṇa, nava nava kṣaṇe kṣaṇa,*
*tāra āge kṛṣṇera mādhurya*
*doṅhe kare huḍāhuḍi, bāḍe, mukha nāhi muḍi,*
*nava nava doṅhāra prācurya*

### SYNONYMS

*gopī-bhāva-darapaṇa*—the *gopīs'* ecstasy is like a mirror; *nava nava kṣaṇe kṣaṇa*—newer and newer at every moment; *tāra āge*—in front of that; *kṛṣṇera mādhurya*—the sweetness of Kṛṣṇa's beauty; *doṅhe*—both; *kare*—do; *huḍāhuḍi*—struggling together; *bāḍe*—increases; *mukha nāhi muḍi*—never turning away the faces; *nava nava*—newer and newer; *doṅhāra*—of both of them; *prācurya*—abundance.

### TRANSLATION

**"Both the gopīs and Kṛṣṇa are complete. The gopīs' ecstatic love is like a mirror that becomes newer and newer at every moment and reflects Kṛṣṇa's bodily luster and sweetness. Thus competition increases. Since neither give up, their pastimes become newer and newer, and both sides constantly increase.**

### TEXT 119

কর্ম, তপ, যোগ, জ্ঞান, বিধি-ভক্তি, জপ, ধ্যান,
ইহা হৈতে মাধুর্য দুর্লভ।
কেবল যে রাগমার্গে, ভজে কৃষ্ণে অনুরাগে,
তারে কৃষ্ণমাধুর্য সুলভ ॥ ১১৯ ॥

*karma, tapa, yoga, jñāna, vidhi-bhakti, japa, dhyāna,*
*ihā haite mādhurya durlabha*
*kevala ye rāga-mārge, bhaje kṛṣṇe anurāge,*
*tāre kṛṣṇa-mādhurya sulabha*

### SYNONYMS

*karma*—fruitive activities; *tapa*—austerities; *yoga*—the practice of mystic *yoga; jñāna*—speculative cultivation of knowledge; *vidhi-bhakti*—regulative principles in devotional service; *japa*—chanting; *dhyāna*—meditation; *ihā haite*—from these things; *mādhurya*—the sweetness of Kṛṣṇa; *durlabha*—very difficult to perceive; *kevala*—only; *ye*—one; *rāga-mārge*—by the path of spontaneous ecstatic love; *bhaje*—worships; *kṛṣṇe*—Lord Kṛṣṇa; *anurāge*—with transcendental feeling; *tāre*—unto him; *kṛṣṇa-mādhurya*—the sweetness of Kṛṣṇa's; *sulabha*—very easily appreciated.

### TRANSLATION

**"The transcendental mellows generated from the dealings between the gopīs and Kṛṣṇa cannot be tasted by fruitive activity, yogic austerities,**

**speculative knowledge, regulative devotional service, mantra-yoga or meditation. This sweetness can be tasted only through the spontaneous love of liberated persons who chant the holy names with great ecstatic love.**

### TEXT 120

সেইরূপ ব্রজাশ্রয়, ঐশ্বর্য-মাধুর্যময়,
দিব্যগুণগণ-রত্নালয় ।
আনের বৈভব-সত্তা, কৃষ্ণদত্ত ভগবত্তা,
কৃষ্ণ—সর্ব-অংশী, সর্বাশ্রয় ॥ ১২০॥

*sei-rūpa vrajāśraya, aiśvarya-mādhuryamaya,*
*divya-guṇa-gaṇa-ratnālaya*
*ānera vaibhava-sattā, kṛṣṇa-datta bhagavattā,*
*kṛṣṇa——sarva-aṁśī, sarvāśraya*

### SYNONYMS

*sei-rūpa*—that supernatural beauty; *vraja-āśraya*—whose abode is in Vṛndāvana; *aiśvarya-mādhurya-maya*—full of opulence and the sweetness of love; *divya-guṇa-gaṇa*—of transcendental qualities; *ratna-ālaya*—the source of all the gems; *ānera*—of others; *vaibhava-sattā*—the presence of opulences; *kṛṣṇa-datta*—all bestowed by Kṛṣṇa; *bhagavattā*—qualities of the Supreme Personality of Godhead; *kṛṣṇa*—Lord Kṛṣṇa; *sarva-aṁśī*—the original source of all of them; *sarva-āśraya*—the shelter of all of them.

### TRANSLATION

**"Such ecstatic transactions between Kṛṣṇa and the gopīs are only possible in Vṛndāvana, which is full of the opulences of transcendental love. The form of Kṛṣṇa is the original source of all transcendental qualities. It is like a mine of gems. The opulences belonging to all the personal expansions of Kṛṣṇa are to be understood to be bestowed by Kṛṣṇa; therefore Kṛṣṇa is the original source and shelter of everyone.**

### TEXT 121

শ্রী, লজ্জা, দয়া, কীর্তি, ধৈর্য, বৈশারদী মতি,
এই সব কৃষ্ণে প্রতিষ্ঠিত ।
সুশীল, মৃদু, বদান্য, কৃষ্ণ-সম নাহি অন্য,
কৃষ্ণ করে জগতের হিত ॥ ১২১ ॥

*śrī, lajjā, dayā, kīrti, dhairya, vaiśāradī mati,*
*ei saba kṛṣṇe pratiṣṭhita*
*suśīla, mṛdu, vadānya, kṛṣṇa-sama nāhi anya,*
*kṛṣṇa kare jagatera hita*

### SYNONYMS

*śrī*—beauty; *lajjā*—humility; *dayā*—mercy; *kīrti*—merit; *dhairya*—patience; *vaiśāradī*—very expert; *mati*—intelligence; *ei saba*—all these; *kṛṣṇe*—in Lord Kṛṣṇa; *pratiṣṭhita*—situated; *su-śīla*—well behaved; *mṛdu*—mild; *vadānya*—magnanimous; *kṛṣṇa-sama*—like Kṛṣṇa; *nāhi*—there is no one; *anya*—else; *kṛṣṇa*—Lord Kṛṣṇa; *kare*—does; *jagatera*—of the world; *hita*—welfare.

### TRANSLATION

**"Beauty, humility, mercy, merit, patience and expert intelligence are all manifest in Kṛṣṇa. But besides these, Kṛṣṇa has other qualities like good behavior, mildness and magnanimity. He also performs welfare activities for the whole world. All these qualities are not visible in expansions like Nārāyaṇa.**

### PURPORT

Śrīla Bhaktivinoda Ṭhākura mentions that the qualities of beauty, humility, mercy, merit, patience and expert intelligence are brilliant qualities, and when they are exhibited in the person of Nārāyaṇa, one should know that they are bestowed upon Nārāyaṇa by Kṛṣṇa. Good behavior, mildness and magnanimity are found only in Kṛṣṇa. Only Kṛṣṇa performs welfare activities for the whole world.

### TEXT 122

কৃষ্ণ দেখি' নানা জন, কৈল নিমিষে নিন্দন,
ব্রজে বিধি নিন্দে গোপীগণ ।
সেই সব শ্লোক পড়ি', মহাপ্রভু অর্থ করি',
সুখে মাধুর্য করে আস্বাদন ॥ ১২২ ॥

*kṛṣṇa dekhi' nānā jana, kaila nimiṣe nindana,*
*vraje vidhi ninde gopī-gaṇa*
*sei saba śloka paḍi', mahāprabhu artha kari',*
*sukhe mādhurya kare āsvādana*

### SYNONYMS

*kṛṣṇa*—Lord Kṛṣṇa; *dekhi'*—seeing; *nānā jana*—various persons; *kaila*—did; *nimiṣe*—due to the blinking of the eyes; *nindana*—blaming; *vraje*—in

Vṛndāvana; *vidhi*—Lord Brahmā; *ninde*—blame; *gopī-gaṇa*—all the *gopīs; sei saba*—all those; *śloka*—verses; *paḍi'*—reciting; *mahāprabhu*—Śrī Caitanya Mahāprabhu; *artha kari'*—explaining the meaning; *sukhe*—in happiness; *mādhurya*—transcendental sweetness; *kare*—does; *āsvādana*—tasting.

### TRANSLATION

**"After seeing Kṛṣṇa, various people criticize the blinking of their eyes. In Vṛndāvana, especially, all the gopīs criticize Lord Brahmā because of this defect in the eyes." Then Śrī Caitanya Mahāprabhu recited some verses from Śrīmad-Bhāgavatam and explained them vividly, thus enjoying the taste of transcendental sweetness with great happiness.**

### TEXT 123

যস্যাননং মকরকুণ্ডলচারুকর্ণ-
ভ্রাজৎকপোলসুভগং সবিলাসহাসম্ ।
নিত্যোৎসবং ন ততৃপুর্দৃশিভিঃ পিবন্ত্যো
নার্যো নরাশ্চ মুদিতাঃ কুপিতা নিমেশ্চ ॥ ১২৩ ॥

*yasyānanaṁ makara-kuṇḍala-cāru-karṇa-*
*bhrājat-kapola-subhagaṁ savilāsa-hāsam*
*nityotsavaṁ na tatṛpur dṛśibhiḥ pibantyo*
*nāryo narāś ca muditāḥ kupitā nimeś ca*

### SYNONYMS

*yasya*—of Kṛṣṇa; *ānanam*—face; *makara-kuṇḍala*—by earrings resembling sharks; *cāru*—beautified; *karṇa*—the ears; *bhrājat*—shining; *kapola*—cheeks; *subhagam*—delicate; *sa-vilāsa-hāsam*—smiling with an enjoying spirit; *nitya-utsavam*—in which there are eternal festivities of joy; *na*—not; *tatṛpuḥ*—satisfied; *dṛśibhiḥ*—by the eyes; *pibantyaḥ*—drinking; *nāryaḥ*—all the women; *narāḥ*—the men; *ca*—and; *muditāḥ*—very pleased; *kupitāḥ*—very angry; *nimeḥ*—at the creator of the blinking of the eyes; *ca*—also.

### TRANSLATION

**" 'All men and women were accustomed to enjoying the beauty of the shining face of Lord Kṛṣṇa, as well as His sharklike earrings swinging on His ears. His beautiful features, His cheeks and His playful smiles all combined to form a constant festival for the eyes, and the blinking of the eyes became obstacles that impeded one from seeing that beauty. For this reason, men and women became very angry at the creator [Lord Brahmā].'**

### PURPORT

This is a verse from *Śrīmad-Bhāgavatam* (9.24.65).

### TEXT 124

অটতি যদ্ভবানহ্নি কাননং ত্রুটির্যুগায়তে ত্বামপশ্যতাম্ ।
কুটিলকুন্তলং শ্রীমুখঞ্চ তে জড় উদীক্ষতাং পক্ষ্মকৃদ্দৃশাম্ ॥১২৪॥

*aṭati yad bhavān ahni kānanaṁ*
*truṭir yugāyate tvām apaśyatām*
*kuṭila-kuntalaṁ śrī-mukhaṁ ca te*
*jaḍa udīkṣatāṁ pakṣma-kṛd dṛśām*

### SYNONYMS

*aṭati*—goes; *yat*—when; *bhavān*—Your Lordship; *ahni*—in the day; *kānanam*—to the forest; *truṭiḥ*—half a second; *yugāyate*—appears like a *yuga; tvām*—You; *apaśyatām*—of those not seeing; *kuṭila-kuntalam*—adorned with curled hair; *śrī-mukham*—beautiful face; *ca*—and; *te*—Your; *jaḍaḥ*—stupid; *udīkṣatām*—looking at; *pakṣma-kṛt*—the maker of eyelashes; *dṛśām*—of the eyes.

### TRANSLATION

**" 'O Kṛṣṇa, when You go to the forest during the day and we do not see Your sweet face, which is surrounded by beautiful, curling hair, half a second becomes as long as an entire age for us. And we consider the creator, who has put eyelids on the eyes we use for seeing You, to be simply a fool.'**

### PURPORT

This verse is spoken by the *gopīs* in *Śrīmad-Bhāgavatam* (10.31.15).

### TEXT 125

কামগায়ত্রী-মন্ত্ররূপ, হয় কৃষ্ণের স্বরূপ,
সার্ধ-চব্বিশ অক্ষর তার হয় ।
সে অক্ষর 'চন্দ্র' হয়, কৃষ্ণে করি' উদয়,
ত্রিজগৎ কৈলা কামময় ॥ ১২৫ ॥

*kāma-gāyatrī-mantra-rūpa, haya kṛṣṇera svarūpa,*
*sārdha-cabbiśa akṣara tāra haya*
*se akṣara 'candra' haya, kṛṣṇe kari' udaya,*
*trijagat kailā kāmamaya*

### SYNONYMS

*kāma-gāyatrī-mantra-rūpa*—the hymn known as *kāma-gāyatrī; haya*—is; *kṛṣṇera svarūpa*—identical with Kṛṣṇa; *sārdha-cabbiśa*—twenty-four and a half; *akṣara*—syllables; *tāra*—of that; *haya*—are; *se akṣara*—these syllables; *candra haya*—are like the moon; *kṛṣṇe*—Lord Kṛṣṇa; *kari' udaya*—awakening; *tri-jagat*—the three worlds; *kailā*—made; *kāma-maya*—full of desire.

### TRANSLATION

**"Kṛṣṇa, the Supreme Personality of Godhead, is identical with the Vedic hymn known as the kāma-gāyatrī, which is composed of twenty-four and a half syllables. Those syllables are compared to moons that arise in Kṛṣṇa. Thus all three worlds are filled with desire.**

### TEXT 126

সখি হে, কৃষ্ণমুখ—দ্বিজরাজ-রাজ।
কৃষ্ণবপু-সিংহাসনে, বসি' রাজ্য-শাসনে,
করে সঙ্গে চন্দ্রের সমাজ ॥ ১২৬ ॥ ধ্রু ॥

*sakhi he, kṛṣṇa-mukha——dvija-rāja-rāja*
*kṛṣṇa-vapu-siṁhāsane, vasi' rājya-śāsane,*
*kare saṅge candrera samāja*

### SYNONYMS

*sakhi he*—O dear friend; *kṛṣṇa-mukha*—the face of Lord Kṛṣṇa; *dvija-rāja-rāja*—the king of moons; *kṛṣṇa-vapu*—of the transcendental body of Kṛṣṇa; *siṁhāsane*—on the throne; *vasi'*—sitting; *rājya-śāsane*—ruling of the kingdom; *kare*—does; *saṅge*—in the company of; *candrera samāja*—the society of moons.

### TRANSLATION

**"The face of Kṛṣṇa is the king of all moons, and the body of Kṛṣṇa is the throne. Thus the king governs a society of moons.**

### PURPORT

The entire face is called the king of moons. The mouth is another moon, the left cheek is a moon, and the right cheek is a moon. The spots of sandalwood pulp on Kṛṣṇa's face are also considered different moons, and His fingernails and toenails are also different moons. His forehead is considered a half moon, His face is considered the king of moons, and His body is considered the throne. All the other *candras* (moons) are considered to be subordinate moons.

### TEXT 127

দুই গণ্ড সুচিক্কণ, জিনি' মণিসুদর্পণ,
সেই দুই পূর্ণচন্দ্র জানি ।
ললাটে অষ্টমী-ইন্দু, তাহাতে চন্দন-বিন্দু,
সেহ এক পূর্ণচন্দ্র মানি ॥ ১২৭ ॥

*dui gaṇḍa sucikkaṇa, jini' maṇi-sudarpaṇa,*
*sei dui pūrṇa-candra jāni*
*lalāṭe aṣṭamī-indu, tāhāte candana-bindu,*
*sei eka pūrṇa-candra māni*

### SYNONYMS

*dui*—two; *gaṇḍa*—cheeks; *su-cikkaṇa*—very shiny; *jini'*—conquering; *maṇi-su-darpaṇa*—glowing gems; *sei dui*—those two; *pūrṇa-candra*—full moons; *jāni*—I consider; *lalāṭe*—on the forehead; *aṣṭamī-indu*—eighth-day moon (half moon); *tāhāte*—on that; *candana-bindu*—the drop of sandalwood pulp; *sei*—that; *eka*—one; *pūrṇa-candra*—full moon; *māni*—I consider.

### TRANSLATION

**"Kṛṣṇa has two cheeks that shine like glowing gems. Both are considered full moons. His forehead is considered a half moon, and His spots of sandalwood are considered full moons.**

### TEXT 128

করনখ-চান্দের হাট, বংশী-উপর করে নাট,
তার গীত মুরলীর তান ।
পদনখ-চন্দ্রগণ, তলে করে নর্তন,
নূপুরের ধ্বনি যার গান ॥ ১২৮ ॥

*kara-nakha-cāndera hāṭa, vaṁśī-upara kare nāṭa,*
*tāra gīta muralīra tāna*
*pada-nakha-candra-gaṇa, tale kare nartana,*
*nūpurera dhvani yāra gāna*

### SYNONYMS

*kara-nakha*—of the nails on the hands; *cāndera*—of the full moons; *hāṭa*—the bazaar; *vaṁśī*—the flute; *upara*—on; *kare*—do; *nāṭa*—dancing; *tāra*—of them;

*gīta*—the song; *muralīra tāna*—the melody of the flute; *pada-nakha*—of the nails on the toes; *candra-gaṇa*—the different full moons; *tale*—on the ground; *kare*—do; *nartana*—dancing; *nūpurera*—of the ankle bells; *dhvani*—the sound; *yāra*—whose; *gāna*—musical song.

### TRANSLATION

**"His fingernails are many full moons, and they dance on the flute on His hands. Their song is the melody of that flute. His toenails are also many full moons, and they dance on the ground. Their song is the jingling of His ankle bells.**

### TEXT 129

নাচে মকর-কুণ্ডল, নেত্র—লীলা-কমল,
বিলাসী রাজা সতত নাচায় ।
ভ্রূ—ধনু, নেত্র—বাণ, ধনুর্গুণ—দুই কাণ,
নারীমন-লক্ষ্য বিন্ধে তায় ॥ ১২৯ ॥

*nāce makara-kuṇḍala, netra——līlā-kamala,*
*vilāsī rājā satata nācāya*
*bhrū——dhanu, netra——bāṇa, dhanur-guṇa——dui kāṇa,*
*nārī-mana-lakṣya vindhe tāya*

### SYNONYMS

*nāce*—dance; *makara-kuṇḍala*—the earrings shaped like sharks; *netra*—the eyes; *līlā*—for play; *kamala*—like lotus flowers; *vilāsī*—the enjoyer; *rājā*—the king; *satata nācāya*—always causes to dance; *bhrū*—two eyebrows; *dhanu*—just like bows; *netra*—the eyes; *bāṇa*—just like arrows; *dhanuḥ-guṇa*—the string of the bow; *dui kāṇa*—the two ears; *nārī-mana*—the minds of the *gopīs; lakṣya*—the target; *vindhe*—pierces; *tāya*—there.

### TRANSLATION

**"Kṛṣṇa's face is the enjoyer king. That full-moon face makes His shark-shaped earrings and lotus eyes dance. His eyebrows are like bows, and His eyes are like arrows. His ears are fixed on the string of that bow, and when His eyes spread to His ears, He pierces the hearts of the gopīs.**

### TEXT 130

এই চান্দের বড় নাট, পসারি' চান্দের হাট,
বিনিমূলে বিলায় নিজামৃত ।

কাহোঁ স্মিত-জ্যোৎস্নামৃতে, কাঁহারে অধরামৃতে,
সব লোক করে আপ্যায়িত ॥ ১৩০ ॥

*ei cāndera baḍa nāṭa, pasāri' cāndera hāṭa,*
*vinimūle vilāya nijāmṛta*
*kāhoṅ smita-jyotsnāmṛte, kāṅhāre adharāmṛte,*
*saba loka kare āpyāyita*

**SYNONYMS**

*ei cāndera*—of this moon of the face; *baḍa*—big; *nāṭa*—dancing; *pasāri'*—expanding; *cāndera hāṭa*—the marketplace of full moons; *vinimūle*—without a price; *vilāya*—distributes; *nija-amṛta*—its personal nectar; *kāhoṅ*—to some; *smita-jyotsnā-amṛte*—by the nectar of the sweetly smiling moonrays; *kāṅhāre*—to someone; *adhara-amṛte*—by the nectar of the lips; *saba loka*—all people; *kare āpyāyita*—pleases.

**TRANSLATION**

**"The dancing features of His face surpass all other full moons and expand the marketplace of full moons. Although priceless, the nectar of Kṛṣṇa's face is distributed to everyone. Some purchase the moonrays of His sweet smiles, and others purchase the nectar of His lips. Thus He pleases everyone.**

**TEXT 131**

বিপুলায়তারুণ, মদন-মদ-ঘূর্ণন,
মন্ত্রী যার এ দুই নয়ন ।
লাবণ্যকেলি-সদন, জন-নেত্র-রসায়ন,
সুখময় গোবিন্দ-বদন ॥ ১৩১ ॥

*vipulāyatāruṇa, madana-mada-ghūrṇana,*
*mantrī yāra e dui nayana*
*lāvaṇya-keli-sadana, jana-netra-rasāyana,*
*sukhamaya govinda-vadana*

**SYNONYMS**

*vipula-āyata*—broad and spread; *aruṇa*—reddish; *madana-mada*—the pride of Cupid; *ghūrṇana*—bewildering; *mantrī*—ministers; *yāra*—whose; *e*—these; *dui*—two; *nayana*—eyes; *lāvaṇya-keli*—of pastimes of beauty; *sadana*—home; *jana-netra-rasa-āyana*—very pleasing to the eyes of everyone; *sukha-maya*—full of happiness; *govinda-vadana*—the face of Lord Kṛṣṇa.

### TRANSLATION

**"Kṛṣṇa has two reddish, widely spread eyes. These are ministers of the king, and they subdue the pride of Cupid, who also has beautiful eyes. That face of Govinda, which is full of happiness, is the home of the pastimes of beauty, and it is very pleasing to everyone's eyes.**

### TEXT 132

যাঁর পুণ্যপুঞ্জফলে, সে-মুখ-দর্শন মিলে,
দুই আঁখি কি করিবে পানে ?
দ্বিগুণ বাড়ে তৃষ্ণা-লোভ, পিতে নারে—মনঃক্ষোভ,
দুঃখে করে বিধির নিন্দনে ॥ ১৩২ ॥

*yāṅra puṇya-puñja-phale, se-mukha-darśana mile,*
*dui āṅkhi ki karibe pāne?*
*dviguṇa bāḍe tṛṣṇā-lobha, pite nāre——manaḥ-kṣobha,*
*duḥkhe kare vidhira nindane*

### SYNONYMS

*yāṅra*—whose; *puṇya-puñja-phale*—by the result of many pious activities; *se-mukha*—of that face; *darśana*—seeing; *mile*—if one gets to do; *dui āṅkhi*—two eyes; *ki*—how; *karibe*—will do; *pāne*—drinking; *dvi-guṇa*—twice; *bāḍe*—increases; *tṛṣṇā-lobha*—greed and thirst; *pite*—to drink; *nāre*—not able; *manaḥ-kṣobha*—agitation of the mind; *duḥkhe*—in great distress; *kare*—does; *vidhira*—of the creator; *nindane*—criticizing.

### TRANSLATION

**"If by devotional service one gets the results of pious activities and sees Lord Kṛṣṇa's face, he can relish the Lord with his eyes. His greed and thirst then increase twofold by seeing the nectarean face of Kṛṣṇa. Due to one's inability to sufficiently drink that nectar, one becomes very unhappy and criticizes the creator for not having given more than two eyes.**

### TEXT 133

না দিলেক লক্ষ-কোটি, সবে দিলা আঁখি দুটি,
তাতে দিলা নিমিষ-আচ্ছাদন ।
বিধি—জড় তপোধন, রসশূন্য তার মন,
নাহি জানে যোগ্য স্বজন ॥ ১৩৩ ॥

*nā dileka lakṣa-koṭi, sabe dilā āṅkhi duṭi,*
*tāte dilā nimiṣa-ācchādana*
*vidhi——jaḍa tapodhana, rasa-śūnya tāra mana,*
*nāhi jāne yogya sṛjana*

### SYNONYMS

*nā dileka*—did not award; *lakṣa-koṭi*—thousands and millions; *sabe*—only; *dilā*—gave; *āṅkhi duṭi*—two eyes; *tāte*—in them; *dilā*—gave; *nimiṣa-ācchādana*—covering of the eyelids; *vidhi*—creator; *jaḍa*—dull; *tapaḥ-dhana*—assets of austerities; *rasa-śūnya*—without juice; *tāra*—his; *mana*—mind; *nāhi jāne*—does not know; *yogya*—suitable; *sṛjana*—creating.

### TRANSLATION

**"When the onlooker of Kṛṣṇa's face becomes dissatisfied in this way, he thinks, 'Why didn't the creator give me thousands and millions of eyes? Why has he given me only two? Even these two eyes are disturbed by blinking, which keeps me from continuously seeing Kṛṣṇa's face.' Thus one accuses the creator of being dry and tasteless due to engaging in severe austerities. 'The creator is only a dry manufacturer. He does not know how to create and set things in their proper places.**

## TEXT 134

যে দেখিবে কৃষ্ণানন, তার করে দ্বি-নয়ন,
বিধি হঞা হেন অবিচার ।
মোর যদি বোল ধরে, কোটি আঁখি তার করে,
তবে জানি যোগ্য সৃষ্টি তার ॥ ১৩৪ ॥

*ye dekhibe kṛṣṇānana, tāra kare dvi-nayana,*
*vidhi hañā hena avicāra*
*mora yadi bola dhare, koṭi āṅkhi tāra kare,*
*tabe jāni yogya sṛṣṭi tāra*

### SYNONYMS

*ye*—anyone who; *dekhibe*—will see; *kṛṣṇa-ānana*—the face of Kṛṣṇa; *tāra*—of him; *kare*—make; *dvi-nayana*—two eyes; *vidhi*—an authority in creation; *hañā*—being; *hena*—such; *avicāra*—lack of consideration; *mora*—my; *yadi*—if; *bola*—instruction; *dhare*—accepts; *koṭi āṅkhi*—millions of eyes; *tāra*—of him; *kare*—would create; *tabe jāni*—then I would understand; *yogya*—suitable; *sṛṣṭi*—creation; *tāra*—his.

### TRANSLATION

**" 'The creator says, "Let those who will see Kṛṣṇa's beautiful face have two eyes." Just see the lack of consideration exhibited by this person posing as a creator. If the creator took my advice, he would give millions of eyes to the person who intends to see Śrī Kṛṣṇa's face. If the creator will accept this advice, then I would say that he is competent in his work.'**

### TEXT 135

কৃষ্ণাঙ্গ-মাধুর্য—সিন্ধু, সুমধুর মুখ—ইন্দু,
অতি-মধু স্মিত—সুকিরণে ।
এ-তিনে লাগিল মন, লোভে করে আস্বাদন,
শ্লোক পড়ে স্বহস্ত-চালনে ॥ ১৩৫ ॥

*kṛṣṇāṅga-mādhurya——sindhu, sumadhura mukha——indu,*
*ati-madhu smita——sukiraṇe*
*e-tine lāgila mana, lobhe kare āsvādana,*
*śloka paḍe svahasta-cālane*

### SYNONYMS

*kṛṣṇa-aṅga*—of the transcendental body of Kṛṣṇa; *mādhurya*—of sweetness; *sindhu*—the ocean; *su-madhura*—very sweet; *mukha*—face; *indu*—like the full moon; *ati-madhu*—extraordinarily sweet; *smita*—smiling; *su-kiraṇe*—beam of moonlight; *e-tine*—these three; *lāgila mana*—attracted the mind; *lobhe*—with more and more greed; *kare āsvādana*—relished; *śloka paḍe*—recites a verse; *sva-hasta-cālane*—moving His own hand.

### TRANSLATION

**"The transcendental form of Lord Śrī Kṛṣṇa is compared to an ocean. A particularly extraordinary vision is the moon above that ocean, and another vision is His smile, which is sweeter than sweet and is like shining beams of moonlight." While speaking of these things with Sanātana Gosvāmī, Śrī Caitanya Mahāprabhu began to remember one thing after another. Moving His hands in ecstasy, He recited a verse.**

### TEXT 136

মধুরং মধুরং বপুরস্য বিভোর্মধুরং মধুরং বদনং মধুরম্ ।
মধুগন্ধি মৃদুস্মিতমেতদহো মধুরং মধুরং মধুরং মধুরম্ ॥১৩৬॥

*madhuraṁ madhuraṁ vapur asya vibhor*
*madhuraṁ madhuraṁ vadanaṁ madhuram*
*madhu-gandhi mṛdu-smitam etad aho*
*madhuraṁ madhuraṁ madhuraṁ madhuram*

### SYNONYMS

*madhuram*—sweet; *madhuram*—sweet; *vapuḥ*—the transcendental form; *asya*—His; *vibhoḥ*—of the Lord; *madhuram*—sweet; *madhuram*—sweet; *vadanam*—face; *madhuram*—more sweet; *madhu-gandhi*—the fragrance of honey; *mṛdu-smitam*—soft smiling; *etat*—this; *aho*—O; *madhuram*—sweet; *madhuram*—sweet; *madhuram*—sweet; *madhuram*—still more sweet.

### TRANSLATION

**" 'O my Lord, the transcendental body of Kṛṣṇa is very sweet, and His face is even sweeter than His body. The soft smile on His face, which is like the fragrance of honey, is sweeter still.'**

### PURPORT

This is a verse quoted from *Kṛṣṇa-karṇāmṛta* by Bilvamaṅgala Ṭhākura.

## TEXT 137

সনাতন, কৃষ্ণমাধুর্য—অমৃতের সিন্ধু ।
মোর মন—সন্নিপাতি, সব পিতে করে মতি,
দুর্দৈব-বৈদ্য না দেয় এক বিন্দু ॥ ১৩৭ ॥ ধ্রু ॥

*sanātana, kṛṣṇa-mādhurya——amṛtera sindhu*
*mora mana——sannipāti, saba pite kare mati,*
*durdaiva-vaidya nā deya eka bindu*

### SYNONYMS

*sanātana*—O My dear Sanātana; *kṛṣṇa-mādhurya*—the sweetness of Lord Kṛṣṇa; *amṛtera sindhu*—an ocean of ambrosia; *mora mana*—my mind; *sannipāti*—a disease of convulsions; *saba*—all; *pite*—to drink; *kare*—does; *mati*—desire; *durdaiva-vaidya*—a physician who suppresses; *nā*—not; *deya*—gives; *eka*—one; *bindu*—drop.

### TRANSLATION

**"My dear Sanātana, the sweetness of Kṛṣṇa's personality is just like an ocean of ambrosia. Although My mind is now afflicted by convulsive diseases**

**and I wish to drink that entire ocean, the repressive physician does not allow Me to drink even one drop.**

### PURPORT

When there is a combination of *kapha, pitta* and *vāyu,* the three bodily elements, there occurs *sannipāti,* or a convulsive disease. "This disease is caused by the personal features of Lord Kṛṣṇa. The three elements are the beauty of Kṛṣṇa's body, the beauty of His face, and the beauty of His smile. Stricken by these three beauties, My mind goes into convulsions. It wishes to drink the ocean of Kṛṣṇa's beauty, but because I am undergoing convulsions, My physician, who is Śrī Kṛṣṇa Himself, does not even allow Me to take a drop of water from that ocean." Śrī Caitanya Mahāprabhu was ecstatic in this way because He was presenting Himself in the mood of the *gopīs.* The *gopīs* wanted to drink the ocean of sweetness arising from the bodily features of Kṛṣṇa, but Kṛṣṇa did not allow them to come near. Consequently their desire to meet Kṛṣṇa increased, and being unable to drink the ambrosia of Kṛṣṇa's bodily features, they became very unhappy.

### TEXT 138

**কৃষ্ণাঙ্গ—লাবণ্যপূর, মধুর হৈতে সুমধুর,**
**তাতে যেই মুখ সুধাকর ।**
**মধুর হৈতে সুমধুর, তাহা হইতে সুমধুর,**
**তার যেই স্মিত জ্যোৎস্না-ভর ॥ ১৩৮ ॥**

*kṛṣṇāṅga——lāvaṇya-pūra, madhura haite sumadhura,*
*tāte yei mukha sudhākara*
*madhura haite sumadhura, tāhā ha-ite sumadhura,*
*tāra yei smita jyotsnā-bhara*

### SYNONYMS

*kṛṣṇa-aṅga*—the bodily features of Kṛṣṇa; *lāvaṇya-pūra*—the city of attractive beauty; *madhura*—sweetness; *haite*—than; *su-madhura*—still more sweet; *tāte*—in that body; *yei*—that; *mukha*—face; *sudhākara*—like the moon; *madhura haite su-madhura*—sweeter than sweetness; *tāhā ha-ite*—than that; *su-madhura*—still more sweet; *tāra*—of which; *yei*—that; *smita*—smiling; *jyotsnā-bhara*—like the moonshine.

### TRANSLATION

**"Kṛṣṇa's body is a city of attractive features, and it is sweeter than sweet. His face, which is like the moon, is sweeter still, and the gentle smile on that moonlike face is like rays of moonshine.**

## PURPORT

The smile on Kṛṣṇa's face is just like the smiling of the moon, which generates greater and greater happiness for the *gopīs*.

## TEXT 139

মধুর হৈতে সুমধুর, তাহা হৈতে সুমধুর,
তাহা হৈতে অতি সুমধুর ।
আপনার এক কণে, ব্যাপে সব ত্রিভুবনে,
দশদিক্ ব্যাপে যার পূর ॥ ১৩৯ ॥

*madhura haite sumadhura, tāhā haite sumadhura,*
*tāhā haite ati sumadhura*
*āpanāra eka kaṇe, vyāpe saba tribhuvane,*
*daśa-dik vyāpe yāra pūra*

## SYNONYMS

*madhura haite su-madhura*—sweeter than sweet; *tāhā haite*—than that; *su-madhura*—still sweeter; *tāhā haite*—than that; *ati su-madhura*—still much more sweet; *āpanāra*—of Himself; *eka kaṇe*—by one particle; *vyāpe*—spreads; *saba*—all; *tri-bhuvane*—throughout the three worlds; *daśa-dik*—ten directions; *vyāpe*—spreads; *yāra*—whose; *pūra*—the city of Kṛṣṇa's beauty.

## TRANSLATION

**"The beauty of Kṛṣṇa's smile is the sweetest feature of all. His smile is like a full moon that spreads its rays throughout the three worlds—Goloka Vṛndāvana, the spiritual sky of the Vaikuṇṭhas, and Devī-dhāma, the material world. Thus Kṛṣṇa's shining beauty spreads in all ten directions.**

## TEXT 140

স্মিত-কিরণ-সুকর্পূরে, পৈশে অধর-মধুরে,
সেই মধু মাতায় ত্রিভুবনে ।
বংশীছিদ্র আকাশে, তার গুণ শব্দে পৈশে,
ধ্বনিরূপে পাঞা পরিণামে ॥ ১৪০ ॥

*smita-kiraṇa-sukarpūre, paiśe adhara-madhure,*
*sei madhu mātāya tribhuvane*
*vaṁśī-chidra ākāśe, tāra guṇa śabde paiśe,*
*dhvani-rūpe pāñā pariṇāme*

### SYNONYMS

*smita-kiraṇa*—the shining of Kṛṣṇa's smile; *su-karpūre*—compared to camphor; *paiśe*—enters; *adhara-madhure*—within the sweetness of the lips; *sei madhu*—that ambrosia; *mātāya*—maddens; *tri-bhuvane*—the three worlds; *vaṁśī-chidra*—of the holes in the flute; *ākāśe*—in the space; *tāra guṇa*—the quality of that sweetness; *śabde*—in sound vibration; *paiśe*—enters; *dhvani-rūpe*—the form of sound vibration; *pāñā*—obtaining; *pariṇāme*—by transformation.

### TRANSLATION

**"His slight smiling and fragrant illumination are compared to camphor, which enters the sweetness of the lips. That sweetness is transformed and enters into space as vibrations from the holes of His flute.**

## TEXT 141

**সে ধ্বনি চৌদিকে ধায়,  অণ্ড ভেদি' বৈকুণ্ঠে যায়,**
**বলে পৈশে জগতের কাণে ।**
**সবা মাতোয়াল করি',  বলাৎকারে আনে ধরি',**
**বিশেষতঃ যুবতীর গণে ॥ ১৪১ ॥**

*se dhvani caudike dhāya,  aṇḍa bhedi' vaikuṇṭhe yāya,*
*bale paiśe jagatera kāṇe*
*sabā mātoyāla kari',  balātkāre āne dhari',*
*viśeṣataḥ yuvatīra gaṇe*

### SYNONYMS

*se dhvani*—that vibration; *cau-dike*—in the four directions; *dhāya*—runs; *aṇḍa bhedi'*—piercing the coverings of the universe; *vaikuṇṭhe yāya*—goes to the spiritual sky; *bale*—by force; *paiśe*—enters; *jagatera*—of the three worlds; *kāṇe*—in the ears; *sabā*—everyone; *mātoyāla kari'*—making drunk; *balātkāre*—by force; *āne*—brings; *dhari'*—catching; *viśeṣataḥ*—specifically; *yuvatīra gaṇe*—all the young damsels of Vrajabhūmi.

### TRANSLATION

**"The sound of Kṛṣṇa's flute spreads in four directions. Even though Kṛṣṇa vibrates His flute within this universe, its sound pierces the universal covering and goes to the spiritual sky. Thus the vibration enters the ears of all inhabitants. It especially enters Goloka Vṛndāvana-dhāma and attracts the minds of the young damsels of Vrajabhūmi, bringing them forcibly to where Kṛṣṇa is present.**

## TEXT 142

ধ্বনি—বড় উদ্ধত, পতিব্রতার ভাঙ্গে ব্রত,
পতি-কোল হৈতে টানি' আনে।
বৈকুণ্ঠের লক্ষ্মীগণে, যেই করে আকর্ষণে,
তার আগে কেবা গোপীগণে ॥ ১৪২ ॥

*dhvani——baḍa uddhata, pativratāra bhāṅge vrata,*
*pati-kola haite ṭāni' āne*
*vaikuṇṭhera lakṣmī-gaṇe, yei kare ākarṣaṇe,*
*tāra āge kebā gopī-gaṇe*

## SYNONYMS

*dhvani*—vibration; *baḍa*—very much; *uddhata*—aggressive; *pati-vratāra*—of chaste wives; *bhāṅge*—breaks; *vrata*—the vow; *pati*—of the husband; *kola*—the lap; *haite*—from; *ṭāni'*—taking; *āne*—brings; *vaikuṇṭhera*—of the Vaikuṇṭha planets; *lakṣmī-gaṇe*—all the goddesses of fortune; *yei*—that which; *kare ākarṣaṇe*—attracts; *tāra*—of that; *āge*—in front; *kebā*—what to speak of; *gopī-gaṇe*—the *gopīs* of Vṛndāvana.

## TRANSLATION

**"The vibration of Kṛṣṇa's flute is very aggressive, and it breaks the vows of all chaste women. Indeed, its vibration takes them forcibly from the laps of their husbands. The vibration of His flute attracts even the goddesses of fortune in the Vaikuṇṭha planets, to say nothing of the poor damsels of Vṛndāvana.**

## TEXT 143

নীবি খসায় পতি-আগে, গৃহধর্ম করায় ত্যাগে,
বলে ধরি' আনে কৃষ্ণস্থানে।
লোকধর্ম, লজ্জা, ভয়, সব জ্ঞান লুপ্ত হয়,
ঐছে নাচায় সব নারীগণে ॥ ১৪৩ ॥

*nīvi khasāya pati-āge, gṛha-dharma karāya tyāge,*
*bale dhari' āne kṛṣṇa-sthāne*
*loka-dharma, lajjā, bhaya, saba jñāna lupta haya,*
*aiche nācāya saba nārī-gaṇe*

### SYNONYMS

*nīvi*—the knots of the underwear; *khasāya*—loosens; *pati-āge*—even in front of the husbands; *gṛha-dharma*—household duties; *karāya tyāge*—causes to give up; *bale*—by force; *dhari'*—catching; *āne*—brings; *kṛṣṇa-sthāne*—before Lord Kṛṣṇa; *loka-dharma*—social etiquette; *lajjā*—shame; *bhaya*—fear; *saba*—all; *jñāna*—such knowledge; *lupta haya*—becomes hidden; *aiche*—in that way; *nācāya*—causes to dance; *saba*—all; *nārī-gaṇe*—the women.

### TRANSLATION

**"The vibration of His flute slackens the knots of their underwear even in front of their husbands. Thus the gopīs are forced to abandon their household duties and come before Lord Kṛṣṇa. In this way all social etiquette, shame and fear are vanquished. The vibration of His flute causes all women to dance.**

### TEXT 144

কাণের ভিতর বাসা করে, আপনে তাঁহা সদা স্ফুরে,
অন্য শব্দ না দেয় প্রবেশিতে।
আন কথা না শুনে কাণ, আন বলিতে বোলয় আন,
এই কৃষ্ণের বংশীর চরিতে ॥ ১৪৪ ॥

*kāṇera bhitara vāsā kare, āpane tāṅhā sadā sphure,*
*anya śabda nā deya praveśite*
*āna kathā nā śune kāṇa, āna balite bolaya āna,*
*ei kṛṣṇera vaṁśīra carite*

### SYNONYMS

*kāṇera*—the hole of the ear; *bhitara*—within; *vāsā kare*—makes a residence; *āpane*—personally; *tāṅhā*—there; *sadā*—always; *sphure*—is prominent; *anya*—other; *śabda*—sounds; *nā*—not; *deya*—allows; *praveśite*—to enter; *āna kathā*—other talks; *nā*—not; *śune*—hears; *kāṇa*—the ear; *āna*—something else; *balite*—to speak; *bolaya*—speaks; *āna*—another thing; *ei kṛṣṇera*—of Lord Kṛṣṇa; *vaṁśīra*—of the flute; *carite*—characteristics.

### TRANSLATION

**"The vibration of His flute is just like a bird that creates a nest within the ears of the gopīs and always remains prominent there, not allowing any other sound to enter their ears. Indeed, the gopīs cannot hear anything else, nor are they able to concentrate on anything else, not even to give a suitable reply. Such are the effects of the vibration of Lord Kṛṣṇa's flute."**

## PURPORT

The vibration of Kṛṣṇa's flute is always prominent in the ears of the *gopīs.* Naturally they cannot hear anything else. Constant remembrance of the holy sound of Kṛṣṇa's flute keeps them enlightened and enlivened, and they do not allow any other sound to enter their ears. Since their attention is fixed on Kṛṣṇa's flute, they cannot divert their minds to any other subject. In other words, a devotee who has heard the sound of Kṛṣṇa's flute forgets to talk or hear of any other subject. This vibration of Kṛṣṇa's flute is represented by the Hare Kṛṣṇa *mahā-mantra.* A serious devotee of the Lord who chants and hears this transcendental vibration becomes so accustomed to it that he cannot divert his attention to any subject matter not related to Kṛṣṇa's blissful characteristics and paraphernalia.

## TEXT 145

পুনঃ কহে বাহ্যজ্ঞানে, আন কহিতে কহিলুঁ আনে,
কৃষ্ণ-কৃপা তোমার উপরে ।
মোর চিত্ত-ভ্রম করি', নিজৈশ্বর্য-মাধুরী,
মোর মুখে শুনায় তোমারে ॥ ১৪৫ ॥

*punaḥ kahe bāhya-jñāne, āna kahite kahiluṅ āne,*
*kṛṣṇa-kṛpā tomāra upare*
*mora citta-bhrama kari', nijaiśvarya-mādhurī,*
*mora mukhe śunāya tomāre*

## SYNONYMS

*punaḥ*—again; *kahe*—He says; *bāhya-jñāne*—in external consciousness; *āna*—something else; *kahite*—to speak; *kahiluṅ*—I have spoken; *āne*—another thing; *kṛṣṇa-kṛpā*—the mercy of Lord Kṛṣṇa; *tomāra*—you; *upare*—upon; *mora*—My; *citta-bhrama*—mental concoction; *kari'*—making; *nija-aiśvarya*—His personal opulence; *mādhurī*—sweetness; *mora mukhe*—through My mouth; *śunāya*—causes to hear; *tomāre*—you.

## TRANSLATION

**Resuming His external consciousness, Śrī Caitanya Mahāprabhu told Sanātana Gosvāmī, "I have not spoken of what I intended. Lord Kṛṣṇa is very merciful to you because by bewildering My mind, He has exposed His personal opulence and sweetness. He has caused you to hear all these things from Me for your understanding.**

### PURPORT

Śrī Caitanya Mahāprabhu admitted that He was speaking like a madman, which He should not have done for the understanding of those who are externally situated. Statements about Kṛṣṇa's body, His characteristics and His flute would appear like a madman's statements to a mundane person. It was actually a fact that Kṛṣṇa wanted to expose Himself to Sanātana Gosvāmī due to His specific mercy upon him. Somehow or other, Kṛṣṇa explained Himself and His flute to Sanātana Gosvāmī through the mouth of Śrī Caitanya Mahāprabhu, who appeared as though mad. Śrī Caitanya Mahāprabhu admitted that He wanted to tell Sanātana Gosvāmī something else, but somehow or other, in a transcendental ecstasy, He spoke of a different subject matter.

### TEXT 146

আমি ত' বাউল, আন কহিতে আন কহি।
কৃষ্ণের মাধুর্যামৃতস্রোতে যাই বহি' ॥ ১৪৬ ॥

*āmi ta' bāula, āna kahite āna kahi*
*kṛṣṇera mādhuryāmṛta-srote yāi vahi'*

### SYNONYMS

*āmi ta' bāula*—I am a madman; *āna kahite*—to speak something; *āna kahi*—I speak on something else; *kṛṣṇera*—of Lord Kṛṣṇa; *mādhurya-amṛta*—of the nectar of the sweetness; *srote*—in the waves of; *yāi*—I go; *vahi'*—being carried away.

### TRANSLATION

**"Since I have become a madman, I am saying one thing instead of another. This is because I am being carried away by the waves of the nectarean ocean of Lord Kṛṣṇa's transcendental sweetness."**

### TEXT 147

তবে মহাপ্রভু ক্ষণেক মৌন করি' রহে।
মনে এক করি' পুনঃ সনাতনে কহে ॥ ১৪৭ ॥

*tabe mahāprabhu kṣaṇeka mauna kari' rahe*
*mane eka kari' punaḥ sanātane kahe*

### SYNONYMS

*tabe*—thereupon; *mahāprabhu*—Śrī Caitanya Mahāprabhu; *kṣaṇeka*—for a moment; *mauna*—silence; *kari'*—making; *rahe*—remained; *mane*—within His mind; *eka kari'*—adjusting things; *punaḥ*—again; *sanātane*—unto Sanātana Gosvāmī; *kahe*—instructs.

## TRANSLATION

**Śrī Caitanya Mahāprabhu then remained silent for a moment. Finally, adjusting things within His mind, He again spoke to Sanātana Gosvāmī.**

## TEXT 148

কৃষ্ণের মাধুরী আর মহাপ্রভুর মুখে।
ইহা যেই শুনে, সেই ভাসে প্রেমসুখে ॥ ১৪৮ ॥

*kṛṣṇera mādhurī āra mahāprabhura mukhe*
*ihā yei śune, sei bhāse prema-sukhe*

## SYNONYMS

*kṛṣṇera*—of Lord Kṛṣṇa; *mādhurī*—the sweetness; *āra*—and; *mahāprabhura mukhe*—in the mouth of Śrī Caitanya Mahāprabhu; *ihā*—this statement; *yei*—anyone who; *śune*—hears; *sei*—that person; *bhāse*—floats; *prema-sukhe*—in the transcendental bliss of love of Godhead.

## TRANSLATION

**I now summarize these teachings of Śrī Caitanya Mahāprabhu. If anyone gets an opportunity to hear about the sweetness of Kṛṣṇa in this chapter of Śrī Caitanya-caritāmṛta, he will certainly be eligible to float in the transcendentally blissful ocean of love of God.**

## TEXT 149

শ্রীরূপ-রঘুনাথ-পদে যার আশ।
চৈতন্যচরিতামৃত কহে কৃষ্ণদাস ॥ ১৪৯ ॥

*śrī-rūpa-raghunātha-pade yāra āśa*
*caitanya-caritāmṛta kahe kṛṣṇadāsa*

## SYNONYMS

*śrī-rūpa*—Śrīla Rūpa Gosvāmī; *raghunātha*—Śrīla Raghunātha dāsa Gosvāmī; *pade*—at the lotus feet; *yāra*—whose; *āśa*—expectation; *caitanya-caritāmṛta*—the book named *Caitanya-caritāmṛta;* *kahe*—describes; *kṛṣṇadāsa*—Śrīla Kṛṣṇadāsa Kavirāja Gosvāmī.

## TRANSLATION

**Praying at the lotus feet of Śrī Rūpa and Śrī Raghunātha, always desiring their mercy, I, Kṛṣṇadāsa, narrate Śrī Caitanya-caritāmṛta, following in their footsteps.**

*Thus end the Bhaktivedanta purports to the* Śrī Caitanya-caritāmṛta, Madhya-līlā, *Twenty-first Chapter, describing the blissful characteristics of Kṛṣṇa.*

CHAPTER 22

# The Process of Devotional Service

In this Twenty-second Chapter, Śrī Caitanya Mahāprabhu describes the process of devotional service. In the beginning He describes the truth about the living entity and the superexcellence of devotional service. He then describes the uselessness of mental speculation and mystic *yoga*. In all circumstances the living entity is recommended to accept the path of devotional service as personally explained by Śrī Caitanya Mahāprabhu. The speculative method of the so-called *jñānīs* is considered a waste of time, and that is proved in this chapter. An intelligent person should abandon the processes of *karma-kāṇḍa, jñāna-kāṇḍa* and mystic *yoga*. One should give up all these useless processes and take seriously to the path of Kṛṣṇa consciousness. In this way one's life will be successful. If one takes to Kṛṣṇa consciousness fully, even though he may sometimes be agitated due to having previously practiced mental speculation and yogic mysticism, he will be saved by Lord Kṛṣṇa Himself. The fact is that devotional service is bestowed by the blessings of a pure devotee (*sa mahātmā sudurlabhaḥ*). A pure devotee is the supreme transcendentalist, and one has to receive his mercy for one's dormant Kṛṣṇa consciousness to be awakened. One has to associate with pure devotees. If one has firm faith in the words of a great soul, pure devotional service will awaken.

In this chapter Śrī Caitanya Mahāprabhu has differentiated between a pure devotee and others. He also describes the characteristics of a pure devotee. A devotee's most formidable enemy is association with women in an enjoying spirit. Association with nondevotees is also condemned because it is also a formidable enemy on the path of devotional service. One has to fully surrender unto the lotus feet of Kṛṣṇa and give up attraction for women and nondevotees.

The six symptoms of fully surrendered souls are also described in this chapter. Devotional service has been divided into two categories—regulative devotional service and spontaneous love. There are sixty-four items listed in regulative devotional service, and out of these sixty-four the last five are considered very important. By practicing even one of the nine processes of devotional service, one can become successful. Speculative knowledge and mystic *yoga* can never help one in devotional service. Pious activity, nonviolence, sense control and regulation are not separate from devotional service in its pure form. If one engages in devotional service, all good qualities follow. One does not have to cultivate them separately. Spontaneous devotional service arises when one follows a pure devotee who is awakened to spontaneous love of God. Śrī Caitanya Mahāprabhu has described the symptoms of devotees who are already situated in spontaneous love of God. He has also described the devotees who are trying to follow in the footsteps of the pure devotees.

### TEXT 1

**বন্দে শ্রীকৃষ্ণচৈতন্যদেবং তং করুণার্ণবম্ ।**
**কলাবপ্যতিগূঢ়েয়ং ভক্তির্যেন প্রকাশিতা ॥ ১ ॥**

*vande śrī-kṛṣṇa-caitanya-*
*devaṁ taṁ karuṇārṇavam*
*kalāv apy ati-gūḍheyaṁ*
*bhaktir yena prakāśitā*

### SYNONYMS

*vande*—I offer my respectful obeisances; *śrī-kṛṣṇa-caitanya-devam*—unto Lord Śrī Caitanya Mahāprabhu; *tam*—unto Him; *karuṇa-arṇavam*—who is an ocean of mercy; *kalau*—in this age of Kali; *api*—even; *ati*—very; *gūḍhā*—confidential; *iyam*—this; *bhaktiḥ*—devotional service; *yena*—by whom; *prakāśitā*—manifested.

### TRANSLATION

**I offer my respectful obeisances unto Lord Śrī Caitanya Mahāprabhu. He is an ocean of transcendental mercy, and although the subject matter of bhakti-yoga is very confidential, He has nonetheless manifested it so nicely, even in this age of Kali, the age of quarrel.**

### TEXT 2

**জয় জয় শ্রীকৃষ্ণচৈতন্য নিত্যানন্দ ।**
**জয়াদ্বৈতচন্দ্র জয় গৌরভক্তবৃন্দ ॥ ২ ॥**

*jaya jaya śrī-kṛṣṇa-caitanya nityānanda*
*jayādvaita-candra jaya gaura-bhakta-vṛnda*

### SYNONYMS

*jaya jaya*—all glories; *śrī-kṛṣṇa-caitanya nityānanda*—to Śrī Kṛṣṇa Caitanya Mahāprabhu and Nityānanda Prabhu; *jaya*—all glories; *advaita-candra*—to Advaita Prabhu; *jaya*—all glories; *gaura-bhakta-vṛnda*—to the devotees of Śrī Caitanya Mahāprabhu.

## TRANSLATION

**All glories to Śrī Caitanya Mahāprabhu! All glories to Nityānanda Prabhu! All glories to Advaitacandra! All glories to all the devotees of Śrī Caitanya Mahāprabhu!**

## TEXT 3

এইত কহিলুঁ সম্বন্ধ-তত্ত্বের বিচার ।
বেদশাস্ত্রে উপদেশে, কৃষ্ণ—এক সার ॥ ৩ ॥

*eita kahiluṅ sambandha-tattvera vicāra*
*veda-śāstre upadeśe, kṛṣṇa——eka sāra*

## SYNONYMS

*eita*—thus; *kahiluṅ*—I have described; *sambandha-tattvera vicāra*—consideration of one's relationship with Kṛṣṇa; *veda-śāstre*—all Vedic literature; *upadeśe*—instructs; *kṛṣṇa*—Lord Kṛṣṇa; *eka sāra*—the only essential point.

## TRANSLATION

**Śrī Caitanya Mahāprabhu said, "I have described one's relation with Kṛṣṇa in various ways. This is the subject matter of all the Vedas. Kṛṣṇa is the center of all activities.**

## TEXT 4

এবে কহি, শুন, অভিধেয়-লক্ষণ ।
যাহা হৈতে পাই—কৃষ্ণ, কৃষ্ণপ্রেমধন ॥ ৪ ॥

*ebe kahi, śuna, abhidheya-lakṣaṇa*
*yāhā haite pāi——kṛṣṇa, kṛṣṇa-prema-dhana*

## SYNONYMS

*ebe*—now; *kahi*—I shall explain; *śuna*—please hear; *abhidheya-lakṣaṇa*—one's prime business (devotional service); *yāhā haite*—from which; *pāi*—one can get; *kṛṣṇa*—Lord Kṛṣṇa; *kṛṣṇa-prema-dhana*—and the wealth of transcendental love for Him.

## TRANSLATION

**"Now I shall speak about the characteristics of devotional service, by which one can attain the shelter of Kṛṣṇa and His loving transcendental service.**

### TEXT 5

কৃষ্ণভক্তি—অভিধেয়, সর্বশাস্ত্রে কয়।
অতএব মুনিগণ করিয়াছে নিশ্চয়॥ ৫॥

*kṛṣṇa-bhakti——abhidheya, sarva-śāstre kaya*
*ataeva muni-gaṇa kariyāche niścaya*

### SYNONYMS

*kṛṣṇa-bhakti*—devotional service to Lord Kṛṣṇa; *abhidheya*—the real activity of life; *sarva-śāstre*—all Vedic literatures; *kaya*—say; *ataeva*—therefore; *muni-gaṇa*—all saintly persons; *kariyāche*—have made; *niścaya*—ascertainment.

### TRANSLATION

**"A human being's activities should be centered only about devotional service to Lord Kṛṣṇa. That is the verdict of all Vedic literatures, and all saintly people have ascertained this.**

### TEXT 6

শ্রুতির্মাতা পৃষ্টা দিশতি ভবদারাধনবিধিং
যথা মাতুর্বাণী স্মৃতিরপি তথা বক্তি ভগিনী।
পুরাণাদ্যা যে বা সহজনিবহাস্তে তদনুগা
অতঃ সত্যং জ্ঞাতং মুরহর ভবানেব শরণম্॥ ৬॥

*śrutir mātā pṛṣṭā diśati bhavad-ārādhana-vidhiṁ*
*yathā mātur vāṇī smṛtir api tathā vakti bhaginī*
*purāṇādyā ye vā sahaja-nivahās te tad-anugā*
*ataḥ satyaṁ jñātaṁ murahara bhavān eva śaraṇam*

### SYNONYMS

*śrutiḥ*—Vedic knowledge; *mātā*—like a mother who is affectionate to her children; *pṛṣṭā*—when questioned; *diśati*—she directs; *bhavat*—of You; *ārādhana*—worship; *vidhim*—the process; *yathā*—just as; *mātuḥ vāṇī*—the instructions of the mother; *smṛtiḥ*—*smṛti-śāstras,* which explain the Vedic literatures; *api*—also; *tathā*—similarly; *vakti*—express; *bhaginī*—like a sister; *purāṇa-ādyāḥ*—headed by the *Purāṇas; ye*—which; *vā*—or; *sahaja-nivahāḥ*—like brothers; *te*—all of them; *tat*—of the mother; *anugāḥ*—followers; *ataḥ*—therefore; *satyam*—the truth; *jñātam*—known; *mura-hara*—O killer of the demon Mura; *bhavān*—Your Lordship; *eva*—only; *śaraṇam*—the shelter.

## TRANSLATION

**" 'When the mother Vedas [śruti] is questioned as to whom to worship, she says that You are the only Lord and worshipable object. Similarly, the corollaries of the śruti-śāstras, the smṛti-śāstras, give the same instructions, just like sisters. The Purāṇas, which are like brothers, follow in the footsteps of their mother. O enemy of the demon Mura, the conclusion is that You are the only shelter. Now I have understood this in truth.'**

## PURPORT

This quotation from the Vedic literature was spoken by great sages.

## TEXT 7

অদ্বয়জ্ঞান-তত্ত্ব কৃষ্ণ —স্বয়ং ভগবান্ ।
'স্বরূপ -শক্তি'রূপে তাঁর হয় অবস্থান ॥ ৭ ॥

*advaya-jñāna-tattva kṛṣṇa——svayaṁ bhagavān*
*'svarūpa-śakti' rūpe tāṅra haya avasthāna*

## SYNONYMS

*advaya-jñāna*—of nondual knowledge; *tattva*—the principle; *kṛṣṇa*—Lord Kṛṣṇa; *svayam bhagavān*—Himself the Supreme Personality of Godhead; *svarūpa*—personal expansions; *śakti*—of potencies; *rūpe*—in the form; *tāṅra*—His; *haya*—there is; *avasthāna*—existence.

## TRANSLATION

**"Kṛṣṇa is the nondual Absolute Truth, the Supreme Personality of Godhead. Although He is one, He maintains different personal expansions and energies for His pastimes.**

## PURPORT

The Lord has many potencies, and He is nondifferent from all these potencies. Because the potencies and the potent cannot be separated, they are identical. Kṛṣṇa is described as the source of all potencies, and He is also identified with the external potency, the material energy. Kṛṣṇa also has internal potencies, or spiritual potencies, which are always engaged in His personal service. His internal potency is different from His external potency. Kṛṣṇa's internal potency and Kṛṣṇa Himself, who is the potent, are always identical.

## TEXT 8

স্বাংশ-বিভিন্নাংশ-রূপে হঞা বিস্তার।
অনন্ত বৈকুণ্ঠ-ব্রহ্মাণ্ডে করেন বিহার ॥ ৮ ॥

*svāṁśa-vibhinnāṁśa-rūpe hañā vistāra*
*ananta vaikuṇṭha-brahmāṇḍe karena vihāra*

### SYNONYMS

*sva-aṁśa*—of personal expansions; *vibhinna-aṁśa*—of separated expansions; *rūpe*—in the forms; *hañā*—becoming; *vistāra*—expanded; *ananta*—unlimited; *vaikuṇṭha*—in the spiritual planets known as Vaikuṇṭhas; *brahmāṇḍe*—in the material universes; *karena vihāra*—performs His pastimes.

### TRANSLATION

**"Kṛṣṇa expands Himself in many forms. Some of them are personal expansions, and some are separate expansions. Thus He performs pastimes in both the spiritual and material worlds. The spiritual worlds are the Vaikuṇṭha planets, and the material universes are brahmāṇḍas, gigantic globes governed by Lord Brahmā.**

## TEXT 9

স্বাংশ-বিস্তার—চতুর্ব্যূহ, অবতারগণ।
বিভিন্নাংশ জীব—তাঁর শক্তিতে গণন ॥ ৯ ॥

*svāṁśa-vistāra——catur-vyūha, avatāra-gaṇa*
*vibhinnāṁśa jīva——tāṅra śaktite gaṇana*

### SYNONYMS

*sva-aṁśa-vistāra*—the expansion of His personal forms; *catuḥ-vyūha*—His quadruple form; *avatāra-gaṇa*—the incarnations; *vibhinna-aṁśa*—His separated forms; *jīva*—the living entities; *tāṅra*—His; *śaktite*—in the category of potency; *gaṇana*—calculating.

### TRANSLATION

**"Expansions of His personal self—like the quadruple manifestations of Saṅkarṣaṇa, Pradyumna, Aniruddha and Vāsudeva—descend as incarnations from Vaikuṇṭha to this material world. The separated expansions are living entities. Although they are expansions of Kṛṣṇa, they are counted among His different potencies.**

## PURPORT

The personal expansions are known as *viṣṇu-tattva,* and the separated expansions are known as *jīva-tattva.* Although the *jīvas* (living entities) are part and parcel of the Supreme Personality of Godhead, they are still counted among His multi-potencies. This is fully described in *Bhagavad-gītā:*

*apareyam itas tv anyāṁ*
*prakṛtiṁ viddhi me parām*
*jīva-bhūtāṁ mahā-bāho*
*yayedaṁ dhāryate jagat*

"Besides this inferior nature, O mighty-armed Arjuna, there is a superior energy of Mine, which consists of all living entities who are struggling with material nature and are sustaining the universe." (Bg. 7.5)

Although the living entities are Kṛṣṇa's parts and parcels, they are *prakṛti,* not *puruṣa.* Sometimes *prakṛti* (a living entity) attempts to imitate the activities of the *puruṣa.* Due to a poor fund of knowledge, living entities conditioned in this material world claim to be God. They are thus illusioned. A living entity cannot be on the level of a *viṣṇu-tattva,* or the Personality of Godhead, at any stage; therefore it is ludicrous for a living entity to claim to be God. Advanced spiritualists would never accept such a thing. Such claims are made to cheat ordinary, foolish people. The Kṛṣṇa consciousness movement declares war against such bogus incarnations. The bogus propaganda put out by people claiming to be God has killed God consciousness all over the world. Members of the Kṛṣṇa consciousness movement must be very alert to defy these rascals who are presently misleading the whole world. One such rascal, known as Pauṇḍraka, appeared before Lord Kṛṣṇa, and the Lord immediately killed him. Of course, those who are Kṛṣṇa's servants cannot kill such imitation gods, but they should try their best to defeat them through the evidence of *śāstra,* authentic knowledge received through the disciplic succession.

## TEXT 10

সেই বিভিন্নাংশ জীব—দুই ত' প্রকার ।
এক—'নিত্যমুক্ত', এক—'নিত্য-সংসার' ॥ ১০ ॥

*sei vibhinnāṁśa jīva——dui ta' prakāra*
*eka——'nitya-mukta', eka——'nitya-saṁsāra'*

## SYNONYMS

*sei vibhinna-aṁśa*—that separated part and parcel of Kṛṣṇa; *jīva*—the living entity; *dui ta' prakāra*—two categories; *eka*—one; *nitya-mukta*—eternally liberated; *eka*—one; *nitya-saṁsāra*—perpetually conditioned.

### TRANSLATION

**"The living entities [jīvas] are divided into two categories. Some are eternally liberated, and others are eternally conditioned.**

### TEXT 11

'নিত্যমুক্ত' – নিত্য কৃষ্ণচরণে উন্মুখ ।
'কৃষ্ণ-পারিষদ' নাম, ভুঞ্জে সেবা-সুখ ॥ ১১ ॥

*'nitya-mukta'——nitya kṛṣṇa-caraṇe unmukha*
*'kṛṣṇa-pāriṣada' nāma, bhuñje sevā-sukha*

### SYNONYMS

*nitya-mukta*—eternally liberated; *nitya*—always; *kṛṣṇa-caraṇe*—the lotus feet of Lord Kṛṣṇa; *unmukha*—turned toward; *kṛṣṇa-pāriṣada*—associates of Lord Kṛṣṇa; *nāma*—known as; *bhuñje*—enjoy; *sevā-sukha*—the happiness of service.

### TRANSLATION

**"Those who are eternally liberated are always awake to Kṛṣṇa consciousness, and they render transcendental loving service at the feet of Lord Kṛṣṇa. They are to be considered eternal associates of Kṛṣṇa, and they are eternally enjoying the transcendental bliss of serving Kṛṣṇa.**

### TEXT 12

'নিত্যবদ্ধ'—কৃষ্ণ হৈতে নিত্য-বহির্মুখ ।
'নিত্যসংসার', ভুঞ্জে নরকাদি দুঃখ ॥ ১২ ॥

*'nitya-bandha'——kṛṣṇa haite nitya-bahirmukha*
*'nitya-saṁsāra', bhuñje narakādi duḥkha*

### SYNONYMS

*nitya-bandha*—perpetually conditioned; *kṛṣṇa haite*—from Kṛṣṇa; *nitya*—eternally; *bahiḥ-mukha*—averse; *nitya-saṁsāra*—perpetually conditioned in the material world; *bhuñje*—enjoy; *naraka-ādi duḥkha*—the tribulations of hellish conditions of life.

### TRANSLATION

**"Apart from the ever-liberated devotees, there are the conditioned souls who always turn away from the service of the Lord. They are perpetually conditioned in this material world and are subjected to the material tribulations brought about by different bodily forms in hellish conditions.**

### TEXT 13

সেই দোষে মায়া-পিশাচী দণ্ড করে তারে।
আধ্যাত্মিকাদি তাপত্রয় তারে জারি' মারে ॥ ১৩ ॥

*sei doṣe māyā-piśācī daṇḍa kare tāre*
*ādhyātmikādi tāpa-traya tāre jāri' māre*

### SYNONYMS

*sei doṣe*—because of this fault; *māyā-piśācī*—the witch known as the external energy; *daṇḍa kare*—gives punishment; *tāre*—unto him; *ādhyātmika-ādi*—beginning with those pertaining to the body and mind; *tāpa-traya*—the threefold miseries; *tāre*—him; *jāri'*—burning; *māre*—gives pain.

### TRANSLATION

**"Due to his being opposed to Kṛṣṇa consciousness, the conditioned soul is punished by the witch of the external energy, māyā. He is thus ready to suffer the threefold miseries—miseries brought about by the body and mind, the inimical behavior of other living entities and natural disturbances caused by the demigods.**

### TEXTS 14-15

কাম-ক্রোধের দাস হঞা তার লাথি খায়।
ভ্রমিতে ভ্রমিতে যদি সাধু-বৈদ্য পায় ॥ ১৪ ॥

তাঁর উপদেশ-মন্ত্রে পিশাচী পলায়।
কৃষ্ণভক্তি পায়, তবে কৃষ্ণ-নিকট যায় ॥ ১৫ ॥

*kāma-krodhera dāsa hañā tāra lāthi khāya*
*bhramite bhramite yadi sādhu-vaidya pāya*

*tāṅra upadeśa-mantre piśācī palāya*
*kṛṣṇa-bhakti pāya, tabe kṛṣṇa-nikaṭa yāya*

### SYNONYMS

*kāma*—of lusty desires; *krodhera*—and of anger; *dāsa*—the servant; *hañā*—becoming; *tāra*—by them; *lāthi khāya*—is kicked; *bhramite bhramite*—wandering and wandering; *yadi*—if; *sādhu*—a devotee; *vaidya*—physician; *pāya*—he gets; *tāṅra*—his; *upadeśa-mantre*—by instruction and hymns; *piśācī*—the witch (the external energy); *palāya*—flees; *kṛṣṇa-bhakti*—devotional service to Kṛṣṇa; *pāya*—obtains; *tabe*—in this way; *kṛṣṇa-nikaṭa yāya*—he goes to Kṛṣṇa.

## TRANSLATION

**"In this way the conditioned soul becomes the servant of lusty desires, and when these are not fulfilled, he becomes a servant of anger and continues to be kicked by the external energy, māyā. Wandering and wandering throughout the universe, he may by chance get the association of a devotee physician, whose instructions and hymns make the witch of external energy flee. The conditioned soul thus gets into touch with the devotional service of Lord Kṛṣṇa, and in this way he can approach nearer and nearer to the Lord.**

## PURPORT

An explanation of verses 8 through 15 is given by Śrīla Bhaktivinoda Ṭhākura in his *Amṛta-pravāha-bhāṣya.* The Lord is spread throughout the creation in His quadruple expansions and incarnations. Kṛṣṇa is fully represented with all potencies in each and every personal extension, but the living entities, although separated expansions, are also considered one of the Lord's energies. The living entities are divided into two categories—the eternally liberated and eternally conditioned. Those who are ever-liberated never come in contact with *māyā,* the external energy. The ever-conditioned are always under the clutches of the external energy. This is described in *Bhagavad-gītā:*

*daivī hy eṣā guṇamayī*
*mama māyā duratyayā*

"This divine energy of Mine, consisting of the three modes of material nature, is difficult to overcome." (Bg. 7.14)

The *nitya-baddhas* are always conditioned by the external energy, and the *nitya-muktas* never come in contact with the external energy. Sometimes an ever-liberated personal associate of the Supreme Personality of Godhead descends into this universe just as the Lord descends. Although working for the liberation of conditioned souls, the messenger of the Supreme Lord remains untouched by the material energy. Generally ever-liberated personalities live in the spiritual world as associates of Lord Kṛṣṇa, and they are known as *kṛṣṇa-pāriṣada,* associates of the Lord. Their only business is enjoying Lord Kṛṣṇa's company, and even though such eternally liberated persons come within this material world to serve the Lord's purpose, they enjoy Lord Kṛṣṇa's company without stoppage. The ever-liberated person who works on Kṛṣṇa's behalf enjoys Lord Kṛṣṇa's company through his engagement. The ever-conditioned soul, provoked by lusty desires to enjoy the material world, is subjected to transmigrate from one body to another. Sometimes he is elevated to higher planetary systems, and sometimes he is degraded to hellish planets and subjected to the tribulations of the external energy.

Due to being conditioned by the external energy, the conditioned soul within this material world gets two kinds of bodies—a gross material body and a subtle body composed of mind, intelligence and ego. Due to the gross and subtle bodies, he is subjected to the threefold miseries (*ādhyātmika, ādhibhautika* and *ādhidaivika*), miseries arising from the body and mind, other living entities, and natural disturbances caused by demigods from higher planetary systems. The conditioned soul subjected to the threefold material miseries is ceaselessly kicked by *māyā,* and this is his disease. If by chance he meets a saintly person who works on Kṛṣṇa's behalf to deliver conditioned souls, and if he agrees to abide by his order, he can gradually approach the Supreme Personality of Godhead, Kṛṣṇa.

## TEXT 16

কামাদীনাং কতি ন কতিধা পালিতা দুর্নিদেশা-
স্তেষাং জাতা ময়ি ন করুণা ন ত্রপা নোপশান্তিঃ ।
উৎসৃজ্যৈতানথ যদুপতে সাম্প্রতং লব্ধবুদ্ধি-
স্ত্বামায়াতঃ শরণমভয়ং মাং নিযুঙ্ক্ষ্বাত্মদাস্যে ॥ ১৬ ॥

*kāmādīnāṁ kati na katidhā pālitā durnideśās*
*teṣāṁ jātā mayi na karuṇā na trapā nopaśāntiḥ*
*utsṛjyaitān atha yadu-pate sāmpratam labdha-buddhis*
*tvām āyātaḥ śaraṇam abhayaṁ māṁ niyuṅkṣvātma-dāsye*

## SYNONYMS

*kāma-ādīnām*—of my masters such as lust, anger, greed, illusion and envy; *kati*—how many; *na*—not; *katidhā*—in how many ways; *pālitāḥ*—obeyed; *durnideśāḥ*—undesirable orders; *teṣām*—of them; *jātā*—generated; *mayi*—unto me; *na*—not; *karuṇā*—mercy; *na*—not; *trapā*—shame; *na*—not; *upaśāntiḥ*—desire to cease; *utsṛjya*—giving up; *etān*—all these; *atha*—herewith; *yadu-pate*—O best of the Yadu dynasty; *sāmpratam*—now; *labdha-buddhiḥ*—having awakened intelligence; *tvām*—You; *āyātaḥ*—approached; *śaraṇam*—who are the shelter; *abhayam*—fearless; *mām*—me; *niyuṅkṣva*—please engage; *ātma-dāsye*—in Your personal service.

## TRANSLATION

**" 'O my Lord, there is no limit to the unwanted orders of lusty desires. Although I have rendered them so much service, they have not shown any mercy to me. I have not been ashamed to serve them, nor have I even desired to give them up. O my Lord, O head of the Yadu dynasty, recently, however, my intelligence has been awakened, and now I am giving them up. Due to transcendental intelligence, I now refuse to obey the unwanted orders of these desires, and I now come to You to surrender myself at Your fearless lotus feet. Kindly engage me in Your personal service and save me.'**

### PURPORT

This verse is also quoted in *Bhakti-rasāmṛta-sindhu* (3.2.35). When we chant the Hare Kṛṣṇa *mahā-mantra* we are saying, "Hare! O energy of the Lord! O my Lord Kṛṣṇa!" In this way we are simply addressing the Lord and His spiritual potency represented as Rādhā-Kṛṣṇa, Sītā-Rāma, or Lakṣmī-Nārāyaṇa. The devotee always prays to the Lord and His internal energy (consort) so that he may engage in Their transcendental loving service. When the conditioned soul attains his real spiritual energy and fully surrenders unto the Lord's lotus feet, he tries to engage in the Lord's service. This is the real constitutional position of the living entity.

### TEXT 17

**কৃষ্ণভক্তি হয় অভিধেয়-প্রধান ।**
**ভক্তিমুখ-নিরীক্ষক কর্ম-যোগ-জ্ঞান ॥ ১৭ ॥**

*kṛṣṇa-bhakti haya abhidheya-pradhāna*
*bhakti-mukha-nirīkṣaka karma-yoga-jñāna*

### SYNONYMS

*kṛṣṇa-bhakti*—devotional service to Lord Kṛṣṇa; *haya*—is; *abhidheya-pradhāna*—the chief function of the living entity; *bhakti-mukha*—of the face of devotional service; *nirīkṣaka*—observers; *karma-yoga-jñāna*—fruitive activities, mystic *yoga* and speculative knowledge.

### TRANSLATION

**"Devotional service to Kṛṣṇa is the chief function of the living entity. There are different methods for the liberation of the conditioned soul—karma, jñāna, yoga and bhakti—but all are dependent on bhakti.**

### TEXT 18

**এই সব সাধনের অতি তুচ্ছ বল ।**
**কৃষ্ণভক্তি বিনা তাহা দিতে নারে ফল ॥ ১৮ ॥**

*ei saba sādhanera ati tuccha bala*
*kṛṣṇa-bhakti vinā tāhā dite nāre phala*

### SYNONYMS

*ei saba*—all these; *sādhanera*—of methods of spiritual activities; *ati*—very; *tuccha*—insignificant; *bala*—strength; *kṛṣṇa-bhakti*—devotional service to Lord Kṛṣṇa; *vinā*—without; *tāhā*—all these; *dite*—to deliver; *nāre*—are not able; *phala*—the desired result.

## TRANSLATION

**"But for devotional service, all other methods for spiritual self-realization are weak and insignificant. Unless one comes to the devotional service of Lord Kṛṣṇa, jñāna and yoga cannot give the desired results.**

## PURPORT

In Vedic scriptures, stress is sometimes given to fruitive activity, speculative knowledge and the mystic *yoga* system. Although people are inclined to practice these processes, they cannot attain the desired results without being touched by *kṛṣṇa-bhakti,* devotional service. In other words, the real desired result is to invoke dormant love for Kṛṣṇa. *Śrīmad-Bhāgavatam* (1.2.6) states:

*sa vai puṁsāṁ paro dharmo*
*yato bhaktir adhokṣaje*
*ahaituky apratihatā*
*yayātmā suprasīdati*

*Karma, jñāna* and *yoga* cannot actually awaken love of Godhead. One has to take to the Lord's devotional service, and the more one is inclined to devotional service, the more he loses interest in other so-called achievements. Dhruva Mahārāja went to practice mystic *yoga* to see the Lord personally face to face, but when he developed an interest in devotional service, he saw that he was not being benefited by *karma, jñāna* and *yoga.*

## TEXT 19

নৈষ্কর্ম্যমপ্যচ্যুতভাব-বর্জিতং
ন শোভতে জ্ঞানমলং নিরঞ্জনম্ ।
কুতঃ পুনঃ শশ্বদভদ্রমীশ্বরে
ন চার্পিতং কর্ম যদপ্যকারণম্ ॥ ১৯ ॥

*naiṣkarmyam apy acyuta-bhāva-varjitaṁ*
*na śobhate jñānam alaṁ nirañjanam*
*kutaḥ punaḥ śaśvad abhadram īśvare*
*na cārpitaṁ karma yad apy akāraṇam*

## SYNONYMS

*naiṣkarmyam*—which does not produce enjoyment of the resultant action; *api*—although; *acyuta-bhāva*—of devotional service to the Supreme Personality of Godhead; *varjitam*—devoid; *na*—not; *śobhate*—looks beautiful; *jñānam*—speculative knowledge; *alam*—exceedingly; *nirañjanam*—which is without material contamination; *kutaḥ*—how much less; *punaḥ*—again; *śaśvat*—always (at the time of practicing and at the time of achieving the goal); *abhadram*—inauspicious; *īśvare*—to the Supreme Personality of Godhead; *na*—not; *ca*—also; *arpitam*—dedicated; *karma*—activities; *yat*—which; *api*—although; *akāraṇam*—causeless.

## TRANSLATION

**" 'When pure knowledge is beyond all material affinity but is not dedicated to the Supreme Personality of Godhead [Kṛṣṇa], it does not appear very beautiful, although it is knowledge without a material tinge. What, then, is the use of fruitive activities—which are naturally painful from the beginning and transient by nature—if they are not utilized for the devotional service of the Lord? How can they be very attractive?'**

## PURPORT

This is a quotation from *Śrīmad-Bhāgavatam* (1.5.12). Even after writing many Vedic literatures, Vyāsadeva felt very morose. Therefore his spiritual master, Nāradadeva, told him that he could be happy by writing about the activities of the Supreme Personality of Godhead. Up to that time, Śrīla Vyāsadeva had written the *karma-kāṇḍa* and *jñāna-kāṇḍa* sections of the *Vedas,* but he had not written about *upāsanā-kāṇḍa,* or *bhakti*. Thus his spiritual master, Nārada, chastised him and advised him to write about the activities of the Supreme Personality of Godhead. Therefore Vyāsadeva began writing *Śrīmad-Bhāgavatam.*

## TEXT 20

তপস্বিনো দানপরা যশস্বিনো
মনস্বিনো মন্ত্রবিদঃ সুমঙ্গলাঃ ।
ক্ষেমং ন বিন্দন্তি বিনা যদর্পণং
তস্মৈ সুভদ্রশ্রবসে নমো নমঃ ॥ ২০ ॥

*tapasvino dāna-parā yaśasvino*
*manasvino mantra-vidaḥ sumaṅgalāḥ*
*kṣemaṁ na vindanti vinā yad-arpaṇaṁ*
*tasmai subhadra-śravase namo namaḥ*

## SYNONYMS

*tapasvinaḥ*—those engaged in severe austerities and penances; *dāna-parāḥ*—those engaged in giving his possessions as charity; *yaśasvinaḥ*—those famous in society; *manasvinaḥ*—experts in mental speculation or meditation; *mantra-*

*vidaḥ*—experts in reciting the Vedic hymns; *su-maṅgalāḥ*—very auspicious; *kṣemam*—real, eternal auspiciousness; *na*—never; *vindanti*—obtain; *vinā*—without; *yat-arpaṇam*—dedicating unto whom (the Supreme Personality of Godhead); *tasmai*—unto that Supreme Personality of Godhead; *su-bhadra śravase*—whose glory is very auspicious; *namaḥ namaḥ*—I offer my repeated respectful obeisances.

## TRANSLATION

**"'Those who perform severe austerities and penances, those who give away all their possessions out of charity, those who are very famous for their auspicious activity, those who are engaged in meditation and mental speculation, and even those who are very expert in reciting the Vedic mantras, are not able to obtain any auspicious results, although they are engaged in auspicious activities, if they do not dedicate their activities to the service of the Supreme Personality of Godhead. I therefore repeatedly offer my respectful obeisances unto the Supreme Personality of Godhead, whose glories are always auspicious.'**

## PURPORT

This is also a quotation from *Śrīmad-Bhāgavatam* (2.4.17).

## TEXT 21

কেবল জ্ঞান 'মুক্তি' দিতে নারে ভক্তি বিনে ।
কৃষ্ণোন্মুখে সেই মুক্তি হয় বিনা জ্ঞানে ॥ ২১ ॥

*kevala jñāna 'mukti' dite nāre bhakti vine*
*kṛṣṇonmukhe sei mukti haya vinā jñāne*

## SYNONYMS

*kevala*—only; *jñāna*—speculative knowledge; *mukti*—liberation; *dite*—to deliver; *nāre*—is not able; *bhakti vine*—without devotional service; *kṛṣṇa-unmukhe*—if one is attached to the service of Lord Kṛṣṇa; *sei mukti*—that liberation; *haya*—appears; *vinā*—without; *jñāne*—knowledge.

## TRANSLATION

**"Speculative knowledge alone, without devotional service, is not able to give liberation. On the other hand, even without knowledge one can obtain liberation if one engages in the Lord's devotional service.**

## PURPORT

One cannot attain liberation simply by speculative knowledge. Even though one may be able to distinguish between Brahman and matter, one's liberation will be hampered if one is misled into thinking that the living entity is as good as the Supreme Personality of Godhead. Indeed, one falls down again onto the material platform because considering oneself the Supreme Person, the Supreme Absolute Truth, is offensive. When such a person comes in contact with a pure devotee, he can actually become liberated from material bondage and engage in the Lord's service. A prayer by Bilvamaṅgala Ṭhākura is relevant here:

*bhaktis tvayi sthiratarā bhagavan yadi syād*
*daivena naḥ phalati divya-kiśora-mūrtiḥ*
*muktiḥ svayaṁ mukulitāñjaliḥ sevate 'smān*
*dharmārtha-kāma-gatayaḥ samaya-pratīkṣāḥ*

"O my Lord, if one engages in Your pure devotional service with determination, You become visible in Your original transcendental youthful form as the Supreme Personality of Godhead. As far as liberation is concerned, she stands before the devotee with folded hands waiting to render service. Religion, economic development and sense gratification are all automatically attained without separate endeavor."

## TEXT 22

শ্রেয়ঃস্মৃতিং ভক্তিমুদস্য তে বিভো
ক্লিশ্যন্তি যে কেবলবোধলব্ধয়ে।
তেষামসৌ ক্লেশল এব শিষ্যতে
নান্যদ্ যথা স্থূলতুষাবঘাতিনাম্ ॥ ২২ ॥

*śreyaḥ-sṛtiṁ bhaktim udasya te vibho*
*kliśyanti ye kevala-bodha-labdhaye*
*teṣām asau kleśala eva śiṣyate*
*nānyad yathā sthūla-tuṣāvaghātinām*

## SYNONYMS

*śreyaḥ-sṛtim*—the auspicious path of liberation; *bhaktim*—devotional service; *udasya*—giving up; *te*—of You; *vibho*—O my Lord; *kliśyanti*—accept increased difficulties; *ye*—all those persons who; *kevala*—only; *bodha-labdhaye*—for obtaining knowledge; *teṣām*—for them; *asau*—that; *kleśalaḥ*—trouble; *eva*—only; *śiṣyate*—remains; *na*—not; *anyat*—anything else; *yathā*—as much as; *sthūla*—bulky; *tuṣa*—husks of rice; *avaghātinām*—of those beating.

### TRANSLATION

**" 'My dear Lord, devotional service unto You is the only auspicious path. If one gives it up simply for speculative knowledge or the understanding that these living beings are spirit souls and the material world is false, he undergoes a great deal of trouble. He only gains troublesome and inauspicious activities. His endeavors are like beating a husk that is already devoid of rice. One's labor becomes fruitless.'**

### PURPORT

This is a verse from *Śrīmad-Bhāgavatam* (10.14.4).

### TEXT 23

দৈবী হ্যেষা গুণময়ী মম মায়া দুরত্যয়া।
মামেব যে প্রপদ্যন্তে মায়ামেতাং তরন্তি তে ॥ ২৩ ॥

*daivī hy eṣā guṇamayī*
*mama māyā duratyayā*
*mām eva ye prapadyante*
*māyām etāṁ taranti te*

### SYNONYMS

*daivī*—belonging to the Supreme Lord; *hi*—certainly; *eṣā*—this; *guṇa-mayī*—made of the three modes; *mama*—My; *māyā*—external energy; *duratyayā*—very difficult to surpass; *mām*—unto Me; *eva*—certainly; *ye*—those who; *prapadyante*—surrender fully; *māyām*—illusory energy; *etām*—this; *taranti*—cross over; *te*—they.

### TRANSLATION

**" 'This divine energy of Mine, consisting of the three modes of material nature, is difficult to overcome. But those who have surrendered unto Me can easily cross beyond it.'**

### PURPORT

This is a quotation from *Bhagavad-gītā* (7.14).

### TEXT 24

**'কৃষ্ণ-নিত্যদাস'—জীব তাহা ভুলি' গেল।**
**এই দোষে মায়া তার গলায় বান্ধিল ॥ ২৪ ॥**

*'kṛṣṇa-nitya-dāsa'——jīva tāhā bhuli' gela*
*ei doṣe māyā tāra galāya bāndhila*

### SYNONYMS

*kṛṣṇa-nitya-dāsa*—eternal servant of Kṛṣṇa; *jīva*—the living entity; *tāhā*—that; *bhuli'*—forgetting; *gela*—went; *ei doṣe*—for this fault; *māyā*—the material energy; *tāra*—his; *galāya*—on the neck; *bāndhila*—has bound.

### TRANSLATION

**"The living entity is bound around the neck by the chain of māyā because he has forgotten that he is eternally a servant of Kṛṣṇa.**

## TEXT 25

**তাতে কৃষ্ণ ভজে, করে গুরুর সেবন।**
**মায়াজাল ছুটে, পায় কৃষ্ণের চরণ ॥ ২৫ ॥**

*tāte kṛṣṇa bhaje, kare gurura sevana*
*māyā-jāla chuṭe, pāya kṛṣṇera caraṇa*

### SYNONYMS

*tāte*—therefore; *kṛṣṇa bhaje*—if one worships Lord Kṛṣṇa; *kare*—performs; *gurura sevana*—service to his spiritual master; *māyā-jāla chuṭe*—gets free from the binding net of *māyā; pāya*—gets; *kṛṣṇera caraṇa*—shelter at the lotus feet of Kṛṣṇa.

### TRANSLATION

**"If the conditioned soul engages in the service of the Lord and simultaneously carries out the orders of his spiritual master and serves him, he can get out of the clutches of māyā and become eligible for shelter at Kṛṣṇa's lotus feet.**

### PURPORT

It is a fact that every living entity is eternally a servant of Kṛṣṇa. This is forgotten due to the influence of *māyā,* which induces one to believe in material happiness. Being illusioned by *māyā,* one thinks that material happiness is the only desirable object. This material consciousness is like a chain around the neck of the conditioned soul. As long as he is bound to that conception, he cannot get out of *māyā's* clutches. However, if by Kṛṣṇa's mercy he gets in touch with a bona fide spiritual master, abides by his order and serves him, engaging other conditioned souls in the Lord's service, he then attains liberation and Lord Śrī Kṛṣṇa's shelter.

### TEXT 26

**চারি বর্ণাশ্রমী যদি কৃষ্ণ নাহি ভজে ।**
**স্বকর্ম করিতে সে রৌরবে পড়ি' মজে ॥ ২৬ ॥**

*cāri varṇāśramī yadi kṛṣṇa nāhi bhaje*
*svakarma karite se raurave paḍi' maje*

### SYNONYMS

*cāri varṇa-āśramī*—followers of the four social and spiritual orders of life; *yadi*—if; *kṛṣṇa*—Lord Kṛṣṇa; *nāhi*—not; *bhaje*—serve; *sva-karma karite*—performing his duty in life; *se*—that person; *raurave*—in a hellish condition; *paḍi'*—falling down; *maje*—becomes immersed.

### TRANSLATION

**"The followers of the varṇāśrama institution accept the regulative principles of the four social orders [brāhmaṇa, kṣatriya, vaiśya and śūdra] and four spiritual orders [brahmacarya, gṛhastha, vānaprastha and sannyāsa]. However, if one carries out the regulative principles of these orders but does not render transcendental service to Kṛṣṇa, he falls into the hellish condition of material life.**

### PURPORT

One may be a *brāhmaṇa, kṣatriya, vaiśya* or *śūdra,* or one may perfectly follow the spiritual principles of *brahmacarya, gṛhastha, vānaprastha* and *sannyāsa,* but ultimately one falls down into a hellish condition unless one becomes a devotee. Without developing one's dormant Kṛṣṇa consciousness, one cannot be factually elevated. The regulative principles of *varṇāśrama-dharma* in themselves are insufficient for attainment of the highest perfection. That is confirmed in the following two quotations from *Śrīmad-Bhāgavatam* (11.5.2-3).

### TEXT 27

মুখবাহূরুপাদেভ্যঃ পুরুষস্যাশ্রমৈঃ সহ ।
চত্বারো জজ্ঞিরে বর্ণা গুণৈর্বিপ্রাদয়ঃ পৃথক্ ॥ ২৭ ॥

*mukha-bāhūru-pādebhyaḥ*
*puruṣasyāśramaiḥ saha*
*catvāro jajñire varṇā*
*guṇair viprādayaḥ pṛthak*

### SYNONYMS

*mukha*—the mouth; *bāhu*—the arms; *ūru*—the waist; *pādebhyaḥ*—from the legs; *puruṣasya*—of the Supreme Person; *āśramaiḥ*—the different spiritual orders; *saha*—with; *catvāraḥ*—the four; *jajñire*—appeared; *varṇāḥ*—social orders; *guṇaiḥ*—with particular qualifications; *vipra-ādayaḥ*—*brāhmaṇas* and so on; *pṛthak*—separately.

### TRANSLATION

**" 'From the mouth of Brahmā, the brahminical order has come into existence. Similarly, from his arms the kṣatriyas have come, from his waist the vaiśyas have come, and from his legs the śūdras have come. These four orders and their spiritual counterparts [brahmacarya, gṛhastha, vānaprastha and sannyāsa] combine to make human society complete.**

### TEXT 28

য এষাং পুরুষং সাক্ষাদাত্মপ্রভবমীশ্বরম্ ।
ন ভজন্ত্যবজানন্তি স্থানাদ্ভ্রষ্টাঃ পতন্ত্যধঃ ॥ ২৮ ॥

*ya eṣāṁ puruṣaṁ sākṣād-*
*ātma-prabhavam īśvaram*
*na bhajanty avajānanti*
*sthānād bhraṣṭāḥ patanty adhaḥ*

### SYNONYMS

*ye*—anyone who; *eṣām*—of those divisions of social and spiritual orders; *puruṣam*—the Supreme Personality of Godhead; *sākṣāt*—directly; *ātma-prabhavam*—the source of everyone; *īśvaram*—the supreme controller; *na*—not; *bhajanti*—worship; *avajānanti*—or who neglect; *sthānāt*—from their proper place; *bhraṣṭāḥ*—being fallen; *patanti*—fall; *adhaḥ*—downward into hellish conditions.

### TRANSLATION

**" 'If one simply maintains an official position in the four varṇas and āśramas but does not worship the Supreme Lord Viṣṇu, he falls down from his puffed-up position into a hellish condition.'**

### TEXT 29

জ্ঞানী জীবন্মুক্তদশা পাইনু করি' মানে ।
বস্তুতঃ বুদ্ধি 'শুদ্ধ' নহে কৃষ্ণভক্তি বিনে ॥ ২৯ ॥

*jñānī jīvan-mukta-daśā pāinu kari' māne*
*vastutaḥ buddhi 'śuddha' nahe kṛṣṇa-bhakti vine*

## SYNONYMS

*jñānī*—the speculative philosophers; *jīvan-mukta-daśā*—the stage of liberation even while in this body; *pāinu*—I have gotten; *kari'*—taking; *māne*—considers; *vastutaḥ*—factually; *buddhi*—intelligence; *śuddha*—purified; *nahe*—not; *kṛṣṇa-bhakti vine*—without devotional service to Kṛṣṇa.

## TRANSLATION

**"There are many philosophical speculators [jñānīs] belonging to the Māyāvāda school who consider themselves liberated and call themselves Nārāyaṇa. However, their intelligence is not purified unless they engage in Kṛṣṇa's devotional service.**

## TEXT 30

যেঽন্যেঽরবিন্দাক্ষ বিমুক্তমানিন-
স্ত্বয্যস্তভাবাদবিশুদ্ধবুদ্ধয়ঃ ।
আরুহ্য কৃচ্ছ্রেণ পরং পদং ততঃ
পতন্ত্যধোঽনাদৃতযুষ্মদঙ্ঘ্রয়ঃ ॥ ৩০ ॥

*ye 'nye 'ravindākṣa vimukta-māninas*
*tvayy asta-bhāvād aviśuddha-buddhayaḥ*
*āruhya kṛcchreṇa paraṁ padaṁ tataḥ*
*patanty adho 'nādṛta-yuṣmad-aṅghrayaḥ*

## SYNONYMS

*ye*—all those who; *anye*—others (nondevotees); *aravinda-akṣa*—O lotus-eyed one; *vimukta-māninaḥ*—who consider themselves liberated; *tvayi*—unto You; *asta-bhāvāt*—without devotion; *aviśuddha-buddhayaḥ*—whose intelligence is not purified; *āruhya*—having ascended; *kṛcchreṇa*—by severe austerities and penances; *param padam*—to the supreme position; *tataḥ*—from there; *patanti*—fall; *adhaḥ*—down; *anādṛta*—without respecting; *yuṣmat*—Your; *aṅghrayaḥ*—lotus feet.

## TRANSLATION

**" 'O lotus-eyed one, those who think they are liberated in this life but do not render devotional service to You must be of impure intelligence. Although they accept severe austerities and penances and rise to the spiritual position,**

**to impersonal Brahman realization, they fall down again because they neglect to worship Your lotus feet.'**

## PURPORT

This verse is quoted from *Śrīmad-Bhāgavatam* (10.2.32).

## TEXT 31

কৃষ্ণ—সূর্যসম ; মায়া হয় অন্ধকার ।
যাহাঁ কৃষ্ণ, তাহাঁ নাহি মায়ার অধিকার ॥ ৩১ ॥

*kṛṣṇa——sūrya-sama; māyā haya andhakāra*
*yāhāṅ kṛṣṇa, tāhāṅ nāhi māyāra adhikāra*

## SYNONYMS

*kṛṣṇa*—Kṛṣṇa, the Supreme Personality of Godhead; *sūrya-sama*—like the sun planet; *māyā*—the illusory energy; *haya*—is; *andhakāra*—darkness; *yāhāṅ kṛṣṇa*—wherever there is Kṛṣṇa; *tāhāṅ*—there; *nāhi*—not; *māyāra*—of *māyā,* or the darkness of illusion; *adhikāra*—the jurisdiction.

## TRANSLATION

**"Kṛṣṇa is compared to sunshine, and māyā is compared to darkness. Wherever there is sunshine, there cannot be darkness. As soon as one takes to Kṛṣṇa consciousness, the darkness of illusion (the influence of the external energy) will immediately vanish.**

## PURPORT

In *Śrīmad-Bhāgavatam* (2.9.34) it is stated:

*ṛte 'rthaṁ yat pratīyeta*
*na pratīyeta cātmani*
*tad vidyād ātmano māyāṁ*
*yathābhāso yathā tamaḥ*

Wherever there is light, there cannot be darkness. When a living entity becomes Kṛṣṇa conscious, he is immediately relieved of all material lusty desires. Lusty desires and greed are associated with *rajas* and *tamas,* darkness and passion. When one becomes Kṛṣṇa conscious, the modes of darkness and passion immediately vanish, and the remaining mode, *sattva-guṇa* (goodness), remains. When one is situated in the mode of goodness, he can make spiritual advancement and understand things clearly. This position is not possible for everyone.

When a person is Kṛṣṇa conscious, he continuously hears about Kṛṣṇa, thinks about Him, worships Him and serves Him as a devotee. If he remains in Kṛṣṇa consciousness in this way, the darkness of *māyā* certainly will not be able to touch him.

## TEXT 32

বিলজ্জমানয়া যস্য স্থাতুমীক্ষাপথেঽমুয়া ।
বিমোহিতা বিকত্থন্তে মমাহমিতি দুর্ধিয়ঃ ॥ ৩২ ॥

*vilajjamānayā yasya*
*sthātum īkṣā-pathe 'muyā*
*vimohitā vikatthante*
*mamāham iti durdhiyaḥ*

## SYNONYMS

*vilajjamānayā*—being ashamed; *yasya*—of whom; *sthātum*—to remain; *īkṣā-pathe*—in the line of sight; *amuyā*—by that (*māyā*); *vimohitāḥ*—bewildered; *vikatthante*—boast; *mama*—my; *aham*—I; *iti*—thus; *durdhiyaḥ*—having poor intelligence.

## TRANSLATION

**" 'The external illusory energy of Kṛṣṇa, known as māyā, is always ashamed to stand in front of Kṛṣṇa, just as darkness is ashamed to remain before the sunshine. However, that māyā bewilders unfortunate people who have no intelligence. Thus they simply boast that this material world is theirs and that they are its enjoyers.'**

## PURPORT

The entire world is bewildered because people are thinking, "This is my land," "America is mine," "India is mine." Not knowing the real value of life, people think that the material body and the land where it is produced are all in all. This is the basic principle behind nationalism, socialism and communism. Such thinking, which simply bewilders the living being, is nothing but rascalism. It is due to the darkness of *māyā,* but as soon as one becomes Kṛṣṇa conscious, he is immediately relieved from such misconceptions. This verse is quoted from *Śrīmad-Bhāgavatam* (2.5.13). There is also another appropriate verse in *Śrīmad-Bhāgavatam* (2.7.47):

*śaśvat praśāntam abhayaṁ pratibodha-mātraṁ*
*śuddhaṁ samaṁ sad-asataḥ paramātma-tattvam*
*śabdo na yatra puru-kārakavān kriyārtho*

*māyā paraity abhimukhe ca vilajjamānā*
*tad vai padaṁ bhagavataḥ paramasya puṁso*
*brahmeti yad vidur ajasra-sukhaṁ viśokam*

"What is realized as the Absolute Brahman is full of unlimited bliss without grief. That is certainly the ultimate phase of the supreme enjoyer, the Personality of Godhead. He is eternally void of all disturbances, fearless, completely conscious as opposed to matter, uncontaminated and without distinctions. He is the principal, primeval cause of all causes and effects, in whom there is no sacrifice for fruitive activities and in whom the illusory energy does not stand."

This verse was spoken by Lord Brahmā when he was questioned by the great sage Nārada. Nārada was surprised to see the creator of the universe meditating, for he was doubting whether there was someone greater than Lord Brahmā. While answering the great sage Nārada, Lord Brahmā described the position of *māyā* and the bewildered living entities. This verse was spoken in that connection.

### TEXT 33

**'কৃষ্ণ, তোমার হও' যদি বলে একবার ।**
**মায়াবন্ধ হৈতে কৃষ্ণ তারে করে পার ॥ ৩৩ ॥**

*'kṛṣṇa, tomāra haṅa' yadi bale eka-bāra*
*māyā-bandha haite kṛṣṇa tāre kare pāra*

### SYNONYMS

*kṛṣṇa*—O my Lord Kṛṣṇa; *tomāra haṅa*—I am Yours; *yadi*—if; *bale*—someone says; *eka-bāra*—once; *māyā-bandha haite*—from the bondage of conditional life; *kṛṣṇa*—Lord Kṛṣṇa; *tāre*—him; *kare pāra*—releases.

### TRANSLATION

**"One is immediately freed from the clutches of māyā if he seriously and sincerely says, 'My dear Lord Kṛṣṇa, although I have forgotten You for so many long years in the material world, today I am surrendering unto You. I am Your sincere and serious servant. Please engage me in Your service.'**

### TEXT 34

সকৃদেব প্রপন্নো যস্তবাস্মীতি চ যাচতে ।
অভয়ং সর্বদা তস্মৈ দদাম্যেতদ্‌ব্রতং মম ॥ ৩৪ ॥

*sakṛd eva prapanno yas*
*tavāsmīti ca yācate*

*abhayaṁ sarvadā tasmai*
*dadāmy etad vrataṁ mama*

## SYNONYMS

*sakṛt*—once only; *eva*—certainly; *prapannaḥ*—surrendered; *yaḥ*—anyone who; *tava*—Yours; *asmi*—I am; *iti*—thus; *ca*—also; *yācate*—prays; *abhayam*—fearlessness; *sarvadā*—always; *tasmai*—unto him; *dadāmi*—I give; *etat*—this; *vratam*—vow; *mama*—My.

## TRANSLATION

**" 'It is My vow that if one only once seriously surrenders unto Me, saying, "My dear Lord, from this day I am Yours," and prays to Me for courage, I shall immediately award courage to that person, and he will always remain safe from that time on.'**

## PURPORT

This is a quotation from the *Rāmāyaṇa.*

## TEXT 35

ভুক্তি-মুক্তি-সিদ্ধিকামী 'সুবুদ্ধি' যদি হয় ।
গাঢ়-ভক্তিযোগে তবে কৃষ্ণেরে ভজয় ॥ ৩৫ ॥

*bhukti-mukti-siddhi-kāmī 'subuddhi' yadi haya*
*gāḍha-bhakti-yoge tabe kṛṣṇere bhajaya*

## SYNONYMS

*bhukti*—of material enjoyment; *mukti*—of impersonal liberation; *siddhi*—of achieving mystic power; *kāmī*—desirous; *su-buddhi*—actually intelligent; *yadi*—if; *haya*—he is; *gāḍha*—deep; *bhakti-yoge*—by devotional service; *tabe*—then; *kṛṣṇere bhajaya*—worships Lord Kṛṣṇa.

## TRANSLATION

**"Due to bad association, the living entity desires material happiness, liberation or merging into the impersonal aspect of the Lord, or he engages in mystic yoga for material power. If such a person actually becomes intelligent, he takes to Kṛṣṇa consciousness by engaging himself in intense devotional service to Lord Śrī Kṛṣṇa.**

## TEXT 36

অকামঃ সর্বকামো বা মোক্ষকাম উদারধীঃ ।
তীব্রেণ ভক্তিযোগেন যজেত পুরুষং পরম্ ॥ ৩৬ ॥

*akāmaḥ sarva-kāmo vā*
*mokṣa-kāma udāra-dhīḥ*
*tīvreṇa bhakti-yogena*
*yajeta puruṣaṁ param*

### SYNONYMS

*akāmaḥ*—a pure devotee with no desire for material enjoyment; *sarva-kāmaḥ*—one who has no end to his desires for material enjoyment; *vā*—or; *mokṣa-kāmaḥ*—one who desires to merge into the existence of Brahman; *udāra-dhīḥ*—being very intelligent; *tīvreṇa*—firm; *bhakti-yogena*—by devotional service; *yajeta*—should worship; *puruṣam*—the person; *param*—supreme.

### TRANSLATION

**" 'Whether one desires everything or nothing, or whether he desires to merge into the existence of the Lord, he is intelligent only if he worships Lord Kṛṣṇa, the Supreme Personality of Godhead, by rendering transcendental loving service.'**

### PURPORT

This is a verse from *Śrīmad-Bhāgavatam* (2.3.10).

## TEXT 37

অন্যকামী যদি করে কৃষ্ণের ভজন ।
না মাগিতেহ কৃষ্ণ তারে দেন স্ব-চরণ ॥ ৩৭ ॥

*anya-kāmī yadi kare kṛṣṇera bhajana*
*nā māgiteha kṛṣṇa tāre dena sva-caraṇa*

### SYNONYMS

*anya-kāmī*—one who desires many other things; *yadi*—if; *kare*—he performs; *kṛṣṇera bhajana*—devotional service to Lord Kṛṣṇa; *nā māgiteha*—although not asking; *kṛṣṇa*—Lord Kṛṣṇa; *tāre*—to him; *dena*—gives; *sva-caraṇa*—the shelter of His lotus feet.

### TRANSLATION

**"If those who desire material enjoyment or merging into the existence of the Absolute Truth engage in the Lord's transcendental loving service, they will immediately attain shelter at Kṛṣṇa's lotus feet, although they did not ask for it. Kṛṣṇa is therefore very merciful.**

### TEXT 38

কৃষ্ণ কহে,– 'আমা ভজে, মাগে বিষয়-সুখ ।
অমৃত ছাড়ি' বিষ মাগে,- এই বড় মূর্খ ॥ ৩৮ ॥

*kṛṣṇa kahe,—'āmā bhaje, māge viṣaya-sukha*
*amṛta chāḍi' viṣa māge,—ei baḍa mūrkha*

### SYNONYMS

*kṛṣṇa kahe*—Kṛṣṇa says; *āmā bhaje*—he worships Me; *māge*—but requests; *viṣaya-sukha*—material happiness; *amṛta chāḍi'*—giving up the nectar; *viṣa māge*—he begs for poison; *ei baḍa mūrkha*—he is a great fool.

### TRANSLATION

**"Kṛṣṇa says, 'If one engages in My transcendental loving service but at the same time wants the opulence of material enjoyment, he is very, very foolish. Indeed, he is just like a person who gives up ambrosia to drink poison.**

### TEXT 39

আমি—বিজ্ঞ, এই মূর্খে 'বিষয়' কেনে দিব ?
স্ব-চরণামৃত দিয়া 'বিষয়' ভুলাইব ॥ ৩৯ ॥

*āmi—vijña, ei mūrkhe 'viṣaya' kene diba?*
*sva-caraṇāmṛta diyā 'viṣaya' bhulāiba*

### SYNONYMS

*āmi*—I; *vijña*—all-intelligent; *ei mūrkhe*—unto this foolish person; *viṣaya*—material enjoyment; *kene diba*—why should I give; *sva-caraṇa-amṛta*—the nectar of shelter at My lotus feet; *diyā*—giving; *viṣaya*—the idea of material enjoyment; *bhulāiba*—I shall make him forget.

### TRANSLATION

**" 'Since I am very intelligent, why should I give this fool material prosperity? Instead I shall induce him to take the nectar of the shelter of My lotus feet and make him forget illusory material enjoyment.'**

### PURPORT

Those who are interested in material enjoyment are known as *bhukti.* One who is interested in merging into the effulgence of Brahman or perfecting the mystic *yoga* system is not a devotee at all. Devotees do not have such desires. However, if a *karmī, jñānī* or *yogī* somehow contacts a devotee and renders devotional service, Kṛṣṇa immediately awards him love of God and gives him shelter at His lotus feet, although he may have no idea how to develop love of Kṛṣṇa. If a person wants material profit from devotional service, Kṛṣṇa condemns such materialistic desires. To desire material opulence while engaging in devotional service is foolish. Although the person may be foolish, Kṛṣṇa, being all-intelligent, engages him in His devotional service in such a way that he gradually forgets material opulence. The point is that we should not try to exchange loving service for material prosperity. If we are actually surrendered to the lotus feet of Kṛṣṇa, our only desire should be to satisfy Kṛṣṇa. That is pure Kṛṣṇa consciousness. Surrender does not mean that we demand something from the Lord but that we completely depend on His mercy.

## TEXT 40

সত্যং দিশত্যর্থিতমর্থিতো নৃণাং
নৈবার্থদো যৎ পুনরর্থিতা যতঃ ।
স্বয়ং বিধত্তে ভজতামনিচ্ছতা-
মিচ্ছাপিধানং নিজপাদপল্লবম্ ॥ ৪০ ॥

*satyaṁ diśaty arthitam arthito nṛṇāṁ*
*naivārthado yat punar arthitā yataḥ*
*svayaṁ vidhatte bhajatām anicchatām*
*icchā-pidhānaṁ nija-pāda-pallavam*

## SYNONYMS

*satyam*—it is true; *diśati*—He awards; *arthitam*—that which is desired; *arthitaḥ*—being requested; *nṛṇām*—by human beings; *na*—not; *eva*—certainly; *artha-daḥ*—giving desired things; *yat*—which; *punaḥ*—again; *arthitā*—request; *yataḥ*—from which; *svayam*—Himself; *vidhatte*—He gives; *bhajatām*—of those engaged in devotional service; *anicchatām*—even though not desiring; *icchā-pidhānam*—covering all other desires; *nija-pāda-pallavam*—the shelter of His own lotus feet.

## TRANSLATION

**" 'Whenever Kṛṣṇa is requested to fulfill one's desire, He undoubtedly does so, but He does not award anything which, after being enjoyed, will cause someone to petition Him again and again to fulfill further desires. When one has other desires but engages in the Lord's service, Kṛṣṇa forcibly gives one shelter at His lotus feet, where one will forget all other desires.'**

## PURPORT

This is a quotation from *Śrīmad-Bhāgavatam* (5.19.26).

## TEXT 41

**কাম লাগি' কৃষ্ণে ভজে, পায় কৃষ্ণ-রসে ।**
**কাম ছাড়ি' 'দাস' হৈতে হয় অভিলাষে ॥ ৪১ ॥**

*kāma lāgi' kṛṣṇe bhaje, pāya kṛṣṇa-rase*
*kāma chāḍi' 'dāsa' haite haya abhilāṣe*

## SYNONYMS

*kāma lāgi'*—for fulfillment of one's material desires; *kṛṣṇe bhaje*—one engages in the transcendental service of Lord Kṛṣṇa; *pāya*—he gets; *kṛṣṇa-rase*—a taste of the lotus feet of Lord Kṛṣṇa; *kāma chāḍi'*—giving up all desires for material enjoyment; *dāsa haite*—to be an eternal servant of the Lord; *haya*—there is; *abhilāṣe*—aspiration.

## TRANSLATION

**"When someone engages in Lord Kṛṣṇa's devotional service for the satisfaction of the senses and instead acquires a taste to serve Kṛṣṇa, he gives up his material desires and willingly offers himself as an eternal servant of Kṛṣṇa.**

## TEXT 42

স্থানাভিলাষী তপসি স্থিতোঽহং
ত্বাং প্রাপ্তবান্ দেবমুনীন্দ্রগুহ্যম্ ।
কাচং বিচিন্বন্নপি দিব্যরত্নং
স্বামিন্ কৃতার্থোঽস্মি বরং ন যাচে ॥ ৪২ ॥

*sthānābhilāṣī tapasi sthito 'haṁ*
*tvāṁ prāptavān deva-munīndra-guhyam*
*kācaṁ vicinvann api divya-ratnaṁ*
*svāmin kṛtārtho 'smi varaṁ na yāce*

## SYNONYMS

*sthāna-abhilāṣī*—desiring a very high position in the material world; *tapasi*—in severe austerities and penances; *sthitaḥ*—situated; *aham*—I; *tvām*—You; *prāptavān*—have obtained; *deva-muni-indra-guhyam*—difficult to achieve even for great demigods, saintly persons and kings; *kācam*—a piece of glass; *vicinvan*—searching for; *api*—although; *divya-ratnam*—a transcendental gem; *svāmin*—O my Lord; *kṛta-arthaḥ asmi*—I am fully satisfied; *varam*—any benediction; *na yāce*—I do not ask.

### TRANSLATION

**[When he was being benedicted by the Supreme Personality of Godhead, Dhruva Mahārāja said] " 'O my Lord, because I was seeking an opulent material position, I was performing severe types of penance and austerity. Now I have gotten You, who are very difficult for the great demigods, saintly persons and kings to attain. I was searching after a piece of glass, but instead I have found a most valuable jewel. Therefore I am so satisfied that I do not wish to ask any benediction from You.'**

### PURPORT

This verse is from the *Hari-bhakti-sudhodaya* (7.28).

### TEXT 43

সংসার ভ্রমিতে কোন ভাগ্যে কেহ তরে।
নদীর প্রবাহে যেন কাষ্ঠ লাগে তীরে ॥ ৪৩ ॥

*saṁsāra bhramite kona bhāgye keha tare*
*nadīra pravāhe yena kāṣṭha lāge tīre*

### SYNONYMS

*saṁsāra bhramite*—wandering throughout the universe; *kona bhāgye*—by some good fortune; *keha tare*—someone crosses the ocean of nescience; *nadīra pravāhe*—in the flow of the river; *yena*—just as; *kāṣṭha*—wood; *lāge*—sticks; *tīre*—on the bank.

### TRANSLATION

**"There are unlimited conditioned souls who are bereft of Lord Kṛṣṇa's service. Not knowing how to cross the ocean of nescience, they are scattered by waves, time and tide. However, some are fortunate to contact devotees, and by this contact they are delivered from the ocean of nescience, just as a log, floating down a river, accidentally washes upon the bank.**

### TEXT 44

নৈবং মমাধমস্যাপি স্যাদেবাচ্যুতদর্শনম্।
হ্রিয়মাণঃ কালনদ্যা ক্বচিত্তরতি কশ্চন ॥ ৪৪ ॥

*maivaṁ mamādhamasyāpi*
*syād evācyuta-darśanam*
*hriyamāṇaḥ kāla-nadyā*
*kvacit tarati kaścana*

### SYNONYMS

*mā*—not; *evam*—thus; *mama*—of me; *adhamasya*—who is the most fallen; *api*—although; *syāt*—there may be; *eva*—certainly; *acyuta-darśanam*—seeing of the Supreme Personality of Godhead; *hriyamāṇaḥ*—being carried; *kāla-nadyā*—by the stream of time; *kvacit*—sometimes; *tarati*—crosses over; *kaścana*—someone.

### TRANSLATION

**" ' "Because I am so fallen, I shall never get a chance to see the Supreme Personality of Godhead." This was my false apprehension. Rather, by chance a person as fallen as I am may get to see the Supreme Personality of Godhead. Although one is being carried away by the waves of the river of time, one may eventually reach the shore.'**

### PURPORT

This is a quotation from *Śrīmad-Bhāgavatam* (10.38.5).

### TEXT 45

কোন ভাগ্যে কারো সংসার ক্ষয়োন্মুখ হয়।
সাধুসঙ্গে তবে কৃষ্ণে রতি উপজয় ॥ ৪৫ ॥

*kona bhāgye kāro saṁsāra kṣayonmukha haya*
*sādhu-saṅge tabe kṛṣṇe rati upajaya*

### SYNONYMS

*kona bhāgye*—by fortune; *kāro*—of someone; *saṁsāra*—conditioned life; *kṣaya-unmukha*—on the point of destruction; *haya*—is; *sādhu-saṅge*—by association with devotees; *tabe*—then; *kṛṣṇe*—to Lord Kṛṣṇa; *rati*—attraction; *upajaya*—awakens.

### TRANSLATION

**"By good fortune, one becomes eligible to cross the ocean of nescience, and when one's term of material existence decreases, one may get an opportunity to associate with pure devotees. By such association, one's attraction to Kṛṣṇa is awakened.**

## PURPORT

Śrīla Bhaktivinoda Ṭhākura explains this point. Is this *bhāgya* (fortune) the result of an accident or something else? In the scriptures, devotional service and pious activity are considered fortunate. Pious activities can be divided into three categories—pious activities that awaken one's dormant Kṛṣṇa consciousness are called *bhakty-unmukhī sukṛti.* Pious activities that bestow material opulence are called *bhogonmukhī,* and pious activities that enable the living entity to merge into the existence of the Supreme are called *mokṣonmukhī.* These last two awards of pious activity are not actually fortunate. Pious activities are fortunate when they help one become Kṛṣṇa conscious. The good fortune of *bhakty-unmukhī* is attainable only when one comes in contact with a devotee. By associating with a devotee willingly or unwillingly, one advances in devotional service, and thus one's dormant Kṛṣṇa consciousness is awakened.

## TEXT 46

ভবাপবর্গো ভ্রমতো যদা ভবে-
জ্জনস্য তর্হ্যচ্যুত সৎসমাগমঃ ।
সৎসঙ্গমো যর্হি তদৈব সদ্‌গতৌ
পরাবরেশে ত্বয়ি জায়তে রতিঃ ॥ ৪৬ ॥

*bhavāpavargo bhramato yadā bhavej*
*janasya tarhy acyuta sat-samāgamaḥ*
*sat-saṅgamo yarhi tadaiva sad-gatau*
*parāvareśe tvayi jāyate ratiḥ*

## SYNONYMS

*bhava-apavargaḥ*—liberation from the nescience of material existence; *bhramataḥ*—wandering; *yadā*—when; *bhavet*—should be; *janasya*—of a person; *tarhi*—at that time; *acyuta*—O Supreme Personality of Godhead; *sat-samāgamaḥ*—association with devotees; *sat-saṅgamaḥ*—association with devotees; *yarhi*—when; *tadā*—at that time; *eva*—only; *sat-gatau*—the highest goal of life; *parāvareśe*—the Lord of the universe; *tvayi*—to You; *jāyate*—appears; *ratiḥ*—attraction.

## TRANSLATION

**"'O my Lord! O infallible Supreme Person! When a person wandering throughout the universes becomes eligible for liberation from material existence, he gets an opportunity to associate with devotees. When he associates with devotees, his attraction for You is awakened. You are the Supreme Personality of Godhead, the highest goal of the supreme devotees and the Lord of the universe.'**

### PURPORT

This is a quotation from *Śrīmad-Bhāgavatam* (10.51.53).

### TEXT 47

কৃষ্ণ যদি কৃপা করে কোন ভাগ্যবানে ।
গুরু-অন্তর্যামি-রূপে শিখায় আপনে ॥ ৪৭ ॥

*kṛṣṇa yadi kṛpā kare kona bhāgyavāne*
*guru-antaryāmi-rūpe śikhāya āpane*

### SYNONYMS

*kṛṣṇa*—Lord Kṛṣṇa; *yadi*—if; *kṛpā kare*—shows His mercy; *kona bhāgyavāne*—to some fortunate person; *guru*—of the spiritual master; *antaryāmi*—of the Supersoul; *rūpe*—in the form; *śikhāya*—teaches; *āpane*—personally.

### TRANSLATION

**"Kṛṣṇa is situated in everyone's heart as caitya-guru, the spiritual master within. When He is kind to some fortunate conditioned soul, He personally gives one lessons to progress in devotional service, instructing the person as the Supersoul within and the spiritual master without.**

### TEXT 48

নৈবোপযন্ত্যপচিতিং কবয়স্তবেশ
ব্রহ্মায়ুষাপি কৃতমৃদ্ধমুদঃ স্মরন্তঃ ।
যোঽন্তর্বহিস্তনুভৃতামশুভং বিধুন্ব-
ন্নাচার্যচৈত্ত্যবপুষা স্বগতিং ব্যনক্তি ॥ ৪৮ ॥

*naivopayanty apacitiṁ kavayas taveśa*
*brahmāyuṣāpi kṛtam ṛddha-mudaḥ smarantaḥ*
*yo 'ntar bahis tanu-bhṛtām aśubhaṁ vidhunvann*
*ācārya-caittya-vapuṣā sva-gatiṁ vyanakti*

### SYNONYMS

*na eva*—not at all; *upayanti*—are able to express; *apacitim*—their gratitude; *kavayaḥ*—learned devotees; *tava*—Your; *īśa*—O Lord; *brahma-āyuṣā*—with a lifetime equal to Lord Brahmā's; *api*—in spite of; *kṛtam*—magnanimous work; *ṛddha*—increased; *mudaḥ*—joy; *smarantaḥ*—remembering; *yaḥ*—who; *antaḥ*—within; *bahiḥ*—outside; *tanu-bhṛtām*—of those who are embodied; *aśubham*—

misfortune; *vidhunvan*—dissipating; *ācārya*—of the spiritual master; *caittya*—of the Supersoul; *vapuṣā*—by the forms; *sva*—own; *gatim*—path; *vyanakti*—shows.

### TRANSLATION

**" 'O my Lord! Transcendental poets and experts in spiritual science could not fully express their indebtedness to You, even if they were endowed with the prolonged lifetime of Brahmā, for You appear in two features—externally as the ācārya and internally as the Supersoul—to deliver the embodied living being by directing him how to come to You.'**

### PURPORT

This is a verse from *Śrīmad-Bhāgavatam* (11.29.6). It was spoken by Uddhava after he had been instructed in *yoga* by Śrī Kṛṣṇa.

### TEXT 49

**সাধুসঙ্গে কৃষ্ণভক্ত্যে শ্রদ্ধা যদি হয় ।**
**ভক্তিফল 'প্রেম' হয়, সংসার যায় ক্ষয় ॥ ৪৯ ॥**

*sādhu-saṅge kṛṣṇa-bhaktye śraddhā yadi haya*
*bhakti-phala 'prema' haya, saṁsāra yāya kṣaya*

### SYNONYMS

*sādhu-saṅge*—by the association of devotees; *kṛṣṇa-bhaktye*—in discharging devotional service to Kṛṣṇa; *śraddhā*—faith; *yadi*—if; *haya*—there is; *bhakti-phala*—the result of devotional service to Kṛṣṇa; *prema*—love of Godhead; *haya*—awakens; *saṁsāra*—the conditioned life in material existence; *yāya kṣaya*—becomes vanquished.

### TRANSLATION

**"By associating with a devotee, one awakens his faith in devotional service to Kṛṣṇa. Because of devotional service, one's dormant love for Kṛṣṇa awakens, and thus one's material, conditional existence comes to an end.**

### TEXT 50

যদৃচ্ছয়া মৎকথাদৌ জাতশ্রদ্ধস্তু যঃ পুমান্ ।
ন নির্বিণ্ণো নাতিসক্তো ভক্তিযোগোঽস্য সিদ্ধিদঃ ॥ ৫০ ॥

*yadṛcchayā mat-kathādau*
*jāta-śraddhas tu yaḥ pumān*

*na nirviṇṇo nātisakto*
*bhakti-yogo 'sya siddhidaḥ*

### SYNONYMS

*yadṛcchayā*—by some good fortune; *mat-kathā-ādau*—in talk about Me; *jāta-śraddhaḥ*—has awakened his attraction; *tu*—but; *yaḥ pumān*—a person who; *na nirviṇṇaḥ*—not falsely detached; *na atisaktaḥ*—not attached to material existence; *bhakti-yogaḥ*—the process of devotional service; *asya*—for such a person; *siddhi-daḥ*—bestowing perfection.

### TRANSLATION

**" 'Somehow or other, if one is attracted to talks about Me and has faith in the instructions I have set forth in Bhagavad-gītā, and if one is actually detached from material things and material existence, his dormant love for Me will be awakened by devotional service.'**

### PURPORT

This verse from *Śrīmad-Bhāgavatam* (11.20.8) was spoken by Kṛṣṇa at the time of His departure from this material world. It was spoken to Uddhava.

### TEXT 51

মহৎ-কৃপা বিনা কোন কর্মে 'ভক্তি' নয় ।
কৃষ্ণভক্তি দূরে রহু, সংসার নহে ক্ষয় ॥ ৫১ ॥

*mahat-kṛpā vinā kona karme 'bhakti' naya*
*kṛṣṇa-bhakti dūre rahu, saṁsāra nahe kṣaya*

### SYNONYMS

*mahat-kṛpā*—the mercy of great devotees; *vinā*—without; *kona karme*—by some other activity; *bhakti naya*—there is not devotional service; *kṛṣṇa-bhakti*—love of Kṛṣṇa or devotional service to Kṛṣṇa; *dūre rahu*—leaving aside; *saṁsāra*—the bondage of material existence; *nahe*—there is not; *kṣaya*—destruction.

### TRANSLATION

**"Unless one is favored by a pure devotee, he cannot attain the platform of devotional service. To say nothing of kṛṣṇa-bhakti, one cannot even be relieved from the bondage of material existence.**

### PURPORT

Pious activities bring about material opulence, but one cannot acquire devotional service by any amount of material pious activity, not by giving charity, opening big hospitals and schools or working philanthropically. Devotional service can be attained only by the mercy of a pure devotee. Without a pure devotee's mercy, one cannot even escape the bondage of material existence. The word *mahat* in this verse means "a pure devotee." As confirmed in *Bhagavad-gītā:*

*mahātmānas tu māṁ pārtha*
*daivīṁ prakṛtim āśritāḥ*
*bhajanty ananya-manaso*
*jñātvā bhūtādim avyayam*

"O son of Pṛthā, those who are not deluded, the great souls, are under the protection of the divine nature. They are fully engaged in devotional service because they know Me as the Supreme Personality of Godhead, original and inexhaustible." (Bg. 9.13)

One also has to associate with such a *mahātmā* who has accepted Kṛṣṇa as the supreme source of the entire creation. Without being a *mahātmā,* one cannot understand Kṛṣṇa's absolute position. A *mahātmā* is rare and transcendental, and he is a pure devotee of Lord Kṛṣṇa. Foolish people consider Kṛṣṇa a human being, and they consider Lord Kṛṣṇa's pure devotee an ordinary human being also. Whatever one may be, one must take shelter at the lotus feet of a devotee *mahātmā* and treat him as the most exalted well-wisher of all human society. We should take shelter of such a *mahātmā* and ask for his causeless mercy. Only by his benediction can one be relieved from attachment to a materialistic way of life. When one is thus relieved, he can engage in the Lord's transcendental loving service through the mercy of the *mahātmā.*

### TEXT 52

রহূগণৈতত্তপসা ন যাতি
ন চেজ্যয়া নির্বপণাদ্গৃহাদ্বা ।
ন চ্ছন্দসা নৈব জলাগ্নিসূর্যৈ-
র্বিনা মহৎপাদরজোঽভিষেকম্ ॥ ৫২ ॥

*rahūgaṇaitat tapasā na yāti*
*na cejyayā nirvapaṇād gṛhād vā*
*na cchandasā naiva jalāgni-sūryair*
*vinā mahat-pāda-rajo-'bhiṣekam*

### SYNONYMS

*rahūgaṇa*—O King Rahūgaṇa; *etat*—this; *tapasā*—by severe austerities and penances; *na yāti*—one does not obtain; *na*—neither; *ca*—also; *ijyayā*—by gorgeous worship; *nirvapaṇāt*—by renounced order of life; *gṛhāt*—by sacrifices while living in the home; *vā*—or; *na chandasā*—nor by scholarly study of the *Vedas; na*—nor; *eva*—certainly; *jala-agni-sūryaiḥ*—by those who worship water, fire or scorching sunshine; *vinā*—without; *mahat-pāda-rajaḥ*—of the dust of the lotus feet of a *mahātmā; abhiṣekam*—the sprinkling.

### TRANSLATION

**" 'O King Rahūgaṇa, without taking upon one's head the dust from the lotus feet of a pure devotee [a mahājana or mahātmā], one cannot attain devotional service. Devotional service is not possible to attain simply by undergoing severe austerities and penances, by gorgeously worshiping the Deity, or by strictly following the rules and regulations of the sannyāsa or gṛhastha order, nor by studying the Vedas, submerging oneself in water, or exposing oneself to fire or scorching sunlight.'**

### PURPORT

This verse appears in *Śrīmad-Bhāgavatam* (5.12.12). Jaḍa Bharata herein tells King Rahūgaṇa how he attained the *paramahaṁsa* stage. Mahārāja Rahūgaṇa, the King of Sindhu-sauvīra, had asked Jaḍa Bharata how he had attained the *paramahaṁsa* stage. The King had called him to carry his palanquin, but when the King heard from *paramahaṁsa* Jaḍa Bharata about the supreme philosophy, he expressed surprise and asked Jaḍa Bharata how he had attained such great liberation. At that time Jaḍa Bharata informed the King how to become detached from material attraction.

### TEXT 53

নৈষাং মতিস্তাবদুরুক্রমাঙ্ঘ্রিং
স্পৃশত্যনর্থাপগমো যদর্থঃ ।
মহীয়সাং পাদরজোঽভিষেকং
নিষ্কিঞ্চনানাং ন বৃণীত যাবৎ ॥ ৫৩ ॥

*naiṣāṁ matis tāvad urukramāṅghriṁ*
*spṛśaty anarthāpagamo yad-arthaḥ*
*mahīyasāṁ pāda-rajo-'bhiṣekaṁ*
*niṣkiñcanānāṁ na vṛṇīta yāvat*

## SYNONYMS

*na*—not; *eṣām*—of those who are attached to household life; *matiḥ*—the interest; *tāvat*—that long; *urukrama-aṅghrim*—the lotus feet of the Supreme Personality of Godhead, who is credited with uncommon activities; *spṛśati*—touches; *anartha*—of unwanted things; *apagamaḥ*—vanquishing; *yat*—of which; *arthaḥ*—result; *mahīyasām*—of the great personalities, devotees; *pāda-rajaḥ*—of the dust of the lotus feet; *abhiṣekam*—sprinkling on the head; *niṣkiñcanānām*—who are completely detached from material possessions; *na vṛṇīta*—does not do; *yāvat*—as long as.

## TRANSLATION

**" 'Unless human society accepts the dust of the lotus feet of great mahātmās—devotees who have nothing to do with material possessions—mankind cannot turn its attention to the lotus feet of Kṛṣṇa. Those lotus feet vanquish all the unwanted miserable conditions of material life.'**

## PURPORT

This verse appears in the *Śrīmad-Bhāgavatam* (7.5.32). When the great sage Nārada was giving instructions to Mahārāja Yudhiṣṭhira, he narrated the activities of Prahlāda Mahārāja. This verse was spoken by Prahlāda Mahārāja to his father, Hiraṇyakaśipu, the king of demons. Prahlāda Mahārāja informed his father of the nine basic processes of *bhakti-yoga*. Whoever takes to these processes is to be considered a highly learned scholar. Hiraṇyakaśipu, however, did not like his son to talk about devotional service; therefore he immediately called his teacher, Ṣaṇḍāmarka. The teacher explained that he did not teach devotional service to Prahlāda but that the boy was naturally inclined that way. At that time Hiraṇyakaśipu became very angry and asked Prahlāda why he had become a Vaiṣṇava. In answer to this question, Prahlāda Mahārāja recited this verse to the effect that one cannot become the Lord's devotee without receiving the mercy and blessings of another devotee.

## TEXT 54

**'সাধুসঙ্গ', 'সাধুসঙ্গ'—সর্বশাস্ত্রে কয় ।**
**লবমাত্র সাধুসঙ্গে সর্বসিদ্ধি হয় ॥ ৫৪ ॥**

*'sādhu-saṅga', 'sādhu-saṅga'——sarva-śāstre kaya*
*lava-mātra sādhu-saṅge sarva-siddhi haya*

## SYNONYMS

*sādhu-saṅga sādhu-saṅga*—association with pure devotees; *sarva-śāstre*—all the revealed scriptures; *kaya*—say; *lava-mātra*—even for a moment; *sādhu-saṅge*—by association with a devotee; *sarva-siddhi*—all success; *haya*—there is.

### TRANSLATION

**"The verdict of all revealed scriptures is that by even a moment's association with a pure devotee, one can attain all success.**

### PURPORT

According to astronomical calculations, *lava* is one eleventh of one second.

### TEXT 55

তুলয়াম লবেনাপি ন স্বর্গং নাপুনর্ভবম্ ।
ভগবৎসঙ্গিসঙ্গস্য মর্ত্যানাং কিমুতাশিষঃ ॥ ৫৫ ॥

*tulayāma lavenāpi*
*na svargaṁ nāpunar-bhavam*
*bhagavat-saṅgi-saṅgasya*
*martyānāṁ kimutāśiṣaḥ*

### SYNONYMS

*tulayāma*—we make equal; *lavena*—with one instant; *api*—even; *na*—not; *svargam*—heavenly planets; *na*—nor; *apunaḥ-bhavam*—merging into the existence of the Supreme; *bhagavat-saṅgi-saṅgasya*—of the association of devotees who are always associated with the Supreme Personality of Godhead; *martyānām*—of persons destined to die; *kim uta*—what; *āśiṣaḥ*—the blessings.

### TRANSLATION

**" 'The value of a moment's association with a devotee of the Lord cannot even be compared to the attainment of heavenly planets or liberation from matter, and what to speak of worldly benedictions in the form of material prosperity, which is for those who are meant for death.'**

### PURPORT

This is a quotation from *Śrīmad-Bhāgavatam* (1.18.13). This verse concerns the Vedic rites and sacrifices performed by the great sages of Naimiṣāraṇya, headed by Śaunaka Ṛṣi. The sages pointed out that association with a devotee for even less than a second is beyond comparison to a thousand Vedic rituals and sacrifices, elevation to heavenly planets or merging into the existence of the Supreme.

### TEXT 56

**কৃষ্ণ কৃপালু অর্জুনেরে লক্ষ্য করিয়া ।**
**জগতেরে রাখিয়াছেন উপদেশ দিয়া ॥ ৫৬ ॥**

*kṛṣṇa kṛpālu arjunere lakṣya kariyā*
*jagatere rākhiyāchena upadeśa diyā*

## SYNONYMS

*kṛṣṇa*—Lord Kṛṣṇa; *kṛpālu*—merciful; *arjunere*—Arjuna; *lakṣya kariyā*—aiming at; *jagatere*—the whole world; *rākhiyāchena*—has protected; *upadeśa diyā*—giving instructions.

## TRANSLATION

**"Kṛṣṇa is so merciful that simply by aiming His instructions at Arjuna, He has given protection to the whole world.**

## TEXTS 57-58

সর্বগুহ্যতমং ভূয়ঃ শৃণু মে পরমং বচঃ ।
ইষ্টোঽসি মে দৃঢ়মিতি ততো বক্ষ্যামি তে হিতম্ ॥ ৫৭ ॥
মন্মনা ভব মদ্ভক্তো মদ্যাজী মাং নমস্কুরু।
মামেবৈষ্যসি সত্যং তে প্রতিজানে প্রিয়োঽসি মে ॥৫৮॥

*sarva-guhyatamaṁ bhūyaḥ*
*śṛṇu me paramaṁ vacaḥ*
*iṣṭo 'si me dṛḍham iti*
*tato vakṣyāmi te hitam*

*man-manā bhava mad-bhakto*
*mad-yājī māṁ namaskuru*
*mām evaiṣyasi satyaṁ te*
*pratijāne priyo 'si me*

## SYNONYMS

*sarva-guhya-tamam*—most confidential of all; *bhūyaḥ*—again; *śṛṇu*—hear; *me*—My; *paramam vacaḥ*—supreme instruction; *iṣṭaḥ*—beloved; *asi*—you are; *me*—My; *dṛḍham iti*—very firmly; *tataḥ*—therefore; *vakṣyāmi*—I shall speak; *te*—to you; *hitam*—words of benediction; *mat-manāḥ*—whose mind is always on Me; *bhava*—become; *mat-bhaktaḥ*—My devotee; *mat-yājī*—My worshiper; *mām*—unto Me; *namaskuru*—offer obeisances; *mām eva*—to Me only; *eṣyasi*—you will come; *satyam*—truly; *te*—to you; *pratijāne*—I promise; *priyaḥ asi*—you are dear; *me*—My.

### TRANSLATION

**" 'Because you are My very dear friend, I am speaking to you the most confidential part of knowledge. Hear this from Me, for it is for your benefit. Always think of Me and become My devotee, worship Me and offer obeisances unto Me. Thus you will come to Me without fail. I promise you this because you are My very dear friend.'**

### PURPORT

This is a quotation from *Bhagavad-gītā* (18.64-65).

### TEXT 59

পূর্ব আজ্ঞা,—বেদ-ধর্ম, কর্ম, যোগ, জ্ঞান।
সব সাধি' শেষে এই আজ্ঞা—বলবান্ ॥ ৫৯ ॥

*pūrva ājñā,——veda-dharma, karma, yoga, jñāna*
*saba sādhi' śeṣe ei ājñā——balavān*

### SYNONYMS

*pūrva ājñā*—previous orders; *veda-dharma*—performance of Vedic ritualistic ceremonies; *karma*—fruitive activities; *yoga*—mystic *yoga* practice; *jñāna*—speculative knowledge; *saba sādhi'*—executing all these processes; *śeṣe*—at the end; *ei ājñā*—this order; *balavān*—powerful.

### TRANSLATION

**"Although Kṛṣṇa has previously explained the proficiency of executing Vedic rituals, performing fruitive activity as enjoined in the Vedas, practicing yoga and cultivating jñāna, these last instructions are most powerful and stand above all the others.**

### TEXT 60

এই আজ্ঞাবলে ভক্তের 'শ্রদ্ধা' যদি হয়।
সর্বকর্ম ত্যাগ করি' সে কৃষ্ণ ভজয় ॥ ৬০ ॥

*ei ājñā-bale bhaktera 'śraddhā' yadi haya*
*sarva-karma tyāga kari' se kṛṣṇa bhajaya*

### SYNONYMS

*ei ājñā-bale*—on the strength of this supreme order of the Supreme Personality of Godhead; *bhaktera*—of the devotees; *śraddhā*—faith; *yadi*—if; *haya*—there is; *sarva-karma*—all other activities, material and spiritual; *tyāga kari'*—leaving aside; *se*—he; *kṛṣṇa bhajaya*—serves Lord Kṛṣṇa.

### TRANSLATION

**"If the devotee has faith in the strength of this order, he worships Lord Kṛṣṇa and gives up all other activities.**

### TEXT 61

তাবৎ কর্মাণি কুর্বীত ন নির্বিদ্যেত যাবতা ।
মৎকথাশ্রবণাদৌ বা শ্রদ্ধা যাবন্ন জায়তে ॥ ৬১ ॥

*tāvat karmāṇi kurvīta*
*na nirvidyeta yāvatā*
*mat-kathā-śravaṇādau vā*
*śraddhā yāvan na jāyate*

### SYNONYMS

*tāvat*—up to that time; *karmāṇi*—fruitive activities; *kurvīta*—one should execute; *na nirvidyeta*—is not satiated; *yāvatā*—as long as; *mat-kathā*—of discourses about Me; *śravaṇa-ādau*—in the matter of *śravaṇam, kīrtanam,* and so on; *vā*—or; *śraddhā*—faith; *yāvat*—as long as; *na*—not; *jāyate*—is awakened.

### TRANSLATION

**" 'As long as one is not satiated by fruitive activity and has not awakened his taste for devotional service by śravaṇaṁ kīrtanaṁ viṣṇoḥ, one has to act according to the regulative principles of the Vedic injunctions.'**

### PURPORT

This is a quotation from *Śrīmad-Bhāgavatam* (11.20.9).

### TEXT 62

**'শ্রদ্ধা'-শব্দে—বিশ্বাস কহে সুদৃঢ় নিশ্চয় ।**
**কৃষ্ণে ভক্তি কৈলে সর্বকর্ম কৃত হয় ॥ ৬২ ॥**

*'śraddhā'-śabde——viśvāsa kahe sudṛḍha niścaya*
*kṛṣṇe bhakti kaile sarva-karma kṛta haya*

### SYNONYMS

*śraddhā-śabde*—by the word *śraddhā; viśvāsa*—faith; *kahe*—is said; *su-dṛḍha*—firm; *niścaya*—certain; *kṛṣṇe*—unto Lord Kṛṣṇa; *bhakti*—devotional service; *kaile*—by executing; *sarva-karma*—all activities; *kṛta*—completed; *haya*—are.

## TRANSLATION

**"By rendering transcendental loving service to Kṛṣṇa, one automatically performs all subsidiary activities. This confident, firm faith, favorable to the discharge of devotional service, is called śraddhā.**

## PURPORT

Firm faith and confidence are called *śraddhā*. When one engages in the Lord's devotional service, he is to be understood to have performed all his responsibilities in the material world. He has satisfied his forefathers, ordinary living entities, and demigods and is free from all responsibility. Such a person does not need to meet his responsibilities separately. It is automatically done. Fruitive activity (*karma*) is meant to satisfy the senses of the conditioned soul. However, when one awakens to Kṛṣṇa consciousness, he does not have to work separately for pious activity. The best achievement of all fruitive activity is detachment from material life, and this detachment is spontaneously enjoyed by the devotee firmly engaged in the Lord's service.

## TEXT 63

যথা তরোর্মূলনিষেচনেন
তৃপ্যন্তি তৎস্কন্ধভুজোপশাখাঃ ।
প্রাণোপহারাচ্চ যথেন্দ্রিয়াণাং
তথৈব সর্বার্হণমচ্যুতেজ্যা ॥ ৬৩ ॥

*yathā taror mūla-niṣecanena*
*tṛpyanti tat-skandha-bhujopaśākhāḥ*
*tṛpyanti tat-skandha-bhujopaśākahāḥ*
*prāṇopahārāc ca yathendriyāṇāṁ*
*tathaiva sarvārhaṇam acyutejyā*

## SYNONYMS

*yathā*—as; *taroḥ*—of a tree; *mūla*—on the root; *niṣecanena*—by pouring water; *tṛpyanti*—are satisfied; *tat*—of the tree; *skandha*—trunk; *bhuja*—branches; *upaśākhāḥ*—sub-branches; *prāṇa*—to the living force; *upahārāt*—from offering food; *ca*—also; *yathā*—as; *indriyāṇām*—of all the senses; *tathā*—similarly; *eva*—indeed; *sarva*—of all; *arhaṇam*—worship; *acyuta*—of the Supreme Personality of Godhead; *ijyā*—worship.

### TRANSLATION

**" 'By pouring water on the root of a tree, one automatically satisfies the trunk, branches and twigs. Similarly, by supplying food to the stomach, where it nourishes the life air, one satisfies all the senses. In the same way, by worshiping Kṛṣṇa and rendering Him service, one automatically satisfies all the demigods.'**

### PURPORT

This is a quotation from *Śrīmad-Bhāgavatam* (4.31.14).

### TEXT 64

শ্রদ্ধাবান্ জন হয় ভক্তি-অধিকারী ।
'উত্তম', 'মধ্যম', 'কনিষ্ঠ'—শ্রদ্ধা-অনুসারী ॥ ৬৪ ॥

*śraddhāvān jana haya bhakti-adhikārī*
*'uttama', 'madhyama', 'kaniṣṭha'——śraddhā-anusārī*

### SYNONYMS

*śraddhāvān jana*—a person with faith; *haya*—is; *bhakti-adhikārī*—eligible for discharging transcendental loving service to the Lord; *uttama*—first class; *madhyama*—intermediate; *kaniṣṭha*—the lowest class; *śraddhā-anusārī*—according to the proportion of faith.

### TRANSLATION

**"A faithful devotee is a truly eligible candidate for the loving service of the Lord. According to one's faith, one is classified as a topmost devotee, an intermediate devotee or an inferior devotee.**

### PURPORT

The word *śraddhāvān* (faithful) means understanding Kṛṣṇa to be the *summum bonum,* the eternal truth and absolute transcendence. If one has full faith in Kṛṣṇa and confidence in Him, one becomes eligible to discharge devotional service confidentially. According to one's faith, one is a topmost, intermediate or inferior devotee.

### TEXT 65

শাস্ত্রযুক্ত্যে সুনিপুণ, দৃঢ়শ্রদ্ধা যাঁর ।
'উত্তম-অধিকারী' সেই তারয়ে সংসার ॥ ৬৫ ॥

*śāstra-yuktye sunipuṇa, dṛḍha-śraddhā yāṅra*
*'uttama-adhikārī' sei tāraye saṁsāra*

### SYNONYMS

*śāstra-yuktye*—in argument and logic; *su-nipuṇa*—very expert; *dṛḍha-śraddhā*—firm faith and confidence in Kṛṣṇa; *yāṅra*—whose; *uttama-adhikārī*—the topmost devotee; *sei*—he; *tāraye saṁsāra*—can deliver the whole world.

### TRANSLATION

**"One who is expert in logic, argument and the revealed scriptures and who has firm faith in Kṛṣṇa is classified as a topmost devotee. He can deliver the whole world.**

### TEXT 66

শাস্ত্রে যুক্তৌ চ নিপুণঃ সর্বথা দৃঢ়নিশ্চয়ঃ ।
প্রৌঢ়শ্রদ্ধোঽধিকারী যঃ স ভক্তাবুত্তমো মতঃ ॥ ৬৬ ॥

*śāstre yuktau ca nipuṇaḥ*
*sarvathā dṛḍha-niścayaḥ*
*prauḍha-śraddho 'dhikārī yaḥ*
*sa bhaktāv uttamo mataḥ*

### SYNONYMS

*śāstre*—in the revealed scriptures; *yuktau*—in logic; *ca*—also; *nipuṇaḥ*—expert; *sarvathā*—in all respects; *dṛḍha-niścayaḥ*—who is firmly convinced; *prauḍha*—deep; *śraddhaḥ*—who has faith; *adhikārī*—eligible; *yaḥ*—who; *saḥ*—he; *bhaktau*—in devotional service; *uttamaḥ*—highest; *mataḥ*—is considered.

### TRANSLATION

**" 'One who is expert in logic and understanding of revealed scriptures, and who always has firm conviction and deep faith that is not blind, is to be considered a topmost devotee in devotional service.'**

### PURPORT

This verse appears in the *Bhakti-rasāmṛta-sindhu* (1.2.17) by Śrīla Rūpa Gosvāmī.

### TEXT 67

শাস্ত্র-যুক্তি নাহি জানে দৃঢ়, শ্রদ্ধাবান্ ।
'মধ্যম-অধিকারী' সেই মহা-ভাগ্যবান্ ॥ ৬৭ ॥

*śāstra-yukti nāhi jāne dṛḍha, śraddhāvān*
*'madhyama-adhikārī' sei mahā-bhāgyavān*

### SYNONYMS

*śāstra-yukti*—logical arguments on the basis of revealed scripture; *nāhi*—not; *jāne*—knows; *dṛḍha*—firmly; *śraddhāvān*—faithful; *madhyama-adhikārī*—second-class devotee; *sei*—he; *mahā-bhāgyavān*—very fortunate.

### TRANSLATION

**"One who is not very expert in argument and logic based on revealed scriptures but who has firm faith is considered a second-class devotee. He also must be considered most fortunate.**

### TEXT 68

যঃ শাস্ত্রাদিষ্বনিপুণঃ শ্রদ্ধাবান্ স তু মধ্যমঃ ॥ ৬৮ ॥

*yaḥ śāstrādiṣv anipuṇaḥ*
*śraddhāvān sa tu madhyamaḥ*

### SYNONYMS

*yaḥ*—anyone who; *śāstra-ādiṣu*—in the revealed scriptures; *anipuṇaḥ*—not very expert; *śraddhāvān*—full of faith; *saḥ*—he; *tu*—certainly; *madhyamaḥ*—second-class or middle-class devotee.

### TRANSLATION

**" 'He who does not know scriptural argument very well but who has firm faith is called an intermediate or second-class devotee.'**

### PURPORT

This verse appears in the *Bhakti-rasāmṛta-sindhu* (1.2.18).

### TEXT 69

**যাহার কোমল শ্রদ্ধা, সে 'কনিষ্ঠ' জন ।**
**ক্রমে ক্রমে তেঁহো ভক্ত হইবে 'উত্তম' ॥ ৬৯ ॥**

*yāhāra komala śraddhā, se 'kaniṣṭha' jana*
*krame krame teṅho bhakta ha-ibe 'uttama'*

### SYNONYMS

*yāhāra*—whose; *komala śraddhā*—soft faith; *se*—such a person; *kaniṣṭha jana*—a neophyte devotee; *krame krame*—by a gradual progression; *teṅho*—he; *bhakta*—devotee; *ha-ibe*—will become; *uttama*—first class.

### TRANSLATION

**"One whose faith is soft and pliable is called a neophyte, but by gradually following the process, he will rise to the platform of a first-class devotee.**

## TEXT 70

যো ভবেৎ কোমলশ্রদ্ধঃ স কনিষ্ঠো নিগদ্যতে ॥ ৭০ ॥

*yo bhavet komala-śraddhaḥ*
*sa kaniṣṭho nigadyate*

### SYNONYMS

*yaḥ*—anyone who; *bhavet*—may be; *komala*—soft; *śraddhaḥ*—having faith; *saḥ*—such a person; *kaniṣṭhaḥ*—neophyte devotee; *nigadyate*—is said to be.

### TRANSLATION

**" 'One whose faith is not very strong, who is just beginning, should be considered a neophyte devotee.'**

### PURPORT

This verse also appears in the *Bhakti-rasāmṛta-sindhu* (1.2.19).

## TEXT 71

**রতি-প্রেম-তারতম্যে ভক্ত—তর-তম ।**
**একাদশ স্কন্ধে তার করিয়াছে লক্ষণ ॥ ৭১ ॥**

*rati-prema-tāratamye bhakta——tara-tama*
*ekādaśa skandhe tāra kariyāche lakṣaṇa*

### SYNONYMS

*rati*—of attachment; *prema*—and love; *tāratamye*—by comparison; *bhakta*—devotee; *tara-tama*—superior and superlative; *ekādaśa skandhe*—in the Eleventh Canto of *Śrīmad-Bhāgavatam; tāra*—of him; *kariyāche*—has made; *lakṣaṇa*—symptoms.

## TRANSLATION

**"A devotee is considered superlative and superior according to his attachment and love. In the Eleventh Canto of Śrīmad-Bhāgavatam, the following symptoms have been ascertained.**

## PURPORT

Śrīla Bhaktivinoda Ṭhākura has stated that if one has developed faith in Kṛṣṇa consciousness, he is to be considered an eligible candidate for further advancement in Kṛṣṇa consciousness. Those who have faith are divided into three categories—*uttama, madhyama* and *kaniṣṭha* (first-class, second-class and neophyte). A first-class devotee has firm conviction in the revealed scriptures and is expert in arguing according to the *śāstras.* He is firmly convinced of the science of Kṛṣṇa consciousness. The *madhyama-adhikārī,* or second-class devotee, has firm conviction in Kṛṣṇa consciousness, but he cannot support his conviction by citing śāstric references. The neophyte devotee does not yet have firm faith. In this way the devotees are typed.

The standard of devotion is also categorized in the same way. A neophyte believes that only love of Kṛṣṇa or Kṛṣṇa consciousness is very good, but he may not know the basis of pure Kṛṣṇa consciousness or how one can become a perfect devotee. Sometimes in the heart of a neophyte there is attraction for *karma, jñāna* or *yoga.* When he is free and transcendental to mixed devotional activity, he becomes a second-class devotee. When he becomes expert in logic and can refer to the *śāstras,* he becomes a first-class devotee. The devotees are also described as positive, comparative and superlative, in terms of their love and attachment for Kṛṣṇa.

It should be understood that a *madhyama-adhikārī,* a second-class devotee, is fully convinced of Kṛṣṇa consciousness but cannot support his convictions with śāstric reference. A neophyte may fall down by associating with nondevotees because he is not firmly convinced and strongly situated. The second-class devotee, even though he cannot support his position with śāstric reference, can gradually become a first-class devotee by studying the *śāstras* and associating with a first-class devotee. However, if the second-class devotee does not advance himself by associating with a first-class devotee, he makes no progress. There is no possibility that a first-class devotee will fall down, even though he may mix with nondevotees to preach. Conviction and faith gradually increase to make one an *uttama-adhikārī,* a first-class devotee.

## TEXT 72

সর্বভূতেষু যঃ পশ্যেদ্ভগবদ্ভাবমাত্মনঃ ।
ভূতানি ভগবত্যাত্মন্যেষ ভাগবতোত্তমঃ ॥ ৭২ ॥

*sarva-bhūteṣu yaḥ paśyed*
*bhagavad-bhāvam ātmanaḥ*
*bhūtāni bhagavaty ātmany*
*eṣa bhāgavatottamaḥ*

## SYNONYMS

*sarva-bhūteṣu*—in all objects (in matter, spirit, and combinations of matter and spirit); *yaḥ*—anyone who; *paśyet*—sees; *bhagavat-bhāvam*—the ability to be engaged in the service of the Lord; *ātmanaḥ*—of the supreme spirit soul or the transcendence beyond the material conception of life; *bhūtāni*—all beings; *bhagavati*—in the Supreme Personality of Godhead; *ātmani*—the basic principle of all existence; *eṣaḥ*—this; *bhāgavata-uttamaḥ*—a person advanced in devotional service.

## TRANSLATION

**" 'A person advanced in devotional service sees within everything the soul of souls, the Supreme Personality of Godhead, Śrī Kṛṣṇa. Consequently he always sees the form of the Supreme Personality of Godhead as the cause of all causes and understands that all things are situated in Him.**

## PURPORT

This is a quotation from *Śrīmad-Bhāgavatam* (11.2.45).

## TEXT 73

ঈশ্বরে তদধীনেষু বালিশেষু দ্বিষৎসু চ।
প্রেম-মৈত্রী-কৃপোপেক্ষা যঃ করোতি স মধ্যমঃ ॥ ৭৩ ॥

*īśvare tad-adhīneṣu*
*bāliśeṣu dviṣatsu ca*
*prema-maitrī-kṛpopekṣā*
*yaḥ karoti sa madhyamaḥ*

## SYNONYMS

*īśvare*—unto the Supreme Personality of Godhead; *tat-adhīneṣu*—to persons who have taken fully to Kṛṣṇa consciousness; *bāliśeṣu*—unto the neophytes or the ignorant; *dviṣatsu*—to persons envious of Kṛṣṇa and the devotees of Kṛṣṇa; *prema*—love; *maitrī*—friendship; *kṛpā*—mercy; *upekṣā*—negligence; *yaḥ*—anyone who; *karoti*—does; *saḥ*—he; *madhyamaḥ*—a second-class devotee.

### TRANSLATION

**" 'An intermediate, second-class devotee shows love for the Supreme Personality of Godhead, is friendly to all devotees and is very merciful to neophytes and ignorant people. The intermediate devotee neglects those who are envious of devotional service.**

### PURPORT

This is a quotation from *Śrīmad-Bhāgavatam* (11.2.46). This statement was made by the great sage Nārada while he was speaking to Vasudeva about devotional service. This subject was originally discussed between Nimi, the King of Videha, and the nine Yogendras.

### TEXT 74

অর্চায়ামেব হরয়ে পূজাং যঃ শ্রদ্ধয়েহতে ।
ন তদ্ভক্তেষু চান্যেষু স ভক্তঃ প্রাকৃতঃ স্মৃতঃ ॥ ৭৪ ॥

*arcāyām eva haraye*
*pūjāṁ yaḥ śraddhayehate*
*na tad-bhakteṣu cānyeṣu*
*sa bhaktaḥ prākṛtaḥ smṛtaḥ*

### SYNONYMS

*arcāyām*—in the temple worship; *eva*—certainly; *haraye*—for the pleasure of the Supreme Personality of Godhead; *pūjām*—worship; *yaḥ*—anyone who; *śraddhayā*—with faith and love; *īhate*—executes; *na*—not; *tat-bhakteṣu*—to the devotees of the Lord; *ca anyeṣu*—and to others; *saḥ*—he; *bhaktaḥ*—a devotee; *prākṛtaḥ*—materialistic; *smṛtaḥ*—is considered.

### TRANSLATION

**" 'A prākṛta, or materialistic devotee does not purposefully study the śāstra and try to understand the actual standard of pure devotional service. Consequently he does not show proper respect to advanced devotees. He may, however, follow the regulative principles learned from his spiritual master or from his family who worships the Deity. He is to be considered on the material platform, although he is trying to advance in devotional service. Such a person is a bhakta-prāya [neophyte devotee], or bhaktābhāsa, for he is a little enlightened by Vaiṣṇava philosophy.'**

## PURPORT

This verse is from *Śrīmad-Bhāgavatam* (11.2.47). Śrīla Bhaktivinoda Ṭhākura says that one who has full love for the Supreme Personality of Godhead and who maintains a good friendship with the Lord's devotees is always callous to those who envy Kṛṣṇa and Kṛṣṇa's devotees. Such a person is to be considered an intermediate devotee. He becomes a first-class devotee when, in the course of advancing in devotional service, he feels an intimate relationship with all living entities, seeing them as part and parcel of the Supreme Person.

## TEXT 75

**সর্ব মহা-গুণগণ বৈষ্ণব-শরীরে ।**
**কৃষ্ণভক্তে কৃষ্ণের গুণ সকলি সঞ্চারে ॥ ৭৫ ॥**

*sarva mahā-guṇa-gaṇa vaiṣṇava-śarīre*
*kṛṣṇa-bhakte kṛṣṇera guṇa sakali sañcāre*

## SYNONYMS

*sarva*—all; *mahā*—great; *guṇa-gaṇa*—transcendental qualities; *vaiṣṇava-śarīre*—in the bodies of Vaiṣṇavas; *kṛṣṇa-bhakte*—in the devotees of Lord Kṛṣṇa; *kṛṣṇera*—of Lord Kṛṣṇa; *guṇa*—the qualities; *sakali*—all; *sañcāre*—appear.

## TRANSLATION

**"A Vaiṣṇava is one who has developed all good transcendental qualities. All the good qualities of Kṛṣṇa gradually develop in Kṛṣṇa's devotee.**

## TEXT 76

যস্যাস্তি ভক্তির্ভগবত্যকিঞ্চনা
সর্বৈর্গুণৈস্তত্র সমাসতে সুরাঃ ।
হরাবভক্তস্য কুতো মহদ্‌গুণা
মনোরথেনাসতি ধাবতো বহিঃ ॥ ৭৬ ॥

*yasyāsti bhaktir bhagavaty akiñcanā*
*sarvair guṇais tatra samāsate surāḥ*
*harāv abhaktasya kuto mahad-guṇā*
*mano-rathenāsati dhāvato bahiḥ*

## SYNONYMS

*yasya*—of whom; *asti*—there is; *bhaktiḥ*—devotional service; *bhagavati*—unto the Supreme Personality of Godhead; *akiñcanā*—without material desires; *sarvaiḥ*—all; *guṇaiḥ*—with good qualities; *tatra*—there; *samāsate*—live; *surāḥ*—the demigods; *harau*—unto the Lord; *abhaktasya*—of the nondevotee; *kutaḥ*—where; *mahat-guṇāḥ*—the high qualities; *manaḥ-rathena*—by mental concoction; *asati*—to temporary material happiness; *dhāvataḥ*—running; *bahiḥ*—externally.

## TRANSLATION

**" 'In one who has unflinching devotional faith in Kṛṣṇa, all the good qualities of Kṛṣṇa and the demigods are consistently manifest. However, he who has no devotion to the Supreme Personality of Godhead has no good qualifications because he is engaged by mental concoction in material existence, which is the external feature of the Lord.'**

## PURPORT

This was spoken by Bhadraśravā and his followers, who were offering prayers to Nṛsiṁhadeva (*Śrīmad-Bhāgavatam* 5.18.12).

## TEXT 77

সেই সব গুণ হয় বৈষ্ণব-লক্ষণ ।
সব কহা না যায়, করি দিগ্‌দরশন ॥ ৭৭ ॥

*sei saba guṇa haya vaiṣṇava-lakṣaṇa*
*saba kahā nā yāya, kari dig-daraśana*

## SYNONYMS

*sei saba guṇa*—all those transcendental qualities; *haya*—are; *vaiṣṇava-lakṣaṇa*—the symptoms of a Vaiṣṇava; *saba*—all; *kahā nā yāya*—cannot be explained; *kari*—I shall do; *dik-daraśana*—a general review.

## TRANSLATION

**"All these transcendental qualities are the characteristics of pure Vaiṣṇavas, and they cannot be fully explained, but I shall try to point out some of the important qualities.**

## TEXTS 78-80

কৃপালু, অকৃতদ্রোহ, সত্যসার সম ।
নিদোষ, বদান্য, মৃদু, শুচি, অকিঞ্চন ॥ ৭৮ ॥

সর্বোপকারক, শান্ত, কৃষ্ণৈকশরণ ।
অকাম, অনীহ, স্থির, বিজিত-ষড়্গুণ ॥ ৭৯ ॥
মিতভুক্, অপ্রমত্ত, মানদ, অমানী ।
গম্ভীর, করুণ, মৈত্র, কবি, দক্ষ, মৌনী ॥ ৮০ ॥

*kṛpālu, akṛta-droha, satya-sāra sama*
*nidoṣa, vadānya, mṛdu, śuci, akiñcana*

*sarvopakāraka, śānta, kṛṣṇaika-śaraṇa*
*akāma, anīha, sthira, vijita-ṣaḍ-guṇa*

*mita-bhuk, apramatta, mānada, amānī*
*gambhīra, karuṇa, maitra, kavi, dakṣa, maunī*

### SYNONYMS

*kṛpālu*—merciful; *akṛta-droha*—not defiant; *satya-sāra*—thoroughly true; *sama*—equal; *nidoṣa*—faultless; *vadānya*—magnanimous; *mṛdu*—mild; *śuci*—clean; *akiñcana*—without material possessions; *sarva-upakāraka*—working for the welfare of everyone; *śānta*—peaceful; *kṛṣṇa-eka-śaraṇa*—exclusively surrendered to Kṛṣṇa; *akāma*—desireless; *anīha*—indifferent to material acquisitions; *sthira*—fixed; *vijita-ṣaṭ-guṇa*—completely controlling the six bad qualities (lust, anger, greed, etc.); *mita-bhuk*—eating only as much as required; *apramatta*—without inebriation; *māna-da*—respectful; *amānī*—without false prestige; *gambhīra*—grave; *karuṇa*—compassionate; *maitra*—a friend; *kavi*—a poet; *dakṣa*—expert; *maunī*—silent.

### TRANSLATION

**"Devotees are always merciful, humble, truthful, equal to all, faultless, magnanimous, mild and clean. They are without material possessions, and they perform welfare work for everyone. They are peaceful, surrendered to Kṛṣṇa and desireless. They are indifferent to material acquisitions and are fixed in devotional service. They completely control the six bad qualities—lust, anger, greed and so forth. They eat only as much as required, and they are not inebriated. They are respectful, grave, compassionate and without false prestige. They are friendly, poetic, expert and silent.**

### TEXT 81

তিতিক্ষবঃ কারুণিকাঃ সুহৃদঃ সর্বদেহিনাম্ ।
অজাতশত্রবঃ শান্তাঃ সাধবঃ সাধুভূষণাঃ ॥ ৮১ ॥

*titikṣavaḥ kāruṇikāḥ*
*suhṛdaḥ sarva-dehinām*
*ajāta-śatravaḥ śāntāḥ*
*sādhavaḥ sādhu-bhūṣaṇāḥ*

### SYNONYMS

*titikṣavaḥ*—very forebearing; *kāruṇikāḥ*—merciful; *suhṛdaḥ*—who are well-wishers; *sarva-dehinām*—to all living entities; *ajāta-śatravaḥ*—without enemies; *śāntāḥ*—peaceful; *sādhavaḥ*—following the injunctions of the *śāstra; sādhu-bhūṣaṇāḥ*—who are decorated with good character.

### TRANSLATION

**" 'Devotees are always tolerant, forebearing and very merciful. They are the well-wishers of every living entity. They follow the scriptural injunctions, and because they have no enemies, they are very peaceful. These are the decorations of devotees.'**

### PURPORT

This is a quotation from *Śrīmad-Bhāgavatam* (3.25.21). When the sages, headed by Śaunaka, inquired about Kapiladeva, the incarnation of Godhead, Suta Gosvāmī, who was the topmost devotee of the Lord, quoted talks about self-realization between Maitreya, a friend of Vyāsadeva, and Vidura. It was then that the topic of Lord Kapila came up and His discussions with His mother, wherein He stated that attachment to material things is the cause of conditional life. When a person becomes attached to transcendental things, he is on the path of liberation.

### TEXT 82

মহৎসেবাং দ্বারমাহুর্বিমুক্তে-
স্তমোদ্বারং যোষিতাং সঙ্গিসঙ্গম্ ।
মহান্তস্তে সমচিত্তাঃ প্রশান্তা
বিমন্যবঃ সুহৃদঃ সাধবো যে ॥ ৮২ ॥

*mahat-sevāṁ dvāram āhur vimuktes*
*tamo-dvāraṁ yoṣitāṁ saṅgi-saṅgam*
*mahāntas te sama-cittāḥ praśāntā*
*vimanyavaḥ suhṛdaḥ sādhavo ye*

### SYNONYMS

*mahat-sevām*—the service of the pure devotee spiritual master; *dvāram*—door; *āhuḥ*—they said; *vimukteḥ*—of liberation; *tamaḥ-dvāram*—the door to darkness; *yoṣitām*—of women and money; *saṅgi-saṅgam*—association with those who enjoy the association; *mahāntaḥ*—great souls; *te*—they; *sama-cittāḥ*—equally disposed to all; *praśāntāḥ*—very peaceful; *vimanyavaḥ*—without anger; *suhṛdaḥ*—well-wishers of everyone; *sādhavaḥ*—who are endowed with all good qualities, or who do not look for faults in others; *ye*—those who.

### TRANSLATION

**" 'It is the verdict of all śāstras and great personalities that by serving a pure devotee, one attains the path of liberation. However, by associating with materialistic people who are attached to material enjoyment and women, one attains the path of darkness. Those who are actually devotees are broadminded, equal to everyone and very peaceful. They never become angry, and they are friendly to all living entities.'**

### PURPORT

This verse is from *Śrīmad-Bhāgavatam* (5.5.2).

### TEXT 83

*kṛṣṇa-bhakti-janma-mūla haya 'sādhu-saṅga'*
*kṛṣṇa-prema janme, teṅho punaḥ mukhya aṅga*

### SYNONYMS

*kṛṣṇa-bhakti*—of devotional service to Kṛṣṇa; *janma-mūla*—the root cause; *haya*—is; *sādhu-saṅga*—association with advanced devotees; *kṛṣṇa-prema*—love of Kṛṣṇa; *janme*—awakens; *teṅho*—that same association with devotees; *punaḥ*—again; *mukhya aṅga*—the chief principle.

### TRANSLATION

**"The root cause of devotional service to Lord Kṛṣṇa is association with advanced devotees. Even when one's dormant love for Kṛṣṇa awakens, association with devotees is still most essential.**

### TEXT 84

ভবাপবর্গো ভ্রমতো যদা ভবে-
জ্জনস্য তর্হ্যচ্যুত সৎসমাগমঃ ।

সৎসঙ্গমো যর্হি তদৈব সদ্গতৌ
পরাবরেশে ত্বয়ি জায়তে রতিঃ ॥ ৮৪ ॥

*bhavāpavargo bhramato yadā bhavej*
*janasya tarhy acyuta sat-samāgamaḥ*
*sat-saṅgamo yarhi tadaiva sad-gatau*
*parāvareśe tvayi jāyate ratiḥ*

## SYNONYMS

*bhava-apavargaḥ*—liberation from the nescience of material existence; *bhramataḥ*—wandering; *yadā*—when; *bhavet*—should be; *janasya*—of a person; *tarhi*—at that time; *acyuta*—O Supreme Personality of Godhead; *sat-samāgamaḥ*—association with devotees; *sat-saṅgamaḥ*—association with the devotees; *yarhi*—when; *tadā*—at that time; *eva*—only; *sat-gatau*—the highest goal of life; *parāvareśe*—the Lord of the universe; *tvayi*—to You; *jāyate*—appears; *ratiḥ*—attraction.

## TRANSLATION

**"'O my Lord! O infallible Supreme Person! When a person wandering throughout the universes becomes eligible for liberation from material existence, he gets an opportunity to associate with devotees. When he associates with devotees, his attraction for You is awakened. You are the Supreme Personality of Godhead, the highest goal of the supreme devotees and the Lord of the universe.'**

## PURPORT

This is a quotation from *Śrīmad-Bhāgavatam* (10.51.53).

## TEXT 85

অত আত্যন্তিকং ক্ষেমং পৃচ্ছামো ভবতোঽনঘাঃ ।
সংসারেঽস্মিন্ ক্ষণার্ধোঽপি সৎসঙ্গঃ সেবধির্নৃণাম্ ॥ ৮৫ ॥

*ata ātyantikaṁ kṣemaṁ*
*pṛcchāmo bhavato 'naghāḥ*
*saṁsāre 'smin kṣaṇārdho 'pi*
*sat-saṅgaḥ sevadhir nṛṇām*

## SYNONYMS

*ataḥ*—therefore (due to the rareness of seeing pure devotees of the Lord); *ātyantikam*—supreme; *kṣemam*—auspiciousness; *pṛcchāmaḥ*—we are asking;

*bhavataḥ*—you; *anaghāḥ*—O sinless ones; *saṁsāre*—in the material world; *asmin*—this; *kṣaṇa-ardhaḥ*—lasting half a moment; *api*—even; *sat-saṅgaḥ*—association with devotees; *sevadhiḥ*—a treasure; *nṛṇām*—for human society.

### TRANSLATION

**" 'O devotees! O you who are free from all sins! Let me inquire from you about that which is supremely auspicious for all living entities. Association with a pure devotee for even half a moment in this material world is the greatest treasure for human society.'**

### PURPORT

This is a quotation from *Śrīmad-Bhāgavatam* (11.2.30).

### TEXT 86

সতাং প্রসঙ্গান্মম বীর্যসম্বিদো

ভবন্তি হৃৎকর্ণরসায়নাঃ কথাঃ ।

তজ্জোষণাদাশ্বপবর্গবর্ত্মনি

শ্রদ্ধা রতির্ভক্তিরনুক্রমিষ্যতি ॥ ৮৬ ॥

*satāṁ prasaṅgān mama vīrya-saṁvido*
*bhavanti hṛt-karṇa-rasāyanāḥ kathāḥ*
*taj-joṣaṇād āśv apavarga-vartmani*
*śraddhā ratir bhaktir anukramiṣyati*

### SYNONYMS

*satām*—of the devotees; *prasaṅgāt*—by the intimate association; *mama*—of Me; *vīrya-saṁvidaḥ*—talks full of spiritual potency; *bhavanti*—appear; *hṛt*—to the heart; *karṇa*—and to the ears; *rasa-āyanāḥ*—a source of sweetness; *kathāḥ*—talks; *tat*—of them; *joṣaṇāt*—from proper cultivation; *āśu*—quickly; *apavarga*—of liberation; *vartmani*—on the path; *śraddhā*—faith; *ratiḥ*—attraction; *bhaktiḥ*—love; *anukramiṣyati*—will follow one after another.

### TRANSLATION

**" 'The spiritually powerful message of Godhead can be properly discussed only in a society of devotees, and it is greatly pleasing to hear in that association. If one hears from devotees, the way of transcendental experience quickly opens, and gradually one attains firm faith that in due course develops into attraction and devotion.'**

### PURPORT

This is a quotation from *Śrīmad-Bhāgavatam* (3.25.25). For an explanation see *Ādi-līlā* (1.60).

### TEXT 87

**অসৎসঙ্গত্যাগ,—এই বৈষ্ণব-আচার ।**
**'স্ত্রীসঙ্গী'—এক অসাধু, কৃষ্ণাভক্ত' আর ॥ ৮৭ ॥**

*asat-saṅga-tyāga,——ei vaiṣṇava-ācāra*
*'strī-saṅgī'——eka asādhu, 'kṛṣṇābhakta' āra*

### SYNONYMS

*asat-saṅga-tyāga*—rejection of the association of nondevotees; *ei*—this; *vaiṣṇava-ācāra*—the behavior of a Vaiṣṇava; *strī-saṅgī*—who associates with women for sense gratification; *eka*—one; *asādhu*—unsaintly person; *kṛṣṇa-abhakta*—one who is not a devotee of Lord Kṛṣṇa; *āra*—another.

### TRANSLATION

**"A Vaiṣṇava should always avoid the association of ordinary people. Common people are very much materially attached, especially to women. Vaiṣṇavas should also avoid the company of those who are not devotees of Lord Kṛṣṇa.**

### TEXTS 88-90

সত্যং শৌচং দয়া মৌনং বুদ্ধির্হ্রীঃ শ্রীর্যশঃ ক্ষমা ।
শমো দমো ভগশ্চেতি যৎসঙ্গাদ্যাতি সংক্ষয়ম্ ॥ ৮৮ ॥
তেষ্বশান্তেষু মূঢ়েষু খণ্ডিতাত্মস্বসাধুষু ।
সঙ্গং ন কুর্যাচ্ছোচ্যেষু যোষিৎক্রীড়ামৃগেষু চ ॥ ৮৯ ॥
ন তথাস্য ভবেন্মোহো বন্ধশ্চান্যপ্রসঙ্গতঃ ।
যোষিৎসঙ্গাদ্যথা পুংসো যথা তৎসঙ্গিসঙ্গতঃ ॥ ৯০ ॥

*satyaṁ śaucaṁ dayā maunaṁ*
*buddhir hrīḥ śrīr yaśaḥ kṣamā*
*śamo damo bhagaś ceti*
*yat-saṅgād yāti saṅkṣayam*

*teṣv aśānteṣu mūḍheṣu*
*khaṇḍitātmasv asādhuṣu*
*saṅgaṁ na kuryāc chocyeṣu*
*yoṣit-krīḍā-mṛgeṣu ca*

*na tathāsya bhaven moho*
*bandhaś cānya-prasaṅgataḥ*
*yoṣit-saṅgād yathā puṁso*
*yathā tat-saṅgi-saṅgataḥ*

## SYNONYMS

*satyam*—truthfulness; *śaucam*—cleanliness; *dayā*—mercy; *maunam*—silence; *buddhiḥ*—intelligence; *hrīḥ*—modesty; *śrīḥ*—beauty; *yaśaḥ*—fame; *kṣamā*—forgiveness; *śamaḥ*—controlling the mind; *damaḥ*—controlling the senses; *bhagaḥ*—opulence; *ca*—and; *iti*—thus; *yat*—of whom; *saṅgāt*—by the association; *yāti*—goes to; *saṅkṣayam*—complete destruction; *teṣu*—among them; *aśānteṣu*—who are restless; *mūḍheṣu*—among the fools; *khaṇḍita-ātmasu*—whose self-realization is spoiled; *asādhuṣu*—not saintly; *saṅgam*—association; *na*—not; *kuryāt*—should do; *śocyeṣu*—who are full of lamentation; *yoṣit*—of women; *krīḍā-mṛgeṣu*—who are like toy animals; *ca*—also; *na*—not; *tathā*—so much; *asya*—of him; *bhavet*—there may be; *mohaḥ*—illusion; *bandhaḥ*—binding; *ca*—and; *anya*—other types; *prasaṅgataḥ*—from association; *yoṣit-saṅgāt*—by association with women; *yathā*—as; *puṁsaḥ*—of the man; *yathā*—as well as; *tat-saṅgi-saṅgataḥ*—by association with persons attached to women.

## TRANSLATION

**" 'By association with worldly people, one becomes devoid of truthfulness, cleanliness, mercy, gravity, spiritual intelligence, shyness, austerity, fame, forgiveness, control of the mind, control of the senses, fortune and all opportunities. One should not at any time associate with a coarse fool who is bereft of the knowledge of self-realization and who is no more than a toy animal in the hands of a woman. The illusion and bondage that accrue to a man from attachment to any other object are not as complete as that resulting from association with a woman or with men too attached to women.'**

## PURPORT

These verses, quoted from *Śrīmad-Bhāgavatam* (3.31.33-35), were spoken by Kapiladeva, an incarnation of the Supreme Personality of Godhead, to His mother. Herein Kapiladeva discusses pious and impious activities and the symptoms of those who are devoid of devotional service to Kṛṣṇa. Generally people do not know about the miserable conditions within the womb of a mother in any species of life. Due to bad association, one gradually falls into lower species. Association with women is greatly stressed in this regard. When one becomes attached to women or to those who are attached to women, one falls down into the lower species.

*puruṣaḥ prakṛti-stho hi*
*bhuṅkte prakṛti-jān guṇān*
*kāraṇaṁ guṇa-saṅgo 'sya*
*sad-asad-yoni-janmasu*

"The living entity in material nature thus follows the ways of life, enjoying the three modes of nature. This is due to his association with that material nature. Thus he meets with good and evil among various species." (*Bhagavad-gītā* 13.22)

According to Vedic civilization, one's association with women should be very much restricted. In spiritual life there are four *āśramas—brahmacarya, gṛhastha, vānaprastha* and *sannyāsa.* The *brahmacārī, vānaprastha* and *sannyāsī* are completely forbidden to associate with women. Only *gṛhasthas* are allowed to associate with women under certain very restricted conditions—that is, one associates with women to propagate nice children. Other reasons for association are condemned.

## TEXT 91

বরং হুতবহজ্বালা-পঞ্জরান্তর্ব্যবস্থিতিঃ ।
ন শৌরিচিন্তাবিমুখ-জনসংবাসবৈশসম্ ॥ ৯১ ॥

*varaṁ huta-vaha-jvālā-*
*pañjarāntar-vyavasthitiḥ*
*na śauri-cintā-vimukha-*
*jana-saṁvāsa-vaiśasam*

## SYNONYMS

*varam*—better; *huta-vaha*—of fire; *jvālā*—in the flames; *pañjara-antaḥ*—inside a cage; *vyavasthitiḥ*—abiding; *na*—not; *śauri-cintā*—of Kṛṣṇa consciousness, or thought of Kṛṣṇa; *vimukha*—bereft; *jana*—of persons; *saṁvāsa*—of the association; *vaiśasam*—the calamity.

## TRANSLATION

**" 'It is better to accept the miseries of being encaged within bars and surrounded by burning flames than to associate with those bereft of Kṛṣṇa consciousness. Such association is a very great hardship.'**

## PURPORT

This is a quotation from the *Kātyāyana-saṁhitā.*

### TEXT 92

মা দ্রাক্ষীঃ ক্ষীণপুণ্যান্ ক্বচিদপি
ভগবদ্ভক্তিহীনান্ মনুষ্যান্ ॥ ৯২ ॥

*mā drākṣīḥ kṣīṇa-puṇyān kvacid api*
*bhagavad-bhakti-hīnān manuṣyān*

### SYNONYMS

*mā*—do not; *drākṣīḥ*—see; *kṣīṇa-puṇyān*—who are bereft of all piety; *kvacit api*—at any time; *bhagavat-bhakti-hīnān*—who are bereft of Kṛṣṇa consciousness and devotional service; *manuṣyān*—persons.

### TRANSLATION

**" One should not even see those who are bereft of devotional service in Kṛṣṇa consciousness and who are therefore devoid of pious activities.**

### TEXT 93

এত সব ছাড়ি' আর বর্ণাশ্রম-ধর্ম ।
অকিঞ্চন হঞা লয় কৃষ্ণৈক-শরণ ॥ ৯৩ ॥

*eta saba chāḍi' āra varṇāśrama-dharma*
*akiñcana hañā laya kṛṣṇaika-śaraṇa*

### SYNONYMS

*eta saba*—all these; *chāḍi'*—giving up; *āra*—and; *varṇa-āśrama-dharma*—the regulative principle of four *varṇas* and four *āśramas; akiñcana*—without any attachment for anything material; *hañā*—becoming; *laya*—he takes; *kṛṣṇa-eka-śaraṇa*—exclusive shelter at the lotus feet of the Lord.

### TRANSLATION

**"Without hesitation, one should take the exclusive shelter of Lord Kṛṣṇa with full confidence, giving up bad association and even neglecting the regulative principles of the four varṇas and four āśramas. That is to say, one should abandon all material attachment.**

### TEXT 94

সর্বধর্মান্ পরিত্যজ্য মামেকং শরণং ব্রজ ।
অহং ত্বাং সর্বপাপেভ্যো মোক্ষয়িষ্যামি মা শুচঃ ॥ ৯৪ ॥

*sarva-dharmān parityajya*
*māṁ ekaṁ śaraṇaṁ vraja*
*ahaṁ tvāṁ sarva-pāpebhyo*
*mokṣayiṣyāmi mā śucaḥ*

## SYNONYMS

*sarva-dharmān*—all kinds of occupational duties; *parityajya*—giving up; *mām ekam*—unto Me only; *śaraṇam*—as shelter; *vraja*—go; *aham*—I; *tvām*—unto you; *sarva-pāpebhyaḥ*—from all the reactions of sinful life; *mokṣayiṣyāmi*—will give liberation; *mā*—don't; *śucaḥ*—worry.

## TRANSLATION

**" 'After giving up all kinds of religious and occupational duties, if you come to Me, the Supreme Personality of Godhead, and take shelter, I shall give you protection from all of life's sinful reactions. Do not worry.'**

## PURPORT

This is a quotation from *Bhagavad-gītā* (18.66) spoken by Lord Kṛṣṇa. For an explanation, refer to *Madhya-līlā* (8.63).

## TEXT 95

ভক্তবৎসল, কৃতজ্ঞ, সমর্থ, বদান্য ।
হেন কৃষ্ণ ছাড়ি' পণ্ডিত নাহি ভজে অন্য ॥ ৯৫ ॥

*bhakta-vatsala, kṛtajña, samartha, vadānya*
*hena kṛṣṇa chāḍi' paṇḍita nāhi bhaje anya*

## SYNONYMS

*bhakta-vatsala*—very kind to the devotees; *kṛta-jña*—grateful; *samartha*—full of all abilities; *vadānya*—magnanimous; *hena*—such; *kṛṣṇa*—Lord Kṛṣṇa; *chāḍi'*—giving up; *paṇḍita*—a learned man; *nāhi*—does not; *bhaje*—worship; *anya*—anyone else.

## TRANSLATION

**"Lord Kṛṣṇa is very kind to His devotees. He is always very grateful and magnanimous, and He possesses all abilities. A learned man does not give up Kṛṣṇa to worship anyone else.**

## PURPORT

An intelligent person gives up the company of those who are attached to women and bereft of Kṛṣṇa consciousness. One should be free from all kinds of material attachment and should take full shelter under the lotus feet of Kṛṣṇa. Kṛṣṇa is very kind to His devotees. He is always grateful, and He never forgets the service of a devotee. He is also completely opulent and all-powerful. Why, then, should one take shelter of a demigod and leave Lord Kṛṣṇa's shelter? If one worships a demigod and leaves Kṛṣṇa, he must be considered the lowest fool.

## TEXT 96

কঃ পণ্ডিতস্ত্বদপরং শরণং সমীয়া-
ভ্তক্তপ্রিয়াদৃতগিরঃ সুহৃদঃ কৃতজ্ঞাৎ ।
সর্বান্ দদাতি সুহৃদো ভজতোঽভিকামা-
নাত্মানমপ্যুপচয়াপচয়ৌ ন যস্য ॥ ৯৬ ॥

*kaḥ paṇḍitas tvad-aparaṁ śaraṇaṁ samīyād*
*bhakta-priyād ṛta-giraḥ suhṛdaḥ kṛtajñāt*
*sarvān dadāti suhṛdo bhajato 'bhikāmān*
*ātmānam apy upacayāpacayau na yasya*

## SYNONYMS

*kaḥ*—what; *paṇḍitaḥ*—learned man; *tvat-aparam*—other than Your Lordship; *śaraṇam*—shelter; *samīyāt*—would take; *bhakta-priyāt*—who are affectionate to Your devotees; *ṛta-giraḥ*—who are truthful to the devotees; *suhṛdaḥ*—who are the friend of the devotees; *kṛta-jñāt*—who are grateful to the devotees; *sarvān*—all; *dadāti*—gives; *suhṛdaḥ*—to Your well-wishers; *bhajataḥ*—who worship You by devotional service; *abhikāmān*—desires; *ātmānam*—Yourself; *api*—even; *upacaya*—increase; *apacayau*—and diminution; *na*—not; *yasya*—of whom.

## TRANSLATION

**" 'My dear Lord, You are very affectionate to Your devotees. You are also a truthful and grateful friend. Where is that learned man who would give You up and surrender to someone else? You fulfill all the desires of Your devotees, so much so that sometimes You even give Yourself to them. Still, You neither increase nor decrease by such activity.'**

## PURPORT

This is a verse from *Śrīmad-Bhāgavatam* (10.48.26).

## TEXT 97

বিজ্ঞ-জনের হয় যদি কৃষ্ণগুণ-জ্ঞান ।
অন্য ত্যজি' ভজে, তাতে উদ্ধব—প্রমাণ ॥ ৯৭ ॥

*vijña-janera haya yadi kṛṣṇa-guṇa-jñāna*
*anya tyaji', bhaje, tāte uddhava——pramāṇa*

### SYNONYMS

*vijña-janera*—of an experienced person; *haya*—there is; *yadi*—if; *kṛṣṇa-guṇa-jñāna*—knowledge of Kṛṣṇa's transcendental qualities; *anya*—others; *tyaji'*—giving up; *bhaje*—he engages in devotional service; *tāte*—in that connection; *uddhava*—Uddhava; *pramāṇa*—the evidence.

### TRANSLATION

**"Whenever an experienced person develops real knowledge of Kṛṣṇa and His transcendental qualities, he naturally gives up all other engagements and renders service to the Lord. Uddhava gives evidence concerning this.**

### TEXT 98

অহো বকী যং স্তনকালকূটং
জিঘাংসয়াপায়য়দপ্যসাধ্বী ।
লেভে গতিং ধাত্র্যুচিতাং ততোঽন্যং
কং বা দয়ালুং শরণং ব্রজেম ॥ ৯৮ ॥

*aho bakī yaṁ stana-kāla-kūṭaṁ*
*jighāṁsayāpāyayad apy asādhvī*
*lebhe gatiṁ dhātry-ucitāṁ tato 'nyaṁ*
*kaṁ vā dayāluṁ śaraṇaṁ vrajema*

### SYNONYMS

*aho*—how wonderful; *bakī*—Pūtanā, the sister of Bakāsura; *yam*—whom; *stana*—on the two breasts; *kāla-kūṭam*—the deadly poison; *jighāṁsayā*—with a desire to kill; *apāyayat*—forced to drink; *api*—although; *asādhvī*—dangerously inimical to Kṛṣṇa; *lebhe*—achieved; *gatim*—the destination; *dhātrī*—for a nurse; *ucitām*—suitable; *tataḥ*—than Him; *anyam*—other; *kam*—to whom; *vā*—or; *dayālum*—the most merciful; *śaraṇam*—shelter; *vrajema*—shall take.

### TRANSLATION

**" 'Oh, how wonderful it is! Pūtanā, the sister of Bakāsura, wanted to kill Kṛṣṇa by smearing deadly poison on her breasts and having Kṛṣṇa take it. Nonetheless, Lord Kṛṣṇa accepted her as His mother, and thus she attained the destination befitting Kṛṣṇa's mother. Of whom should I take shelter but Kṛṣṇa, who is most merciful?'**

## PURPORT

This is a quotation from *Śrīmad-Bhāgavatam* (3.2.23).

## TEXT 99

**শরণাগতের, অকিঞ্চনের —একই লক্ষণ ।**
**তার মধ্যে প্রবেশয়ে 'আত্মসমর্পণ' ॥ ৯৯ ॥**

*śaraṇāgatera, akiñcanera——eka-i lakṣaṇa*
*tāra madhye praveśaye 'ātma-samarpaṇa'*

## SYNONYMS

*śaraṇāgatera*—of a person who has fully taken shelter of Kṛṣṇa; *akiñcanera*—of a person who is free of all material desires; *eka-i lakṣaṇa*—the symptoms are one and the same; *tāra madhye*—of them all; *praveśaye*—enters; *ātma-samarpaṇa*—full surrender.

## TRANSLATION

**"There are two kinds of devotees—those who are fully satiated and free from all material desires and those who are fully surrendered to the lotus feet of the Lord. Their qualities are one and the same, but those who are fully surrendered to Kṛṣṇa's lotus feet are qualified with another transcendental quality—ātma-samarpaṇa, full surrender without reservation.**

## TEXT 100

আনুকূল্যস্য সঙ্কল্পঃ প্রাতিকূল্যস্য বর্জনম্ ।
রক্ষিষ্যতীতি বিশ্বাসো গোপ্তৃত্বে বরণং তথা ।
আত্মনিক্ষেপ-কার্পণ্যে ষড়্‌বিধা শরণাগতিঃ ॥ ১০০ ॥

*ānukūlyasya saṅkalpaḥ*
*prātikūlyasya varjanam*
*rakṣiṣyatīti viśvāso*
*goptṛtve varaṇaṁ tathā*
*ātma-nikṣepa-kārpaṇye*
*ṣaḍ-vidhā śaraṇāgatiḥ*

## SYNONYMS

*ānukūlyasya*—of anything that assists devotional service to the Lord; *saṅkalpaḥ*—acceptance; *prātikūlyasya*—of anything that hinders devotional service; *varjanam*—complete rejection; *rakṣiṣyati*—He will protect; *iti*—thus; *viśvāsaḥ*—strong conviction; *goptṛtve*—in being the guardian, like the father or husband, master or maintainer; *varaṇam*—acceptance; *tathā*—as well as; *ātma-nikṣepa*—full self-surrender; *kārpaṇye*—humility; *ṣaṭ-vidhā*—sixfold; *śaraṇa-āgatiḥ*—process of surrender.

### TRANSLATION

**" 'The six divisions of surrender are the acceptance of those things favorable to devotional service, the rejection of unfavorable things, the conviction that Kṛṣṇa will give protection, the acceptance of the Lord as one's guardian or master, full self-surrender and humility.**

### PURPORT

One who is fully surrendered is qualified with the six following characteristics. (1) The devotee has to accept everything that is favorable for the rendering of transcendental loving service to the Lord. (2) He must reject everything unfavorable to the Lord's service. This is also called renunciation. (3) A devotee must be firmly convinced that Kṛṣṇa will give him protection. No one else can actually give one protection, and being firmly convinced of this is called faith. This kind of faith is different from the faith of an impersonalist who wants to merge into the Brahman effulgence in order to benefit by cessation of repeated birth and death. A devotee wants to remain always in the Lord's service. In this way, Kṛṣṇa is merciful to His devotee and gives him all protection from the dangers found on the path of devotional service. (4) The devotee should accept Kṛṣṇa as his supreme maintainer and master. He should not think that he is being protected by a demigod. He should depend only on Kṛṣṇa, considering Him the only protector. The devotee must be firmly convinced that within the three worlds he has no protector or maintainer other than Kṛṣṇa. (5) Self-surrender means remembering that one's activities and desires are not independent. The devotee is completely dependent on Kṛṣṇa, and he acts and thinks as Kṛṣṇa desires. (6) The devotee is meek and humble. As stated in *Bhagavad-gītā:*

*sarvasya cāhaṁ hṛdi sanniviṣṭo*
*mattaḥ smṛtir jñānam apohanaṁ ca*
*vedaiś ca sarvair aham eva vedyo*
*vedānta-kṛd veda-vid eva cāham*

"I am seated in everyone's heart, and from Me come remembrance, knowledge and forgetfulness. By all the *Vedas* am I to be known; indeed I am the compiler of Vedānta, and I am the knower of the *Vedas.*" (Bg. 15.15)

Situated in everyone's heart, Kṛṣṇa deals differently according to the living entity's position. The living entity's position is to be under the protection of the illusory energy or under Kṛṣṇa's personal protection. When a living entity is fully surrendered, he is under the direct protection of Kṛṣṇa, and Kṛṣṇa gives him all intelligence by which he can advance in spiritual realization. The nondevotee, however, being under the protection of the illusory energy, increasingly forgets his relationship with Kṛṣṇa. Sometimes it is asked how Kṛṣṇa causes one to forget. Kṛṣṇa causes His devotee to forget material activities, and through the agency of *māyā,* Kṛṣṇa causes the nondevotee to forget his devotional service to the Lord. This is called *apohana.*

## TEXT 101

তবাস্মীতি বদন্ বাচা তথৈব মনসা বিদন্ ।
তৎস্থানমাশ্রিতস্তন্বা মোদতে শরণাগতঃ ॥ ১০১ ॥

*tavāsmīti vadan vācā*
*tathaiva manasā vidan*
*tat-sthānam āśritas tanvā*
*modate śaraṇāgataḥ*

## SYNONYMS

*tava*—His; *asmi*—I am; *iti*—thus; *vadan*—saying; *vācā*—by words; *tathā*—so; *eva*—certainly; *manasā*—with the mind; *vidan*—knowing; *tat-sthānam*—His place; *āśritaḥ*—taken shelter of; *tanvā*—by the body; *modate*—he enjoys; *śaraṇa-āgataḥ*—fully surrendered.

## TRANSLATION

**" 'One whose body is fully surrendered takes shelter at the holy place where Kṛṣṇa had His pastimes, and he prays to the Lord, "My Lord, I am Yours." Understanding this with his mind, he enjoys spiritual bliss.**

## PURPORT

These last two verses appear in the *Hari-bhakti-vilāsa* (11.417, 418).

## TEXT 102

শরণ লঞা করে কৃষ্ণে আত্মসমর্পণ ।
কৃষ্ণ তারে করে তৎকালে আত্মসম ॥ ১০২ ॥

*śaraṇa lañā kare kṛṣṇe ātma-samarpaṇa*
*kṛṣṇa tāre kare tat-kāle ātma-sama*

## SYNONYMS

*śaraṇa lañā*—taking shelter; *kare*—does; *kṛṣṇe*—unto Kṛṣṇa; *ātma-samarpaṇa*—fully surrendering; *kṛṣṇa*—Lord Kṛṣṇa; *tāre*—him; *kare*—makes; *tat-kāle*—immediately; *ātma-sama*—one of His confidential associates.

## TRANSLATION

**"When a devotee thus fully surrenders unto Kṛṣṇa's lotus feet, Kṛṣṇa accepts him as one of His confidential associates.**

## TEXT 103

মর্ত্যো যদা ত্যক্তসমস্তকর্মা
নিবেদিতাত্মা বিচিকীর্ষিতো মে ।
তদামৃতত্বং প্রতিপদ্যমানো
ময়াত্মভূয়ায় চ কল্পতে বৈ ॥ ১০৩ ॥

*martyo yadā tyakta-samasta-karmā*
*niveditātmā vicikīrṣito me*
*tadāmṛtatvaṁ pratipadyamāno*
*mayātma-bhūyāya ca kalpate vai*

## SYNONYMS

*martyaḥ*—the living entity subjected to birth and death; *yadā*—as soon as; *tyakta*—given up; *samasta*—all; *karmā*—fruitive activities; *nivedita-ātmā*—a fully surrendered soul; *vicikīrṣitaḥ*—desired to act; *me*—by Me; *tadā*—at that time; *amṛtatvam*—immortality; *pratipadyamānaḥ*—attaining; *mayā*—with Me; *ātma-bhūyāya*—for becoming of a similar nature; *ca*—also; *kalpate*—is eligible; *vai*—certainly.

## TRANSLATION

**" 'The living entity who is subjected to birth and death attains immortality when he gives up all material activities, dedicates his life to the execution of My order, and acts according to My directions. In this way he becomes fit to enjoy the spiritual bliss derived from exchanging loving mellows with Me.'**

## PURPORT

This is a quotation from *Śrīmad-Bhāgavatam* (11.29.34). Kṛṣṇa was advising His most confidential servant, Uddhava, about *sambandha, abhidheya* and *prayojana.* These concern one's relationship with the Supreme Personality of Godhead and the activities of that relationship, as well as the perfection of life. The Lord also described the characteristics of confidential devotees.

### TEXT 104

**এবে সাধনভক্তি-লক্ষণ শুন, সনাতন ।**
**যাহা হৈতে পাই কৃষ্ণপ্রেম-মহাধন ॥ ১০৪ ॥**

*ebe sādhana-bhakti-lakṣaṇa śuna, sanātana*
*yāhā haite pāi kṛṣṇa-prema-mahā-dhana*

### SYNONYMS

*ebe*—now; *sādhana-bhakti*—regulative principles for executing devotional service; *lakṣaṇa*—the symptoms; *śuna*—please hear; *sanātana*—My dear Sanātana; *yāhā haite*—from which; *pāi*—one can get; *kṛṣṇa-prema-mahā-dhana*—the most valuable treasure of love for Kṛṣṇa.

### TRANSLATION

**"My dear Sanātana, please now hear about the regulative principles for the execution of devotional service. By this process, one can attain the highest perfection of love of Godhead, which is the most desirable treasure.**

### TEXT 105

কৃতিসাধ্যা ভবেৎ সাধ্যভাবা সা সাধনাভিধা ।
নিত্যসিদ্ধস্য ভাবস্য প্রাকট্যং হৃদি সাধ্যতা ॥ ১০৫ ॥

*kṛti-sādhyā bhavet sādhya-*
*bhāvā sā sādhanābhidhā*
*nitya-siddhasya bhāvasya*
*prākaṭyaṁ hṛdi sādhyatā*

### SYNONYMS

*kṛti-sādhyā*—which is to be executed by the senses; *bhavet*—should be; *sādhya-bhāvā*—by which love of Godhead is acquired; *sā*—that; *sādhana-abhidhā*—called *sādhana-bhakti,* or devotional service in practice; *nitya-siddhasya*—which is eternally present; *bhāvasya*—of love of Godhead; *prākaṭyam*—the awakening; *hṛdi*—in the heart; *sādhyatā*—potentiality.

### TRANSLATION

**" 'When transcendental devotional service by which love for Kṛṣṇa is attained is executed by the senses, it is called sādhana-bhakti, or the regulative discharge of devotional service. Such devotion eternally exists within the heart of every living entity. The awakening of this eternal devotion is the potentiality of devotional service in practice.'**

### PURPORT

This verse is found in *Bhakti-rasāmṛta-sindhu* (1.2.2). Because living entities are minute, atomic parts and parcels of the Lord, devotional service is already present within them in a dormant condition. Devotional service begins with *śravaṇa kīrtana,* hearing and chanting. When a man is sleeping, he can be awakened by sound vibration; therefore every conditioned soul should be given the chance to hear the Hare Kṛṣṇa *mantra* chanted by a pure Vaiṣṇava. One who hears the Hare Kṛṣṇa *mantra* thus vibrated is awakened to spiritual consciousness, or Kṛṣṇa consciousness. In this way one's mind gradually becomes purified, as stated by Śrī Caitanya Mahāprabhu (*ceto-darpaṇa-mārjanam*). When the mind is purified, the senses are also purified. Instead of using the senses for sense gratification, the awakened devotee employs the senses in the transcendental loving service of the Lord. This is the process by which dormant love for Kṛṣṇa is awakened.

### TEXT 106

শ্রবণাদি-ক্রিয়া—তার 'স্বরূপ'-লক্ষণ ।
'তটস্থ'-লক্ষণে উপজায় প্রেমধন ॥ ১০৬ ॥

*śravaṇādi-kriyā——tāra 'svarūpa'-lakṣaṇa*
*'taṭastha'-lakṣaṇe upajāya prema-dhana*

### SYNONYMS

*śravaṇa-ādi-kriyā*—the process of hearing, chanting and so forth; *tāra*—of that; *svarūpa-lakṣaṇa*—symptoms of the nature; *taṭastha-lakṣaṇe*—marginal symptoms; *upajāya*—awakens; *prema-dhana*—love of Godhead.

### TRANSLATION

**"The spiritual activities of hearing, chanting, remembering and so forth are the natural characteristics of devotional service. The marginal characteristic is that it awakens pure love for Kṛṣṇa.**

### TEXT 107

নিত্যসিদ্ধ কৃষ্ণপ্রেম 'সাধ্য' কভু নয়।
শ্রবণাদি-শুদ্ধচিত্তে করয়ে উদয়॥ ১০৭॥

*nitya-siddha kṛṣṇa-prema 'sādhya' kabhu naya*
*śravaṇādi-śuddha-citte karaye udaya*

### SYNONYMS

*nitya-siddha*—eternally proved; *kṛṣṇa-prema*—love of Kṛṣṇa; *sādhya*—to be gained; *kabhu*—at any time; *naya*—not; *śravaṇa-ādi*—by hearing, etc.; *śuddha*—purified; *citte*—in the heart; *karaye udaya*—awakens.

### TRANSLATION

**"Pure love for Kṛṣṇa is eternally established in the hearts of living entities. It is not something to be gained from another source. When the heart is purified by hearing and chanting, the living entity naturally awakens.**

### TEXT 108

এই ত সাধনভক্তি— দুই ত' প্রকার।
এক 'বৈধী ভক্তি', 'রাগানুগা-ভক্তি' আর॥ ১০৮॥

*ei ta sādhana-bhakti——dui ta' prakāra*
*eka 'vaidhī bhakti', 'rāgānugā-bhakti' āra*

### SYNONYMS

*ei ta*—this; *sādhana-bhakti*—process of devotional service; *dui ta' prakāra*—two kinds; *eka*—one; *vaidhī bhakti*—the regulative devotional service; *rāgānugā-bhakti*—spontaneous devotional service; *āra*—and.

### TRANSLATION

**"There are two processes of practical devotional service. One is regulative devotional service, and the other is spontaneous devotional service.**

### TEXT 109

রাগহীন জন ভজে শাস্ত্রের আজ্ঞায়।
'বৈধী ভক্তি' বলি' তারে সর্বশাস্ত্রে গায়॥ ১০৯॥

*rāga-hīna jana bhaje śāstrera ājñāya*
*'vaidhī bhakti' bali' tāre sarva-śāstre gāya*

## SYNONYMS

*rāga-hīna*—who are without spontaneous attachment to Kṛṣṇa; *jana*—persons; *bhaje*—execute devotional service; *śāstrera ājñāya*—according to the principles and regulations described in the revealed scriptures; *vaidhī bhakti*—regulative devotional service; *bali'*—calling; *tāre*—that; *sarva-śāstre*—all revealed scriptures; *gāya*—sing.

## TRANSLATION

**"Those who have not attained the platform of spontaneous attachment in devotional service render devotional service under the guidance of a bona fide spiritual master according to the regulative principles mentioned in the revealed scriptures. According to the revealed scriptures, this kind of devotional service is called vaidhī bhakti.**

## PURPORT

In the beginning, one has to hear from a bona fide spiritual master. This is favorable for advancing in devotional service. According to this process, one hears, chants, remembers and engages in Deity worship, acting under the directions of the spiritual master. These are the essential primary activities of devotional service. Devotional service must not be executed for some material purpose. One should not even have a desire to merge into the Absolute Truth. One has to render such service out of love only. *Ahaitukī, apratihatā.* Devotional service must be without ulterior motives; then material conditions cannot check it. Gradually one can rise to the platform of spontaneous loving service. A child is sent to school by force to receive an education, but when he gets a little taste of education at an advanced age, he automatically participates and becomes a learned scholar. One cannot force a person to become a scholar, but sometimes force is used in the beginning. A child is forced to go to school and read and write according to the instructions of his teachers. Such is the difference between *vaidhī bhakti* and spontaneous *bhakti.* Dormant love for Kṛṣṇa exists in everyone's heart, and it simply has to be awakened by the regulative process of devotional service. One has to learn to use a typewriter by following the regulative principles of the typing book. One has to place his fingers on the keys in such a way and practice, but when one becomes adept, he can type swiftly and correctly without even looking at the keys. Similarly, one has to follow the rules and regulations of devotional service as they are set down by the spiritual master; then one can come to the point of spontaneous loving service. This love is already there within the heart of everyone (*nitya-siddha kṛṣṇa-prema*).

Spontaneous service is not artificial. One simply has to come to that platform by rendering devotional service according to the regulative principles. Thus one has to practice hearing and chanting and follow the other regulative principles by washing the temple, cleansing oneself, rising early in the morning, attending *maṅgala-ārati* and so on. If one does not come to the platform of spontaneous service in the beginning, he must adopt regulative service according to the instructions of the spiritual master. This regulative service is called *vaidhī bhakti.*

## TEXT 110

তস্মাদ্ভারত সর্বাত্মা ভগবান্ হরিরীশ্বরঃ।
শ্রোতব্যঃ কীর্তিতব্যশ্চ স্মর্তব্যশ্চেচ্ছতাভয়ম্ ॥ ১১০ ॥

*tasmād bhārata sarvātmā*
*bhagavān harir īśvaraḥ*
*śrotavyaḥ kīrtitavyaś ca*
*smartavyaś cecchatābhayam*

## SYNONYMS

*tasmāt*—therefore; *bhārata*—O descendant of Bharata; *sarva-ātmā*—the all-pervasive Lord, who is situated in everyone's heart; *bhagavān*—the Supreme Personality of Godhead; *hariḥ*—Lord Hari, who takes away all the miserable conditions of material existence; *īśvaraḥ*—the supreme controller; *śrotavyaḥ*—to be heard about (from bona fide sources); *kīrtitavyaḥ*—to be glorified (as one has heard); *ca*—also; *smartavyaḥ*—to be remembered; *ca*—and; *icchatā*—by a person desiring; *abhayam*—freedom from the fearful condition of material existence.

## TRANSLATION

**" 'O descendant of Bharata! O Mahārāja Parīkṣit! The Supreme Personality of Godhead, who is situated in everyone's heart as Paramātmā, who is the supreme controller and who always removes the miseries of living entities, must always be heard about from reliable sources, and He must be glorified and remembered by one who wishes to become fearless.'**

## PURPORT

This is a quotation from *Śrīmad-Bhāgavatam* (2.1.5). It is one's duty to understand the Supreme Personality of Godhead through the hearing process. This is called *śrotavyaḥ.* If one has heard properly about the Supreme Personality of Godhead, his duty is to glorify the Lord and preach His glories. This is called *kīrtitavyaḥ.* When one hears about the Lord and glorifies Him, it is natural to think of Him. This is called *smartavyaḥ*. All this must be carried out if one actually wants to be immune from fear.

## TEXT 111

মুখবাহূরুপাদেভ্যঃ পুরুষস্যাশ্রমৈঃ সহ ।
চত্বারো জজ্ঞিরে বর্ণা গুণৈর্বিপ্রাদয়ঃ পৃথক্ ॥ ১১১ ॥

*mukha-bāhūru-pādebhyaḥ*
*puruṣasyāśramaiḥ saha*
*catvāro jajñire varṇā*
*guṇair viprādayaḥ pṛthak*

## SYNONYMS

*mukha*—the mouth; *bāhu*—the arms; *ūru*—the waist; *pādebhyaḥ*—from the legs; *puruṣasya*—of the supreme person; *āśramaiḥ*—the different spiritual orders; *saha*—with; *catvāraḥ*—the four; *jajñire*—appeared; *varṇāḥ*—social orders; *guṇaiḥ*—with particular qualifications; *vipra-ādayaḥ*—*brāhmaṇas,* etc.; *pṛthak*—separately.

## TRANSLATION

**" 'From the mouth of Brahmā, the brahminical order has come into existence. Similarly, from his arms the kṣatriyas have come, from his waist the vaiśyas have come and from his legs the śūdras have come. These four orders and their spiritual counterparts [brahmacarya, gṛhastha, vānaprastha and sannyāsa] combine to make human society complete.**

## PURPORT

This verse and the next are quotations from *Śrīmad-Bhāgavatam* (11.5.2-3).

## TEXT 112

য এষাং পুরুষং সাক্ষাদাত্ম-প্রভবমীশ্বরম্ ।
ন ভজন্ত্যবজানন্তি স্থানাদ্ ভ্রষ্টাঃ পতন্ত্যধঃ ॥ ১১২ ॥

*ya eṣāṁ puruṣaṁ sākṣād*
*ātma-prabhavam īśvaram*
*na bhajanty avajānanti*
*sthānād bhraṣṭāḥ patanty adhaḥ*

## SYNONYMS

*ye*—those who; *eṣām*—of those divisions of social and spiritual orders; *puruṣam*—the Supreme Personality of Godhead; *sākṣāt*—directly; *ātma-prabhavam*—the source of everyone; *īśvaram*—the supreme controller; *na*—not; *bhajanti*—worship; *avajānanti*—or who neglect; *sthānāt*—from their proper place; *bhraṣṭāḥ*—being fallen; *patanti*—fall; *adhaḥ*—downward into hellish conditions.

## TRANSLATION

**" 'If one simply maintains an official position in the four varṇas and āśramas but does not worship the Supreme Lord Viṣṇu, he falls down from his puffed-up position into a hellish condition.'**

## TEXT 113

স্মর্তব্যঃ সততং বিষ্ণুর্বিস্মর্তব্যো ন জাতুচিৎ ।
সর্বে বিধিনিষেধাঃ স্যুরেতয়োরেব কিঙ্করাঃ ॥ ১১৩ ॥

*smartavyaḥ satataṁ viṣṇur*
*vismartavyo na jātucit*
*sarve vidhi-niṣedhāḥ syur*
*etayor eva kiṅkarāḥ*

## SYNONYMS

*smartavyaḥ*—to be remembered; *satatam*—always; *viṣṇuḥ*—Lord Viṣṇu; *vismartavyaḥ*—to be forgotten; *na*—not; *jātucit*—at any time; *sarve*—all; *vidhi-niṣedhāḥ*—rules and prohibitions mentioned in the revealed scripture or given by the spiritual master; *syuḥ*—should be; *etayoḥ*—of these two principles (always to remember Kṛṣṇa or Viṣṇu and never to forget Him); *eva*—certainly; *kiṅkarāḥ*—the servants.

## TRANSLATION

**" 'Kṛṣṇa is the origin of Lord Viṣṇu. He should always be remembered and never forgotten at any time. All the rules and prohibitions mentioned in the śāstras should be the servants of these two principles.'**

## PURPORT

This verse is a quotation from the *Padma Purāṇa*. There are many regulative principles in the *śāstras* and directions given by the spiritual master. These regulative principles should act as servants of the basic principle—that is, one should always remember Kṛṣṇa and never forget Him. This is possible when one chants the Hare Kṛṣṇa *mantra.* Therefore one must strictly chant the Hare Kṛṣṇa *mahā-mantra* twenty-four hours daily. One may have other duties to perform under the direction of the spiritual master, but he must first abide by the spiritual master's order to chant a certain number of rounds. In our Kṛṣṇa consciousness movement, we have recommended that the neophyte chant at least sixteen rounds. This chanting of sixteen rounds is absolutely necessary if one wants to remember Kṛṣṇa and not forget Him. Of all the regulative principles, the spiritual master's order to chant at least sixteen rounds is most essential.

One may sell books or enlist life members or render some other service, but these duties are not ordinary duties. These duties serve as an impetus for remembering Kṛṣṇa. When one goes with a *saṅkīrtana* party or sells books, he naturally remembers that he is going to sell Kṛṣṇa's books. In this way, he is remembering Kṛṣṇa. When one goes to enlist a life member, he talks about Kṛṣṇa and thereby remembers Him. *Smartavyaḥ satataṁ viṣṇur vismartavyo na jātucit.* The conclusion is that one must act in such a way that he will always remember Kṛṣṇa, and one must refrain from doing things that make him forget Kṛṣṇa. These two principles form the basic background of Kṛṣṇa consciousness.

## TEXT 114

বিবিধাঙ্গ সাধনভক্তির বহুত বিস্তার ।
সংক্ষেপে কহিয়ে কিছু সাধনাঙ্গ-সার ॥ ১১৪ ॥

*vividhāṅga sādhana-bhaktira bahuta vistāra*
*saṅkṣepe kahiye kichu sādhanāṅga-sāra*

## SYNONYMS

*vividha-aṅga*—varieties of limbs (regulative principles); *sādhana-bhaktira*—of regulative devotional service; *bahuta*—many; *vistāra*—expansions; *saṅkṣepe*—in brief; *kahiye*—I shall speak; *kichu*—something; *sādhana-aṅga-sāra*—the essential parts of the practice of devotional service.

## TRANSLATION

**"I shall say something about the various practices of devotional service, which is expanded in so many ways. I wish to speak briefly of the essential practices.**

## TEXT 115

গুরুপাদাশ্রয়, দীক্ষা, গুরুর সেবন ।
সদ্ধর্মশিক্ষা-পৃচ্ছা, সাধুমার্গানুগমন ॥ ১১৫ ॥

*guru-pādāśraya, dīkṣā, gurura sevana*
*sad-dharma-śikṣā, pṛcchā, sādhu-mārgānugamana*

### SYNONYMS

*guru-pāda-āśraya*—shelter at the feet of a bona fide spiritual master; *dīkṣā*—initiation by the spiritual master; *gurura sevana*—service to the spiritual master; *sat-dharma-śikṣā*—instruction in the transcendental process of devotional service; *pṛcchā*—and inquiry; *sādhu-mārga*—the path of transcendental devotional service; *anugamana*—following strictly.

### TRANSLATION

**"On the path of regulative devotional service, one must observe the following items: (1) One must accept a bona fide spiritual master. (2) Accept initiation from him. (3) Serve him. (4) Receive instructions from the spiritual master and make inquiries in order to learn devotional service. (5) Follow in the footsteps of the previous ācāryas and follow the directions given by the spiritual master.**

### TEXT 116

কৃষ্ণপ্রীত্যে ভোগত্যাগ, কৃষ্ণতীর্থে বাস ।
যাবন্নির্বাহ-প্রতিগ্রহ, একাদশ্যুপবাস ॥ ১১৬ ॥

*kṛṣṇa-prītye bhoga-tyāga, kṛṣṇa-tīrthe vāsa*
*yāvan-nirvāha-pratigraha, ekādaśy-upavāsa*

### SYNONYMS

*kṛṣṇa-prītye*—for satisfaction of Kṛṣṇa; *bhoga-tyāga*—acceptance and rejection of something; *kṛṣṇa-tīrthe vāsa*—residence in a place where Kṛṣṇa is situated; *yāvat-nirvāha*—as much as required to keep the body and soul together; *pratigraha*—acceptance of gifts; *ekādaśī-upavāsa*—observance of fasting on the Ekādaśī day.

### TRANSLATION

**"The next steps are as follows: (6) One should be prepared to give up everything for Kṛṣṇa's satisfaction, and one should also accept everything for Kṛṣṇa's satisfaction. (7) One must live in a place where Kṛṣṇa is present—a city like Vṛndāvana or Mathurā or a Kṛṣṇa temple. (8) One should acquire a livelihood that is just sufficient to keep body and soul together. (9) One must fast on Ekādaśī day.**

## TEXT 117

ধাত্র্যশ্বত্থগোবিপ্র-বৈষ্ণব-পূজন ।
সেবা-নামাপরাধাদি দূরে বিসর্জন ॥ ১১৭ ॥

*dhātry-aśvattha-go-vipra-vaiṣṇava-pūjana*
*sevā-nāmāparādhādi dūre visarjana*

## SYNONYMS

*dhātrī*—a type of tree; *aśvattha*—the banyan trees; *go*—the cows; *vipra*—the *brāhmaṇas; vaiṣṇava*—the devotees of Lord Viṣṇu; *pūjana*—worshiping; *sevā*—in devotional service; *nāma*—in chanting of the holy name; *aparādha-ādi*—the offenses; *dūre*—far away; *visarjana*—giving up.

## TRANSLATION

**"One should worship dhātrī trees, banyan trees, cows, brāhmaṇas and devotees of Lord Viṣṇu. One should avoid offenses against devotional service and the holy name.**

## PURPORT

There are ten items in the beginning of devotional service, up to the point of worshiping the *dhātrī* tree, banyan tree, cow, *brāhmaṇa* and devotee of Lord Viṣṇu. The eleventh item is to avoid offenses when rendering devotional service and chanting the holy names.

## TEXT 118

অবৈষ্ণব-সঙ্গ-ত্যাগ, বহুশিষ্য না করিব ।
বহুগ্রন্থ-কলাভ্যাস-ব্যাখ্যান বর্জিব ॥ ১১৮ ॥

*avaiṣṇava-saṅga-tyāga, bahu-śiṣya nā kariba*
*bahu-grantha-kalābhyāsa-vyākhyāna varjiba*

## SYNONYMS

*avaiṣṇava*—of one who is not a devotee of the Lord; *saṅga*—the association; *tyāga*—giving up; *bahu-śiṣya*—an unlimited number of disciples; *nā kariba*—should not accept; *bahu-grantha*—of many different types of scriptures; *kalā-abhyāsa*—studying a portion; *vyākhyāna*—and explanation; *varjiba*—we should give up.

## TRANSLATION

**"The twelfth item is to give up the company of nondevotees. (13) One should not accept an unlimited number of disciples. (14) One should not partially study many scriptures just to be able to give references and expand explanations.**

## PURPORT

Accepting an unlimited number of devotees or disciples is very risky for one who is not a preacher. According to Śrīla Jīva Gosvāmī, a preacher has to accept many disciples to expand the cult of Śrī Caitanya Mahāprabhu. This is risky because when a spiritual master accepts a disciple, he naturally accepts the disciple's sinful activities and their reactions. Unless he is very powerful, he cannot assimilate all the sinful reactions of his disciples. Thus if he is not powerful, he has to suffer the consequences, for one is forbidden to accept many disciples.

One should not partially study a book just to pose oneself as a great scholar by being able to refer to scriptures. In our Kṛṣṇa consciousness movement we have therefore limited our study of Vedic literatures to *Bhagavad-gītā, Śrīmad-Bhāgavatam, Caitanya-caritāmṛta* and *Bhakti-rasāmṛta-sindhu.* These four works are sufficient for preaching purposes. They are adequate for the understanding of the philosophy and the spreading of missionary activities all over the world. If one studies a particular book, he must do so thoroughly. That is the principle. By thoroughly studying a limited number of books, one can understand the philosophy.

## TEXT 119

**হানি-লাভে সম, শোকাদির বশ না হইব।**
**অন্যদেব, অন্যশাস্ত্র নিন্দা না করিব ॥ ১১৯ ॥**

*hāni-lābhe sama, śokādira vaśa nā ha-iba*
*anya-deva, anya-śāstra nindā nā kariba*

## SYNONYMS

*hāni*—in loss; *lābhe*—in gain; *sama*—equal; *śoka-ādira*—of lamentation and so on; *vaśa*—under the control; *nā ha-iba*—we should not be; *anya-deva*—other demigods; *anya-śāstra*—other scriptures; *nindā*—criticizing; *nā kariba*—we should not do.

## TRANSLATION

**"Fifteen: The devotee should treat loss and gain equally. (16) The devotee should not be overwhelmed by lamentation. (17) The devotee should not**

**worship demigods, nor should he disrespect them. Similarly, the devotee should not study or criticize other scriptures.**

### TEXT 120

বিষ্ণুবৈষ্ণব-নিন্দা, গ্রাম্যবার্তা না শুনিব ।
প্রাণিমাত্রে মনোবাক্যে উদ্বেগ না দিব ॥ ১২০ ॥

*viṣṇu-vaiṣṇava-nindā, grāmya-vārtā nā śuniba*
*prāṇi-mātre manovākye udvega nā diba*

### SYNONYMS

*viṣṇu-vaiṣṇava-nindā*—blaspheming of Lord Viṣṇu and His devotee; *grāmya-vārtā*—ordinary talks; *nā śuniba*—we should not hear; *prāṇi-mātre*—to any living entity however insignificant; *manaḥ-vākye*—by mind or by words; *udvega*—anxiety; *nā diba*—we should not give.

### TRANSLATION

**"Eighteen: The devotee should not hear Lord Viṣṇu or His devotees blasphemed. (19) The devotee should avoid reading or hearing newspapers or mundane books that contain stories of love affairs between men and women or subjects palatable to the senses. (20) Neither by mind nor words should the devotee cause anxiety to any living entity, regardless how insignificant he may be.**

### PURPORT

The first ten items are dos and the second ten items are don'ts. Thus the first ten items give direct action, and the second ten items give indirect action.

### TEXT 121

শ্রবণ, কীর্তন, স্মরণ, পূজন, বন্দন ।
পরিচর্যা, দাস্য, সখ্য, আত্মনিবেদন ॥ ১২১ ॥

*śravaṇa, kīrtana, smaraṇa, pūjana, vandana*
*paricaryā, dāsya, sakhya, ātma-nivedana*

### SYNONYMS

*śravaṇa*—hearing; *kīrtana*—chanting; *smaraṇa*—remembering; *pūjana*—worshiping; *vandana*—praying; *paricaryā*—serving; *dāsya*—accepting servitorship; *sakhya*—friendship; *ātma-nivedana*—surrendering fully.

## TRANSLATION

**"After one is established in devotional service, the positive actions are (1) hearing, (2) chanting, (3) remembering, (4) worshiping, (5) praying, (6) serving, (7) accepting servitorship, (8) becoming a friend and (9) surrendering fully.**

## TEXT 122

অগ্রে নৃত্য, গীত, বিজ্ঞপ্তি, দণ্ডবন্নতি ।
অভ্যুত্থান, অনুব্রজ্যা, তীর্থগৃহে গতি ॥ ১২২ ॥

*agre nṛtya, gīta, vijñapti, daṇḍavan-nati*
*abhyūtthāna, anuvrajyā, tīrtha-gṛhe gati*

## SYNONYMS

*agre nṛtya*—dancing before the Deity; *gīta*—songs; *vijñapti*—opening the mind; *daṇḍavat-nati*—offering obeisances; *abhyūtthāna*—stand up; *anuvrajyā*—following; *tīrtha-gṛhe gati*—going to temples and places of pilgrimage.

## TRANSLATION

**"One should also (10) dance before the Deity, (11) sing before the Deity, (12) open one's mind to the Deity, (13) offer obeisances to the Deity, (14) stand up before the Deity and the spiritual master just to show them respect, (15) follow the Deity or the spiritual master and (16) visit different places of pilgrimage or go see the Deity in the temple.**

## TEXT 123

পরিক্রমা, স্তবপাঠ, জপ, সঙ্কীর্তন ।
ধূপ-মাল্য-গন্ধ-মহাপ্রসাদ-ভোজন ॥ ১২৩ ॥

*parikramā, stava-pāṭha, japa, saṅkīrtana*
*dhūpa-mālya-gandha-mahāprasāda-bhojana*

## SYNONYMS

*parikramā*—circumambulation; *stava-pāṭha*—recitation of different prayers; *japa*—chanting softly; *saṅkīrtana*—chanting congregationally; *dhūpa*—incense; *mālya*—flower garlands; *gandha*—scents; *mahā-prasāda*—remnants of food offered to Viṣṇu; *bhojana*—eating or enjoying.

### TRANSLATION

**"One should (17) circumambulate the temple, (18) recite various prayers, (19) chant softly, (20) chant congregationally, (21) smell the incense and flower garlands offered to the Deity, and (22) eat the remnants of food offered to the Deity.**

### TEXT 124

আরাত্রিক-মহোৎসব-শ্রীমূর্তি-দর্শন ।
নিজপ্রিয়-দান, ধ্যান, তদীয়-সেবন ॥ ১২৪ ॥

*ārātrika-mahotsava-śrīmūrti-darśana*
*nija-priya-dāna, dhyāna, tadīya-sevana*

### SYNONYMS

*ārātrika*—ārati; *mahotsava*—festivals; *śrīmūrti-darśana*—seeing the Deity; *nija-priya-dāna*—to present to the Lord something very dear to oneself; *dhyāna*—meditation; *tadīya-sevana*—rendering service to those related to the Lord.

### TRANSLATION

**"One should (23) attend ārati and festivals, (24) see the Deity, (25) present what is very dear to oneself to the Deity, (26) meditate, and (27) serve those related to the Lord.**

### TEXT 125

'তদীয়'—তুলসী, বৈষ্ণব, মথুরা, ভাগবত ।
এই চারির সেবা হয় কৃষ্ণের অভিমত ॥ ১২৫ ॥

*'tadīya'——tulasī, vaiṣṇava, mathurā, bhāgavata*
*ei cārira sevā haya kṛṣṇera abhimata*

### SYNONYMS

*tadīya*—related to the Lord; *tulasī*—*tulasī* leaves; *vaiṣṇava*—devotees; *mathurā*—the birthplace of Kṛṣṇa; *bhāgavata*—*Śrīmad-Bhāgavatam; ei cārira*—of these four; *sevā*—the service; *haya*—is; *kṛṣṇera abhimata*—the desire of Kṛṣṇa.

### TRANSLATION

**"Tadīya means the tulasī leaves, the devotees of Kṛṣṇa, the birthplace of Kṛṣṇa, Mathurā, and the Vedic literature Śrīmad-Bhāgavatam. Kṛṣṇa is very eager to see His devotee serve tulasī, Vaiṣṇavas, Mathurā and Bhāgavatam.**

## PURPORT

After item twenty-six (meditation), the twenty-seventh is to serve *tulasī,* the twenty-eighth is to serve the Vaiṣṇava, the twenty-ninth is to live in Mathurā, the birthplace of Lord Kṛṣṇa, and the thirtieth is to read *Śrīmad-Bhāgavatam* regularly.

## TEXT 126

কৃষ্ণার্থে অখিল-চেষ্টা, তৎকৃপাবলোকন ।
জন্ম-দিনাদি-মহোৎসব লঞা ভক্তগণ ॥ ১২৬ ॥

*kṛṣṇārthe akhila-ceṣṭā, tat-kṛpāvalokana*
*janma-dinādi-mahotsava lañā bhakta-gaṇa*

## SYNONYMS

*kṛṣṇa-arthe*—for the sake of Kṛṣṇa; *akhila-ceṣṭā*—all activity; *tat-kṛpā-avalokana*—looking for His mercy; *janma-dina-ādi*—the appearance day and so on; *mahotsava*—festivals; *lañā bhakta-gaṇa*—with devotees.

## TRANSLATION

**"Thirty-one: One should perform all endeavors for Kṛṣṇa. (32) One should look forward to His mercy. (33) One should partake of various ceremonies with devotees, ceremonies like Lord Kṛṣṇa's birthday or Rāmacandra's birthday.**

## TEXT 127

সর্বথা শরণাপত্তি, কার্তিকাদি-ব্রত ।
'চতুঃষষ্টি অঙ্গ' এই পরম-মহত্ত্ব ॥ ১২৭ ॥

*sarvathā śaraṇāpatti, kārtikādi-vrata*
*'catuḥ-ṣaṣṭi aṅga' ei parama-mahattva*

## SYNONYMS

*sarvathā*—in all respects; *śaraṇa-āpatti*—surrender; *kārtika-ādi-vrata*—to observe special vows in the month of Kārttika; *catuḥ-ṣaṣṭi aṅga*—sixty-four parts; *ei*—this; *parama-mahattva*—very important items.

## TRANSLATION

**"Thirty-four: One should surrender to Kṛṣṇa in all respects. (35) One should observe particular vows like kārtika-vrata. These are some of the sixty-four important items of devotional service.**

### TEXT 128

সাধুসঙ্গ, নামকীর্তন, ভাগবতশ্রবণ ।
মথুরাবাস, শ্রীমূর্তির শ্রদ্ধায় সেবন ॥ ১২৮ ॥

*sādhu-saṅga, nāma-kīrtana, bhāgavata-śravaṇa*
*mathurā-vāsa, śrī-mūrtira śraddhāya sevana*

### SYNONYMS

*sādhu-saṅga*—association with devotees; *nāma-kīrtana*—chanting the holy name; *bhāgavata-śravaṇa*—hearing *Śrīmad-Bhāgavatam; mathurā-vāsa*—living at Mathurā; *śrī-mūrtira śraddhāya sevana*—worshiping the Deity with faith and veneration.

### TRANSLATION

**"One should associate with devotees, chant the holy name of the Lord, hear Śrīmad-Bhāgavatam, reside at Mathurā and worship the Deity with faith and veneration.**

### TEXT 129

সকলসাধন-শ্রেষ্ঠ এই পঞ্চ অঙ্গ ।
কৃষ্ণপ্রেম জন্মায় এই পাঁচের অল্প সঙ্গ ॥ ১২৯ ॥

*sakala-sādhana-śreṣṭha ei pañca aṅga*
*kṛṣṇa-prema janmāya ei pāṅcera alpa saṅga*

### SYNONYMS

*sakala-sādhana*—of all items for executing devotional service; *śreṣṭha*—the best; *ei pañca aṅga*—these five limbs; *kṛṣṇa-prema*—love of Kṛṣṇa; *janmāya*—awakens; *ei*—these; *pāṅcera*—of the five; *alpa saṅga*—slight association with or performance.

### TRANSLATION

**"These five limbs of devotional service are the best of all. Even a slight performance of these five awakens love for Kṛṣṇa.**

### PURPORT

Śrīla Bhaktivinoda Ṭhākura points out that there are thirty-five items up to the point of observing special vows in the month of Kārttika. To these thirty-five items, another four are added—namely marking *tilaka* on different parts of the body, writing the names of the Lord all over the body, accepting the Deity's garland and accepting *caraṇāmṛta.* These four items are understood to be included by Kavirāja Gosvāmī within *arcana,* worship of the Deity. Although these items are not mentioned here, they are to be added to the previous thirty-five items. Thus the total number becomes thirty-nine. To these thirty-nine should be added five others: association with devotees, chanting the Hare Kṛṣṇa *mahā-mantra,* reading *Śrīmad-Bhāgavatam* regularly, residing in Mathurā, the birthplace of Kṛṣṇa, and worshiping the Deity with great respect and veneration. The thirty-nine items plus these five come to a total of forty-four. If we add the previous twenty items to these forty-four, the total number becomes sixty-four. The five items mentioned above repeat previously mentioned items. In the *Bhakti-rasāmṛta-sindhu,* Śrīla Rūpa Gosvāmī states:

*aṅgānāṁ pañcakasyāsya*
*pūrva-vilikhitasya ca*
*nikhila-śraiṣṭhya-bodhāya*
*punar apy atra śaṁsanam*

"The glorification of these five items [association with devotees, chanting the holy name and so on] is to make known the complete superiority of these five practices of devotional service."

The sixty-four items of devotional service include all the activities of the body, mind and senses. Thus the sixty-four items engage one in devotional service in all respects.

## TEXT 130

শ্রদ্ধা বিশেষতঃ প্রীতিঃ শ্রীমূর্তের়ঙ্ঘ্রিসেবনে ॥ ১৩০ ॥

*śraddhā viśeṣataḥ prītiḥ*
*śrī-mūrter aṅghri-sevane*

## SYNONYMS

*śraddhā*—faith; *viśeṣataḥ*—particularly; *prītiḥ*—love; *śrī-mūrteḥ*—of the Deity form of the Lord; *aṅghri-sevane*—in service of the lotus feet.

## TRANSLATION

**" 'One should have full faith and love in worshiping the lotus feet of the Deity.**

## PURPORT

This verse and the following two verses are found in *Bhakti-rasāmṛta-sindhu* (1.2.90-92).

## TEXT 131

শ্রীমদ্ভাগবতার্থানামাস্বাদো রসিকৈঃ সহ ।
সজাতীয়াশয়ে স্নিগ্ধে সাধৌ সঙ্গঃ স্বতো বরে ॥ ১৩১ ॥

*śrīmad-bhāgavatārthānām*
*āsvādo rasikaiḥ saha*
*sajātīyāśaye snigdhe*
*sādhau saṅgaḥ svato vare*

## SYNONYMS

*śrīmad-bhāgavata*—of the *Śrīmad-Bhāgavatam; arthānām*—of the meanings; *āsvādaḥ*—enjoying the taste; *rasikaiḥ saha*—with the devotees; *sa-jātīya*—similar; *āśaye*—endowed with a desire; *snigdhe*—advanced in devotional affection; *sādhau*—with a devotee; *saṅgaḥ*—association; *svataḥ*—for one's self; *vare*—better.

## TRANSLATION

**" 'One should taste the meaning of Śrīmad-Bhāgavatam in the association of pure devotees, and one should associate with the devotees who are more advanced than oneself and endowed with a similar type of affection for the Lord.**

## PURPORT

The words *sajātīyāśaye snigdhe sādhau saṅgaḥ svato vare* are very important items. One should not associate with professional *Bhāgavatam* reciters. A professional *Bhāgavatam* reciter is one who is not in the disciplic succession or one who has no taste for *bhakti-yoga.* Simply on the strength of grammatical knowledge and word jugglery, professional reciters maintain their bodies and their desires for sense gratification by reading *Śrīmad-Bhāgavatam.* One should also avoid those who are averse to Lord Viṣṇu and His devotees, those who are Māyāvādīs, those who offend the chanting of the Hare Kṛṣṇa *mantra,* those who simply dress as Vaiṣṇavas or so-called *gosvāmīs,* and those who make a business by selling Vedic *mantras* and reciting *Śrīmad-Bhāgavatam* to maintain their families. One should not try to understand *Śrīmad-Bhāgavatam* from such materialistic people. According to the Vedic injunctions: *yasya deve parā bhaktiḥ.* The *Śrīmad-*

*Bhāgavatam* can only be recited by one who has unflinching faith in the lotus feet of Kṛṣṇa and His devotee, the spiritual master. One should try to understand *Śrīmad-Bhāgavatam* from the spiritual master. The Vedic injunction states: *bhaktyā bhāgavataṁ grāhyaṁ na buddhyā na ca ṭīkayā.* One has to understand *Śrīmad-Bhāgavatam* through the process of devotional service and by hearing the recitation of a pure devotee. These are the injunctions of Vedic literature—*śruti* and *smṛti.* Those who are not in the disciplic succession and who are not pure devotees cannot understand the real mysterious objective of *Śrīmad-Bhāgavatam* and *Śrīmad Bhagavad-gītā.*

### TEXT 132

নামসংকীর্তনং শ্রীমন্মথুরামণ্ডলে স্থিতিঃ ॥ ১৩২ ॥

*nāma-saṅkīrtanaṁ śrīman-*
*mathurā-maṇḍale sthitiḥ*

### SYNONYMS

*nāma-saṅkīrtanam*—chanting the Hare Kṛṣṇa *mahā-mantra; śrīman-mathurā-maṇḍale*—in Mathurā, where Kṛṣṇa specifically performs His pastimes; *sthitiḥ*—residence.

### TRANSLATION

**" 'One should congregationally chant the holy name of the Lord and reside in Vṛndāvana.'**

### PURPORT

Navadvīpa-dhāma, Jagannātha Purī-dhāma and Vṛndāvana-dhāma are considered to be identical. If one goes to Mathurā-maṇḍala-bhūmi for sense gratification or to make a livelihood, he commits an offense and is condemned. Whoever does so must be penalized in the next life by becoming a hog or a monkey in Vṛndāvana-dhāma. After taking on such a body, the offender is liberated in the next life. Śrīla Bhaktisiddhānta Sarasvatī Ṭhākura remarks that residing in Vṛndāvana with a view to enjoy sense gratification surely leads a so-called devotee to a lower species.

### TEXT 133

দুরূহাদ্ভুতবীর্যেঽস্মিন্ শ্রদ্ধা দূরেঽস্তু পঞ্চকে ।
যত্র স্বল্পোঽপি সম্বন্ধঃ সদ্ধিয়াং ভাবজন্মনে ॥ ১৩৩ ॥

*durūhādbhuta-vīrye 'smin*
*śraddhā dūre 'stu pañcake*
*yatra svalpo 'pi sambandhaḥ*
*sad-dhiyāṁ bhāva-janmane*

## SYNONYMS

*durūha*—difficult to be reconciled; *adbhuta*—wonderful; *vīrye*—in the power; *asmin*—in this; *śraddhā*—faith; *dūre*—far away; *astu*—let it be; *pañcake*—in the above-mentioned five principles; *yatra*—in which; *svalpaḥ*—a little; *api*—even; *sambandhaḥ*—connection; *sat-dhiyām*—of those who are intelligent and offenseless; *bhāva-janmane*—to awaken one's dormant love for Kṛṣṇa.

## TRANSLATION

**" 'The power of these five principles is very wonderful and difficult to reconcile. Even without faith in them, a person who is offenseless can experience dormant love of Kṛṣṇa simply by being a little connected with them.'**

## PURPORT

This verse is also found in *Bhakti-rasāmṛta-sindhu* (1.2.238).

## TEXT 134

'এক' অঙ্গ সাধে, কেহ সাধে 'বহু' অঙ্গ ।
'নিষ্ঠা' হৈলে উপজয় প্রেমের তরঙ্গ ॥ ১৩৪ ॥

*'eka' aṅga sādhe, keha sādhe 'bahu' aṅga*
*'niṣṭhā' haile upajaya premera taraṅga*

## SYNONYMS

*eka*—one; *aṅga*—portion; *sādhe*—executes; *keha*—someone; *sādhe*—executes; *bahu*—many; *aṅga*—portions; *niṣṭhā*—firm faith; *haile*—if there is; *upajaya*—awaken; *premera*—of love of Godhead; *taraṅga*—the waves.

## TRANSLATION

**"When one is firmly fixed in devotional service, whether he executes one or many processes of devotional service, the waves of love of Godhead will awaken.**

## PURPORT

The processes of devotional service are *śravaṇaṁ kīrtanaṁ viṣṇoḥ smaraṇaṁ pāda-sevanam/ arcanaṁ vandanaṁ dāsyaṁ sakhyam ātma-nivedanam.*

### TEXT 135

'এক' অঙ্গে সিদ্ধি পাইল বহু ভক্তগণ ।
অম্বরীষাদি ভক্তের 'বহু' অঙ্গ-সাধন ॥ ১৩৫ ॥

*'eka' aṅge siddhi pāila bahu bhakta-gaṇa*
*ambarīṣādi bhaktera 'bahu' aṅga-sādhana*

### SYNONYMS

*eka aṅge*—by one portion; *siddhi*—perfection; *pāila*—achieved; *bahu*—many; *bhakta-gaṇa*—devotees; *ambarīṣa-ādi*—King Ambarīṣa Mahārāja and others; *bhaktera*—of devotees; *bahu aṅga-sādhana*—execution of many processes of devotional service.

### TRANSLATION

**"There are many devotees who execute only one of the nine processes of devotional service. Nonetheless, they get ultimate success. Devotees like Mahārāja Ambarīṣa execute all nine items and they also get ultimate success.**

### TEXT 136

শ্রীবিষ্ণোঃ শ্রবণে পরীক্ষিদভবদ্বৈয়াসকিঃ কীর্তনে
প্রহ্লাদঃ স্মরণে তদঙ্ঘ্রিভজনে লক্ষ্মীঃ পৃথুঃ পূজনে ।
অক্রূরস্ত্বভিবন্দনে কপিপতির্দাস্যেঽথ সখ্যেঽর্জুনঃ
সর্বস্বাত্মনিবেদনে বলিরভূৎ কৃষ্ণাপ্তিরেষাং পরা ॥ ১৩৬ ॥

*śrī-viṣṇoḥ śravaṇe parīkṣid abhavad vaiyāsakiḥ kīrtane*
*prahlādaḥ smaraṇe tad-aṅghri-bhajane lakṣmīḥ pṛthuḥ pūjane*
*akrūras tv abhivandane kapi-patir dāsye 'tha sakhye 'rjunaḥ*
*sarvasvātma-nivedane balir abhūt kṛṣṇāptir eṣāṁ parā*

### SYNONYMS

*śrī-viṣṇoḥ*—of Lord Śrī Viṣṇu; *śravaṇe*—in hearing; *parīkṣit*—King Parīkṣit, known also as Viṣṇurāta, or one who is protected by Lord Viṣṇu; *abhavat*—was; *vaiyāsakiḥ*—Śukadeva Gosvāmī; *kīrtane*—in reciting *Śrīmad-Bhāgavatam; prahlādaḥ*—Mahārāja Prahlāda; *smaraṇe*—in remembering; *tat-aṅghri*—of Lord Viṣṇu's lotus feet; *bhajane*—in serving; *lakṣmīḥ*—the goddess of fortune; *pṛthuḥ*—Mahārāja Pṛthu; *pūjane*—in worshiping the Deity of the Lord; *akrūraḥ*—Akrūra; *tu*—but; *abhivandane*—in offering prayers; *kapi-patiḥ*—Hanumānjī, or Vajrāṅgajī; *dāsye*—in servitude to Lord Rāmacandra; *atha*—moreover; *sakhye*—in friendship; *arjunaḥ*—Arjuna; *sarvasva-ātma-nivedane*—in fully dedicating oneself; *baliḥ*—Mahārāja Bali; *abhūt*—was; *kṛṣṇa-āptiḥ*—the achievement of the lotus feet of Lord Kṛṣṇa; *eṣām*—of all of them; *parā*—transcendental.

### TRANSLATION

**" 'Mahārāja Parīkṣit attained the highest perfection, shelter at Lord Kṛṣṇa's lotus feet, simply by hearing about Lord Viṣṇu. Śukadeva Gosvāmī attained perfection simply by reciting Śrīmad-Bhāgavatam. Prahlāda Mahārāja attained perfection by remembering the Lord. The goddess of fortune attained perfection by massaging the transcendental legs of Mahā-Viṣṇu. Mahārāja Pṛthu attained perfection by worshiping the Deity, and Akrūra attained perfection by offering prayers unto the Lord. Vajrāṅgajī [Hanumān] attained perfection by rendering service to Lord Rāmacandra, and Arjuna attained perfection simply by being Kṛṣṇa's friend. Bali Mahārāja attained perfection by dedicating everything to the lotus feet of Kṛṣṇa.'**

### PURPORT

This verse appears in the *Padyāvalī* (53) and the *Bhakti-rasāmṛta-sindhu* (1.2.265).

### TEXTS 137-139

স বৈ মনঃ কৃষ্ণপদারবিন্দয়ো-
র্বচাংসি বৈকুণ্ঠগুণানুবর্ণনে ।
করৌ হরের্মন্দিরমার্জনাদিষু
শ্রুতিঞ্চকারাচ্যুত-সৎকথোদয়ে ॥ ১৩৭ ॥
মুকুন্দলিঙ্গালয়দর্শনে দৃশৌ
তদ্ভৃত্যগাত্রস্পরশেঽঙ্গসঙ্গমম্ ।
ঘ্রাণঞ্চ তৎপাদসরোজসৌরভে
শ্রীমত্তুলস্যা রসনাং তদর্পিতে ॥ ১৩৮ ॥
পাদৌ হরেঃ ক্ষেত্রপদানুসর্পণে
শিরো হৃষীকেশ-পদাভিবন্দনে ।
কামঞ্চ দাস্যে ন তু কামকাম্যয়া
যথোত্তমঃশ্লোকজনাশ্রয়া রতিঃ ॥ ১৩৯ ॥

*sa vai manaḥ kṛṣṇa-padāravindayor*
*vacāṁsi vaikuṇṭha-guṇānuvarṇane*
*karau harer mandira-mārjanādiṣu*
*śrutiṁ cakārācyuta-sat-kathodaye*

*mukunda-liṅgālaya-darśane dṛśau*
*tad-bhṛtya-gātra-sparaśe 'ṅga-saṅgamam*
*ghrāṇaṁ ca tat-pāda-saroja-saurabhe*
*śrīmat-tulasyā rasanāṁ tad-arpite*

*pādau hareḥ kṣetra-padānusarpaṇe*
*śiro hṛṣīkeśa-padābhivandane*
*kāmaṁ ca dāsye na tu kāma-kāmyayā*
*yathottamaḥśloka-janāśrayā ratiḥ*

## SYNONYMS

*saḥ*—he (Mahārāja Ambarīṣa); *vai*—certainly; *manaḥ*—the mind; *kṛṣṇa-pada-aravindayoḥ*—on the two lotus feet of Kṛṣṇa; *vacāṁsi*—words; *vaikuṇṭha-guṇa-anuvarṇane*—in describing the transcendental character of Kṛṣṇa; *karau*—the two hands; *hareḥ*—of Lord Kṛṣṇa or Viṣṇu; *mandira-mārjana-ādiṣu*—in cleansing the temple of Hari and similar other duties; *śrutim*—the ears; *cakāra*—engaged; *acyuta*—of the Lord; *sat-kathā-udaye*—in the arising of transcendental topics; *mukunda-liṅga*—of the Deities of the Lord; *ālaya*—temples; *darśane*—in visiting; *dṛśau*—the two eyes; *tat-bhṛtya*—of the servants of the Lord; *gātra*—the bodies; *sparaśe*—in touching; *aṅga-saṅgamam*—bodily contact such as embracing or touching the lotus feet; *ghrāṇam*—the sensation of smell; *ca*—and; *tat-pāda-saroja*—of the Lord's lotus feet; *saurabhe*—in the fragrance; *śrīmat*—most auspicious; *tulasyāḥ*—of *tulasī* leaves; *rasanām*—the tongue; *tat-arpite*—in food offered to the Lord; *pādau*—the two feet; *hareḥ*—of the Lord; *kṣetra*—the place of pilgrimage; *pada-anusarpaṇe*—in walking to; *śiraḥ*—the head; *hṛṣīkeśa*—of the Lord of the senses, the Personality of Godhead; *pada-abhivandane*—in offering prayers at the lotus feet; *kāmam*—all desires; *dāsye*—in serving the Lord; *na*—not; *tu*—but; *kāma-kāmyayā*—with a desire for sense gratification; *yathā*—as much as; *uttamaḥ-śloka*—of the Lord, who is worshiped by selected poems; *jana*—in the devotee; *āśrayā*—having shelter; *ratiḥ*—attachment.

## TRANSLATION

**" 'Mahārāja Ambarīṣa always engaged his mind at the lotus feet of Kṛṣṇa, his words in describing the spiritual world and the Supreme Personality of Godhead, his hands in cleansing and washing the Lord's temple, his ears in hearing topics about the Supreme Lord, his eyes in seeing the Deity of Lord Kṛṣṇa in the temple, his body in touching the lotus feet of Vaiṣṇavas and embracing them, his nostrils in smelling the aroma of the tulasī leaves offered to Kṛṣṇa's lotus feet, his tongue in tasting food offered to Kṛṣṇa, his legs in going to places of pilgrimage like Vṛndāvana and Mathurā or to the Lord's temple, and his head in touching the lotus feet of the Lord and offering Him**

**prayers. Thus Mahārāja Ambarīṣa desired only to serve the Lord faithfully. In this way he engaged his senses in the transcendental loving service of the Lord. As a result, he awakened his dormant loving propensity for the Lord's service.'**

### PURPORT

This is a quotation from *Śrīmad-Bhāgavatam* (9.4.18-20).

### TEXT 140

**কাম ত্যজি' কৃষ্ণ ভজে শাস্ত্র-আজ্ঞা মানি' ।**
**দেব-ঋষি-পিত্রাদিকের কভু নহে ঋণী ॥ ১৪০ ॥**

*kāma tyaji' kṛṣṇa bhaje śāstra-ājñā māni'*
*deva-ṛṣi-pitrādikera kabhu nahe ṛṇī*

### SYNONYMS

*kāma*—material desires; *tyaji'*—giving up; *kṛṣṇa*—Lord Kṛṣṇa; *bhaje*—worships; *śāstra-ājñā*—the direction of the revealed scripture; *māni'*—accepting; *deva*—demigods; *ṛṣi*—great sages; *pitṛ-ādikera*—of the forefathers and so on; *kabhu*—at any time; *nahe*—not; *ṛṇī*—a debtor.

### TRANSLATION

**"If a person gives up all material desires and completely engages in the transcendental loving service of Kṛṣṇa, as enjoined in revealed scriptures, he is never indebted to demigods, sages or forefathers.**

### PURPORT

After birth, every man is indebted in so many ways. He is indebted to the demigods for their supplying necessities like air, light and water. When one takes advantage of Vedic literatures, one becomes indebted to great sages like Vyāsadeva, Nārada, Devala and Asita. When one takes birth in a particular family, he becomes indebted to his forefathers. We are even indebted to common living entities like cows, from whom we take milk. Because we accept service from so many animals, we become indebted. However, if one is completely engaged in the Lord's devotional service, he is absolved of all debts. This is confirmed in the following verse, quoted from *Śrīmad-Bhāgavatam* (11.5.41).

### TEXT 141

দেবর্ষিভূতাপ্তনৃণাং পিতৄণাং
ন কিঙ্করো নায়মৃণী চ রাজন্ ।

সর্বাত্মনা যঃ শরণং শরণ্যং
গতো মুকুন্দং পরিহৃত্য কর্তম্ ॥ ১৪১ ॥

*devarṣi-bhūtāpta-nṛṇāṁ pitṝṇāṁ*
*na kiṅkaro nāyam ṛṇī ca rājan*
*sarvātmanā yaḥ śaraṇaṁ śaraṇyaṁ*
*gato mukundaṁ parihṛtya kartam*

**SYNONYMS**

*deva*—of the demigods; *ṛṣi*—of the sages; *bhūta*—of ordinary living entities; *āpta*—of friends and relatives; *nṛṇām*—of ordinary men; *pitṝṇām*—of the forefathers; *na*—not; *kiṅkaraḥ*—the servant; *na*—nor; *ayam*—this one; *ṛṇī*—debtor; *ca*—also; *rājan*—O King; *sarva-ātmanā*—with his whole being; *yaḥ*—a person who; *śaraṇam*—shelter; *śaraṇyam*—the Supreme Personality of Godhead, who affords shelter to all; *gataḥ*—approached; *mukundam*—Mukunda; *parihṛtya*—giving up; *kartam*—duties.

**TRANSLATION**

**" 'One who has given up all material duties and taken full shelter at the lotus feet of Mukunda, who gives shelter to all, is not indebted to the demigods, great sages, ordinary living beings, relatives, friends, mankind or even one's forefathers who have passed away.'**

**PURPORT**

It is said:

*adhyāpanaṁ brahma-yajñaḥ*
*pitṛ-yajñas tu tarpaṇam*
*homo daivo balir bhauto*
*nṛ-yajño 'tithi-pūjanam*

"By performing oblations with ghee, the demigods are satisfied. By studying the *Vedas, brahma-yajña* is performed, and by this the great sages are satisfied. Offering libations of water before one's forefathers is called *pitṛ-yajña.* By offering tribute, *bhūta-yajña* is performed. By properly receiving guests, *nṛ-yajña* is performed." There are five *yajñas* and five kinds of indebtedness—indebtedness to the demigods, great sages, forefathers, living entities and common men. Therefore one has to perform five kinds of *yajñas,* but when one takes to *saṅkīrtana-yajña* (the chanting of the Hare Kṛṣṇa *mantra*) one doesn't have to perform any other *yajña.* In *Śrīmad-Bhāgavatam,* Nārada Muni made a statement about the systematic performance of *bhāgavata-dharma* in connection with statements previously made by the nine Yogendras before Mahārāja Nimi. The sage Karabhājana Ṛṣi explained the four incarnations of the four *yugas,* and at the end, in this verse (text 141), he explained the position of Kṛṣṇa's pure devotee and how he is absolved of all debts.

### TEXT 142

**বিধি-ধর্ম ছাড়ি' ভজে কৃষ্ণের চরণ।**
**নিষিদ্ধ পাপাচারে তার কভু নহে মন ॥ ১৪২ ॥**

*vidhi-dharma chāḍi' bhaje kṛṣṇera caraṇa*
*niṣiddha pāpācāre tāra kabhu nahe mana*

### SYNONYMS

*vidhi-dharma chāḍi'*—giving up all regulative principles of the *varṇa* and *āśrama* institution; *bhaje*—worships; *kṛṣṇera caraṇa*—the lotus feet of Lord Kṛṣṇa; *niṣiddha*—forbidden; *pāpa-ācāre*—in sinful activities; *tāra*—his; *kabhu*—at any time; *nahe*—not; *mana*—the mind.

### TRANSLATION

**"Although the pure devotee does not follow all the regulative principles of varṇāśrama, he worships the lotus feet of Kṛṣṇa. Therefore he naturally has no tendency to commit sin.**

### PURPORT

The *varṇāśrama* institution is planned in such a way that one will not commit sinful activities. Material existence continues due to sinful activity. When one acts sinfully in this life, he gets a suitable body for the next life. When one again acts sinfully, he takes on another material body. In this way one is continuously under the influence of material nature.

*puruṣaḥ prakṛti-stho hi*
*bhuṅkte prakṛti-jān guṇān*
*kāraṇaṁ guṇa-saṅgo 'sya*
*sad-asad-yoni-janmasu*

"The living entity in material nature thus follows the ways of life, enjoying the three modes of material nature. This is due to his association with that material nature. Thus he meets with good and evil among various species." (Bg. 13.22)

Due to our association with the modes of material nature, we get different types of bodies—good and bad. One cannot be liberated from the cycle of birth and death, known as transmigration of the soul, unless one is completely freed from all sinful activities. The best process, therefore, is to take to Kṛṣṇa consciousness. One cannot take to Kṛṣṇa consciousness without being freed from all sinful activities. Naturally one who is very serious about Kṛṣṇa consciousness is freed from all sinful activity. Consequently a devotee is never inclined to commit sins. If one is pressured by the law or obligations to give up sinful activity, one cannot do so. However, if one takes to Kṛṣṇa consciousness, he can very easily give up all sinful activity. This is confirmed herein.

## TEXT 143

অজ্ঞানে বা হয় যদি 'পাপ' উপস্থিত ।
কৃষ্ণ তাঁরে শুদ্ধ করে, না করায় প্রায়শ্চিত্ত ॥ ১৪৩ ॥

*ajñāne vā haya yadi 'pāpa' upasthita*
*kṛṣṇa tāṅre śuddha kare, nā karāya prāyaścitta*

## SYNONYMS

*ajñāne*—by ignorance; *vā*—or; *haya*—there are; *yadi*—if; *pāpa*—sinful activities; *upasthita*—present; *kṛṣṇa*—Lord Kṛṣṇa; *tāṅre*—him (the devotee); *śuddha kare*—purifies; *nā karāya*—does not cause; *prāyaścitta*—atonement.

## TRANSLATION

**"If, however, a devotee accidentally becomes involved in a sinful activity, Kṛṣṇa purifies him. He does not have to undergo the regulative form of atonement.**

## PURPORT

Kṛṣṇa purifies from within as *caitya-guru,* the spiritual master within the heart. This is described in the following verse from *Śrīmad-Bhāgavatam* (11.5.42).

## TEXT 144

স্বপাদমূলং ভজতঃ প্রিয়স্য
ত্যক্তান্যভাবস্য হরিঃ পরেশঃ ।
বিকর্ম যচ্চোৎপতিতং কথঞ্চিৎ
ধুনোতি সর্বং হৃদি সন্নিবিষ্টঃ ॥ ১৪৪ ॥

*svapāda-mūlaṁ bhajataḥ priyasya*
*tyaktānya-bhāvasya hariḥ pareśaḥ*

*vikarma yac cotpatitaṁ kathañcit*
*dhunoti sarvaṁ hṛdi sanniviṣṭaḥ*

## SYNONYMS

*sva-pāda-mūlam*—the lotus feet of Kṛṣṇa, the shelter of the devotees; *bhajataḥ*—who is engaged in worshiping; *priyasya*—who is very dear to Kṛṣṇa; *tyakta*—given up; *anya*—for others; *bhāvasya*—of one whose disposition or inclination; *hariḥ*—the Supreme Personality of Godhead; *para-īśaḥ*—the Supreme Lord; *vikarma*—sinful activities; *yat*—whatever; *ca*—and; *utpatitam*—occurred; *kathañcit*—somehow; *dhunoti*—removes; *sarvam*—everything; *hṛdi*—in the heart; *sanniviṣṭaḥ*—entered.

## TRANSLATION

**" 'One who has given up everything and taken full shelter at the lotus feet of Hari, the Supreme Personality of Godhead, is very dear to Kṛṣṇa. If he is involved in some sinful activity by accident, the Supreme Personality of Godhead, who is seated within everyone's heart, removes his sins without difficulty.'**

## TEXT 145

জ্ঞান-বৈরাগ্যাদি – ভক্তির কভু নহে 'অঙ্গ' ।
অহিংসাযম-নিয়মাদি বুলে কৃষ্ণভক্ত-সঙ্গ ॥ ১৪৫ ॥

*jñāna-vairāgyādi——bhaktira kabhu nahe 'aṅga'*
*ahiṁsā-yama-niyamādi bule kṛṣṇa-bhakta-saṅga*

## SYNONYMS

*jñāna*—the path of knowledge; *vairāgya-ādi*—the path of renunciation and so on; *bhaktira*—of devotional service; *kabhu*—at any time; *nahe*—not; *aṅga*—a part; *ahiṁsā*—nonviolence; *yama*—controlling the senses and the mind; *niyama-ādi*—restrictions and so on; *bule*—roam; *kṛṣṇa-bhakta-saṅga*—in the association of a devotee of Lord Kṛṣṇa.

## TRANSLATION

**"The path of speculative knowledge and renunciation is not very essential for devotional service. Indeed, good qualities such as nonviolence and mind and sense control automatically accompany a devotee of Lord Kṛṣṇa.**

## PURPORT

Sometimes a neophyte devotee or ordinary person thinks highly of speculative knowledge, austerity, penances and renunciation, thinking them the only path for advancement in devotional service. Actually this is not a fact. The path of knowledge, mystic *yoga* and renunciation has nothing to do with the pure soul. When one is temporarily in the material world, such processes may help a little, but they are not necessary for a pure devotee of Kṛṣṇa. In the material world, such activities end in material enjoyment or merging into the effulgence of the Supreme. They have nothing to do with the eternal loving service of the Lord. If one abandons speculative knowledge and simply engages in devotional service, he has attained his perfection. The devotee has no need for speculative knowledge, pious activity or mystic *yoga*. All these are automatically present when one renders the Lord transcendental loving service.

## TEXT 146

তস্মান্মদ্ভক্তিযুক্তস্য যোগিনো বৈ মদাত্মনঃ ।
ন জ্ঞানং ন চ বৈরাগ্যং প্রায়ঃ শ্রেয়ো ভবেদিহ ॥ ১৪৬ ॥

*tasmān mad-bhakti-yuktasya*
*yogino vai mad-ātmanaḥ*
*na jñānaṁ na ca vairāgyaṁ*
*prāyaḥ śreyo bhaved iha*

## SYNONYMS

*tasmāt*—therefore; *mat-bhakti*—in My devotional service; *yuktasya*—of one who is engaged; *yoginaḥ*—the first-class *yogī* or mystic; *vai*—certainly; *mat-ātmanaḥ*—whose mind is always engaged in Me; *na*—not; *jñānam*—speculative knowledge; *na*—not; *ca*—also; *vairāgyam*—dry renunciation; *prāyaḥ*—for the most part; *śreyaḥ*—beneficial; *bhavet*—would be; *iha*—in this world.

## TRANSLATION

**" 'For one who is fully engaged in My devotional service, whose mind is fixed on Me in bhakti-yoga, the path of speculative knowledge and dry renunciation is not very beneficial.'**

## PURPORT

The path of devotional service is always independent of other activity. The path of speculative knowledge or mystic *yoga* may be a little beneficial in the beginning, but it cannot be considered part of devotional service. This verse (*Śrīmad-Bhāgavatam* 11.20.31) was spoken by Lord Kṛṣṇa when He was speaking to Uddhava before His departure from this material world. These are important instructions given directly by Lord Kṛṣṇa. Śrī Uddhava asked the Lord about the two kinds of instructions given in the *Vedas*. One instruction is called *pravṛtti-mārga,* and the other is called *nivṛtti-mārga.* These are directions for enjoying the material world according to regulative principles and then giving up the material world for higher spiritual understanding. Sometimes one does not know whether to practice speculative knowledge or mystic *yoga* for advancement in spiritual knowledge. Kṛṣṇa explains to Uddhava that the mechanical process of speculative knowledge and *yoga* is not necessary for advancing in devotional service. Devotional service is completely spiritual; it has nothing to do with material things. It is awakened by hearing and chanting in the association of devotees. Because devotional service is always transcendental, it has nothing to do with material activity.

### TEXT 147

এতে ন হ্যদ্ভুতা ব্যাধ তবাহিংসাদয়ো গুণাঃ ।
হরিভক্তৌ প্রবৃত্তা যে ন তে স্যুঃ পরতাপিনঃ ॥ ১৪৭ ॥

*ete na hy adbhutā vyādha*
*tavāhiṁsādayo guṇāḥ*
*hari-bhaktau pravṛttā ye*
*na te syuḥ paratāpinaḥ*

### SYNONYMS

*ete*—all these; *na*—not; *hi*—certainly; *adbhutāḥ*—wonderful; *vyādha*—O hunter; *tava*—your; *ahiṁsā-ādayaḥ*—nonviolence and others; *guṇāḥ*—qualities; *hari-bhaktau*—in devotional service; *pravṛttāḥ*—engaged; *ye*—those who; *na*—not; *te*—they; *syuḥ*—are; *paratāpinaḥ*—envious of other living entities.

### TRANSLATION

**" 'O hunter, good qualities like nonviolence, which you have developed, are not very astonishing, for those who are engaged in the Lord's devotional service are never inclined to give pain to others because of envy.'**

### PURPORT

This is a quotation from the *Skanda Purāṇa.*

### TEXT 148

বৈধীভক্তি-সাধনের কহিলুঁ বিবরণ ।
রাগানুগা-ভক্তির লক্ষণ শুন, সনাতন ॥ ১৪৮ ॥

*vaidhī-bhakti-sādhanera kahiluṅ vivaraṇa*
*rāgānugā-bhaktira lakṣaṇa śuna, sanātana*

## SYNONYMS

*vaidhī-bhakti*—of devotional service according to the regulative principles; *sādhanera*—of the execution; *kahiluṅ*—I have made; *vivaraṇa*—description; *rāgānugā-bhaktira*—of spontaneous devotional service; *lakṣaṇa*—the symptoms; *śuna*—please hear; *sanātana*—O Sanātana.

## TRANSLATION

**"My dear Sanātana, I have now in detail described devotional service according to the regulative principles. Now hear from Me about spontaneous devotional service and its characteristics.**

## TEXT 149

রাগাত্মিকা-ভক্তি—'মুখ্যা' ব্রজবাসি-জনে ।
তার অনুগত ভক্তির 'রাগানুগা'-নামে ॥ ১৪৯ ॥

*rāgātmikā-bhakti——'mukhyā' vraja-vāsi-jane*
*tāra anugata bhaktira 'rāgānugā'-nāme*

## SYNONYMS

*rāgātmikā-bhakti*—spontaneous devotional service; *mukhyā*—preeminent; *vraja-vāsi-jane*—in the inhabitants of Vraja, or Vṛndāvana; *tāra*—that; *anugata*—following; *bhaktira*—of devotional service; *rāgānugā-nāme*—named *rāgānugā* or following after spontaneous devotional service.

## TRANSLATION

**"The original inhabitants of Vṛndāvana are attached to Kṛṣṇa spontaneously in devotional service. Nothing can compare to such spontaneous devotional service, which is called rāgātmikā bhakti. When a devotee follows in the footsteps of the devotees of Vṛndāvana, his devotional service is called rāgānugā bhakti.**

## PURPORT

In his *Bhakti-sandarbha,* Jīva Gosvāmī states:

*tad evaṁ tat-tad-abhimāna-lakṣaṇa-bhāva-viśeṣveṇa svābhāvika-rāgasya vaiśiṣṭye sati tat-tad-rāga-prayuktā śravaṇa-kīrtana-smaraṇa-pāda-sevana-vandanātma-nivedana-prāyā bhaktis teṣāṁ rāgātmikā bhaktir ity ucyate.... tatas tadīyaṁ rāgaṁ rucyānugacchantī sā rāgānugā.*

When a pure devotee follows the footsteps of a devotee in Vṛndāvana, he develops *rāgānugā bhakti.*

## TEXT 150

ইষ্টে স্বারসিকী রাগঃ পরমাবিষ্টতা ভবেৎ।
তন্ময়ী যা ভবেদ্ভক্তিঃ সাত্র রাগাত্মিকোদিতা ॥ ১৫০ ॥

*iṣṭe svārasikī rāgaḥ*
*paramāviṣṭatā bhavet*
*tanmayī yā bhaved bhaktiḥ*
*sātra rāgātmikoditā*

### SYNONYMS

*iṣṭe*—unto the desired object of life; *svārasikī*—appropriate for one's own original aptitude of love; *rāgaḥ*—attachment; *parama-āviṣṭatā*—absorption in the service of the Lord; *bhavet*—is; *tat-mayī*—consisting of that transcendental attachment; *yā*—which; *bhavet*—is; *bhaktiḥ*—devotional service; *sā*—that; *atra*—here; *rāgātmikā-uditā*—called *rāgātmikā,* or spontaneous devotional service.

### TRANSLATION

**" 'When one becomes attached to the Supreme Personality of Godhead, his natural inclination to love is fully absorbed in thoughts of the Lord. That is called transcendental attachment, and devotional service according to that attachment is called rāgātmikā, or spontaneous devotional service.'**

### PURPORT

This verse is found in *Bhakti-rasāmṛta-sindhu* (1.2.272).

## TEXT 151

ইষ্টে 'গাঢ়-তৃষ্ণা'—রাগের স্বরূপ-লক্ষণ।
ইষ্টে 'আবিষ্টতা' —এই তটস্থ-লক্ষণ ॥ ১৫১ ॥

*iṣṭe 'gāḍha-tṛṣṇā'——rāgera svarūpa-lakṣaṇa*
*iṣṭe 'āviṣṭatā'——ei taṭastha-lakṣaṇa*

### SYNONYMS

*iṣṭe*—in the desired object, the Supreme Personality of Godhead; *gāḍha-tṛṣṇā*—deep attachment; *rāgera*—of spontaneous love; *svarūpa-lakṣaṇa*—the primary symptom; *iṣṭe*—unto the Supreme; *āviṣṭatā*—absorption; *ei*—this; *taṭastha-lakṣaṇa*—the marginal symptom.

## TRANSLATION

**"The primary characteristic of spontaneous love is deep attachment for the Supreme Personality of Godhead. Absorption in Him is a marginal characteristic.**

## TEXT 152

রাগময়ী-ভক্তির হয় 'রাগাত্মিকা' নাম ।
তাহা শুনি' লুব্ধ হয় কোন ভাগ্যবান্ ॥ ১৫২ ॥

*rāgamayī-bhaktira haya 'rāgātmikā' nāma*
*tāhā śuni' lubdha haya kona bhāgyavān*

## SYNONYMS

*rāga-mayī*—consisting of attachment; *bhaktira*—of devotional service; *haya*—is; *rāgātmikā*—spontaneous love; *nāma*—the name; *tāhā śuni'*—hearing this; *lubdha*—covetous; *haya*—becomes; *kona bhāgyavān*—some fortunate person.

## TRANSLATION

**"Thus devotional service which consists of rāga [deep attachment] is called rāgātmikā, spontaneous loving service. If a devotee covets such a position, he is considered to be most fortunate.**

## TEXT 153

লোভে ব্রজবাসীর ভাবে করে অনুগতি ।
শাস্ত্রযুক্তি নাহি মানে—রাগানুগার প্রকৃতি ॥ ১৫৩ ॥

*lobhe vraja-vāsīra bhāve kare anugati*
*śāstra-yukti nāhi māne——rāgānugāra prakṛti*

## SYNONYMS

*lobhe*—in such covetousness; *vraja-vāsīra bhāve*—in the moods of the inhabitants of Vṛndāvana, Vraja; *kare anugati*—follows; *śāstra-yukti*—injunctions or reasonings of the *śāstras; nāhi māne*—does not abide by; *rāgānugāra*—of spontaneous love; *prakṛti*—the nature.

## TRANSLATION

**"If one follows in the footsteps of the inhabitants of Vṛndāvana out of such transcendental covetousness, he does not care for the injunctions or reasonings of śāstra. That is the way of spontaneous love.**

## PURPORT

Śrīla Bhaktisiddhānta Sarasvatī Ṭhākura says that a devotee is attracted by the service of the inhabitants of Vṛndāvana—namely the cowherd men, Mahārāja Nanda, mother Yaśodā, Rādhārāṇī, the *gopīs,* and the cows and calves. An advanced devotee is attracted by the service rendered by an eternal servitor of the Lord. This attraction is called spontaneous attraction. Technically it is called *svarūpa-upalabdhi.* This stage is not achieved in the beginning. In the beginning one has to render service strictly according to the regulative principles set forth by the revealed scriptures and spiritual master. By continuously rendering service through the process of *vaidhī bhakti,* one's natural inclination is gradually awakened. That is called spontaneous attraction, or *rāgānugā bhakti.*

An advanced devotee situated on the platform of spontaneity is already very expert in śāstric instruction, logic and argument. When he comes to the point of eternal love for Kṛṣṇa, no one can deviate him from that position, neither by argument nor by śāstric evidence. An advanced devotee has realized his eternal relationship with the Lord, and consequently he does not accept the logic and arguments of others. Such an advanced devotee has nothing to do with the *sahajiyās,* who manufacture their own way and commit sins by indulging in illicit sex, intoxication and gambling, if not meat-eating. Sometimes the *sahajiyās* imitate advanced devotees and live in their own whimsical way, avoiding the principles set down in the revealed scriptures. Unless one follows the six Gosvāmīs—Śrī Rūpa, Sanātana, Raghunātha Bhaṭṭa, Śrī Jīva, Gopāla Bhaṭṭa and Raghunātha dāsa—one cannot be a bona fide spontaneous lover of Kṛṣṇa. In this connection, Śrīla Narottama dāsa Ṭhākura says: *rūpa-raghunātha-pade haibe ākuti kabe hāma bujhaba se yugala pirīti.* The *sahajiyās'* understanding of the love affairs between Rādhā and Kṛṣṇa is not bona fide because they do not follow the principles laid down by the six Gosvāmīs. Their illicit connection and their imitation of the dress of Rūpa Gosvāmī as well as their avoidance of the prescribed methods of revealed scriptures will lead them to the lowest regions of hell. These imitative *sahajiyās* are cheated and unfortunate. They are not equal to advanced devotees (*paramahaṁsas*). Debauchees and *paramahaṁsas* are not on the same level.

## TEXT 154

বিরাজন্তীমভিব্যক্তাং ব্রজবাসিজনাদিষু ।
রাগাত্মিকামনুসৃতা যা সা রাগানুগোচ্যতে ॥ ১৫৪ ॥

*virājantīm abhivyaktāṁ*
*vraja-vāsi-janādiṣu*
*rāgātmikām anusṛtā*
*yā sā rāgānugocyate*

## SYNONYMS

*virājantīm*—shining intensely; *abhivyaktām*—fully expressed; *vraja-vāsi-jana-ādiṣu*—among the eternal inhabitants of Vṛndāvana; *rāgātmikām*—devotional service consisting of spontaneous love; *anusṛtā*—following; *yā*—which; *sā*—that; *rāgānugā*—devotional service following in the wake of spontaneous love; *ucyate*—is said.

## TRANSLATION

**" 'Devotional service in spontaneous love is vividly expressed and manifested by the inhabitants of Vṛndāvana. Devotional service that accords with their devotional service is called rāgānugā bhakti, or devotional service following in the wake of spontaneous loving service.'**

## PURPORT

This verse is found in *Bhakti-rasāmṛta-sindhu* (1.2.270).

## TEXT 155

তত্তদ্ভাবাদিমাধুর্যে শ্রুতে ধীর্যদপেক্ষতে ।
নাত্র শাস্ত্রং ন যুক্তিঞ্চ তল্লোভোৎপত্তিলক্ষণম্ ॥ ১৫৫ ॥

*tat-tad-bhāvādi-mādhurye*
*śrute dhīr yad apekṣate*
*nātra śāstraṁ na yuktiṁ ca*
*tal lobhotpatti-lakṣaṇam*

## SYNONYMS

*tat-tat*—respective; *bhāva-ādi-mādhurye*—the sweetness of the loving moods (namely *śānta-rasa, dāsya-rasa, sakhya-rasa, vātsalya-rasa* and *mādhurya-rasa*) of the inhabitants of Vṛndāvana; *śrute*—when heard; *dhīḥ*—the intelligence; *yat*—which; *apekṣate*—depends on; *na*—not; *atra*—here; *śāstram*—revealed scriptures; *na*—not; *yuktim*—logic and argument; *ca*—also; *tat*—that; *lobha*—of covetousness to follow in the footsteps; *utpatti-lakṣaṇam*—the symptom of awakening.

## TRANSLATION

**" 'When an advanced realized devotee hears about the affairs of the devotees of Vṛndāvana—in the mellows of śānta, dāsya, sakhya, vātsalya and mādhurya—he becomes inclined in that way, and his intelligence becomes attracted. Indeed, he begins to covet that particular type of devotion. When**

**such covetousness is awakened, one's intelligence no longer depends on the instruction of śāstra, revealed scripture, logic or argument.'**

### PURPORT

This verse is found in *Bhakti-rasāmṛta-sindhu* (1.2.292).

### TEXTS 156-157

**বাহ্য, অন্তর,– ইহার দুই ত' সাধন।**
**'বাহ্যে' সাধক-দেহে করে শ্রবণ-কীর্তন ॥ ১৫৬ ॥**
**'মনে' নিজ-সিদ্ধদেহ করিয়া ভাবন।**
**রাত্রি-দিনে করে ব্রজে কৃষ্ণের সেবন ॥ ১৫৭ ॥**

*bāhya, antara,——ihāra dui ta' sādhana*
*'bāhye' sādhaka-dehe kare śravaṇa-kīrtana*

*'mane' nija-siddha-deha kariyā bhāvana*
*rātri-dine kare vraje kṛṣṇera sevana*

### SYNONYMS

*bāhya*—externally; *antara*—internally; *ihāra*—of this spontaneous love of Godhead; *dui*—two; *ta'*—indeed; *sādhana*—such processes of execution; *bāhye*—externally; *sādhaka-dehe*—with the body of an advanced devotee; *kare*—does; *śravaṇa-kīrtana*—hearing and chanting; *mane*—the mind; *nija*—own; *siddha-deha*—eternal body or self-realized position; *kariyā bhāvana*—thinking of; *rātri-dine*—night and day; *kare*—executes; *vraje*—in Vṛndāvana; *kṛṣṇera*—of Lord Kṛṣṇa; *sevana*—service.

### TRANSLATION

**"There are two processes by which one may execute this rāgānugā bhakti—external and internal. When self-realized, the advanced devotee externally remains like a neophyte and executes all the śāstric injunctions, especially hearing and chanting. However, within his mind, in his original purified self-realized position, he serves Kṛṣṇa in Vṛndāvana in his particular way. He serves Kṛṣṇa twenty-four hours, all day and night.**

### TEXT 158

সেবা সাধকরূপেণ সিদ্ধরূপেণ চাত্র হি।
তদ্ভাবলিপ্সুনা কার্যা ব্রজলোকানুসারতঃ ॥ ১৫৮ ॥

*sevā sādhaka-rūpeṇa*
*siddha-rūpeṇa cātra hi*
*tad-bhāva-lipsunā kāryā*
*vraja-lokānusārataḥ*

### SYNONYMS

*sevā*—service; *sādhaka-rūpeṇa*—with the external body as a devotee practicing regulative devotional service; *siddha-rūpeṇa*—with a body suitable for eternal, self-realized service; *ca*—also; *atra*—in this connection; *hi*—certainly; *tat*—of that; *bhāva*—the mood; *lipsunā*—desiring to obtain; *kāryā*—to be executed; *vraja-loka*—of the particular servant of Kṛṣṇa in Vṛndāvana; *anusārataḥ*—by following in the footsteps.

### TRANSLATION

**" 'The advanced devotee who is inclined to spontaneous loving service should follow the activities of a particular associate of Kṛṣṇa in Vṛndāvana. He should execute service externally as a regulative devotee as well as internally from his self-realized position. Thus he should perform devotional service both externally and internally.'**

### PURPORT

This verse is found in *Bhakti-rasāmṛta-sindhu* (1.2.295).

### TEXT 159

নিজাভীষ্ট কৃষ্ণপ্রেষ্ঠ পাছেত' লাগিয়া।
নিরন্তর সেবা করে অন্তর্মনা হঞা ॥ ১৫৯ ॥

*nijābhīṣṭa kṛṣṇa-preṣṭha pācheta' lāgiyā*
*nirantara sevā kare antarmanā hañā*

### SYNONYMS

*nija-abhīṣṭa*—one's own choice; *kṛṣṇa-preṣṭha*—the servitor of Kṛṣṇa; *pācheta' lāgiyā*—following; *nirantara*—twenty-four hours a day; *sevā*—service; *kare*—executes; *antarmanā*—within the mind; *hañā*—being.

### TRANSLATION

**"Actually the inhabitants of Vṛndāvana are very dear to Kṛṣṇa. If one wants to engage in spontaneous loving service, he must follow the inhabitants of Vṛndāvana and constantly engage in devotional service within his mind.**

### TEXT 160

কৃষ্ণং স্মরন্ জনঞ্চাস্য প্রেষ্ঠং নিজসমীহিতম্ ।
তত্তৎকথা-রতশ্চাসৌ কুর্যাদ্বাসং ব্রজে সদা ॥ ১৬০ ॥

*kṛṣṇaṁ smaran janaṁ cāsya*
*preṣṭhaṁ nija-samīhitam*
*tat-tat-kathā-rataś cāsau*
*kuryād vāsaṁ vraje sadā*

### SYNONYMS

*kṛṣṇam*—Lord Kṛṣṇa; *smaran*—thinking of; *janam*—a devotee; *ca*—and; *asya*—of His; *preṣṭham*—very dear; *nija-samīhitam*—chosen by oneself; *tat-tat-kathā*—to those respective topics; *rataḥ*—attached; *ca*—and; *asau*—that; *kuryāt*—should do; *vāsam*—living; *vraje*—in Vṛndāvana; *sadā*—always.

### TRANSLATION

**" 'The devotee should always think of Kṛṣṇa within himself, and one should choose a very dear devotee who is a servitor of Kṛṣṇa in Vṛndāvana. One should constantly engage in topics about that servitor and his loving relationship to Kṛṣṇa, and one should live in Vṛndāvana. However, if one is physically unable to go to Vṛndāvana, he should mentally live there.'**

### PURPORT

This verse is found in *Bhakti-rasāmṛta-sindhu* (1.2.294).

### TEXT 161

দাস-সখা-পিত্রাদি-প্রেয়সীর গণ ।
রাগমার্গে নিজ-নিজ-ভাবের গণন ॥ ১৬১ ॥

*dāsa-sakhā-pitrādi-preyasīra gaṇa*
*rāga-mārge nija-nija-bhāvera gaṇana*

### SYNONYMS

*dāsa*—servants; *sakhā*—friends; *pitṛ-ādi*—parents; *preyasīra gaṇa*—conjugal lovers; *rāga-mārge*—on the path of spontaneous loving service; *nija-nija*—of one's own choice; *bhāvera*—of the ecstasy; *gaṇana*—counting.

### TRANSLATION

**"Kṛṣṇa has many types of devotees—some are servants, some are friends, some are parents, and some are conjugal lovers. Those who are situated in one**

**of these attitudes of spontaneous love according to their choice are considered to be on the path of spontaneous loving service.**

## TEXT 162

ন কর্হিচিন্মৎপরাঃ শান্তরূপে
নঙ্ক্ষ্যন্তি নো মেঽনিমিষো লেঢ়ি হেতিঃ ।
যেষামহং প্রিয় আত্মা সুতশ্চ
সখা গুরুঃ সুহৃদো দৈবমিষ্টম্ ॥ ১৬২ ॥

*na karhicin mat-parāḥ śānta-rūpe*
*naṅkṣyanti no me 'nimiṣo leḍhi hetiḥ*
*yeṣām ahaṁ priya ātmā sutaś ca*
*sakhā guruḥ suhṛdo daivam iṣṭam*

## SYNONYMS

*na*—not; *karhicit*—at any time; *mat-parāḥ*—devotees of Me; *śānta-rūpe*—O mother, the symbol of peacefulness; *naṅkṣyanti*—will perish; *no*—nor; *me*—My; *animiṣaḥ*—time; *leḍhi*—licks up (destroys); *hetiḥ*—weapon; *yeṣām*—of whom; *aham*—I; *priyaḥ*—dear; *ātmā*—the Supersoul; *sutaḥ*—the son; *ca*—and; *sakhā*—friend; *guruḥ*—spiritual master; *suhṛdaḥ*—well-wisher; *daivam*—the Deity; *iṣṭam*—chosen.

## TRANSLATION

**" 'My dear mother, Devahūti! O emblem of peace! My weapon, the disc of time, never vanquishes those for whom I am very dear, for whom I am the Supersoul, the son, friend, spiritual master, well-wisher, worshipable Deity and desired goal. Since the devotees are always attached to Me, they are never vanquished by the agents of time.'**

## PURPORT

This was spoken by Kapiladeva to His mother Devahūti and is recorded in *Śrīmad-Bhāgavatam* (3.25.38). Kapiladeva instructed His mother in *sāṅkhya-yoga,* but the importance of *bhakti-yoga* is mentioned here. Later *sāṅhkya-yoga* was imitated by atheists, whose system was founded by a different Kapiladeva, Ṛṣi Kapiladeva.

## TEXT 163

পতিপুত্রসুহৃদ্ভ্রাতৃপিতৃবন্মিত্রবদ্ধরিম্ ।
যে ধ্যায়ন্তি সদোদ্যুক্তাস্তেভ্যোঽপীহ নমো নমঃ ॥ ১৬৩ ॥

*pati-putra-suhṛd-bhrātṛ-*
*pitṛvan mitravad dharim*
*ye dhyāyanti sadodyuktās*
*tebhyo 'pīha namo namaḥ*

### SYNONYMS

*pati*—a husband; *putra*—a son; *suhṛt*—a friend; *bhrātṛ*—a brother; *pitṛ*—a father; *vat*—like; *mitra*—an intimate friend; *vat*—like; *harim*—on the Supreme Personality of Godhead; *ye*—all those who; *dhyāyanti*—meditate; *sadā*—always; *udyuktāḥ*—full of eagerness; *tebhyaḥ*—unto them; *api*—also; *iha*—here; *namaḥ namaḥ*—repeated respectful obeisances.

### TRANSLATION

**" 'Let me offer my respectful obeisances again and again to those who always eagerly meditate upon the Supreme Personality of Godhead as a husband, son, friend, brother, father or intimate friend.'**

### PURPORT

This verse appears in the *Bhakti-rasāmṛta-sindhu* (1.2.308).

### TEXT 164

এই মত করে যেবা রাগানুগা-ভক্তি ।
কৃষ্ণের চরণে তাঁর উপজয় 'প্রীতি' ॥ ১৬৪ ॥

*ei mata kare yebā rāgānugā-bhakti*
*kṛṣṇera caraṇe tāṅra upajaya 'prīti'*

### SYNONYMS

*ei mata*—in this way; *kare*—executes; *yebā*—anyone who; *rāgānugā-bhakti*—spontaneous devotional service to Kṛṣṇa; *kṛṣṇera caraṇe*—to the lotus feet of Kṛṣṇa; *tāṅra*—his; *upajaya*—awakens; *prīti*—affection.

### TRANSLATION

**"If one engages in spontaneous loving service to the Lord, his affection at the lotus feet of Kṛṣṇa gradually increases.**

### TEXT 165

প্রীত্যঙ্কুরে 'রতি', 'ভাব'—হয় দুই নাম ।
যাহা হৈতে বশ হন শ্রীভগবান্ ॥ ১৬৫ ॥

*prīty-aṅkure 'rati', 'bhāva'——haya dui nāma*
*yāhā haite vaśa hana śrī-bhagavān*

## SYNONYMS

*prīti-aṅkure*—in the seed of affection; *rati*—attachment; *bhāva*—emotion; *haya*—there are; *dui nāma*—two names; *yāhā haite*—from which; *vaśa*—controlled; *hana*—is; *śrī-bhagavān*—the Supreme Personality of Godhead.

## TRANSLATION

**"In the seed of affection, there is attachment which goes by two names, rati and bhāva. The Supreme Personality of Godhead comes under the control of such attachment.**

## PURPORT

Śrīla Bhaktisiddhānta Sarasvatī Ṭhākura comments on this verse. Externally a devotee performs all the items of devotional service—*śravaṇa* and *kīrtana*—in nine different ways, and within his mind he always thinks of his eternal relationship with Kṛṣṇa and follows in the footsteps of the devotees of Vṛndāvana. If one engages himself in the service of Rādhā and Kṛṣṇa in this way, he can transcend the regulative principles enjoined in the *śāstras* and, through his spiritual master, fully engage in rendering spontaneous love to Kṛṣṇa. In this way, he attains affection at the lotus feet of Kṛṣṇa. Kṛṣṇa actually comes under the control of such spontaneous feelings, and ultimately one can attain association with the Lord.

## TEXT 166

**যাহা হৈতে পাই কৃষ্ণের প্রেম-সেবন ।**
**এইত' কহিলুঁ 'অভিধেয়'-বিবরণ ॥ ১৬৬ ॥**

*yāhā haite pāi kṛṣṇera prema-sevana*
*eita' kahiluṅ 'abhidheya'-vivaraṇa*

## SYNONYMS

*yāhā haite*—from which; *pāi*—I can get; *kṛṣṇera*—of Lord Kṛṣṇa; *prema-sevana*—affectionate service; *eita'*—this; *kahiluṅ*—I have done; *abhidheya-vivaraṇa*—description of the means (devotional service) in detail.

## TRANSLATION

**"That by which one can attain loving service to the Lord I have described in detail as the execution of devotional service called abhidheya.**

## TEXT 167

অভিধেয়, সাধন-ভক্তি এবে কহিলুঁ সনাতন ।
সংক্ষেপে কহিলুঁ, বিস্তার না যায় বর্ণন ॥ ১৬৭ ॥

*abhidheya, sādhana-bhakti ebe kahiluṅ sanātana*
*saṅkṣepe kahiluṅ, vistāra nā yāya varṇana*

### SYNONYMS

*abhidheya*—the means of obtaining the desired object; *sādhana-bhakti*—devotional service performed by means of the body and senses; *ebe*—now; *kahiluṅ*—I have described; *sanātana*—My dear Sanātana; *saṅkṣepe*—in short; *kahiluṅ*—I have described; *vistāra*—expansion; *nā yāya*—is not possible; *varṇana*—describing.

### TRANSLATION

**"My dear Sanātana, I have briefly described the process of devotional service in practice, which is the means for obtaining love of Kṛṣṇa. It cannot be described broadly."**

## TEXT 168

অভিধেয় সাধনভক্তি শুনে যেই জন ।
অচিরাৎ পায় সেই কৃষ্ণপ্রেমধন ॥ ১৬৮ ॥

*abhidheya sādhana-bhakti śune yei jana*
*acirāt pāya sei kṛṣṇa-prema-dhana*

### SYNONYMS

*abhidheya*—necessary duty; *sādhana-bhakti*—devotional service in practice; *śune*—hears; *yei jana*—anyone who; *acirāt*—very soon; *pāya*—gets; *sei*—that person; *kṛṣṇa-prema-dhana*—the treasure of love of Kṛṣṇa.

### TRANSLATION

**Whoever hears the process of practical devotional service very soon attains shelter at the lotus feet of Kṛṣṇa in love and affection.**

## TEXT 169

শ্রীরূপ-রঘুনাথ-পদে যার আশ ।
চৈতন্যচরিতামৃত কহে কৃষ্ণদাস ॥ ১৬৯ ॥

*śrī-rūpa-raghunātha-pade yāra āśa*
*caitanya-caritāmṛta kahe kṛṣṇadāsa*

## SYNONYMS

*śrī-rūpa*—Śrīla Rūpa Gosvāmī; *raghunātha*—Śrīla Raghunātha dāsa Gosvāmī; *pade*—at the lotus feet; *yāra*—whose; *āśa*—expectation; *caitanya-caritāmṛta*—the book named *Caitanya-caritāmṛta; kahe*—describes; *kṛṣṇadāsa*—Śrīla Kṛṣṇadāsa Kavirāja Gosvāmī.

## TRANSLATION

**Praying at the lotus feet of Śrī Rūpa and Śrī Raghunātha, always desiring their mercy, I, Kṛṣṇadāsa, narrate Śrī Caitanya-caritāmṛta, following in their footsteps.**

*Thus end the Bhaktivedanta purports to the* Śrī Caitanya-caritāmṛta, Madhya-līlā, *Twenty-second Chapter, describing the execution of devotional service.*

# References

The statements of *Śrī Caitanya-caritāmṛta* are all confirmed by standard Vedic authorities. The following authentic scriptures are quoted in this book on the pages listed. Numerals in bold type refer the reader to *Śrī Caitanya-caritāmṛta's* translations. Numerals in regular type are references to its purports.


*Aitareya Upaniṣad,* 152

*Amṛta-pravāha-bhāṣya* (Bhaktivinoda Ṭhākura), 328

*Bhagavad-gītā,* 5, 30, 32, 41, **63,** 65, 67, 70, 71, 77, 84, 88, **92,** 98, 137, 150, 151, 152, 153, 195, 204, 211, 213, 224, 241, 279, 325, 328, **335,** 354, 359, 378, **380,** 384

*Bhakti-rasāmṛta-sindhu* (Rūpa Gosvāmī), 200, 215, 363, 364, 365, **403-405,** 406, **408, 418, 421-422, 423, 426**

*Bhakti-sandarbha* (Jīva Gosvāmī), 417

*Brahma-saṁhitā,* **86, 89,** 93, 142, 150, 152, 159, **170,** 174, 178, 217, 241, **254, 258**

*Bṛhan-nāradīya Purāṇa,* **52,** 195

*Caitanya-caritāmṛta* (Kṛṣṇadāsa Kavirāja), 149, 152, 199

*Gīta-bhāṣya* (Śaṅkarācārya), 175

*Hari-bhakti-sudhodaya,* **31, 348**

*Hari-bhakti-vilāsa* (Sanātana Gosvāmī), **28, 385**

*Hayaśīrṣa-pañcarātra,* **130**

*Laghu-bhāgavatāmṛta* (Rūpa Gosvāmī), 93, 104-105, 133, 139, 212, **262**

*Lalita-mādhava* (Rūpa Gosvāmī), 102, 103

*Kaṭha Upaniṣad,* 155

*Kātyāyana-saṁhitā,* **378**

*Kṛṣṇa-karṇāmṛta* (Bilvamaṅgala Ṭhākura), 309

# Glossary

## A

*Abhidheya*—the regulated activities of the soul for reviving his relationship with the Lord.
*Ācārya*—a bona fide spiritual master who teaches by his own example.
*Ādhibhautika*—miseries inflicted by other living entities.
*Ādhidaivika*—natural disturbances caused by the demigods.
*Ādhyātmika*—miseries arising from one's own body and mind.
*Ahaitukī*—without cheating motivation.
*Ahaṅkāra*—false ego.
*Ākāśa*—sky.
*Anādi*—beginningless.
*Antaryāmī*—indwelling; the Supersoul.
*Apratihatā*—uninterrupted.
*Ārati*—the ceremony of offering lamps and other items to the Deity.
*Avidhi-pūrvaka*—without properly following rules and regulations.
*Avyakta*—the material creation when it is not yet manifested from the *mahat-tattva*.
*Arcā-mūrti*—the worshipable Deity form of the Lord.
*Aṣṭāṅga-yoga*—the mystic *yoga* system to control the senses.
*Ātmā*—the soul or living entity.
*Ātma-samarpaṇa*—full surrender to Kṛṣṇa without reservation.
*Āvaraṇātmikā*—*māyā's* power by which a conditioned soul feels satisfied in any condition of life.
*Avatāras*—incarnations of Kṛṣṇa.
*Āveśa-rūpa*—a living entity who is specifically empowered by the Lord with knowledge or strength.

## B

*Bhāgavata-dharma*—the science of devotional service.
*Bhāgya*—good fortune.
*Bhakta-prāya*—an "almost" devotee.
*Bhakti-śakti*—the power to distribute devotional service.
*Bhakti-yoga*—devotional service.
*Bhakty-unmukhī sukṛti*—pious activities that awaken one's dormant Kṛṣṇa consciousness.
*Bhāva*—the preliminary stage of transcendental love of Godhead.
*Bhogonmukhī*—pious activities that bestow material opulence.
*Bhū-dhāraṇa-śakti*—the power to hold up the planets within the universe.
*Bhukti*—interest in material enjoyment.
*Brahmacarya*—the vow of strict abstinence from sex indulgence.
*Brāhmaṇa*—the intelligent class of men.
*Brahmāṇḍas*—the material universes.
*Brahma-yajña*—studying the *Vedas*.

## C

*Caitya-guru*—Kṛṣṇa as the spiritual master within the heart.
*Caṇḍāla*—a person accustomed to eating dogs.
*Caraṇāmṛta*—water offered to the lotus feet of the Lord, which is mixed with the seed of the *tulasī* tree.
*Caturvyūha*—the first four-handed expansions of Kṛṣṇa—Vāsudeva, Saṅkarṣaṇa, Aniruddha and Pradyumna.
*Cira-loka-pālas*—permanent governors of the universe.
*Cit-kaṇas*—particles of spirit; the living entities.

## D

*Dāsya-rasa*—the eternal relation of servitorship with the Supreme Lord.
Devī-dhāma—the material planets.
*Duṣṭa-damana-śakti*—the power to cut down rogues and demons.
*Dvīpa*—island; planet.

## G

Gaurasundara—Lord Caitanya Mahāprabhu, who has a beautiful golden form.
*Gṛhastha*—Kṛṣṇa conscious householder stage of life.
*Guṇa-avatāras*—incarnations who control material qualities.
*Guru*—the spiritual master.

## H

*Hari-nāma-saṅkīrtana*—congregational chanting of the holy names of the Lord.
*Hiraṇmaya-mahat-tattva*—the total material energy.

## J

*Jīva-tattva*—the separated expansions of the Lord; minute living entities.
*Jñāna-kāṇḍa*—section of the *Vedas* describing the process of mental speculation.
*Jñāna*—knowledge. Material *jñāna* does not go beyond the material body. Transcendental *jñāna* discriminates between matter and spirit. Perfect *jñāna* is knowledge of the body, the soul and the Supreme Lord.
*Jñāna-śakti*—the power to distribute transcendental knowledge.
*Jñānī*—one who is engaged in the cultivation of speculative knowledge. Upon attaining perfection, a *jñānī* surrenders to Kṛṣṇa.

## K

*Kaiśora*—Kṛṣṇa's age from the eleventh to the fifteenth year.
*Kaitava-dharma*—a cheating religion.

*Kaivalyam*—the state of realization of one's constitutional position as part and parcel of the Supreme Lord, which is preliminary to manifestation of activities on the platform of devotional service.

*Kalpa*—a millennium.

*Kalpa-avatāras*—*līlā-avatāras* appearing in each day of Brahmā.

Kāma-gāyatrī—a Vedic hymn which is composed of twenty-four and a half syllables.

*Kaniṣṭha-adhikārī*—the third-class devotee, who recognizes only the Deity and himself, but not other devotees.

*Kapha*—mucus, one of the three major elements of the gross body.

*Karma*—(1) material action performed according to scriptural regulations; (2) action pertaining to the development of the material body; (3) any material action which will incur a subsequent reaction; (4) the material reaction one incurs due to fruitive activities.

*Karma-kāṇḍa*—section of the *Vedas* describing the process of fruitive activity.

*Khaṇḍa*—a valley between two mountains.

*Kṛṣṇa-pāriṣada*—associates of the Lord.

*Kṣatriya*—the administrative or protective class.

*Kṣetra-jñā-śakti*—the living entities.

## L

*Līlā-avatāras*—incarnations who perform pastimes.

*Līlās*—Kṛṣṇa's pastimes.

*Loka-pālas*—predominating deities of the universe.

## M

Madana-mohana—Kṛṣṇa, the attractor of Cupid.

*Mādhukarī*—a saintly mendicant who takes a little food from each householder's place, like a bee gathering honey.

*Mādhurya-rasa*—the eternal relationship of conjugal love with the Lord.

*Madhyama-adhikārī*—second-class devotee who recognizes four types of persons—the Lord, the devotees, the innocent and the demons—and treats each appropriately.

*Mahā-bhāgavata*—a great devotee.

*Mahā-mantra*—the great chanting for deliverance: Hare Kṛṣṇa, Hare Kṛṣṇa, Kṛṣṇa Kṛṣṇa, Hare Hare/ Hare Rāma, Hare Rāma, Rāma Rāma, Hare Hare.

*Mahāraurava*—a hell wherein animal killers are sent.

*Mahātmā*—a great soul.

*Mahat-tattva*—the total material energy.

*Maheśvara*—the supreme proprietor.

*Mantra*—(*manas*—mind; *tṝ*—to deliver) a pure sound vibration to deliver the mind from its material inclinations.

*Manvantara-avatāras*—incarnations of the Manus.

*Mauṣala-līlā*—the pastimes of the annihilation of the Yadu dynasty and Lord Kṛṣṇa's disappearance.

*Mokṣonmukhī*—pious activities that enable the living entity to merge into the existence of the Supreme.
*Mūrti*—some form of the Lord.

## N

*Nava-yauvana*—the eternal transcendental form of Kṛṣṇa as pre-youth.
*Nija-dharma*—one's constitutional position.
*Nitya-baddhas*—souls who are always conditioned by the external energy.
*Nitya-līlā*—Kṛṣṇa's eternally present pastimes.
*Nitya-muktas*—souls who never come in contact with the external energy.
*Nivṛtti-mārga*—directions for giving up the material world for higher spiritual understanding.
*Nṛ-yajña*—the proper reception of guests.

## P

*Pālana-śakti*—the power to rule and maintain the living entities.
*Parabrahman*—the Supreme Brahman, the Personality of Godhead, Śrī Kṛṣṇa.
*Paramahaṁsa*—a person on the highest platform of spiritual realization, above all material designations.
*Paramaṁ padam*—the Lord's transcendental abode.
*Paravyoma*—the spiritual sky.
*Pitṛ-yajña*—offering oblations of water before one's forefathers.
*Pitta*—bile, one of the three major elements of the gross body.
in which His form is unchanged.
*Pradhāna*—the ingredients from which the cosmic manifestation is created.
*Praharas*—three-hour period, eight of which make up each day.
*Prajāpatis*—the progenitors of living entities, chief of whom is Lord Brahmā.
*Prākṛta-bhakta*—a materialistic devotee.
*Prakṛti*—nature (lit., that which is predominated).
*Prakṣepātmikā-śakti*—*māyā's* power to throw one into the material world.
*Pravṛtti-mārga*—directions for enjoying the material world according to regulative principles.
*Prayojana*—the ultimate goal of life.
*Puruṣa*—the enjoyer.
*Puruṣa-avatāras*—expansions of Kṛṣṇa who are Lords of universal creation; the three Viṣṇus.

## R

*Rāga*—deep attachment.
*Rāgānugā bhakti*—devotional service following the spontaneous loving service of the inhabitants of Vṛndāvana.
*Rāgātmikā bhakti*—spontaneous devotional service of the inhabitants of Vṛndāvana according to their transcendental attachment.
*Rāja-pāla*—the governor of the state.

*Rajas*—the material mode of passion.
*Rājasa-ahaṅkāra*—egotism in passion.
*Rajo-guṇa*—the mode of passion.
*Rati*—strong attraction.

## S

*Śabda-pramāṇa*—evidence from the Vedic literature.
*Śabda-tanmātra*—the material element of sound vibration.
*Ṣaḍ-aiśvarya*—Kṛṣṇa's six opulences.
*Sādhaka*—a devotee preparing for perfection.
*Sādhana-bhakti*—the regulative discharge of devotional service.
*Sādhu*—a saintly person.
*Sakhya-rasa*—the eternal relationship of friendship with the Lord.
*Śakti-tattva*—persons who are plenary expansions of the Lord's internal potency.
*Śaktyāveśa-avatāras*—empowered living entities who serve as incarnations of the Lord.
*Sambandha*—the soul's relationship with the Lord.
*Saṅkīrtana-yajña*—the sacrifice prescribed for the age of Kali; congregational chanting of the name, fame and pastimes of the Supreme Personality of Godhead.
*Sannipāti*—a convulsive disease caused by combination of *kapha, pitta, vāyu.*
*Sannyāsa*—the renounced order of life.
*Śānta-rasa*—passive or neutral relationship with the Lord.
*Sarva-kāraṇa-kāraṇam*—Kṛṣṇa, the cause of all causes.
*Sarva-loka*—all the three worlds.
*Śāstras*—the revealed scriptures.
*Sattva-guṇa*—the material mode of goodness.
*Sāttvika-ahaṅkāra*—egotism in goodness.
*Siddha*—a devotee who is already perfect.
*Siddhi-kāṇḍa*—*See: Jñāna-kāṇḍa.*
*Smṛti-śāstras*—the corollaries of the *Vedas.*
*Śraddhā*—firm faith and confidence.
*Śravaṇaṁ kīrtanaṁ viṣṇoḥ*—hearing and chanting about Kṛṣṇa.
*Sṛṣṭi-śakti*—the power to create the cosmic manifestation.
*Śūdra*—the laborer class of men.
*Sūrya*—the sun-god.
*Svāṁśaka*—expansions of Kṛṣṇa's personal potency.
*Svāṅga-viśeṣābhāsa-rūpe*—the form by which the Lord begets living entities in the material world.
*Śva-paca*—dog-eater.
*Svārājya-lakṣmī*—the personal spiritual potency of the Lord.
*Svarūpa-upalabdhi*—one's having become established in his eternal service relationship with the Lord.
*Sva-sevana-śakti*—the power to perform the personal service of the Supreme Lord.
*Svayaṁ-rūpa*—Kṛṣṇa's original form as a cowherd boy in Vṛndāvana.

## T

*Tad-ekātma-rūpa*—forms of the Lord which are nondifferent from His original form, but which have different bodily features and specific activities.
*Tamas*—the material mode of ignorance.
*Tāmasa*—egotism in ignorance.
*Tamo-guṇa*—*See: Tamas.*
*Tilaka*—sacred clay used to mark Viṣṇu temples on twelve places on the body of a devotee.
Tryadhīśvara—the proprietor of the three worlds.

## V

*Vaidhī-bhakti*—following devotional service regulative principles by the order of the spiritual master and in accordance with revealed scripture.
Vaikuṇṭha—(lit., without anxiety) the eternal planets of the spiritual sky.
*Vaiśya*—the class of men involved in business and farming.
*Vānaprastha*—retired life, in which one quits home and travels to holy places in preparation for the renounced order of life.
*Vātsalya-rasa*—parental relationship with the Lord.
*Vāyu*—air, one of the three major elements of the gross body.
*Vibhūti*—a secondary incarnation indirectly empowered by the Supreme Lord.
*Viṣṇu-tattva*—the personal expansions of Kṛṣṇa, each of whom is also God.
*Vyakta*—material creation when it is manifested from the total energy of *mahat-tattva.*

## Y

*Yoga*—linking of the consciousness of the infinitesimal living entity with the supreme living entity, Kṛṣṇa.
*Yogamāyā*—the internal potency of the Lord.
*Yuga*—one of four ages of the universe.
*Yuga-avatāras*—incarnations of the Lord in different millenniums.

# Bengali Pronunciation Guide

## BENGALI DIACRITICAL EQUIVALENTS AND PRONUNCIATION

### Vowels

অ a  আ ā  ই i  ঈ ī  উ u  ঊ ū  ঋ ṛ

ৠ ṝ  এ e  ঐ ai  ও o  ঔ au

ং ṁ *(anusvāra)*  ঁ ṅ *(candra-bindu)*  ঃ ḥ *(visarga)*

### Consonants

| | | | | | |
|---|---|---|---|---|---|
| **Gutterals:** | ক ka | খ kha | গ ga | ঘ gha | ঙ ṅa |
| **Palatals:** | চ ca | ছ cha | জ ja | ঝ jha | ঞ ña |
| **Cerebrals:** | ট ṭa | ঠ ṭha | ড ḍa | ঢ ḍha | ণ ṇa |
| **Dentals:** | ত ta | থ tha | দ da | ধ dha | ন na |
| **Labials:** | প pa | ফ pha | ব ba | ভ bha | ম ma |
| **Semivowels:** | য ya | র ra | ল la | ব va | |
| **Sibilants:** | শ śa | ষ ṣa | স sa | হ ha | |

### Vowel Symbols

The vowels are written as follows after a consonant:

া ā  ি i  ী ī  ু u  ূ ū  ৃ ṛ  ৄ ṝ  ে e  ৈ ai  ো o  ৌ au

For example: কা kā  কি ki  কী kī  কু ku  কূ kū  কৃ kṛ

কৄ kṝ  কে ke  কৈ kai  কো ko  কৌ kau

The letter *a* is implied after a consonant with no vowel symbol.

The symbol *virāma* (्) indicates that there is no final vowel. क् k

The letters above should be pronounced as follows:

a –like the *o* in h*o*t; sometimes like the *o* in go; final *a* is usually silent.
ā –like the *a* in f*a*r.
i, ī –like the *ee* in m*ee*t.
u, ū –like the *u* in r*u*le.
ṛ –like the *ri* in *ri*m.
ṝ –like the *ree* in *ree*d.
e –like the *ai* in p*ai*n; rarely like *e* in b*e*t.
ai –like the *oi* in b*oi*l.
o –like the *o* in g*o*.
au –like the *ow* in *ow*l.
ṁ –*(anusvāra)* like the *ng* in so*ng*.
ḥ –*(visarga)* a final *h* sound like in Ah.
ṅ –*(candra-bindu)* a nasal *n* sound like in the French word *bon*.
k –like the *k* in *k*ite.
kh –like the *kh* in Ec*kh*art.
g –like the *g* in *g*ot.
gh –like the *gh* in bi*g-h*ouse.
ṅ –like the *n* in ba*n*k.
c –like the *ch* in *ch*alk.
ch –like the *chh* in mu*ch-h*aste.
j –like the *j* in *j*oy.
jh –like the *geh* in colle*ge-h*all.
ñ –like the *n* in bu*n*ch.
ṭ –like the *t* in *t*alk.
ṭh –like the *th* in ho*t-h*ouse.
ḍ –like the *d* in *d*awn.
ḍh –like the *dh* in goo*d-h*ouse.
ṇ –like the *n* in g*n*aw.
t–as in *t*alk but with the tongue against the the teeth.
th–as in ho*t-h*ouse but with the tongue against the teeth.
d–as in *d*awn but with the tongue against the teeth.
dh–as in goo*d-h*ouse but with the tongue against the teeth.
n–as in *n*or but with the tongue against the teeth.
p –like the *p* in *p*ine.
ph –like the *ph* in *ph*ilosopher.
b –like the *b* in *b*ird.
bh –like the *bh* in ru*b-h*ard.
m –like the *m* in *m*other.
y –like the *j* in *j*aw. য
y –like the *y* in *y*ear. য়
r –like the *r* in *r*un.
l –like the *l* in *l*aw.
v –like the *b* in *b*ird or like the *w* in d*w*arf.
ś, ṣ –like the *sh* in *sh*op.
s –like the *s* in *s*un.
h–like the *h* in *h*ome.

This is a general guide to Bengali pronunciation. The Bengali transliterations in this book accurately show the original Bengali spelling of the text. One should note, however, that in Bengali, as in English, spelling is not always a true indication of how a word is pronounced. Tape recordings of His Divine Grace A. C. Bhaktivedanta Swami Prabhupāda chanting the original Bengali verses are available from the International Society for Krishna Consciousness, 3764 Watseka Ave., Los Angeles, California 90034.

# Index of Bengali and Sanskrit Verses

This index constitutes a complete alphabetical listing of the first and third line of each four-line erse and both lines of each two-line verse in *Śrī Caitanya-caritāmṛta.* In the first column the transteration is given, and in the second and third columns respectively the chapter-verse references nd page number for each verse are to be found.

## A

## C



## D

## E

## N

## R



## S

## T

## U



## V



## Y

# General Index

Numerals in bold type indicate references to *Śrī Caitanya-caritāmṛta's* verses. Numerals in regular type are references to its purports.

## A


*Abhidheya*
described, **66-67**
Absolute Truth
as source of all emanations, 151
Kṛṣṇa as nondual, **323**
three features of, **87-88**
*See also:* Kṛṣṇa, Supreme Lord
*Ācārya*
followed by intelligent, 199
one must follow in footsteps of, 395
*See also:* Spiritual master
*Acintya-bhedābheda-tattva*
position of Rudra as, 173
Activities
*arcā-mūrtis* increase spiritual, 122
devotional service always independent of material, 416
incarnations can be known by uncommon, **202**
Kṛṣṇa performs welfare, **299**
of body, mind and senses included in sixty-four items, 403
of humans should be centered about devotional service, **322**
of Kṛṣṇa very grave, **32**
of *yogamāyā* absent in spiritual sky, 287
required for creation, **140**
results of spiritual performed in *yugas,* **193-196**
Acyuta
as form of Personality of Godhead, 99
as pastime expansion, **114-115**
position of weapons of, **128**
Adhokṣaja
as pastime expansion, **114-115**
position of weapons of, **130**
*Adhyāpanaṁ brahma-yajñaḥ*
verses quoted, 411
*Advaitam acyutam anādim ananta-rūpaṁ*
quoted, 85, 217
*Agnir mahī gaganam ambu*
verse quoted, 150
Agrahāyana
Keśava predominating Deity of, **111**
*Aitareya Upaniṣad*
quoted on Mahā-Viṣṇu's glancing, 152
Ajita
as *avatāra* in *Cākṣuṣa-manvantara,* **183**
Akrūra
attained perfection by prayers, **408**
Ambarīṣa Mahārāja
perfected nine processes of devotional service, **409**
*Amṛta-pravāha-bhāṣya*
cited on two kinds of living beings, 328
*Ānanda-cinmaya-rasa-pratibhāvitābhiḥ*
quoted, 241
Ānandāraṇya
as residence of Vāsudeva, etc. **119**
Ananta
can't describe Kṛṣṇa forms, **227**
can't reach end of Lord's transcendental qualities, **237-238**
empowered to bear planets within universe, 135, **211**
Gokula created by will of, **142**
Anantadeva
*See:* Ananta
*Anayāpekṣi yad rūpaṁ syayaṁ-rūpaḥ*
quoted, 93
*Aṅgānāṁ pañcakasyāsya*
verses quoted, 403
*Aṅgāni yasya sakalendriya*
verse quoted, 152
Anger
conditioned souls as servant of, 64, **328**-329
Animals
pastime incarnations as,**166-167**
Aniruddha
as expansion in Dvārakā Purī, **132**
as expansion of Supreme Lord, **190, 324**

## B

## H

## I

## L

# O

## S

## U



## V

## Y



## Z

# The Author

His Divine Grace A. C. Bhaktivedanta Swami Prabhupāda appeared in this world in 1896 in Calcutta, India. He first met his spiritual master, Śrīla Bhaktisiddhānta Sarasvatī Gosvāmī, in Calcutta in 1922. Bhaktisiddhānta Sarasvatī, a prominent devotional scholar and the founder of sixty-four Gauḍīya Maṭhas (Vedic Institutes), liked this educated young man and convinced him to dedicate his life to teaching Vedic knowledge. Śrīla Prabhupāda became his student, and eleven years later (1933) at Allahabad he became his formally initiated disciple.

At their first meeting, in 1922, Śrīla Bhaktisiddhānta Sarasvatī Ṭhākura requested Śrīla Prabhupāda to broadcast Vedic knowledge through the English language. In the years that followed, Śrīla Prabhupāda wrote a commentary on the *Bhagavad-gītā,* assisted the Gauḍīya Maṭha in its work and, in 1944, without assistance, started an English fortnightly magazine, edited it, typed the manuscripts and checked the galley proofs. He even distributed the individual copies freely and struggled to maintain the publication. Once begun, the magazine never stopped; it is now being continued by his disciples in the West.

Recognizing Śrīla Prabhupāda's philosophical learning and devotion, the Gauḍīya Vaiṣṇava Society honored him in 1947 with the title "Bhaktivedanta." In 1950, at the age of fifty-four, Śrīla Prabhupāda retired from married life, and four years later he adopted the *vānaprastha* (retired) order to devote more time to his studies and writing. Śrīla Prabhupāda traveled to the holy city of Vṛndāvana, where he lived in very humble circumstances in the historic medieval temple of Rādhā-Dāmodara. There he engaged for several years in deep study and writing. He accepted the renounced order of life (*sannyāsa*) in 1959. At Rādhā-Dāmodara, Śrīla Prabhupāda began work on his life's masterpiece: a multivolume translation and commentary on the eighteen thousand verse *Śrīmad-Bhāgavatam* (*Bhāgavata Purāṇa*). He also wrote *Easy Journey to Other Planets.*

After publishing three volumes of *Bhāgavatam,* Śrīla Prabhupāda came to the United States, in 1965, to fulfill the mission of his spiritual master. Since that time, His Divine Grace has written over forty volumes of authoritative translations, commentaries and summary studies of the philosophical and religious classics of India.

In 1965, when he first arrived by freighter in New York City, Śrīla Prabhupāda was practically penniless. It was after almost a year of great difficulty that he established the International Society for Krishna Consciousness in July of 1966. Under his careful guidance, the Society has grown within a decade to a worldwide confederation of almost one hundred *āśramas,* schools, temples, institutes and farm communities.

In 1968, Śrīla Prabhupāda created New Vṛndāvana, an experimental Vedic community in the hills of West Virginia. Inspired by the success of New Vṛndāvana, now a thriving farm community of more than one thousand acres, his students have since founded several similar communities in the United States and abroad.

In 1972, His Divine Grace introduced the Vedic system of primary and secondary education in the West by founding the *Gurukula* school in Dallas, Texas. The school began with 3 children in 1972, and by the beginning of 1975 the enrollment had grown to 150.

Śrīla Prabhupāda has also inspired the construction of a large international center at Śrīdhāma Māyāpur in West Bengal, India, which is also the site for a planned Institute of Vedic Studies. A similar project is the magnificent Kṛṣṇa-Balarāma Temple and International Guest House in Vṛndāvana, India. These are centers where Westerners can live to gain firsthand experience of Vedic culture.

Śrīla Prabhupāda's most significant contribution, however, is his books. Highly respected by the academic community for their authoritativeness, depth and clarity, they are used as standard textbooks in numerous college courses. His writings have been translated into eleven languages. The Bhaktivedanta Book Trust, established in 1972 exclusively to publish the works of His Divine Grace, has thus become the world's largest publisher of books in the field of Indian religion and philosophy. Its latest project is the publishing of Śrīla Prabhupāda's most recent work: a seventeen-volume translation and commentary—completed by Śrīla Prabhupāda in only eighteen months—on the Bengali religious classic *Śrī Caitanya-caritāmṛta.*

In the past ten years, in spite of his advanced age, Śrīla Prabhupāda has circled the globe twelve times on lecture tours that have taken him to six continents. In spite of such a vigorous schedule, Śrīla Prabhupāda continues to write prolifically. His writings constitute a veritable library of Vedic philosophy, religion, literature and culture.